THE BEST OF

LONDON

Editor-in-Chief
André Gayo

Managing Edi
Mary Anne Eva

Editor
Sharon Boorstin

Contributing Editors
Hugo Arnold, Lindsay Bareham, Louis Charles,
Guy Dimond, George Dorgan, David Evans, Carole Hirschhorn,
Ossi Laurila, Sandrae Lawrence, Michael North, Sudi Piggott,
Stuart Walton, Ian Wisniewski, David Wolfe

Coordination
Sophie Gayot

Publisher
Alain Gayot

GAULT MILLAU

Paris ▪ Los Angeles ▪ New York ▪ London ▪ Munich ▪ San Francisco

GAYOT PUBLICATIONS

The Best of Beverly Hills
The Best of Chicago
The Best of Florida
The Best of France
The Best of Germany
The Best of Hawaii
The Best of Hong Kong
The Best of Italy
The Best of London
The Best of Los Angeles
The Best of New England
The Best of New Orleans
The Best of New York
The Best of Paris
Paris, Ile-de-France & The Loire Valley
Paris & Provence
The Best of San Francisco
The Best of Thailand
The Best of Toronto
The Best of Washington, D.C.
The Best Wineries of North America

LA Restaurants, NYC Restaurants, SF Restaurants
The Food Paper, Tastes Newsletter
http://www.gayot.com

Published by Gault Millau, Inc.
5900 Wilshire Blvd.
Los Angeles, CA 90036

Please address all comments regarding
THE BEST OF LONDON to:
GaultMillau, Inc.
P.O. Box 361144
Los Angeles, CA 90036
E-mail: gayots@aol.com

Advertising Sales:
Debbie Eskew
5900 Wilshire Blvd.
Los Angeles, CA 90036
323-965-4841 Fax 323-936-2883

Production: Walter Mladina
Page Layout and Design: Mad Macs Communications

ISSN 1520-3514

Printed in the United States of America

Contents

Cool Britannia

London, like most major cities, is in a constant state of change and growth. But in the past two years or so, the capital has seen some of the most exciting developments for centuries. The rest of the world has been quick to recognise London's status, and when *Newsweek* declared England 'Cool Britannia', the seal was set.

But what is it that makes London such a global magnet; what is it that draws young Europeans to London; international financial businesses to the City and Docklands; the top fashion houses to those two great meccas for shoppers, Bond Street in Mayfair, and Sloane Street in Knightsbridge; and those star names who come to enjoy what is now universally acknowledged as the 'coolest city on the planet'?

The attractions of London are endless, and continually evolving, involving so many threads and strands of human achievement. Some of her attractions are immediately obvious. You only have to stroll around Whitehall, walk up the Mall to Buckingham Palace, explore the streets of nearby St. James's to appreciate the most glorious and varied city architecture in the world. If you want to probe further, there are enough buildings open for the most curious spectator. Buckingham Palace is currently open to view each summer; so is the charming, small former home of the writer and historian, Thomas Carlyle. An afternoon spent in the Victoria and Albert, the British Museum, or the Maritime Museum is time spent appreciating the greatest art - and artifacts - you can find anywhere, offering what is in effect a succinct tour of the world's great civilisations. Walk down Cork Street, Bruton Street or St. James's, or venture further out to the East End and you'll be rewarded with contemporary art that is challenging all our pre-conceptions of what is art. An evening at the theatre will entertain or it will provoke profound emotions; London boasts the most varied theatre in the western world, offering a play for everyone. You can shop until you drop in Chelsea, Knightsbridge, Sloane Street and Bond Streets, or just window shop, one of life's great treats. You return to your hotel, chosen because it's the most luxurious you can find...or it offers a home-from-home in a gracious townhouse setting...or is a family home run for a select number of guests in leafy residential Chiswick or splendid Kensington. Then it's off to a restaurant for dinner. But which restaurant? London offers every cuisine at every level and every price, and the choice is difficult.

For choice is what London is all about, and what is so exciting about the city today. There is something for every taste, for every age and for every budget in this great metropolis. As with our last guide, we have set out to present London in all its various forms, to suggest, inform and intrigue. We have explored and written about the best of London - in every possible aspect. We have included the very best shopping to be had, and we comprehensively cover London's vibrant restaurant scene, from the most expensive to the places where you get real value-for-money.

In this edition of The Best of London, we bring together all those elements which attract the rest of the world to London, elements which will take 'the coolest city on the planet' into the new century.

THE BEST OF LONDON

RIGHTS

SPECIAL SALES

Gayot Publications are available at discounts for bulk purchases, direct sales or premiums.

- Makes a great gift that will put your name in front of important clients over and over again—and at a small cost.
- Links your firm with internationally respected publications.
- Orders over 1,000 can be customized with your logo on the cover at no extra charge.

Call our toll-free number for information and orders:

1 (800) 532-3781

OR WRITE US:
Gayot Publications
5900 Wilshire Blvd.
Los Angeles, CA 90036

E-mail: gayots@aol.com

DISCLAIMER

Readers are advised that prices and conditions change over the course of time. The restaurants, shops and other businesses reviewed in this book have been reviewed over a period of time, and the reviews reflect the personal experiences and opinions of the reviewers. The reviewers and publishers cannot be held responsible for the experiences of the reader related to the establishments reviewed. Readers are invited to write the publisher with ideas, comments and suggestions for future editions.

RESTAURANTS

CONTENTS

INTRODUCTION

A BUOYANT SCENE

The London restaurant world is changing, like the world itself. So what's new? The large, well-designed restaurant is here to stay, with Sir Terence Conran once more leading the way. Now he is taking his ideas to Paris and to New York. Other leading players include Marco Pierre White, who backed by the leading hotel group, Granada, is set to take charge of more hotel restaurants both in and outside London. With the move of Pierre Koffmann to The Berkeley, and the constant presence of Nico Ladenis at Chez Nico at Ninety, Michel Roux at Le Gavroche, and outside London top chefs like Raymond Blanc at Le Manoir aux Quat' Saisons, the hotel dining room is once again coming into its own, holding a place in the gastronomic league rather as it did at the turn of this century. But, conversely, the small, individual, often family-run restaurant still thrives. Indeed, with the opening of more mega-restaurants comes a yearning for the intimate, and those small places that survive are once again full. The 'gastro-pub' is going strong as well, thanks to the thoroughly laudable practice of young enthusiastic chefs taking over former pubs with small overheads and turning out excellent meals at reasonable prices. And overall in most of London's restaurants, value for money generally is still an important and much welcome factor, with stiff competition being the chief cause.

On the downside is the constant drain on expertise, with the pool of experienced chefs still too low to be able to sustain yet more significant expansion of London's restaurants. As with chefs, so with waiting staff, and standards of service are still generally down, particularly when considering the expense of eating out. Another deplorable aspect of London's restaurant scene is the insistence by restaurateurs on tables being turned over in two hours to maximise profit while minimising the diner's enjoyment. There is nothing more depressing than being told that the restaurant must have the table back at a certain time, and when that is compounded as it can be, by slow and sloppy service, it is totally unacceptable. All these complaints, which are frequent, are a result of the booming restaurant scene, which is as buoyant as ever. A scene which in turn is fuelled by the big breweries and by large companies who are seemingly paying over the odds to buy individual enterprises and small chains.

All these comments could describe many cities. But there is no doubt that London remains one of the world's great gastronomic capitals, attracting young chefs from everywhere into our kitchens, and diners eager to enjoy the experience. London with its huge mix of cultures and therefore of cuisines, continues to offer an unparalleled choice of dining, for all purses and for all tastes. Bon appetit!

RESTAURANT SAVVY

You will have to book the top restaurants in advance, and some might require a few weeks' notice. Be prepared to give your telephone number and expect the restaurant to reconfirm the booking. There have been so many cases of no-shows in the past that restaurants have found themselves with empty tables on busy nights that they can ill afford.

Dress is fairly casual, though at the better restaurants women may feel out of place in pantsuits. Men also, might prefer to wear a jacket and tie. Although there is seldom any formal dress code, many people these days dress up for an evening out, so you may feel out of place if too casually dressed.

At any of the top restaurants, it is always a good idea to ask the head waiter for suggestions. Remember, too, that the wine waiter is there to offer expert advice, so never be afraid to ask.

Lunch is generally served from 12.30pm to around 2.30pm; dinner usually from 7pm onwards. However, many restaurants now offer pre- or post-theatre menus. These can be very good value. Another established practice (though centuries-old in Chinese restaurants) is the prix-fixe menu, which can offer good value and often the best efforts of the chef.

Some restaurants add a service charge (this should be printed on the menu); others will leave the service charge up to you. Fifteen percent has become the norm. But always double check your bill as cases are often recorded of the practice of adding on the service charge but leaving the final total free in the hopes that the unsuspecting customer will add yet more to what should be a final total.

In today's rapidly changing world, chefs change too, which means a restaurant might not be as described in this book. Chef-owned restaurants are generally more stable, though they can also change. If you experience any of this, please don't hold us responsible.

ABOUT THE REVIEWS

USING OUR RATING SYSTEM

Our rating system works as follows: restaurants are ranked in the same manner that French students are graded, on a scale of one to twenty.

THE RANKINGS REFLECT ONLY OUR OPINION OF THE FOOD. THE DECOR, SERVICE, AMBIENCE AND WINE LIST ARE COMMENTED UPON WITHIN EACH REVIEW.

Restaurants that are ranked 13/20 and above are distinguished with toques (chef's hats) according to the table below.

Exceptional *(4 Toques)*
(ratings of 19/20)
Excellent *(3 Toques)*
(ratings of 17/20 and 18/20)
Very good *(2 Toques)*
(ratings of 15/20 and 16/20)
Good *(1 Toque)*
(ratings of 13/20 and 14/20)

Keep in mind that we are comparing London's restaurants to the very best in the world. Also, these ranks are relative. A 13/20 (one toque) may not be a superlative ranking for a highly reputed (and very expensive) restaurant, but it is quite complimentary for a small place without much culinary pretension. We know that diners often choose a restaurant for reasons other than the quality of the food because of its location, type of cuisine or just because it's a fun place to spend an evening.

OUR PRICING SYSTEM

PRICES for a three-course meal for one with coffee and service, but no beverages:

£—under £25 **£££—£35-£50**
££—£25-£35 **££££—over £50**

SYMBOLS:

All credit cards taken . . . . A
Visa . . . . VISA
MasterCard . . . . MasterCard
American Express . . . .
Diners Club . . . . Diners Club International
Discover . . . . DISCOVER
Reservations suggested . . . .
Valet parking . . . .
Ties suggested . . . .
Romantic setting . . . .
Heart-healthy dishes . . . .
View . . . .
Outdoor dining . . . .

Sample Review

The following key explains the information provided in our reviews.

Top Restaurants: Food Rating

TOQUE TALLY

19/20

La Tante Claire (Knightsbridge)
Le Manoir aux Quat'Saisons (Oxford)
The Oak Room (Piccadilly)

18/20

Gordon Ramsay (Chelsea)
Chez Nico at Ninety (Mayfair)
The Square (Mayfair)

17/20

Tatsuso (The City)
Waterside Inn (Bray-on-Thames)

16/20

The Capital (Knightsbridge)
City Rhodes (The City)
The Connaught Grill Room & Restaurant (Mayfair)
Le Gavroche (Mayfair)
Lettonie (Bath)
L'Ortolan (Shinfield)
Nobu (Mayfair)
Pied-à-Terre (Tottenham Court Road)
River Café (Hammersmith)
Sabras (Willesden)

THE TOQUE, CIRCA 1700

Have you ever wondered about the origin of that towering, billowy (and slightly ridiculous) white hat worn by chefs all over the world? Chefs have played an important role in society since the fifth century B.C., but the hats didn't begin to appear in kitchens until around the eighteenth century A.D. The toque is said to be of Greek origin; many famous Greek cooks, to escape persecution, sought refuge in monasteries and continued to practice their art. The chefs donned the tall hats traditionally worn by Orthodox priests, but to distinguish themselves from their fellows, they wore white hats instead of black. The custom eventually was adopted by chefs from Paris to Peking.

15/20

Alastair Little Lancaster Road (Notting Hill Gate)
Aroma (Chinatown)
Bibendum (South Kensington)
Café Royal Grill Room (Piccadilly)
Chavot (Fulham)
Clarke's (Kensington)
The Fifth Floor (Knightsbridge)
Fung Shing (Chinatown)
Leith's (Notting Hill Gate)
L'Oranger (St. James's)
Mandarin Kitchen (Bayswater)
Mirabelle (Mayfair)
Moro (Clerkenwell)
Quo Vadis (Soho)
Rhodes in the Square (Pimlico)
Richard Corrigan at Lindsay House (Soho)
Stephano Cavallini at The Halkin (Belgravia)
Tatsuso Teppan Room (The City)
Vong (Knightsbridge)
Windows Roof Restaurant (Mayfair)
Zen Garden (Mayfair)

14/20

Al Hamra (Mayfair)
Alastair Little (Soho)
Assaggi at The Chepstow (Notting Hill Gate)
Bali Sugar (Notting Hill Gate)
Bank (Covent Garden)
The Birdcage (Tottenham Court Road)
Boisdale (Victoria)
The Brackenbury (Shepherd's Bush)
Café du Jardin (Covent Garden)
Café Spice Namaste (Battersea)
Cambio de Tercio (Knightsbridge)
The Canteen (Chelsea)
Chez Bruce (Wandsworth)
Chez Max (Fulham)
Chez Moi (Holland Park)
Chinon (Shepherd's Bush)
Claridge's (Mayfair)
Coast (Mayfair)
The Dining Room (Kensington)
Ebury Wine Bar (Victoria)
1837 (Mayfair)
The Greenhouse (Mayfair)
Hilaire (South Kensington)
Ibla (Marylebone)
Interlude (Tottenham Court Road)
The Ivy (Covent Garden)
La Ciboulette (Chelsea)
Le Caprice (St. James's)
L'Escargot (Soho)
Le Pont de la Tour (Tower Bridge)
Le Soufflé (Mayfair)
Leith's Soho (Soho)
Les Saveurs de Jean-Christophe Novelli (Mayfair)
MPW (The City)
Mr Kong (Chinatown)
Novelli EC1 (Clerkenwell)
Novelli W8 (Kensington)
Odette's (Primrose Hill)
One Lawn Terrace (Blackheath)
Orrery (Marylebone)
Oxo Tower Restaurant, Bar & Brasserie (South Bank)
Ransome's Dock (Battersea)
Rasa (Stoke Newington)
Restaurant One-O-One (Knightsbridge)
The Ritz Restaurant (St. James's)
Riva (Barnes)
The River Restaurant (Strand)
The Room at The Halcyon (Holland Park)
Saga Sushi Bar (Mayfair)
Saigon Times (The City)
St. John (Clerkenwell)
Sartoria (Piccadilly)
Snows on the Green (Shepherd's Bush)
Stephen Bull St. Martin's Lane (Covent Garden)
Stephen Bull (Marylebone)
The Stepping Stone (Battersea)
Sugar Club (Soho)
Tentazioni (Tower Bridge)
The Tenth (Kensington)
Turner's (South Kensington)
The Vineyard at Stockcross (Near Newbury)
Woz (Notting Hill Gate)

13/20

Abero & Grana (Chelsea)
Al San Vincenzo (Marble Arch)
The Avenue (St. James)
Belair House (Dulwich)
Bertorelli's (Tottenham Court Road)
Blue Print Café (Tower Bridge)
Busabong Tree (Chelsea)
Brasserie St. Quentin (Knightsbridge)
The Chiswick (Chiswick)
Chutney Mary (Fulham)
Circus (Soho)
Criterion Marco Pierre White (Piccadilly)
Delfina Studio Café (Bermondsey)
Dorchester Grill (Mayfair)
First Floor (Notting Hill Gate)
French House (Soho)
Ginnan (Clerkenwell)
Granita (Islington)
Gresslin's (Hampstead)
The Grill Room (Strand)

Grissini (Knightsbridge)
Ho Ho (Mayfair)
Inaho (Bayswater)
Kensington Place (Kensington)
Langan's Brasserie (Mayfair)
Livebait (Covent Garden)
Lola's (Islington)
Lou Pescadou (South Kensington)
Ma Goa (Richmond)
Matsuri Sushi Bar (St. James's)
Mezzo (Soho)
New Diamond (Chinatown)
New Hoo Wah (Chinatown)
Nico Central (Marylebone)
192 (Notting Hill Gate)
The Oriental (Mayfair)
Pharmacy (Notting Hill Gate)
Phoenicia (Kensington)
Quaglino's (St. James's)
Quality Chop House (Clerkenwell)
RSJ (South Bank)
Saga (Mayfair)
Searcy's at the Barbican (The City)
Simply Nico (Pimlico)
Sonny's (Barnes)
The Stafford (St. James's)
Star of India (South Kensington)
Suntory (St. James's)
Tamarind (Mayfair)
Ten (The City)
The Terrace (Kensington)
Union Café (Marylebone)
Veeraswamy (Piccadilly)
Wilton's (St. James's)
Zafferano (Belgravia)
Zen Central (Mayfair)
Zujuma's (Wimbledon)

RESTAURANTS BY CUISINE

There are so many cross-overs in modern cooking that it is difficult to pinpoint the inspiration behind many restaurants. However we have taken the predominant tastes to classify restaurants by their cuisine.

AMERICAN

Christopher's American Grill (Covent Garden)
Clarke's (Kensington)
Joe Allen (Covent Garden)

BELGIAN

Belgo Noord (Camden Town/Chalk Farm)

BRITISH

Dorchester Grill (Mayfair)
French House Dining Room (Soho)
Green's Restaurant and Oyster Bar (St. James's)
The Grill Room, The Savoy (Strand)
Leith's (Notting Hill Gate)
St. John, (Clerkenwell)
Simpson's-in-the-Strand (Strand)
Wiltons (St. James's)

BURMESE

Mandalay (Marylebone)

CHINESE

Aroma (Chinatown)
Fung Shing (Chinatown)
Ho Ho (Mayfair)
Hunan (Pimlico)
London Jade Garden (Chinatown)
Mandarin Kitchen (Bayswater)
Mr Kong (Chinatown)
New Diamond (Chinatown)
New Hoo Wah (Chinatown)
The Oriental (Mayfair)
Poons in the City (City)
Zen Central (Mayfair)
Zen Garden (Mayfair)

FRENCH

Aubergine (Chelsea)
Bath Place (Oxford)
Brasserie St. Quentin (Knightsbridge)
Café Royal Grill Room (Piccadilly)
Camden Brasserie (Camden Town/Chalk Farm)
Chavot (Fulham)
Chez Bruce (Wandsworth)
Chez Gérard at the Opera Terrace (Covent Garden)
Chez Max (Fulham)
Chez Moi (Holland Park)
Chez Nico at Ninety (Mayfair)
Chinon (Shepherd's Bush)
La Ciboulette (Chelsea)
Clos du Roy (Bath)
Criterion Marco Pierre White (Piccadilly)
The Dining Room (Kensington)
1837 (Mayfair)
L'Escargot (Soho)
Fat Duck (Bray-on-Thames, see Windsor)
Frederick's (Islington)
Le Gavroche (Mayfair)
Lettonie (Bath)
Lou Pescadou (South Kensington)
Le Manoir aux Quat'Saisons (Great Milton, see Oxford)
Mirabelle (Mayfair)
Nico Central (Marylebone)
Novelli EC1 (Clerkenwell)
Novelli W8 (Kensington)

The Oak Room (Piccadilly)
L'Oranger (St. James's)
L'Ortolan (Shinfield, see Windsor)
Le Palais du Jardin (Covent Garden)
Pied-à-Terre (Tottenham Court Road)
Le Pont de la Tour (Tower Bridge)
Mon Plaisir (Covent Garden)
Restaurant 101 (Knightsbridge)
The Ritz (St. James's)
The River Restaurant (Strand)
Les Saveurs de Jean-Christophe Novelli (Mayfair)
Simply Nico (Pimlico)
Simply Nico Chelsea (Chelsea)
Snows on the Green (Shepherd's Bush)
Le Soufflé (Mayfair)
Le Suquet (South Kensington)
La Tante Claire (Belgravia)
Turner's (South Kensington)
Waterside Inn (Bray-on-Thames, see Windsor)
Windows Restaurant (Mayfair)

FRENCH/THAI
The Birdcage (Tottenham Court Road)
Vong (Knightsbridge)

FRENCH/BRITISH
Claridge's (Mayfair)
The Connaught Restaurant and Grill (Mayfair)
Langan's Brasserie (Mayfair)

FRENCH/ORIENTAL
Saigon Times (City)

INDIAN
Bombay Brasserie (South Kensington)
Café Spice Namaste (Battersea)
Chutney Mary (Fulham)
Ma Goa (Richmond)
Rasa (Stoke Newington)
Red Fort (Soho)
Sabras (Willesden)
Star of India (South Kensington)
Tamarind (Mayfair)
Veeraswmay (Piccadilly)
Zujuma's (Wimbledon)

INTERNATIONAL
Atlantic Bar & Grill (Piccadilly)
The Avenue (St. James's)
Bali Sugar (Notting Hill Gate)
Browns (Oxford)
Café du Jardin (Covent Garden)
Coast (Mayfair)
The Collection (South Kensington)
Dakota (Notting Hill Gate)
Ebury Wine Bar (Victoria)
Euphorium (Islington)
First Floor (Notting Hill Gate)
Granita (Islington)
Gresslin's (Hampstead)
Interlude (Tottenham Court Road)
Livebait (Covent Garden)
Lola's (Islington)
MPW (The City)
Melton's (York)
L'Odéon (Piccadilly)
Odette's (Primrose Hill)
Old Parsonage (Oxford)
Pomegranates (Pimlico)
Searcy's at the Barbican (The City)
The Sugar Club (Soho)
The Tenth (Kensington)
Vong (Knightsbridge)

IRISH
Richard Corrigan at Lindsay House (Soho)

ITALIAN
L'Accento (Notting Hill Gate)
Al San Vincenzo (Marble Arch)
Assaggi at The Chepstow (Notting Hill Gate)
Bertorelli's (Tottenham Court Road)
Cibo (Kensington)
Daphne's (Chelsea)
Del Buongustaio (Putney)
Grissini (Knightsbridge)
Ibla (Marylebone)
Olivo (Belgravia)
Orsino (Notting Hill Gate)
Orso (Covent Garden)
Osteria Antica Bologna (Battersea)
Riva (Barnes)
River Café (Hammersmith)
San Lorenzo (Knightsbridge)
San Martino (South Kensington)
Sartoria (Piccadilly)
Stephano Cavallini at The Halkin (Knightsbridge)
Tentazioni (Tower Bridge)
Zafferano (Belgravia)

JAPANESE/SUSHI
Ginnan (Clerkenwell)
Inaho (Bayswater)
Matsuri (St. James's)
Miyama (Mayfair)
Saga (Mayfair)
Suntory (St. James's)
Tatsuso (The City)

JAPANESE/INTERNATIONAL
Nobu (Mayfair)

LEBANESE
Al Hamra (Mayfair)
Phoenicia (Kensington)

MEDITERRANEAN
Cantina del Ponte (Tower Bridge)
Fredericks (Islington)
Moro (Clerkenwell)
Nicole's (Mayfair)
Soho Soho (Soho)
Woz (Notting Hill Gate)

MODERN BRITISH
Alastair Little (Soho)
Alastair Little Lancaster Road (Notting Hill Gate)
Alfred (Bloomsbury)
Bank (Covent Garden)
Belair House (Dulwich)
Bibendum (South Kensington)
Bibendum Oyster Bar (South Kensington)
Bluebird (Chelsea)
Blue Print Café (Tower Bridge)
The Brackenbury (Shepherd's Bush)
Butlers Wharf Chop House (Tower Bridge)
The Canteen (Chelsea)
The Capital (Knightsbridge)
Le Caprice (St. James's)
Cherwell Boathouse (Oxford)
The Chiswick (Chiswick)
Circus (Soho)
City Rhodes (The City)
Clarke's (Kensington)
Delfina Studio Café (Bermondsey)
Euphorium (Islington)
The Feathers Hotel (Oxford)
The Fifth Floor Restaurant (Knightsbridge)
First Floor (Notting Hill Gate)
The Fish Restaurant at 190 Queensgate (South Kensington)
Gee's (Oxford)
Gordon Ramsey (Chelsea)
The Greenhouse (Mayfair)
Hilaire (South Kensington)
Hole in the Wall (Bath)
The Ivy (Covent Garden)
Kensington Place (Kensington)
Langan's Brasserie (Mayfair)
Launceston Place (Kensington)
Leith's Soho (Soho)
The Lexington (Soho)
Mezzo (Soho)
Middlethorpe Hall (York)
Moon & Sixpence (Bath)
Nicole's (Mayfair)
One Lawn Terrace (Blackheath)
192 (Notting Hill Gate)
19 Grape Lane (York)
The Orrery (Marylebone)
Le Petit Blanc (Oxford)
Pharmacy (Notting Hill Gate)
Royal Crescent Hotel (Bath)
Le Pont de la Tour (Tower Bridge)
Putney Bridge (Putney)
Quaglino's (St. James's)
Quality Chop House (Clerkenwell)
Queensbury Hotel (Bath)
Quo Vadis (Soho)
Ransome's Dock (Battersea)
The Room at the Halcyon (Holland Park)
RSJ (South Bank)
Snows on the Green (Shepherd's Bush)
Sonny's (Barnes)
The Square (Marylebone)
The Stafford (St. James's)
Stephen Bull (Marylebone)
Stephen Bull St. Martin's Lane (Covent Garden)
Stephen Bull Smithfield (Clerkenwell)
The Stepping Stone (Battersea)
Ten (The City)
The Terrace (Kensington)
Union Café (Marylebone)
Villandry (Marylebone)
Woods (Bath)
Zinc Bar & Grill (Piccadilly)

MOROCCAN
Agadir (Notting Hill Gate)
Pasha (South Kensington)

NORTH AFRICA
Momo (Piccadilly)

PAKISTANI
Salloos (Belgravia)

RUSSIAN/FRENCH
Caviar Kaspia (Mayfair)

SCOTTISH
Boisdale (Victoria)

SPANISH
Albero & Grana (Chelsea)
Cambio de Tercio (Knightsbridge)

SWEDISH

Anna's Place (Islington)

THAI

Bahn Thai (Soho)
Blue Elephant (Fulham)
Busabong Tree (Chelsea)
Esarn Kheaw (Shepherd's Bush)

RESTAURANTS BY NOTABLE FEATURES

FISH

Restaurants serving exclusively or predominantly fish.

Bibendum Oyster Bar (South Kensington)
The Fish Restaurant at 190 Queen's Gate (South Kensington)
Green's Restaurant & Oyster Bar (Piccadilly)
Lou Pescadou (South Kensington)
Restaurant One-0-One (Knightsbridge)
Le Suquet (South Kensington)

LATE-NIGHT

Last orders at or by 11pm during the week. Check when you book. Most restaurants close much earlier on Sunday.

L'Accento (Notting Hill Gate)
Alastair Little (Soho)
Assaggi at The Chepstow (Notting Hill Gate)
Alfred (Bloomsbury)
Bahn Thai (Soho)
Bank (Covent Garden)
Belgo (Camden Town/Chalk Farm)
Bertorelli's (Tottenham Court Road)
Bibendum (South Kensington)
The Birdcage (Tottenham Court Road)
Bluebird (Chelsea)
Blue Print Café (Tower Bridge)
Boisdale (Victoria)
Brasserie St. Quentin (Knightsbridge)
Busabong Tree (Chelsea)
Butlers Wharf Chop House (Tower Bridge)
Café Royal Grill Room (Piccadilly)
Café Spice Namaste (Battersea)
The Canteen (Chelsea)
The Capital (Knightsbridge)
Caviar Kaspia (Mayfair)
Chez Gérard at the Opera Terrace (Covent Garden)
Chez Max (Fulham)
Chez Moi (Holland Park)
Chinon (Shepherd's Bush)
The Chiswick (Chiswick)
Cibo (Kensington)
Daphne's (South Kensington)
Del Buongustaio (Putney)
Dorchester Grill (Mayfair)
Ebury Wine Bar (Victoria)
Esarn Kheaw (Shepherd's Bush)
L'Escargot (Soho)
First Floor (Notting Hill Gate)
The Fish Restaurant at 190 Queen's Gate (South Kensington)
French House Dining Room (Soho)
Fung Shing (Chinatown)
Le Gavroche (Mayfair)
The Greenhouse (Mayfair)
Inaho (Bayswater)
Interlude (Tottenham Court Road)
Leith's Soho (Soho)
Lou Pescadou (South Kensington)
Leith's (Notting Hill Gate)
Livebait (Covent Garden)
Lola's (Islington)
London Jade Garden (Chinatown)
Lou Pescadou (South Kensington)
Mandalay (Marylebone)
Mandarin Kitchen (Bayswater)
Momo (Piccadilly)
Mon Plaisir (Covent Garden)
New Hoo Wah (Chinatown)
Nico Central (Marylebone)
Novelli EC1 (Clerkenwell)
Novelli W8 (Kensington)
The Oak Room (Piccadilly)
Odette's (Primrose Hill)
Olivo (Belgravia)
Restaurant One-0-One (Knightsbridge)
L'Oranger (St. James's)
The Oriental (Mayfair)
Orsino (Notting Hill Gate)
Osteria Antica Bologna (Battersea)
Oxo Tower Restaurant Bar & Brasserie, (South Bank)
Pomegranates (Pimlico)
Putney Bridge (Putney)
Ransome's Dock (Battersea)
Red Fort (Soho)
The Ritz Restaurant (St. James's)
Riva (Barnes)
The River Restaurant (Strand)
RSJ (South Bank)
Salloos (Belgravia)
Simply Nico (Pimlico)
Simpson's-in-the-Strand (Strand)
Sonny's (Barnes)
Stephano Cavallini at The Halkin (Belgravia)
The Stepping Stone (Battersea)

The Sugar Club (Soho)
Tamarind (Mayfair)
Turner's (South Kensington)
Vong (Knightsbridge)
Windows Restaurant (Mayfair)
Zafferano (Belgravia)
Zen Central (Mayfair)
Zen Garden (Mayfair)
Zujuma's (Wimbledon)

LATE-LATE NIGHT

Restaurants with last orders at 11.30pm or later, though double-check. If it's a quiet night, the restaurant may close earlier than its stated time.

Agadir (Notting Hill Gate)
Albero & Grana (Chelsea)
Al Hamra (Mayfair)
Aroma (Chinatown)
Atlantic Bar & Grill (Piccadilly)
The Avenue (St. James's)
Belgo Noord (Camden Town/Chalk Farm)
Blue Elephant (Fulham)
Bombay Brasserie (South Kensington)
Café du Jardin (Covent Garden)
Camden Brasserie (Camden Town/Chalk Farm)
Le Caprice (St. James's)
Chez Gérard at the Opera Terrace (Covent Garden)
Christopher's American Grill (Covent Garden)
Chutney Mary (Fulham)
Circus (Soho)
The Collection (South Kensington)
Coast (Mayfair)
Criterion Marco Pierre White (Piccadilly)
The Fifth Floor (Knightsbridge)
Fredericks (Islington)
Hilaire (South Kensington)
The Ivy (Covent Garden)
Joe Allen (Covent Garden)
Kensington Place (Kensington)
Langan's Brasserie (Mayfair)
Launceston Place (Kensington)
Mezzo (Soho)
Mirabelle (Mayfair)
Mr Kong (Chinatown)
New Diamond (Chinatown)
L'Odéon (Piccadilly)
192 (Notting Hill Gate)
Orso (Covent Garden)
Le Palais du Jardin (Covent Garden)
Pasha (South Kensington)
Phoenicia (Kensington)
Le Pont de la Tour (Tower Bridge)
Quaglino's (St. James's)
Quality Chop House (Clerkenwell)
Quo Vadis (Soho)
St. John (Clerkenwell)
San Martino (South Kensington)
Soho Soho (Soho)
Star of India (South Kensington)
Stephen Bull St. Martin's Lane (Covent Garden)
Stephen Bull Smithfield (Clerkenwell)
Le Suquet (South Kensington)
Tentazioni (Tower Bridge)
Veeraswamy (Piccadilly)
Windows Restaurant (Mayfair)
Zinc Bar & Grill (Piccadilly)

VEGETARIAN

Most restaurants have one or two dishes for appetisers and main courses. We have listed here only restaurants serving a substantial number of vegetarian dishes or with a separate vegetarian menu.

Al Hamra (Mayfair)
The Blue Elephant (Fulham)
Bombay Brasserie (South Kensington)
Ma Goa (Richmond)
The Room at the Halcyon (Holland Park)
Sabras (Willesden)
Star of India (South Kensington)

OPEN ON A SUNDAY

(L) means lunch only, (D) means dinner only.

L'Accento (Notting Hill Gate)
Agadir (Notting Hill Gate)
Al Hamra (Mayfair)
Albero & Grana (Chelsea)
Aroma (Chinatown)
Assaggi at The Chepstow (D) (Notting Hill Gate)
Atlantic Bar & Grill (D) (Piccadilly)
The Avenue (St. James's)
Bahn Thai (D) (Soho)
Bali Sugar (Notting Hill Gate)
Bank (Covent Garden)
Belair House (L) (Dulwich)
Belgo (Camden Town/Chalk Farm)
Bibendum (South Kensington)
Bibendum Oyster Bar (South Kensington)
The Birdcage (Tottenham Court Road)
Bluebird (Chelsea)
Blue Elephant (Fulham)
Blue Print Café (L) (Tower Bridge)
Bombay Brasserie (South Kensington)
The Brackenbury (L) (Shepherd's Bush)
Brasserie St. Quentin (Knightsbridge)
Busabong Tree (L) (Chelsea)
Butlers Wharf Chop House (L) (Tower

Bridge)
Café Spice Namaste (Battersea)
Café du Jardin (Covent Garden)
Cambio de Tercio (Knightsbridge)
Camden Brasserie (Camden Town/Chalk Farm)
The Canteen (L) (Chelsea)
Cantina del Ponte (Tower Bridge)
The Capital (Knightsbridge)
Le Caprice (St. James's)
Chez Bruce (L) (Wandsworth)
Chez Gérard at The Opera Terrace (Covent Garden)
The Chiswick (L) (Chiswick)
Christopher's American Grill (L) (Covent Garden)
Chutney Mary (Fulham)
Cibo (L) (Kensington)
La Ciboulette (L) (Chelsea)
Circus (Soho)
Claridge's (Mayfair)
Coast (D) (Mayfair)
The Connaught Restaurant and Grill (Mayfair)
Criterion Marco Pierre White (Piccadilly)
Dakota (Notting Hill Gate)
Daphne's (South Kensington)
Del Buongustaio (Putney)
Dorchester Grill (Mayfair)
Ebury Wine Bar (Victoria)
Esarn Kheaw (D) (Shepherd's Bush)
The Fifth Floor (L) (Knightsbridge)
First Floor (Notting Hill Gate)
The Fish Restaurant at 190 Queen's Gate (South Kensington)
Fung Shing (Chinatown)
Granita (Islington)
The Greenhouse (Mayfair)
Green's Restaurant and Oyster Bar (L) (St. James's)
Gresslin's (L) (Hampstead)
Grissini (L) (Knightsbridge)
Ibla (L) (Marylebone)
The Ivy (Covent Garden)
Joe Allen (Covent Garden)
Kensington Place (Kensington)
Launceston Place (L) (Kensington)
Lola's (L) (Islington)
London Jade Garden (Chinatown)
Lou Pescadou (South Kensington)
Mandarin Kitchen (Bayswater)
Ma Goa (Richmond)
Mezzo (Soho)
Mirabelle (Mayfair)
Mr Kong (Chinatown)
Miyama (D) (Mayfair)
New Diamond (Chinatown)
New Hoo Wah (Chinatown)
Novelli W8 (Kensington)
Olivo (D) (Belgravia)
One Lawn Terrace (Blackheath)
Orrery (Marylebone)
192 (Notting Hill Gate)
Orso (Covent Garden)
Orsino (Notting Hill Gate)
Osteria Antica Bologna (Battersea)
Oxo Tower Restaurant, Bar & Brasserie (South Bank)
Le Palais du Jardin (Covent Garden)
Phoenicia (Kensington)
Le Pont de la Tour (Tower Bridge)
Putney Bridge (Putney)
Quaglino's (St. James's)
Quality Chop House (D) (Clerkenwell)
Quo Vadis (D) (Soho)
Ransome's Dock (L) (Battersea)
Rasa (Stoke Newington)
Red Fort (Soho)
Restaurant One-O-One (Knightsbridge)
The Ritz Restaurant (St. James's)
Riva (Barnes)
River Café (L) (Hammersmith)
The River Restaurant (Strand)
The Room at the Halcyon (Holland Park)
Sabras (D) (Willesden)
San Martino (South Kensington)
Sartoria (L) (Piccadilly)
Searcy's at the Barbican (City)
Simply Nico Chelsea (L) (Chelsea)
Simpson's-in-the-Strand (Strand)
Snows on the Green (L) (Shepherd's Bush)
Soho Soho (Soho)
Sonny's (L) (Barnes)
The Square (D) (Mayfair)
The Stafford (D) (St. James's)
Star of India (South Kensington)
Stephano Cavallini at The Halkin (D) (Belgravia)
The Stepping Stone (L) (Battersea)
The Sugar Club (Soho)
Le Suquet (South Kensington)
Tamarind (Mayfair)
The Tenth (Kensington)
The Terrace (L) (Kensington)
Turner's (South Kensington)
Veeraswamy (Piccadilly)
Vong (D) (Knightsbridge)
Wiltons (St. James's)
Woz (L) (Notting Hill Gate)
Zen Central (Mayfair)
Zen Garden (Mayfair)
Zinc Bar & Grill (D) (Piccadilly)
Zujuma's (Wimbledon)

RESTAURANTS BY PRICE

Prices for a three-course meal for one with coffee and service, but no beverages.

UNDER £25

L'Accento (Notting Hill Gate)
Agadir (Notting Hill Gate)
Alfred (Bloomsbury)
Anna's Place (Islington)
Aroma (Chinatown)
The Brackenbury (Shepherd's Bush)
The Busabong Tree (Chelsea)
Café du Jardin (Covent Garden)
Café Spice Namaste (Battersea)
Camden Brasserie (Camden Town/Chalk Farm)
Chez Gérard at The Opera Terrace (Covent Garden)
Chinon (Shepherd's Bush)
The Chiswick (Chiswick)
Delfina Studio Café (Bermondsey)
Ebury Wine Bar (Victoria)
Esarn Kheaw (Shepherd's Bush)
First Floor (Notting Hill Gate)
The French House Dining Room (Soho)
Fung Shing (Chinatown)
Ginnan (Clerkenwell)
Gresslin's (Hampstead)
Ho Ho (Mayfair)
Hunan (Pimlico)
Ibla (Marylebone)
Inaho (Bayswater)
Joe Allen (Covent Garden)
London Jade Garden (Chinatown)
Ma Goa (Richmond)
Mandalay (Marylebone)
Mon Plaisir (Covent Garden)
Moro (Clerkenwell)
Mr Kong (Chinatown)
New Diamond (Chinatown)
New Hoo Wah (Chinatown)
192 (Notting Hill Gate)
Osteria Antica Bologna (Battersea)
Poons in the City (The City)
Rasa (Stoke Newington)
RSJ (South Bank)
St. John (Clerkenwell)
Sabras (Willesden)
Saigon Times (The City)
Simply Nico Chelsea (Chelsea)
Stephen Bull Smithfield (Clerkenwell)
The Sugar Club (Notting Hill Gate)
Veeraswamy (Piccadilly)
Woz (Notting Hill Gate)
Zinc Bar & Grill (Piccadilly)

BETWEEN £25 & £35

Al Hamra (Mayfair)
Al San Vincenzo (Marble Arch)
Alastair Little (Soho)
Alastair Little, Lancaster Road (Notting Hill Gate)
Albero & Grana (Chelsea)
Assaggi at The Chepstow (Notting Hill Gate)
Atlantic Bar & Grill (Piccadilly)
Bahn Thai (Soho)
Bali Sugar (Notting Hill Gate)
Bank (Covent Garden)
Belair House (Dulwich)
Belgo Noord (Camden Town/Chalk Farm)
Bertorelli's (Tottenham Court Rd)
Bibendum Oyster Bar (South Kensington)
Bluebird (Chelsea)
The Birdcage (Tottenham Court Rd)
Blue Print Café (Tower Bridge)
Bombay Brasserie (South Kensington)
Brasserie St. Quentin (Knightsbridge)
Cambio de Tercio (Knightsbridge)
Cantina del Ponte (Tower Bridge)
Le Caprice (St. James's)
Chez Bruce (Wandsworth)
Chez Max (Fulham)
Chez Moi (Holland Park)
Chinon (Shepherd's Bush)
Christopher's American Grill (Covent Garden)
Chutney Mary (Fulham)
Cibo (Kensington)
La Ciboulette (Chelsea)
Circus (Soho)
City Rhodes (The City)
Coast (Mayfair)
The Collection (South Kensington)
Criterion Marco Pierre White (Piccadilly)
Dakota (Notting Hill Gate)
Daphne's (Notting Hill Gate)
Del Buongustaio (Putney)
L'Escargot (Soho)
Euphorium (Islington)
The Fish Restaurant at 190 Queen's Gate (South Kensington)
Frederick's (Islington)
Granita (Islington)
Green's Restaurant and Oyster Bar (St. James's)
Grissini (Knightsbridge)
Hilaire (South Kensington)
Interlude (Tottenham Court Rd)
The Ivy (Covent Garden)
Kensington Place (Kensington)
Launceston Place (Kensington)
Leith's Soho (Soho)
Livebait (Covent Garden)
Lola's (Islington)
Lou Pescadou (South Kensington)

MPW (The City)
Mandarin Kitchen (Bayswater)
Matsuri (St. James's)
Mirabelle (Mayfair)
Miyama (Mayfair)
Momo (Piccadilly)
Nico Central (Marylebone)
Nicole's (Mayfair)
Novelli EC1 (Clerkenwell)
Novelli W8 (Kensington)
L'Odéon (Piccadilly)
Odette's (Primrose Hill)
Olivo (Belgravia)
One Lawn Terrace (Blackheath)
Orsino (Notting Hill Gate)
Orso (Covent Garden)
Le Palais du Jardin (Covent Garden)
Pasha (South Kensington)
Pharmacy (Notting Hill Gate)
Phoenicia (Kensington)
Pomegranates (Pimlico)
Putney Bridge (Putney)
Quality Chop House (Clerkenwell)
Quaglino's (St. James's)
Ransome's Dock (Battersea)
Red Fort (Soho)
Richard Corrigan at Lindsay House (Soho)
Riva (Barnes)
Saga (Mayfair)
Salloos (Belgravia)
San Martino (South Kensington)
Sartoria (Piccadilly)
Searcy's at the Barbican (The City)
Simply Nico (Pimlico)
Simpson's-in-the-Strand (Strand)
Snow's on the Green (Shepherd's Bush)
Soho Soho (Soho)
Sonny's (Barnes)
The Stafford (St. James's)
Star of India (South Kensington)
Stephen Bull St. Martin's Lane (Covent Garden)
The Stepping Stone (Battersea)
Sugar Club (Notting Hill Gate)
Le Suquet (South Kensington)
Tatsuso (The City)
Ten (The City)
Tentazioni (Tower Bridge)
The Terrace (Kensington)
Turner's (South Kensington)
Union Cafe (Marylebone)
Villandry (Marylebone)
Zafferano (Belgravia)

£35-£50

The Avenue (St. James's)
Blue Elephant (Fulham)
Boisdale (Victoria)
Butlers Wharf Chop House (Tower Bridge)
The Canteen (Chelsea)
Caviar Kaspia (Mayfair)
Chavot (Fulham)
Clarke's (Kensington)
The Dining Room (Kensington)
Dorchester Grill (Mayfair)
The Fifth Floor (Knightsbridge)
The Greenhouse (Mayfair)
The Grill Room (Strand)
Langan's Brasserie (Mayfair)
Leith's (Notting Hill Gate)
Mezzo (Soho)
Nobu (Mayfair)
L'Oranger (St. James's)
The Oriental (Mayfair)
Quo Vadis (Soho)
The Room at The Halcyon (Holland Park)
The Square (Mayfair)
Stefano Cavallini at The Halkin (Belgravia)
Suntory (St. James's)
Tamarind (Mayfair)
Tatsuso (The City)
Tatsuso Teppan Room (The City)
The Tenth (Kensington)
Vong (Knightsbridge)
Wilton's (St. James's)
Windows Roof Restaurant (Mayfair)
Zen Central (Mayfair)
Zen Garden (Mayfair)

ABOVE £50

Bibendum (South Kensington)
Café Royal Grill Room (Piccadilly)
The Capital (Knightsbridge)
Claridge's (Mayfair)
The Connaught (Mayfair)
1837 (Mayfair)
Gordon Ramsey (Chelsea)
Le Gavroche (Mayfair)
Nico at Ninety (Mayfair)
The Oak Room (Piccadilly)
The Orrerry (Marylebone)
Le Pont de la Tour (Tower Bridge)
The Ritz (St. James's)
River Café (Hammersmith)
The River Restaurant (Strand)
Les Saveurs de Jean-Christophe Novelli (Mayfair)
Le Soufflé (Mayfair)
La Tante Claire (Belgravia)

BARNES

Riva

ITALIAN 14/20

169 CHURCH RD, SW13, 0181-748 0434
Lunch Sun.-Fri., Dinner daily. ££ BR: Barnes Bridge.

The neighbourhood Italian restaurant from heaven. Intimate, friendly and expertly overseen by owner Andrea Riva. Pale decor and a sea-grass carpet lend it a homey air. The cuisine is defiantly north Italian, more specifically Lombardy and the Adriatic coast. Fish features strongly in the cooking of chef Francesco Zanchetta squid, grilled and served with fresh herbs, sea bass baked in a 'bag', or pasta with clams, mussels and bottarga (the salted and dried roe of tuna or grey mullet). The simplicity of the menu's terminology hides a sure hand in the kitchen. Antipasto for two is a delicate feast of salumi, while rabbit might come with spätzli, calf's liver with polenta and a rich mushroom ragoût. Dishes alternate from the rustic charms of quail with sausages, cabbage and lentils to the more delicate pigeon roasted and served with mash and a gravy rich in onions and raisins. Desserts are on a par and include unusual items like sweet milk gnocchi. Wines are all Italian, and favour the north. If you like grappa, feast your eyes on this haul.

Sonny's

MODERN BRITISH 13/20

94 CHURCH RD, SW13, 0181-748 0393,
FAX 0181 748 2698
Lunch daily, Dinner Mon.-Sat. ££
BR: Barnes Bridge.

Sonny's, under the capable leadership of Rebecca Mascarenhas, continues to please both locals and those from further afield. Chefs have come and go, with slight dips in consistency, but the cooking now, under Leigh Diggins, combines intelligent use of modish ingredients with appropriate and sensible interpretation. Tomato and oregano soup is given an extra boost with a confit of red onions; seared scallops come with vanilla risotto which works well as a counter-taste. Equally as well executed are dishes like the light feuilleté of steamed halibut with orange and olive oil sauce, and a delicious ballotine of rabbit with sage pasta and trompette mushrooms. Desserts continue in similar vein, as in a lemon grass crème brûlée with a basil tuile, though the steamed date and ginger pudding with vanilla ice cream was a lesson in traditional British cooking. The room, long and narrow and decorated in white, is slightly stark but full of odd artefacts. Service is friendly, the wine list short but reasonable. Sonny's should continue to draw in the punters. Set lunch £12.

BATTERSEA

Café Spice Namaste

INDIAN 14/20

247 LAVENDER HILL, SW11, 0171-738 1717,
FAX 0171-738 1666
Lunch Sat. & Sun., Dinner daily. £
BR: Clapham Junction.

Cyrus Todiwala cooks in his original City kitchen and on television, and the absence of the master's touch here in this, his second restaurant, occasionally shows in slightly less vivid flavours. The same applies to the South Indian decor; or possibly we are now used to this multi-coloured, near psychedelic style. The menu ranges from North India, Gwalior, Kashmir and the Punjab to Madras, even Thailand, but Parsee and Goanese dishes predominate. Tandooris include venison, monkfish, Barbary duck, Goanese chicken piri-piri, and galinha cafreal. Other rare ingredients are queen scallops, tilapia, mussels and beef in Goanese chilli carne de vaca. Spicing is more subtle than fiery, but lively homemade chutneys and pickles add hotness as required. Among desserts, note warm carrot halva, kulfis, and the house speciality Parsee apricot toffee ice-cream. There is a well-chosen wine list and a leaflet 'Wines & Spice' with useful suggestions about complementing Indian food. Set 2-course lunch, & 6pm-8pm Thurs.-Sun. £8.50, 3 courses £10. **Also at 16 Prescot Street, E1, 0171-488 9242, Fax 0171-488 9339.**

Osteria Antica Bologna

ITALIAN 12/20

23 NORTHCOTE RD, SW11, 0171-978 4771

Lunch & Dinner daily. £ BR: Clapham Junction.

The Osteria has begun casting its culinary net wider of late than co-proprietor Aurelio Spagnuolo's native Bologna. Classic Roman dishes now crop up; they may not quite rise to the extravagances of the Satyricon, but are possessed of a certain flair nonetheless. The feasting takes place in a wood-beamed cocoon of a room, and may begin with a robust and plentiful soup incorporating hot Bolognese sausage, before proceeding to grills and roasts of impeccable Italian authenticity. Lamb is a favoured main-course meat, perhaps slow-cooked with barley and prunes, or fashioned into meatballs with capers and Parmesan that are simmered in red wine. Tiramisù is a stalwart on dessert menus of all ethnic origins these days, but the version here is gutsier than most, not stinting on either alcohol or caffeine. Homely service and a thoughtfully composed list of modern Italian wines add to the allure. Set lunch £7.50.

Ransome's Dock

MODERN BRITISH 14/20

35 PARKGATE RD, SW11,
0171-223 1611/924 2462, FAX 0171-924 2614

Lunch daily, Dinner Mon.-Sat. ££. U: None nearby.

A

Chef Martin Lam scouts the world for inspiration, but brings to the execution of his dishes an assured touch and intelligent approach. His confidence and skill make what at first seems like an eclectic menu remarkably solid and comforting. While sirloin steak comes simply with a red wine jus, a fillet of brill is served on a pea, rocket and broad bean risotto. Thai spicing figures alongside confident use of chilli, while credited classics like Elizabeth David's lamb and aubergine stew comfort in just the right way. Desserts follow a classic theme, prune and armagnac soufflé being a regular and successful example. Many other restaurants would do well to look at Mr Lam's wine list and his mark-ups. He brings an intelligence which encourages experimentation. The room is a bright blue, making up for the lack of river frontage, the dock in the title being a somwhat grim inlet to one side. Windows make for bright dining in the summer, but can be slightly chilly in the winter. Lunch is superb value, and at weekends the brunch theme figures strongly. Set lunch is priced at £11.50.

Dining and Dancing

Tripping the light fantastic in London's restaurants has always been popular. The best evenings are, naturally, at the end of the week and some restaurants restrict their dinner dances to those times. Telephone for information, and it is best to book.

Claridges, Brook St, W1, 0171-629 8860.

The Conservatory, The Lanesborough, Hyde Park Corner, SW1, 0171-259 5599.

Diva, 43 Thurloe St, SW7, 0171-584 2000.

The Landmark London, 222 Marylebone Rd, NW1, 0171-631 8000.

Memories Restaurant, Langham Hilton, 1 Portland Pl, W1, 0171-636 1000.

The Savoy Hotel, Strand, WC2, 0171-836 4343.

Windows Restaurant, London Hilton on Park Lane, W1, 0171-493 8000.

The Stepping Stone

MODERN BRITISH 14/20

123 QUEENSTOWN RD, SW8, 0171-622 0555, FAX 0171-622 4230

Lunch Sun.-Fri., Dinner Mon.-Sat. ££. U: None nearby.

A

While this restaurant has plenty of visitors from the other side of the river, it is also a prime example of a neighbourhood restaurant. Indeed, it's a favourite with all the locals who have gentrified Battersea, and who enjoy the

Stepping Stone as a West End equivalent on their own doorstep. Decor is 'user-friendly minimalism,' with a streamlined but inviting look which relies principally on contrasting colours like bright blue and white, rather than 'features'. The walls are hung with occasional artworks for sale; the friendly service is also professional and astute. Dishes are a pleasant surprise when they arrive, being more interesting than they sound on the menu, with clear, harmonising flavours and a range of textures. Crab salad comes with deliciously prepared mixed leaves and herbs, while roast chicken, chorizo and potato rösti means succulent chicken, spicy chorizo and accompanying greenery that is an attraction in its own right, not a mere accessory. Cheeses from Neal's Yard make no secret of their distinguished provenance, though dairy products are equally superlative when prepared on the premises—try the home-made ice creams. Set lunch £10.75.

BAYSWATER

Inaho

JAPANESE/SUSHI 13/20

4 HEREFORD RD, W2, 0171-221 8495

Lunch Mon.-Fri., Dinner Mon.-Sat. £ U: Bayswater.

Friendly, small restaurant with a homely decor (there's even a working cuckoo clock which catches newcomers by surprise), and a loyal local clientele who are rarely disappointed in a menu which ranges from appetisers of the likes of yakitori to soba and udon noodles, from edamame lightly salted green soy beans to tempura and braised tuna. There are specials written on wooden notice boards supplementing the main menu, but all the dishes come up to scratch here. If there's anything that confuses or intrigues you can always ask the owner's advice; Mr Nakamura now serves instead of cooking, but the kitchen remains as good as before. Set lunches at £8 or £10 for six dishes. Set dinners £20 and £22.

Mandarin Kitchen

CHINESE 15/20

14-16 QUEENSWAY, W2, 0171-727 9012

Open Lunch & Dinner daily. ££ U: Queensway.

The name is deceptive for this kitchen's cooking is almost exclusively Cantonese. The emphasis is on seafood which many consider the best in London—there are six ways with Scottish lobster, four with crab. Of these, pot of crab, with bean noodles and dry shrimps in chilli sauce, exemplifies the most refined of peasant dishes. Of eight fish usually offered, carp is an oriental favourite, but few can resist almost overwhelmingly rich eel with pork and straw mushrooms. Meat is not neglected, and veal appears in several dishes. Booking is essential, but does not guarantee the table being ready. While efficient, service is not notably friendly, and may even be brusque for small groups; but they react positively to those prepared to investigate the specialities. Neither crowded, closely spaced tables, nor inelegant decor deter Chinese gourmets and their families, and occidental bons viveurs who appreciate cuisine equalled only by Chinatown's best. Set meal £10.

BELGRAVIA

Olivo

ITALIAN 12/20

21 ECCLESTON ST, SW1, 0171-730 2505, FAX 0171-824 8190

Lunch Mon.-Fri., Dinner daily. ££ U: Victoria.

At this predominantly Sardinian restaurant you'll find a simple, warm blue-and-yellow decor, a superb selection of Sardinian wines, friendly service, and a menu which often hits the spot. One dish which never fails is the classic Sardinian bottarga, where dried red mullet roe is grated over a bowl of spaghetti. It's pungent and fishy—a taste, which if you haven't tried before, grows on you. Other specialities might include smoked pork neck or another regular dish, the soup of clams and couscous. More mainstream Italian dishes also make an appearance for those whose tastes are a little milder. Service is friendly and helpful, the atmosphere relaxed. Olivo is a bright spot in this mostly dull area around Victoria. Set lunches £14 and £16.

Salloos

PAKISTANI 12/20

62-64 KINNERTON ST, SW1, 0171-235 6845, FAX 0171-259 5703

Lunch & Dinner Mon.-Sat. ££ U: Knightsbridge.

There were few luxurious 'Indian' restaurants when Salloos opened over 20 years ago;

even fewer were Pakistani. Neither chef nor ownership has changed since, although a new generation of the Salahuddin (Saloo) family now warmly welcomes diners. Only in service does this fine restaurant sometimes fail to live up to its otherwise high standards, and good, if expensive, wines may not receive the respect they deserve. The food differs from Indian in that curries are secondary to tandoori roasts, and sizzling dishes served on an iron karahi. Vegetable dishes are few, the emphasis is on prawns, chicken, lamb all Halal. Examples of fine ingredients are tandoori-marinated lamb chops (off the bone); and jheenga masala, prawns with what the menu accurately calls a 'subtly spiced sauce'. Rice is cooked in aromatic stock; tandoori breads are light and tasty. Set lunch £16.

Stephano Cavallini at The Halkin

ITALIAN 15/20

HALKIN ST, SW1, 0171-333 1000,
FAX 0171-333 1100
Lunch Mon.-Fri., Dinner daily. £££
U: Hyde Park Corner.

A ☎

While the rest of the world seems hell-bent on rustic Italian food, Stefano Cavallini concentrates on refined Italian cuisine. There is little frippery here however, though certainly elaboration—but always with a purpose: i.e. the richness of foie gras offset by the exquisite earthiness of Castelluccio lentils; perfectly grilled scallops with spinach, olive oil and a generous shaving of black truffles. Dishes can tend towards the complex as in mashed cod with potatoes and olive oil, or roasted quail with radicchio and broccoli sauce, but are balanced by more straightforward offerings like langoustines with a ragoût or pulses for example. Desserts tend toward the classic. The room is gloriously minimalist, with generous spacing between the tables and views on to a slim 'garden'. The wine list majors on Italy and France and is very fine indeed. Service is earnest and while à la carte prices may seem steep, service is included. The set 5-course dinner is £45. The fixed-price lunch menu at £25 makes for some welcome relief.

Zafferano

ITALIAN 13/20

15 LOWNDES ST, SW1, 0171-235 5800,
FAX 0171-325 1971
Lunch & Dinner Mon.-Sat. ££
U: Knightsbridge.

Simple, straight-forward Italian cooking at its best in a corner of London renowned more for expense than bargains. Giorgio Locatelli remains loyal to his origins, scanning the regions of Italy for what he likes best, but also taking in a little of France where he worked for some time. Decoration is minimal—bare tiles on the floor and cream or brick walls depending on which of the two street-level rooms you sit in. But prices are very reasonable (and fixed depending on the number of courses eaten at both lunch and dinner) and have remained that way, a big attraction even for the well-heeled of Belgravia. The menu concentrates on prime ingredients and minimal interference: beef carpaccio with a drizzling of truffle oil, a salad of octopus and potatoes, pasta with broad beans and rocket, the latter dressed with butter, a welcome reminder that not everything in Italy is dressed with olive oil. Fish is deftly handled: cod is roasted and served with lentils; John Dory comes with accompanying potatoes and olives; salmon, served with nothing more than its juices and spinach is a case of serene simplicity. Offal is well handled: kidneys with artichokes and lentils had all the earthiness required. Desserts follow the modern Italian theme: tiramisù, amaretto ice cream and are well executed. Drink Champagne from France, but everything else, including some well-aged reds, is from Italy. Service has attitude, but not always of the correct kind. Set lunch £16.50-£19.50, Set dinner £21.50-£28.50.

BERMONDSEY

Delfina Studio Café

MODERN BRITISH 13/20

50 BERMONDSEY ST, SE1, 0171-357 0244,
FAX 0171-357 9157
Lunch Mon.-Fri. £ U: London Bridge.

A ☎

Bermondsey is a restaurant desert; most people seeking a decent lunch head for the clutch of Conran restaurants at nearby Butlers Wharf. But the Delfina, only open at lunch times, is a brilliant alternative for those in the know. The interior of this former chocolate factory looks like a bare, white-painted art gallery—because that's exactly what it has become. The gallery restaurant serves surprisingly good food from a short menu which changes frequently. Starters might include roasted tomato and cumin-spiked soup, smoked sardines and houmous with green olive tapenade, or char-grilled prawns on avocado—this latter dish was artfully presented, a feast for the eyes as well as the palate. Main courses usually play safe with the likes of char-grilled red snapper, but sometimes other fare feels the searing heat of the char-grill—perhaps tuna steak or scallops. Portion sizes tend to be generous even with the desserts—lime ice cream sandwiched in frozen chocolate sheets was too filling to finish.

BLACKHEATH

One Lawn Terrace

MODERN BRITISH 14/20

BLACKHEATH VILLAGE, SE3, 0181-355 1110

Lunch & Dinner daily. ££ BR: Blackheath.

Blackheath used to be a place to walk the dog or fly a kite, but having to eat there as well was an inevitable compromise. Fortunately, One Lawn Terrace has actually provided an incentive to go to Blackheath, and leave the dog or kite at home. Ironically, it was while walking their dogs that the respective owners of One Lawn Terrace first met on Blackheath. The restaurant's striking interiors exemplify 'post-industrial chic,' capitalising on the imposing scale and the existing features (such as exposed beams and pipes) of this former printing works. In fact, the space extends to 4,400 sq ft, providing plenty of room for a separate bar and large dining area with a mezzanine gallery in the centre. The sense of space always works in the restaurant's favour, and you won't be subjected to diner's agoraphobia. Indeed, plenty of white wall space features retro-modern art. International influences infuse the food with clarity and balance rather than having the world collide on your plate. Subtle and elegant flavours are handled as skilfully as their bold and robust counterparts, with simple but thoughtful presentation adding great visual appeal. Triumphs include the likes of sashimi of tuna, salmon, tempura of tiger prawns, shredded carrots and mouli; mustard-crusted calf's liver, crispy polenta and Dolcelatte slab, Italian spinach and pancetta; pistachio nut and bay-leaf crème brûée. Set lunch £12.95, and £16.50.

BLOOMSBURY

Alfred

MODERN BRITISH 12/20

245 SHAFTESBURY AVE, WC2, 0171-240 2566, FAX 0171-497 0672

Lunch and Dinner Mon.-Sat. £

U: Tottenham Court Rd.

Bare and basic describes both the decor and the food, but this is all to the good in this unashamedly neo-British establishment sitting on a tree-covered traffic island at the 'wrong' end of Oxford Street. Formica-topped tables and straightforward café-style cutlery introduces a menu that falls somwhere between bistro and pub: ham, potato salad, mixed leaves and chutney; calf's liver with bubble and squeak, or roast belly of pork with root vegetables and mash. Side salads come well dressed and with a decent assortment of leaves; starters are somewhat minimalist—mussels perhaps, or straightforward carrot-and-coriander soup. Puds follow the bread-and-butter pudding route. The drinks list is impressive and refreshing, a host of British microbeers plus Guinness along with lemonade and cider before you even get to the wines.

CAMDEN TOWN/CHALK FARM

Belgo Noord

BELGIAN 11/20

72 CHALK FARM RD, NW1, 0171-267 0718, FAX 0171-267 7508

Lunch & Dinner daily. ££

U: Chalk Farm.

Belgo continues to pack in the punters, and so it should. The decor is pretty wild—concrete walls carved with various names and sayings, twisted stainless steel pipes, wooden tables and chairs, and fast, friendly and furious service from waiters dressed as monks. Most people come here for the mussels and frites for which the two Belgos have become famous. Mussels come as platters, served every which way and a few more—meunière, à l'escargot, pizza, Ardennaises, or in kilo pots. Marinières, and Provençales are recognisable, but when did you last try them done in coconut cream and lemon grass (Congo), or in Leffe beer and bacon (Blonde/Bacon)? Frites and mayo accompany. If the quality of the mussels occasionally leaves something to be desired, go for other Belgian specialities—wild boar sausages with Belgian mash and sharp forest fruits; Belgian chicken with a vegetable julienne cooked in a lemon, black pepper and cream sauce. The desserts will deliciously sink you. The beer list is a dream, but beware, some of the Trappist-brewed varieties are unbelievably strong. Finish with a sharp schnapps. When the original Belgo opened, it was an instant but by no means obvious success. Now the company is part of Pizza Express and has bought Mogens Tholstrup's three restaurants, Daphne's, The Collection and Pasha. **Also Belgo Centraal, 50 Earlham St, WC2, 0171-813 2233.**

Camden Brasserie

FRENCH 11/20

216 CAMDEN HIGH ST, NW1, 0171-482 2114

Open Lunch & Dinner daily. £

U: Camden Town.

The Camden Brasserie has been here since the early days of Camden Market which is now such a great weekend draw, but it remains (except at Saturday and Sunday lunch), the archetypal local restaurant. It's a well-executed formula: starters of merguez sausage served with coriander and cumin yoghurt; seared tuna tataki on rocket with a sesame-soy dressing; main dishes of grilled salmon on new potatoes treated with watercress and dill mustard; wild boar sausages with potato mash and onion marmalade—fashionable enough to keep the cleintele happy. Charcoal grilling is their forte and used on fresh ingredients it's a winner. The short, well-chosen wine list runs from house wine at £9.50 to a Premier Cru Rully at £19. And the owners are still there in the evenings which is all to the good.

CHELSEA

Albero & Grana

SPANISH 13/20

CHELSEA CLOISTERS, 89 SLOANE AVE, SW3, 0171-225 1048, FAX 0171-581 3259

Lunch & Dinner daily. ££ Tapas bar open daily.

U: South Kensington.

A

The interior has been toned down somewhat and money invested in the kitchen so paella is now offered, either for one or more if a group so wishes. The bright L-shaped room is inviting and airy. Gone too, is the somewhat rigid application of the bar and tapas menu versus the main dining menu. Which is all to the good. Angel Garcia's excellent Spanish food raises this often misunderstood cuisine to new heights. Tapas are an integral part of the bar, but can also start a meal in the slightly raised dining room. Lasagne of black pudding is a signature dish and rightly so, the spicy pudding working well in this format. Dishes can surprise in presentation, over-elaborate refinement being the culprit, so it is as well to seek advice, though this is not necessary for the Segovian-style suckling pig, vibrant salads and much sea food. Spanish wines deserve greater attention on the list and the presentation of sherry is lamentable. Desserts rightly slip over the border into France. The bar can get crowded towards the weekend.

Aubergine

MODERN BRITISH NO RATING

68 ROYAL HOSPITAL RD, SW3

Lunch Mon.-Fri, Dinner Mon.-Sat. ££££

U: Sloane Square.

A

As we go to press, Gordon Ramsay is opening in Pierre Koffman's former La Tante Claire, calling the new restaurant Gordon Ramsay. Plans for the former Aubergine have not been finalized.

Bluebird Restaurant

MODERN BRITISH 12/20

350 KING'S RD, SW3, 0171-559 1000,
FAX 0171-559 1111
Lunch & Dinner daily. ££
U: Sloane Sq.

The increasing Conran-isation of London also includes a growing choice of highly individual venues in ever-more postal codes. Far more than just a restaurant, Bluebird is a gastro-complex domiciled within an inspired refurbishment of what was originally one of London's grandest garages (during the 1920s). The food hall is fully comprehensive, being stocked with normalities as well as luxuries, while the café has great-value staples, such as grilled vegetables on focaccia. Located on the first floor, the restaurant has a bar area, which is just that, an area within the restaurant rather than thriving as an independent entity—and this doesn't help in raising anticipation before moving on to the restaurant. Dishes such as salt cod cakes with salsa verde; duck breast with wood-roasted parsnips and onions; chocolate semi-freddo with toronne and honey, are well-prepared and professionally served. Nevertheless, the experience can seem like the latest product off a very slick, and very long, production line. The private dining room is one of London's most unusual—perched under the eaves, it provides a panorama over the central 'nave' of the restaurant. Whether the Bluebird stretches its wings and really takes flight remains to be seen. We all want it to. Set lunch Mon.-Fri. £12.75, £15.75, Sun. £17.75.

Busabong Tree

THAI 13/20

112 CHEYNE WALK, SW10, 0171-352 7534,
FAX 0171-352 6661
Lunch daily, Dinner Mon.-Sat. £
U: None nearby.

Thai charm marches with—no, dances with—Chelsea chic in this oddly shaped, prettily decorated restaurant. Little changes except for new, smarter national costumes for the waiters and a few more eye-pleasing artefacts adorning the inner rooms. The conservatory remains a luxuriance of plants and flowers. Some details of the cooking have improved such as less sugar in the sauces accompanying chunky beef and chicken sateh. The menu's claims of hotness are now realistic; triple-starred beef jungle curry is actually too fiery for many western palates, while even one-star aromatic pork spicy-fried noodles with sweet basil has an arresting touch of chilli. Many oriental specialities are famously aphrodisiac but a dish of king prawns sautéed in fish sauce with crushed garlic, coriander roots and black pepper is called 'Passion Killer'. Fortunately a variety of great occidental aphrodisiacs appear in a short carefully chosen wine list. Set lunch £9.95, set dinners £22 and £27.

The Canteen

MODERN BRITISH 14/20

UNIT G4, HARBOUR YARD, CHELSEA HARBOUR,
SW10, 0171-351 7330, FAX 0171-351 6189
Lunch Sun.-Fri., Dinner Mon.-Sat. £££
U: None nearby.

With views over Chelsea Harbour, the subtle playing-card theme of the room and much light and space, the Canteen works well both at lunchtime and in the evening when the crowd tends to be more local. The brasserie atmosphere is well complemented by the menu, which seeks inspiration in France, but can drift with success further south into the Mediterranean. Marco Pierre White was once involved in this venture and shades of his style remain, despite the sure hand of chef David Ali. First courses might include a rich rabbit terrine with pear chutney, or a suitably intense ballottine of foie gras with duck rillette and a grape chutney. Risotti come in for praise too, admirable in what is certainly a large dining room. Main courses are strong and straightforward—cod roasted with clams, garlic and chilli; or calf's liver with Alsace bacon and pomme purée. Desserts are dramatic, both in presentation and content: chocolate soufflé and sauce, exemplary tart Tatin. The wine list concentrates on Bordeaux to the detriment of other areas and there could be more on offer by the glass. Service can be abrupt and somewhat challenging, but underneath is well meaning. Set lunches £15.50 and 19.50.

Gordon Ramsay

MODERN BRITISH 18/20

68 ROYAL HOSPITAL RD, SW3, 0171-352 4441
Lunch Mon.-Fri, Dinner Mon.-Sat. ££££
U: Sloane Square.

The trajectory described by Gordon Ramsay's performance at Aubergine was little short of spectacular. When he opened in his pleasant Chelsea location a few short years ago, high hopes were vested in this Marco Pierre White protegé, but the first few months were slightly marred by indistinct flavours and combinations that seemed to be striving for novelty for its own sake. It's never worth writing off a Marco star, though, as the man himself passed from adolescence into a positively sedate maturity, his skill at training chefs and spotting talent has been shown to be without peer in the capital. Now Gordon Ramsay has taken over the former La Tante Claire and renamed it Gordon Ramsay, as Pierre Koffmann moves to a larger dining room at The Berkeley.

La Ciboulette

FRENCH 14/20

138A KING'S RD, SW3, 0171-823 7444,
FAX 0171-823 7457
Open Lunch daily, Dinner Mon.-Sat. ££
U: Sloane Sq.

A ☎

This is a classic example of the 'little neighbourhood place in a basement which you have to know is there in order to find it' sort of restaurant, and of its type it is very good. La Ciboulette is discreet, personable, friendly, attractively done in light yellow with dark green chairs and some mirrors to make the small space seem larger. The cooking is very superior-grade bistro food. So the terrine of potatoes and foie gras nicely balances earthy and rich (even if the portion is over-generous), although the cep cream did not really add any lustre to the flavour mix. A special of scrambled egg feuilleté had properly creamy eggs on a pastry base with well separated leaves, but a tomato coulis was misjudged saucing. Roast red mullet with aubergine pancake and pistou olive oil was every bit as appealing as it sounds, the fish skin just beginning to frizzle and the previously misapplied tomato coulis aptly pulling the dish together, demonstrating that the chef is capable of excellence. Baked stuffed quail with foie gras, crozet Savoyard was a good, classic combination of flavours. Cold soufflés, like the chilled tear of mandarin imperial, are well prepared, and pear and almond tatin had a lovely caramelised and frangipane-rich character.Very popular with locals. Set lunches £13, £15, set dinner £21.50.

Simply Nico Chelsea

FRENCH 12/20

7 PARK WALK, SW1, 0171-349 8866
Lunch Tues.-Fri., Sun., Dinner Mon.-Sat. £
U: South Kensington.

A ☎

This is one of the first in the Simply Nico chain on which Nico Landenis—award-winning eminence grise of British kitchens—is now placing his impramuter. It serves evolved bistro fare, and for the most part succeeds on its own terms. The menu is shortish: about eight choices for main courses and starters, split equally between meat and fish, or game. Our plate of charcuterie was okay; better was the home-cured salmon on blini with caviar. Other choices such as smoked haddock and potato soup, or gammon ravioli with parsley broth would have tested kitchen skills more measurably. Our mains were seared cod on a purée of beans and white bean velouté-which was delicate and flavoursome-and a nicely meaty monkfish with bacon, sage and shallots. Desserts included the eponymous tart tatin; a lemony crème brûlée, and a delicious chocolat fondant-a soufflé cooked to order taking twenty minutes but worth the wait. A beautifully scented Gewurtzraminer was somewhat spoilt by bits of floating cork. The food is prettily presented, likewise the place itself-tables with thick napery, walls a glossy yellow, floors of stripped pine, a stained-glass skylight in the rear room. Young French staff move around solicitously. Wine is sensibly served by the glass and half bottle. Diners shoudn't approach S N Chelsea as a temple of gastronomy, expecting a faithful emulation of the master. It's simply good food.

CHINATOWN

Aroma

CHINESE 15/20

11 GERRARD ST, W1, 0171-439 2720
Lunch & Dinner daily. £
U: Leicester Sq.

A ☎

Only vampires and doppelgangers can avoid being reflected from the multi-faceted mirrors dominating the back of this brightly lit restaurant. Others need not be deterred from enjoying its exciting Cantonese food

(Szechuan-Hunan dishes are less interesting). Seekers after authenticity relish the flavour and texture of deep-fried pig intestines (which sound better as andouillettes), and, from the 'Aroma special menu', sea-slug (which sounds much better as sea-cucumber). More conventional palates enjoy equally well prepared Dover sole, grouper, scallop, mussels or lobster. At the other end of the Cantonese spectrum, the Aroma House Special Noodles menu offers a wide range of home-style dishes, variously cooked, sauced and garnished, as well as rice and congee. They come from a 'noodle kitchen' in the window and demonstrate the virtues of la cuisine grandpère for it is the father of owner Mrs. Lee who makes the feather-light won ton and dumplings. Menus £9 to £21.50

Fung Shing

CHINESE 15/20

15 Lisle St, WC2, 0171-437 1539,
Fax 0171-734 0284
Lunch & Dinner daily. £
U: Leicester Sq.

A ☎

Mr. Wu, respected Fung Shing's founder and chef, has sadly passed on, to cook for blessed departed gastronomes. While the restaurant upholds his classic standards, some changes—even improvements—have come. Expansion into a pleasant high-ceilinged back room and fewer seats in front give more comfort for diners and space for smoother service. The ambience is now well above the Chinatown norm, well suited to superlatively cooked and presented classic Cantonese, and modern Hong Kong cuisines. Ostrich seems to be replacing beef on Chinese menus—at least this one. It is similar in flavour, lean and usually more tender. Here it succeeds with onion and a little chilli in a light coating of yellow bean sauce. A short supplement to the printed menu lists mussels, fresh abalone, frogs' legs and an amazing stuffed squid with seafood. Its body, filled with finely chopped fish, shrimp, scallops, water chestnut and much else is steamed then braised in a delicate sauce. Replacing the head are the crisp fried tentacles and coriander leaves. Fresh abalone is served whole and eaten with knife and fork—even by Chinese who admit that this is better than cooking pieces to be picked up by chopsticks. Note the well-chosen wine list. Menus £12.50 to £35.

London Jade Garden

CHINESE 12/20

15 Wardour St, W1, 0171-437 5065
Lunch & Dinner daily. £
U: Piccadilly Circus.

A ☎

Lunch early for a table by the balcony rail overlooking the frantic ground floor. This may divert attention from the service which is neither speedy nor particularly friendly. But the excellent dim sum are worth a wait, even if menu descriptions don't always correspond with what arrives. For example bamboo stick steamed rice comes not on a skewer but in a cylindrical pot—a bamboo stem-filled with rice layered and topped with meat and mushrooms. The filling of ultra-crisp fried shredded chicken pancake roll seems to be mainly prawn, while in seafood and asparagus dumplings, unidentifiable green fragments add a subtle savour. Wonderful special teas, super ti guan yin or silver needle shou mei, match the food better than faded jasmine. The very long, reasonably priced, main menu holds few surprises but is also cooked with care and skill. Set menus for a minimum of 2 people £10.50 £26.

Mr Kong

CHINESE 14/20

21 Lisle St, WC2, 0171-437 7341
Lunch & Dinner daily. £
U: Leicester Sq.

Chinatown newcomers may have overtaken Mr. Kong's service, decor and general ambience, but in quality of ingredients and skill in cooking, it is still in the top echelon. Even everyday dishes are very capably prepared. Mixed meat and rice include tasty 'springy' beef balls, while Szechuan beef-far from Cantonese but an adopted favourite son in Chinatown is cut a tad thicker than usual to preserve its tender-chewy texture with its chilli content well judged. Baked lobster with ginger and spring onion sometimes fails to justify its price, but typically Cantonese stuffed dry beancurd skin with meat and stuffed vegetables is impeccable crisp beancurd rolls, a fine filling, egg-white sauce, all surrounded by bok choy 'stuffed' on top with minced prawn. As always in serious Chinese restaurants, a word with the manager may help ensure getting the best out of a distinguished kitchen. Set menus range from £15 to £22 for minimum of 4 people.

New Diamond

CHINESE 13/20

23 LISLE ST, WC2, 0171-437 2517

Lunch & Dinner daily. £

U: Leicester Sq.

A

The revival—even resurrection—of Chinatown is signalled here by the white walls with decorative black wooden panels and well-spaced tables. Service is polite, occasionally even friendly. Richly flavoured, homely Cantonese cooking shows in a dish as simple as baked turbot in spicy salt, succulent inside, crunchy-crisp outside, discreetly seasoned with chopped green chilli. The earthiness of stewed duck with yam in hot-pot is lifted by dried tangerine peel—a Chinese twist on caneton à l'orange. Fresh ginger enlivens a soup of algae with salted egg and pork. And 'Chinese' mushrooms on the menu means real dried black mushrooms, not tasteless straw mushrooms. To finish there is a little plate of fruit-grape, melon and orange slices—replacing the once-universal orange segments. This may or may not be an improvement. But it demonstrates that in at least this Chinatown restaurant change is no longer unthinkable. Set menus £10 to £16.

New Hoo Wah

CHINESE 13/20

37-38 GERRARD ST, W1, 0171-434 0540

Lunch & Dinner daily. £

U: Leicester Sq.

A

Chinese and Europeans fill this large, bustling Chinatown restaurant for excellent, modestly priced, dim sum served until 5pm. Most are cooked to order including standard fried and steamed dumplings from £1.60, and specials, many of seafood, from £2.20. The 'snack stall' in the window provides stewed ox tripe or pork knuckle from a bainmarie; also pan-fried noodle rolls, stuffed tofu and vegetables; the counter displays more specials and tempting slices of vegetable pastes—try turnip, infinitely more exciting than it sounds. The 'lunch special menu' runs from familiar noodle dishes, £4.50, to such exotics as sautéed slice of snakehead fish with lily-bud, wood fungi and red dice, £11.80; and home-made snake soup, £5. The main menu holds no surprises but 'promotional menus' of remarkable seasonal banquets are £88 for 4 persons to £488 for 10 (wine and soft drinks included). One menu is named after Monk Jump Over Wall—abalone, other seafoods and meat in a delicate broth 'double cooked for at least 5 hours'. Also included is asparagus stuffed fresh bamboo pith in crab meat sauce; and quick fried fillet of Dover sole served in its deep-fried skin and fins. Impersonal service does not quite match the ambitions of the kitchen, but show your interest and consult manager Philip Chan for a gastronomic adventure. Set menus £10 to £20.

CHISWICK

The Chiswick

MODERN BRITISH 13/20

131 CHISWICK HIGH RD, W4, 0181-994 6887

Lunch Sun.-Fri., Dinner Mon.-Sat. £

U: Turnham Green.

When Ian Bates left The Chiswick (to cook for Sir Terence Conran's Bluebird Club), there was a collective groan throughout Chiswick. After a short sticky patch while Mark Broadbent came to grips with a menu that owed much to Bates' days with Simon Hopkinson at Bibendum, he moved up a gear and the food just goes on getting better and better. The menu changes slightly each day and the two-course set lunch and early supper menu is stunning value at £9.50. Regular favourites include caponata with home-made rosemary focaccia; smoked haddock, spinach, poached egg and hollandaise; steak frites with Béarnaise sauce, and, in season, roast pheasant with parsnips and bread sauce. As ever the menu cuts across fashion with a hard core of tried—and—tested classic bistro dishes whilst appearing very up-to-date with dishes such as roast cod with couscous salad, saffron risotto with wilted greens and ricotta fritters with lemon sorbet. The room has been given a new moodier look with dark green walls and smart new up-lights. In summer the windows fold back and tables are set on the deep pavement. Set lunch and pre-theatre dinner £9.50.

THE CITY

City Rhodes

MODERN BRITISH 16/20

1 NEW STREET SQUARE, EC4, 0171-583 1313, FAX 0171-353 1662

Lunch & Dinner Mon.-Fri. ££

U: Chancery Lane.

Opening in an area that has always lacked a distinguished restaurant was strategically a good move, though City Rhodes would be in a class of its own even if the area was already gastronomically well-endowed. And what a show the restaurant is! All those gentlemen (and ladies) in black, sipping their Champagne to worship Mammon. That is on Fridays if the Footsie has climbed a few more rungs on the stock exchange ladder. The more rungs, the more Champagne. The restaurant is cleverly segmented to provide you with a sense of personal space, though you can still check out who's operating on whom in any area. The occasional Victor Passmore print has more impact for being hung on a cool background. Chairs upholstered with a houndstooth check fabric take you straight to the man himself, as this is the preferred trouser style of 'Gazza Gastro' Gary Rhodes. As a child, Gary discovered the quaint and unusual taste of a prawn, and the idea that something had to be done for the traditional British steak-and-kidney pie entered his mind. Many prawns later, after moderning those traditional British dishes, he also discovered the chaos of modern cooking with its floods of spices and flavours, its monsoon of lemon grass and lime leaves. He believes in simplicity and sincerity. So he cooks simply what he believes in. That is why the exalted taste of the fruit in his tomato cakes with peppered goats' cheese, and his terrine of salmon confit with caramelised shallots and capers—the salmon not diluted into a bland mish-mash—is so enjoyable. In the main dishes, cabbage sustains beautifully the flavour of steamed halibut and the 'poivre' just enhances the tuna fish tournedos. If another reference to British influence is found in the final act with a superb bread-and-butter pudding, this place is really more modern than British. Service is classy and the wine list offers many reasonable opportunities. You needn't wait until the Down Jones goes through the roof to pay your check (around £50), and don't forget to visit the state-of-the-art awesome restrooms.

MPW

INTERNATIONAL 14/20

2ND FLOOR, CABOT PLACE EAST, CANARY WHARF, E14, 0171-513 0513, FAX 0171-513 0551

Lunch & Dinner Mon.-Fri. ££

DLR: Canary Wharf.

This latest expansion of the Marco Pierre White empire opened in summer 1997. Visiting it offers a crash course in the Canary Wharf experience. Alighting from the Docklands Light Railway, you ascend on escalators to the celestial glass heights where MPW sits nonchalantly among fast-food joints. Not that there is anything high-falutin' about the menus here which offer tried-and-true retro cooking, some of it almost provocatively familiar (thickly sliced gravad lax, abundantly garliced chicken Kiev); some of it less so (veal Holstein is a breaded escalope with a fried egg on top). The quality shows in the accompanying stocks and sauces, as well as in the care in presentation. Glasses are a favoured vehicle for the food: our deeply flavoured crab cocktail and agreeably rich vanilla cream with summer fruits both came in vessels designed for martinis. Sombre formality is the tone of the service, and the wine list is packed with modern classics at reasonable prices. Set dinner £12.95.

Poons in the City

CHINESE 12/20

2 MINSTER PAVEMENT, MINSTER COURT, MINCING LANE, EC3, 0171-626 0126, FAX 0171-626 0526

Mon.-Fri. noon-10.30pm. £

U: Monument.

After founding the original 'little Poon's' in Lisle St, Chinatown, chef Bill Poon and family set up their Poons mini-empire. His luxurious city flagship is in the unpromising basement atrium of a modern office block. Generously sized, well spaced tables and comfortable thrones match Chinese panelling, fine calligraphy and pictures. A quick-service snack bar offers more basic ambience and food. Mr. Poon's greatest contribution to London Chinese gastronomy, wind-dried food, appears here in lap yuk soom, a sort of moo shu rou (chopped meat and vegetables) with lettuce—its deep smoky flavour contrasts with the freshness of the leaves. Cantonese mixed cold meats comprise pork, roast duck, chicken and cucumber salad. For main dishes consider 'Bill Poon's Specials' such as Cantonese beef hot-pot; prawn-wrapped aubergines; and the vegetarian 'honeycomb' specials. Duck with pancakes—both classic kam ling in three courses, and the simpler 'crispy, aromatic' version, is artfully prepared. Set menus £22 £30.

Saigon Times

FRENCH ORIENTAL 14/20

20-22 LEADENHALL MARKET, EC3,
0171-621 0022, FAX 0171-623 0028
Breakfast & Lunch Mon.-Fri. £
U: Bank/Monument.

A

On street level, there's a lively brasserie/bar serving a scaled-down version of the restaurant menu. The downstairs restaurant is a Franco-Oriental emporium with barrel-vaulted ceilings, modern uplighters and fantastic collections on the walls of old French-Indo-Chinese shipping posters and fascinating Chinese apparel: tiny, embroidered shoes and amazing robes, one of which was used in *The Last Emperor.* Menus include both French (often with a Moroccan twist) and Vietnamese items, but the taste of the Orient is what makes the trip worthwhile. The tremblingly delicate pork-and-crab timbale is a marvellously aromatic steamed mousse. Then try the banana leaf parcel of monkfish marinated in coconut milk and lemon grass—and there's no extra charge for the clouds of fragrant steam when you open it up. Stay with the theme for desserts with délice of chua (banana) in coconut milk with roast sesame seeds; or if you must, the crème brûlée with confit ginger. A short, well-chosen wine list with enough choice under £20 a bottle, features some New Worlders among mostly French bottles. Set dinner £15.

Searcy's at the Barbican

INTERNATIONAL 13/20

BARBICAN CENTRE, LEVEL 2, SILK ST, EC2,
0171-588 3008, FAX 0171-382 7247
Lunch Sun.-Fri. Dinner nightly (to 6.30pm Sun). ££
U: Barbican.

A

The Barbican this may be, but every effort has been made to move away from the institutional approach. Pale wood and brushed steel, with screening to break up the L-shaped room looking out over the gardens to St. Giles Church, has done much to change things. So too, has the decision to bring Richard Corrigan on board (see Lindsay House, where he cooks). Corrigan's role as executive chef, working alongside chef Tom Illic, has done much to raise the standards of what previously fell into the feed-the-theatre-and-concert-goers trap. First courses of crab ravioli, the pasta sitting in an intense broth, or goat's cheese and potato terrine, bring flavours and textures to the fore. Main courses are serious and often show Mr Corrigan's Irish roots, as in pork fillet, crubeen, black pudding and pig's cheek with sauerkraut; or mackerel, roasted and served with cabbage and a butter sauce intense with smoky bacon. Desserts deliver punch, but standards can fluctuate—a brownie served with pear sorbet sitting rather too heavily as a round-off. The wine list is well-chosen and wide-ranging. Service needs attention. Set lunch and dinner menus £18.50 and £21.50.

Tatsuso

JAPANESE 17/20

32 BROADGATE CIRCLE, EC2, 0171-638 5863;
FAX 0171-638 5864
Lunch & Dinner Mon.-Fri. £££
U: Liverpool St.

A

The knowledgeable leave it to the chef to choose a superlative meal in classic oriental restaurants. This chef's assorted sashimi might include sea bass and ama-ebi, fresh water prawns, as well as hirame usuzukuri, thinly sliced turbot with a soya, ponzu and chive sauce—no wasabi. Mild vinegar-sauced sunamono with jellyfish, and mackerel rolled in seaweed, paradoxically combine luxury and everyday ingredients. In a variation on chawan-mushi, a savoury egg custard, foie gras discreetly underlies the delicate flavour while other garnishes include chicken, pork and soya bean, and as always, garishly dyed fish cake. Even carnivores appreciate a nimono, boiled dish, of winter vegetables including yam and sweet potato. Other unexpected delights are satoimo mangu, a bun stuffed with shrimp and fish in a delicious gelatinous gravy; and ichikiku (figs mashed into a semi-sweet 'doughnut'). More conventional sushi and tempura are prepared with equal care, and those who prefer a set menu will find a wide range here. Those who enjoy being cooked at, rather than cooked for, admire the upper teppan room, where choice meat and shellfish is sizzled on gleaming steel plates. A superb house saké—origoroshi—is soft and rich in flavour yet fully dry. Set price menus range from £28 to £75, but note that lunch is not the cheapest menu.

Tatsuso Teppan Room

JAPANESE 15/20

32 BROADGATE CIRCLE, EC2, 0171-638 5863

Lunch & Dinner Mon.-Fri.

U: Liverpool St.

For set menus see above.

Ten

MODERN BRITISH 13/20

10 CUTLERS GARDENS ARCADE, DEVONSHIRE SQ, EC2, 0171-283 7888, FAX 0171-626 4859

Lunch & Dinner Mon.-Fri. ££

U: Liverpool St.

On the site of the long-running Le Champenois, the design has been updated by Julyan Wickham who designed the original 14 years ago, and Mark Wickham has expanded and updated his original Seurat-style murals. These give a view to the basement dining room which is further brightened by a (somewhat disorienting) mirrored wall. The group behind the project are the owners of Bank (also a Wyckham design), and the chef is from The Ivy. Not surprisingly then, the emphasis is on contemporary British comfort food, some of which works quite nicely, some of which doesn't. Sushi, sashimi and tataki admittedly fall outside this category, but there are a number of oriental-ish dishes and this one succeeds with quality ingredients and good presentation. Less successful was a crab risotto, which had good flavour but gloopy rice. Duck hot pot is rich, sweet, tangy/gingery and well served in a big bowl with noodles and Chinese greens. Ham knuckle is rarely encountered in restaurants, but this one could lead the way as it was so well flavoured with chilli, honey, soy and ginger. Good twists on nursery desserts, like Armagnac prunes with the baked rice pudding.

CLERKENWELL

Ginnan

JAPANESE 13/20

1-2 ROSEBERRY CT, ROSEBERRY AVE, EC1, 0171-278 0008

Lunch Mon.-Fri., Dinner Mon.-Sat. £

U: Farringdon.

Filling the gap between expensive classical Japanese restaurants and canteens, Ginnan offers good value set lunches from £8 and set dinners at £25. The speciality is kushiyaki—little bamboo skewers of chicken—plain, minced, or with onion, also chicken skin, chicken gizzard, or vegetables. They can be enjoyed at the table or at the kushiyaki bar which here replaces the usual sushi bar. Other homely dishes include various noodle soups and oden—boiled fish cake, egg and vegetables. This is a meaty Japanese menu with accurately cooked Chinese chives and chicken liver; grilled loin of pork; diced pork belly in soy sauce; and an oriental delicacy we did not try, shallow-fried cabbage and corned beef. The usual grilled and fried fish are offered too, and unusually the full range of enticing appetisers is listed in both Japanese and English. Service is skilled and helpful. Set lunch menus £7.50 to £21, set dinner menu £25.

Moro

MEDITERRANEAN 15/20

34-36 EXMOUTH MARKET, EC1, 0171-833 8336, FAX 0171-833 9338

Lunch & Dinner Mon.-Fri. £

U: Farringdon.

Only in Cordoba's mediaeval Jewish quarter can one find anything like Moro's Spanish-Moorish cuisine. The combination of intense sensuality and earthy goodness recalls another Spanish-Arabic cultural fusion—flamenco. Not effete cabaret versions but real cante jondo. The joy of encountering it here becomes jubilation when it is so superbly executed. On the blackboard listing 'mezes-raciones', bar-snacks more substantial than tapas, you may find mojama, wind-dried tuna 'ham' or potted spiced lamb as well as familiar items. Starters may include pastel de bacalhau, salt cod and potato croquettes with aïoli and tomato sauce, or whole artichokes with dill, tarragon egg and caper sauce. Subtly, but ardently sauced, wood-roasted chicken comes with sumac, roast squash and ferik-smoked wheat. Malaga raisin ice cream with Pedro Ximenez 'essence' of sweet sherry is a hedonist's dream. Fortunately our toques and marks relate only to cooking, not to the appearance of the restaurant. For in this extreme example of '90s brutality, with institutional green-and-cream walls, the only decoration is the sloped mirrors over the bar. Tables are close, the floor is bare wood, the noise level is high. But it is all acceptable to a host of diners, mostly youngish but not juvenile. Proximity to Islington may account for many Tony Blair look-alikes amongst them. First-class service with a smile, a thorough knowledge of the menu's unfamiliar ingredients, and a superb modern wine list are yet more attractions of one of London's most exciting newcomers.

Bagels

This great Jewish staple is making quite a stir in London; in fact packets have even hit the supermarkets, which is a sure sign of arrival, if not neccessarily of quality. But for the best, particularly with good fillings like the echt smoked salmon and cream cheese, check out:

Angel Bagel, 53 Goodge St, W1, 0171-636 0561; **Brick Lane Beigel Bake**, 159 Brick Lane, E1, 0171-729 0606; **Carmelli Bakeries**, 126-128 Golders Green Rd, NW11, 0181-455 2074; **Great American Bagel Factory**, 18 Endell St, Wc2, 0171-497 1115; **Hip Bagel**, 323 Fulham Rd, SW10, 0171-376 8984.

Novelli EC1

FRENCH 14/20

29 CLERKENWELL GREEN, EC1, 0171-251 6606, FAX 0171-490 1083

Lunch and Dinner Mon.-Sat. ££

U: Farringdon.

Jean-Christophe Novelli's base in the City of London was once simply Maison Novelli, but has now bifurcated and doubles as that and EC1, the latter a bustling compact dining room offering modern brasserie cooking under the aegis of head chef Jean-Marie Lenfant. It's an à la carte menu with great breadth of choice, and with most dishes demonstrating the kinds of fresh, vibrant—and occasionally off-the-wall—flavours that a restaurant needs to be cognisant with if it is to compete these days. Start with something like black pudding, lambs' tongues and a poached egg on warm frisée, or smoked stuffed goose neck and gésiers with pistachio oil to get the tastebuds singing. Then it's on to roast grey mullet with polenta in a sauce of carrot juice, vanilla and mustard seeds, or honey-glazed lamb knuckle with chickpea salsa. This level of experimentation is what's known as raising the stakes, and the odd dish does fail to achieve lift-off, but there are more hits than misses, and at the end you may be rewarded for your persistence by tiramisù flavoured with juniper, tarte tatin of quinces with walnut ice cream or caramelised rice pudding with rhubarb compôte. Extra charges must be paid for the vegetables, and even—shame!—for bread and butter. The pace is hectic, but service is capable, and the wine list offers a good modern international selection.

Quality Chop House

MODERN BRITISH 13/20

94 FARRINGDON RD, EC1, 0171-837 5093

Lunch Mon.-Fri., Sun. Dinner nightly. ££

U: Farringdon.

You have to take your hat off to Charles Fontaine. It is nearly ten years since he left Le Caprice and restored the Quality Chop House to its former glory as a Victorian café. Despite, or perhaps because of, the bleak plain decor, uncomfortable (original) bench seats and the inevitability of sharing a table, people flock back for the excellent nineties equivalent of a 'progressive working-class caterer'. The menu is a happy mix of favourites such as Caesar salad, bang bang chicken and salmon fish cakes with sorrel sauce that he perfected at Le Caprice, and French as well as English classics. Hence roast snails with garlic butter; corned beef hash with fried egg; grilled calf's liver and bacon; and rice pudding. The wine list is short and sweet but the drinks list encompasses Roedere Brut, Nut Brown Ale and traditional English tea. The Chop House has expanded next door with around 20 more covers.

St. John

BRITISH 14/20

26 ST. JOHN ST, EC1, 0171-251 0848,
FAX 0171-251 4090
Lunch Mon.-Fri., Dinner Mon.-Sat. £
U: Farringdon.

Meat-eaters weary of the ubiquitous blandness of the prime cuts—those who relish a brain or a trotter above breast of chicken or fillet steak—should set a course for St. John. Before the street of the same name became quite so drop-dead trendy, Fergus Henderson was already regaling the denizens of Clerkenwell with such delicacies, and the popularity of this blinding-white warehouse-like space suggests his aim remains true. Roasted bone marrow with dressed flat parsley, the fibrously appetising pork rillettes with crusty bread, and main courses like skate with proper black butter have convinced us that this is about more than mere fashion. Government regulations may have banished the beloved oxtail of yesteryear, but the tripe and onions hold their own. Portions, especially of vegetables, are on the wolfish side of generous, but spare room for echt British puddings such as rhubarb fool or mincemeat tart. A fair spread of suitably robust wines is offered at prices that don't insult.

Stephen Bull Smithfield

MODERN BRITISH 12/20

71 ST JOHN ST, EC1, 0171-490 1750,
FAX 0171-490 3127
Lunch Mon.-Fri., Dinner Mon.-Sat. £
U: Angel.

The giant barracuda hanging over the repositioned, enlarged bar is not entanked so may not be homage to the great gastronome and artist, Damien Hirst. Otherwise the bright, piscine decor remains unchanged. But the old uncomfortable seating has been replaced. The short, reasonably priced à la carte, mainly British, also offers intriguing notions from elsewhere. Here the 'delicacies from . . .' platter of charcuterie, Bull's signature dish, is Spanish. Spiced aubergine and courgette risotto, and blackened salmon with char-grilled bok choy show judicious eclecticism, but marinated pike with wild mushroom cream, very much 'on-the-bone', should not have left Hungary. Wallow in such sensual desserts as chocolate and orange indulgence, or pecan pie with vanilla ice cream. The notable wine list arranged according to style, not geography, will please wine buffs as much as those just beginning to explore the world of wine.

COVENT GARDEN

Bank

MODERN BRITISH 14/20

1 KINGSWAY, WC2, 0171-379 9797,
FAX 0171-379 9014
Breakfast Mon.-Fri., Lunch & Dinner daily. ££
U: Covent Garden/Holborn.

With its high ceilings and its stainless steel, the large bar at Bank, crowded in the evenings, leads towards the open-plan linear kitchen. Diners walk down its length and into the spacious eating area, dominated on one wall by a mural, the other by a window. This Julyan Wickham-designed interior is bold, modern and rather relaxing, although some are not so keen on the vertically hung shards of glass that hang down from the ceiling. The menu is diverse, running from classic French-inspired cooking to more modern interpretations. After a terrine of chicken livers, the wok-fried lobster with Thai spices was a delight. Dishes like chicken Kiev and fish and chips figure frequently alongside steaks, risottos and pastas. Desserts are good—ices, tarts and old English favourites like treacle and bread-and-butter puddings. The wine list is large, grouped by style and fairish in price. Brunch at weekends is popular, as is breakfast during the week. Service is very efficient. Set lunch £12.50 and £16.50, also available until 7pm.

Café du Jardin

INTERNATIONAL 14/20

28 WELLINGTON ST, WC2, 0171-836 8769,
FAX 0171-836 4123
Lunch & Dinner daily. £
U: Covent Garden.

It is pleasantly surprising to find a Covent Garden restaurant with so many old-fashioned virtues. It attracts a mature clientele with a modern but not noisy ambience. Downstairs there is live piano music. Windows on two sides make the ground floor, with its copper ceiling, light and airy. Service is relaxed. The menu, in English, is happily almost free of kitchen-ese. It is eclectic, with ingredients daringly combined by a chef who understands which flavours marry well-grilled breast of pigeon on bubble and squeak with a kim chee salad for example, although the kim chee as served was red cabbage. Mediterranean influence is strong as in grilled loin of tuna niçoise with a basil pesto infusion; and tube pasta with a sauté of spinach, chorizo sausage and ricotta cheese. Desserts are equally imaginative; a not entirely successful peach tatin was redeemed by its accompanying black pepper sorbet. Set lunch and pre- and post- theatre menus £9.95, £13.50.

Chez Gérard at the Opera Terrace

FRENCH 11/20

FIRST FLOOR, THE MARKET, THE PIAZZA, WC2, 0171-379 0666, FAX 0171-497 9060

Lunch & Dinner daily. £
U: Covent Garden.

The Chez Gérard group is expanding fast, and two more have just opened. This one, on the first floor in the Covent Garden market, has a huge bar, a wonderful terrace and a restaurant to one side with a railway carriage decor—stainless steel luggage racks, and banquette seating. Chez Gérards run to a formula, and a mighty successful one it is at that, at least in terms of popularity and price. It's just what you'd expect, onion soups coming with croûtons and Gruyère cheese toppings, moules marinières, grills running from lamb cutlets to Chateaubriand as well as confit de canard and a vegetarian concession. Salads, pommes frites and sauce Béarnaise accompany; desserts like tarte tatin or petit pot au chocolat finish. This is not haute cuisine, but humble bistro fare and the cooking can be inconsistent. The best bet is their good value three-course prix fixe menu at £15 which runs through the evening and at weekday lunches. The Chez Gérards are useful and generally fun, with decent reasonably priced wine lists. 3 course meal £15. **Also 31 Dover St, W1, 0171-499 8171; 119 Chancery Ln, WC2, 0171-405 0290; 64 Bishopsgate, EC2, 0171-588 1200; 8 Charlotte St, W1, 0171-636 4975, 84 Roseberry Ave, EC1 (no tel no. yet); 3 Yeomans Row, SW3, 0171-581 8377.**

Christopher's American Grill

AMERICAN 11/20

18 WELLINGTON ST, WC2, 0171-240 4222, FAX 0171-240 3357

Lunch Mon.-Fri., dinner Mon.-Sat., brunch noon-3pm Sat.-Sun. ££ U: Covent Garden.

The dining room is reached via a twisting stone staircase on the majestic scale (this was a bank building when such edifices were unabashed temples of money), but all pomp ends there as the informal bustle of the restaurant extends before you. East Coast American classics are the kitchen's trade, with Maryland crabcakes, strip steak with tobacco onions and New York cheesecake setting the sights higher than just burgers and fries. The occasional experiment is essayed, but this is one of those places where the established repertoire is definitely worth sticking to. Weekend brunchers may opt for Caesar salad with grilled chicken, or a textbook version of eggs Benedict. Portions may not be quite as generous as New Yorkers would expect, but enough for London to be going on with. Service moves at lightning pace, which may be welcome if you're eating before the theatre, as many do. California wines are supplemented by some surprisingly top-flight French offerings. Pre- and post-theatre dinner £15.

The Ivy

MODERN BRITISH 14/20

1 WEST ST, WC2, 0171-836 4751, FAX 0171-240 0333

Lunch & Dinner daily. ££
U: Leicester Sq.

Just behind the Ivy, The Mousetrap continues its endless run. As West End institutions go, however, the restaurant makes for a more diverting evening. Long known as a star-spotter's paradise, it offers the throwback ambience of an older theatrical London, with stained-glass windows in rainbow hues contrasting with dark wooden screens. The menu covers the known culinary world from bang bang chicken to baked Alaska, taking in shepherd's pie on the way. Indian and oriental dishes may tempt you away from the British domestic axis, but these days they amount to the same thing. All are rendered with the same precise attention to detail, a particularly impressive feat given the relentless press of business, and the staff are more than equal to the task of keeping everybody happy. Side orders of potatoes and vegetables done in various ways should not be missed, and nor—in season—should the Scandinavian berries with white chocolate sauce. Wines are expensive, but many are offered by the glass. Set weekend lunch is £17.

Joe Allen

AMERICAN 11/20

13 EXETER ST, WC2, 0171-836 0651

Lunch & Dinner daily. £

U: Covent Garden.

Joe Allen lives on, mighty busy and great fun. With its tiny entrance easily missed by those who don't know it, its bare brick walls, dark wood, piano and pictures, and of course, given the location, its noisy theatre crowd, it takes you straight to New York. And it has that indefinable but oh-so-necessary ingredient for success; it makes you feel part of the action, whoever you might be. Some seriously trendy people alongside ordinary mortals up from the country and a few fashion victims consume a short menu running from black bean soup or the ubiquitous Caesar salad, grilled ribeye steak with fries, lamb cutlets beautifully grilled, to some pretty ordinary ice cream. The cooking is straightforward and mainly succeeds where char-grilling is brought into play. But the cooking is not really the point here; it's the atmosphere that counts. Set lunches £11 and £13.

Le Palais du Jardin

FRENCH 11/20

136 LONG ACRE, WC2, 0171-379 5353,
FAX 0171-379 1846

Lunch & Dinner daily. ££

U: Covent Garden.

Open all day, this 350-seater Parisian brasserie happens to be in London. In front of the towering bar is the café opening onto bustling Long Acre. Service in the invariably busy restaurant is usually friendly, but sometimes overwhelmed. Foreground music plays all the time. The menu, in French, English and Kitchen French, is spectacularly misspelled in all three languages-and oysters are offered by the 1\2 (sic) dozen. Plateaux of fruits de mer include crab, lobster, oysters, prawns, scallops, langoustine plus clams and mussels, in a biting horseradish-tomato sauce. Rubbery whelks and unrewarding winkles are wisely eschewed. The basically French menu incorporates some oriental and Mediterranean ingredients as in seared tuna on tabbouleh with lemon oil and fennel. But pavé (translated as fillet!) de boeuf comes with celeriac and horseradish purée; and huge steak tartare with French fries. Diverse wines include some sound bottles.

Livebait

INTERNATIONAL 13/20

21 WELLINGTON ST, WC2, 0171-836 7161,
FAX 0171-836 7141

Lunch and Dinner Mon.-Sat. ££

U: Covent Garden.

When the second Livebait restaurant opened in Covent Garden, London held its breath. The rapidly growing Groupe Chez Gérard had bought the original, much loved and well respected restaurant in Waterloo and with this second one, made clear its intention to spawn a whole lot more Livebaits. The original chef, Theodore Kyriakou, is also an original, who had taken a fresh, innovative look at the cooking of fish. Would his style, occasionally downright anarchic, transfer? Both the Covent Garden and Waterloo Livebait are thriving, though the chef has now departed. Starters range from the simple as in crustacea, perhaps crevettes served with mayonnaise or a bowl of winkles, to the type of dish for which Kyriakou became famous. Perhaps a baked smoked haddock with a pilaff of porcini mushrooms, black winter truffles and a fried egg, sunny side up; or a less successful, but nonetheless interesting, Dover sole grilled and coming with duck's live paté, a heavy thyme and feta koukourtopita and watercress. Mains continue to explore the mixing of tastes, as in a baked bream with steamed mussels in a delicately Thai scented coconut broth, or barbecued whole red mullet with roasted fennel, oranges and black olives—a masterly combination. The dessert list is long but satisfying—orange mousse and chocolate Genoise terrine with delicate passion fruit ice cream, pistachio and chocolate ice cream. The Covent Garden Livebait champions British beers; the wine list is short but good. Both restaurants have the look of a former eel and pie shop, with tiled walls and floors in dark greens, white, functional wooden tables and chairs, and globe lights. Pre-theatre 2-course menu £14.50. **Also 43 The Cut, SE1, 0171-928 7211.**

Mon Plaisir

FRENCH 11/20

21 MONMOUTH ST, WC2, 0171-836 7243,
FAX 0171-379 0121

Lunch Mon.-Fri., Dinner Mon.-Sat. £
U: Covent Garden/Tottenham Court Rd.

'Rustic French' conjures up Mon Plaisir exactly. There are the brick walls, the wooden floors, the accordion music (which the affable owner, Alain Lhermitte threatens to make live, rather than piped as it is at the moment), Monsieur Bibendum surveying all from the bar, and a menu which is properly French bistro. Lots of well cooked, authentic French dishes here—snails with garlic butter; soup of the day; grilled entrecôte with those excellent small French fries; steak tartare; red mullet in parsley juice with a sweetcorn pancake; crème brûlée; truffe au chocolat, and an excellent French cheese board. Tout va bien at this excellent French outpost in London. Set lunch £14.50.

Orso

ITALIAN 12/20

27 WELLINGTON ST, WC2, 0171-240 5269,
FAX 0171-497 2148

Lunch & Dinner daily. ££
U: Covent Garden.

The fashion for simple rustic Italian food has caught up with Orso's no-nonsense approach. This basement restaurant—tiled walls and low ceiling—can seem a little grim on sunny days, but the food makes an effort to shine. Pizzette are the speciality—small pizzas with toppings like spinach and pancetta, or aubergine and caper. Precursors might be the antipasti of bresaola with watercress and olives, or a warm salad of broad beans, peas and artichoke. For more substantial eating, try roast suckling pig stuffed with pancetta and fennel, or veal kidneys with garlic, parsley and white wine. Orso remains popular, but somehow seems to have lost an edge. Some good Italian cheeses are offered alongside a standard range of desserts. The Italian wine list spans a good range. House drinking is from jugs. Pre-theatre menus £13, £15, Sat.-Sun. lunch £14, £16.

Stephen Bull St. Martin's Lane

MODERN BRITISH 14/20

12 UPPER ST MARTIN'S LANE, WC2,
0171-379 7811, FAX 0171-490 3128

Lunch Mon.-Fri, Dinner Mon.-Sat. ££
U: Leicester Sq.

Like a perverse general, Stephen Bull lays a minefield then advances triumphantly through it. The mines here are the oddly shaped room, its coldness in winter, and the austere decor-although paintings have added a welcome touch of colour. Bull's skill as chef-restaurateur, and in choosing cooks, shows first in ultra-crisp cheese puff appetisers, then in such original, yet classical, dishes as salt cod soufflé, with spinach, aïoli and mussels. Ingredients and ideas come from all of Europe, but without resort to the East and presentation is unfussy. Roast calf's liver would have been better grilled but the accompanying Swiss chard and sage butter was a revelation. Boned skate wing, roast potatoes, chorizo and persillade seems odd but works well. Crème fraîche sorbet made a romantic gastronomic marriage with fresh grenadine and orange. Cleverly chosen wines, many by the glass, are listed by style; nearly all are below £25. Pre-theatre menu offers starters for £5.50 and main courses for £10.

DULWICH

Belair House

MODERN BRITISH 13/20

GALLERY RD, SE21M 0181-299 9788,
FAX 0181-693 3230

Lunch Mon.-Sun., Dinner Mon.-Sat. ££
BR: Dulwich West.

Forget modern minimalism, Belair House, as its name suggests, is a Georgian house built in 1785 which now houses a restaurant and separate bar. The approach via the small driveway is magnificent, the grand staircase as you enter a joy to behold, but the bright yellow dining room itself is strangley proportioned and lacks the drama and character you expect. Excitement, however, comes in the cooking from Colin Barnett who has done stints at a couple of good restaurants that have closed, victims of the economics of running small, classy operations. Starters of gravlax marinated in beetroot with an avocado salsa, and a terrine of foie gras and smoked duck were punchy; main dishes of grey mullet with ratatouille and spinach, and risotto of artichokes with rocket salad satisfying. The lemon tart with a black currant sorbet was the equal of anywhere; a light toffee mousse came with crème brûlée ice cream. The wine list is even-handed in its choice of European and New World wines, with enough good wines under £20, though to judge from the well-heeled locals of Dulwich who make up the majority of the diners, expense is a secondary consideration here. Set lunches, Mon.-Sat. £10 and £14.75, set dinner Mon.-Thurs. £24.95.

FULHAM

Blue Elephant

THAI 11/20

4-6 FULHAM BROADWAY, SW6, 0171-385 6595, FAX 0171-386 7665

Lunch Sun.-Fri., Dinner nightly. £££

U: Fulham Broadway.

The Blue Elephant might not offer the best or most authentic Thai food in town, but it's served in one of the most exotic settings. Each year the surrounding walls recede further in this large space as the greenery grows lusher, trailing down from above (ceiling seems the wrong word in such a tropical setting where small 'streams' divide the various dining areas). Beautifully dressed staff glide to and fro, adding a formal air. Formality extends to the presentation, with intricately carved vegetables adding to the beauty of the food, much of which is served in small blue-and-white dishes. The menu is long but for those unfamiliar with the cuisine, there are suggestions and the temptation of the Royal Thai banquet menu. Explanations accompany each dish, though often promise more than they deliver. Thai fish cakes 'mixed with spices and red curry paste' were remarkably characterless, while a hot yellow curry of prawns in coconut milk just had too much coconut milk; on the other hand 'Sweet Melody', stir-fried pork with mushroom, tomatoes and baby corn in a sweet and sour sauce was delicious, the separate tastes coming through, and the Muslim South Thai dish of slowly braised lamb had been cooked to just the right consistency. The cooking here can be inconsistent and it's pricey, but much is forgiven in such a setting and the service pleases. Sun brunch buffet £16.75, set dinners £29 and £34.

Chavot

FRENCH 15/20

257-259 FULHAM RD, SW3, 0171-351 7823, FAX 0171-376 4971

Lunch Mon.-Fri., Dinner Mon.-Sat. £££

U: South Kensington.

Formerly called Fulham Road, the new name is the same as that of the current chef, Eric Crouillère-Chavot. Eric was formerly in residence at Interlude de Chavot, where he won numerous accolades. Chavot is one of those restaurants that thrives on that particular Parisian brand of Frenchness which is apparent the moment you arrive—and that's not a criticism. The trés elegant staff are polished, and they know it; but they also care—and you will know it. The restaurant is divided into two sections, both of course equally chic, with a subtly varied colour scheme that is cleverly lit, providing the essential 'features'. The cuisine exemplifies an equal degree of contemporary sophistication. Indeed, one of Chavot's outstanding signature dishes is the foie gras with endive tarte tatin with butter orange sauce—amazing: subtle yet intense, and beautifully balanced. Other creations are equally creative and subject to impeccable quality control: salad of duck confit with truffle vinaigrette; stuffed leg of rabbit with squid and barley risotto; liquorice fondant with vanilla ice cream. The mise-en-place of this haute cuisine is as perfectly co-ordinated as haute couture, while the flavours have unexpected depth. Indeed, familiar ingredients can be a revelation, as though sampled for the first time. Set lunches £15.50 and £18.50.

Chez Max

FRENCH 14/20

168 IFIELD RD, SW10, 0171-835 0874, FAX 0181-947 4461

Lunch Tues.-Fri., Dinner Tues.-Sat. ££

U: West Brompton.

Another of those neighbourhood restaurants from heaven, Chez Max also merits a detour for non-locals. Just off the Fulham

Road, it's a small basement restaurant reached via a spiral staircase with a faintly 60s feel to it—all wood, closely packed tables, old wine lists and menus on the walls and faint lighting, relieved by natural light at one end. Originally owned by Max Renzland, its fortunes over the last two years or so have waxed and waned as chefs of varying degrees of competence have come and gone. However, fingers crossed for proprietor and customers alike, things now seem set fair. The style takes inspiration from the original owner, producing those French favourites like quail salad with Puy lentils and foie gras, Perigord salad, mullet, monkfish, lamb and pot au feu, prepared and cooked with exactly the right degree of accuracy and inspiration. Take the snails and mussels poached in a light broth with watercress; that red mullet which is poached in a tomato consommé and coming with saffron noodles; or fillet of beef à la ficelle—not on the menu when we went, but offered, so ask if there are any hidden treasures. The beef had been cooked at a rolling boil in a bouillon, becoming tender and retaining a full rich flavour. The pastry chef is pretty hot stuff too, so anything on a pastry base in the first two courses and the most desirable desserts will tempt. The wine list is predominantly French, service is erratically friendly and Chez Max should be encouraged. Menu Vite! Tues.-Fri. lunch and dinner £10, Menu du Jour £20.50 and £23.50.

Chutney Mary

INDIAN 13/20

535 King's Rd, SW10, 0171-351 3113, Fax 0171-351 7694

Lunch & Dinner daily. ££

U: None nearby.

Delightful Anglo-Indian decor in the far reaches of Chelsea with a brilliant bar upstairs, a buzzy restaurant downstairs, and the best seats in the conservatory. Regular food festivals maintain a level of excitement on the menu, as with a recent one from Kerala. Firsts and lasts were a real high point, so it's a pity that main courses generally weren't up to it. Starters from the Kerala menu really shine and have joined the regular menu: prawns stir-fried with coconut, served with steamed rick cakes (idlis) were exotic even for Indian food; and the fragrant lamb chilli fry is cooled down by accompanying spiced vermicelli. From the regular menu, minced chicken breast kebabs are moist and tasty. Malabar chicken curry, lamb kurma and roast duck curry each had a flavour of their own, but in the sauce only and not in the meat; the prawn and cashew curry with fresh coconut milk had a more integral, rounded flavour. Desserts come into their own: the Hill Station bread-and-butter pudding is an evergreen, and the almond paste-filled samosas with ice cream are an inventive finish. Wines are sensible and well chosen; service is good. Good set menu jazz brunch on Sundays at £16. Set lunches £12.50 and £15, Sun. brunch £16, set menu 4 courses £31.50.

HAMMERSMITH

River Café

ITALIAN 16/20

Thames Wharf Studios, Rainville Rd, W6, 0171-381 8824, Fax 0171-381 6217

Lunch daily, Dinner Mon.-Sat. ££££

U: Hammersmith.

There are only ever two complaints about the River Café: the cost (a conservative £60 a head) and the difficulty of getting a table. No-one minds that the restaurant is hidden away in a Fulham backwater, that parking can be difficult (despite a caped car jockey providing valet parking), or that there are no real views of the river. What is important is the excellence of the food and the understated chic of the room. These days, a wood-fuelled oven dominates the menu and the smell of the burning wood mingling with home-made Pugliese sourdough and wafer-thin pizzas loaded with wild mushrooms, asparagus and prosciutto di San Daniele, is almost too much to bear. Sourcing the very best and freshest ingredients is what drives Rose Gray and Ruthie Rogers, and their daily changing menu is a testament to their good taste. Char-grilled squid with fresh red chilli and rocket has become a modern classic, as has grilled fillet of sea bass with salsa verde, and their way of serving wafer-thin slices of entrecôte draped over grilled vegetables. Despite two successful recipe books (another planned, plus a TV series), the River Café remains London's hottest ticket.

HAMPSTEAD

Gresslin's

INTERNATIONAL 13/20

13 HEATH ST, NW3, 0171-794 8386,
FAX 0171-433 3282

Lunch Tues.-Sun., Dinner Mon.-Sat. £
U: Hampstead.

At last, a decent restaurant in Hampstead which the local population is delighted with. Michael Gresslin trained with Anton Mosimann and brings a modern French approach, tempered with Asian influences, to his menus. The restaurant itself is small, a long narrow room with good photographs on the walls and efficient waiting staff. A pleasant atmosphere in which to enjoy imaginative dishes like a starter of grilled duck liver with tabouleh and teriyaki sauce; or a risotto of roasted butternut squash with Amarone; followed by sautéed calf's liver with pancetta, stewed apples and potatoes; barbecued chump of lamb with braised celery and black olive jus; then baked cheese cake with stewed prunes, or a pear tarte tatin with saffron and stem-ginger cream. The combination of robust tastes works well together in the hands of this most competent chef. All in all, a very pleasant addition to this leafy part of London. Tues.-Sat. lunch £7.95, Sun. £13.95.

HOLLAND PARK

Chez Moi

FRENCH 14/20

1 ADDISON AVE, W11, 0171-603 8267,
FAX 0171-603 3898

Lunch Mon.-Fri., Dinner Mon.-Sat. ££
U: Holland Park.

Restaurants come n'go, but this one has lasted 30 years so they must be doing something right, and indeed they are. Splendid cooking by the joint proprietors, chef Richard Walton, and Colin Smith who cossets front-of-house, entices devoted regulars and delights newcomers to a menu which parallels 'old fashioned' favourites beside 'something different'. These might include Dutch veal kidneys in mustard sauce with mash, or currently fashionable Pacific Rim or North African dishes such as tagine with the tenderest lamb—one of Chez Moi's hallmarks. Our confit of Gressingham ducks' legs with celeriac purée and port sauce was beautifully rendered. Of the desserts, the chocolate-flavoured orange pot had few equals in toothsomeness. The knowledgeable wine list is strong on classic Burgundies and Bordeaux, but expect to pay for them. However the very drinkable house and affordable halves do not short-change, and neither does meticulous service. The three-course set lunch menu at £15 must be one of London's bargains. Enjoy all this in two striking blood-red rooms with gilt mirrors and tiger skin banguettes. Chez Moi is a delight. Set lunch £15.

The Room at The Halcyon

MODERN BRITISH 14/20

THE HALCYON, 129 HOLLAND PARK AVE, W11,
0171-221 5411, FAX 0171-229 8516

Lunch Sun.-Fri., Dinner daily. £££
U: Holland Park.

Luxurious ingredients and a suitably stylish interior opening on to a garden make this Holland Park hotel dining room suitably exclusive. Eating—let alone staying—here, implies a certain kudos. Efficient, formal service, well-spaced tables and a style of cooking which is modern without constant recourse to the char-grill. Martin Hadden's cooking is based on haute cuisine, but the execution is suitably confident not to be a slave to it. Starters might be lobster ravioli, or marinated salmon on warm potatoes with sour cream and caviar. Main courses are strong throughout: squab might be roasted and served with morels, or perhaps red currants; sea bass with celeriac purée, or pigs' trotter with judicious use of truffle oil. Desserts are refreshingly light, a gratin of red fruits perhaps, or delicious lemon tart. The short wine list scores notable hits, although you pay dearly for the high ones. The room is a delight in summer. Set lunch £22.50, Sun. £25.

ISLINGTON

Anna's Place

SWEDISH 11/20

90 MILDMAY PARK, NEWINGTON GREEN
N1, 0171-249 9379

Lunch & Dinner Tues.-Sat. £ BR: Canonbury.

Sufficiently focused on the cooking of Sweden, while at the same time triumphing as a neighbourhood restaurant. Tables are certainly packed in, but it only adds to the feeling of bonhomie. Essentially the ground floor of a Victorian house off Newington Green, the garden room at the back is rightly popular. Well-cured gravlax comes with a punchy mustard-and-dill dressing; smoked fish features strongly. Main courses are led by the legendary Biff Strindberg, no relation to the playwright, but fillet marinated in mustard and sautéed. For those unenthusiastic about Swedish cooking, there is a pasta dish and vegetarians are also catered for. Portions are generous, vegetables decidedly pedestrian, although praise is deserved for the dumplings and potatoes, particularly the latter in dauphinois style. Desserts concentrate on berries and home baking. The wine list is short and to the point, price being a major consideration. Set menus for lunch and dinner £21 and £23.

Euphorium

INTERNATIONAL 12/20

203 UPPER ST, N1, 0171-704 6909,
FAX 0171-226 0241
Lunch daily, Dinner Mon.-Sat. ££
U: Angel.

Once small, minimalist and modern, Euphorium has maintained the theme while expanding into premises both to left and right, though the pale wood and concrete combination remains. Bright young things of Islington pack what has grown to become restaurant, bar and shop. Chefs have changed a number of times, but the guiding hand of owner Marwan Badram has provided some consistency in what is already a fairly eclectic menu. Descriptions focus on light, salady ingredients—sweetbreads with a polenta crust served with tabouleh for example. Main courses might be pappardelle with broad beans, cep and truffle oil; or rack of lamb with butter bean and rosemary purée. Fish, char-grilled or roasted, might come with spinach or tapenade. Desserts look to England and France, the latter for the tarts, the former for the likes of date, almond and chocolate pudding. The wine list is suitably modern, from the New World, Italy and the lesser known regions of France. Set lunch £13.50.

Frederick's

FRENCH 11/20

106 CAMDEN PASSAGE, N1, 0171-359 2888,
FAX 0171-359 5173
Lunch & Dinner Mon.-Sat. ££
U: Angel.

Redesigned a few years ago and with a new chef installed, the restaurant's intention was clearly to move what had been a rather relaxed if chaotic Islington refuge upmarket. The food is certainly more adventurous—duck with tabbouleh and plum sauce; char-grilled Dover sole with foie gras and pasta—but the decor leaves one with a curiously disjointed feeling. The bar area—also known as country house hotel—leads into a dining room-cum-conservatory-cum-patio area. Walls are of brick and hung with gilt-framed pictures and tapestries; chairs are wooden. The mismatch approach extends to the service, and while everyone aims to please, the whole doesn't really hang together. Prices encourage high expectations, as does the menu: lamb kleftiko with flageolet beans and roasted vegetables; duck breast with green beans and garlic cream, but on delivery, can fail to match up. The wine list fits the bill. Set lunch and early dinner £12, Sat. lunch £13.50.

Granita

INTERNATIONAL 13/20

127 UPPER ST, N1, 0171-226 3222,
FAX 0171-226 4833
Lunch Wed.-Sun., Dinner Tues.-Sun. ££
U: Angel.

Austere and minimalist as the room certainly is—not a picture in sight, the only relief the flower arrangement on the end of the beaten metal bar—Granita has maintained a consistency and freshness since the day it opened. Chef and co-owner Ahmed Kharshoum scans the world but brings a sharp eye to focus on the plate. Dishes are described as a list of their component parts, thus you may start with tagliatelle, roasted aubergine, marjoram and Parmesan; or something as simple as scallops with spiced lentils and rocket. Main courses might be char-grilled tuna with avocado and red onion relish, roasted potatoes and green beans; or lamb, butter beans, tomato and rosemary. Salading is much in evidence and olive oil is given much prominence. Tarts, cakes and ices make up the puddings. Seasonal shopping drives the menu and everything is made on the day, including the excellent bread. Service is efficient, sometimes to the point of over-enthusiasm. The wine list is carefully thought out, and although concise, knows where its heart is—that is, with the customer. Set lunches £11.95 and £13.95, Sun. lunches £12.50 and £14.50.

Lola's

INTERNATIONAL 13/20

THE MALL BUILDING, 359 UPPER ST, N1, 0171-359 1932, FAX 0171-359 2209

Lunch daily, Dinner Mon.-Sat. ££

U: Angel.

Climb the stairs to this airy first-floor room and lose yourself in some of the more unusual European dishes: socca, a kind of pancake made with chickpea flour, or harira, a rather generous medly of squid, scallops, crabs, prawns and lentils flavoured with coriander and cumin. Service is exemplary and while the nomenclature on the menu can sometimes frustrate (why not just say Greek salad instead of horiatiki), there is always someone willing to explain. Cooking is of a high standard. A favourite starter is the spinach soup, dahl, rava dosa and raita, and rightly so, the spicing is spot on, the textures close but providing variation. Mains might be calf's liver and bacon with split-pea croquettes and mustard sauce, or lamb chump with ratatouille and olive oil mash. Desserts are strong, as in hot chocolate mousse cake, or rhubarb and pistachio trifle. The wine list pays homage to France, but shuffles around the rest of the world with care and attention. Set lunches £12 and courses £16.50.

KENSINGTON

Cibo

ITALIAN 11/20

3 RUSSELL GDNS, W14, 0171-371 6271, FAX 0171-602 1371

Lunch Sun.-Fri., Dinner Mon.-Sat. ££

U: Kensington (Olympia).

Tucked away in a side street, Cibo has a relaxed air to it, amusingly off-set by the unusual bas reliefs and Italianate naked ladies. This rather eclectic approach does not follow through to the food however, which is firmly Italian. Go for the fish and seafood, which is dictated by the market and on the whole, handled well. Cibo was once at the cutting edge, so to speak, of London's love affair with Italy. Others followed and as is so often the case, passed the likes of Cibo by. Relax and enjoy a starter of sautéed broad beans with melting goat's cheese, or duck ravioli with wild mushroom sauce. Main courses might be grilled swordfish with olives and rosemary, or seafood with tomatoes, garlic and herbs and a slight chilli kick. Sea bass will come simply baked with a salad of rocket perhaps; octopus will be meltingly stewed with tomatoes and herbs. Desserts are Italian through and through, as is the wine list. Miniature pastries come with coffee. Set lunch £12.50.

Clarke's

15/20 

CALIFORNIAN/MODERN BRITISH

124 KENSINGTON CHURCH ST, W8, 0171-221 9225, FAX 0171-229 4564

Lunch & Dinner Mon.-Fri. £££

U: Notting Hill Gate.

It is over a decade now since Sally Clarke first launched her mission to bring cool California culinary style to this bijou part of Kensington. The trend is now rampant, of course, all over the capital, but here it is still done with the minimum of self-promotion and with the quiet, confident ability that comes with long experience. Readers who have visited the ground-breaking Chez Panisse in Berkeley, California, where Sally Clarke once worked, will instantly recognise the same tone of direct simplicity in the cooking here. The drill is a four-course no-choice dinner menu at £40 (the week's menus are posted in advance if you happen to be passing, otherwise ring ahead or wait to be surprised), with a short carte at lunchtime. A light, often pasta-based first course that may incorporate marinated vegetables or some strong herb is followed by main-course meat or fish that is as often as not subject to quick, careful cooking on the char grill, whether it be lamb cutlets or plump Scottish scallops. The excellence of the raw materials is left to speak for itself rather than being over-garnished or swamped in a sauce. Cheese follows, and comes with fine oatmeal biscuits baked in-house, and the dessert is always designed not to outface. Poached pear is a favourite, perhaps annointed with a delicately spiced syrup and a drop of cream. Service is highly professional and welcoming. California's finest head the concise wine list, as may be expected. Prices are not low, but the quality is irreproachable. Set dinner £40.

The Dining Room

FRENCH 14/20

MILESTONE HOTEL, 1 KENSINGTON COURT, W1, 0171-917 1000, FAX 0171-917 1010
Lunch & Dinner Mon.-Fri. £££
U: High St Kensington.

This is English country-house style in the middle of Kensington, a red-brick Victorian building with a delightfully unexpected baronnial interior. Drinks in the elegant, comfortable drawing room, and a formally served dinner in the small dining room, with its elaborate carved plaster ceiling, small gothic windows and apparently flickering candles, is rather a different experience from either the normal hotel dining room or the echoing spaces of minimalist brasseries. The cooking, too, harks back to elegant, more leisured days, with a menu from young chef Simon Rogan that is a lesson in classic French style given a lighter contemporary treatment. So expect object lessons in dishes like sea scallops grilled and served with a purée of fennel and lemon and parsley sauce; an exquisite sabayon of shellfish with chives and ginger for starters; fillets of red mullet with langoustine tempura, a ginger purée in a wonderfully reduced lie de vin sauce; pave of Angus beef with a tatin of potatoes, and fondant of foiegras with a rich red wine sauce. Deserts are just as good, as in a gratin of caramel with Valrhona chocolate and lemon; or nougatine of blackcurrant parfait with liquorice. The wine list is very manageable and includes well known names at good prices; service is very willing. The as yet, relatively unknown Milestone Dining Room is doing everything right.

Kensington Place

MODERN BRITISH 13/20

205 KENSINGTON CHURCH ST, W8, 0171-727 3184, FAX 0171-229 2025
Lunch & Dinner daily. ££
U: Notting Hill Gate.

Quite what keeps KP so successful is hard to quantify. It opened nearly fifteen years ago, around the same time as The River Café, Bibendum and Alastair Little in Soho, and like all these places it is invariably full. It is big and noisy, the chairs are uncomfortable, the bar is small, the food is usually good but isn't reliable and there is no privacy. Nevertheless, the sum of its parts-and that includes some of London's most attractive and stroppy waiting staff, unisex loos, and dining in a gold fish bowl (it is a place to see and be seen), makes it work. The menu changes slightly each day but certain dishes such as cod and chips; scallops with a minted pea vinaigrette; sweet corn pancakes with foie gras; and grilled tamarillos with vanilla ice cream, rarely leave it. Daily specials, such as roast grouse with bread sauce; lamb couscous with harissa; and sole with Puy lentils and salsa verde, are often the best choice. Set lunch Mon.-Fri. £14.50, Sun. £16.50.

Launceston Place

MODERN BRITISH 12/20

1A LAUNCESTON PL, W8, 0171-937 6912, FAX 0171-938 2412
Lunch Sun.-Fri., Dinner Mon.-Sat. ££
U: High St Kensington.

This may be a leafy backwater of Kensington, but Launceston Place is at the forefront of modern British cooking. The bright cream-coloured room, with its nooks and crannies, is deceptively large and benefits from a wall of windows wrapping around the corner site. The kitchen delivers ingredients-led cooking, with a sideways glance to the English establishment as in the roast meats for Sunday lunch, or poached haddock with parsley sauce. Its heart, however, is in a more gutsy approach: Thai fish soup, black pudding with apple and potato rösti; or seared foie gras with grilled sourdough bread for starters. Main courses might include cotechino with calf's liver, lentils and salsa verde; or roast poussin with ceps. Desserts are in the bread-and-butter pudding or tart mould, and the wine list, although short, is well focused. The set lunch (and dinner from 7pm to 8pm) at £14.50 to £17.50 is good value.

Novelli W8

FRENCH 14/20

122-124 PALACE GARDENS TERRACE, W8, 0171-229 4024, FAX 0171-243 1826

Lunch Tues.-Sun., Dinner nightly. ££

U: Farringdon.

Jean-Christophe Novelli is one of those chefs intent on making their mark all over London, and this venue—once a timewarp restaurant called the Ark—is his Kensington bolthole. The seriously limited space is deceptively enhanced with mirrors, but foreclosed again by an unsubtle colour—scheme of advancing inky blue. Expansive menus offer what has become the recognisable Novelli idiom: earthy dishes such as cassoulet ingredients fashioned into a terrine; frothy soups like green pea enriched with foie gras, and oriental seasonings used with shellfish. Pig's trotter is always there, cooked à ma façon each day, while the slow-cooking may also be extended to stuffed rabbit leg, done in a thick sauce incorporating tomatoes and coriander. Brandy snap cornets of ice cream garnished with summer fruits were an amusing and well executed dessert. Staff cope admirably, given the lack of room for manoeuvre, and the wine list is unostentatiously serviceable. Set lunch £14.50.

Phoenicia

LEBANESE 13/20

11-13 ABINGDON RD, W8, 0171-937 0120, FAX 0171-937 7668

Lunch & Dinner daily. ££

U: High St Kensington.

The Lebanese decor is restrained with well-spaced, comfortable seating. Equally suited to the Kensington location just off the High Street is friendly, unobtrusive service. Prices are reasonable, especially for set meals, and the cooking maintains high standards. The £16.80 per head mezze of 15 dishes for four people includes arayess—pita stuffed with meat, sesame cream, and grilled; shankleesh—cheese in thyme, with tomatoes, onion parsley and olive oil; batata harra—potato sautéed in garlic, onion, coriander and chilli; mouhammara-mixed crushed nuts, capsicum, olive oil and spices; and better known dishes such as hummus, tabbouleh, vine leaves, moutabel, grilled chicken wings and kafta kebab—minced lamb on a skewer. Most main course grills and stews come with rice and there are baked fish dishes and vegetarian choices. Finish with home-made pastries and Lebanese coffee or mint tea. Buffet lunch £10.95 (Mon.-Sat.); £12.95 (Sun./Bank Hol); menus £16.50 £30.95.

The Tenth

INTERNATIONAL 14/20

ROYAL GARDEN HOTEL, 2-24 KENSINGTON HIGH ST, W8, 0171-361 1910, FAX 0171-361 1909

Lunch & Dinner daily. £££

U: High St Kensington.

The Tenth is, as you might expect from the name, on the tenth floor of the Royal Garden Hotel, which gives a stupendous view during the day over the green expanses of Kensington Gardens and Hyde Park. Get a table as near the windows as possible, as the decor is from the hotel-dining-room school, which is uninspiring to say the least. The same however cannot be said about the food, which delights with its freshness, inventiveness and style. The new chef, Derek Baker, has been promoted from within, after doing stints with Paul Gayler and John Torode. He displays a sure touch on a thoroughly modern menu—crispy duck spring roll with a tagliatelle of cucumber and a plum dressing; spiced barbecued quail on a beetroot cabbage with baby corn beignets for starters; Thai-flavoured risotto with flamed tiger prawns and coconut crisps; pan-fried fillet of beef with pommes Anna, wild mushroom galette and morel sauce for mains. This mixing of ingredients can be dangerous territory, but is beautifully handled here. Dishes marked NYT indicate that £1 is given to the National Youth Theatre. This is not a public relations gesture however, the hotel's general manager, Graham Bamford is a man with a mission—to encourage young talent in the theatre and music world. This translates into Saturday evenings when the John Wilson Band plays some very good music indeed, using young musicians from the Guildhall School of Music. The first Saturday of the month is a real winner—proper big band music from the likes of Irving Berlin, Cole Porter and George Gershwin. Set lunches £16.50 and £21.

The Terrace

MODERN BRITISH 13/20

33C HOLLAND ST, W8, 0171-937 3224
Lunch daily, Dinner Mon.-Sat. ££
U: High St. Kensington.

This was previously Mon Petit Plaisir, the moderately successful offshoot of Mon Plaisir in Covent Garden. Taken over by Steven Loveridge, whose first venture in restaurants this is, it has blossomed into a perfect neighbourhood place, offering great cooking in a pretty venue. It's a sensible menu, offering something for every taste, from a seemingly simple but perfectly balanced Jerusalem artichoke soup flavoured with coriander and balsamic vinegar to heavily garliced pan-fried prawns with celeriac and basil coleslaw. Main dishes are equally well cooked, a dish of scallops, grilled to perfection, coming with roast parsnips and field mushrooms, and black beans and sesame seeds. The char-grilled rump of lamb came with pease pudding and coriander and mustard oil. Desserts are tops: for a true British experience try the Bakewell tart; for a dish that should become a classic, go for the steamed stem ginger and lemon sponge with custard, a challenge to anyone with memories of how mother made such a steamed sponge. The wine list is adequate, the service friendly. You must book. Set lunches £12.50 and £14.50.

KNIGHTSBRIDGE

Brasserie St. Quentin

FRENCH 13/20

243 BROMPTON RD, SW3, 0171-581 5131,
FAX 0171-584 6064
Lunch & Dinner daily. ££
U: South Kensington.

The selling of the Brasserie St Quentin by the Savoy group to Groupe Chez Gérard was a logical move, and that move has apparently been seamless. But why tinker with a well-established institution with a loyal local French following? The restaurant is relatively small, lightened by mirrors on the walls and very much as you would expect to find in Paris. The clientele is sophisticated, well travelled enough to know their terrine de foie gras from their assiette de charcuterie de Gascogne, their cuisse de lapin au ragoût de celeri from their magret de canard de Barbarie, sauce foie gras, but sensibly the menu offers an exact English translation of these tried-and-tested French classics. And very good they are too, examples of the kind of traditional French cooking which once expected to find in every small French provincial town. Grilled Scotch fillet comes with a piquant tarragon sauce and excellent French fries, that aforementioned breast of duck with a wonderful foie gras sauce, creamed Savoy cabbage and white beans; desserts are particularly good, and the ever popular lemon tart holds its own beautifully. The wine list is French, the service ditto, that is in this case, efficient and fast. Set lunch £12.50, also available before 7.30pm.

Cambio de Tercio

SPANISH 14/20

163 OLD BROMPTON RD, SW5, 0171-244 8970
Lunch & Dinner daily. ££
U: Knightsbridge.

Blood-and-sand-coloured walls, with matadors' capes and hats, and colourful, if soft focus, photographs of bull fights make this uncongenial for vegetarians. But add live guitar music and lively Spanish service and you have an ambience which—to judge by the adoring couples dining there, is romantic, even erotic. The brilliant Spanish-Basque cooking is equal to the occasion. Start with the sweetest, most succulent mountain ham. Continue with ostras gratinadas, warm oysters in a sort of savoury sabayon or endivias rellenas, chicory stuffed with ham in a leek sauce. Then suckling pig Segovian-style, crisp and moist as the best Chinese; or solomillo de avestruz Cordobesa, fillet of ostrich—well why not? They feel at home in the Spanish desert too. Fine cheeses come with membrillo and the ninety Spanish wines offer abundant choice. Here sophisticated Kensingtonians may utter 'viva España!' and even be forgiven an 'olé!'

The Capital

MODERN BRITISH 16/20

22-24 BASIL ST, SW3, 0171-589 5171,
FAX 0171-225 0011
Open Lunch & Dinner daily. ££££
U: Knightsbridge.

A

Just perusing the menu at this intimate hotel dining room is a pleasure indeed, for it abounds in modern, elegant creations that have earned the continually improving chef, Philip Britten, our highest admiration. Amazingly, the prices of the set dinner haven't gone up since the last edition of this book: the 'Temptation' costs £55, the 'Seduction' and understandably higher £75. Both are sumptuous feasts and allow substitutions from the à la carte menu. Seduced we were by the nine-course 'Seduction,' whose dishes included a garlic-haunted tomato pot-au-feu; an asparagus tuile on a sabayon of Sauternes with truffle and lime; langoustine risotto with caviar, boudin of foie gras; scalded lobster with sage pasta, and seared scallops with Savoy cabbage and apples—all refreshing, exciting combinations of flavours and textures. Throughout the meal, ingredients were of a uniformly high level of quality and freshness, and dessert was not an afterthought but a crowning moment—a butterscotch soufflé on a compôte of oranges, with fromage-blanc sorbet. The simple yet well-built wine list is committed to high quality, a reflection of owner David Levin's other lifeas a winemaker. Set lunch £23.50 and £28. Set dinners £55 for 7 courses, £75 for 9 courses.

The Fifth Floor

MODERN BRITISH 15/20

HARVEY NICHOLS, KNIGHTSBRIDGE, SW1,
0171-235 5250, FAX 0171-235 5020
Lunch daily, Dinner Mon.-Sat. £££
U: Knightsbridge.

A

It's all happening on the top floor at Harvey Nichols. Many consider the food hall to rival certain of its Knightsbridge neighbours in offering the recherché and the remarkable: there is a bustling café, where worn-out gourmet shoppers may pause to fortify themselves, an excellent wine department, and the Fifth Floor restaurant, where Henry Harris has forged himself quite a reputation. It's a long, spacious room, the arched windows along one side allowing for furtive peeps on to the Knightsbridge bustle below, the armchair seating inviting cosy snuggling without hindering our powers of digestion.

The menus pursue an essentially modern British idiom, although they allow themselves the freedom to dip into the classic French mode as the fancy takes them. Oeufs en meurette, cooked in Burgundy with mushrooms, are not much seen in London, and we fell upon them with glee. Oysters in the Bordelais manner with spiced sausages have been sighted, but there are gleanings from further afield too, as in the Spanish ham made from black pigs fed on acorns that comes authentically dressed with quince jelly. Roast rabbit is always good, timed to a nicety to retain succulence, while monkfish has received the Indian spice treatment, accompanied by a salad of cucumber and mint in distant suggestion of raita. The dessert menu tempts by virtue of its thoughtful suggestions for sweet wines that are keyed to each dish, and for the quality of raw materials in such dishes as the chocolate tart with pistachio ice cream. Wines reflect the pedigree of the adjacent wine shop, and the spread of prices is nothing like as intimidating as one might expect. Set lunch £19.50 and £23.50.

Grissini

ITALIAN 13/20

HYATT CARLTON TOWER, SLOANE ST, SW1,
0171-235 1234, FAX 0171-2456570
Lunch Mon.-Fri., Brunch Sun., Dinner Mon.-Sat. ££ U: Knightsbridge.

A

As the name of a clichéd Italian speciality—that delightful little breadstick—Grissini is also the name of a chic Italian restaurant. Maybe it's supposed to act as an ironic contradistinction, because the food (and decor) is far from clichéd, or even derivative, which is getting harder to achieve as our Mediterranean-mania continues to run riot. Indeed, north Italian specialities include the likes of pesto risotto with pan-fried scallops and crisp zucchini flowers, which may sound like gilding the lily, but the flavours do actually reinforce each other. The same applies to deep-fried monkfish medallions flavoured with lime zest, and it's obvious that the chocolate cake with hazlenut ice cream and vanilla sorbet is going to exemplify the genre. The restaurant is idylically positioned overlooking Cadogan

Gardens, with a 'full frontal' of the nearby greenery ensured by conservatory-style windows, while a domed area also provides an al fresco feel. It is a perfect fit with the sophisticated, modern north Italian style, featuring some clever bronzework and just enough of the signature lavender colour to create maximum effect. Only set menus: Set lunches £19.50 and £22.50, set dinners £24.50 and £28.50.

La Tante Claire

FRENCH 19/20

THE BERKELEY HOTEL, WILTON PLACE, SW1
0171-352 6045/235 6000, FAX 0171-352 3257
Please telephone for opening times. ££££
U: Hyde Park Corner.

Pierre Koffmann of La Tante Claire has transferred his famous restaurant from Chelsea to this prestigious address, which opens early September 1998. Anyone who has been kept on the waiting list because the place was too small must rejoice. From September, La Tante Claire doubles its capacity as the restaurant sits 70 gastronomes with more space for each one. This expansion was the new challenge for Pierre Koffmann, it being the maximum number that he was sure he could handle while still maintaining the perfection of his cooking. After dominating the London scene from his intimate, almost hidden, blue and yellow dining room, inspiring an entire generation of British chefs, the great and tranquil Koffman was ready for a well thought-out move. What else could it have been? Being a cook from top to toe and not a businessman, he is not the kind to start a chain of Tante Claires. When he is not with his family, his life is entirely devoted to his kitchen where he continues to cook dishes that he invented, making them better and better over the years, while also inventing new ones. Besides being a creator, he is a true artisan in love with his work, finding his satisfaction in the daily accomplishment of cooking. After all these years—we first discovered him in 1980—we are even more enthusiastic for his signature dishes such as the garbure de turbot aux haricots Tarbais (ragout of turbot with beans from Tarbes); saumon à la graisse d'oie (salmon in goose fat); pieds de cochon aux morilles (pig's trotters stuffed with morels); canard de Challans à la presse et herbes sèches (pressed Challans duck with dried herbs); and the saddle of venison with strawberry vinegar and bitter chocolate. To crown these dishes, originally inspired by the south western 'terroir' of Pierre, the new pastry chef shoots an unforgettable firework with the assiette de parfum aux deux agrumes (fragrance around two citrus fuits), and trois desserts Gascons (three desserts from Gascony). The service is aerial. Of course the wine list is impressive, but intelligently enough, very affordable varietal wines are offered like Marsanne and Viognier mostly from the Southwest, Camargue and Minervois. Set lunch £28.

Restaurant One-O-One

SEAFOOD 14/20

WILLIAM ST, SW1, 0171-290 7101,
FAX 0171-235 6196
Lunch & Dinner daily. £££
U: Knightsbridge

For long, Pascal Proyart, the young French chef at the Sheraton Park Tower, has been one of the unsung heroes of fish cuisine. He has consistently been cooking some of the best fish dishes in town, producing delicate flavours and beautiful patterns on the plate. He's worked with Michel Belys at L'Orangerie in Brussels and at The Sea Grill Restaurant Le Divellec in Paris, and has always made much of his Brittany upbringing, to good effect. Now he has a setting worthy of his talents. The former dining room of the hotel has been transformed, with its own entrance in William Street, and a coulour décor of—guess what-navy blue, jade and aquamarine. Dominating the interior is a fourteen-foot sculpture of a fish, as striking, but not quite as eccentric, as a Damien Hirst creation, which would not suit the clientele. Complex ingredients are beautifully treated. Fillet of sea bass comes with a layer of caviar and is served with a shallot cream sauce which complements rather than overhwelms; grilled grey and red mullet comes with a bright flash of coulour in a coulis of red peppers and a vegetable couscous, the flavours producing an explosion of taste. Clearly Pascal Proyart loves sea bass—he spreads it with caviar and serves it with a shallot cream sauce; he roasts it on its skin, first covering it with a soft crust of olive tapenade and serving it with an artichoke barigoule sauce. This is inventive, confident cooking. Service is attentive; the wine list extensive. Set lunches £21 and £25; Set Dinners £32 and £42, Menu Discovery £45, Menu Gourmandise £55.

Vong

FRENCH-THAI 15/20

KNIGHTSBRIDGE, SW1, 0171-235 1010,
FAX 0171-235 1011
Lunch Mon.-Sat., Dinner nightly. £££
U: Knightsbridge.

The Berkeley Hotel is so keen that Vong should be perceived as a separate restaurant (as opposed to a hotel restaurant) that it has its own entrance and identity. The restaurant is sleek, slick and modern, providing no distractions for the exotically presented menu of French-Thai crossover food. These days, Jean-Georges Vongerichten is an occasional visitor, leaving the execution of his innovative, complex dishes in the capable hands of Shaun Gilmore. The menu bargain is undoubtedly the Black Plate (£15), available as a shared starter for two or a lunch menu. Highlights include prawn satay bound with mousse, breadcrumbed and served with fresh oyster sauce; lobster daikon roll made with transparent rice pancakes and eaten with a rosemary ginger dip; and quail rubbed with Thai spices accompanied by a crunchy cress salad. Main dishes are complex to a fault and often bamboozle the palette. Lobster with Thai herbs sounds light and elegant but comes in a rich cream sauce garnished with apple. Valrhona chcocolate cake alone is worth a visit. Set menus £15—£45.

MARBLE ARCH

Al San Vincenzo

ITALIAN 13/20

30 CONNAUGHT ST, W2, 0171-262 9623
Lunch Mon.-Fri., Dinner Mon.-Sat. ££
U: Marble Arch.

A small, compact and friendly room, this family-run restaurant has somehow bypassed the current Renaissance for all things Italian and continues to do its own thing. The regionality of Italy is thrown aside in favour of a more general approach: the chilli-heat of the south rubbing shoulders with the pig's trotters, cotechino and lentils of the north. What it lacks in edge, it more than makes up for in its solid approach, although vegetables continue to appear rather as an afterthought. Dishes as simple as tongue and salsa verde, borlotti bean soup or stewed octopus have the required earthiness. Attention is paid to the seasons, so lamb comes with peas; sea bass with a generous seasoning of spring herbs. Refreshingly untrendy, which for some is a relief. Desserts move beyond tiramisù and there is a delicious version of bread-and-butter pudding using panettone and mascarpone. The wine list is short and good.

MARYLEBONE

Ibla

ITALIAN 14/20

89 MARYLEBONE HIGH ST, W1, 0171-224 3799
Lunch daily, Dinner Tues.-Sat. £
U: Baker St.

Charming, unpretentious and understated, you can choose from the rear dining room or the front area, the latter more shop than restaurant, where you can select cheese, dried pastas and salami to take away. The green paintwork is certainly distinctive and strangely calming but this may have more to do with the homely atmosphere. Ingredients shine on unfussy plates, a salad of chicken livers perhaps, or chickpea soup, the latter with a smooth intensity. Pasta is superb, dressed with punchy rabbit, or duck rendered silky from long, slow cooking. Calf's liver looks deceptively the same as elsewhere, but has just the right intensity. Tarts are impressive, both savoury and sweet, desserts generally having a finesse more French than Italian. Service is charming and efficient and the all-Italian wine list is unusual and rewarding if lacking somewhat in more heavyweight contenders. Set lunches £13 and £16.

Mandalay

BURMESE 12/20

444 EDGWARE RD, W2, 0171-258 3696
Lunch & Dinner Mon.-Sat. £
U: Edgware Rd.

London's only fully-fledged Burmese restaurant does an exemplary job as an ambassador of that beleaguered nation's cuisine. As you might expect, the food shares common elements with Indian food, but with the inclusion of south-east Asian flavours (such as lemon grass), and some Chinese ingredients (especially noodle dishes). The dishes, served by the utterly charming Ally family, use very fresh ingredients and are prepared with great care. Try the 'rice noodles in fish soup', which is mohingar, the Burmese national dish, and genuinely different. If you prefer something more mainstream, there is plenty of choice of lamb, vegetarian and chicken dishes, plus soups and salads. Be warned that the restaurant is no palace; it's a converted shop unit on a busy trunk road, but the warm welcome makes up for any lack of expensive interior design (a move may be on the cards). The set lunches are a complete steal. Set lunches £3.50 and £5.40.

Nico Central

FRENCH 13/20

35 GT PORTLAND ST, W1, 0171-436 8846,
FAX 0171-436 0134
Lunch Mon.-Fri., Dinner Mon.-Sat. ££
U: Gt. Portland St.

Nico Ladenis is no longer involved (except through family connections) and occasionally the master's touch is noticeably lacking. In pressed ham and artichoke terrine with foie gras the meat was stringy, and the fond d'artichaut carelessly prepared. But velouté of celeriac with truffle oil was a soup-lover's dream; better still was roast fillet of cod with fresh capers and a spring onion mash of which Nico would be proud. And he would be more than content with the chips. Crisp apple crumble with iced crème fraîche nearly lived up to its alliterative name but critics might cry for louder crepitation. Nico Central is a gastronomic oasis for local rag-traders and media people. They, and many others, cherish the unpretentious English language menu, the bright decor and ambience. Decently priced bottles in the interesting wine list include the magnificent Cape Mentelle Semillon Sauvignon at £25. Prices are set: 2 course lunch is £22, 3 courses is £25. Dinner is £27 for 3 courses and service is included in all prices.

Orrery

MODERN BRITISH 14/20

55-57 MARYLEBONE HIGH ST, NW1,
0171-616-8000, FAX 0171-616-8080
Lunch & Dinner daily. ££££
U: Regent's Park.

Sir Terence Conran has been making much of the running in London's increasingly-frenetic food scene in recent years. Whenever he opens a restaurant (which he does with great frequency), the rush is on to get a booking, and in the case of the critics, to be as sharply critical as possible. All to the good, for he is a powerful force. At Orrery, happily, he is on top form, for this is everything a Conran restaurant should be. It's extremely comfortable, with seating seemingly designed to accommodate every shape and size from the largest corporation to the tiniest model; the details of the cool decor in this long room are impeccable; the service is friendly and professional; the wine list formidable; and the attention to design detail perfect. And the cooking is first-rate. The whole reminds us of the younger sister of Bibendum. First courses might include a perfectly rendered terrine of foie gras with toasted brioche; a seemingly simple but beautifully prepared lobster bisque; or a wild mushroom risotto to rival Milan's best (a dish which can appear as a main vegetarian course with truffles). Main courses follow in the same vein: seared scallops coming with garlic mash and a red wine and basil sauce; a satisfying venison loin with red pepper, caramelised onions and sauce poivrade. The dessert list is short, but save room, if you can, for the hot chocolate fondant with vanilla ice cream or the tarte fine of apples coming with the obligatory Granny Smith sorbet. Set lunches £22.50 and £26.50.

Stephen Bull

MODERN BRITISH 14/20

5-7 BLANDFORD ST, W1, 0171-486 9696
Lunch Mon.-Fri., Dinner Mon.-Sat. ££
U: Baker St.

The ambience here, once trend-setting in its severity, is now softer, multi-coloured, and even includes comfortable banquettes. White-clothed tables are small, glass and cutlery simple and elegant. New chef Robert Jones has brought interest to the short daily-changing menu. Brief descriptions lead to such pleasant surprises as the salsa which lifted twice-baked goat's cheese soufflé, or the bed—no, cushion—of spinach which supported perfectly cooked rump of lamb with artichokes and butter beans. A fashion which we hope he will moderate is for using Mediterranean ingredients inappropriately—here it is olive oil instead of butter in mashed potatoes. Imaginative desserts include a fine peach ice cream and a pear feuilleté with butterscotch, its pastry as crisp as the cheese puffs on the table when you arrive.

Union Café

MODERN BRITISH 13/20

96 MARYLEBONE LANE, W1, 0171-486 4860

Lunch & Dinner Mon.-Sat. ££

U: Bond St.

Impeccably sourced raw ingredients are given a confident treatment that knows when to leave well alone. Judicious use of the chargrill renders sea bass crispy on the outside, moist inside; tuna, sufficiently seared, is served with a punchy lime and chilli salsa. The room is bare wooden boards, lots of windows and an open-plan kitchen, more Californian than the back of Oxford Street. Baking is a strong point, whether bread, tart or pizza. The charcuterie is superb, while soups have a solid earthiness. Smoked haddock will get a classic treatment of spinach and Hollandaise, while veal—organic and English—might be braised with sweet and succulent carrots. Desserts might be biscotti with dessert wine, or pears on fine shortcrust pastry. The wine list is short but confident and other drinks, whether it be lemonade or elderflower cordial, are given due attention. Breakfast—scrambled eggs, toast and pancetta—is a delight.

Villandry

MODERN BRITISH 12/20

170 GT PORTLAND ST, W1, 0171-631 3131

Lunch & Dinner Mon.-Sat. ££

U: Oxford Circus.

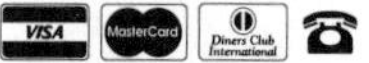

The good news about the new Villandry is that the restaurant (and stunning food shop) is more than double the size of the old dining room in Marylebone High Street. The bad news is that a meal can (still) be painfully slow. This is not so much due to the fact that all the food is cooked to order, but more to do with a lack of control at the helm. Although owner Jean-Charles Carrarini is often to be seen stalking distractedly round the large, very noisy dining rooms, he doesn't take charge as a host. Nevertheless, as before, when the food does arrive it is fresh and seasonal, wholesome and nicely presented. Incidentals, such as butter and fresh bread and large cotton napkins, can't be faulted. The four choices per course change with every meal and great store is set by using the finest ingredients. Hence the taste and texture of the smoked salmon (wild and from Ireland) is noticeably superior. Thin, carefully cooked slices of calf's liver arrive draped over a well-seasoned stew of peas, broad beans, braised cabbage and prosciutto; a small but perfectly cooked tranche of cod came with lentils, chick peas, preserved lemon and salsa verde. Great puds such as quince and almond tart, and bread-and-butter pudding with orange sauce.

MAYFAIR

Al Hamra

LEBANESE 14/20

31 SHEPHERD MARKET, W1, 0171-493 1954, FAX 0171-493 1044

Open Lunch & Dinner daily. ££

U: Green Park.

Al Hamra is in keeping with Mayfair's legendary opulence. It comfortably seats 75 at large tables even if some are intimately close together. But some seclusion is provided by moveable wooden partitions holding plants at table-top level. Terrace tables benefit from infra-red heaters and the liveliness of Shepherd Market makes the ambience as animated outside as in. High prices are justified by friendly service and fine food. The long list of cold and hot meze includes several ways of preparing aubergines: as moutabal they are grilled and pounded to a subtly seasoned paste; as moussakaa batinjan, they are fried with chick peas and tomatoes; and as makdous batinjan, pickled baby aubergines are stuffed with walnuts, spices and garlic. Lamb and offal are well represented while fish include Dover sole, mullet, and trout. Arak and Lebanese wine head the list of otherwise mainly French wines at £16.50 to £57.

Caviar Kaspia

RUSSIAN/FRENCH 12/20

18/18A BRUTON PL, W1, 0171-493 2612

Lunch & Dinner Mon.-Sat. £££

U: Green Park.

The sister of the Paris caviar shop, Caviar Kaspia continues to ply its trade in a mews off Berkeley Square, discreetly feeding the British upper crust, local business people and visitors. Caviar, vodkas and Champagne are the main reason to come here, the famous fish eggs starting at a modest £10 for 30g of pressed caviar up to a whopping and wonderful £297 for 125g of best Beluga. In case you don't know your caviars, the menu has delightful explanations and a few choice sayings, such as James Bond's remark in Casino Royale to Vesper that 'The trouble always is...not how to get enough caviar but how to get enough toast with it'. Should you not want caviar, there are some good alternatives at remarkably modest prices: vegetable borscht and mushroom piroshjki at £5; avocado, smoked chicken and prawn salad at £10.50; Kaspia's special gravlax marinated in spices and blueberries with a dill mustard sauce at £12.50; a large smoked salmon and scrambled egg on toasted brioche at £12.50. Or mix the peasant with the prince in a potato with caviar. It all reinforces the restaurant's general outlook on life: the ultra-rich can afford to do anything they like without embarrassment. Caviar Kaspia is surprisingly good entertainment and can be good value, all in a rather formal setting with pre-revolutionary Russian pictures on the walls, some beautiful china and silver. Set menus £32, £59.50 and £99.

Chez Nico at Ninety

FRENCH 18/20

GROSVENOR HOUSE, 90 PARK LANE, W1,
0171-409 1290, FAX 0171-355 4877
Lunch Mon.-Fri., Dinner Mon.-Sat. ££££
U: Hyde Park Corner.

We like Nico Ladenis—he is a great restaurateur and an outspoken person. You can't be more European—even universal—than this Greco-Anglo-French godfather of fine dining in London. There's nothing more enjoyable than hearing him chastising the charlatans and self-promoted cooks who sprinkle coriander on couscous with a lemon grass, taro and coconut salad marinated in a saké and soya sauce and then try to make believe that they have reconstructed the universe of Marco Polo and repaved the road to Mandalay. As there is only one Parthenon, so there is only (at least in the Western world) respectable kitchen: the one of Escoffier and of the great French masters. In his elegant-without-ostentation restaurant facing Hyde Park, Nico maintains this tradition at its highest level. The whims of fashion have no hold here and it's immensely reassuring to know that in this fickle world, a few pillars of wisdom stand firm. Dining here brings the pleasure of returning to the roots, though roots which have been rejuvenated; respecting tradition does not mean repeating the same story. It is the strict adjustments to changing times and tastes that keep this house so strong. The quality of the products speaks for the rest. No-one serves such large, moist, tender grilled scallops from Scotland on buttered leeks, or fresher Dover soles with an impeccable tartar sauce. His foie gras flavoured with girottines, black truffles and green peppercorns is tops. The baked turbot with artichokes and mushrooms could serve as a cooking school model. But Nico excels in meat and offal courses: calf's sweetbreads are wrapped in a brique pastry with boudin blanc; foie gras renders the Bresse pigeon even more tender on his bed of cabbage. Of course the chickens are corn-fed and the veal milk-fed. Only the best of the farm is good enough for Nico's pans. This is also true of the wine list with its superb bottles, seducing us this time with a voluptuous Santenay premier cru La Maladiéreat at a relatively affordable price. Set lunch £34, Set dinner £64.

Claridge's

FRENCH/BRITISH 14/20

CLARIDGE'S HOTEL, BROOK ST, W1,
0171-629 8860, FAX 0171-499 2210
Lunch & Dinner daily. ££££
U: Bond St.

Claridge's has always catered to aristocratic tastes and continues to do so, so you're likely to encounter the odd dowager with her grandchildren beautifully dressed up, as well as captains of industry. It's very formal, from the string quartet playing in the drawing room as the occasional liveried footman passes by and you sip your aperitif, to the dome-lifting that predominates in the dining room. Some people might call it a time warp, but it's amazingly popular and when you do it this well, why change. John Williams does a remarkably good job, producing classic dishes but with enough innovation to satisfy more forward-looking souls. So the Cornish lobster and crab salad comes with peppered pineapple dressing; a trio of foie gras with elderflower sauce and spiced bread, though the aniseed scented courgettes and fennel confit that accompanied a red mullet overpowered rather than complemented the fish. Strong tastes that worked well came in a duck with braised Savoy cabbage and a green pepper sauce, and a roast fillet of lamb on a vegetable tartlet with a pungent mustard and thyme essence. Homesick North Americans can order the maple syrup crème brûlée; we went for iced apple soufflé with cinnamon biscuit and a great Calvados caramel, and a good old-fashioned strawberry Romanoff. Suitably grand wine list and suitably grand service. A true British experience not to be missed even if you have to save hard for it. Set lunches £29 and £38, set dinner £38 and chef's special Sonata menu £58, £85 with wine. All include service.

Coast

INTERNATIONAL 14/20

26B ALBEMARLE ST, W1, 0171-495 5999, FAX 0171-495 2999

Lunch Mon.-Fri., Dinner daily. ££

U: Green Park.

Oliver Peyton is one of London's headline-hitting restaurateurs. Owner also of the Atlantic Bar and Grill, he designs eateries in the boldest style, and in the case of this Mayfair address (once a car showroom), with almost ruthless simplicity. A bright airy box with goldfish-bowl window and unadorned walls forms the backdrop for cooking that has improved immeasurably after a shaky start. The culinary ideas bring a whole new meaning to the over-used description 'eclectic', essaying daring turns such as the herb-scented waffle doused in maple syrup that supported a beautifully timed slice of foie gras, or the appealingly rich crab 'won-ton' that was sandwiched between crisp potato wafers. When cooking is as adventurous as this, the inevitable miss is occasionally recorded, but most dishes are brought off with nerveless panache. An Italian accent runs through desserts that may take in sweet versions of cannelloni filled with ice cream, or risotto flavoured with apple. Wines are well-chosen, with France a strong suit, but prices are Mayfair-stiff.

The Connaught Grill Room and Restaurant

BRITISH/FRENCH 16/20

CARLOS PL, W1, 0171-499 7070, FAX 0171-495 3262

Restaurant: Lunch & Dinner daily; Grill: Lunch Sun.-Fri., Dinner daily. ££££

U: Bond St.

The Connaught continues in its inimitable way, the only change seemingly being the appearance of a menu displayed just outside the hotel, which is probably the nearest the Connaught will ever get to advertising. The miracle is wrought by Michel Bourdin, Maître Cuisinier de France, the chef who has presided here for nearly 25 years and through whose capable kitchens so many top chefs have passed. In a world of rapid and confusing change, The Connaught remains the place to return to again and again, to reassure you of the excellence of classic British and French cooking and give you a yardstick against which to judge so many newcomers. The Connaught has two dining rooms, the smaller more intimate Grill Room, and the very grand, but very comfortable Restaurant where the oak still gleams, the roast beef is still served on a Wednesday, and the boiled silverside appears on a Thursday. Should these stalwarts not be to your taste, there is enough on the long menu for everyone. From the hors d'oeuvres, perhaps the freshest oysters; terrine of goose foie gras in a port gelée; Prince of Wales consommé with a crisp pastry crust. From the main course, only the best ingredients are used in turbot poached, grilled or roasted in the oven with a beurre Nantais; a perfectly cooked wild duck with peaches; Kentish lamb 'Forestière'; cold Scottish salmon. For dessert, perhaps a simple iced raspberry mousse, or a proper bread-and-butter pudding. All will be perfectly cooked, and served with the confidence that comes with a hundred year-old tradition of fine dining and very fine drinking, in a discreet but oh-so-elegant setting. The Connaught is one of our favourites. Plus, of course, a very splendid wine list. Lunch Mon.-Sat. 27.50, Sun. £30.50. Set dinner £55.

Dorchester Grill

BRITISH 13/20

THE DORCHESTER, PARK LANE, W1, 0171-629 8888, FAX 0171-317 6464

Lunch & Dinner daily. £££

U: Hyde Park Corner.

The mention of a 'grill room' immediately conjures up visions of a grand, traditionally English dining room, whereas the Dorchester Grill leaves this element to the menu—the decor is far more individual, having been modelled on a traditional Spanish palace. The proportions and features are indeed palatial, with gilt galore, tapestries and chandeliers, not to mention a coffered ceiling. The usual crowd is equally gilded, being a cosmopolitan, soignée combination of traditional good taste. Service is immaculate, in the old-school tradition, which incorporates impressive culinary chariots cruising the room. Moreover service is not stiff-upper-lipped, with amicable conversation served up should you encourage it. The menu makes the most of British ingredients, serving them up within contemporized regional specialities and traditional favourites. Presentation is traditional, while also managing to avoid the usual regimented hotel look, with the forte of Willi Elsenser's cooking being an overall harmony between varying flavours; they add up to give a result which is far greater than the sum total of the individual parts. Feast on warm Stilton and leek tart; Hereford duck breast and sausage with quince-flavoured gravy; flambé crèpes Suzette. Coffee and sublime petit fours are such an indulgence that they are effectively a course in their own right.

1837

FRENCH 14/20

BROWN'S HOTEL, ALBERMARLE ST, W1, 0171-408 1837

Lunch Mon.-Fri, Dinner Mon.-Sat. ££££
U: Green Park.

A

1837 is not the address, it's the date London's first public restaurant opened, at Brown's Hotel. It's also the date Queen Victoria ascended the throne. As such a date indicates, 1837 has a venerable interior—lots of beautiful, mellow wood panelling, heavy oil paintings of people long dead, a roaring fireplace, lots of space between tables covered in heavy linen. But it is also quite pristine after a sensitive renovation. Much the same could be said of chef Gregory Nicholson's cooking which, for lack of a better term might be called nouvelle vielle; traditional dishes with a modern twist. For some, like the hand-dived scallops steamed in their shell with herbs and vermouth, this means delicacy and slight undercooking so these children of Venus retain their texture and flavour, then serving them under a puff pastry lid. Other dishes, like the rock oysters and smoked salmon in a Muscadet saffron jelly, could have come straight out of Escoffier, as could the main course of tournedos Rossini. Veal sweetbreads coated in parsley and tarragon with braised leeks and a Meaux mustard cream sauce was exquisitely judged. The well-chosen selection of French and English cheeses are properly ripened. Desserts, like the tart of caramelised puff pastry and pears with fromage blanc sorbet, or the selection of petit lemon desserts, are tempting even after a large meal. The wine list is an exhaustive trawl through the world's great wines with a concentration on France, but also including exceptional wines from the rest of Europe and the New World. Fortunately, as it runs to 53 pages and over 750 wines, the sommelier and wine waiters know their wines and share their knowledge, rather than using it as a weapon. Set lunch £27, dégustation menu £55.

The Greenhouse

MODERN BRITISH 14/20

27A HAYS MEWS, W1, 0171-499 3331, FAX 0171-499 5368

Lunch Sun.-Fri., Dinner daily. £££
U: Green Park.

A

Tucked away in a mews in the herbaceous heart of Mayfair, the Greenhouse feels like the kind of improbable grand restaurant one sometimes comes across in an otherwise unassuming simple French village. A walkway leads through a rocky garden to the entrance, and inside is a bustling, cheerful dining room with a slightly clubby feel. Once confined to renditions of British-heritage cooking, the menus are now a sight more innovative. Offal is used to stimulating effect, as in the poached veal tongue that comes with beetroot and horseradish purée, and fish too is given piquancy, as witness the razor-sharp dressing that annointed carpaccio of tuna. Some of the old sweet dishes remain, so devotees of the richly custardy bread-and-butter pudding need shed no tears, but the chocolate tart enlivened with raspberry purée was immensely impressive too. Service is keen to make friends with you, although the short wine list still looks as cursory as it always has done. Set Sunday lunch is good value at £19.50.

Ho Ho

CHINESE 13/20

29 MADDOX ST, W1, 0171-493 1228

Lunch Mon.-Fri., Dinner Mon.-Sat. £
U: Oxford Circus.

A

Cool but not cold with mainly white walls, bright but not gaudy with pictures and coloured panels, small but not cramped, this is a civilised Mayfair restaurant. Skilful friendly service makes it easy to enjoy its eclectic Chinese (and wider) cuisine, which is carefully prepared. A free-ranging selection might start with Peking pancakes stuffed with scallions; beef salad in a spicy Vietnamese dressing; Szechuan crispy lamb with pungent soy and garlic dip; then rempah—white fish fillets in a rich, Malaysian sauce of lemon grass, shallots and lime peel; Thai green chicken curry; Cantonese roast duck on pickled vegetables; nasi goreng—Indonesian fried rice; finally Chinese 'profiterolles' with red bean filling. More conventional are set regional menus—Peking and Szechuan-and a meat-free lobster feast. Busy at lunchtime, a little quieter in the evening, ideal for high-powered entertaining. Wines are well chosen to match the food. Menus are £17.85 to £23.

Langan's Brasserie

BRITISH/FRENCH 13/20

STRATTON ST, W1, 0171-491 8822,
FAX 0171-493 8309
Lunch Mon.-Fri., Dinner Mon.-Sat. £££
U: Green Park.

A ☎

There are those who like to knock Langan's Brasserie but many more who think of it as one of London's greatest restaurants. The glamour of the place and its reputation as a hang-out for the rich and famous help keep it full, but it is the consistency of the food that is the real key to its success. The menu changes very slightly every now and again but remains the perfect compromise of sound British classics and French brasserie dishes. Hence roast chicken dinner with all the trimmings, and fish and chips with mushy peas and treacle tart sit alongside carré d'agneau rôti aux herbes de Provence, and crème caramel. Everything is cooked with care, and certain dishes, including spinach soufflé with anchovy sauce and oeufs pochés au haddock fumé, have achieved cult status. Service can be clubby. The wine list, in direct contrast to the menu, is short. Both lists offer good value for money.

Le Gavroche

FRENCH 16/20

43 UPPER BROOK ST, W1, 0171-408 0881,
FAX 0171-409 0939
Lunch & Dinner Mon.-Fri. ££££
U: Bond St.

A ☎

The British press made much in the spring of 1998 of the story of a group of corporate diners congratulating themselves on some particularly skilful bit of profit-making by splashing out at Le Gavroche. Their bill for three came to £13,000. We knew this place was expensive, but that final tally would even look a touch pricey in Tokyo. But fear not. Most of that outlay went on vintage wines and armagnac, and while the wine list is certainly no stranger to the art of marking up, you can get away with drinking for a little less than that.

If it hadn't happened in one of the grand hotels, such a story could only have emerged from Le Gavroche. To call the place an institution captures something of the gentlemen's club ambience of the dignified green basement dining room, as well as acknowledging the dynastic longevity of this section of the Roux family business (Michel Roux jr, son of the great Albert Roux, maintains the classical standards well). But the institutional tag might suggest dullness too, and that would be to traduce the supremely conscientious approach to cuisine that has always been the hallmark of this kitchen. In our last edition we were constrained to report on a disappointing lunch. This time, happier things have come our way. Mousses may not be fashionable elsewhere right now, but the power and perfection of the lobster mousse generously garnished with caviar and sauced with Champagne butter was a sensual triumph, and lacked nothing in sheer concentration of flavour. Another good hors d'oeuvre was the quail fillets in a salad dressed with walnut oil and a foundation of green Puy lentils, earthiness and lightness combining to memorable effect. Main courses offer luxury treatments of the prime cuts, but also the imaginative flourish of calf's sweetbreads crisply fried and given a sauce aigre-doux. Desserts can be as traditional as the trio of sablés with various fruit fillings, or as innovative as an iced aniseed soufflé, served with warm cherry sponge. Service is discreet, composed and ultra-professional, and the wine list is encyclopaedic, at least in France. The menu exceptionnel is a seven-course blowout of great elaboration, while for £40 a head, there is a lunch menu that offers three courses plus coffee and a half-bottle of pre-selected wine. Set lunch £40 with a 1/2 bottle of wine and canapés. Set dinner £65, £85.

Le Soufflé

FRENCH 14/20

INTER-CONTINENTAL HOTEL, 1 HAMILTON PL, HYDE PARK CORNER, W1, 0171-409 3131, FAX 0171-409 7460

Lunch Tues.-Fri., Dinner Tues.-Sat. ££££

U: Hyde Park Corner.

Pierre Kromberg, the maître here, continues to offer fine hotel dining at a level of consistency that is praiseworthy. A selection of menus, and several of what are called 'Healthy Heart' dishes which are low in fat, calories and carbohydrates and high in fibre, acknowledge late twentieth-century concerns over indulgence and indicate the hotel's international clientele, but those after a really good experience should eschew these in favour of the splendid seven-course dinner which demonstrates the skill of the chef. After the amuse bouche, choices might include lobster ravioli with freshly herbed cauliflower; pan-fried monkfish and langoustine with a little creamed spinach; almond-encrusted lamb with an omelette of Swiss chard and lardons; cheeses; crème brûlée with black truffles; the soufflé for which the chef is so well known, coffee and petits fours. This is one of London's great feasts, and remarkably good value. The service is impeccable, and the wine list, inevitably expensive, is superb, particularly favouring mature clarets. Set lunches £25, £29.50, £33.50, Sun. lunch 4 courses £29. Set dinners £35 and £50.

Les Saveurs de Jean-Christophe Novelli

FRENCH 14/20

37A CURZON ST, W1, 0171-491 8919

Lunch Tues.-Fri. Dinner Mon.-Sat. ££££

U: Green Park.

When Novelli, who is spawning restaurants all over the capital at a rate of knots, took over in this Mayfair basement dining room in the spring of 1998, he created one of the more cumbersomely titled dining experiences in London. Whereas the other venues are just a surname and postcode, here we have the full double-barrelled splendour. Thus are we left in no doubt that this is intended to be the flagship of the mini-empire. Why then does a sigh of disappointment attend our early visits? There are flashes of brilliance here that recall Novelli's high-rolling days at the Four Seasons, in dishes such as the pipérade of squid and langoustine with red pepper sauce, or the multi-layering of flavours in daube of beef with shiitake mushrooms cooked as a lasagne and served with puréed leeks and a liquorice sauce. But in the multi-layering lies the possibility for pitfalls, and the risk of presenting a dish that leaves the palate confused. Attention to detail has not always been precise. When the cooking scores, though, we are reminded that the potential for greatness is not lost, only in need of a period of stability after all the openings and launches. Meanwhile, enjoy the excellent desserts, which include a tarte fine of figs with pistachio ice cream, or a white chocolate cup of crème brûlée spiked with amaretto. Service is smooth and professional, and the wine list well-chosen and full of obvious pedigree. The base price of the menu is restrained indeed for Mayfair, but watch out: it is sprinkled with supplements and extra charges for vegetables, and is not inclusive of service. Set dinner £29.50, Menu Degustation £75 (5 courses, inc glass of Champagne).

Mirabelle

FRENCH 15/20

56 CURZON ST, W1, 0171-499 4636, FAX 0171-499 5449

Daily Lunch & Dinner. ££

U: Green Park.

The Mirabelle in its former life was, in its heyday, one of London's grand restaurants. The Mirabelle in its present re-incarnation, looks set to regain that position. Masterminded by Marco Pierre White, with joint head chefs Charlie Rushton and Lee Bunting, it's been beautifully redecorated. Two private rooms give the possibility of dining in an intimate wood-panelled room with carvings à la Grinling Gibbons or in a room where the silver Chinese wallpaper shimmers. The main dining room is long and elegant, almost austere in its whiteness, but alleviated by Bugatti sculptures, and with windows in the ceiling which give light in the winter and can be retracted in the summer. Opening off the end of this is a large terrace shaded with huge white parasols and with planters running all around at shoulder height full of lavender, overlooked by towering modern buildings but big enough to hold its own. Affordable luxury is how Marco Pierre White describes the place: the set lunch menus at £14.95 or £17.95 are a steal, and the à la carte prices are exceptional for the address. All this would be irrelevant if the cooking did not display all the sure touches of the master. The menu echoes MPW's classics; it's an object lesson in deceptive simplicity. Take the foie gras, gelée au Sauternes with toasted brioche (at £14.95 understandably the most expensive starter); a parsley soup with bacon broth from the fixed price menu; the tenderest grilled scallops; sea bream enlivened by sharp citrus fruits, and coriander; a perfectly simply cooked roast lamb with Provençale vegetables and a lavender jus. The sommelier, Claude Douard used to oversee the Oak Room, his knowledge and the imparting of it is just as valuable in this new venture where everything combines in perfect harmony. Set lunches £14.95 and £17.95.

Miyama

JAPANESE 12/20

38 CLARGES ST, W1, 0171-499 2443, FAX 0171-493 1573

Lunch Mon.-Fri., Dinner daily. ££

U: Green Park.

A ☎

Little changes at this smart Mayfair restaurant, whose 'modern' Italian-Japanese decor now looks somewhat dated. But reception and service now seems warmer and more welcoming, for both Japanese and foreigners. Although sashimi and sushi are offered, chef-patron Fumio Miyama's strong point is cooked dishes. Those listed as 'One more step forward selection of unusual but healthy minded starters, side or main dishes' are hard to distinguish from those in the main menu. Outstanding mens sana items are nasu agedashi, aubergine 'battered and deep fried' in soya broth, with mushroom, courgette and julienne of spring onion; and tori teba yaki, grilled, salted, chicken wings, plump, moist and tasting as chicken did 50 years ago. One of the happier results of Japan's economic problems is that restaurants like this no longer add inflated service charges. Another is that Japanese businessmen can indulge in a homely bowl of noodle soup even in this civilised ambience. The sister restaurant is **City Miyama, 17 Godliman St, EC4, 0171-489 1937.**

Nicole's

MODERN BRITISH 12/20

158 NEW BOND ST, W1, 0171-499 8408, FAX 0171-409 0381

Lunch Mon.-Sat., Dinner Mon.-Fri. ££

U: Green Park.

A ☎

This is more than just a café and restaurant in the basement of a posh frock shop; this is the place for Bond Street Girls to 'do lunch', when it becomes mobbed with couture types pushing salads around their plates. It's a modern, chic restaurant, from the beautifully understated architecture of the sand-coloured interior, through the extensive list of wines by the glass, to the impossibly handsome and well-groomed staff. Nicole's serves dinner as well as lunch, and on our evening visit it was emptier than a fashion editor's head; a great bonus in this put-you-on-hold, three-sittings-a-night city. The cooking is good but expensive—a starter of deep-fried vegetables with tarragon mayonnaise might be pleasant but costs £6.25; grilled brill was brill, but £14.50 is a lot to pay when tiny side dishes of vegetables cost an extra £2-£3.75. Still, it's cheaper than a mere trinket from the Nicole Farhi shop upstairs, and much better than other better publicised (and over-hyped) gastrodomes.

Nobu 16/20

JAPANESE/INTERNATIONAL

METROPOLITAN HOTEL, 19 OLD PARK LANE, W1, 0171-447 4747, FAX 0171-447 4749

Lunch Mon.-Fri., Dinner Mon.-Sat. £££

U: Hyde Park Corner.

A ☎

The ultimate in New York minimalist chic, yet also thoroughly cosmopolitan—an effect which is accentuated by the typical diner (who is of course far from being typical in the usual scheme of things). Indeed, while views of Hyde Park are great from this first-floor location, the internal panorama is far more interesting. The 'Nobu effect' owes it all to a culinary sandwich of celebrated Japanese chef Noboyuki Matsushia, Hollywood superstar Robert De Niro and Christina Ong, who currently owns the Metropolitan Hotel as well as The Halkin Hotel, Alberto & Grano and so on. Nobu's culinary style is best described as a combination of classic sushi training with South American influences, and it's a case of two into one will go—brilliantly. In fact, this genre has yielded post-modern signature dishes like sashimi salad with Matsuhisa soy-sauce dressing; black cod in miso, asparagus with egg sauce and salmon roe; sea urchin tempura and monkfish pâté with caviar. The sense of innovation is based on sterling principles, a careful balance of the familiar with the unexpected. To call Nobu an East-meets-West triumph is a simplification; it's more a case of global gourmet genius. Ingredients hitherto unfamiliar with each other achieve amazing combinations of texture and flavour, which is in a different league from much of the 'fusion' cooking that is currently served up. Dishes arrive in splendid isolation: one by one, whereas, you might prefer to have all your sushi together and eat it as an ensemble piece. If you prefer, you can pull up a stool at the sushi counter. Set lunch £28, set dinner £37.

The Oriental

CHINESE 13/20

THE DORCHESTER, PARK LANE, W1,
0171-629 8888, Fax 0171-409 0114
Lunch Mon.-Fri., Dinner Mon.-Sat. £££
U: Hyde Park Corner.

A ☎

Opulent in its purple and gold decor, the Oriental is about as far from Chinatown as you can get without going all the way to a five-star Hong Kong hotel, which it somewhat resembles. Ornate Chinese furniture, deepest pile carpets and elegant table furniture leaves you in no doubt. The style is Cantonese, which in some hands can be somewhat bland. Here delicacy reigns in the sauces which use the freshest of spices. In keeping with the surroundings are exotic offerings like braised abalone with oyster sauce; lobster with ginger and spring onions, and shark's fin (superior-grade) soup. Synchronised dome-lifting is much in evidence and forget any ideas of making up your own Peking Duck—the waiters do that for you so there is little chance of adding extra meat to your pancake. As to the overall quality, it is undoubtedly good, although prices would lead you to expect nothing but the best. Desserts are rather more hit-and-miss: red-bean paste puffs, chilled mango pudding. The wine list draws on the hotel's excellent cellar. Set menus £38 to £86.

Saga

JAPANESE 13/20

SUSHI BAR 14/20

43 SOUTH MO3LTON ST, W1, 0171-408 2236,
FAX 0171-629 7507
Lunch & Dinner Mon.-Sat. ££
U: Bond St.

A ☎

Fashionable ladies (and businessmen) lunch in the ground floor sushi bar whose à la carte lists 35 different fish nigiri; most are also offered as sushi rolls or portions of sashimi. Classically prepared by the (Thai) chef and his assistants, they also offer such rarities as warm shiitake mushroom elegantly trimmed to look like a tiny slipper. Intriguing 'small appetisers' have included a squid and cucumber cocktail; a nimono (boiled dish) of sea bass with shiitake and matsutake mushrooms; and hotate tobiko ae—scallop and flying fish roe sashimi. The warren of downstairs rooms decorated in Japanese rustic style may be as authentic as English 'Jacobean', but pleases nonetheless. Charming and helpful service especially from Anglo-French manager Mr. Leroy. Here are all the Japanese standards—tempura, fried or grilled meat, fish and tofu. And table-cooked sukiyaki and its poached equivalent, shabu-shabu. Lunch menus £7 to £16, Dinner menus £35 to £42.

The Square

MODERN BRITISH 18/20

6-10 BRUTON ST, W1, 0171 495 7100,
FAX 0171-495 7150
Lunch Mon.-Fri., Dinner nightly. £££
U: Bond St/Green Park.

A ☎

If there is a restaurant we would not want to miss in London, this is the one. Everything is so polished, so engaging that you immediately realise that you are in good hands. The decor is not of the extravagant modern style that will not last, and this distinctive sobriety seems to percolate to the audience. You feel so good in the deep, comfortable chairs that life tastes sweeter. In addition, The Square is probably one of the best value restaurants in London, almost equalling the great ones, but at a much lower price. The cooking is excellent, why then is Philip Howard's name not yet on everyone's lips? In fact, Philip Howard is something of an enigma, for this young man in his thirties is an almost totally self-taught chef. If he did spend a limited time with the Roux brothers and with Marco Pierre White, most of his knowledge comes apparently from the facility of learning quickly. In fact he did a degree in biology and then decided that pans were better companions than microscopes. His cooking is not of the boring intellectual type, but with great precision, he integrates all the parameters into the right place. We loved the fragrant assiette of red mullet with fennel and pesto, and the sauté of scallops and langoustines with chanterelles. The oriental touch of steamed turbot with coriander risotto and a light curry sauce was played with discretion, and the loin of venison in a Shiraz sauce showed a well-controlled technique. In fact the latest menu concocted by Philip Howard uses less of the trendy exotic spices and veers towards classicism with a hint of Provence: pigeon from Bresse with pommes Rossini, shellfish bisque with a steamed courgette flower. The assiette de desserts is well worth restraining your appetite for. Service is perfectly mastered by maître Jacques, and the extensive wine list offers some very affordable options like a delicious floral Merlot from Chile. Set dinner £45.

Tamarind

INDIAN 13/20

20 QUEEN ST, W1, 0171-629 3561,
FAX: 0171-499 5034
Lunch Sun.-Fri., Dinner daily. £££
U: Green Park.

A ☎

The advantage of naming restaurants after fruits (Pomegranates is London's only other example) is that when it appears on a rival's menu you get a free advertisement. We eagerly anticipate the openings of Carambola, Dangleberry and Wampee. Meanwhile Tamarind satisfies its multi-national clientele with decor, ambience, service and food in keeping with the smart Mayfair location. The menu, much shorter than most, is northern Indian. The longest section is tandoori dishes which are cooked behind a glass plate in view of diners. As well as fish, chicken and lamb there are vegetarian options. Appetisers and curries are generously spiced but for chilli-hotness take green chillies as a side dish. Vegetables include amazingly rich, meaty dal bukhari—black lentils which show how pulses can replace meat. Varied breads include missi roti—a thin naan gently spiced with chilli, onion and ginger. Wines include full-flavoured reds ideal with this cuisine. Set lunch and post-theatre dinner £16.50.

Windows Roof Restaurant

FRENCH 15/20

LONDON HILTON ON PARK LANE, 22 PARK LANE, W1, 0171-493 8000, FAX 0171-208 4142
Lunch & Dinner Mon.-Sat. £££
U: Hyde Park Corner.

A ☎

The views are stupendous from the 28th-floor restaurant at the Hilton, and chef Jacques Rolancy has deservedly been awarded the Meilleur Ouvrier de France en Cuisine. Two good reasons to spend a most enjoyable evening in London. Start with the oysters in Champagne granita and fried shallots, or sweet-and-sour rice cakes with a beetroot vinaigrette. Proceed with the 'best selling' roasted tronçon of sole with a ragoût of shellfish and herbs—an extra light, but oh-so-tasty dish created especially for health-conscious diners who can also indulge (with no pangs) in a rack of lamb with vegetables cooked en cocotte. It seems that Jacques has modernised his classical roots and kept the calory count at a reasonable level in the rest of the menu. Cooked in a jus, the monk fish—pot-roasted with potatoes, artichokes, baby onions and bacon; the braised leg of rabbit glazed with mustard and tomato, and with vegetables simmered Provençal-style; the sea bass on a bed of gingered fennel; a tartar of lobster with asparagus, all combine a solid technique with a hint of adventure. Sheer classicism appears in the noisette of venison with Brussel sprouts, radishes, Swiss chard and foie gras and Chinon sauce. There's an impressive cheese platter and delicate desserts like an almond mousse with a raspberry coulis and dried fruits. Although the attraction is more outside than inside, a comprehensive refurbishment is planned to jazz up the decor. From the extensive wine list, we chose an affordable and delectable Volnay 1992 Clos de la Rougeotte. Good value at lunchtime with set menus. Set lunch incl. wine £34 and £36.50. Set dinner £38.50. No cover charge Mon.-Wed., £6 Thurs.-Sat.

Zen Central

CHINESE 13/20

20 QUEEN ST, W1, 0171-629 8089/8103,
FAX 0171-493 6181
Lunch and Dinner daily. £££
U: Green Park.

In the heart of Mayfair, the 'hard' decor, in green and white, was so ahead of the field when Zen Central opened in 1987 that it still looks modern-except for the deep carpet which keeps the noise down in a busy room seating 100. The clientele, mainly westerners from nearby hotels and businesses, appreciate impeccable service and cuisine in the modern Hong-Kong style. While some western ingredients are used, powerful, punchy flavours prevail. The varied tastes of jellyfish, abalone, prawns and scallops in classic Imperial hors d'oeuvres are intensified by mustard; while veal 'cutlets', really slices of tender escalope with a vibrant black pepper sauce, exemplify the modern style. High, but not unjustified, prices soar for specials such as supreme shark's fin, whole abalone, lobster, or whole suckling pig. Desserts include a dazzling ginger sorbet. Wines are mainly expense account French, but house red, a southern French Merlot, is good value at £16.

Zen Garden

CHINESE 15/20

15/16 BERKELEY ST, W1, 0171-493 1381,
FAX 0171-491 2655
Lunch & dinner daily. £££
U: Green Park.

Located between the Ritz and Berkeley Square, Zen Garden justifies astronomic prices with superior Chinese food, suave service and luxurious decor. There is a koi pool and an aquarium in the reception area, fine Chinese pottery and robes in glass cases, and framed embroideries; but some details, like the pendant lights, recall the premises' past as the Embassy nightclub. Astonishing finesse and polish characterise Cantonese cuisine based on superlative ingredients, sometimes simply, always classically, prepared. Shark's fin is offered in three grades—standard, superior and supreme. There are five ways with lobster and three braised abalone dishes, one with venison tendon. The chef shows equal skills in dim sum which are quite different from their stronger tasting, if sometimes earthy, Chinatown counterparts. If delicate flavours occasionally seem to verge on blandness, this may reflect occidental tastes unused to such refined haute cuisine. Set menus are from £25 to £138.

NOTTING HILL GATE

Agadir

MOROCCAN 11/20

84 WESTBOURNE GROVE, W2, 0171-792 2207
Lunch & Dinner daily. £
U: Notting Hill Gate.

The vogue for Mahgrebian cuisine means that this is no longer London's only Moroccan restaurant. But it still offers agreeable, if unsophisticated service and ambience not unlike modest eating houses in north Africa. The decor is red and bright green—red reflecting the warm, rich flavour of a tagine, green the intense aroma of the mint tea which traditionally ends the meal. It may also stimulate the appetite if your arrival coincides with its being served at a nearby table. Start with briouat, tiny 'spring rolls' of filo pastry filled with spiced, but not peppery, meat, or feather-light maakouda, mashed potato fried with egg in parsley and spices, or margaze (better known as merguez), delicately spiced sausages. Continue with couscous, a tagine or a kebab. Drink north African rosé wine, finish with pastries—and that mint tea.

Alastair Little Lancaster Road

MODERN BRITISH 15/20

136A LANCASTER RD, W11, 0171-243 2220
Lunch & Dinner Mon-Sat. ££.
U: Ladbroke Grove.

The small local restaurant that everyone should have at the end of their road. White walls and pale wooden floors make for a bright and breezy atmosphere, while the cooking follows Mr Little's well-judged, gutsy approach, leaning heavily on Italy for inspiration, France for technique and Japan for occasional flurries of interest. Mr Little flits between this and his Soho premises so his hand may not always be at the stove, but his watchful eye keeps things on the straight and narrow. The menu tends to be short and succinct: skate wing with broccoli and anchovies, the broccoli purple and sprouting; roast plaice with rocket, baked tomatoes and olive dressing; lamb's fillets and sweetbreads, peas, onions and mint. Starters follow a similar theme: squid with a spicy piquant tomato dressing; pasta e fagioli with mussels. Desserts are to the point: cherry and almond tart; tiramisù; orange ice cream. The wine list is short, the selection sensible and price-conscious. Service has charm and willingness. Set dinner £25.

Assaggi at The Chepstow

ITALIAN 14/20

39 CHEPSTOW PLACE, W2, 0171-792 5501
Lunch Tues.-Sat., Dinner Tues.-Sun. ££
U: Notting Hill Gate.

A charming first-floor room above The Chepstow pub—wooden floors, squares of vivid colours on the walls—looks out through three west-facing floor-to-ceiling windows on this wide Notting Hill street. Chef Nino Sassu and partner Pietro Fraccari cook some of the most honest Italian food in London. From the bread—either foccacia or wafer-thin Sardinian carta da musica—to the pasta, perhaps ricotta-stuffed tortelloni, or the ever popular Swiss-roll style loaf, the emphasis is on quality and simplicity, the very essence of rustic Italian cooking. Starters tend to the simple—excellent bresaola and prosciutto, and light and salady-tomato, rocket and basil; crab with assorted salad leaves. Pasta dishes come in main-course portions and prices, or you can head for fish and meat, which tends to be grilled or pan-fried and simply served: swordfish perhaps with rocket, or beef with wild mushrooms and truffle oil. Desserts are fine: pannacotta, chocolate tart or sorbet. The wine list is short and Italian. Service, led by Pietro Fraccari, is enthusiastic and polished.

Bali Sugar

INTERNATIONAL 14/20

33A ALL SAINTS RD, W11, 0171-221 3844,
FAX 0171-229 2759
Lunch & Dinner daily. ££
U: Westbourne Park/Notting Hill Gate.

The fabulously successful Sugar Club has moved on to Soho, and in its place is Bali Sugar with a new head chef, Claudio Aprile from Zoom in Toronto, a new senior sous chef, Simon Fenwick from Sydney, though the sous chef Sharon Deer remains from the original Sugar Club staff. The restaurant has always produced some pretty dramatic cooking and culinary surprises and there's no reason to think this will change. In fact the style remains very Sugar Club. So expect the unexpected in dishes like sashimi ceviche of tuna and prawn with a radish salad and wasabi aïoli; seared foie gras with sautéed Asian pear, lotus chips and red onion marmalade; grilled Mahi Mahi with smoked oyster dumplings, chop stick spinach (!) and lemongrass broth; crispy Asian-style duck breast with slow roasted duck leg, sweet potatoes and plum sauce. And if your taste buds are still crying out for innovation, go for coconut pannacotta with espresso dates.

Dakota

INTERNATIONAL 11/20

127 LEDBURY RD, W11, 0171-792 9191
Lunch & Dinner daily. ££
U: Ladbroke Grove.

The room is a bright corner site facing north and east, the decor understated, except perhaps for the wall of tree trunks at the back of the room which sits somewhat incongruously with the rest of the decor. Dishes tend to be long on description and rather shorter on delivery. A grilled pumpkin and jalapeño polenta, New World vegetables, sage, smoked tomato oil and Yerba Santa goat's cheese (and yes, that is one dish), was fine. Other starters included roasted duck carnita, chestnuts, Napa cabbage, pear and serrano salsa; and swordfish, wood-smoked mussels, mesclun and fennel salad with lime dressing. Even the main course of grilled rib-eye steak comes with buttermilk onion rings and chimichurri sauce. The dessert list calms down a bit and the wine list is satisfactory. Set lunch £10.

First Floor

INTERNATIONAL 13/20

186 PORTOBELLO RD, W11, 0171-243 0072,
FAX 0171-221 9440
Lunch & Dinner daily. £
U: Notting Hill Gate.

The Portobello Road may not be London's loveliest thoroughfare, but it runs through a happening part of town. This stripped-down room above a pub—climb the worn wooden staircase—is currently showcasing some of the most excitingly innovative cooking in the capital. Dishes may sound utterly bemusing in their mixing and matching of often obscure ingredients, but the results on the palate can be sensational. That was the case with our black pudding slice that was garnished with jellied crab and sauced with a chillied-up tomato relish. Interesting meats have included roast bison, while even a fish as forthright as smoked haddock is topped pizza-fashion with anchovies and capers and sits in a lake of astringent watercress purée. If you think you're going to get away with something simple like crème brûlée to finish, be prepared for the rhubarb and Chinese spice that lift it into the realms of the exotic. Wines are rather humdrum compared to the food. Set lunch £10.50, set dinner £30.

L'Accento

ITALIAN 11/20

16 Garway Rd, W2, 0171-243 2201,
Fax 0171-243 2201
Lunch & Dinner daily. £
U: Bayswater/Queensway.

Terracotta tiles on the floor, bare walls and tightly packed tables make for a bustling, uncompromising atmosphere and the food more than keeps pace. A set two-course menu has been maintained for some years now at £11.50 (up £1 since it opened), and certainly draws the crowds. Dishes tend to reside in northern Italy: osso buco with saffron risotto; calf's liver, balsamic vinegar and polenta; and rabbit marinated in rosemary. The quality is generally good, but at times it lacks a certain edge. Pasta is a smart way to start, taglioni with lobster perhaps, or a more general seafood version. Desserts are Italian and straightforward, as is the wine list. Set menu £11.50.

Leith's

BRITISH 15/20

92 Kensington Park Rd, W11, 0171-229 4481,
Fax 0171-221 1246
Lunch Tues.-Fri., Dinner Mon.-Sat. £££
U: Notting Hill Gate.

A

Down a short alleyway off one of Notting Hill's leafier streets, lies the calm and order of one of London's more welcoming dining rooms. Cream walls and bright blue chairs provide the backdrop to cooking supervised by Alex Floyd which is classically assured with well-judged modern flurries. Roasting, either of meat or fish, is exemplary; game is spot on. None of this is to the detriment of vegetarians, however, who are treated with equal seriousness. If you would like something cooked differently from the way it is presented on the menu, then pay heed to the note: 'certain dishes can be altered or cooked more plainly if preferred.' The sentiment is with the customer, whether you take the offer up, or are happy to start with, say, roasted scallops layered up with artichokes, thin potato slices and served with couscous and curry butter, or a selection of vegetarian hors d'oeuvres. Main courses are a delight: duckling for two, the orange sauce light and properly unsweetened; perfectly roasted rump of lamb with a Stilton and herb tart, or roasted salmon served on meat juices with wild mushrooms and lentils. The classical theme is continued with the desserts, but the modern twists are even more evident: mascarpone with a rhubarb crème brûlée, or banana fritters with a liquorice ice cream. The cheese board is worthy of considerable attention, the wine list even more so, although expect to pay dearly for delights. Set lunches £16.50 and £19.50, set dinners £27.50 and £35.

192

MODERN BRITISH 13/20

192 Kensington Park Rd, W11, 0171-229 0482,
Fax 0171-229 0033
Lunch & Dinner daily. £
U: Notting Hill Gate.

A

Suitably of-the-moment without being a slave to fashion and style, 192 has fed Notting Hill residents for years with panache and commitment. The decor manages to be modern, homely and welcoming, the staff efficient and charming. The menu changes twice a day and majors on salads and composed dishes like duck confit with beetroot and poached egg; calf's liver with potato gratin; lamb with wild garlic mash and spinach. Salads might be Caesar or Greek, or the constant seasonal—the ingredients of which change daily according to what is good and available. Non-salad starters might include potato pancake with smoked salmon and salmon caviar, or grilled

Mediterranean vegetables with mozzarella and pesto. For desserts, the menu heads back home with bread-and-butter pudding; crumbles; French-style tarts, and chocolate pots. The wine list shines under £20 with lots of choices by the glass. Set lunch £10.50, Sun. lunch £12.50.

Orsino

ITALIAN 12/20
119 PORTLAND RD, W11, 0171-221 3299,
FAX 0171-229 9414
Lunch & Dinner daily. ££
U: Holland Park.

First there was Joe Allen (1977), then Orso (1985), and last but not least Orsino (1993). Like the rest of its well-respected family, Orsino doesn't scream its presence from the rooftops but keeps itself to itself. Once through the discreet swing door, the long, narrow restaurant snakes to the right with windows hidden behind stylish giant Venetian blinds on both sides. Upstairs is a smaller, cosier room. Lighting is subtle (from wonderful folded parchment wall lights) whatever the time of day or night, and service is discreet and slick. The Italian food is similar to Orso, with super-thin small pizzas a speciality, and pasta, risotto and the char-grill providing the cornerstones of a short daily changing menu. The food is always pretty good but can be outstanding. Grilled lamb fillet with tomato, black olives and rosemary; pumpkin ravioli with sage and butter; apricot and almond tart with vanilla sauce. Useful opening hours, sensible wine list with small jugs available and great set Sunday lunch at £11.50 for two courses, £15.50 for three.

Pharmacy

MODERN FRENCH 13/20
150 NOTTING HILL GATE, W11, 0171-221 2442
Lunch & Dinner daily. ££
U: Notting Hill Gate.

A

How far can concepts for concept restaurants go? If for a joke you want to disguise yourself with a white coat, or if fantasies of syringes and other operating room devices turn you on, this place might suit you. Otherwise your appetite might balk at the sight of receptionists dressed like nurses, along with the diplays of antibiotics and Band Aids used as wall paper. Is the idea, by any chance, to shock the bourgeoisie and whip up controversy to generate publicity? The medical environment is depressing enough to encourage a call for a doctor rather than a waiter. Needless to say the place is like a honey-pot, with a bouncer on the door controlling the queues for the bar, and a restaurant waiting list. The menu—or perhaps prescription—is decorated with the attractive hands of a doctor, but when you can turn the page, surprise: at last a quite decent and tempting bill of fare to restore your blood pressure to normal and revive your taste buds. The food, from an Alan Ducasse protégé, the half Korean and half Norwegian Sonja Lee, is modern French with a few surprises. Choose your tonic from the tian of Dorset crab, foie gras cooked en sel with shaved fennel; chargrilled sea bass with red wine sauce; or spit-roast Landes duck with apple juice and greens. All of this is rather well executed. And if you over-indulge, well this is the place to be, isn't it? A 'toasts' menu is seved in the bar. Set lunches £13.50, and £15.50.

Woz

MEDITERRANEAN 14/20
46 GOLBORNE RD, W10, 0181-968 2200,
FAX 0181-968 0550
Lunch Tues.-Sun., Dinner Mon.-Sat. £
U: Ladbroke Grove.

Antony Worrall Thompson's inventive flair, and understanding of enjoyable dining, show in every aspect of his own restaurant. The deeply unfashionable location contributes to its modest pricing—the fixed price five-course dinner (£24.95) includes mineral water and coffee. As in a friend's dining room there is no choice, but when you book they ask if anything should be avoided. Bread, olives, oil and balsamic vinegar precede five or six starters typically including rabbit rillettes; bean purée with capers and rosemary; and surprisingly delicious carrot and pineapple rissoles. Pasta or risotto follows, then a main roast or stew. Cheese with membrillo or pickled walnuts precedes dessert and coffee. Relaxed, friendly staff encourage you to eat at your own pace; the table is yours for the evening. The ground floor is bright and noisy, downstairs feels softer and warmer. Lunch or brunch available all day. Exceptional decently priced wines. Set lunch £15, set dinner £24.95 inc wine and mineral water.

PICCADILLY

Atlantic Bar & Grill

INTERNATIONAL 12/20

20 GLASSHOUSE ST, W1, 0171-734 4888

Lunch Mon.-Sat., Dinner nightly. ££

U: Piccadilly Circus.

A ☎

Despite the proliferation of trendy bars and restaurants, the queues of those who have not booked remain hopefully outside the Atlantic, while the young and beautiful, or perhaps merely the prudent, troop downstairs to fill this cavernous space. It's a rich mix on the menu as well, mixing and matching much as fashion demands. But it does it well. Warm chestnut, ricotta and Roquefort tart (naturally using organic leaf salad); tuna tartar with smoked and pan-fried prawns; Beluga caviar with blinis and sour cream at £40 for those who really have arrived; or a simple salad, followed by perhaps seared tuna with stir-fried vegetables, chilli, ginger and flat parsley; or pan-fried calf's liver with colcannon, shallot confit and a sage sauce; then something in the style of banana fritters. The wine list is surprisingly good, given the preference for cocktails at the bar, with good New World bottles. Set lunch £11.50.

Café Royal Grill Room

FRENCH 15/20

68 REGENT ST, W1, 0171-437 9090

Lunch Mon.-Fri., Dinner Mon.-Sat. ££££

U: Piccadilly Circus.

A ☎

Step into the Edwardian splendour of this opulent room and leave the 1990s behind. Gilt-edged mirrors adorn the walls with statuettes and painted nymphs to lighten the load. Starched white collars meet and greet, but underneath the formality there is a charm and willingness to please. The menu surprises in the simplicity of some dishes—rack of lamb, say, or rib of beef—but at the same time pulls no punches over more elaborate offerings. Foie gras, hardly terrined at all, and served with celeriac, truffle and parsley oil was heavenly; and lobster with asparagus and a ginger butter perfectly judged to cut the richness equally so. Main courses remain firmly French and classical, but with the odd twist: turbot and crayfish cooked as a pot au feu and served with grain mustard and horseradish, for example. Desserts follow a soufflé and pithivier path, executed with exemplary precision. The wine list is daunting in its extent and pricing, but advice from the sommelier is always on hand. Set lunch £24.50, pre-theatre menu between 6pm-6.30pm is £27.

Criterion Marco Pierre White

FRENCH 13/20

PICCADILLY CIRCUS, W1, 0171-930 0488,
FAX 0171-930 8380

Lunch & Dinner daily. ££

U: Piccadilly Circus.

A ☎

This must be one of the most stunning dining rooms in London, with gold mosaics, elegant potted plants, much gilt and mirrors, and suitably grand proportions. It should be romantic, but it is so successful and crowded that there is no chance to linger over the long menu or the extravagant—in terms of price—wine list. New World excels, not much is left out, but take care of your cheque book. You are left in no doubt that this prime site is being made to work flat out. Dishes read well and are competent: gazpacho with basil and courgette cream; salad Lyonnaise with poached egg; grilled sea bream with artichoke; roast wing of skate with snails. Desserts come in for particular praise, good lemon tart, cadeaux of white chocolate and raspberries, or good crème brûlée. The set lunches are excellent. Set lunches £14.95 and £17.95.

L'Odéon

INTERNATIONAL 12/20

65 REGENT ST, W1, 0171-287 1400

Lunch Mon.-Fri., Sun. Dinner Mon.-Sat. ££

U: Piccadilly Circus.

A ☎

Bruno Loubet has now departed the kitchens, but his erstwhile deputy tends the flame at this restaurant with its sleek post-modern decor. There is a unifying thread of earthy robustness running through the food, even in summer, that may test the frail appetite, but offers gutsy, satisfying cooking to those in the mood. Pork knuckle with prunes and mashed roots is indicative of the style, and the Loubet fascination with north African dishes is preserved in the pairing of best end of lamb with spicy merguez sausage. A favourite that deserved to stay is roast scallops with fried black pudding and mashed potato, almost a signature dish of the restaurant. Exotic ice creams such as aniseed or pineapple and coconut are the mainstay of the dessert suggestions. It all takes place in a long, light, curving, noisy first-floor room a short hop from the statue of Eros. The international wine list is resourceful and fairly priced. Set weekday lunch £18, Sun. lunch £16.50. Pre-theatre menus are also available.

Momo

NORTH AFRICAN 12/20
25 HEDDON ST, W1, 0171-434-4040,
FAX 0171-287-0404
Lunch Mon.-Fri., Dinner daily. ££
U: Piccadilly Circus.

The premises used to be a supermarket, but it's hard to believe. Down the left-hand side runs an enormous stainless steel bar. The kitchen, complete with wood-burning oven, sits across the rear wall, and the southern-Spain-meets-north-Africa theme comes into play in the bench running the length of the right-hand wall complete with tubular cushions. As to the menu, cumin, coriander and harissa along with yoghurt, dates, cinnamon and cloves point to an often delightful interpretation of Moorish food. The spiced fish soup with dried limes and yoghurt was bright and intense; the pan-fried sweetbreads with wilted herb salad and yoghurt slightly off-centre, but nonetheless good. The main course char-grilled monkfish with pistachio sauce and pink fir potatoes was overcooked, but otherwise good; the wood-roasted chicken marinated in yoghurt with lentils, chard and beetroot a resounding success. Desserts are refreshingly different: almond tart with quince and oloroso; pumpkin tart with cinnamon and cloves. The wine list focuses on Spain, but doesn't forget France and Italy. The real delight, however, is the seriousness of the sherries (every third glass served at the bar is sherry according to the owners). The bar also serves tapas for those not wanting to sit to dinner. Service is enthusiastic.

The Oak Room

FRENCH 19/20
LE MERIDIEN, 21 PICCADILLY, W1,
0171-734 8000
Lunch Mon.-Fri., Dinner Mon.-Sat. ££££
U: Piccadilly Circus.

While some chefs are stars, Marco Pierre White is a comet and his incandescent and numerous streaks of the last decade have marked the London culinary galaxy. We admire his entrepreneurship while at times being disconcerted by the magnitiude of his orbit. At a recent count he was involved in the Café Royal Grill Room, MPW, Quo Vadis, The Criterion, Mirabelle and Pharmacy, and the number keeps growing. So what? As our reviewers found, they all work extremely well. What about the Oak Room? This is where the love story begins. An art connoisseur, MPW first fell for its beauty and the grandeur. But you can't eat decor. To make the Oak Room the best restaurant in London, you also need a great chef. And who else than the flamboyant MPW? He swears that he will be faithful and steer the Oak Room firmly. But doesn't the genius of the artist also lie in being able to infuse some of his talent and enthusiasm into other brains and hands? If this is the case, and the chef de cuisine Robert Reid is the right man, then MPW has accomplished another tour de force.

In this magnificent sculpted wooden decor, a gigantic carte reveals the many facets of his art, with inspiration mainly from the French heritage, and paying an honest tribute to the great predecessors and even to contemporary masters like Pierre Koffmann. All of this revisited à la Marco. His overwhelming and passionate personality is shown on a menu that evokes more a torrent than a quiet river. So be prepared to be swept away by the subtlety of the marinière of shellfish with caramelized calamaris and fresh basil, and the complex lightness of the aspic of oysters with watercress en gelée de Champagne. A bit of a rest comes with the simplicity of foie gras with green pepper en gelée de Sauternes which isolates and sharpens its savour. The common salmon finds sophistication in the brilliant company of crayfish in a wild sorrel sauce and of caviar. Simple or elaborate, the choice is wide open, from mille-feuilles of crab and tomato; vinaigrette of leeks and langoustine en gelée to the Bresse pigeon and foie gras, Savoy cabbage, fumet of truffles. Hard to save some appetite for the original and refreshing caramelized pineapple with ginger and vanilla. The wine list is as comprehensive as possible, but also offers a few bargains like the Chateau Lyonnat or the Côtes du Rhone Guerin. The set lunch at £29.50 is unbelievably good value. Set lunch £29.50, set dinner £75.

Sartoria

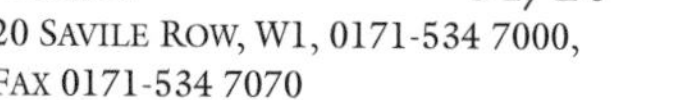

ITALIAN 14/20

20 SAVILE ROW, W1, 0171-534 7000,
FAX 0171-534 7070

Lunch daily, Dinner Mon.-Sat. ££
U: Piccadilly Circus.

Sir Terence Conran appears to have done it again, and produced a restaurant which fits seamlessly into its surroundings. Forgive the pun, but the main design theme is bespoke tailoring, it's on the corner of Savile Row, one of the most famous tailoring streets in the world, and the word sartoria means tailor in Italian. It's an elegant restaurant, a long, good-height room with windows that open along one side and a large room at the back which can be shut off with glass screens. The colour scheme is muted, the chairs are large, the tables well-spaced—the whole place exudes a feeling of expensive comfort. The cooking, too, is solidly good from chef Darren Simpson, who latterly was at the River Café and before that with Richard Corrigan, at Bibiendum and Le Gavroche. Flavours, as you might expect from such a background, are robust, and the cooking is confident in a menu which combines classic antipasti—di mare or verdure; pastas; risottos, and main dishes like roast suckling pig cooked with aromatic herbs and garlic, with contemporary Italian offerings like quail with zucchini and grapes, and desserts of poached cherries with ricotta cheese, and green tomato tart with zabaglione. The wine list contains some good, relatively little known Italian wines, service is charming, and the tailors of Savile Row, and more particularly their customers, are enthusiastic.

Veeraswamy

INDIAN 13/20

VICTORY HOUSE, 101 REGENT ST, W1,
0171-734 1401

Lunch & dinner daily. £
U: Piccadilly Circus.

We all love a good make-over, and this is a perfect example of what was latterly an old favourite showing its age being relaunched as a microcosm of modern India. Vivid colour schemes, embracing mustard yellows and moss greens, may seem like Veeraswamy jumping onto the contemporary bandwagon, but these are traditional sari colours. For all the modernity, the interior features antique highlights: a dancing Shiva, historic door locks set in glass mounts like works of art, a beautifully inlaid console table. The pick of the tables overlook Regent Street. The menu is a combination of dishes from southern Indian, particularly Hyderabad, and specialities from the courts and bourgeois homes of north India. The results include malai murgh—white chicken curry flavoured with cinnamon, cinnamon leaf, cardamom and green chillies, and battir kofta—minced quail wrapped around quail's eggs cooked in a golden aromatic creamy curry. Subtlety is achieved as effectively as boldness, with the composition of dishes always based on authenticity. Indian street food is served up at the Sunday brunch menu, with the likes of biryani prepared with lamb shanks, and potato-stuffed pancakes with lentil curry, accompanied by a live jazz band. Set lunches £11 £13, Sat. jazz brunch £14.50.

Zinc Bar and Grill

MODERN BRITISH 12/20

21 HEDDON ST, W1, 0171-255 8899

Mon.-Wed. noon-11pm, Thurs.-Sat. noon-midnight, Sun. noon-6pm. £.
U: Oxford Circus.

Sir Terence Conran's Zinc Bar & Grill is set in a narrow side street parallel to Regent Street, along with the north African Momo. With its pavement tables and awnings, long frontage, very long bar inside, wooden tables and chairs, Zinc, you feel, should be on a main drag in Paris, the perfect place to sit and people-watch. The menu fortifies that sentiment, with its Bayonne ham and artichoke remoulade; goat's cheese and aubergine tart for starters; its piles of crustacea (of course, this is a Conran restaurant); salads; sandwiches; grills; dishes from the rôtisserie; main dishes like roast cod, pipérade and pesto, and copious pommes frites. The cooking is okay bistro standard, but is not really the main point here. It's the great atmosphere, the buzz of youth, good service and as always the impeccable design details, that are the attractions in an essentially fun place. Sat., Sun. lunches £10 £12.50 inc glass of juice and tea or coffee.

PIMLICO

Pomegranates

INTERNATIONAL 12/20

95 GROSVENOR RD, SW1, 0171-828 6560

Lunch Mon-Fri, Dinner Mon-Sat. ££

U: Pimlico.

A ☎

As we noted in the last guide, Pomegranates is a hardy survivor, still overseen by the genial Patrick Gwynn-Jones. Opened in 1974, it attracted a celebrity clientele who came to eat in its comfortable interior with its feeling of Edwardian decadence. It's the kind of place where you can easily imagine a large number of them remaining in their chairs after a good lunch, sipping their port and staying on for another meal in the evening. Certainly any who still do will find themselves easily slipping back to their gilded youth as the menu has remained remarkably similar over the years. Gravlax with dill and mustard was pioneered, according to Mr Gwynn-Jones, here at Pomegranates, and it's still here, along with lime-pickled raw salmon with spring onions and parsley dressing and those unfairly neglected pickled herrings with rye bread. Dishes like crispy breast of lamb with Sechuan sauce, Welsh salt duck with white onion sauce; or breast of wild duck with apple and Calvados will bring memories flooding back. Patrick Gwynn-Jones despises the present beef ban and proudly declares himself a member of the Scotch Beef Club, then lists seven Aberdeen Angus beef dishes, including carpetbag steak and that nostalgic dish, beef Wellington. English cheeses are great; desserts are filling, but wait, there is still the 'bottomless' coffee pot and chocolates. Crudités, aïoli, homemade bread and vegetables, rice, salads, etc are all included in the price. Mr Gwynn-Jones' generosity and bonhomie lives on. Set lunch es£10.95 and £13.95, set dinners £14.95 and £17.95.

Rhodes in the Square

MODERN BRITISH 15/20

DOLPHIN SQUARE, CHICHESTER ST., SW1, 0171-798 6767

Lunch Sun.-Fri., Dinner daily. £££.

U: Pimlico.

A ☎

Dolphin Square in Pimlico was originally opened in 1937 as a huge complex of apartments, plus hotel, leisure facility and conference center. It seems logical to have an upmarket restaurant here, but this particular site has not been blessed by great good fortune in recent years. But if anyone can make this work, it has to be Gary Rhodes, whose reputation precedes his new venture in this elegant, Art Deco room, and should ensure full tables every night. The cooking is echt Rhodes-a gutsy mix of flavours, where British tradition has been assaulted by a vivid imagination. Take fillet of smoked haddock, a classic ingredient which is then glazed with welsh rarebit and presented on a tomato-and-chive salad. The delicate scallop, usually treated with a vast amount of veneration, is seared and served with a hot mustard-shallot sauce. Main dishes are treated with similar innovation, as in lamb confit with aubergine and tomatoes that have been flavoured with anchovy; or halibut which is steamed and served with braised flageolet beans, garlic and tarragon. In less skilled hands, such combinations could herald disaster; here they reinvent the vocabulary. If you're looking for a clone of City Rhodes, you'll be disappointed. Only two of his signature dishes are served here, bread-and-butter pudding and the unfortunate Jaffa cake pudding, over which a large veil should be drawn. Instead try grilled rhubarb trifle with extra thick cream. Service is good, friendly and solicitous, the wine list full of delights.

Simply Nico

FRENCH 13/20

48A ROCHESTER ROW, SW1, 0171-630 8061

Lunch Mon-Fri, Dinner Mon-Sat. ££

U: Pimlico.

A ☎

There are restaurants where the owner of the name adorning the facia occasionally appears to try, sometimes successfully, to lift the cooking above mediocrity. Simply Nico is not one of them. Nico Ladenis still influences this rapidly growing chain, although the link is now only a family one. Fixed price menus in English, and simply presented accomplished French cooking are the keynotes. A faithful following—politicians, business people and top civil servants—accept the not particularly attractive decor, and tables too close for discreet plotting. They relish such starters as gratin of pasta and scallops with chive velouté, or stuffed cabbage with sweetbreads, foie gras, bacon and tomato. Main dishes include roasted breast of duck with Sicilian green olives and wild mushrooms; and sea bass stuffed with basil mousse on red pepper coulis. Desserts, imaginative as caramelised apples with cinnamon vanilla ice cream, or conventional lemon tart, are perfectly executed. Set lunches £22 and £25, set dinner £27.

PRIMROSE HILL

Odette's

INTERNATIONAL 14/20

130 REGENT'S PARK RD, NW1, 0171-586 5486, FAX 0171-586 0508

Lunch Mon-Fri, Dinner Mon.-Sat., Sat., Sun., ££ Lunch Wine Bar only.

U: Chalk Farm.

Like a Georgian house surrounded, but not overwhelmed, by some modern buildings, this is a charming, unpretentious place. Service is unobtrusive but flawless, and the menu is in plain English. Eight first and main courses are cleverly balanced in ingredients and cooking methods, so choosing is difficult. Classic simplicity does not exclude lasagne of crab and Swiss chard with tomato and hazelnut vinaigrette, or warm salad of char-grilled Jerusalem artichokes, roasted tomatoes, garlic and rocket. Main dishes include '60's fillet of beef Rossini, and '90's breast of Barbary duck, with Puy lentils and juniper wrapped in Savoy cabbage. Desserts such as glazed goat's curd and lemon tart, and warm chocolate espresso tart with crème fraîche match visual splendour to spectacular flavours. The long wine list offers well-chosen classics and delicious rarities such as Gros Manseng from Gascony and Piedmont's Moscato d'Asti make the perfect accompaniment to ice cream. Set lunch £10.

PUTNEY

Del Buongustaio

ITALIAN 12/20

283 PUTNEY BRIDGE RD, SW15, 0181-780 9361, FAX 0181-789 9659

Lunch Sun-Fri, Dinner daily. ££

U: Putney Bridge.

Modelled on the osterias or inns traditionally found throughout Italy, Del Buongustaio ranges throughout the country for inspiration, drawing on peasant dishes and some of the more refined cuisine of the north. Panzanella is well handled, alongside bresaola with artichokes and Parmesan. At times hot and smoky, the atmosphere is usually intense and exciting, partly driven by the food, but also by enthusiastic locals. Cream-coloured walls, terracotta tiles on the floor and basic table furniture lends a relaxed air to the long but smallish room. The menu changes monthly, featuring dishes like grilled octopus and Mediterranean vegetable salad, bruscheta di mare. Main courses might be duck stuffed with chicken livers, mushrooms and truffles; or pork loin, cooked in milk and served with baked fennel. Desserts follow the sorbet and panna cotta route with perhaps an almond tart. Wines step outside Italy to good effect. Set lunch Mon.-Fri. £9.50, Sun. £15.50 and £24.50 for 6 courses.

Putney Bridge

MODERN BRITISH 12/20

EMBANKMENT, SW15, 0181-780 1811, FAX 0181-780 1211

Restaurant Lunch & Dinner daily. Bar Servery/Patisserie Mon.-Thurs. 10am-10pm, Fri. to 9pm, Sat., Sun. to 6pm. ££

U: Putney Bridge.

Set by the river beside Putney Bridge, this is the first purpose-built, stand-alone restaurant to open since 1953 when the now long-gone Serpentine Pavilion took that honour. The two-storey Putney Bridge has won various architectural awards, but whether you love or hate its sleek modern lines, red granite blocks, stainless steel and glass, you can't miss it. Once inside it becomes less exciting; after all we've got used to airy, cool, minimalist interiors using light wood. But it has the enormous advantage of huge windows overlooking the Thames at one of the river's most beautiful points. The modern European menu steers a modish course—starters perhaps of miso soup with three seaweeds and udon noodles; or a plain smoked eel salad with celeriac remoulade not particularly tasty pieces of smoked eel on celeriac with a bland dressing. Main courses improved with a fillet of sea bass, delicately cooked and colourfully presented on marsh samphire with a pungent ratatouille vinaigrette; venison sausage was suitably gamey and went well with truffle mash and onion jus. It got better, with excellent desserts of a truly tart lime madelaine offset by a sweeter lemon curd ice cream, and winter fruit tartlet packed with berries with fresh pear sorbet. Putney Bridge got a lot of praise and publicity when it first opened in 1997, and has settled into a groove which while not knocking your taste buds for six, manages to satisfy. And the view is terrific. Set lunches £13.50, and £17.50.

RICHMOND

Ma Goa

INDIAN 13/20

244 UPPER RICHMOND RD, SW15,
0181-780 1767, FAX 0181-246 6878
Lunch Tues.-Fri., Sun., Dinner Tues.-Sun. £
BR: Barnes.

The new back room provides more space and a bright, simple background for equally brilliant, but far from simple Goanese cooking by the Kapur family. A sensibly short, but wide-ranging menu is supplemented by a blackboard offering a main dish of the day, and half a dozen fresh vegetables. These may include aubergine in pickling sauce, while chick peas in roasted spices are soft, even sensual, which that pulse rarely is. Follow authentically hot Goan sausage with even hotter pork vindaloo or milder Aunty Bella's lamb kodi. Exceptional rice and breads. A whole new meaning is brought to 'salad' 'Indian' cuisine by Fernandez onion-and-chilli salad. Desserts include Goan bibique (coconut cake), and alozma (figs and apricots). Well-chosen wines include soft, full-bodied reds ideal with richly spiced food. Friendly service by the younger Kapurs, Dee and Ela (sic). Set lunch £7, Mon.-Thurs. Set dinner 7pm-8pm is £8.50.

ST. JAMES'S

The Avenue

INTERNATIONAL 13/20

7-9 ST. JAMES'S ST, SW1, 0171-321 2111,
FAX 0171-321 2500
Lunch & Dinner daily. £££
U: Green Park.

A long bar, opposite which a bank of video screens keeps you company should you need it, opens out into a cavernous, largely white and bright room lit, during the day, by an ingenious skylight down one side. Designed by architect Rick Mather, hard edges abound, matched by the Nicole Farhi-designed uniforms of the efficient staff. Dark suits predominate among the well-heeled customers, but after that everything softens. The food plays on the Mediterranean theme—seared tuna with red pepper couscous and coriander; sea bass with a Provençal herb crust; coq au vin with garlic and parsley mash. Starters might be a selection of antipasti or risotto, while desserts might be baked cheesecake with blueberry compôte, or apple and walnut cake with spiced ice cream. The wine list is exemplary, with plenty by the glass and sensible mark-ups. And a tie-up with Christies auction house around the corner has brought grand crus on to the list with invitingly small mark-ups. Set lunch £17.50 and £19.50, pre-theatre menus £13.50 and £ 15.50.

Green's Restaurant and Oyster Bar

BRITISH 12/20

36 DUKE ST, SW1, 0171-930 4566,
FAX 0171-930 1383
Lunch & Dinner Mon.-Sat. ££
U: Green Park.

Clubby is the most apt description for Green's, tucked away in Duke Street among the fine art dealers of St. James's. It's wood-panelled with booths for four people running down one side, a bar in the centre, and old English prints, cartoons and caricatures on the walls. Many of the customers, too, seem to regard it as their own particular dining club, spurred on by the presence of the charming owner, Simon Parker Bowles, who started the venture in 1982 after running a City wine merchants. But rest assured, clubby does not translate here as exclusive, and everyone is treated to the same delightful welcome and service. There's a new chef, Patrick Williams who cooked at The Ivy and The Canteen before coming here. The menu has always been traditional, the place to come to for native oysters; smoked Scottish salmon; smoked eel fillets, or lobster cocktail as starters; salmon fishcakes, native crab, grilled fillet of beef or even those stalwarts of fish and chips, and bangers and mash, and Bakewell tart as well as spotted dick with custard. The freshest of ingredients simply cooked have suited the captains of industry for some 16 years and will continue to do so well into the next century when something hitherto unknown has replaced lemongrass on the menus of those new, 'cutting-edge' eateries. The wine list is, naturally, very good.

Le Caprice

MODERN BRITISH 14/20

ARLINGTON HOUSE, ARLINGTON ST, SW1, 0171-629 2239, FAX 0171-493 9040

Lunch & Dinner daily. ££

U: Green Park.

It may be situated in the heart of staid old St. James's, but Le Caprice is an island of friendly informality in a monochrome pin-stripe sea. Many relish the chance of sitting at the bar for a plate of eggs Benedict and a grade-A Bloody Mary, but even seated at a table, you won't be expected to stand on ceremony. The cooking on offer is modern brasserie fare, similar to that at sister restaurant, The Ivy. Even if you aren't properly dressed, the Cornish crab will be, and we have also thoroughly approved the ink-black risotto nero; the delicately constructed salmon fish-cake with sorrel sauce; and the grilled scallops with correctly crisped bacon. Two-tone chocolate mousse, and canonical crème brûlée are the stars of the pudding show. Good strong espresso rounds things off in style. People return for the smiling service and the palpable sense of value. The wine list won't fire the imagination, but just about suits the purpose.

L'Oranger

FRENCH 15/20

5 ST. JAMES'S ST, SW1, 0171-839 3774, FAX 0171-839 4330

Lunch & Dinner Mon.-Sat. £££

U: Green Park.

The atrium roof ensures a soft bright light falls into this wood-panelled and mirrored room. Crisp linen and French service of the correct formality sit comfortably with the St. James address. Marcus Wareing sticks to the French theme, but Asian influences and a modern eye lift the predictable to the often exceptional. First courses like marinated tuna salad with crushed peppercorns; or a ham hock and parsley terrine with gazpacho sauce were well executed and with just the right light touch. Braised rabbit with spring vegetables; or perfectly pink pigeon with choucroûte and a wild mushroom sauce had punch and direction. Mr Wareing likes stacks, and plates impress on arrival. Desserts return firmly to France: lemon tart; crème brûlée; chocolate mousse with raspberry sauce, and are good. The wine list favours France and the better producers, but not to the detriment of the rest of the world. Set lunches £19.50 and £22.50. Dinner £33.50.

Matsuri

JAPANESE/SUSHI BAR 13/20

TEPPAN ROOM 12/20

15 BURY ST, SW1, 0171-839 1101, FAX 0171-930 7010

Lunch & Dinner Mon.-Sat. ££

U: Green Park.

The giant devil mask which greets diners on entry is no longer illuminated, and the food too is a tad less brilliant than before. But the traditional ten-seat sushi bar justifies high prices for nigiri sushi with generous morsels of a wide range of fresh seafood on perfect rice—every grain lying in the same direction'. Shiso leaves aromatise cucumber, o-shinko (pickled mooli) and burdock rolls, and garnish sashimi. Intriguing grilled 'Japanese appetisers' include smoky aubergine or shisamo, tiny smelts eaten whole like large whitebait. In the 120-seat teppan room, careful cooking of choice ingredients takes precedence over displays of knife-juggling and there are modestly priced pre-theatre menus too. Lunch sushi or teppan-yaki £5.50-£20, set lunch £40. Dinner set menus £35 to £55.

Quaglino's

MODERN BRITISH 13/20

16 BURY ST, SW1, 0171-930 6767,
FAX 0171-836 2866
Lunch & Dinner daily. ££
U: Green Park.

When the Conran empire re-opened Quaglino's as its central London flagship, it was heralded as the way ahead for mass catering. Forsake dull burgers, pizzas and ribs, come and partake of calf's liver and bacon, groaning seafood platters and smoked haddock in mustard sauce. Although the final bill must weigh heavy on the common pocket, Quaglino's has undoubtedly found its niche. It is packed every night, as much perhaps for the marble-pillared splendour of the ambience with the seafood shrine occupying pride of place at the far end, as for the textbook brasserie cooking. We enjoyed a salad of pork with dandelion leaves and oriental seasonings, as well as a hefty dish of lamb with sausages and haricot beans, whilst finding the desserts well short of the mark. The seafood selections are expensive, especially if lobster is included, but won't disappoint the true devotee. Every table is time-limited, so expect to be hassled if you linger over the cappuccino. The wine list is costly but good. Set lunches and pre-theatre dinner (5.30pm-6.30pm) £15.50 and £19.

The Ritz Restaurant

FRENCH 14/20

THE RITZ, PICCADILLY, W1, 0171-493 8181,
FAX 0171-493 2687
Lunch & Dinner daily. ££££
U: Green Park.

One of the more spectacular dining rooms in London, particularly if you either gaze at the ceiling with its magnificent trompe l'oeil, or out through the floor-to-ceiling windows of this tall room onto St. James's Park. In summer it is a delight, with its grand chandeliers and many mirrors and terrace dining. The cooking is solidly French, but with more of a modern twist than you might expect in an institution as grand as this—risotto with Pecorino in place of the more usual Parmesan perhaps, or roasted sea bass with a minestrone sauce. The chef is new too, so the style may alter somewhat over the coming months, although desserts are likely to continue in the excellent tart and crème brûlée mode. The wine list here used to be superb, but has fallen into the adequate but hardly sensational trap. Plenty of fairly priced Champagne and unimaginative clarets, should you want to show off. The Palm Court in the reception area continues to provide delicious and substantial afternoon teas and now light lunches. Set lunch £34, set dinner Sun.-Wed. £49.

The Stafford

MODERN BRITISH 13/20

ST. JAMES'S PLACE, SW1, 0171-493 0111,
FAX 0171-493 7121
Lunch Sun.-Fri., Dinner nightly. ££
U: Green Park.

American visitors suffused with home thoughts from abroad should make straight for the Stafford. Set in a quiet St James's backwater, it boasts a bar that is bedecked with pennants, scarves and other Stateside sporting memorabilia, a comfort perhaps while you nurse a whisky sour. In the frescoed and crystalline dining room, old England takes over once more, both in the glitzy formality of the ambience and in the heritage menu that forms one eating option. Expect smoked salmon, fillet steaks and treacle tart. Alongside this, Christopher Oakes offers a more far-reaching slate of inventive dishes that may look to France for inspiration—we wholeheartedly applauded the guinea fowl with smoked bacon, mushrooms and parisienne potatoes—or take the modern British route for pigeon and black pudding in a sharply dressed first-course salad. Cambridge burnt cream is what the English did to crème brûlée—it appears here with intense and plentiful fresh raspberry sauce. The wine list is a weighty tome in the grand hotel manner, impressive in its way. Set lunch £23.50, Set dinners £20.95, £26.25.

Suntory

JAPANESE 13/20

72 ST. JAMES'S ST, SW1, 0171-409 0201,
FAX 0171-499 0208
Lunch & Dinner Mon.-Sat. £££
U: Green Park.

A feminist writer dining in dungarees at Claridges is as unlikely as a girls' night out at

Suntory; but the former has been seen, so the latter might be too. Ladies who lunch should consider 'Lady's Bento' at £25, including a glass of wine with sashimi salad, broiled dish, fried dish, braised dish, pressed smoked salmon sushi, miso soup and dessert. Dishes described only by cooking method are customary; in any menu each will be different. 'Chef's suggestions' might include braised broad beans, deep-fried lotus root with mustard paste, mixed seafood cooked on hot stone, and varied noodles, one flavoured with the magical shiso herb. More conventional are sushi, tempura, grilled fish, sukiyaki—and ice cream tempura to finish. In the teppan room excellent ingredients are sizzled before you on the steel plates. Smooth service with restaurant manager Eric whose fluent English is combined with sound knowledge of the cuisine. Set lunch £15, set dinner £50.

Wiltons

BRITISH 13/20

55 JERMYN ST, W1, 0171-629 9955,
FAX 0171-495 6233
Lunch & Dinner Sun.-Fri. £££
U: Green Park.

Tradition still rules in this old-established (1742) St. James's restaurant. The decor is all you could hope for—etched glass, fishing pictures on the walls, carpets and comfort. The emphasis in the kitchen remains on traditional British cooking, using the finest ingredients. Come here to savour Loch Fyne oysters; smoked salmon and crab mousse with a gribiche sauce; real turtle soup; breast of smoked turkey with brandy peach. Even potted shrimps make an appearance. Move on to simply grilled or poached plaice, turbot or halibut, or a properly cooked grilled steak; continue with pear belle Helene or sherry trifle, and finish with savouries which are rarely found nowadays in restaurants: Welsh rarebit, or angels on horseback. It's all very Edwardian, though there's a nod to modern modish ingredients in the odd dish like chargrilled tuna with a tomato, coriander and red onion salad. The wine list is as you might expect in St. James's, heavy on good French wines. The service is old-fashioned and delightful. Sun. lunch £19.75.

SHEPHERD'S BUSH

The Brackenbury

MODERN BRITISH 14/20

129-131 BRACKENBURY RD, W6, 0181-748 0107,
FAX 0181-741 0905
Lunch Tues.-Fri., Sun., Dinner Mon.-Sat. £
U: Goldhawk Rd.

The change of ownership—Adam Robinson sold out to the Kensington Place boys in May 1997—has been smooth and almost undetectable. A new colour scheme—now aquamarine—a bit of tidying up around the bar area, and attention to al fresco dining are the outward signs. In the kitchen, Marcia Chang-Hong (ex-Kensington Place) continues the tradition of eclectic continental and modern British food pioneered by the Robinsons. Hence serrano ham with potato pancake, poached egg and Hollandaise; Cheddar omelette with chips and salad; pan-fried turbot with aubergine purée, peas and mint; and buttermilk pudding with grilled white peaches. Sadly, the old regime of cooking with modest, seasonal ingredients and cheaper cuts of meat and unfashionable seafood is less evident. Hence prices have crept up—they now average £25—and meals at the Brackenbury are no longer the bargain they were: a gap admirably filled by the nearby Anglesea Arms (see Quick Bites). Set lunches £8.50 and £10.50.

Chinon

FRENCH 14/20

23 RICHMOND WAY, W14, 0171-602 5968,
FAX 0171 602 4082
Lunch Mon.-Fri., Dinner Mon.-Sat. ££
U: Shepherd's Bush.

Chinon nestles down a lacklustre residential street and it shines like a gem. Its decor is nice enough: restful yellow walls, calm lighting, well-spaced tables, and a floor-to-ceiling window overlooking a leafy courtyard. This sets the scene for cooking which if not exactly secret, should be appreciated by more than the culinary cognoscenti, or lucky locals. The owners cook and manage the place and it's clearly a labour of love: he's in the kitchen, she's front-of-house. Both have been trained in classical French cuisine, but the repertoire extends beyond it. There is a bias towards fish, crustacea and game—the imperative being perfect extraction of flavours, strong or subtle. Recent first courses have included ravioli of crab and leeks with salmon caviar, followed by roast saddle of hare, prunes and salsify—every part of both dishes perfectly judged. We would have greedily returned the next day to try filleted whole sea bass, saffron cream sauce and crispy potatoes. Desserts get marvellous care, too. A thoughtful wine list complements the frequently changing menu. There is a good value 3-course set dinner for £18 which might include stuffed squid and pesto oil followed by breasts of pigeon, black pudding and parsnip purée. Chinon is more than a neighbourhood restaurant—it's worth crossing town for. Set dinner £18.

Esarn Kheaw

THAI 12/20

314 UXBRIDGE RD, W12, 0181-743 8930

Lunch Mon.-Fri, Dinner daily. £

U: Shepherd's Bush.

Thailand's economic problems have dramatically cut the number of Thai customers, but the cooking is still probably the most authentic in London—so some dishes may be too powerful for European palates. Fish sauce elsewhere used so discreetly that one is often unaware of its presence, can be overwhelming; in spiced papaya salad northeast style it was too much even for a Thai taste. Its chilli content was another challenge. Usually mild and creamy tom kha kai, chicken soup with coconut, is here as strong as many tom yum soups. More generally accessible are moist, garlicky Esarn Kheaw sausages with fresh young ginger and peanuts. The sweetness of pineapple and grapes in gaeng pet pedyang, succulent roast duck with coconut milk, makes a mild red curry even more agreeable. Large portions make meals for four (or more) much less expensive than a glance at the menu suggests.

Snows on the Green

MODERN BRITISH 14/20

166 SHEPHERD'S BUSH RD, W6, 0171-603 2142

Lunch Sun.-Fri., Dinner Mon.-Sat. ££

U: Hammersmith.

Sebastian Snow no longer has his second Battersea restaurant and is now concentrating once again on this, his first and most successful restaurant, which brings a dash of Provence to the local residents. Sunny yellows and lavender walls with bright pictures of the South of France set the tone for a menu which delivers the same optimism and joy. A pressed terrine of mozzarella, courgette and tomato with tapenade toasts; a warm herring, new potato, boiled egg and rocket salad might be followed by a flavourful braised knuckle of lamb in brioche crumbs with flageoloet beans and spinach, or that favourite, stuffed saddle of rabbit which comes here en croûte flavoured with soy and coriander and accompanied by gnocchi. Desserts continue to sing;:try the steamed pear and ginger pudding with custard, or a very successful variant of bread-and-butter pudding using croissant and with a crème anglaise. Good wine list concentrating on France and the New World. Set lunches £12.50 and £15.50.

SOHO

Alastair Little

MODERN BRITISH 14/20

49 FRITH ST, W1, 0171-734 5183

Lunch Mon.-Fri., Dinner Mon.-Sat. ££

U: Tottenham Court Rd.

These days, the most splash-making restaurants in London look the most understated, so if you're expecting layers of napery and a sommelier in a bow-tie here, think again. Alastair Little's Soho eatery is provocatively plain, with pale green walls and lightweight tables, and staff who look like they might be about to go clubbing. The food, too, is refreshingly unpretentious, mixing Mediterranean and oriental moods in the contemporary vein, bringing on oily pizzetta bianca piled with rocket and potato, and farinaceous stews to support something like a blackened, salted leg of duck confit. Çountry cooking in the heart of Medialand. Breads are excellent, as is the muscular treatment of fish dishes, but puddings let the side down on our last visit. The strawberry pavlova was a collapsed and painfully sugary mess. Prices have eased considerably, though, since the restaurant's eighties heyday, so this is a good time to go. Make the most of the short but imaginative wine list. Set lunch £15-£25, Set dinner £30.

Bahn Thai

THAI 12/20

21A FRITH ST, W1, 0171-437 8504,
FAX 0171-439 0340
Lunch Mon.-Sat., Dinner nightly. ££
U: Piccadilly Circus.

A ☎

Bahn Thai was a pioneer among Thai restaurants long before the boom of the last few years, and has long been considered one of the best. In recent years, this three-floor Soho eaterie has been variable in both service and meal quality, but on a recent visit, both were very much on form. The menu is far more extensive than the usual Thai top fifty, with many unusual dishes, and the best quality Thai ingredients are always used. Our papaya salad had the full complement of green papaya (no ingredient substitution here), and tiny, salty Thai shrimps, just like you'll find in Thailand. A green vegetable curry contained two kinds of Thai aubergine (golfball and pea), and the curry sauce was wonderfully fresh and aromatic. The pad Thai (stir-fried noodles) was a generous amount and packed with goodies. Make this your first choice for Thai in Soho. Set menus £22-£35.

Circus

MODERN BRITISH 13/20

1 UPPER JAMES ST, W1, 0171-534 4000,
FAX 0171-534 4010
Lunch daily, Dinner Mon.-Sat. ££
U: Piccadilly Circus.

A ☎

Circus is amongst the latest to join the mega-restaurant formula, following in the footsteps of the owners' other successful venture, The Avenue in St. James. The decor is stark, white and minimalist: it is certainly of the moment. The downstairs bar has become a trendy hang-out whilst the restaurant itself crackles with chic. When we visited it was half-empty and felt strangely flat: we blamed it on a cold wet Monday night. Would we be warmed by the modern European cooking? Our first courses augured well enough: pan-fried foie gras burst enticingly on the palate, but the risotto, though tasty, had a glutinous rather than unctuous quality. We progressed to scallops with aïoli and bacon—a nicely balanced contrast—but were really smitten by the first-rate succulent rabbit with leek mash and spinach. Puddings were good: flavoursome and creamy amaretto cheesecake, and nicely piquant apple fritters. We washed everything down with a crisp Sancerre. Service was helpful if a bit undirected. There are pre- and post-theatre set menus to keep prices down (Beluga caviar with blinis is a fearsome £50 by the way!). Designer-led concepts run a heavy risk of fashion fickleness, but on a positive note the Circus kitchen resists clowning around. Set lunch menu, pre- and post-theatre and in the bar two courses £13.50, three courses £15.50.

French House

BRITISH 13/20

49 DEAN ST, W1, 0171-437 2477,
FAX 0171-287 9109
Lunch & Dinner Mon.-Sat. £
U: Leicester Sq.

A ☎

The French House is a room above a pub in the lubricious heart of Soho. Here is where leaders of the French resistance met during the war (hence the nickname), and the rough-and-ready feel is retained. Get a window table if you can, but get any table; there aren't many and they book up well in advance. What you're in for is domestic British cookery of unashamed simplicity served in muscle-building portions with a minimum of ceremony. Nourishing soups such as chestnut and apple, or thick green watercress are followed by main-course ingredients chosen with an eye to economy, so it's lemon sole, not Dover (with great chunky chips to boot), and onglet—or skirt steak—rather than sirloin. Offal is given a fair say as well: the ox tongue is superbly tender. The Britishness of it all extends to jelly and blancmange for afters, but grown-up, intensely flavoured versions, while old-school steamed puddings test any remaining appetite. The French wines are well selected and not expensive.

Leith's Soho

MODERN BRITISH 14/20

41 BEAK ST, W1, 0171-287 2057,
FAX 0171-287 1767
Mon.-Sat. Lunch & Dinner. ££
U: Oxford Circus.

A ☎

Leith's Soho has opened in the former Atelier and been given a cool, modern appearance with pale blond-wood floors and furniture, and some rather natty wood and glass panels which normally lie flush with one wall, but which can swing out to give more intimate spaces to this long, narrow restaurant. Surfaces might be hard, but the noise level is delightfully low, and there are only around 65 seats here. Alex Floyd who was at Leith's in Notting Hill has transferred here for the moment, and is clearly relishing the change. The menu zings with inventiveness and imagination. Hence a tuna carpaccio which came with additional tuna mashed with capers, lime and coriander and salad; or an apparently modest Vichyssoise which challenged the taste buds with marvelous smoked haddock and mustard. Salmon and crab cakes with a tomato and caper butter sauce were more flavourful than the norm; a rump of English lamb, beautifully cooked and tender, came on an aubergine and garlic risotto with cumin, with extra roast garlic for the brave. Sensibly, salads like bitter leaf salad with grain mustard, or rocket and Roquefort, come either as a side order or as a starter; there are extra vegetables, but these are hardly necessary. Of the desserts, a rhubarb and mascarpone crème brûlée was masterly, the sweet and the tart setting each other off brilliantly; home-made ice creams and sorbets will calm you down. The wine list is good. Altogether this is a notably addition to Soho. Let's hope that Leith's in Notting Hill will spawn a few more such promising offspring.

L'Escargot

FRENCH 14/20

48 GREEK ST, W1, 0171-437 6828,
FAX 0171-437 0790
Ground floor Restaurant: Lunch Mon.-Fri., Dinner Mon.-Sat. ££ Picasso Room Lunch Tues.-Fri., Dinner Tues.-Sat. ££
U: Leicester Sq.

A ☎

L'Escargot, with its refurbished interiors and cooking now in the hands of Billy Reid, is once more setting quite a pace in London's restaurant scene. Downstairs there are a couple of tables at the front dominated by two large paintings—one a Hockney still life, the other a Mirò, and a fireplace, looking out onto Greek Street. The bar stretches the length of the room into what is now called the Ground Floor Restaurant, refurbished in beautiful Mediterranean colours and sporting quite an art collection on the walls. Upstairs, the Picasso Room is aptly named, full of Picasso plates and Art Deco bronzes. The ground floor restaurant offers a slightly more modest menu, perhaps starting with a parfait of foie gras and chicken livers, or a terrine of pheasant with Agen prunes that really zinged, all at £6.95. Main courses, at £12.95, might range from a disarmingly simple chump of lamb with a rosemary Dauphinoise and roasted root vegetables, to a wonderfully cooked sea bass with creamed leeks and a startlingly pungent essence of cepes (which carried a £3 supplement). Desserts run from lemon tart to a very good ginger brûlée with a warm orange compôte. Up in the Picasso Room, things are a little more elaborate and expensive, so expect dishes like wild mushroom potage with rabbit tortellini and a truffle Chantilly to start; medallions of monkfish with poached oysters, noodles and curry sauce, or a Bresse pigeon which comes with confit cabbage and foie gas ravioli in thyme jus. This is self-confident, good cooking in a wonderful couple of rooms. The wine list is good, and very extensive. Pre-theatre menus £14.95 and £17.95. Picasso Room lunches £25, and £30, dinner 3 courses £42.

Mezzo

MODERN BRITISH 13/20

100 WARDOUR ST, W1, 0171-314 4000,
FAX 0171-314 4040
Lunch & Dinner daily. £££
U: Piccadilly Circus.

A ☎

Mezzo has all the virtues and vices of a Conran restaurant, depending on who you speak to. The place is big, bustling and noisy, has a booking policy with attitude, and an attendant in the ladies who offers fragrances and towels and expects a tip. Pretentious? Overhyped? Or the place to be seen at, one of London's hippest places that is teaching the rest of the world a thing or two about restaurant life? Mezzo itself is the more expensive, up-market basement part of a complex which embraces Mezzonine, a bar which heaves at all times, and the next door café. While Mezzonine serves the likes of tom yum soup with wok-fried prawns to a predominantly young clientele, Mezzo downstairs caters to the more serious, with dishes like seared salmon salad with green papaya and lime; duck liver parfait with a fig chutney; roast cod, spinach and rouille; and fillet of beef with fried salsify and a Béarnaise sauce. It used to be

John Terode presiding over the kitchens, which are open-plan and can be seen through a vast glass wall. But he has departed to help Bluebird fly a little higher. Still, Mezzo is on the whole pretty good: the cooking is consistent, prices are reasonable, there's a long wine list and service is friendly. But beware the arbitrary £5 music cover charge if you happen to hit a time when there's a festival on, whether you knew or not and whether you like the music or not. Like the time-limited table policy, it's these small details that annoy. Upstairs in Mezzonine South-East Asian-Pacific set lunch £8.50 and downstairs in the main restaurant set lunches £12.50 and £15.50. Pre-theatre 3 courses 6pm-7pm, £14.

Richard Corrigan at Lindsay House

MODERN BRITISH/IRISH 15/20

21 ROMILLY STREET, W1, 0171-439 0450

Lunch Mon.-Fri., Dinner Mon.-Sat. ££

U: Leicester Sq.

A smile on the radiant face of Richard Corrigan, a much-travelled chef within London, was enough to make us instant supporters of the Lindsay House band. His talents have long deserved a fitting and firmly grounded showcase, and here at last, in this elegantly converted 1790 townhouse in Soho, he may have found his niche. We were seduced by the rusticity and authenticity of the place with its crooked, narrow staircase and wooden floors worn to the thinness of old parchment by generations of feet. Irish by birth, he is one of those who has taken pride in restoring a sense of earthiness and robustness to cooking in the nineties, using ingredients that would once have been scorned as infra dig, and presenting them in deft and original combinations. The menu is concise, offering a choice of six starters, six main courses and six desserts. His style may be seen to vibrant effect in the lobster and potato salad. Tiny discs of new potato sandwiched together with creamy mayonnaise and lobster of exemplary freshness and deep, eloquent flavour impressed enormously. The terrine of foie gras conceals just enough of the sweetness of prunes to lighten the strength of the walnuts; salty cured sea bass offsets the sweetness of the bavarois of beetroot glazed with raspberry vinegar. A main course of rabbit leg stuffed with black pudding, supported by a richly sticky, nutritious, stock-based sauce, demonstrated just how rustic the cooking can be. Italian and Chinese accents are brought in willy-nilly (sometimes, defiantly enough, in the same dish) and the smoulder of chilli is a favoured seasoning. Refreshingly, Corrigan avoids today's cop-out dessert options of straight crème brûlée or toffee pudding, and offers us instead a thickly textured sorbet of Granny Smith apples adorned with a nutty tuile and surrounded by sweet-skinned Muscat grapes, mango and papaya canelloni with lemon curd. Although there is a smartness to the atmosphere, the service is delightfully straightforward, and the wine list, a broad-minded international collection, is very affordable—from £12 upwards and well explained. Lunch from about half-a-dozen choices is £21.

Quo Vadis

MODERN BRITISH 15/20 

26 DEAN STREET, W1, 0171-437 9585,
FAX 0171-434 9972

Lunch Mon.-Fri., Dinner daily. £££

U: Leicester Sq.

This old Soho stager was hauled out of faded obscurity by the combined talents of Marco Pierre White and British bratpack conceptual artist Damien Hirst. Formerly Leoni's, London's first Italian restaurant, it relaunched in spring 1997 with a lengthy and instantly identifiable Marco menu and some classically diverting new British art objects—most notoriously in the shape of a pair of flayed cow's heads in formaldehyde that glare balefully down on drinkers in the top-floor bar. The cooking is indelibly the master's style: many of the dishes will have a Name-That-Tune familiarity to those who have eaten Marco's creations all around the capital. Thickly silky parsley velouté, given resonance with truffle oil, is the kind of thing to begin with (the poached egg that floats in it creates a deliciously sickening colour collision as it bursts), but there is also the waggishness of a plate of Beluga caviar with blinis for £250. The glutinous risotto—bright yellow and pungently aromatic with saffron—is a flawless creation. Scallops are sautéed until just toasty on the surface and partnered with deep-fried squid rings and tiny puddles of ink. Main courses satisfy for gutsiness and quantity: the stuffed rabbit leg was a succulent miracle of timing, while the spit-roasted suckling pig with apple sauce is a dish to fortify. Desserts mine the classic French seam of short pastry tarts, ice creams of deeply concentrated flavour, chocolate truffle and nougat glacé, with raspberry coulis. Service is plentiful and attentive, and the wine list stuffed with classics at central London prices. Set lunches £14.95 and £17.95.

Red Fort

INDIAN 12/20

77 DEAN ST, W1, 0171-437 2115

Lunch & Dinner daily. ££

U: Leicester Sq.

A ☎

This handsome restaurant is dominated by its huge bar, which unusually for Soho isn't open to non-diners. The warm Indian decor does not overstress its ethnicity and the soft lighting pleases romantics but can make reading the menu difficult. The basement, with secretive alcoves, is equally pleasant despite its low ceiling. The cooking maintains a high standard, and is no longer influenced by fat-free notions foreign to Indian food, which dimmed its spice flavours. Sadly service doesn't do it justice; we trust it will improve. The menu, a straightforward à la carte specifies dishes as their own 'original', 'regional and 'regional adaptations' for occidental tastes. The last category includes methi kangaroo, a subtle dry curry. An appetising 'reproduction' starter is til ke subz kabab, fried vegetable patties. Rewarding incidentals include crisp spiced poppadums, feather-light naan, and the pearl white boiled rice, chada chawal. Buffet lunch £10, set dinner menus £22.50-£35.

Soho Soho

MEDITERRANEAN 11/20

11-13 FRITH ST, W1, 0171-494 3491,
FAX 0171-251 3091

Lunch & Dinner daily. ££

U: Leicester Sq.

A ☎

Downstairs the rôtisserie jumps without ceasing, a place to meet friends and enjoy a casual meal of perhaps traditional fish soup followed by something from the grill, an omelette or pastas, in a casual laid-back atmosphere. It's helped by the decor, a Provençal-tiled floor, the open rôtisserie to one end and a vibrant Matisse-style bird mural on one wall. Upstairs the restaurant is more serious, a long room with windows down two sides, and brightly coloured chairs which are beginning to show signs of wear and tear. The cooking, too, shows the occasional dip in quality. A Lavandou terrine of pork and chicken liver paté tasted dull, while a grilled goat's cheese and baked tomato with olive-bread toast also did not match expectations. Things improved a little with a tender roast fillet of lamb crusted with herbs and nuts, though the potato gratin was overcooked, and the Soho Soho speciality of wild boar stewed in red wine with sautéed chestnuts and linguine pasta promised much but delivered what appeared to be a rather ordinary pork stew. Desserts rescued an otherwise disappointing meal, with an excellent lemon tart and some good ice creams and sorbets. Let us hope that this is a temporary dip; Soho Soho is an important part of Soho life. Pre- and post-theatre menu 2 courses £12.50, 3 courses £15.50.

Sugar Club

14/20

PACIFIC RIM

21 WARWICK ST, W1, 0171-437 7776,
FAX 0171-437 7772

Lunch & Dinner daily. ££

U: Piccadilly Circus.

A ☎

Don't be fooled by the name into thinking this is a haven for pâtisserie fans. Here New Zealander Peter Gordon sets a cracking pace for Pacific Rim fusion cooking of rare calibre. When the Sugar Club was in Notting Hill, people were beating a path to the door: Madonna was turned away four nights running (she hadn't booked). So why the hubbub? Try a wing of skate with piercing coriander relish to find out, or admire the bravery in partnering squid with sweet red peppers and deep-fried parsnips. Kangaroo has been a favoured meat, the loin grilled in strips to convincing tenderness. Nothing is allowed the sin of being bland. Even the mashed potato is pepped up with horseradish or mustard, and desserts are full of pin-sharp flavours in the likes of a jelly of mixed citrus fruits or crumbly rhubarb tart. The Australian accents of the staff will orient you culturally, although the wines chosen from that region are somewhat perfunctory. Set lunch £16.50.

SOUTH BANK

Oxo Tower Restaurant, Bar & Brasserie 14/20

MODERN BRITISH/INTERNATIONAL
OXO TOWER WHARF, BARGEHOUSE ST, SE1, 9PH, 0171-803 3888, FAX 0171 803 3838
Restaurant Lunch & Dinner daily; Brasserie Mon.-Sat. 11am-11.30pm, Sun. to 10.30pm.
££-£££.
U: Waterloo.

This Harvey Nichols-owned rooftoop restaurant is on the 'wrong' bank of the Thames, but oh what a view of the City! Once you get there, you have to decide which side of the tower you want. In the smaller, more formal restaurant, where Simon Arkless is chef, the cuisine merges traditional British with modern Mediterranean and Pan-Asian twists (whole roast lemon sole with an Indian spiced relish, thyme and onion tarte, and pan-fried calf's liver with shite bean and truffle purée). In the more casual, livelier and more tightly-packed brasserie, Arkless's partner, Cait Mitchelhill, prepares more Italian-accented fare, including such specialties as pan-fried lemon sole with marinated borlotti, cannellini beans and gremolata, and ravioli with pesto, rocket, sundried tomatoes and red peppers. Whichever eatery you choose, you'll be dazzled by the high-style design—leather-clad bars, slate tables and a louvered ceiling where blue neon lights create 'moonlight.' It's all in keeping with the cutting-edge design of the Oxo Tower Wharf development, where high-style clothing and furniture boutiques share the former Oxo Bouillion factory with apartments.

RSJ

MODERN BRITISH 13/20
13A COIN ST, SE1, 0171-928 4554
Lunch Mon.-Fri., Dinner Mon.-Sat. £
U: Waterloo.

This long-established restaurant, close to the South Bank Arts Centre, is very consistent and always full. It is quite rambling with dining areas on several levels. The décor has a calm and serene feel to it which contributes to a pleasant low-key atmosphere, and service is friendly and efficient. Some of the tables for two can be a bit cramped. Set menus are extremely good value with a three-course dinner menu for £16.95. A soup of butternut squash with spinach gnocchi from this menu was as good as their soups invariably are. Beef is always first-class and a rib-eye steak with button mushrooms, bacon lardons, baby onions, sweet potato fondant and tomato fondue with a rosemary jus makes an excellent main course selection from the menu. This was rounded off by chocolate crème brulée. From the à la carte, an interesting carpaccio of venison with pear and plum chutney and tuiles of apple was followed by grilled swordfish with broad bean and lemon risotto, baby fennel and mosaic of vegetables. Risottos feature often on the menu and are always good and inventive. The owner is a well-known aficionado of Loire wines and the choice is remarkable, with very good house wine at modest prices. Set lunch and dinner £16.95.

SOUTH KENSINGTON

Bibendum

MODERN BRITISH 15/20
81 FULHAM RD, SW3, 0171-581 5817, FAX 0171-823 7925
Lunch & Dinner daily. ££££
U: South Kensington.

A stunning room, even on a dark winter's day, marks Bibendum out. The loose-covered chairs—more garden than interior—cosset while service is exemplary. Mr Michelin keeps a watchful eye from the enormous stained-glass window and would, I think, whole-heartedly approve of the understated sureness of the food. Some items remain near fixed, like fish soup; Bresse chicken; deep-fried lemon sole, chips and tartar sauce, while others change depending on availability. A distinctive nod towards the Mediterranean results in dishes like grilled artichokes with tapenade and mozzarella, or grilled rabbit with chickpea purée and aubergine. Desserts include chocolate tart, or peach jelly incorporating the much under-estimated Rivesaltes. The wine list is one of the best in London, although you pay for mainstream indulgence. Set lunch £28.

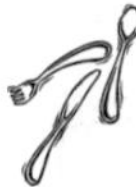

Bibendum Oyster Bar

MODERN BRITISH 12/20

81 FULHAM RD, SW3, 0171-589 1480,
FAX 0171-823 7925
Lunch & Dinner daily. ££
U: South Kensington.

Freshness is all at this perfect spot for an ideal light lunch. Concentrating on cold seafood dishes and salads, the tables and chairs spill out into the hallway entrance to this magnificent building. Sadly what can be commonplace in parts of France—an excellent plateau de fruits de mer—is not so in London, but here is the exception. Well-sourced seafood presented in all its glorious simplicity with bread and excellent unsalted butter. You cannot book, and are likely to have to queue at key times. The wine list is more than a match for the food. Lunch specials about £15.

Bombay Brasserie

INDIAN 11/20

COURTFIELD CLOSE, COURTFIELD RD, SW7,
0171-370 4040, FAX 0171-835 1669
Lunch & Dinner daily. ££
U: Gloucester Rd.

Bombay Brasserie always was fun, with its over-the-top cocktail bar at the front, the main dining room with slowly swinging fans and an Edwardian decor strongly reminiscent of the Raj, and with its conservatory. But now the conservatory has been refurbished and extended, and this really is the place to request a table in. It drips with greenery and hums with conversation, and is particularly romantic at night. The cooking hasn't been refurbished, but remains in the same mould, offering occasional flashes of inspiration, but generally on the predictable side. The lunchtime buffet is deservedly popular, offering a whole range of dishes and unlimited quantities. Otherwise the main menu ranges far and wide, with tandoor specialities from the northwest frontier, which are often the best bet, Goan specialities and royal traditional Mogul cooking. After all, Bombay is the gateway to India. Buffet lunch £15.95.

The Collection

INTERNATIONAL 12/20

264 BROMPTON RD, SW3, 0171-225 1212,
FAX 0171-225 1050
Lunch Wed.-Fri, Dinner daily. ££
U: South Kensington.

Sister restaurant to Daphne's just around the corner, the name of this other venture originally from designer Mogens Tholstrup and now owned by the Pizza Express group, is intended to refer to the fashion world. Glide along an extended glass catwalk over a sea of silver stones, and you'll arrive in a cavernous warehouse conversion at the end of it. Staff are dressed in baggy linen costumes, and the eating is done on a mezzanine floor above the long elegant bar. International eclecticism is the mood of the food, bringing together crab won-tons of exemplary freshness, ravioli of pumpkin with deep-fried sage and shaved Parmesan, and a slice of beautifully concentrated passion fruit tart with a slick of acerbic coulis. Not everything is brought off with quite the same aplomb, but the combination of sharp flavours and weightless textures is what this branch of modern cooking is all about. The wine list is a model of concision and intelligence; most bins are available by the glass for those who want to ring the changes. Set lunches £12.95 and £15.95.

Daphne's

ITALIAN 12/20

112 DRAYCOTT AVE, SW3, 0171-589 4257,
FAX 0171-581 2232
Lunch & Dinner daily. ££
U: South Kensington.

The Mediterranean menus at Daphne's may not be cutting-edge, but that reflects a restaurant that knows what its clientele require. A pleasantly airy pair of rooms leads to a rear extension where the glass roof may be retracted if the sun is smiling on Chelsea. Calorie-counting lightness rules the menus, which major in pasta dishes and leafy salads of unimpeachable freshness. Fish is given star billing, and a fillet of sea bass with red peppers and rocket salsa, or an earthier pairing of sole with girolle mushrooms, are what the crowds are here for. Breaded veal cutlets hark back to older Italian modes, as does the canonically squishy tiramisù. Chocolate brownie accompanied by a blob of whipped cream lightly flavoured with apricot purée suggested to us that the kitchen is at pains to ensure that even the richer desserts won't tax the digestion. Italy leads the wines, followed by French and non-European sections. Choices are sound, but mark-ups offer no favours.

The Fish Restaurant at 190 Queen's Gate

MODERN BRITISH 11/20
190 QUEEN'S GATE, SW7, 0171-581 5666
Lunch & Dinner daily. ££
U: Gloucester Rd.

Windows in two walls look out over tree-lined Kensington streets in this museum-filled corner of London. Furniture is basic and of bistro style and the menu fits in with the fish theme. So fish soup gets the classic treatment with rouillle, Gruyère and croûtons, there are potted shrimps from Salcombe Bay; Dover sole either grilled or meunière, and sea bass roasted with fennel and garlic. Meat eaters are given simple lamb or tournedos Rossini while vegetarians get truffled leek, potato and artichoke tourte. Oysters, mussels, clams, scallops and langoustines are offered in a variety of guises. The formula is as straightforward as the cooking, there is little flair or excitement, but on the whole it is satisfactory. Choose from a range of tarts and ices for dessert.

Hilaire

MODERN BRITISH 14/20
68 OLD BROMPTON RD, SW7, 0171-584 8993,
FAX 0171-581 2949
Lunch Mon.-Fri., Dinner Mon.-Sat. ££
U: South Kensington.

Window tables and those at the back with rounded banquettes are well spaced, but others are too close for comfort. Or would be if the clientele were not as civilized and mature as this charming restaurant with its good, unfussy food, warmly welcoming service, and quiet conversation (no music, carpeted floor). No à la carte, limited choice in the set menus-six to eight in each course. But balanced ingredients, in menus, and in each dish, make choosing a pleasure. Occasional Welsh elements reflect chef-patron Bryan Webb's background, but he wanders no further east than the Mediterranean. His ways with vegetables are masterly. Wild garlic is tamed to make a refined soup; 'broad beans' with sweetbreads are so tiny and tender that the name seems not to fit. Fruit creams, mousses and sorbets tempt and do not disappoint. Wines are listed by style, with many sensibly priced bottles, halves and glasses. Set lunch £18.50 plus dessert at £4.50, set dinner £28.50 plus dessert at £6.50. The lunch menu doubles as a pre- and after-theatre menu 6.30pm-7.30pm and after 10pm.

Le Suquet

FRENCH 12/20
104 DRAYCOTT AVE, SW7, 0171-581 1785,
FAX 0171-225 0838
Lunch & Dinner daily. ££
U: South Kensington.

Sparkingly fresh fish, served in a nautically themed dining room that spills onto the street when the weather allows—you could be in the south of France, except that the prices say you could only be in one of the more fashionable parts of London. While other restaurants have gone minimalist and modern, Le Suquet continues in the old way, tables packed close together and a general bonhomie that keeps everything ticking along. Choose from clams, mussels and scallops, oysters and langoustines—all of which come in a variety of guises. Main courses concentrate on the kings of the sea—turbot, bass, salmon and Dover sole. Lobster of course, and crab too, If you would rather eat meat, steaks, lamb and confit of duck satisfy. Desserts are perfunctory, the wine list exclusively French, as is the service.

Lou Pescadou

FRENCH 13/20
241 OLD BROMPTON RD, SW5, 0171-370 1057,
FAX 0171-244 7545
Lunch & Dinner daily. ££
U: South Kensington.

Unfussy, local and slightly off-beat, Lou Pescadou has been serving up bowls of mussels, fish soup and plateau de fruits de mer to Earl's Court residents keen on a relaxed dinner for years now. The decor is simple and unfussy, somewhat on the kitsch-nautical theme but gets away with it. Bamboo chairs, pink tablecloths and basic cutlery complete the picture. Main courses might be straightforward roast sea bream with garlic, or perhaps a langoustine salad, or something a little more involved like salmon with a mustard sauce, or cuttle fish, the latter cooked in its own intense ink sauce. Desserts follow a French theme, crème brûlée, or a tart, and the wine list remains solidly French. Indeed the restaurant almost pretends the culinary world in London is still much as it was ten years ago, and for a change, there is nothing wrong about that here.

Pasha

MOROCCAN 12/20

1 GLOUCESTER RD, SW7, 0171-589 7969

Lunch & dinner Mon.-Sat. ££

U: Gloucester Rd.

A ☎

Stepping through the door immediately transports you into a Moorish enclave (without any suspension of belief), which is just as well, as the Gloucester Road is hardly an attractive location. The ground floor bar is perfect for an aperitif, while the staircase that greets you on arrival takes you straight down into a traditional, well-appointed Moroccan residence, rather than seeming like a done-up basement. Some details are, however, excessively laboured: a smell of incense which is too strong, even for our Catholic (by which we mean Roman) taste. Service on the other hand can be underdone. We were fine with the slightly dizzy French girl who sometimes looked in on us, but was charming and efficient enough to be a perfect case of less-is Moorish. But our waiter preferred to swish around in ethnic-styled finery. The food is enjoyable enough: an excellent char-grilled squid with aubergine, chilli, coriander and lemon, accompanied by equally good aubergine chips with lemon and mint, though warm salt cod and chickpea salad was not in the same league—bland cod and tough chickpeas. The recipes may be authentic, and the flavours fresh, full and focused, but some of the results can also seem to be yet another example of Modern European as well as Moroccan cooking. Set lunch £12.50.

San Martino

ITALIAN 12/20

103 WALTON ST, SW3, 0171-589 3833,
FAX 0171-244 7545

Lunch and Dinner daily. ££

U: South Kensington.

A ☎

Intimate, charming and cosy, perfect for the area's local residents who are often greeted by name when they arrive at Constanzo Martinucci's restaurant. Pasta is well judged, finished simply with crab perhaps, or smoked salmon and dill. Inspiration is sought from all the regions of Italy to bring the likes of bread soup or suckling pig. Salads are a delight, as they should be, grown as they are by Mr Martinucci. Desserts are solidly Italian as are the wines.

Star of India

INDIAN 13/20

154 OLD BROMPTON RD, SW5, 0171-373 2901,
FAX 0171-373 5664

Lunch & Dinner daily. ££

U: Gloucester Rd.

A ☎

A somewhat outrageous interior—murals of sculptures and pillars, a trompe l'oeil ceiling of an angel heading heavenwards—is a little confusing for the first-time visitor expecting something more normally associated with an Indian restaurant. Flock wallpaper this is not, but then neither is the food from the one-masala school. Seafood in the shape of scallops or mussels, crabs and prawns are spiced with delicacy and accuracy. Vegetables get equal attention, potatoes suffused with a heady mixture of turmeric and meltingly soft garlic, spinach and cheese infused with a complex palette of spices. Game too, when in season, is handled well. The delicate tea is a reminder of how much more suitable a drink it makes over coffee after dinner. Service has a complacency about it.

Turner's

FRENCH 14/20

87-89 WALTON ST, SW3, 0171-584 6711,
FAX 0171-584 4441

Lunch Sun.-Fri., Dinner daily. ££

U: South Kensington.

A ☎

While many of the capital's kitchens are busy assembling dishes, the end result little more than a sum of their component parts, Brian Turner's strength remains in the tradition of grand hotel dining. The room—a warm yellow with comfortable chairs and banquettes, is cosy while at the same time retaining formality. Service is efficient and not without charm. Starters might be a real old-fashioned crab consommé, the colour of oloroso sherry and with a deep, rounded flavour. Salmon might come three ways—smoked, gravlax and cured, ceviche style. Main courses excel in meat, particularly offal—veal kidneys grilled to a perfect pinkness, a sautéed lamb version, rich and full flavoured. Game too, is well handled, as in stuffed saddle of rabbit served with haricot beans. Desserts follow a French theme and if you are unable to decide, you can always go for the selection which is excellent value. So too, is the set lunch. Wines offer good drinking under £20 and some interest above. Set lunches £12.50 to £38.75, set dinners £26.50 to £38.75.

STOKE NEWINGTON

Rasa

INDIAN VEGETARIAN 14/20

55 STOKE NEWINGTON CHURCH ST, N16,
0171-249 0344, FAX 0171-249 8748

Lunch Tues.-Sun., Dinner nightly. £ No smoking restaurant.
U: Stoke Newington.

A

The glowing pink and orange walls of this simple eating house mirror the vivid flavours of its Kerala vegetarian cuisine—plus a few specialities from neighbouring South Indian states. The well-written menu is unlike those of curry and tandoori houses, so newcomers to the style should take advice from owners, Das and Allison. Recommended pre-meal snacks include pappadavadai, battered and fried pappadoms, so crisp they justify the warning that they are not for the noise sensitive. We also warn that what looks like French mustard among the home-made chutneys is pungent chilli; and that Marseilles taxi drivers might find the garlic pickle breath-taking. Don't miss aubergines, sliced and fried as a starter or in bagar baingan, a mild yet intensely flavoured curry. This vegetarian food will satisfy even committed carnivores.

STRAND

The Grill Room

BRITISH 13/20

THE SAVOY, STRAND, WC2, 0171-836 1533,
FAX 0171-379 5421

Lunch Mon.-Fri., Dinner Mon.-Sat. £££
U: Covent Garden/Embankment.

A

Devotees of this Edwardian-style wood-panelled room have been coming for years, drawn by the familiarity of the staff, the overall quality of the food and the sense, one suspects, that nothing has really changed in a world that clearly has. Sink into one of the dark velvet chairs at lunchtime and you could be forgiven for staying there most of the afternoon. City suits dominate and the average age tends towards the latter half of the spectrum, a result in part of relatively high pricing. Each dish from the trolley has its day: Lancashire hot pot on Monday for example, and so it is through the week. Other dishes show a subtle nod towards modernism: cod chowder with Puy lentils and salsa verde, or veal with risotto and chorizo crisps—daring flourishes within the confines of an institution that realises its hallmark is its sameness. Foreigners cannot quite believe it, for regulars it couldn't be otherwise. The English theme works through the puddings, with a little French flavour in the tarts. The wine list, based on stock which also appears in the River Room, remains European, predictable and on the whole, expensive. There is a pre-theatre deal betwen 6pm and 7pm where, if you care for pudding, you can return after the show to take it in the Thames foyer.

The River Restaurant

FRENCH 14/20

THE SAVOY, STRAND, WC2, 0171-836 4343

Lunch & Dinner daily. ££££
U: Covent Garden/Embankment.

A

A window table in this wide open room affords views up and down the Thames over Embankment Gardens. On a warm spring day it is hard to better, the trees outside lending a green tone to the urban setting. At night time a band plays and you can dance, if not until dawn, certainly late into the night. The room oozes establishment, with tail-coated waiters lifting cloches for all they are worth, but always with a sense of calm and order. Despite this most English of settings, chef Anton Edelmann works hard, and largely successfully, to bring the modern world to his dishes. There are a number of menus to choose from, from seasonal to the tasting version. Starters like lobster salad with a light curry dressing may have a Raj ring to them, but modern flurries like pig's trotter with sage and smoked ham, or ravioli de poissons also work well. Main courses too, slide between defiantly traditional-Chateaubriand for two, as near perfect as possible, and the likes of turbot with a butter spiked with wasabi and truffles. Desserts favour the soufflé and apple tart route and are exemplary. The wine list, once a real attraction of the Savoy, has taken a nose dive. This is no place to enjoy aged clarets unless you have a hefty bank balance, and Burgundies are lamentably young.

Simpson's-in-the-Strand

BRITISH 11/20

100 STRAND, WC2, 0171-836 9112,
FAX 0171-836 1381

Lunch & Dinner daily. Breakfast Mon.-Fri. 7am-11am. ££

U: Covent Garden/Embankment.

A ☎

Step through the door into the entrance hall of Simpson's and exhange the noise of traffic for the peace and quiet of an institution largely unchanged over the last 50 years. The English gentleman's club atmosphere draws American and English, mostly gents, alike. Tail-coated waiters, polished wood and a faded grandeur that has an attraction all the more acute in this age of modern minimalist interiors. Roast meats, game and fish form the main courses, the likes of smoked salmon the starters. Play the game and keep it simple and you cannot go wrong: Aylesbury duck with apple sauce, calf's liver and bacon, steak and kidney pie. Desserts follow a sound English route. Breakfast has been introduced and is liable to wipe away any need for lunch. If, by the afternoon, you are feeling peckish once more, tea interprets this English custom in a resolute fashion. The wine list is strong on Burgundies and Clarets and better than might be expected elsewhere.

TOTTENHAM COURT ROAD

Bertorelli's

ITALIAN 13/20

19-23 CHARLOTTE ST, W1, 0171-636 4174,
FAX 0171-631 0216

Lunch & Dinner Mon.-Sat. ££

U: Goodge St.

A ☎

Bertorelli's, founded in 1913, must have changed more in the last few years than over its previous 85 years. Bright white and terracotta decor, pine flooring, and comfortable steel and maroon leather chairs are pure 1990s. Yet traditional virtues are maintained, and its friendly ambience is irresistible. It is no longer a family business and the young, enthusiastic staff may be more Melbournian than Neapolitan, but the kitchen remains the domain of mama, Maddalena Bonino. Her matriarchal attitude towards feeding her 'family' is 'more is better'. So portions vary from generous to enormous. Pastas are big, classics such as veal cutlet Milanese with salsa verde even larger. But much is in today's lighter style—marinated squid on watercress and cucumber with sesame and red pepper salsa for example. Desserts include ice cream confections as elaborate as in Milan. Downstairs the Café Italian is more casual, and there is another larger, branch at **44a Floral St, Covent Garden, WC2, 0171-836 3969.**

The Birdcage

FRENCH/THAI 14/20

110 WHITFIELD ST, W1, 0171-383 5036

Lunch & Dinner daily. ££

U: Goodge St.

VISA MasterCard ☎

An absolute breath of fresh air and a pointed contrast to the neo-brutalism of so many large restaurants bristling with zinc and shoulder pads. The design for this 28-seater was conceived and executed by chef/patron Michael von Hruschka and his partner in warm Thai colours, with lots of Thai sculptural items bought while von Hruschka was in residence at The Oriental in Bangkok. This is a restaurant clearly in touch with its female side, full of touches to amuse and delight, like the origami-bird wine list presented in a small cage. Von Hruschka's cooking is sensual but also technically well prepared. The short menu changes weekly, but has featured items like the tom a lin plate: a soup fragrant with coconut milk, lemon grass, stock and red chilli; unfried carrot spring rolls; and a bean sprout salad. Shishimi salmon had a pepper crust and rested on nori-wrapped sushi rice, served with a ponzu-based dipping sauce and Japanese pickles. Wok-fried tiger prawns in squid ink parcels is a variant of pad Thai, wrapped up like baby aubergines, with a fresh pea and coconut milk sauce and really ignites the pleasure centres. Venetian latte is tiramisù with ginger, and fusion sorbets a stimulating trio of lemon grass, strawberry with chilli, and chocolate with Mekong whisky. The wine list is short, personal and very reasonable. Service is warm and hospitable, but there have been complaints about long waits for food. This is not a perfect restaurant, but it is perfectly delightful.

Interlude

MODERN BRITISH 14/20

5 CHARLOTTE ST, W1, 0171-637 0222,
FAX 0171-637 0224
Open Lunch Mon.-Fri., Dinner Mon.-Sat. ££
U: Tottenham Court Rd.

Various restaurants have operated over the years in this pretty restaurant with four yellow painted rooms. But let's hope for more than an interlude with Paul Merrett, whose cooking is of a high order. Merrett grew up in Zanzibar, and freshly roasted and exotic spices certainly influence some of the dishes of his mostly modern British/European menu. He handles ingredients with real flair. First off were delicious homemade breads, olives and an amuse-gueule of salmon and ginger. Starters of squid and chorizo fritter and flash-fried tuna with tomato and chilli jam were a delightful contrast of textures. Seared sea scallops with crab and coconut milk risotto was lip-smacking with flavour; the cumin-roasted loin of lamb on smoked auburgine with sweet potato sauté and warm mushroom relish tender and triumphant. Fresh wild basil sorbet was redolent of sunny days in Provence. Attention to the palette of colours and presentation on the plate were pictures to behold. The comprehensive wine list reveals a sound knowledge and, luckily, affordability: a Chateau Smith-Haute Lafitte '75 was good value for £40. Service by French waiters is informed and charming. I left Interlude feeling quite uplifted.

Pied-à-Terre

FRENCH 16/20

34 CHARLOTTE ST, W1, 0171-636 1178,
FAX 0171-916 1171
Lunch Mon.-Fri., Dinner Mon.-Sat. £££
U: Goodge St.

The staff at this off-the-beaten-track (by central London standards) eatery are serious, motivated and friendly, from owner-host David Moore, chef Tom Aikens and sommelier Bruno Assoin, to the waitpersons. The dining room may not be one of the most opulent, but the British pop art adds an uplifting feel—as does the cuisine. A readiness to experiment speaks loud and clear in dishes such as the amuse gueule we tried recently: a trio of cucumber aspic, foie gras with quail eggs in caramel and stuffed red mullet, which, had they been in larger portions, would have made an excellent meal in itself! Other memorable dishes include roasted scallops in a tomato juice, confit tomato and fennel with basil, roasted langoustines with sesame filo, avocado salad with langoustine and sesame sauce and roasted sea bass with dill-marinated potatoes, cucumber tagliatelle, caviar and oyster sauce.

Desserts like orange millefeuille and sorbet, confit rhubarb and creamed mano rice, and chestnut and chocolate marquise with caramel ice cream and confit chestnuts, show that culinary daring is held up all the way through. An extensive wine list contains many French treasures, as well as thoughtful choices from elsewhere. Set dinner £32.50, Menu Degustation £60.

TOWER BRIDGE

Blue Print Café

MODERN BRITISH 13/20

SHAD THAMES, BUTLERS WHARF, SE1,
0171-378 7031, FAX 0171-357 8810
Lunch daily, Dinner Mon.-Sat. ££
U: Tower Hill.

Recent changes to this bright, well-lit room include glassing in the balcony overlooking the river and expanding the kitchen. Most diners get a view of the Thames—one of the better river-restaurant views—with Tower Bridge resplendent in all its glory. The whiteness is cooling in summer, and strangely refreshing in winter which makes up for the service which can be irritatingly off-hand. This cannot be said of the food however, which is confidently assured in its Mediterranean theme. Tagliatelle lightly dressed with spring broad beans and asparagus, new potatoes and pancetta, or a confit of new season garlic with tapenade and goat's chese. Chef Jeremy Lee excels at the grill, and when roasting, as in hake with butter, parsley olive and capers. Less successful are more classic offerings, like an oily spinach tart. Desserts mix old and new—trifle looks somewhat out of place, but curiously apt given the amaretti, mascarpone and pistachio ingredients. The wine list is short and well appointed.

Butlers Wharf Chop House

MODERN BRITISH 11/20
BUTLERS WHARF BUILDING, 36 SHAD THAMES, BUTLERS WHARF, SE1, 0171-403 3403, FAX 0171-403 3414
Lunch Sun.-Fri., Dinner Mon.-Sat. £££
U: Tower Hill.

A stunning view, with a well-designed interior where low ceilings disappear against pale walls and equally pale wood. The pine furniture does its job of bringing a homely atmosphere to this quirky establishment peddling all that is British and good: asparagus in season, smoked salmon from Scotland, crab from Dorset all appear much as they would at home and all the better as a result. Main courses excel at steak and kidney pie, bangers and mash, or pork chop, the latter identified as coming from Eastbrook Farm and being organic. Desserts are worth saving room for, crème brûlée comes as burnt cream, while the rhubarb and custard tart was deliciously creamy with just the right bite from this gloriously English fruit. The wine list celebrates the English love of claret, but pays due regard to the wine-growing areas of the New World.

Cantina del Ponte

MEDITERRANEAN 11/20
BUTLERS WHARF BUILDING, 36 SHAD THAMES, SE1, 0171-403 5403, FAX 0171-403 0267
Lunch and Dinner daily. ££
U: Tower Hill.

There is something of a Venetian tone to this quarry-tiled bare wooden-tabled room with its market-place mural running along the back wall. The view out over Tower Bridge only serves to reinforce the nautical theme, but as you would expect in a Conran-owned establishment, the message is subtle. The food is relaxed, more lunch than dinner but actually a delight if what you want is unfussy cooking with a light touch. A Piedmont pepper with mozzarella, asparagus with Parmesan and balsamic vinegar, or something a little more French like a salad of poached Toulouse sausage, egg and mustard dressing. Main courses follow the pasta and pizza, grilled meat and fish route, the emphasis on the latter being sharp, accurate cooking with minimalist dressing—veal escalope with a veal reduction for example. The desserts swing from seasonal berries to baked banana and toffee sauce. The wine list concentrates its efforts on Italy to good effect.

Le Pont de la Tour

FRENCH 14/20
BUTLERS WHARF BUILDING, 36 SHAD THAMES, BUTLERS WHARF, SE1, 0171-403 8403, FAX 0171 403 0267
Lunch Sun.-Fri., Dinner daily. ££££
U: Tower Hill.

Walk past the bar with its seating area and snack menu—good value—and into the dining room. Pale wood and the long windows looking out over the river give this well designed room a distinctly ocean-liner feel, which plays down the serious restaurant theme to good effect. The cooking style is French-based, but with modern interpretation. Fish and seafood tends to come in classic mode: grilled Dover sole and chips; gravlax with mustard sauce; salmon with sauce vierge; oysters au natural. More complex starters might include a roasted pepper stuffed with brandade and served with French beans and tapenade, a wealth of hefty Provençal flavours that works well. Meat is handled well, as is the game as in a pigeon with a well-judged reduction beefed up with morels and truffles. Vegetables come separately, which can be a little confusing given some mains also come with vegetables. At £2 a throw, they can be unnecessary. Desserts vary from a delicious soufflé of prune and armagnac to chocolate brownies or apple tart and ice cream. Service is on the ball, bordering on the brusque. The wine list is extensive, wide ranging and imaginative, although you pay dearly for the choice offerings. Set lunch £27.50, pre- and post-theatre menu £19.50. The bar and grill serve Sat. brunch 11.30am-3pm £14.95 and £17.95.

Tentazioni

ITALIAN 14/20
2 MILL STREET, LLOYDS WHARF, SE1, 0171-237 1100
Lunch Mon.-Fri., Dinner Mon.-Sat. ££ (inc coffee).
U: Tower Hill.

Tentazioni is a comfortably small restaurant on the ground and first floors of a converted warehouse with modern but not austere decor. Service by friendly, but not over-familiar, young people is as sophisticated as the food. This regional Italian haute cuisine does not mimic French fashions, or worse, 'international eclectic' cooking. Its superb ingredients, cooked with consumate skill are almost entirely Italian. The short à la carte-five main courses changes every week or so. Outstanding successes in a single meal included a delicatissimo olive oil with good breads; elegantly presented raw beef salad with asparagus and pecorino cheese; exactly cooked tortelli stuffed with guinea fowl; the blackest of black tagliolini with prawns and asparagus; and feather light polenta gnocchi with navarin of venison. Glorious desserts were taleggio with mostarda, and yoghurt mousse with strawberries in a lightly peppered syrup. Since every dish in each course is the same price, the cost of an à la carte meal can be precisely predicted. The wines are Italian except for Champagne. Great names include Jermann, Isole e Olena, and Gaja. Well-chosen, modest bottles are well worth investigating, while Chardonnay and Montepulciano d'Abruzzo are excellent 'house wines' at £10.50. Set menu 4 course 'degustazione' £24.50 or £29.50 with four glasses of wine (+ coffee £1.50).

VICTORIA

Boisdale

SCOTTISH 14/20

15 ECCLESTON ST, SW1, 0171-730 6922,
FAX 0171-730 0548
Noon-11pm Mon.-Sat. £££
U: Victoria.

In this era of 'star chefs', restaurateurs are under-rated. Ranald Macdonald at Boisdale cooks only in emergencies. But everything—ambience, menus, quality of ingredients, skilful cooking, evinces his control. The Scottish decor is red, green and black with not a square of tartan except in some of the multitudinous pictures. There are tables in a walled garden. The menu features prime Scottish produce—lobsters, salmon and beef—and game in season. The à la carte offers veritable British homemade sausages, steak and kidney pie and fish and offal of the day. From further afield are scallops with fennel and mussels; and lamb with couscous, spinach and minted pesto. There are seven tempting choices in each course of the £16.90 menu. Haggis features at £12.90; it also heads the list of six savouries—a British tradition now being revived. Well chosen wines are a bonus in this outpost of Scottish culture. 2 course menus are £12.90 and £16.90.

Ebury Wine Bar

INTERNATIONAL 14/20

139 EBURY ST, SW1, 0171-730 5447,
FAX 0171-730 0548
Lunch & Dinner daily. £
U: Victoria.

When it comes to originality, Joshua Hampton can give most telly chefs a twelve-ingredient start, and beat them with straightforward good taste. Brandade of salt cod with roasted leeks for example is simply that. Brik is crackling crisp outside, the egg soft inside, and smoked chicken replaces traditional tuna to great effect. Why has no one else thought of uncomplicated fresh pasta with tender chicken livers, bacon, mushrooms and sage? The subtle flavour of lamb, feta and olive meat loaf needs a more elegant name—'angels' haggis' perhaps. The twist on his bread-and-butter pudding is that it is based on panetone. With Mars bar spring roll the chef matches the quirky decor, a trompe l'oeil library of the world's most improbable books. Of some 60 very reasonably priced wines nearly half are available by the glass, and virtually all are excellent examples of their type. Although Joshua cooks at the Ebury he also oversees the kitchens of sister establishments **Carriages, 43 Buckingham Palace Road SW1, 0171-834 0119, and Joe's Brasserie, 130 Wandsworth Bridge Road, SW6, 0171-731 7835.**

WANDSWORTH

Chez Bruce

FRENCH 14/20

2 BELLEVUE RD, SW17, 0181-672 0114,
FAX 0181-767 6648
Lunch daily, Dinner Mon.-Sat. ££
BR: Wandsworth Common.

Found on the edge of Wandsworth Common and right next to the railway station, Chez Bruce is more accessible than its address might suggest. Closely packed tables, a tented ceiling and consistently full houses make for a warm and jolly atmosphere. The walls sport curious but attractive architectural prints. The admirable set-price menus have few supplements and when they appear it is with good reason, like the grande assiette de charcuterie Chez Bruce at £5. What came was an enormous platter with two chutneys, three terrines, a parfait and enough foie gras to satisfy the most committed carnivore. Other starters include home-cured bresaola, herb leaf salad and Parmesan; and a sauté of scallops and squid with noodles and pesto. The cooking is technically assured, with enough classical French input alongside a liking for things Mediterranean. Main courses might include rump of lamb with potato gnocchi, creamed tomatoes and basil; or roast guinea fowl with Puy lentils, wild mushrooms and tarragon. The roast cod with olive oil mash was deceptive in its simplicity—perfectly cooked cod, flaky and squeaky on top of stunning seductive mash. Desserts are strongly French as in St. Emilion au chocolat, tarts and ices. The cheese board is eclectic and good. The wine list is of choice favourites from around the globe.

WILLESDEN

Sabras

INDIAN VEGETARIAN 16/20

263 HIGH RD, NW10, 0181-459 0340

Dinner Tues.-Sun.£

U: Dollis Hill.

Its 25th anniversary has brought minor changes to this simple, exuberantly decorated eating-house. The glass-fronted counter with its Indian pastries, barfi and jilabi has gone. When owner Hemant Desai said it was because they couldn't sell these sweetmeats, it was a reminder that Sabra's is actually a business, rather than Nalinee Desai's home where we go to enjoy her amazing cooking. Her mastery of spices and herbs produces aromas and flavours, subtle and elusive as the fragments of melody which rise and evaporate in Debussy's La Mer. A warning! De-luxe sev puri and pani puri, tiny, crisp filled puffs with tangy sauces may instigate an early visit to the travel agent for tickets to Mumbai (previously Bombay) where, says the menu, they are sold as snacks on Juhu beach. The menu is all-Indian, so next go south for Madras masala dhosa, a rolled pancake topped with chopped onions, tomatoes, coconut, coriander and (optional) green chillies. To Gujerat for seasonal vegetables-spinach, aubergine or (Friday and Saturday only) sakkariya-sweet potato. North Indian Kashmiri kofta, fried, chopped vegetable balls with a nutty lentil sauce are perfect with Kashmiri pulav, rice cooked with steamed vegetables and cashews, garnished with flaked almonds and exquisite pink 'pomegranate pearls'. You should now understand why most people don't need a dessert. But if you do, there is kulfi, shrikhand or basudi, a nutty, chilled milk pudding. Or venturing very far to the north-west, Mövenpick ice cream or sorbet. This is one of London's best bargains; menus range from £6 to £15.

WIMBLEDON

Zujuma's

INDIAN 13/20

58A WIMBLEDON HILL RD, SW19, 0181-879 0916, FAX 0181-944 0861

Lunch & Dinner daily. £

U: Wimbledon.

To eat at Zujuma's is to visit a friend, both a charming hostess, and an accomplished cook. Her homely food, based on that of Hyderabad, is not chilli-hot; even three-flame symbol dishes should not over-excite palates used to conventional curries. But rich spicing, and herbal fragrances will excite those seeking subtlety and delicacy. Shami, finely ground lamb in a skillet, and murgh adrak, chicken with button onions, are enjoyable starters, but some skip this course because similar dishes reappear as side dishes in the mushqaabs. The menu features eight of these complete main courses, including vegetables, dahl and wonderful rice. Consistent excellence makes individual recommendations of main courses unnecessary, but note sabze, shredded green vegetables fit for a rajah. Andon ki peosi, 'golden spongy egg and saffron dessert', resembles, but improves on, gulab jamon. Bright south Indian colours, huge glass spice jars and smartly dressed waiters provide an attractive modern ambience.

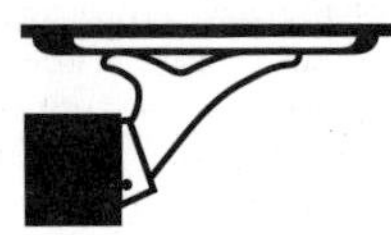

HOTELS

CONTENTS

INTRODUCTION

London's hotel scene is booming. Most of the major top hotels have been refurbished, or are in the process. There has been a move to improve hotels in the moderate price range, and this has resulted in already existing hotels being refurbished and more seriously vetted. We are also seeing the arrival of cheaper chain hotels which are building both in central locations (often around railway stations) and a little further out, particularly in the stretch of land south of the river from Waterloo to the City, an area which is fast becoming the most exciting development in years.

All top hotels now have state-of-the-art equipment, particularly important for business travellers. Business centres are improving, and many are open 24 hours a day. Health clubs have become de rigueur and new swimming pools are being built in many hotels. Even among the smaller hotels, standards are very high indeed, suited for the international traveller.

LONDON HOTEL PRICES

It should be borne in mind that while published rack rates at top hotels appear high, there are many bargains to be had for the intrepid traveller. Check advance purchase packages before departure, investigate corporate rates offered to many businesses, or for the bold, negotiate on the spot. Weekend packages, small group bookings and seasonal savings abound. Our editorial comment will tell you what we think of the hotels, and price does not necessarily mean the best in terms of accommodation, service or ambience. So choose carefully.

RESERVATION SERVICE

If you arrive without having booked an hotel, the **Tourist Information Centres** run by the **London Tourist Board** at **Heathrow Airport, Liverpool Street Station** and at **Victoria Station** can book a room for you, though they do not cover every hotel. There is a credit card booking hotline run by the LTB open Mon-Fri 9.30am-5.30pm, 0171-932 2020, Fax 0171-932 2021. The Evening Standard's *This is London* (www.thisislondon.com) has an agreement with HotelWorld (www.hotelworld.com) for selecting and reserving London hotel accommodation online.

OUR HOTEL RATING SYSTEM

To help you easily find the hotel that best matches your needs and budget, we have listed establishments in sections that reflect price, service and amenities: **Top of the Line**, **Luxury**, **Townhouse** (see explanation below), **Moderate** and **Economy**. We have also listed **Chain Hotels** and **Airport Hotels** at the end of the chapter.

Our ranking of the décor, service, food, amenities and ambience of each hotel is expressed in **Keys**, from one to five. The number of Keys accompanying each review indicates the hotel's ranking according to the following system:

- 1 key — ***Just the basics:*** A clean room and private bath, and that's about it.
- 2 keys — ***Comfortable:*** Adequate rooms, pleasant service and some amenities.
- 3 keys — ***Very comfortable:*** Good rooms, amenities and service; you can't complain.
- 4 keys — ***Everything you need and more:*** Excellent rooms, superb amenities and service—with style.
- 5 keys — ***As good as it gets; pure luxury:*** Where to stay if money is no object and you demand perfection. Among the very best hotels in the world.

TOWNHOUSE HOTELS

The townhouse hotel phenomenon is unique to London, and has seen incredible growth in the last five years. Townhouse hotels are converted private houses in leafy residential areas—Chelsea, South Kensington, Knightsbridge and Notting Hill—that have been joined together and decorated with quality antiques. The service is usually very personal and caring. What townhouse hotels lack in size (most have fewer than 20 rooms), they make up for with charm, style, a very warm welcome and a genuinely personal touch.

RENTING AN APARTMENT

You might also consider the option of renting an apartment, particularly if you are contemplating a longer stay and are quite happy to stock your own fridge and discover your neighbourhood restaurants. Living like a Londoner can be great fun. Renting a house or apartment in London is becoming an increasingly popular option; and greater demand has consequently produced a wider range and choice. The apartments recommended here are only a very few of those available in London. For further advice, contact your local British Tourist Authority office.

The BTA publishes a booklet listing recommended apartments and apartment services. When you enquire about an apartment, try to get as much information as you can, as they vary enormously even within the same apartment block. The rates given here, except where indicated otherwise, are for weekly rentals and are only an indication of the price. There are many options and special breaks, and prices vary according to time of year and availability.

Most apartments also offer daily rates, and do not restrict you to a weekly stay. If you stay longer, rates often decrease. Of the five companies listed first here, all of whom deal with large numbers of apartments, we particularly recommend In **the English Manner** for its delightful townhouses as well as its first-class apartments. They also rent houses outside London.

APARTMENT RENTAL SERVICES:

The Apartment Service

5-6 Francis Grove, Wimbledon, SW19 4DT, 0181-944 1444, Fax 0181-944 6744; in Canada: Bridge Apartments, 1000 Yonge St, Suite 301, Toronto, M4W 2K2, Ontario, 416-923 1000, Fax 416 924 2446; in USA: Keith Prowse & Co, 234 West 44th St, Suite 1000, New York, NY 10036—212-398 1430, 800-669 8687, Fax 212-302 4251.

Barclay International Group

150 East 52nd St, New York NY 10022, 212-832 3777, 800-845 6636, Fax 212-753 1130.

In the English Manner

Lancych, Boncath, Pembrokeshire SA37 0LJ, 0123-969 8444, Fax 0123-969 8686; in USA: 515 South Figueroa St, Suite 1000, Los Angeles, CA 90071, 213-629 1811, 800 422 0799, Fax 213-689 8784 and 4092 North Ivy Rd, NE, Atlanta, GA 30342, 404-231 5837, Fax 404-231 9610.

Park Lane Apartments

48 Curzon St, W1Y 7RE, 0171-629 0763, 1-800 284 7385, Fax 0171-493 1308. Weekly rates £445-£3,500.

Westminster Apartment Services

16 Leinster Sq, W2 4PR, 0171-221 1400, Fax 0171-229 3917. Many apartments all around London at a variety of prices.

RECOMMENDED APARTMENTS

The Ascott Mayfair

49 Hill St, W1X 7FQ, 0171-499 6868, Fax 0171-499 0705. 56 apts Daily £164-£485; weekly £1,095-£3,225. Also rent monthly. Very high standards of both apartments and service here, plus health club, business services, lounge and bar.

Aston's Budget Studios

39 Rosary Gdns, South Kensington, SW7 4NQ, 0171-370 0737, USA 1-800 525 2810, Fax 0171-835 1419. 60 apts nightly rates £43-£135. Recently upgraded and refurbished, these apartments are recommended for budget accommodations in a good Kensington location.

Beaufort House

45 Beaufort Gdns, Knightsbridge, SW3 1PN, 0171-584 2600, Fax 0171-584 6532. 22 apts nightly rates £149-£408, weekly rates £1,008-£2,821. All plus VAT. In pretty Beaufort Gardens near Harrods, these well-decorated and well-equipped suites are in an elegant old building.

Draycott House

10 Draycott Ave, Chelsea, SW3 3AA, 0171-584 4659, Fax 0171-225 3694. 13 apts nightly rate £164-£396, weekly rate £1,037-£2,522. All plus VAT. Friendly welcome here. Located in a charming, old red-brick building, many have their own balconies. Very well decorated in English country style.

Durley House

115 Sloane St, Chelsea, SW1X 9PJ, 0171-235 5537, USA 1-800 553 6674, Fax 0171-259 6977. 11 apts nightly rate £240-£435. All plus VAT. Fashionable address in Sloane Street, delightful, elegant apartments from the owners of Dorset Square, the Pelham Hotel and the new Covent Garden Hotel, thoroughly recommended and all decorated in the English country style at its best. More an all-suite hotel than apartments with the additional comforts.

Flemings Apartments

7 Half Moon St, Mayfair, W1Y 7RA, 0171-493 2088, Fax 0171-629 4063, Ex-USA 800-348-4685, E-mail: reservations @flemings-mayfair.co.uk. 10 apts nightly from £346, inc VAT. Part of Flemings Hotel, they have all the hotel's amenities and a separate entrance. Ideally located in the heart of Mayfair.

Fountains

1 Lancaster Terrace, Hyde Park, W2 3PF, 0171-221 1400, Fax 0171-229 3917. 17 apts nightly from £170-£440, weekly £1,170-£2,990. These are top-of-the-range, beautifully decorated apartments, just north of Hyde Park and overlooking the Italian Water Gardens in the park.

Grosvenor House

Grosvenor House Hotel, Park Lane, W1A 3AA, 0171-499 6363, Fax 0171-493 3342. HYPERLINK http://www.grosvenor-house.co.uk# http://www.grosvenorhouse.co.uk. 46 apts nightly £255-£895. Long lets also. Part of the Grosvenor House Hotel, though with its own entrance, the apartments are well decorated and guests can use the hotel's facilities such as the first-rate health club and pool.

Hyde Park Residence

55 Park Lane, W1Y 3DB, 0171-409 9000, Fax 0171-493 4041, E-mail: lettings @hprapts.demon.co.uk. 120 apts let on weekly basis only £1,000-£6,000. All plus VAT. Superb accommodation on London's Park Lane, some apartments are on long term lets. The building has all the facilities of a five-star hotel.

Nell Gwynn Apartments

Nell Gwynn House, Sloane Ave, SW3 3AX, 0171-584 8317, Fax 0171-823 7133. 127 apts nightly £310-£750. Minimum stay of 22 nights. In an impressive 1930s building, this is a popular location in Chelsea with a health club and garage.

One Thirty

130 Queensgate, South Kensington, SW7 5LE, 0171-581 2322, Fax 0171-823 8488. 54 apts nightly £104.50-£220.50. All plus VAT. In a refurbished Victorian building near the museums and Hyde Park, the apartments are well furnished and some have balconies.

Orion London Apartment Hotel

7-21 Goswell Rd, EC1, 0171-566 8000, Fax 0171-566 8130. 129 ensuite studios and apartments from the large French chain near the Barbican centre, with a Simply Nico restaurant. Well designed, but with fairly ordinary decor, they're all very well run and convenient. Rates per night (which decreases after 7 nights) £84-£126. Also at 94-99 High Holborn, WC1, 0171-395 8800, Fax 0171-395 8799; 18-21 Northumberland Ave, WC2, 0171-766 3700, Fax 0171-766 3766.

23 Greengarden House

23 Greengarden House, St. Christopher's Pl, W1M 5HD, 0171-935 9191, Fax 0171-935 8858, E-mail: greengdnshs@aol.com. 23 apts nightly rates £155-£245, weekly rates £1,085-£1,715. All plus VAT. In a delightful, secluded place behind Oxford Street, some of the apartments are quite small, but well decorated and the management is delightfully helpful.

BED AND BREAKFAST

This is proving a popular and good way to stay in London, in private houses where you are given a warm welcome. Many of the hotels in the Economy section following fit into this category. Contact these companies for vetted accommodations:

At Home in London

70 Black Lion Lane, W6 9BE, 0181-748 1943, Fax 0181-748 2701

Bulldog Club

15 Roland Gardens, SW7 3PE, 0171-0341 9495, Fax 0171-341 9496

Uptown Reservations

50 Christchurch St, SW3 4AR, 0171-351 3445, Fax 0171-351 9383

Wolsey Lodges Ltd.

9 Market Pl, Hadleigh, Ipswich, Suffolk IP7 5DL. Brochure requests: 01473-827500, administration: 01473-822058, Fax 01473 827444, E-mail: wolsey@wolseylo.demon.co.uk, website: www.wolsey-lodges.co.uk

HOTEL SYMBOLS

Before the text of each review, you'll find the following symbols:

- A All credit cards taken
- Visa
- MasterCard
- American Express
- Diners Club
- American Express
- Health club and/or spa
- Tennis
- Golf
- Horseback Riding
- Swimming pool
- P Parking
- In-room faxes
- Meeting rooms
- Business center
- Complimentary continental breakfast

TOP OF THE LINE

The Berkeley

WILTON PL, SW1X 7RL
0171-235 6000, FAX 0171-235 4330
E-mail: info@the-berkeley.co.uk
54stes £415-£1,800, 103rms S £255-£280, D £290-£305 plus VAT. 10 non-smoking suites, 17 non-smoking rooms. Air cond. 24-hr rm service. Limousine service.

A P

Discreet, elegant and superbly and recently refurbished, The Berkeley, which opened in 1972, remains one of London's top hotels. In a wonderful location—a quiet street literally a few seconds from Knightsbridge and Hyde Park—it welcomes its celebrity guests as if they are long-lost friends. The entrance hallway is small but stylish, more in keeping with a grand house than an hotel. The rooms themselves are well sized and impeccably furnished in a grand country-house manner. Two of the top conservatory suites have their own saunas, and service is as good as you would expect. In keeping with the capital's status as a top restaurant city, Vong is one of London's most talked-about new hot spots, with a stylish frontage onto Knightsbridge and an entirely separate entrance (see Restaurant section). From September, the refurbished main restaurant is under the direction of Pierre Koffman of La Tante Claire, giving the Berkeley a real edge on all hotels. The Berkeley Health Club is fully equipped with one of the true pleasures of London—a swimming pool with a retractable roof for fine weather, and great views over London.

Claridge's

BROOK ST, W1A 2JQ
0171-629 8860, FAX 0171-499 2210
E-Mail: info@claridges.co.uk
62stes £460-£2,450, 135rms S £255, D £295-£365 plus VAT. 17 non-smoking suites, 30 non-smoking rooms. Air cond. 24-hr rm, maid and valet service.

A

For over a century, since William Claridge put together six houses in 1853 to let suites as private apartments, Claridge's has been welcoming heads of state, dignitaries and the illustrious from around the world. They come for the discreet welcome, and because this grand and dignified hotel manages so successfully to convey the feel of a private club, though part of the Savoy group. A major refurbishment has transformed parts of the hotel, while still retaining the feeling of old-fashioned comfort and luxury. Two penthouse suites on the seventh floor, both with two bedrooms, two bathrooms and sitting-rooms with terrace, have been created—the Davies Penthouse complete with original fireplace and a barrel-vaulted ceiling, and the Brook Penthouse sporting all the elegance of the Art Deco era. And of course you get a butler. The Royal Suites remain as sumptuous as ever, one complete with the grand piano that belonged to Richard d'Oyly Carte, founder of the Savoy Hotel and the Opera Company. Designed as three, they can make one suite of 50 separate rooms. The facilities are bang up-to-date; the feel however can be Scottish baronial (in winter the smell of wood fires greets you), or 1920s high living. Claridge's Restaurant, originally designed in 1925-26 by Basil Ionides to provide an ambience in keeping with the jazz age, offers some good cooking (see Restaurant section); services include hairdressers for men and women and a society florist.

The Connaught

CARLOS PL, W1Y 6AL

0171-499 7070, FAX 0171-495 3262

E-mail: info@the-connaught.co.uk

24stes £600-£1,160, 66rms S £225-£340, D £310-£340 plus VAT. Air cond in most rms. 24-hr rm service.

Built in 1897 and named after Queen Victoria's third son, The Connaught has always attracted guests for its hushed elegance and feeling of absolute top comfort and quality British service. From the outside with its low height and red brick façade fitting perfectly with its Mayfair neighbours, it doesn't even look very much like a top London hotel. The ratio of staff to guests is very high and it shows. It has never sought to be fashionable; instead it has the feel of a grand country house transplanted to London. Marble fireplaces, oak panelling and wonderfully ornate ceilings in the public areas which are furnished with antiques and paintings, add to the atmosphere. Bedrooms are luxurious and decorated in appropriate English chintzes; bathrooms are marble, and full of toiletries. Every amenity is here. There are two restaurants presided over by top chef Michel Bourdin: **The Connaught Restaurant** (very formal) and **The Grill Room** (Georgian-style), both serving a mix of traditional English and French cuisine (see Restaurant section).

The Dorchester

PARK LANE, W1A 2HJ

0171-629 8888, FAX 0171-409 0114

52stes £400-£1,000, 192rms S £255-£275, D £285-£315 plus VAT. Non-smoking rms on 3rd floor. Air cond. 24-hr rm service.

Just peruse the guest list—Woody Allen, Cindy Crawford, Sigourney Weaver, Karl Lagerfeld, Cecil B de Mille. The Dorchester, built in 1931, is the most spectacular of the great London hotels and one of the most famous. The Rolls Royces, Daimlers and stretch Mercedes parked outside announce a celebrity clientele who frequently want publicity along with tight security and attention. Along with heads of state and international industrialists, they come here for personal service plus the latest technology. The rooms are now among the best in London, restored to the remarkable standards of the past that made the hotel so famous. Triple-glazed bedroom windows, many looking out over Hyde Park, shut out the noise of London. Bedrooms are large and furnished with antiques in grand English country-house style. Some rooms have four-poster beds, swathed in fabrics and silks that are echoed around the windows. Paintings adorn the walls while touches like hand-embroidered cushions scattered around add to the home-from-home—or perhaps palace-to-palace—feel. All the bathrooms, boasting the deepest baths in London, are decorated in white Italian marble and many have windows giving natural light. The Oliver Messel Suite, finished in 1953 and the first luxury suite built in a British hotel, is delightful, with the theatre designer's hand painting in evidence, and the drinks cabinet hidden behind a bookcase. The roof garden suites, restored to their original patterns, are stunning. **The Promenade**, just off the entrance lobby, stretches before you, a sea of marble and opulence perfect for morning coffee, afternoon tea, cocktails and light snacks. The bar is great for cocktails and a menu of light Italian dishes. **The Oriental** offers expensive Chinese food in a spectacular decor, and **The Grill Room** is British (see Restaurant section). After a blow-out, work out in the **Dorchester Spa**.

47 Park Street

47 PARK ST, W1Y 4EB
0171-491 7282, FAX 0171-491 7281
52stes £255-£500 plus VAT. All non-smoking. Air cond. 24-hr rm service from Le Gavroche.

You could describe this as a restaurant with rooms, as **Le Gavroche**, in the capable hands of young Michel Roux (Albert Roux's son), is probably the better known of the two institutions. (See Restaurant section). But what rooms you find in this prestigious Mayfair address, a member of Relais et Châteaux. Each individually designed suite comes with one or two bedrooms plus a sitting room complete with dining table and chairs and a fully equipped kitchen for entertaining or for those on longer stays when even Le Gavroche's attractions might pall. Antiques, interesting fabrics and objets d'art decorate the rooms. The marble bathrooms are all luxury. It's not chance that over sixty percent of their customers represent repeat business.

The Four Seasons Hotel

HAMILTON PL, PARK LANE, W1A 1AZ
0171-499 0888, FAX 0171-493 6629
26stes £440-£1,600, 194rms S £260-£290, D £305-£315 plus VAT. 9 non-smoking suites, 82 non-smoking rms. Two rms for disabled. Air cond. 24-hr rm service.

This may be part of a chain, but the London Four Seasons has managed to make itself highly individual. The plain façade belies a luxurious interior; and this hotel is both grand and welcoming with good views over Hyde Park. From the impressive wood-panelled lobby, a lounge offers light meals and our favourite seasonally changing **Four Seasons Tea** (see Quick Bites section). Apart from the Conservatory rooms which are delightful, and the very well-equipped suites, large bedrooms are decorated with style, many in soft colours. The furnishings are pretty, the sofas comfortable, and the beds are renowned. The hotel has an enviable reputation for professional service and first-rate housekeeping, with baby-listening and baby-sitting services on hand. In the winter of 1998, there will be a new restaurant, called Lanes, using stained glass, marbling and wood panelling and rich colours. There is a spectacular buffet and a new menu adopting many international influences under the chefs Eric Deblonde and Shaun Watling. The fitness club offers state-of-the-art equipment.

The Halkin

5 HALKIN ST, SW1X 7DJ
0171-333 1000, FAX 0171-333 1100
E-mail: res@halkin.co.uk
11stes £395-£550, 30rms S/D £255-£325 plus VAT. Air cond. 24-hr rm service.

One of a kind in London, this stunningly designed hotel tucked away in Belgravia is pure Italian and comes as something of a surprise, from the minimalist decor to the Giorgio Armani-staffed uniforms. From the moment you enter the granite, marble-floored lobbies with Italian-designed leather sofas and chairs, you realise that chintz and the English country-house look have been rejected here in favour of clean, lean and very sophisticated lines. Large bedrooms each have their own seating area and the general scheme is minimal with much wood on the walls and plenty of mirrors. Most of the splendid all-marble bathrooms have their own walk-in showers. Rooms boast all the latest techno-gadgetry, from hand-free telephones and remote control lighting to CD players and videos, plus excellent security. The restaurant, called **Stephano Cavallini at the Halkin**, reflects the esteem this young chef is held in, and focuses on modern Italian cuisine (see Restaurant section). It's first-class, with a handsome adjoining private dining room for parties up to twenty. The small bar adjacent to the lobby is invariably full of designer-clad guests.

The Hempel

LANCASTER GATE, W1
0171-298 9000, FAX 0171-402 4666
E-mail: the-hempel@easynet.co.uk.
12stes from £370-£775, 35rms from from £220. Air cond. 24-hr rm service. Garden.

This is one of those places which you enter and say 'Wow'—that is after you've found the front door of this ultra-discreet, oh-so-talked about hotel designed by Anouska Hempel, the society designer who owns Blake's and her own couture business. Just two minutes from Hyde Park, and stretched over five townhouses which run along an entire garden square (hence the name), it's all lightness, whiteness and sophistication, stone rather than marble, and designed so the fireplaces appear to float in the walls. The rooms are equally sophisticated, some might even say spartan in their approach and a far cry from the glorious rather decadent air of Blake's. All the facilities are here, plus **I-Thai**, serving Italian/South East Asian food. The Shadow Bar with its special cocktail selection attracts a sophisticated clientele. There is a fitness club to keep that figure. Directly opposite, a further townhouse, number 17, is used for fashion shows and shoots and opens onto a Zen garden where peace supposedly reigns. Certainly it's delightfully tucked away.

The Hyatt Carlton Tower

CADOGAN PL, SW1X 9PY

0171-235 1234, FAX 0171-235 9129

60stes £355-£2,750, 160rms £255-£295 plus VAT. 64 non-smoking rms. Air cond. 24-hr rm service.

This is the first modern five-star property to be built in Knightsbridge rather than Park Lane, in 1961. A recent refurbishment has provided the hotel, much used by Far Eastern and Arabic heads of state, with one of the most expensive suites in London—the eighteenth-floor Presidential Suite which is stunning by any standards. From the bullet-proofed glassed-in conservatory style drawing room/dining room you look down over Chelsea's green squares; elsewhere the suite is opulent with a four-poster bed, panic buttons, its own sauna and Jacuzzi with a television built into the wall, plus personal butler with his own pantry area. But you don't have to go quite so high for great views and good-sized rooms. Try room 426 on the fourth floor for its own balcony for breakfast and a delightful gold-starred entrance. On the ninth floor the **Peak Health Club** offers state-of-the-art equipment, work-out classes and an attractive lounge area for light meals. The business centre is impressive. As for restaurants, **Grissini** (see Restaurant section) overlooks leafy Cadogan Square, and **The Rib Room** is good for traditional British beef. Afternoon tea and drinks accompanied by a harpist are fun in the pretty **Chinoiserie Lounge** off the lobby (see Quick Bites section).

The Lanesborough

HYDE PARK CORNER, SW1X 7TA

0171-259 5599, FAX 0171-259 5606

E-mail: info@lanesborough co.uk.

46stes £450-£3,500, 49rms S £225-£255, D £295-£395 plus VAT. 13 non-smoking stes 13 non-smoking rms. Air cond. 24-hr rm and butler service.

You can't miss The Lanesborough. Housed in the former St. George's Hospital, it presents a wonderful white, classical façade to the world that hurries past it at Hyde Park Corner. Marketed as a country stately home in the heart of central London, it's all large-scale antique furniture, acres of marble, yards of impressive fabric and wonderful huge flower arrangements. It may feel like a stately home of the 1820's, but the comforts of the late-20th century are evident. Rooms have triple-glazed windows and are beautifully furnished, containing some of the latest equipment naturally hidden in the furniture. Its arrival policy is singular: guests are taken to the room and introduced to their own butler who will unpack, pack, run baths, and most importantly, explain the high-tech gadgetry which can be confusing—all in a very traditional British manner. **The Conservatory** is in a lavish, over-the-top, mini-Brighton-pavilion style, with massive urns, fountains and trees, particularly right for late evening supper dances, where chef Paul Gaylor cooks an international cuisine. The wood-panelled **Library Bar**, complete with bookshelves, is a real delight and buzzes for drinks and light meals (see Bar Section); tea is served in the formal and rather loftily-named **Withdrawing Room**, which is decorated in wonderful muted gold (see Quick Bites section). Service throughout is faultless, from personalised stationery to complimentary pressing by a 24-hour butler service on arrival. The Royal Suite includes the use of a Bentley and your own 24-hour butler.

The Ritz

PICCADILLY, W1V 9DG

0171-493 8181, FAX 0171-493 2687

14stes £525-£945, 116rms S/D £225-£325 plus VAT. Air cond in stes and executive rms. 24-hr rm service. 3 function rms.

The Ritz is a name to conjure with, and fortunately it is now as glitzy and ritzy (though in the best possible taste) as anyone could want. Built in 1906 by César Ritz, the hotel looks onto Piccadilly and Green Park. It's relatively small, with a mere 130 rooms, each one individually decorated in pretty pastels and gold leaf, full of antique furniture and fireplaces, and with plush marble bathrooms. Suites for private dining are stunning; the Trafalgar Suite looks over Green Park. Afternoon tea in this glorious hotel is a British institution, taken in the opulent **Palm Court** (see Quick Bites section). **The Louis XIV Restaurant**, generally referred to simply as **The Ritz Restaurant**, (see Restaurant section), is probably the most beautiful dining room in London, and in summer has a terrace overlooking a small, artificially created walled garden.

The Savoy

STRAND, WC2R 0EU
0171-836 4343, FAX 0171-240 6040
E-mail: info@the-savoy.co.uk
53stes £365-£1,160, 154rms S £250-£280, D £295-£305 plus VAT. 70% non-smoking rms. Air cond in all rooms. 24-hr rm service.

Ask anyone to name an hotel in London, and nine times out of ten they will cite The Savoy, something of a legend in British life. This grand lady continues to hog the limelight, particularly after her multi-million pound refurbishment which took the suites back to their former glorious furnishings, and removed the clutter of the cathedral-like lobby and brought back the original carvings and shape. Close to both the City and the West End, and within easy walking distance of theatres and Covent Garden, its position facing the Thames and overlooking Embankment Gardens, is spectacular. For this is a view that has inspired and still continues to. From the sought after rooms 310-311, you can see eight bridges over the River Thames. From a nearby suite, French Impressionist Claude Monet produced some 70 paintings of London's bridges on three separate occasions at three different seasons from 1899 to 1901. Thames-side suites with their views over the river come with top service at the touch of a button from maid, waiter or valet; classic furnishings are set off by deep pink velvet curtains; extravagant bathrooms include the famous 10-inch showerheads, and the usual luxurious touches. Since opening in 1889, The Savoy has always been known for restaurants, a recognition continued by chef Anton Edelmann. **The River Restaurant** overlooking the Thames with dancing in the evening, is formal and old-fashioned. The wood-panelled **Grill Room** is good for pre-theatre suppers and serious business lunches and offers an extensive wine list. (See Bar section). **The American Bar** is a great meeting place, afternoon tea or drinks in the **Thames Foyer** provides a good place for people-watching (see Quick Bites section). A Champagne-and-seafood bar is perched above the entrance drive. The elegant **Fitness Gallery** has a swimming pool, massage room, gym and sauna, ladies' and men's hairdresser and beauty treatments.

LUXURY

The Athenaeum

116 PICCADILLY, W1V 0BJ
0171-499 3464, FAX 0171-493 1860
E-mail: info@athenaeum hotel.com.
12stes £375-£650, 111rms S £235-£285, D £255-£305 plus VAT. 8 non-smoking suites, 56 non-smoking rooms. Air cond. 24-hr rm service.

The Athenaeum, found down Piccadilly towards Hyde Park Corner and overlooking the green swathes of Green Park, is now an understatedly elegant, privately owned hotel. Rooms are beautifully lit, and manage to radiate a golden glow with warm fabrics and fine furniture. They also offer all the amenities like two telephone lines, VCRs, CD players and the novelty of heated mirrors in bathrooms that never steam up. **The Windsor Lounge**, good for morning coffee or afternoon tea, has also been redecorated, and the hotel's famous bar continues to stock 56 different malt whiskys. **Bullochs**, named after the ebullient marketing director, Sally Bulloch, serves modern European cuisine in a pretty downstairs room. You're likely to spot the odd celeb here, as it's particularly popular with some of the top film and theatre stars. In addition, they offer self-contained serviced apartments behind the hotel which are very popular, again with stars who are staying in London for any length of time.

Blakes Hotel

33 Roland Gdns, SW7 3PF
0171-370 6701, Fax 0171-373 0442
E-mail: blakes@easynet.co.uk
9stes £475-£695, 42rms S £130, D £155-£300 plus VAT. 3 non-smoking rms. Air cond in large stes and doubles. 24-hr rm service.

Definitely for travel connoisseurs, this theatrical hotel in a series of late-Victorian townhouses was the first venture of Anouska Hempel, aka Lady Weinberg, the wife of Sir Mark Weinberg, a leading city financier. The dramatic results reflect her fashion and acting background. Blake's style is esoteric with strong themes running through each room's decor, from Biedermeier furniture to black Oriental lacquer. There are lots of swagged curtains, trompe l'oeil wall treatments and marble in the bathrooms. Each guest room is different, startling and idiosyncratic, some with painted floorboards, others with fantasy beds. Some might accuse Hempel of over-decoration, and fans of minimalism should definitely steer clear, but it's enormous fun and, not suprisingly, goes down big with the media who make up most of the guests. Downstairs, **Blakes Restaurant** continues Hempel's keen interest in the Orient with Japanese 'Kyoto Country Breakfasts' and an expensive, but beautifully executed, international menu attracting a glamorous clientele.

Brown's Hotel

Albemarle St, W1A 4SW
0171-493 6020, Fax 0171-493 9381
E-mail: brownshotel@ukbusiness.com.
11stes £310-£735, 111rms S/D £235-£265 plus VAT. Air cond. 24-hr rm service.

Perhaps the quintessential English hotel, Brown's has been bought by the group that owns Raffles Hotel in the Far East. Having undergone a quiet refurbishment without changing its character, it remains a delightful, old-fashioned hotel, all stained-glass windows and oak panelling. It was opened by a retired gentleman's valet, and Queen Victoria was a frequent visitor here. Running between Albermarle and Dover Streets, it originally had two entrances. Bedrooms are now done to a good standard and are cosy rather than grand. The Victorian Suite, room 161, for instance, is predominantly blue with chintz furnishings; other executive rooms have small lobbies leading to bedrooms. Some have four-poster beds; all have antiques (some reproduction), and top bathrooms. The refurbishment, renaming and redirecting of the restaurant has been met with enthusiasm. Under the new owners, **1837** looks set to becoming yet another top restaurant which happens to be in a hotel, something in which London excels. (See Restaurant section). Best of all, the **lounge** is delightful for afternoon tea, with comfortable sofas, a fireplace and a palpable feeling of the elegance of a past age; in the winter, particularly, it feels like a time warp with ladies up from the country (See Bar section). The clubby **St. George's Bar** with a stained glass window depicting the English hero, is a popular meeting place.

The Cadogan

75 Sloane St, SW1X 9SG
0171-235 7141, Fax 0171-245 0994
4stes £350, 62rms S £150-£200, D £195-£230. 1 non-smoking floor. 24-hr rm service. Air-cond. most rms.

The Cadogan has plenty of history behind it and uses it to good effect. After all, anyone would be foolish to ignore the fact that Oscar Wilde was arrested here, or that Lily Langtry was a frequent guest. Owned by the excellent small Historic House Hotel group who have properties in Llandudno, Aylesbury and York, the Cadogan is used like a London pied-a-terre. It sits well in Sloane Street, with its red brick façade and stained-glass ground-floor windows, and its refurbishment has left the lady in good order. Halfway between the Sloane Square and Harvey Nichols/Harrods triangle and overlooking Cadogan Gardens, the large rooms have double-glazed windows and are traditionally furnished with antique furniture; the bathrooms, with their colourful Portuguese tiles, make a pleasant change from marble. **The Cadogan Restaurant** is very pretty with floral prints and wood trim, and serves modern British food at respectable prices, while the **Langtry Drawing Room** makes a pleasant afternoon tea break from shopping. Overall, the intimate atmosphere brings to mind an Edwardian country house.

The Capital

28 Basil St, SW3 1AT
0171-589 5171, Fax 0171-225 0011
8stes £320, 40rms S £167, D £217-£280 plus VAT. Air cond. 24-hr rm service.

A member of the Relais et Châteaux group, The Capital is just a few steps from Harrods—delivery of parcels from the store is a facility most guests take advantage of, and is symptomatic of the care and attention provided by the owners, David and Margaret Levin. At this small, intimate hotel, first impressions set the tone—you're welcomed by the doorman into a pretty front hall where a fire burns in the hearth on cold days. The individually designed bedrooms are delightful in a subtle, pretty English-country style; some of the rooms have a more masculine feel, with darker colours and sober oil paintings on the walls. Egyptian cotton bed linens, handmade mattresses, beautiful fabrics at the windows and on the beds, lavish marble bathrooms with power showers, luxury toiletries and robes are all in the package. This is a personally run hotel, and it shows. The French-inspired, first-class, small **Capital Restaurant** under chef Philip Britten, was re-designed by society stylist Nina Campbell and uses, to great effect, mirrors from Viscount Linley; it is among London's best (see Restaurant section). The Levins, who also own L'Hôtel, The Greenhouse Restaurant (see Restaurant section) and **Le Metro Wine Bar** (see Bar section), are firm believers in the good, but elegant, life.

The Chelsea Hotel

17-25 Sloane St, SW1X 9NU
0171-235 4377, Fax 0171-235 3705
7stes £345-£395, 218rms S £180-£200, D £190-£210 plus VAT. 60 non-smoking rms. Air cond. 24-hr rm service.

Bang in the middle of all the top Knightsbridge designer boutiques, the modern Chelsea is glossy enough to keep up with the neighbours. Bedrooms are rather small, but they have been refurbished to a high, modern standard and have smart marble bathrooms. An attractive central atrium has an impressive stairway up to the mezzanine level where you find a cocktail bar and **The First Floor at the Chelsea Restaurant**. An informal brasserie style rules here at lunch which is excellent for Knightsbridge shoppers; there's a more formal air at dinner for the Provençal and Italian mixture of cooking. The lobby area proves popular for afternoon tea, breakfast and snack lunches.

Chelsea Village Hotel

Stamford Bridge, Fulham Rd, SW6 1HS
0171-385 7989, Fax 0171-381 4831
Web Site: http://www.chelseafc.co.uk
160rms £145-£185. Air cond. 24-hr rm service.

Down towards Fulham Broadway and well known to football fans, the Chelsea Village Hotel has been developed by the Chelsea Football Club. It's a massive building, the centrepiece of the £100m redevelopment of the 12-acre Stamford Bridge site. Ken Bates, chairman of the club, reportedly wants to turn the area into the 'Covent Garden of south-west London'. The hotel's entrance—all glass and steel—leads you into the lobby area with restaurants off to different sides. Reception is upstairs. Bedrooms are fairly standard though some are small; bathrooms are good. But prices are reasonable and who knows, you might run into the odd international footballer. You'll certainly get close to them if you book into the massive main meeting and corporate hospitality suite which has an area for conferences and dining leading down to covered seating running the length of the pitch. Of the restaurants, **Fishnets** with al fresco seating, a moderately expensive seafood and crustacean restaurant, is good; **Arkles** serves traditional Irish food; the **King's Brasserie** is the official hotel restaurant; **The Shed Bar** is casual, with banks of TV screens and leather chairs, good for watching sport of all kinds.

The Churchill Inter-Continental

30 Seymour St, Portman Sq, W1A 4ZX
0171-486 5800, Fax 0171-486 1255
E-mail: churchill@interconti.com
34stes £420-£1,800, 414rms S/D £270-£320 plus VAT. 8 non-smoking suites, 108 non-smoking rooms. Air cond. 24-hr rm service.

Run by the Inter-Continental company since 1994, this grand hotel overlooking

Portman Square is extremely comfortable and particular popular with business visitors. Decor in the rooms adopts a British approach, with the overall English country-house hotel look working well. **Clementine's**, appropriately named after Sir Winston Churchill's wife, is an elegant, rather formal room with warm wood panelling, contemporary British art and nattily striped chairs; the food under chef Idris Caldora is modern Mediterranean. The Club Inter-Continental on the eighth floor has its own check-in, concierge and lounge, complimentary continental breakfast and valet service. **The Churchill Bar** is a place you can sink into, with deep, club-like leather sofas, Churchill prints and memorabilia and the air of an interesting private study, concentrating on cigars and Cognac, which again reflects the great man's tastes. There is also a spacious lounge next to the lobby for afternoon tea and informal drinks. Like all Inter-Continental hotels, the guests share all the advantages the group offers to frequent international travellers.

The Conrad

CHELSEA HARBOUR, SW10 0XG

0171-823 3000, FAX 0171-351 6525

159stes S £165-£230, D £175-£260 plus VAT. 50 non-smoking suites. Air cond. 24-hr rm service.

Overlooking Chelsea Harbour, this luxury all-suite hotel is away from the mainstream hotel areas, but with plentiful taxis and many other advantages, this is not really a detraction. The Conrad is a splendid white stone building and part of the riverside Chelsea Harbour complex which includes The Canteen Restaurant, owned by filmstar Michael Caine, and the Viscount Linley-owned Deals. The hotel is very quiet, being in a mainly residential area, and it has a large restful entrance foyer. Of particular appeal is the excellent health club which has gym, sauna, steam bath, massage and swimming pool. Suites are two-roomed and very spacious, and many have wonderful river/harbour views. Within the hotel, **The Brasserie** is a pleasant riverside dining room with modern international cooking—great fun for Sunday brunch. **Drake's Bar** has a terrace and is good for light snacks.

Dukes

ST. JAMES'S PL, SW1A 1NY

0171-491 4840, FAX 0171-493 1264

E-mail: dukeshotel@compuserve.com.

80stes £250-£450, 73 rms S £175, D £190-£225 plus VAT. Air cond. 24-hr rm service.

Most taxi drivers know this address but others might have difficulty finding it without detailed directions. In a private, very quiet, gas-lamped cul-de-sac but just off busy St. James's Street, this red-brick Edwardian building houses a hotel opened in 1908 retaining an old world, almost clublike feel. Since David Naylor Leyland originally took over Dukes, there was a splendid refurbishment and a cut in the prices, all of which is good news. But tradition remains the key element here in St. James, known for its centuries-old shops, tailors and gentlemen's clubs. Many rooms have four-poster beds; all are of different shapes and decors though they all boast good antiques, oil paintings and marble bathrooms. The Penthouse suite has the bonus of a private roof terrace which is used for parties. There is a lobby sitting room with a fireplace, comfortable sofas and newspapers you can read with your morning coffee, afternoon tea or drinks. The restaurant caters only to residents. The small cocktail bar, headed by a barman who reputedly makes the best martinis in the country, also offers the discerning an extensive range of vintage Cognacs.

The Goring

17 BEESTON PL, GROSVENOR GDNS, SW1W 0JW

0171-396 9000, FAX 0171-834 4393

E-mail: reception@goring.

6stes £215-£275, 69rms S £138-£148, D £170-£215 plus VAT. Some rms air cond. 24-hr rm service.

The Goring Hotel is quite right to boast of its personal service, for it has been owned by the same family for three generations, since 1910. Owner George Goring's claim that he has slept in every room and really understands the intricacies of hotel management sums up the delightful and careful approach this hotel epitomises. It's close to Victoria Station and Buckingham Palace, and yet tucked away in a quiet side street. Even the façade with its attractive plants looks inviting. Quality is the buzzword here. Public rooms are delightful—a welcoming entrance area with marble floors and chandeliers, a pretty lounge and bar overlooking gardens (see Quick Bites section) and the more formal *Dining Room* serving good, traditional British meals. Bedrooms are good size, with reproduction and antique furniture, while bathrooms are luxurious and well equipped. Some rooms have private balconies overlooking the pretty gardens at the back of the hotel. This is a delightful hotel, old-fashioned in the sense of offering courteous service and a feeling of comfort and well being.

Grosvenor House

90 Park Lane, W1A 3AA

0171-499 6363, Fax 0171-493 3341

E-mail: gros.house@virgin.net

73stes £450-£980, 589rms S £210-£325, D £235-£645. Some prices inc VAT; 65 non-smoking rooms. Air cond. 24-hour rm service.

On the site of the former home of the Earl of Grosvenor, the Grosvenor House Hotel overlooks Hyde Park on one side and Mayfair on the other. Its enormous, grand ballroom—the Great Room with a capacity of 2,000—attracts major balls and events like the annual June international Grosvenor House Art and Antiques Fair. Its size makes it slightly impersonal, but bedrooms are functional, filled with five-star amenities, and have luxury, well-equipped bathrooms. A hotel of this massive size has a constant refurbishment programme, so check that you've got an up-to-date room when you book. The ground floor entrance now has a cosy wood-panelled library and plenty of armchairs. **Chez Nico at 90** under Nico Ladenis (see Restaurant section) is one of London's top restaurants, and **Café Nico**, set on two floors overlooking Park Lane and Hyde Park, offers breakfast (including a comprehensive Japanese breakfast), lunch and dinner. Go to the Crown Club on the seventh floor for executive perks, including a private boardroom and express check-in. Best rooms are the Sovereign Suites which include limousine service to and from the airport. The health club has a large pool, gym, sauna and massage.

The Halcyon

81 Holland Park, W11 3RZ

0171-727 7288, Fax 0171-229 8516

18stes £295-£650, 25rms S £165-215, D £260 inc VAT. Air cond. 24-hr rm service.

Leafy Holland Park, with its wide streets and air of quiet wealth, is the location for the equally delightful, pink-washed Halcyon Hotel. Created from several grand former private residences, it's reliably private, discreet and luxuriously appointed. All the well-proportioned rooms are furnished with good antiques and delightful fabrics; some rooms have dramatic designs; many boast four-poster beds; and all the marble bathrooms are well appointed. The entrance hallway welcomes with an open fireplace. **The Room at The Halcyon** (see Restaurant section), with its separate entrance, has a Mediterranean-style decor. There's a charming walled outdoor terrace which is perfect for intimate al fresco meals in warmer months; the **Vodka Bar** at the restaurant entrance serves caviar, salmon and lighter meals. Frequently there's a singer to entertain on Sunday evenings. The Halcyon has a place in the country, Fawsley Hall in Nothamptonshire.

Holiday Inn Mayfair

3 Berkeley St W1X 6NE

0171-493 8282, Fax 0171-629 2827

4stes £250-£400, 186rms £200 inc VAT. Non-smoking floor. Air cond.

The flagship of London's Holiday Inns, this hotel occupies a prime site in the heart of Mayfair, between Berkeley Square and Piccadilly. It has undergone extensive refurbishment in recent years, with the introduction of all the modern neccessary facilities like air-conditioning. There is a small entrance foyer with a relaxed atmosphere. The restaurant, **Nightingales**, offers an international menu. Bedrooms are well furnished and superior rooms have spa baths and king-size beds. The standards of service are all that you would expect from a worldwide chain in such a prime location.

The Howard Hotel ££££

TEMPLE PL, STRAND, WC2R 2PR
0171-836 3555, FAX 0171-379 4547
E-mail: reservations@thehowardhotel.co.uk
22stes £305-£565, 265-£495, 114rms S 255, D £285 inc VAT. 15 non-smoking rms. Air cond. 24-hr rm service.

The Howard has one of the lowest profiles of all London's grand hotels, with discretion and privacy the formula for its success among serious captains of industry. Slightly old-fashioned and located on the edge of the City, it is tranquil with sumptuous eighteenth-century decorative touches—friezes, ornate ceilings and marbled pillars. Rooms are well appointed with French marquetry furniture and marble bathrooms. Most have good views of the Thames, and many have twin rather than double beds. The restaurant at the Howard Hotel serves classic food and is formal and comfortable with a predominantly green and pink decor. To emphasise the international business appeal, traditional Japanese breakfasts are available. **The Temple Bar** overlooks the pretty, tiered garden area.

Inter-Continental Hotel ££££

1 HAMILTON PL, W1V 0QY
0171-409 3131, FAX 0171-493 3476
E-mail london@interconti.com
43stes £550-£3,000, 415rms S/D £265-£340 plus VAT. 20 non-smoking suites, 162 non-smoking rms. Air cond. 24-hr rm service.

Situated at the crossroads of Park Lane, Piccadilly and Hyde Park Corner, and the flagship Inter-Continental property in the UK, the hotel has a grand, marbled lobby area with a useful lounge just off it. Bedrooms, which are fair-sized, are comfortably but not ostentatiously decorated, with the top floor rooms having great views over London. All the expected amenities are here, including useful seating areas, and of course double-glazed windows. Luxury suites feature good-sized drawing rooms and have butler service, CD players, videos etc. The penthouse, The Palace, has a large drawing room, master bedroom with marbled bathroom, and private entrance with a lobby. Particularly favoured by business people, the purpose-built Video Conferencing Suite is ideal for top business meetings, and the business centre boasts four private meeting rooms. **Le Soufflé** restaurant under Peter Kromberg is suitably formal and expensive (see Restaurant section). Guests are offered all the advantages of an international hotel group when staying at an Inter-Continental, such as the Six Continents Club, air mile programmes and more. The Club on the dedicated seventh floor has 46 bedrooms and suites, private registration, shower room facilities and lounge with separate meeting space.

The Landmark ££££

222 MARYLEBONE RD, NW1 6JQ
0171-631 8000, FAX 0171-631 8080
13stes £430-£1,083, 298rms S/D £245-£310 plus VAT. Two non-smoking floors. Air cond. R24-hr rm service.

A landmark building (Grade II listed) and former great railway hotel (next door to Marylebone Station), this grand Victorian Gothic architectural landmark was restored to re-open in 1993 as the Regent. Sold in summer 1995, it was re-named The Landmark. The eight-storey central atrium is its most stunning feature, with a mezzanine gallery overlooking the **Winter Garden Lounge** (see Bar section). Also off here is the formal Restaurant, serving good modern British dishes. Similarly, the rooms, in a beige neutral palette, are among the largest in London and are exceptionally well equipped with excellent bathrooms, many with separate shower cubicles. Top suites include the sixth-floor Penthouse suite and the fifth-floor Presidential suite which even has a grand piano. More casual is **The Cellars** bar with a hot snack menu. The fitness facility has a small pool, sauna, steam room, massage and gym.

The Langham Hilton ££££

1 REGENT ST, PORTLAND PL, W1N 3AA
0171-636 1000, FAX 0171-323 2340
18stes £670-£1200, 361rms £250-£330 plus VAT. 12 non-smoking stes, 198 non-smoking rooms. 2 rms for disabled. Air cond. 24-hr rm service.

Originally opened in 1865 and the pinnacle of Victorian style, the Langham played a key role in London society of the day—Oscar Wilde, Toscanini and Mark Twain were once guests. Now, due in part to its close proximity to the BBC opposite, it continues to draw an intriguing crowd of celebrities. Its recent reconstruction after decades as the headquarters of the BBC, is impressive, with marble floors and pillars in public areas and a particularly grand entrance hall, a peach-toned decor and American red oak furniture and fittings in guest rooms. Executive rooms and suites include English breakfast and a complimentary bar. **Memories** restaurant offers a menu of British classics and international influences and is particularly good for breakfast. **Tsar's**, decorated in rich royal Russian greens and golds, is a dark, rather enigmatic bar; it serves 107 types of vodka, caviar and seafood and boasts one of the most comprehensive collections of Louis Roederer Champagne in the world (see Bar section). **The Chukka Bar's** polo scenes and equipment are suitably sporty, and it is packed in the early evening and popular for luncheon buffets. **The Palm Court** is open from 6am to 2am for light refreshments, drinks and afternoon tea (see Quick Bites section). Apart from the sauna, gym, steam room, solarium, hair and beauty salon, shop and theatre desk, there is, surprisingly, a small private garden.

London Bridge Hotel

8-18 LONDON BRIDGE ST, SE1 9SG
0171-407 1717, FAX 0171-357 6475
120rms £140-£175.
Air cond. 24hr rm service.

A

Just opening as we went to press, this new hotel is conceived as 'modern classical' with traditional furnishing but all the latest technology in the bedrooms. It's near the City for business visitors, but at the same time right in the middle of one of London's most exciting developing areas, along the South Bank and near Shakesepare's Globe, HMS Belfast and Butlers Wharf. The restaurant is part of the **Simply Nico** chain, overseen by top chef Nico Ladenis, and offers fixed-price all-inclusive menus, an idea which is proving popular in this chain of restaurants. There's also a traditional English pub.

London Hilton on Park Lane

22 PARK LANE, W1A 2HH
0171-493 8000, FAX 0171-493 4957
53stes £425-£2,200, 399rms S/D £250-£330 plus VAT. 4 floors of non-smoking rms. Air cond. 24-hr rm service.

A P

This was London's first skyscraper hotel, and still has arguably the best views in London. The combination of its splendid Park Lane location and talented management by Rudi Jägersbacher makes this large hotel work beautifully. A massive £35million refurbishment will, over three years, place the London Hilton among London's best hotels, with state-of-the-art facilities. Bedrooms are currently a good size and have traditional mahogany furniture and plush fabrics and furnishings, and the bathrooms are very good. Six floors of executive rooms have their own private check-in, a clubby lounge area for complimentary continental breakfast, tea and drinks as well as a business centre. The Hilton is known for its excellent service and top efficiency, hence its popularity and large number of returning clients. The 28th floor **Windows** restaurant has the best view in town—a panorama of Hyde Park, Buckingham Palace and the rooftops of Mayfair and beyond. In the inspired hands of French chef Jacques Rolancy, the restaurant is gaining a top reputation to add to the stunning views (see Restaurant section). There's a pleasant, welcoming **Brasserie** on the ground floor; **St. George's Bar** is the place for sporting enthusiasts with its six-foot TV screen. **Trader Vic's** Polynesian decor and menu is adventurous, fun, unusual and good value (see Bar section).

London Marriott

GROSVENOR SQ, W1A 4AW
0171-493 1232, FAX 0171-491 3201
17stes £350-£1250, 204rms S £225-£235, D £225-£235 plus VAT. 10 non-smoking suites, 100 non-smoking rooms. Air cond. 24-hr rm service.

A

A splendid position, overlooking impressive Grosvenor Square (although the hotel entrance is in Duke Street), and its proximity to the American Embassy make the London Marriott a popular choice with international travellers. There is always an air of bustle in the public areas where the sofas are set in little alcoves and backed by mirrors. Bedrooms are large, with comfortable armchairs and good writing desks, though bathrooms can be small. Executive rooms and suites have their own lounge. **The Diplomat** plays many dining roles, from offering an informal breakfast and lunch to a comprehensive international dinner menu. The pretty adjacent **Regent Lounge** and **Regent Bar** are good for a sumptuous afternoon tea buffet, drinks and light meals.

Lowndes Hyatt

LOWNDES ST, SW1X 9ES
0171-823 1234, FAX 0171-235 1154
5stes £285-£325, 73rms S £185-£215, D £195-225 plus VAT. 2 non-smoking floors. Air cond.

Very un-Belgravia and definitely un-Hyatt, this intimate, unstuffy, well-run and friendly hotel feels more privately owned than international chain. Bedrooms are decorated in attractive blues, greens and pinks with good wood furniture, and are surprisingly spacious. Five suites offer more luxury and are very well appointed. **Brasserie 21** is informal, with its own bar and an international menu, and it has al fresco tables on the pavement outside in summer for people-watching. If you prefer, you can charge at the restaurants of the neighbouring giant, the Hyatt Carlton Tower. And just next door, the Halkin Arcade is full of shops selling good art, antiques and design.

Mandarin Oriental, Hyde Park

66 KNIGHTSBRIDGE, SW1Y 7LA
0171-235 2000, FAX 0171-235 4552
19stes £650-£1,500, 166rms £260-£450 plus VAT. Non-smoking floor. Air cond. 24-hr rm service.

In 1997, The Mandarin Oriental group took over the Hyde Park—which began as gentlemen's apartments in 1892 and became an hotel in 1908—and is currently refurbishing it. Like all grand hotels, it had its fair share of visiting celebrities, including Rudolph Valentino, who brought the whole of Knightsbridge to a halt when he appeared on the balcony. Today's celebrities include the three world-famous tenors, Pavarotti, Domingo and Carreras, as well as film stars. One of the first tall buildings in London, this splendid red-brick building faces Harvey Nichols department store and is very close to Sloane Street and Harrods. The back and half the bedrooms have a wonderful view over Hyde Park itself. Major works have brought brand-new bathrooms to most of the rooms, beautifully decorated with marble tiles in a gracious style but with all the technology of today. Some of the suites are delightful with their own terraces. All rooms have all the modern equipment expected of a top hotel. Refurbishment in the public rooms has produced the **Park Restaurant**, a beautiful dining room under chef David Nichols which looks out over Hyde Park, an excellent spot particularly in the morning for coffee while watching the Horse Guards pass on their way to changing the guard. The excellent panelled bar has live piano music every night of the week. The lounge offers morning coffee and afternoon tea.

Mayfair Inter-Continental

STRATTON ST, W1A 2AN
0171-629 7777, FAX 0171-629 1459
E-mail: mayfair@interconti.com
31stes £550-£2,000, 258rms S £269-£289, D £289-£299 plus VAT. 1 non-smoking floor. Air cond. 24-hr rm service.

The charming personality of general manager Dagmar Woodward makes this a very personal hotel, full of enthusiastic, professional staff. It's in a good position, tucked in Mayfair and near Piccadilly and Green Park. There's an impressive entrance hall, and bedrooms are a decent size, many with seating areas, comfortably though not lavishly furnished, with very well-equipped bathrooms. Some of the suites like the Penthouse and the Monte Carlo have two bedrooms, a good lounge, dining area and private lift from the street as well as a small roof garden. **Opus 70**, under Michael Coaker, serves an excellent menu and is proving a very popular lunchtime spot for local business people as well as Mayfair shoppers. The small, clubby bar with signed photographs of celebrities reinforces the general impression of friendliness and sophistication. The **Mayfair Café** is open all day, a good place to meet in the evenings, and offers Californian-influenced food. A small health club boasts a gym, solarium and pool. Frequent travellers enjoy all the international Inter-Continental group's facilities.

Le Meridien

21 PICCADILLY, W1V 0BH
0171-734 8000, FAX 0171-437 3574
25stes £405-£550, 266rms S £295-£325, D £325-£355 plus VAT. 2 non-smoking floors. Air cond. 24-hr rm service.

Le Meridien's Piccadilly Circus location is one of the best addresses in London and the hotel is one of the most centrally located. Bedrooms, awash in pastel pinks and turquoise, boast good reproduction furniture, and the chic bathrooms are splendid. Delightful afternoon tea in the lounge features a harpist and 40 different blends of tea (see Quick Bites section). The formal **Oak Room** is now in the hands of Marco Pierre White and as you would expect from such a top chef, is making all the running in London's increasingly competitive restaurant scene (see Restaurant section). Opulent and grand, with splendid carved wood panelling and impeccable service, it's now full of delightful paintings and portraits. The summery fourth-floor **Terrace Garden**, with its glass conservatory ceiling, overlooks Piccadilly and is ideal for grills and light meals. On sunny days, you can eat outside, enjoying the breeze and the view. **The Burlington Bar** is cosy and suitably club-like. To complete the picture, there is a stunning **Champneys** health facility in the basement with gym, pool, squash court, massage and beauty treatments.

Metropolitan

19 Old Park Lane, W1

0171-447 1000, Fax 0171-447 1100

E-mail: sales@metropolitan.co.uk

18 stes, £425-£1,600, 137 rms, S £195-£215, D £245-£285plus VAT. 39 non-smoking rooms. 24-hr rm service.

This luxury hotel (formerly The Londonderry) has been transformed by top interior designer Keith Hobbs into a contemporary masterpiece epitomising simple chic. From the moment you enter the lobby, with its startling space and beautifully arranged pots on the walls, you know that this is aimed at—and is very successful with—a particular clientele. Rooms are well decorated, comfortable and refreshing with their plain light wood fittings; bathrooms are all you would expect. Corner rooms have wonderful views over Hyde Park and Park Lane. Its informal, modern European style appeals to the international set from the advertising, entertainment and fashion worlds who want a London sanctuary which is a complete contrast to standard hotels. **Nobu** is currently one of London's top, fashionable restaurants, owned by Nobuyuki Matsuhisa and Robert de Niro, and offers stunning Japanese food (see Restaurant section). **The Metropolitan Bar** operates a discreet, informal membership policy after 5.30pm, so be warned.

The Milestone

1 Kensington Ct, W8 5DL

0171-917 1000, Fax 0171-917 1010

E-mail: res@themilestone.com

12stes £330-£440, 40rms S £220, D £270 inc VAT. 12 non-smoking rooms. Air cond. 24-hr rm service.

There's an attractive Victorian façade to this very grand late nineteenth-century former private residence which has excellent views of Kensington Palace just opposite. It is also conveniently close to the Knightsbridge shops. Several of the stunning split-level suites and many of the rooms have king-size four-poster beds. All the rooms are spacious, individually decorated and graciously appointed with beautiful antique furniture. As a listed building, its restoration has been meticulously done according to English Heritage standards, which means original fireplaces, carved wood panelling, high ceilings and large ornate windows. Guests also enjoy very attentive, personal service from the staff. **The Milestone Restaurant** is very good indeed, a real find, offering top French cooking. (See Restaurant section). Again, the decor is all Victorian country-house style, with a gothic feel to its plaster ceilings, a small private alcove off the main dining room and flickering candle-style lights. Start with an aperitif in the very comfortable drawing room, full of bookshelves and with a baronnial-style fireplace, and you'll feel far removed from the bustle of Kensington just outside.

Millennium Britannia

Grosvenor Sq, W1A 3AN

0171-629 9400, Fax 0171-629 7736

E-mail: sales@britanniahotel.com

16stes £490-£930, 318rms S £210, D £210-£300 plus VAT. Air cond. 24-hr rm service.

Recently taken over by the Singapore Millennium group, this hotel has always been popular with local embassies and consulates, being in a splendid location at the centre of Mayfair facing Grosvenor Square. The main entrance is behind Grosvenor Square and you step down into a vast well of a main foyer which would benefit from a bit of refurbishment. Superior double rooms are spacious and well-equipped, many with separate stand-up bars, extra seating and massive, very good bathrooms. Furnishings are in an antique style and luxurious. **The Adams Restaurant** serves modern British cuisine, the café has a respectable Anglo-American hot and cold buffet, and the excellent **Shogun** Japanese restaurant has a good sushi bar. There is also a pub called the **Waterloo Dispatch**, named after the announcement of victory at Waterloo on the site; the traditional piano bar is for drinks only and there is a cocktail lounge. You can shop in the Georgian shopping arcade at the florist, confectioner and menswear shop. Front-of-house staff are very friendly and helpful.

The Montcalm

GREAT CUMBERLAND PL, W1A 2LF
0171-402 4288, FAX 0171-724 9180
10stes £285, 110rms S £195, D £215 plus VAT. 27 non-smoking rms. 1 low allergen rm. Air cond. 24-hr rm service.

Named after the eighteenth-century French general, the Marquis de Montcalm, this is something of a retreat, being just north of frenetic Marble Arch in a private Georgian crescent. Owned by the Japanese Nikko Hotels group, it is meticulously maintained and managed. A substantial refurbishment programme has brought the bedroom decor up to scratch, and the duplex suites are comfortably spacious if a bit tricky with narrow connecting spiral staircases. It also has one low-allergen room for the Howard Hughes of this world, where special materials have been used in the furnishings and the cleaning is meticulous. The light and airy conservatory-style **Crescent Restaurant** offers modern British cuisine (and serves Japanese breakfasts to the high proportion of Japanese visitors). The adjacent bar is clubby and cosy with leather chairs, wood panelling, bookcases and a fireplace, and proves a good place for afternoon tea (se Quick Bites section). Service is pleasant and relaxed, though the first impression of the expansive marble lobby can be rather formal. This hotel is certainly a case of reality living up to the promotional material—it is one of London's best-kept secrets!

The Mountbatten

SEVEN DIALS, MONMOUTH ST, WC2H 9HD
0171-836 4300, FAX 0171-240 3540
7stes £375, 120rms S £187, D £208-£226 plus VAT. 3 non-smoking floors. Air cond in public areas. 24-hr rm service.

The Earl Mountbatten of Burma provides the theme for this Covent Garden spot owned by the private group Radisson-Edwardian Hotels, and there are mementoes and tributes to India throughout, creating an eclectic style. Smallish rooms are well equipped with dark wood furniture and all have marble bathrooms. The country-house-style drawing room is good for afternoon tea and informal meetings. **Ad Lib** serves informal French cuisine plus good luncheon specials and pre- and post-theatre suppers; the **Polo Bar** is good for regular cocktails. There's also **Centre Stage**, an after-theatre supper club which begins at around 10pm and goes on until 1am where you dine and listen to excellent cabaret from West End stars.

One Aldwych

1 ALDWYCH, WC2B 4BZ
0171-300 1000, FAX 0171-300 1001
E-mail: sales@onealdwych.co.uk
12stes £395-£995, 93rms S £230-£275, D £245-£295 plus VAT. 4 non-smoking stes, 39 non-smoking rms. Air-cond. 24-hr rm service.

One Aldwych is becoming one of London's most spectacular new luxury hotels. Its location on the edge of Covent Garden, where the West End meets the City, means that it has equal appeal to the theatre-going tourist and the high-powered business executive. The Edwardian building was originally the home of *The Morning Post* newspaper and was designed by Mewès & Davis, the Anglo-French partnership responsible for the Ritz hotels in Paris, London and Madrid; all the period details of the exterior have been retained. The interior design (by owner Gordon Campbell-Gray with society interior designer Mary Fox-Linton) offers something different—contemporary simplicity laced with classicism but 'without an inch of chintz in sight' where 'comfort and function are not sacrificed to design'. The result is a luxury hotel that reflects 'stealth wealth' rather than 'dripping deluxe' with rich colours and plain fabrics. There's a permanent collection of contemporary art and sculpture throughout the hotel and in every bedroom. Flowers take centre stage in public and guest rooms. The modern obsession with fitness and health is met in the health club and pool; some suites feature private gyms. Needless to say, every techno-gadget of modern life is available—fax, modems, CD players as standard and mobile phones on request. The hotel has three restaurants: **Axis** for modern European cuisine, **Indigo** which is less formal and features healthy, creative cooking, and the **Cinnamon Bar** for light meals and coffee.

The Park Lane Hotel

PICCADILLY, W1Y 8EB
0171-499 6321, FAX 0171-499 1965
52stes £300-£350, 253rms S £210-£285, D £230-£305 plus VAT. 9 non-smoking suites, 82 non-smoking rooms. Most rooms air cond. 24-hr rm service.

The Park Lane first opened in 1927 and is now part of the Sheraton group. This splendid Art Deco-influenced hotel, which has provided the location for such period pieces as *Jeeves and Wooster, House of Elliot* and *Brideshead Revisited*, is only eight storeys high. It has some delightful suites like the Lord Peter Whimsey Suite with a large bedroom, study to turn into a second bedroom, and limed-oak drawing room with fireplace and balcony overlooking Green Park. All the bedrooms are individually decorated, and many of the large marble-floored bathrooms have Jacuzzis. Most of the deluxe rooms have separate showers and many have double basins. All six Park Suites look over Green Park. At pretty **Bracewell's Restaurant**, with its Louis XVI style panelling originally from the London home of Pierpont Morgan, the menu is predominantly English. Its eponymous bar is quite clubby, and the expansive, light 1920's inspired **Palm Court Lounge** makes a good meeting spot and is known for its afternoon teas. **The Brasserie on the Park** offers traditional French dishes. There's a men's hair salon and the Daniele Ryman shop sells aromatherapy products, including anti-jet lag potions. The splendid Art Deco ballroom can accommodate up to 600 people for weddings, dinner dances and antiques fairs.

The Radisson Hampshire

31 LEICESTER SQUARE, WC2 7LH
0171-839 9399, FAX 0171-930 8122
7stes £340-£500, 124rms S £243, D £260-£298 inc VAT. 2 non-smoking floors. Air cond. 24-hr rm service.

Though traffic-free, Leicester Square is a non-stop hive of activity with a 24-hour street personality. For cinema and theatregoers, or those who thrive on staying in the heart of a city, the Radisson-Edwardian-owned Hampshire is in the thick of it. Public rooms are quite intimate with an Oriental theme. Bedrooms are pleasant, in English country-house style with pretty chintzes. Bathrooms are well fitted out with Italian marble and mahogany. **Oscars's Café** is lively. **The Drawing Room** is small but good for afternoon tea and provides an invaluable central London meeting place. Suites are spacious, particularly the Penthouse on the seventh floor with its fabulous panoramic views which appeal to celebrities.

Radisson SAS Portman

22 PORTMAN SQ, W1H 9FL
0171-208 6000, FAX 0171-208 6001
E-mail: portman@lon2a.sih.dk
7stes £443-£638, 272rms S/D £209-£226 plus VAT. 130 non-smoking rms. Air cond. 24-hr rm service.

Just behind Marble Arch and very convenient for the Oxford Street shops, the hotel was completely refurbished and streamlined when taken over by Radisson SAS. You are assured of good-sized, standard bedrooms and a reasonable package of services and amenities, including an astute security system and access to the Internet. The deluxe double bedrooms have sofa beds, which make this hotel a favourite with families. Some of the more expensive rooms include breakfast in the price. There is also the novel innovation of the grab-and-run early morning breakfast of coffee and croissants in the lobby. Restaurants include the **Portman Corner**, which in addition to a full à la carte menu features a traditional English roast each day, and the tiny but good **Library Restaurant** with just 20 covers in an intimate wood-panelled room.

Royal Garden Hotel

2-24 Kensington High St, W8 4PT
0171-937 8000, Fax 0171-361 1991
E-mail: guest@royalgdn.co.uk
36stes £335-£1,200, 400rms £195-£320 plus VAT. Air cond. 24-hr rm service.

A P

Re-opened in April 1996, this hotel was transformed under the new ownership of the Singapore-based Goodwood Group. It is now a dramatic building, with some of the best views of London over Kensington Gardens, as well as down Kensington High Street. The marble lobby is impressive, with the raised **Terrace Restaurant** to one end, and the bar and lounge area looking out onto the Gardens. It has, of course, the latest state-of-the-art facilities in each room—in-house movies, two telephone lines, personally controlled air-conditioning and more. Rooms have good wood furniture, and are furnished in a standard style, each one the same. One excellent feature is a seating area by the huge windows, offering both good views and the feeling of being set apart from the main bedroom. Bathrooms are luxurious. **The Tenth** restaurant is creating quite a stir under executive chef Steve Munckley (see Restaurant section). The view is stunning, particularly at night when the lights of London shine in the darkness. Every Saturday there is music, with the first Saturday of the month featuring the big band sounds of Manhattan from the John Wilson band, one of the best evening's entertainment on offer in a London hotel.

Royal Horseguards Thistle

2 Whitehall Ct, SW1A 2EJ
0171-839 3400, Fax 0171-925 2263
4stes £425-£525, 277rms S £179-£220, D £214-£255 inc VAT. 1 non-smoking ste, 193 non-smoking rms. Air cond. 24-hr rm service.

A

Just off Whitehall, another area not associated with hotels, and occupying the very grand former National Liberal Club, this hotel comes as a surprise, particularly as from the outside it has kept its club-like appearance. Walk inside and you're in a large, traditional-looking foyer with beautiful ceilings, again unlike the usual hotel entrance. Recent refurbishments have reduced the number of rooms, which, as a result, now offer substantially more space than before. Executive bedrooms are large and decorated with oak furniture and colourful chintz, and have mini-bars, air conditioning and marble bathrooms; some have a wonderful view of the City. The Library Suite is as it sounds, all leather, chenille and silk; the Egyptian Suite has a suitable black-and-gold colour scheme. Both have private cloakrooms and marble and ebony bathrooms. There's a pretty lounge with chandeliers and paintings, thoroughly in keeping with the general ambience of this pleasant hotel. A rather masculine, clubby restaurant, **Granby's**, has a division bell to summon dining MPs to abandon their meal and go vote in the nearby Houses of Parliament. On summer afternoons, light meals are served in the **Garden Terrace**. Conference facilities for up to 250 people are available in sumptuous One Whitehall Place which adjoins the hotel.

St. James Court

41 Buckingham Gate, SW1E 6AF
0171-834 6655, Fax 0171-630 7587
15stes £253-£325, 350rms S £194-£253, dinner £214-£325 plus VAT. 2 non-smoking floors. Air cond. 24-hr rm service.

A

Owned by the well-regarded Taj group of hotels, who also manage the Bombay Brasserie restaurant (see Restaurant section), the St. James Court is well located in Victoria, close to Buckingham Palace. An impressive open-air courtyard connects the hotel bedrooms with an apartment complex of 80 suites which are ideal for longer stays. There's a splendid lobby with a turn-of-the-century feel to it. Good sized, well-appointed bedrooms have modern furniture and well equipped bathrooms. Many of the tennis stars stay here during Wimbledon fortnight, but there are always a fair number of celebrities to spot. There are three very different restaurants: **Auberge de Provence** (French with a rustic, atmospheric decor and connected with the legendary Oustau de Baumanière in the south of France), the **Inn of Happiness** (Szechuan Chinese in a plush, high-ceilinged room, popular for Sunday lunch) and the **Café Mediterraneé**, an all-day brasserie.

Sheraton Belgravia

20 CHESHAM PL, SW1X 8HQ
0171-235 6040, FAX 0171-259 6243
7stes £295-£450, 82rms S £155-£330, D £295-£450 plus VAT. 3 non-smoking suites, 34 non-smoking rooms. Air cond. 24-hr rm service.

Surrounded by embassies in the heart of Belgravia, this is a relatively small hotel by Sheraton standards. There's distinctively personal service from the moment of check-in, when guests are seated at an antique leather desk in the lobby and served a glass of Champagne—it's hard to imagine the hotel as part of the largest chain in the world! General manager Moyra Beaves is obsessive about detail and runs a tight, professional ship. There are several small public rooms, giving a charming impression of a private residence. Bedrooms are smallish but filled with amenities, even if it means the sofa is crammed into a corner. **Chesham's Restaurant** is a pleasant surprise with an international cuisine, and again designed as a series of rooms, including a conservatory-style area. A friendly bar is an extension of the lobby with little nooks and crannies for private drinks or afternoon tea.

Sheraton Park Tower

101 KNIGHTSBRIDGE, SW1X 7RN
0171-235 8050, FAX 0171-235 8231
23stes £660-£1,990, 266rms S £260-£360, dinner £280-£380 plus VAT. 4 function rms. 12 non-smoking suites, 80 non-smoking rooms. Air cond. 24-hr rm service.

A first-class location, within ambling distance of Harrods and Harvey Nichols and just by Hyde Park, plus Sheraton dependability, makes this hotel a safe choice. Efficiency is the key here which makes the atmosphere rather functional, but it is hard to find fault. Bedrooms and beds are large, security is good and housekeeping impeccable. The executive-floor service, with butlers, is worth the extra cost and includes touches like valet unpacking, two-hour laundering and a special fast check-in service. All rooms have wonderful views from the circular tower, though the higher floors are obviously the best. **Restaurant One-O-One** has recently been refurbished and has a separate entrance on William Street, finally a suitably good setting for the excellent French—mainly fish—cooking of Pascal Proyart (see Restaurant section). There are two comfortable bars, a coffee shop and a hair salon and gift shop.

The Stafford

ST. JAMES'S PL, SW1A 1NJ
0171-493 0111, FAX 0171-493 7121
13stes £330-£400, 67rms S £199, D £220-£310 plus VAT. Air cond in all rms. 24-hr rm service.

The Stafford is another of those small London hotels which people discover and then keep to themselves. Despite this, it's been incredibly popular since World War II, when American and Canadian officers used it as a club. Not surprisingly, anecdotes pepper The Stafford's history, helped and encouraged by Terry Holmes, one of London's most genial general managers. The Stafford is an elegant place, tucked away, like Duke's, behind St. James's. It's all very gracious, with individually furnished rooms in keeping with the traditional style of a refined country house. Some rooms are in the Carriage House, built in the 1700s as stables for the aristocracy and looking out onto a small courtyard full of hanging baskets and tubs. The rooms—many beamed and oddly shaped—do make you feel in the country rather than in the heart of the capital. The Stafford also houses one of the largest wine cellars in London; if you get a chance, ask one of the staff to take you on a tour. **The Stafford Restaurant** under Chris Oakes, is first-rate (see Restaurant section). **The American Bar** is a convenient, convivial luncheon spot or pre-theatre rendezvous point (see Bar section). Crammed with ties, caps and badges, its quirky decor goes down a treat with guests.

Tower Thistle Hotel

ST. KATHARINE'S WAY, E1 9LD
0171-481 2575, FAX 0171-488 4106
18stes £295-£525, 784rms S £155-£185, D £175-£228 inc VAT. 7 non-smoking suites, 392 non-smoking rooms. Air cond. 24-hr rm service.

A P

Part of the expanding Thistle group, this is a massive, modern tower block tucked between Tower Bridge and the colourful St. Katherine's Dock—which means there are spectacular views from both public and guest rooms. City Club executive rooms (on the seventh and eighth floors) include superior, well thought-out amenities like ironing boards, irons, trouser presses and electronic safes, plus separate check-in. The massive multi-level marble foyer is airily attractive. There are three restaurants: the **Princes Room**, named after the little princes murdered in the Tower of London, with an international menu, good views and weekend dining and dancing, a traditional carvery and the **Which Way West** coffee shop/café which becomes a nightclub on Friday and Saturday evenings. **The Thames Bar** again has that wonderful view. The location is handy for both the City and London's number-one tourist attraction, the Tower of London.

The Waldorf Meridien

ALDWYCH, WC2B 4DD

0171-836 2400, FAX 0171-836 7244

6stes £950, 292rms S £205, D £235 plus VAT. Non-smoking rooms. Air cond. 24-hr rm service.

In the heart of theatreland, close to Covent Garden and convenient for the City, The Waldorf recalls the grand days of hotels. Opened in 1908 by King Edward VII, it still maintains a faintly raffish air, mainly due to its over-the-top, but wonderful Edwardian style. A landmark (Grade II listed) building, its rooms echo the Edwardian theme throughout, but it is the public areas which shine—literally—with rich wood panelling and stained-glass windows. Bedrooms have their own entrance lobby and the new decor, traditionally inspired, reflects the hotel's opulent past, with draped curtains and chandeliers. Bathrooms have period-style washbasins. This is an entertaining hotel, reflected in their brochure which gives you fun facts that bring home the huge organisation of a hotel. So '500 scones are served and 1,250 cups of tea poured every weekend, 1,089 pillows are fluffed each day; 15 tons of mineral water are consumed during conferences each year', and so on. **The Palm Court** restaurant is elegant, and on Sundays still holds Tea Dances which go in and out of fashion; otherwise a less energetic afternoon tea is served daily (see Quick Bites section). The informal **Aldwych Brasserie** is ideal for light meals and pre/post theatre dining. Drink either in the oak-panelled **Club Bar** or the rather ordinary **Footlights Bar** which tries hard to be a typical English pub and is always full of broadcasters from the famous World Service just opposite.

The Westbury

CONDUIT ST, W1A 4UH

0171-629 7755, FAX 0171-495 1163

19stes £300-£650, 225rms S £200-£260, D £220-£260 plus VAT. 3 non-smoking floors. Air cond. 24-hr rm service.

Named after the Long Island Polo Ground in New York and built by a keen polo player (Michael Phipps), the Westbury was opened in 1955. Its enviable location—just steps from Bond Street and by the back door of Sotheby's—attracts a well-heeled clientele who love this particular Mayfair patch. Recently bought, it's now being rigorously looked at, and changes for the better are in the offing. Bedrooms are elegant with dark wood furniture and pretty floral touches, though sizes can vary from box-like to spacious. **La Mediterraneanée** serves international fare and offers an excellent fast lunch for Bond Street shoppers; the **Polo Lounge** is open 24 hours for breakfast, lunch, afternoon tea and drinks; and the **Polo Bar** serves drinks. Guests can use the nearby **Metropolitan Club** with its gym, sauna, aerobics classes and pool.

TOWNHOUSE

The Beaufort

33 BEAUFORT GDNS, SW3 1PP

0171-584 5252, FAX 0171-589 2834

7stes £295, 28rms S £150, D £180-£260 plus VAT. Air cond. Modest rm service menu.

There is little from the outside to tell you that this is an hotel, and once inside, you are given your own front-door key and treated as a friend rather than a client. Located on a tree-lined residential square, and ideally situated just 100 yards away from Harrods and Knightsbridge, this privately owned hotel is unusually decorated with hundreds of original, English, twentieth-century floral watercolours. They set the tone for the individually designed rooms, with their mix of English country-house chintz and wood. Prices generously include sherry, chocolates, shortbread and Champagne, breakfast and drinks from the 24-hour bar, and membership at the local Nell Gwynn health club. Service is extremely

friendly and helpful, and this charming hotel, which has won many international awards and accolades, offers a real home-from-home in central London.

The Cliveden Townhouse

26 CADOGAN GDNS, SW3 2RP

0171-730 6466, FAX 0171-730 0236

11suites £310-£820, 24rms S£120-£180, D £210-£250 plus VAT. 1 non-smoking suite, 6 non-smoking rooms. 24-hr rm service. Air cond.

Formerly The Draycott, this handsome townhouse has been taken over by the owners of the top Cliveden hotel in Maidenhead, the former home of the Astors. Their intention was to create a townhouse as an aristocratic family would have enjoyed all those years ago, and on all accounts they have succeeded. There's even a delightful old wooden board used for clocking in and out of the different rooms. The redecorated elegant interior is thoroughbred Victorian with fine antique furniture, prints and oil paintings. It also has two public ground floor rooms, a small library-type room at the front and a large, plush drawing room at the back overlooking gardens that is just right for afternoon tea. Bedrooms, named after actors such as Sheridan and Charles Laughton, vary in size (and some are quite small), have open fireplaces and are carefully decorated to remain in period; some overlook the quiet gardens. They also offer decanters of vodka, whisky and gin, and facilities such as VCRs, CD players, and some have fax machines. Concierge, limousine and nanny service is available twenty-four hours, and they can arrange to meet you at the airport, though there's no restaurant. Service can however sometimes be eratic.

Covent Garden Hotel

10 MONMOUTH ST, WC2H 9 HB

0171-806 1000, FAX 0171-806 1100

E-mail: covent@firmdale.com

3stes £295-£550, 47rms S £175, D £200-£255 plus VAT. Air-cond. 24-hr room service.

If you're feeling theatrical (or really are a thespian), the Covent Garden Hotel will fit you like a glove. This small jewel in Covent Garden, not an area known for its hotels, is one of the creations of Tim ... who have cornered the mark... vidual townhouse hotels with ch... cious entrance hall with a brasserie a... leading off it takes you into the double-heigh... reception area. Up a sweeping stone staircase (great for those entrances and exits), the drawing room with fireplace and adjacent library is the sort of place one dreams of owning. Bedrooms bear all the hallmarks of Kit Kemp's individual style. Handmade embroidered fabrics from China and India fill the rooms, all of which are large and have natural light. Bathrooms are in granite, not the ubiquitous marble. The Loft Suite (Number 303) has entrances on both the third and fourth floors. With its loft-style bedroom overlooking the drawing room, complete with fireplace, two bathrooms, dressing room and separate book-lined study, it is suitably dramatic. All rooms have CD players, VCR's, faxes and computer modem points. **Brasserie Max** provides good light lunches in a long, pleasant room looking out onto the street. The hotel is wonderfully located near theatreland, from where so many of its clients come.

Dorset Square

39/40 DORSET SQ, NW1 6QN

0171-723 7874, FAX 0171-724 3328

E-mail: dorset@firmdale.com

1ste £195, 37rms S £98, D £125-£195 plus VAT. Air cond in some rms. 24-hr rm service.

A former pair of Regency residences, Dorset Square is the intimate and stylish elder sister to the Pelham Hotel, and evokes the same kind of quiet, country-house hotel mood with its pretty drawing rooms with cosy fireplaces. Lots of chintz, swagging, tapestry cushions piled on the beds, good antiques and bountiful floral touches. Private gardens—the original Lord's cricket ground—are accessible to guests, and are particularly pleasant for summertime drinks. **The Potting Shed** restaurant and bar offers modern international food in a pretty setting, decorated with gardening items you might find in a superior kind of...well...potting shed. Otherwise try the Bedroom Picnic in your own room, a pretty tray full of delights like continental meats, cheeses and fruits.

Egerton House

EGERTON TERR, SW3 2BX
0171-589 2412, FAX 0171-584 6540
E-mail: bookings@theegerton.force9.net
1ste from £210, 29rms S from £130, D from £170 plus VAT. Air cond. 24-hr rm service.

A small luxury townhouse true to its description, the privately owned Egerton House was opened in 1990 in the heart of Knightsbridge. Spread over four floors, its rooms embody the English country-house genre, yet it is at the same time unstuffy and intimate. There is no stinting on luxury, with most rooms overlooking private gardens and all with marble bathrooms. Sensible pricing is a major allure, particularly noting its proximity to Harrods, the Beauchamp Place designer shops and the South Kensington museums. An attractive drawing room and study is the ideal venue for afternoon tea or drinks. A dining room downstairs is available for meetings or private dinners up to twenty and is used as a breakfast room.

The Franklin

28 EGERTON GDNS, SW3 2BD
0171-584 5533, FAX 0171-584 5449
E-mail: bookings@thefranklin.force 9.co.uk
10stes £225, 37rms S from £140, D £165-£210 plus VAT. Air cond. 24-hr rm service.

A

In the same ownership as Egerton House and Duke's, the Franklin overlooks a tranquil, leafy garden square. All rooms, which are of good size, have tasteful antique furnishings, original oil paintings, traditional fabrics and marble bathrooms; many also offer four-poster beds. The drawing room has a small bar and opens directly onto the garden. Staff are extraordinarily friendly and professional. The breakfast room is also available as a private function room for up to 20 people.

The Gore

189 QUEEN'S GATE, SW7 5EX
0171-584 6601, FAX 0171-589 8127
E-mail: reservations@gorehotel.co.uk
6stes £225-£245, 48rms S £110-£150, D £150-£225 plus VAT. Day-time rm service.

A

The slightly more sophisticated big sister of Hazlitt's retains its bohemian edge with an intelligent, interesting staff, quirky atmospheric décor—lived-in-look antiques, well-worn Oriental rugs and a fascinating collection of art—and air of comfortable decadence. It's evident as soon as you walk into the long narrow hallway, its walls covered in prints, past the reception desk to the large, comfortable (residents-only) Green Room where sofas are drawn up beside the open fireplace. Club rooms have four-poster beds; the room to beg for is the Tudor Room. In a wide avenue of lesser hotels and minor embassies, The Gore stands out on personality and its restaurants—**Bistrot 190** for breakfast through dinner, and the recently refurbished and re-launched **Fish Restaurant Downstairs at 190** (see Restaurant section).

Hazlitt's

6 FRITH ST, SOHO SQ, W1V 5TZ
0171-434 1771, FAX 0171-439 1524
1ste £235-£265, 23rms S £125, D £163-£193 plus VAT.

A

Quirky is the best way to describe this Bohemian Soho haunt, once owned by painter-turned-essayist William Hazlitt, born in 1778. All the rooms are named after eighteenth- and early nineteenth-century residents or visitors, so you might be Jonathan Swift, Sir Charles Lamb, or the Duke of Portland, as it were. There are creaky stairs, walls jammed with period pictures, antiques, mahogany, oak and pine everywhere, and a general atmosphere of old-fashioned charm and character in this listed building. Rooms vary in size and standards with dark furnishings. Being in the middle of Soho, the clientele is mainly film and music celebrities, but of the low-key sort. Most request specific favourite rooms. They serve an excellent continental breakfast with noteworthy croissants and good coffee. The residents' sitting room is open for light refreshments but there is no liquor license. Nor is there a restaurant, although that would be superfluous—Hazlitt's is located in one of Soho's premier dining streets.

The Leonard

15 SEYMOUR ST, W1H 5AA
0171-935 2010, FAX 0171-935 6700
E-mail: the.leonard@dial.pipex.com
20 stes £225-£390, 8 rms S £160-£225, D £180-£390 inc VAT. 2 non-smoking suites, 2 non-smoking rooms. 24-hr rm service. Air-cond.

Great location just off Portman Square and north of Oxford Street for this small boutique hotel which opened in Spring 1996. It has a delightful entrance, with a good-sized **Café Bar** to the left (excellent for dropping into if shopping in the area, or to meet someone for tea, a drink or a light lunch). The pretty drawing-room comes complete with newspapers to read before the fireplace. Created from several townhouses, the whole place feels like a home-away-from-home. Individually decorated bedrooms and suites have excellent antiques and paintings, pretty chintzes and luxurious curtains and bedspreads. Marble bathrooms are good size and very well appointed. Most impressive are the Grand Suites on the first floor. Number 14, for example, has a very large and comfortable main room, decorated in rich reds and with good antiques, and a large bedroom, luxuriously furnished and equipped with all the latest modern facilities.

L'Hôtel

28 BASIL ST, SW3 1AS
0171-589 6286, FAX 0171-823 7826
1ste £160, 12rms S/D £140 plus VAT.

Just 100 meters from Harrods in a residential street, this charming hotel has rooms that may seem small, but they are fully equipped and decorated in a rural French style. More like an upmarket bed and breakfast hotel, it has a welcoming French pension ambience and the staff treat guests like members of an extended family. The same couple, David and Margeret Levin, own the more lavish Capital Hotel next door where the bar and restaurant are open to L'Hôtel's guests. Some rooms have coal fireplaces. The bustling **Le Metro** wine bar below carries a full menu, from croissants and coffee in the morning to late-evening suppers (see Quick Bites section).

The Pelham

15 CROMWELL PL, SW7 2LA
0171-589 8288, FAX 0171-584 8444
E-mail: dorset@firmdale.com
2stes £350-£550, 44rms S £145, D £175-£225 plus VAT. Air cond. 24-hr rm service.

The Pelham was opened in 1989 by Kit and Tim Kemp, who have a keen design eye for the English country-house genre. The overall effect is cosy and stylish, from the profusion of flower arrangements (both fresh and creatively dried) and traditional floral prints, to fine original antiques and inviting four-poster beds, some of which come with matching teddy bears. Lots of ornaments like clocks, vases, pot pourri and objets d'art are fun, but may make some feel claustrophobic. Bathrooms are attractive and well equipped and concessions to the twentieth century are gently concealed—mini-bars and TVs are hidden under chintz-covered tables. **Kemps Bar and Restaurant**, with a Mediterranean-style cuisine, is very pleasant and a good venue for a meal after visiting the nearby South Kensington museums.

The Portobello Hotel

22 STANLEY GDNS, W11 2NG
0171-727 2777, FAX 0171-792 9641
10stes £195-£240, 12rms S £110, D £150-£160 inc VAT and CB. 6 rms air cond. 24-hr rm service.

Two elegant, six-storey Victorian terraced houses in Kensington were merged to create this eclectic, privately owned hotel, with many rooms overlooking a delightful private garden. Their smallest (cabin) rooms are very small (but inexpensive); other rooms have individual decors, some with delightful floor-to-ceiling windows, one with a Moroccan theme. Not far from Portobello market, it is also a short, pleasant walk away from Kensington Gardens and Holland Park. Extra touches include goose-down duvets, 24-hour breakfasts and lavish room interiors. Sometimes described as a 'sexy' hotel, it appeals to visiting rock stars and celebrities, and one attic room with sloping ceilings boasts a mirror over the bed. The informal restaurant/bar is open 24 hours. The owners also have the extremely popular **Julie's Restaurant and Wine Bar** (see Bar section) in nearby Portland Road.

Sandringham Hotel

3 Holford Rd, NW3 1AD
0171-435 1569, Fax 0171-431 5932
17rms S £70-£90, D £115-£140 inc. breakfast & VAT.

The Sandringham might seem rather a long way out, but Hampstead is a delightful area of London and very easy to get to. Owners Jill and Michael von Grey took over this small hotel to offer a smart country-house style. In a large red-brick Victorian house and close to Hampstead tube, its public rooms overlook a garden. Bedrooms vary in style from pretty blues and florals to a more masculine decor with wood panelling. Many have views over the garden; many look out over the rest of London, giving the visitor a delightfully superior and away-from-it-all feel; doubles have good size bathrooms. Breakfast is excellent, the welcome is friendly from this young couple, and the location—if you want to be out of the city centre—is first-rate.

The Sloane Hotel

29 Draycott Pl, SW3 2SH
0171-581 5757, Fax 0171-584 1348
E-mail: sloanehotel@btinternet.com
3stes £225, 9rms D £140-£225 plus VAT. Air cond. 24-hr rm service.

An absolute gem and the epitome of intimacy, The Sloane Hotel is tucked away near the King's Road and Sloane Square. The lavish decors are transportable too—in other words, you can buy most of the antiques from the bedrooms! The owners are inveterate collectors and decorate the hotel as if it were a private residence. The unusual interior design features vintage Vuitton cases, period military uniforms, beautiful carriage clocks, leopard-print fabrics, extravagant canopied beds and antique lace. The mix of old and modern is ably executed with well-appointed bathrooms, and all suites are split-level with a separate sitting area. Manager Rebecca Maxwell is a disarming combination of efficiency and charm. From the roof-top reception room and terrace, available for breakfast, light meals, afternoon tea or drinks, guests have mesmerising views of the Chelsea neighbourhood.

Sydney House Hotel

9-11 Sydney St, SW3 6PU
0171-376 7711, Fax 0171-376 4233
23rms S £150, D £180-£200 plus VAT. Air cond. 24-hr rm service.

Between the King's Road and Fulham Road, Sydney House Hotel is situated in very trendy quarters indeed and close to the Brompton Cross intersection for shopping and restaurants. In a restored parade of mid-nineteenth-century townhouses, it is managed by the affable Swiss owner Jean-Luc Aeby. Eclecticism reigns as each room is individually designed to a different theme and has unusual details, rich colours and textures, creating a subdued modern mood. Noteworthy are the Chinese Leopard room with Biedermeier furniture, the Royale room with its gilded four-poster bed, the Penthouse with a large terrace, the Paris room with rich reds and toile de Jouy, and the more traditional, pretty Wedgwood Blue room. Attentive service adds to the intimate atmosphere.

22 Jermyn Street

22 Jermyn St, SW1Y 6HL
0171-734 2353, Fax 0171-734 0750
E-mail: office@22jermyn.com
13stes £305.50-£346.63, 5rms S/D £233.83 inc VAT. 24-hour rm service.

This small, clubby, townhouse hotel, which has won more praise than most other hotels in London, and which is being gradually refurbished, remains at the top of our list. Still very much like home as you wish it could be, 22 Jermyn Street is one of London's best private hotel secrets and you could quite easily pass it by in Jermyn Street, for discretion is the key here. No glittering signs, no uniformed valets, no shining Rolls Royces give you any clue as to what is inside. Owner Henry Togna has reshuffled this family property—located near Piccadilly Circus and in historic St. James's—into an hotel of charming suites and studios. Here you experience affordable elegance with antique furniture and granite bathrooms, and gracious but friendly service. The rooms have every modern facility and the desks are the best equipped in town, with every conceivable staple, paper clip and notepad, as well as fresh flowers, monogrammed linen and a glass of Champagne on arrival. Furnishings are comfortable—Country Life-meets-sophisticated-central London but not over-chintzed. Everything is possible—from private fittings by nearby tailors to unobtainable theatre tickets. Guests can use Champney's health club nearby for a nominal fee. Owner-managed, the staff could not be more friendly, professional and helpful, and Henry Togna's personal lists of shops and restaurants are valuable reference documents. A real gem.

MODERATE

Abbey Court

20 PEMBRIDGE GDNS, W2 4DU
0171-221 7518, FAX 0171-792 0858
22rms S £88, D £130-£140. 10 non-smoking rooms. 24 hr rm service.

Ideally placed just near Notting Hill Gate and Portobello Road market, this five-storey hotel (note no lift), has been created from some of the area's splendid white plastered Victorian residences. Fresh flowers add to the country-house feel of the public rooms and there is a charming conservatory breakfast room/bar. Rooms do vary in size; some are small, while the best are spacious and boast four-poster beds. All are furnished with antiques, comfortable chairs (and sofas in the larger rooms) and pretty fabrics and have good, well-equipped marble bathrooms with Jacuzzi baths.

Academy Hotel

17-21 GOWER ST, WC1E 6HG
0171-631 4115, FAX 0171-636 3442
8suites £185, 47rms S £100-£115, D £125-£145 inc. VAT.

Aptly named, with its proximity to London University and the British Museum, its reasonable rates make this hotel a firm favourite with many visitors. Originally three Georgian houses, it's an old-fashioned building, but brought bang-up-to-date. Service is efficient and friendly. Public rooms include the modern designed basement restaurant, **GHQ**, open all day and good for pre- and post-theatre meals, plus a small patio garden for fine days, and a cosy library. Bedrooms, which vary in size, are pretty with pastel shades and hung with good fabrics. Some beds are half-testers with fabrics draped from the wall to both sides of the bed. Bathrooms are en-suite except in a few singles, and are done in marble. Some are very small. If you want a quiet room, ask for a bedroom looking over the back. Luxury rooms are air-conditioned. The owner has a good eye for paintings, which are hung everywhere. All in all this is a very good place in an excellent location.

The Basil Street Hotel

BASIL ST, SW3 1AH
0171-581 3311, FAX 0171-581 3693
E-mail thebasil@aol.com
93rms S £120-£125, D £179-£189 plus VAT. 24-hr rm service.

Privately owned, this small central hotel, just yards from Harrods, was built in 1910. Filled with antiques, rich carpets, tapestries and objets d'art, it has a very liveable feel. Compared to most Knightsbridge hotels, The Basil Street exudes an easy, comfortable and charming personality, rather than smart. Each room is a different size, shape, décor and mood, with lots of interesting nooks and crannies. It is also home to the women-only well established Parrot Club, and a wonderful retreat for female guests and outsiders. The restaurant is open all day for tea, a glass of Champagne, light meals and snacks.

Berners Hotel

10 BERNERS ST, W1A 3BE
0171-666 2000, FAX 0171-666 2001
E-mail: berners@berners.co.uk
3stes £300-£485, 218rms S £150-£220, D £185-£230 inc VAT. 100 non-smoking rms. Air cond. 24-hr rm service.

Being half a block from Oxford Street, and mid-way between Oxford Circus and Tottenham Court Road, might suggest a hectic pace, but this hotel is an oasis of calm. Rooms are a jumble of sizes, but pleasantly decorated with a contemporary country-house theme, with double-glazed windows and bathrooms that have both showers and baths. The new Club Floor has a private lounge where guests check-in and receive complimentary breakfast and a glass of Champagne and canapés every evening. Particularly enjoyable is the **Reflections Restaurant**, a stunning Edwardian dining room with high carved ceilings and a traditional carvery, the original ballroom in the nineteenth-century private home of Joshua Berner. Afternoon tea is served in the lobby, and is accompanied by a pianist. The **Berners Bar** is a good spot to unwind at the end of a hard day's sightseeing.

Blooms Hotel

7 MONTAGUE ST, WC1B 5BP
0171-323 1717, FAX 0171-636 6498
E-mail: blooms@mermaid.co.uk
27rms S £120-£160, D £180-£195 inc breakfast & VAT. 24-hr rm service.

An early eighteenth-century townhouse situated in Bloomsbury, London's literary corner, and very close to the British Museum and the theatre district, Blooms makes an excellent base for those visiting for business or pleasure. Smart planters line the entrance and this theme is continued inside with copious flower arrangements. There is a delightful walled garden where light meals can be taken, looking at the British Museum. The lounge is well decorated in eighteenth-century style and there is an extensive library which guests are invited to use, though no restaurant. A good selection of board games will keep adults and children amused on wet afternoons when even sightseeing seems too wearying. Bedrooms are well furnished and equipped with satellite TV, trouser presses and refreshment trays. A steady refurbishment is underway and it is worth asking for one of the newer rooms.

Cannizaro House

WEST SIDE, WIMBLEDON COMMON, SW19 4UF
0181-879 1464, FAX 0181-879 7338
3stes £310-£435, 43rms S £150-£186, D £173-£249 inc VAT. 6 non-smoking rms. 24-hr rm service.

Officially in the suburbs, Wimbledon is really a smart, upmarket neighbourhood and a wonderful location for this graceful Georgian mansion on the edge of Wimbledon Common, surrounded by pretty Cannizaro Park. Cannizaro House is close to charming Wimbledon Village with its designer boutiques, trendy restaurants, tea shops and riding stables. Though slightly inaccessible to central London, the place is ideal for a retreat, small conference or pleasant experience of local 'village' life. Bedrooms display a tasteful mix of antique and reproduction furniture, but try to book in the original section of the building where the rooms are larger. The executive rooms boast four-poster beds. Public rooms resemble country-house drawing rooms with comfortable couches, fireplaces and huge floral arrangements. The international menu in the **Georgian Dining Room** is strong on fish and game, and Sunday lunch followed by a stroll on the common is popular. Jacket and tie code is observed for gentlemen. Afternoon tea is a delight (see Quick Bites section). Summertime evening concerts in the park, arranged by the local council, are a treat. Inevitably, the hotel is packed during Wimbledon tennis fortnight.

The Cavendish

81 JERMYN ST, SW1Y 6 JF
0171-930 2111, FAX 0171-839 2125
10 stes £240, 240 rms S £150, D £175-£195 inc service & VAT. 75% non-smoking rms. Air cond. 24-hr rm service.

The Cavendish has a great location, being on Jermyn Street, home to London's top shirtmakers and the heart of 'Gentleman's London'. The original Cavendish was where the redoubtable Rosa Lewis (the Duchess of Duke Street) reigned supreme and entertained royalty; the hotel is full of pictures and mementoes of the era and the lady. The building that replaced it has more sixties artefacts and the entrance hall is regrettably gloomy. Bedrooms, however, have been redecorated in a stylish manner with all modern facilities. En-suite bathrooms are marble floored and contain all the extras you expect. The top floor suites have a wonderful view with sitting areas and spa baths, but no lift. This may be inconvenient for some, but it does give a feeling of privacy. **81 Restaurant & Bar** comprises a tapas bar in an elegant corner of the hotel, and a restaurant with a predominantly Spanish cuisine, offering robust and interesting tastes and dishes. Up here is the lounge where you can take tea. On the first floor, window tables have a splendid view over Jermyn Street.

The Chesterfield

35 CHARLES ST, W1X 8LX
0171-491 2622, FAX 0171-491 4793
E-mail: reservations@chesterfield.viewinn.co.uk
9stes £241-£450, 101rms S £112.50-£150, D £135-£190 plus VAT. 16 non-smoking rooms. Air cond in stes. 24-hr rm service.

A

Recent on-going refurbishment is bringing this hotel up to the standards you would expect from such an excellent address. There's lots of wood panelling in the entrance hall and library (where afternoon tea is served), and the bar too has a very masculine clubby feel. The suites and about half of the rooms have found a new lease of life in classic townhouse style with new carpets, antique-look furniture and prints, and it's worth requesting one of these. Little extras are good, with nightly turndown service, bathrobes, pot-pourri sachets and a fine range of toiletries. **The Conservatory** offers late breakfasts, light lunches or pre- and post theatre suppers while there is also a more formal restaurant with dance floor and live music six nights a week. Staff are helpful.

Clifton Ford Hotel

47 WELBECK ST, W1M 8DN
0171-486 6600, FAX 0171-486 7492
4 penthouse stes £192-£270, 186rms S £144-£180, D £160-£200 plus VAT. Air cond. 24-hr rm service.

A P

In a relatively quiet street, just north of Oxford Street, this modern hotel is handy for shops and sightseeing. Bedrooms vary in size but are comfortably kitted out with attractive, although modest, modern decor. The handful of suites, all on the seventh floor with good views, are quite luxurious and highly recommended. **Doyle's** restaurant (a mainstream mix of English and French food, open daily, breakfast through dinner) is informal and staff are very pleasant. **The Howard De Walden Bar** is named after the former aristocrat who lived on the premises.

The Cranley

10-12 BINA GARDENS SW5 OLA
0171-373 0123, FAX 0171-373 9497
6stes £175-£300, 32rms S £120-£140, D £140-£150 inc VAT. All rooms inc kitchenettes.

A

This smart townhouse in South Kensington has recently been very tastefully restored. Public areas have lots of antiques and modish arrangements of fresh and dried flowers. Rooms, each individual, have been decked out with antique furniture and oil paintings, as well as satellite television. For those not wanting to eat out in the area's plethora of excellent restaurants, the Cranley also has kitchenettes in every room with microwaves and refrigerators.

Cranley Gardens Hotel

8 CRANLEY GARDENS, SW7 3DB
0171-373 3232, FAX 0171-373 7944
85rms S £75-£85, D £105-£115, inc service & VAT. 24-hr rm service.

A

In South Kensington, handy for the museums and a short distance from Knightsbridge, this charming hotel represents very good value for money. Originally four Georgian houses in residential Cranley Gardens, it has well decorated bedrooms with built-in desks, TV with in-house movies and telephone. All rooms have en-suite facilities. The restaurant is pretty with swagged curtains and cane chairs, and there is a separate lounge area.

Cumberland Hotel

MARBLE ARCH, W1A 4RF
0171-262 1234, FAX 0171-724 4621
3stes £172, 903rms S £152, D £162 inc VAT. 500 non-smoking rms. Some rms air cond. 24-hr rm service.

A

Long-time stalwart for package-tour operators, the Cumberland is popular for its central location (at the west end of Oxford Street just opposite Marble Arch, Speakers Corner and the wonderful expanse of Hyde Park), and the fact that it has very good housekeeping. It is currently undergoing an extensive renovation programme, with air-conditioning being installed in the Premier Club floors where 200 rooms are specifically designed for the business traveller. The Cumberland's lobby, all stainless steel and maroon carpets, can get hectic in the evening as businessmen arrive in droves to bed down after a hard day in the smoke, but this is one of the largest hotels in the UK and a good bargain if you don't mind anonymous service. There's a mix of restaurants: Chinese (**Sampans**), British (**Original Carvery**) and an all-day coffee shop, plus four decent bars. No points for decor, in spite of the refurbishment. Rooms are functional and have interiors expected from this type of hotel, but with all the usual amenities of hairdryers, trouser presses etc. The Premier Club rooms have well-lit working areas and access to the Premier Lounge with complimentary breakfast and all day snacks.

Durrants

GEORGE ST, W1H 6BJ
0171-935 8131, FAX 0171-487 3510
4stes £250, 92rms S £87.50-£97.50, D £130-£175 inc VAT. 24-hr rm service.

A good and unusual location north of Oxford Street, between Baker Street and Marylebone, and just off Manchester Square where you can browse through the fabulous Wallace Collection, Durrants is a refurbished series of Georgian townhouses giving the overall impression of a clubby, very English welcome. However, some rooms are small and a few do not have private bathrooms, so take care when booking. But the staff make up for any shortcomings (it has been family-run for more than 70 years). **Durrants Restaurant** is informal with a standard international menu selection. **The George Bar** is popular with residents.

Executive Hotel

57 PONT ST, SW1X 0BD
0171-581 2424, FAX 0171-589 9456
27rms S £86, D £108-£128 inc breakfast & VAT.

A stone's throw from Harrods and its situation in elegant turn-of-the-century Pont St makes this hotel very good value for money. The entrance hall is very imposing with its original sweeping staircase, Wedgewood-style medallions and elaborately plastered ceiling. Rooms vary in size and are on the whole well decorated. Bathrooms are a little bit tired but functional and a small defect considering the location and price.

Flemings Mayfair

HALF MOON ST, W1Y 7RA
0171-499 2964, FAX 0171-491 8866
E-mail:enquiries@flemings-mayfair.co.uk
32apt stes £217-£346, 99rms S £165, D from £200 inc VAT. No non-smoking rms. Air cond. 24-hr rm service.

A super location in Mayfair and a snip of a price compared to its glossy Park Lane or Piccadilly neighbours, makes Flemings look like a pretty good bargain. It's a jumble of stairways and nooks and crannies, and some rooms can be a bit poky, but apartments offer good value-for-money and have ensuite kitchens and dining areas. The basement level restaurant has an inexpensive buffet lunch daily, plus there's a small bar and comfortable sitting room next to the lobby for afternoon tea and drinks.

The Forum

97 CROMWELL RD, SW7 4DN
0171-370 5757, FAX 0171-373 1448
E-mail: forum.london@interconti.com
4stes £260-£330, 906rms S £140-£160, D £160-£180 inc VAT. 114 non-smoking rooms. Air cond. 24-hr rm service.

Enormous—in fact, the biggest and tallest hotel in the country—it somehow manages to maintain superb efficiency without being too impersonal. Perhaps it's due to its ownership by Inter-Continental Hotels. Bedrooms may seem functional and modestly equipped but are kept meticulously clean; bathrooms are good. The smart **Tavern Restaurant** offers deli-style food, and the international **Kensington Garden Café** is open all day from buffet breakfast to dinner. **The Tavern** pub offers traditional pub fare and lively Sunday jazz brunches, while **Oliver's Lounge** next to the lobby does afternoon tea, drinks and snacks. Eleven percent of the clientele is Japanese, so there is a good range of specialist menus, including an extensive Japanese breakfast.

Gainsborough

7-11 QUEENSBERRY PLACE SW7 2DL
0171-957 0000 FAX 0171-957 0001
E-mail: gainsborough@eeh.co.uk
4stes £179-£185, 45rms S £65-£85, D £115-£185 plus VAT.

Well located in South Kensington, a couple of minutes from the Natural History, Science and Victoria and Albert museums, not to mention fashionable Brompton Cross and nearby Knightsbridge, this newly refurbished hotel offers excellent value for the money. A deceptively large entrance lobby with lounge area has a welcoming clubby feel and the whole of the reception floor is enhanced by cascades of plants. Reproductions of Gainsborough's paintings are scattered around and the standard of décor is very high, achieving a traditional English elegance. Dashing black and gold stripes adorn the breakfast room/bar where light meals are served all day. Bedrooms are individually decorated and bathrooms are particularly well appointed with a wealth of marble and mahogany.

Gallery Hotel

8-10 Queensberry Pl, SW7 2EA
0171-915 0000, Fax 0171-915 4400
E-mail gallery@eeh.co.uk
2stes £195, 34rms £115 inc breakfast plus VAT. 24hr rm service.

Sister to the Gainsborough (see above) and right opposite, this hotel offers the same good location and exceptional value for money. There is a very welcoming mahogany-panelled lounge/bar area complete with chess set/table. As its name implies, there are art exhibitions in the 'Gallery Room'. All the public rooms have particularly attractive flower arrangements and the team of butlers are exceptionally helpful. Bedrooms are very well furnished with tasteful fabrics and in the main, spacious (a rarity for smaller London hotels). One of the two suites even offers a roof terrace and whirlpool bath and both are air-conditioned. Bathrooms have all been refurbished and feature marble tiles with mahogany woodwork, many have bidets and all have a good array of toiletries. Hair dryers, trouser presses and satellite TV reflect the general care and attention to detail.

George Hotel

1-15 Templeton Pl, SW5 9NB
0171-370 1092, Fax 0171-370 2285
E-mail: hotelgeorge@kkhotels.co.uk
154rms S £125, D £152 inc breakfast & VAT. 28 non-smoking rms. Air cond.

A mid-Victorian exterior makes the 'high-tech', post-modernist interior a complete surprise, but the bright sunshine yellow of the lobby is really very welcoming. The hotel is owned by the Austrian K+K group and the predominantly Austrian staff are extremely helpful and hospitable. Situated very close to Earl's Court Exhibition Centre, the George is just a short tube ride away from the museums of South Kensington and the fashionable shopping of Knightsbridge. Most unusually for a London hotel there is also a large private garden which is overlooked by the breakfast room. The bar area is very relaxed and attracts a number of locals coming in for an 'after-work' drink. Bedrooms are of good size and well appointed with thick down duvets, hairdryers, cable TV, safes and minibars. Bathrooms are similarly well equipped. With breakfast included, this hotel offers very good value for money.

Harrington Hall

5-15 Harrington Gdns, SW7 4JW
0171-396 9696, Fax 0171-396 9090
E-mail: 101752.2030@compuserve.com
4stes £185, 196rms S/D £160 inc service and VAT. 2 non-smoking suites 128 non-smoking rms. 24-hr rm service. Air cond.

In the South Kensington area, this privately-owned hotel lies behind an original period façade. It's now a thoroughly modern hotel, with a formal entrance. There's a lounge bar with a marble fireplace and a well decorated restaurant. Bedrooms are standard but comfortable, with all the facilities such as satellite TV, trouser press, voice-mail etc. With good conference and banqueting facilities, and excellent rates, it's appealing to the business traveller as well as to the tourist.

Knightsbridge Green Hotel

159 Knightsbridge, SW1X 7PD
0171-584 6274, Fax 0171-225 1635
E-mail: thekghotel@aol.com
12stes £160, 27rms S £100, D £135 inc VAT. Air cond.

This small family-owned hotel on the first floor and up, is practically opposite Harrods and is ideal for anyone who wants to be in one of the most expensive areas of London without digging too deeply into the pocket. Barely noticeable from the road with just a small entrance with awning, it opens out quite considerably once inside. On the first floor is a comfortable lounge area with facilities for tea and coffee making and bar service is available from 11am to 8pm. Staircases and corridors are decorated in bold stripes. There is no restaurant but the hotel is happy to recommend or book any of the numerous restaurants within walking distance. Rooms are large and well equipped with phone and fax and satellite TV. All rooms are air-conditioned, a rarity in hotels in this price-range.

London Elizabeth Hotel

LANCASTER TERRACE, W2 3PF
0171-402 6641, FAX 0171-224 8900,
USA 1-800 721 5566
5stes £135-£200, 50rms S £100, D £115-£150 inc VAT and breakfast. 24hr rm service. Deluxe rooms air-conditioned and non-smoking.

A P

Newly renovated, this favourite small hotel, just near Hyde Park, is decorated in traditional style, with comfortable bedrooms, complete with individually controlled central heating, and good bathrooms. Service is excellent as it's family run, and this shows in the friendly welcome. There's one four-poster room, also. **The Rose Garden** restaurant offers imaginative cooking, and provides a good meeting place in an area not particularly well served. There's a cocktail bar and garden terrace.

Millennium Gloucester

4 HARRINGTON GDNS, SW7 4LH
0171-373 6030, FAX 0171-373 0409
8stes £500-£1000, 610rms S £130-£150, D £150-£170 inc VAT. 240 non-smoking rms. Air cond. 24-hr rm service.

A

A large modern hotel in South Kensington which was extensively renovated when Millennium Hotels took it over. The lobby exudes spaciousness and is an impressive focal point awash with marble, wood panelling and a vast chandelier centrepiece. Rooms have been revamped to high standards, with fine fabrics, classic furniture and marble bathrooms. There are also Club rooms for executives, with a private lift, check-out and lounge with complimentary drinks. Italian and Californian-style food is served in the jazzed-up **South West 7** restaurant. There's also the fun **Bugis Street Café** which reflects Millennium's Singapore origins, and a spacious bar in the lobby for tea, drinks and light snacks. The 24-hour business centre is first-rate and the hotel has extensive conference facilities.

Montague on the Gardens

15 MONTAGUE ST, WC1B 5BJ
0171-637 1001, FAX 0171-637 2516
11 stes £350-£420, 93 rms S £140-£160, D £160-£180 plus VAT. 24-hr rm service.

A

Proximity to London's financial district makes this a favourite with businessmen, but it is also very close to the British Museum and the theatre district. Public rooms have been decorated in Victorian style, with tartan wall coverings in the bar and deep leather armchairs. The drawing room, where afternoon tea can be taken, is furnished with antiques and an eclectic collection of upholstered button-back chairs, including a Victorian loveseat. **The Blue Door Restaurant** serves good, light meals. Bedrooms vary in size but all are tastefully furnished and have plush bathrobes, hairdryers and an impressive assortment of toiletries. 'Executive business travel' rooms feature desk space with enhanced lighting, office supplies and speaker phones. Some rooms are specially designed for the female executive.

Number Eleven

11 CADOGAN GDNS, SW3 2RJ
0171-730 7000, FAX 0171-730 5217
6stes £238-£323, 53rms S £127-£144, D £161-£323 inc service and VAT. 24-hr rm service. No direct dial telephone.

A

Number Eleven was one of the first townhouse hotels, and remains delightfully old-world with a clubby atmosphere. In a Victorian red-brick terrace, the oak-pannelled entrance hall leads to a warren of corridors leading to traditionally decked-out rooms, recently upgraded and some now have four-poster beds. The Garden Suite has a splendid large drawing room with grand plaster ceiling and many rooms overlook the gardens. The public drawing room is cosy, with a pretty conservatory off the back, and is excellent for tea in front of the roaring fire in wintertime. They offer complimentary homemade cake at teatime, and sherry and canapés in the evening. In keeping with the area, and the pied-à-terre feeling, there is a chauffeured limousine service available. Most unusually in a small London hotel, there's an excellent state-of-the-art gym for workouts from 6.30am to 10.30pm. They can arrange for a masseur to visit.

Number Sixteen

16 SUMNER PL, SW7 3EG

0171-589 5232, FAX 0171-584 8616

4suites £195 32rms S £75-£120, D £105-£185 inc VAT and CB (served in the rm).

Number Sixteen is undoubtedly the most up-market Bed and Breakfast in Sumner Place, a very smart street in South Kensington and well-placed for the many museums, shops and restaurants of the area. Planters on either side of the pillared entrance hint at the grand interior within. The comfortable drawing room is all chintz and swags and has an elegant fireplace and beautiful fresh flower arrangements. An incredibly trusting honesty system operates in the library bar. The ample-sized rooms feature attractive chintz-covered furniture and include many antiques. Small and intimate, it feels like a private home, and many guests use it as a London pied-à-terre. A conservatory opens onto the secluded walled garden. Three-quarters of the clientele are regulars with a high level of business people.

Pembridge Court Hotel

34 PEMBRIDGE GDNS, W2 4DX

0171-229 9977, FAX 0171-727 4982

20rms S £110-£145, D £135-£175 inc VAT.
Air cond in some rms. 24-hr rm service for light snacks and drinks.

This restored nineteenth-century townhouse faces a quiet, tree-lined garden and is located in the fashionable residential area of Notting Hill Gate, close to Portobello Road. On the ground floor there's a comfortable well-furnished lounge; meals can be taken in **Caps Restaurant** downstairs, and drinks in the **Cellar Bar**. Bedrooms vary in size—some singles can be small—but the rooms on the top floor are spacious. Bathrooms have Italian tiles and are well equipped. Many of the antiques and objets d'art, including a large number of fans and the Victoriana in the rooms, come from nearby antique shops. In addition to an excellent long-standing staff, for whom nothing is too much trouble, guests may well be greeted by the two resident marmalade cats, Spencer and Churchill, who have recently starred in three television shows; they're even feature on the hotel's postcard.

Pippa Pop-ins

430 FULHAM RD, SW6 1DU

0171-385 2458, FAX 0171-385 5706

1 night 5pm-10am £50, 24 hours £75, w/e £145. Accommodates up to 10 children.

Heaven for both parents and children! This bright, west London Georgian townhouse specialises in accommodation for children only (aged two to twelve) and presents a loving, fun-filled environment under Montessori-influenced professional supervision. That means toys galore (teddy bears, clowns, games) for both education and play, and when it's fine, a large private garden area. Arrival late afternoon, pick-up next day late morning, the package includes home-cooked suppers and breakfasts, magic bubble baths in the duck-and-clown bathroom, eight o'clock midnight feasts and bed-time stories. There are night lights and baby-alarm intercoms in each room, and security is tight. Open for proper nursery school during the week in term time, the service is also available for hourly baby-sitting, half-days and full-days. It also takes children, holed up at top hotels while parents work or shop, on their own outings. Even the brochure is fun.

The Regents Plaza Hotel & Suites

PLAZA PARADE, MAIDA VALE, NW6 5RP

0171-543 6000, FAX 0171-543 2100

E-mail: regentsplaza.res@btinternet.com

50stes from £250-£650, 150rms from £150-£175 inc service & VAT.
50% non-smoking rms., Air cond.

P

Opened in summer 1996, this new hotel in Maida Vale, north of Marble Arch, has some 150 rooms (ten for handicapped use) and 50 serviced suites, plus club floors, a club lounge and business centre, 6 banqueting and meeting rooms, health club with swimming pool and car park. It looks spectacular, with a first floor internal landscaped garden to sit in, as well as state-of-the-art technical facilities which attract businessmen. Also on offer are good family packages, taking advantage of the close proximity to Madame Tussauds and London Zoo. **Fratelli's** offers good dining and like the downstairs bar, is popular with locals, adding to the friendly atmosphere here.

Royal Lancaster Hotel

LANCASTER TERR, W2 2TY
0171-262 6737, FAX 0171-724 3191
E-mail: 101645.1307@compuserve.com
20stes from £520, 398rms S £200-£230, D £200-£230 plus VAT. Air cond. Non-smoking rms. 24-hr rm service.

An eighteen-storey modern building overlooking Hyde Park and directly above Lancaster Gate tube station, you enjoy wonderful views over the park from the upper floors. It has recently been refurbished, so from the entrance hall onwards, the feel is luxurious and modern. Rooms, which are standard size, are traditionally, though not spectacularly furnished but have everything necessary for the modern traveller; bathrooms are good and with all the expected amenities. Downstairs the lounge is a favourite place for tea or a drink; **The Park Restaurant** serves English and French food and the **Nipa Restaurant** offers good Thai food. Much used by conferences, the hotel has very good technical back-up.

St. George's Hotel

LANGHAM PL, W1N 8QS
0171-580 0111, FAX 0171-436 7997
8stes £195-£235, 73rms S £150-£170, D £160-£180 inc VAT. 2 non-smoking suites,16 non-smoking rms. Air cond. 24-hr rm service.

Few London hotels can boast panoramic views of the skyline but **The Heights** bar and restaurant on the 15th floor has a stunning view over London (see Bar section). Most bedrooms also offer the same great perspective. The lobby is on the ground floor, and the hotel occupies the ninth to fourteenth floors; external businesses occupy the intervening levels. Its position adjacent to the BBC ensures a regular celebrity clientele, while its proximity to Regent and Oxford Streets makes shopping excursions convenient. Refurbishment has led to updated bedrooms and good bathrooms, although room sizes still vary.

The Selfridge

ORCHARD ST, W1H 0JS
0171-408 2080, FAX 0171-629 8849
4stes £400, 294rms S £110-£175, D £140-£195 inc VAT. 2 non-smoking floors. Air cond. 24-hr rm service.

Shopaholics will appreciate this modern hotel's proximity to Oxford Street and famous Selfridges department store. The approach and driveway are impressive and the busy public rooms are attractive with light wood panelling and leather armchairs. Bedrooms are adequate and well equipped, functional rather than luxurious, though housekeeping standards are good. There's a club-like feel to the first floor where you find a chintz-filled central lounge for tea, light meals and drinks. Also here are the **Stoves Bar** and the **Orchard Terrace**, an informal brasserie open from breakfast through dinner. Shoppers can leave bags at the hotel while they roam Oxford Street.

Sloane Square Moat House

SLOANE SQ, SW1W 8EG
0171-896 9988, FAX 0171-824 8381
3stes £195 105rms S £110-£140, D £110-£165 inc VAT. No air cond. 24-hr rm service.

Sloane Square is an impressive address, and great for the fashion-conscious, being on the corner of the King's Road (known for trendy, youthful fashion) and Sloane Street (with its designer boutiques). Public rooms are comfortable and have a kind of timeless elegance. There is also **Café No 12** (with an English and French menu) and the **Tavern Pub** which gets pretty lively in the evenings and at weekends. Bedrooms are well appointed and have oak furniture and soft colour schemes. Singles, however, remain fairly small. Housekeeping standards are excellent and the staff helpful.

Swiss Cottage Hotel

4 ADAMSON RD, NW3 3HP
0171-722 2281, FAX 0171-483 4588
54rms S £75-£130, D £85-£140 inc VAT. 24 hour room service.

A P

An attractive hotel near Swiss Cottage underground station in terraced houses, the rooms here tend to be small but well furnished, and as is the way with such hotels carved out of residences, there are numerous corridors and passages. But there is a delightful and gracious old-fashioned drawing room furnished with antiques and the view over the surrounding residential streets is leafy and restful. There's a restaurant also; altogether this hotel makes a pleasant alternative to central London.

Topham's Ebury Court Hotel

26 Ebury St, SW1W 0LU

0171-730 8147, Fax 0171-823 5966

4Stes £135, 31rms S£105, D £115-125 inc EB&VAT.

Topham's always reminded us of Agatha Christie's ladies (nothing sinister though). Now this welcoming family-owned-and-run hotel has been completely refurbished and all rooms have bathrooms (2 singles have exclusive use of non-ensuite). There is a pretty lounge area with comfortable armchairs in chintzy fabrics and pastel-coloured walls. The small conference room has a rather odd collection of large bright prints of jungle animals which seem slightly distracting but are rather charming. Bedrooms are newly decorated in pastel colours and are reasonably sized and well equipped with telephone and voice-mail, TV and hairdryers. The new bathrooms are well fitted and have excellent lighting. **Topham's** restaurant is a mix of English and French cooking, with large well-spaced tables. There is a small intimate bar on the lower ground floor which used to be Topham's Club. They have many repeat clients, lots of them British, who swear by its efficiency and genuine convivial atmosphere.

Whites Hotel

90 Lancaster Gate, W2 3NR

0171-262 2711, Fax 0171-262 2147

2stes £395-£425, 52rms S £159-£167, D £215-£220 inc VAT. Air cond. 1 non-smoking suite, 11 non-smoking rms. 24-hr rm service.

A short walk from Kensington Palace, this pretty, gracious building, dating from 1866, is an excellent base from which to explore London. Behind its imposing façade is a relatively unknown charming hotel which carries on the grand feeling of the outside into the reception area, which has a marble fireplace and a panelled writing room. Good-sized bedrooms have comfortable chairs, lots of silk furnishings and well equipped marble bathrooms. **The Grill** restaurant serves good English food, and the bar area is a restful place for a drink.

ECONOMY

Abbey House

11 Vicarage Gate, W8 4AG

0171-727 2594

17 rms S/D £40-£90 inc VAT and breakfast.

An absolutely prime location just off Kensington Church Street, this is a well kept hotel with excellent value prices. Don't expect luxury; bedrooms are simply, sometimes sparsely furnished and the breakfast room is functional. But this is a pretty house, and the public areas, stairways and entrance, are gracious and large. Built in 1860 in this classy residential area, the hotel is welcoming and good for families as it's a charming area close to the South Kensington museums.

Alison House Hotel

82 Ebury St, SW1W 9QD

0171-730 9529, Fax 0171-730 5494

1 ste £60-£85 10rms S £28-£35, D £42-£48, inc VAT.

Though in Belgravia, one of the most expensive districts of London, Ebury Street is filled with small hotels, some good and some mediocre. The decoration here at Alison House, big on pastels such as apricot, may not be inspiring, but the hotel is consistently commendable, clean and tidy, privately owned and popular with an American clientele, many of them businesspeople. All rooms have TVs, hair dryers and basins, though only two rooms have ensuite facilities. There's no restaurant, but plenty in the area.

Amber Hotel

101 Lexham Gdns, W8 6JN
0171-373 8666, Fax 0171-835 1194
40 rms S £55-£85, D £80-£100 inc breakfast & VAT.

In a very smart residential quarter of London, this hotel allows the visitor to be within easy reach of the major sights and yet soak up the feel of living in the city at a very modest price. A generous buffet breakfast is served in the pleasant dining room and service is warm and friendly. Bedrooms are nicely decorated with extremely good bathrooms.

Amsterdam Hotel

7 Trebovir Rd, SW5 9LS
0171-370 5084, Fax 0171-244 7608
8stes £90-£140, 20 rms S £65-£72, D £78-£84 inc breakfast and VAT. 4 non-smoking stes, 10 non-smoking rms.

A small friendly hotel, close to the Earl's Court Exhibition Centre and within easy reach of Knightsbridge and South Kensington. The whole hotel has recently been refurbished and decorated in attractive pastel colours and fabrics. The breakfast room has a pleasant summery feel and continental breakfast is included in the rates. There is a lift and all rooms have TV, telephone and individual heating controls.

Aster House

3 Sumner Pl, SW7 3EE
0171-581 5888, Fax 0171-584 4925
E-mail: asterhouse@btinternet.com
1ste £140-£145, 13rms S £60-£100, D £110-£135 plus VAT. All non-smoking.

Sumner Place has a number of discreet B&B's and this one has been routinely endorsed by the British Tourist Authority as one of the best. It is family run, though beware the occasionally off-hand service. Set in the smart residential area of South Kensington, it features pretty bedrooms, many with four-poster beds, all with fridges and TVs. There is also a well kept garden and a glassed-in conservatory to relax in after a hard day trawling the shops or museums. Good buffet breakfast.

The Claverley

13 Beaufort Gdns, SW3 1PS
0171-589 8541, Fax 0171-584 3410
7stes £160-£195 22rms S £60-£110, D £120-£195 inc VAT.

A short walk from Harrods, this hotel, situated in a quiet garden square, is an elegant base from which to tour the shops of Knightsbridge and the museums in South Kensington. The Claverley is highly recommended by the British Tourist Authority, and has won numerous awards. Rooms are decorated to a high standard, with a country-house feel and a strong emphasis on floral patterns. Good breakfasts and attractive lounge area with complimentary tea, coffee and newspapers.

Elizabeth Hotel

37 Eccleston Sq, SW1V 1PB
0171-828 6812, Fax 0171-828 6814
38rms S £40-£55, D £62-£80, inc VAT. Tennis nearby.

No credit cards.

A simple well run family hotel, the stucco-fronted Elizabeth is well located in the heart of Pimlico on an historic square (the private gardens and tennis court are available to guests) and close to Victoria and Sloane Square. Noteworthy attempts have been made to achieve an authentic mid-nineteenth-century decor with prints and portraits in public rooms which reflect the care that the owners take over detail. Bedrooms are modestly furnished and functional; only four are without bathrooms, but some rooms are very small and family rooms should be checked out for size when booking. They also have longer-stay self-contained fully equipped apartments.

Five Sumner Place

5 Sumner Place, SW7 3EE
0171-584 7586, Fax 0171-823 9962
E-mail: no.5@dial.pipex.com
13rms all non-smoking S £75 D £110-£120 plus VAT.

In the smart residential district of South Kensington, this hotel has long been established as a good, reasonable bed and breakfast, and is recommended by the British Tourist Authority. Recent refurbishments have improved it considerably with each bedroom being individually furnished and decorated to a high standard. There's a lift and all rooms have ensuite bathroom, TV, telephone, trouser presses, hairdryers and refrigerators. It's welcoming and friendly, and there's a Victorian-style conservatory to have breakfast or just relax in.

Generator

COMPTON PLACE, OFF 37 TAVISTOCK PLACE, WC1H 9SD

0171-388 7666, FAX 0171-388 7644

208 rms all non-smoking S £30-£37, D £20-£24.50.

Definitely budget and definitely for the young, and probably back-packers, nevertheless this is a great find. Everything is decorated like a generator, so expect functional decor and bunk beds in double rooms. It's more youth hostel than hotel in feel, but there's a bar and restaurant, staff are friendly and fun, and the place is totally safe so you can send your teenagers here without too much worry.

Hotel 167

167 OLD BROMPTON RD, SW5 0AN

0171-373 0672, FAX 0171-373 3360

19rms S £66-£78, D £82-£90 inc VAT.

This hotel has an excellent location, close to museums like the Victoria & Albert and the Natural History, and to the shops in the Brompton Cross/Fulham Road area. The visitor is greeted by a muted, Scandinavian-influenced decor of soft grey and cream co-ordinating with many good antiques. Rooms are all different with modern, stylish interiors, free from clutter. Double rooms have private baths, although singles only have nearby facilities. Staff are friendly and gracious.

Lincoln House Hotel

33 GLOUCESTER PL, W1H 3PD

0171-486 7630, FAX 01710486 0166

22rms £45-£69, D/T £59-£89 inc EB, service & VAT.

Very handy for the shops of Oxford Street, this small hotel behind a Georgian façade is friendly and welcoming. Bedrooms, though modestly furnished, have facilities like hairdryers and trouser presses, tea and coffee making, and all have en-suite bathrooms. There's a small restaurant for breakfast.

Royal Park Hotel

5 WESTBOURNE TCE, W2 3UL

0171-402 6187, FAX 0171-224 9426

2stes £140, 60rms, S £60, D £81 inc breakfast & VAT.

In Bayswater, just north of Hyde Park, this hotel is taken from three mid-nineteenth century townhouses which have been modernised without losing their original character. The hotel has a free car park for guests, something which is almost unheard of in London, free or otherwise. Public areas consist of two lounges and an attractive bar and there is a lift. Bedrooms are simply furnished and all have ensuite bathroom, TV and telephone.

Rushmore Hotel

11 TREBOVIR RD, SW5 9LS

0171-370 3839, FAX 0171-370 0274

22rms S £59-£69, D £79-£85 inc breakfast & VAT.

Situated in a street of hotels, the Rushmore stands out as being above average both in standards of décor and service. Being very close to the Earl's Court Exhibition Centre, it is very popular with a business clientele but handy for tourists too, just a couple of tube stops from the South Kensington museums and Knightsbridge. Rooms are individually decorated with use of trompe l'oeil to great effect. The breakfast room has a very Mediterranean feel with lots of wrought iron and glass-topped tables. Temporary membership of a local health club can be arranged.

Searcy's Roof Garden Bedrooms

30 PAVILION ROAD, SW1X 0HJ

0171-584 4921, FAX 0171-823 8694

ste £140, 12rms, S £81.50, D £112 inc. VAT.

One of our best new finds, Searcy's will appeal to anyone wanting a very comfortable room in a great location at an affordable price. Situated in a quiet street just behind Harrod's, it doesn't offer the public rooms or amenities of an hotel, though a delicious continental breakfast is served in the rooms. What it does offer is an excellent base from which to explore London's many sights and restaurants. Rooms are extremely well equipped and furnished, decorated tastefully with elegant fabrics and well chosen pictures. Bathrooms are all marble and mahogany with proper cast-iron baths and nice little touches such as bottled water. There is a roof garden and a function centre catering for 20-250 guests. Apartments are also available.

University Women's Club

2 AUDLEY SQUARE, W1
0171-499 2268, FAX 0171-499 7046
23 rms £42 inc VAT.

Just around the corner from the Dorchester, this private club is invaluable. Members and their guests will be accommodated if it is humanly possible, even if it means a sofa in the library as the club policy is committed to the concept of safety for women. London membership is £313, for country members it is £266 and for overseas members, it is only £188 per year. The restaurant for members operates Monday to Friday.

The Wilbraham

WILBRAHAM PLACE, SLOANE ST, SW1X 9AE
0171-730 8296, FAX 0171-730 6815
50rms S £66, D £75-£95.

No credit cards

A first-class location (between Sloane Square and Knightsbridge) at very modest prices justifies our inclusion of this long-established small hotel. It has a certain comfortable old-fashioned charm and one would not be surprised to find Miss Marples sitting in one of the blue-upholstered cane armchairs in the small lounge. There's a panelled bar/buttery area, where breakfast is served. Rooms vary in size and although some have been redecorated, bathrooms are rather small and in need of up-dating. Indeed the whole hotel has an air of slightly faded gentility but will appeal to those seeking an almost 'lost' England. Staff are charming and they have a high proportion of returning guests. Cots are provided as well as a baby-sitting service. All rooms have direct-dial telephones.

Willett Hotel

32 SLOANE GDNS, SW1W 8DJ
0171-824 8415, FAX 0171-730 4830
E-mail: willett@eeh.co.uk
19rms S £61-£75, D £85-£115 inc breakfast plus VAT.

An excellent location, just around the corner from Sloane Square in fashionable Chelsea, makes this small townhouse hotel a very good budget choice. The whole hotel has been renovated to a high standard. Bedrooms are all individually decorated and feature hairdryers, trouser presses, refrigerators and satellite TV.

Windermere Hotel

142 WARWICK WAY, SW1V 4JE
0171-834 5163, FAX 0171-630 8831
20rms S £51-£70, D £64-£99, Family rms £104-£112 inc VAT.

Close to the Victoria Terminal, this welcoming and charming family-run hotel enjoys a high level of routine patronage. Soft drinks are available throughout the day in the pleasant lounge and there is a basement dining room serving light meals. Bedrooms are simply furnished, but comfortable and immaculately kept by housekeeping which is first rate.

THE CHAINS

Holiday Inns

Toll-free central booking 0800 897121. This world-wide chain needs no introduction and as well as the **Mayfair site** (see above), has hotels in **Kensington**, **Kings Cross**, **Docklands**, **Oxford Circus** and **Victoria**. Rates: £69-£180.

Ibis

Part of the French Accor Group, of which Novotel is a part, these are moderately priced hotels with basic ameneties and smaller rooms than Novotels. There are two branches in London: in **Euston**, 0171-388 7777, and at **Greenwich**, 0181-305 1177. Rates £50-£60.

Novotel ££££

Central Bookings 0181-748 3433. Rapidly expanding French chain, with good, reasonably-sized rooms and facilities now has hotels in **Hammersmith** and **Waterloo** (ideal for Eurostar). Rates £100-£125

Radisson Edwardian Hotels

In addition to the three hotels mentioned above—**The Hampshire** (Leicester Square), **The Mountbatten** (Covent Garden) and the **Radisson Edwardian** (Heathrow)—this upscale chain operates seven other country-house-style hotels in central London: **The Berkshire** (Oxford Street), **The Marlborough** (Bloomsbury), **The Pastoria** (Leicester Square), **The Kenilworth** (Bloomsbury), **The Grafton** (Tottenham Court Road), **The Vanderbilt** (Kensington), and **The Savoy Court** (Marble Arch). All are decorated in the charmingly eclectic style of an Edwardian-era English home, and have excellent amenities for business travellers. Radisson Edwardian offers special programs at all their hotels, featuring guaranteed rates in U.S. dollars, full English breakfast, all taxes and service charges—and very reasonable prices. Central reservations: 800-333-3333 in U.S., 0800 37 44 11 in U.K.

AIRPORTS

Room rates vary enormously at the airport hotels, depending on whether you are staying mid week (expensive) or weekend. Corporate rates, as with all hotel rates, vary considerably. Most airport hotels are used for conferences and business meetings, so many have day rates to accommodate international meetings. If you're travelling as a family, enquire about a family room and the possibility of your children staying free in your room. There's often an age limit, usually 16 years old.

GATWICK

Copthorne London Gatwick ££££

COPTHORNE, NR CRAWLEY, WEST SUSSEX, RH10 3PG

01342-714971, FAX 01342-717375

5 Stes £155-£225, 227 rms S £115-£145, D £125-£155 inc service and VAT. Air cond. Garden. 24-hr rm service.

This is a rather different airport hotel, built around an old sixteenth-century farmhouse and set in 100 acres of gardens and woods in the village of Copthorne, just six minutes from the airport. In keeping with its origins, log fires and oak beams grace the public rooms, and many bedrooms are in traditional style, again beamed and with four-poster beds. There are four banqueting suites for business use. The Connoisseur Wing provides extra luxury, and each bathroom has a corner spa bath. There's a formal restaurant, **The Lion d'Or**, the informal **Brasserie**, the **Library Bar and Lounge**, and the **White Swan Pub**. For relaxation there's also a croquet lawn and jogging track, and nearby golf and horse riding. The health club, located in an area away from the hotel, includes a pool.

Gravetye Manor £££££

VOWELS LANE, EAST GRINSTEAD, WEST SUSSEX, RH19 4LJ

01342-810567, FAX 01342-810080

18rms S from £110, D from £165 inc service, but plus VAT.

This is definitely not an airport hotel, but arriving or leaving from Gatwick provides the perfect excuse for a deluxe stay and a delightful dining experience at celebrated Gravetye Manor, a member of the Relais et Châteaux group. One of the first country house hotels in England, this Elizabethan stone mansion was built in 1598, and still retains its baronial feeling. Public downstairs rooms have magnificent panelled walls and moulded ceilings. Bedrooms are large, comfortable and beautifully furnished with antique furniture and glorious fabrics, while books and magazines are scattered around as if in a private home. The welcome given by owner Peter Herbert and his staff is proverbial. The gardens are renowned—1,000 acres of flower beds and lawns invite guests to stroll outside. People come from miles around to eat in the restaurant, from a menu that mixes the traditional with the modern. Set menus run from lunch at £24 to dinner at £30 plus VAT, but the à la carte menu and wine list is expensive. However, if you feel expansive, or want a special treat on arrival or departure, Gravetye Manor is not to be missed.

Le Meridien London Gatwick ££££

NORTH TERMINAL, GATWICK AIRPORT, WEST SUSSEX, RH6 0PH

01293-567070, FAX 01293-567739

9 stes from £250-£400, 468 rms S/D from £145 inc service and VAT. Non-smoking rms. Air cond. 24-hr rm service.

The most notable feature of this large hotel is the eight-storey high atrium with a cocktail bar and café below and a grand piano in the main lobby. Linked to the airport's North Terminal by a short covered walkway, decor is modern and minimal. The hotel has been refurbished; bedrooms are well equipped, and the TV system displays flight information. Restaurants include the **Brasserie** and **Café Montparnasse**. There's a spa and swimming pool.

London Gatwick Hilton

GATWICK, WEST SUSSEX, RH11 0PD
01293-518080, FAX 01293-528980
16 Stes £250-£550, 550 rms S £187-£260 inc VAT. Non-smoking floors. Air cond. 24-hr rm service. Conference facilities for up to 500.

One of the most impressive of Gatwick's hotels, it features a pedestrian walkway connecting to the South Terminal and a four-storey central atrium where a life-size replica of Amy Johnson's biplane hangs from the ceiling. Bedrooms are good size and well equipped and the TVs display the latest flight information. There's a fully equipped health club and pool, **Amy's American Style Diner** and the more formal **Garden Restaurant**, and two bars. Golf, tennis and squash nearby.

HEATHROW

Excelsior Hotel

BATH RD, WEST DRAYTON, MIDDLX, UB7 0DU
0181-759 6611, FAX 0181-759 3421
16 stes from £05-£325, 826 rms S £145, D £155-£185 inc VAT and service. Conference facilities up to 800. Non-smoking rms. Air cond. 24-hr rm service

A huge, modern, recently refurbished hotel offering all the comforts of today. Some bedrooms are equipped for wheelchair-bound guests; there is a pool, and the usual health and beauty facilities. Children under fourteen years old can stay free in their parents' room. A grand entrance lobby greets you, and there are extensive conference facilities. **Wheeler's of St. James's**, the fish restaurant chain, runs one of the restaurants and there is a buffet in **The Original Carvery and Grill**. There are also two bars.

Heathrow Hilton

TERMINAL 4, HOUNSLOW, MIDDLX, TW5 3AF
0181-759 7755, FAX 0181-759 7579
5 Stes £350-£595, 395 rooms S/D £185-£215 inc VAT. Non-smoking rms. Air cond.

Quite the most spectacular of Heathrow's hotels, all steel and glass and a landmark from the outside, you enter via a huge, high atrium which has a lounge and restaurant beneath it. Bedrooms are equipped with all the modern technology international travellers expect. Executive floor includes special check-in, lounge and complimentary breakfast and canapés, and the business facilities are first rate. Direct access to Terminal 4 is via a covered walkway.

Radisson Edwardian Heathrow

140 BATH RD, HAYES, MIDDLX, UB3 5AW
0181-759 6311, FAX 0181-759 4559
17 stes 450-£850, 443 rms S £180, D£200-£235 inc service and VAT. Non-smoking rms. Air cond. 24-hr rm service.

Five minutes from the airport, the Radisson Edwardian Heathrow is a stylish and well equipped hotel with a welcoming foyer. Bedrooms are a good size and well decorated, some with four-poster beds, while suites have spa baths. This is an important residential conference hotel; facilities are excellent for business travellers and include 17 conference suites. Their Business Class, with its hallmark rooms, is aimed at the frequent traveller, with bigger rooms, full English breakfast and more. There is a pool, spa and beauty salon.

Sheraton Skyline

BATH RD, HAYES, MIDDLX, UB3 5BP
0181-759 2535, FAX 0181-759 9150
5 Stes £200-£450, 352 rms S/D £80-£210 inc service and VAT. Non-smoking rms. Air cond. 24-hr rm service.

The Sheraton Skyline is known for the Patio Caribe—a large indoor tropical garden with swimming pool and a bar. Bedrooms are excellently equipped; children up to sixteen years old can stay free in their parents' room, and the banqueting and conference facilities are what you would expect and can accommodate up to 500.

QUICK BITES

CONTENTS

Spots where you can grab a bite and a drink at reasonable prices. Categorized by geographic area.

CAFÉS & ETHNIC RESTAURANTS

ARCHWAY

Paris-London Café

FRENCH

3 JUNCTION RD, N19, 0171-561 0330

Mon.-Sat. 9am-10.30pm. U: Archway.

No cards

French brothers Jerome and Frederic Boileau run this small, though recently extended café-cum-bistro opposite Archway tube in an area that offers nothing more elevated than hamburger chains and greasy-spoon cafés. Tables are close together (and there aren't many of them) but portions are generous and prices are low—£9.95 gives you four courses, and £14.95 five of robust very traditional French bistro cooking—frogs' legs, steaks, duck, lamb, garliced snails etc. The place is much appreciated by locals, particularly hungry and impoverished staff from the nearby Whittington Hospital.

BATTERSEA

Beyoglu

TURKISH

50 BATTERSEA PARK RD, SW11, 0171-627 2052

Lunch Mon.-Sat., Dinner nightly.

BR: Battersea Park.

A bright blue shop front marks this small corner Turkish café on a rather dreary stretch of main road (but close enough to the park). It's welcoming and friendly-and very good with small children—and clearly suits the local population. Seeing it came originally from Stoke Newington, this is a great compliment—the up-and-coming inhabitants of this part of south London are very different from their northern neighbours. Warm pide comes with the meze for scooping up so you can outdo your dining companions with the excellent fava (broad beans puréed with garlic, onions and dill in a little olive oil), and leave them the taramasalata which did not taste homemade. Kebabs are deliciously chargrilled, though the dish of the day, lamb cooked slowly in the oven with tomatoes, onions, peppers and spices was too bland. But prices are excellent (around £3 for starters, from £6 to £8 for main dishes), desserts are sweet and Turkish, and the coffee—which is teeth-tinglingly strong as you filter it through—comes with Turkish delight.

C. Notarianni & Sons

PIZZA

142 BATTERSEA HIGH ST, SW11, 0171-228 7133

Lunch Mon.-Fri., Dinner Mon.-Sat.

BR: Clapham Junction.

Vintage '30s ice cream parlour, still run by the same family, but the emphasis is now on their home-style cooking. There's an original Rock-ola jukebox with '50s, '60s and '70s music to go with honest crunchy pizzas, foccaccia (garlic, tomato or mozzarella) and pastas like a good Italian grandma would make—the one with asparagus, olive oil and garlic is a revelation. House wine is a very gluggable Sicilian; the coffee is good, and they still make their own ice cream. A very real place and a welcome change from chain pizzerias. Around £12 per person.

Duke of Cambridge

PUB/MODERN BRITISH

228 BATTERSEA BRIDGE RD, SW11,
0171-223 5662

Pub: Mon.-Sat. 11am-11pm, Sun. noon-10.30pm. Lunch & Dinner daily.

BR: Clapham Junction.

Once the terminus for horse-drawn omnibuses, this period pub just south of Battersea Bridge has been done-over and turned into a pub-restaurant where dishes like cod stuffed with pesto and chilli with a zucchini-and-potato salad, and crostini of chicken livers with a roasted pepper salad, clearly find favour with the young Battersea crowd. The two owners have done this transformation before, at the Chelsea Ram in Chelsea and the Queen's in Primrose Hill. The more serious menu is around £3 to £6 for starters, main courses from £5 to £11; lighter meals hover around the £4 to £5 mark. The place boasts a good wine list—and all this in a decor of pale coloured walls, dried flowers and hops trailing over the place, old photographs, canvasses and bookcases.

Mason's Arms

PUB/INTERNATIONAL
169 BATTERSEA PARK RD, SW8, 0171-622 2007
Pub: Mon.-Sat 11am-11pm, noon-10.30pm Sun. Lunch & Dinner daily.
BR: Battersea Park.

Made along the model of the Eagle in Farringdon, but with a more modern edge to it—uncluttered, light colours, monthly changing art installations and, of course, a grill behind the bar. Good fun, good wines by the glass or bottle, good food along the lines of big, luscious cheeseburgers and chips, but also items like salmon and sweet potato fishcakes, and a daily changing risotto like slow-roasted tomato, asparagus and Parmesan, all just under £7. Desserts are now homemade and recent favouties included a rhubarb 'crumble' with coconut and pecan which had a lovely chewy texture, and white and dark chocolate mousse; all around £3.50. A very useful oasis in the food dessert near the two British Rail stations in Battersea.

S Bar and Restaurant

PUB/MODERN EUROPEAN
37 BATTERSEA BRIDGE RD, SW11, 0171-223 3322
Bar Sun.-Wed. noon-11pm, Thurs.-Sat. 11am-11pm, Sun. noon-10.30pm. Lunch & Dinner Mon.-Sat. BR: Clapham Junction

A

Energetic yet relaxing, contemporary yet traditional, urban yet country pub atmosphere—but then interesting places always have an element of the paradoxical about them. The upstairs dining room has a lounge bar for pre- and post-prandial drinks with a good assortment of single malts and brandies. The blackboard menu is straightforward but interesting, and changes only as often as the chef thinks it needs to be changed. Look for items like well-prepared quail salad; cod with garlic mash; black pudding risotto; seared salmon; sausage and mash; confit of duck; ribeye steak with chips. It'll cost you around £18 per head, but on Monday night the three-course meal is £12.50, and Sunday lunch is two courses for £10. And there's live jazz on Sunday evenings to set you up for the week.

BAYSWATER

Maison Bouquillon

CAFÉ
41 MOSCOW RD, W2, 0171-727 4897
Daily 8am-8.30pm. U: Bayswater.
No cards

First-rate continental pastries majoring in chocolate, excellent coffee and a European clientele at this popular spot, just around the corner from Queensway so thankfully less crowded than its main road competitors. It's a small place, full of tables and chairs, and with newspapers to read if you're waiting for a friend, and with a definite local feel.

BLOOMSBURY

Coffee Gallery

CAFÉ
23 MUSEUM ST, WC1, 0171-436 0455
Mon.-Fri. 8am-5.30pm, Sat. 10am-5.30pm.
U: Tottenham Court Rd.
No cards

This thoroughly pleasant place, particularly good for vegetarians, has the added attraction of doubling as a small, enthusiastic art gallery. The Italian owner and his English wife serve homemade food of an exceptionally high standard for such a small operation, from breakfast croissants through a lunch that might include homemade soups, salads and changing dishes like courgettes marinated in mint and balsamic vinegar on mixed leaves, or chicken kebabs with courgettes, red onions with marinated grilled pumpkin or just sandwiches on Italian breads. Cakes are first-rate; cappuccinos satisfyingly rich. They also run the Table Café at Habitat but for us this is their best venue, and certainly the best value.

Garden Café

CAFÉ
32 MUSEUM ST, WC1, 0171-637 4309
Mon.-Fri. 9am-5pm. U: Tottenham Court Rd.
No cards

A counter at the front for some of the best French patisseries around, as well as gourmet French chocolates and take away sandwiches, and a small eating area at the back for light lunches of the quiches-and-salad variety, make this a popular spot for visitors to the British

Museum. Good coffee, great ice cream and frozen yoghurt attract hordes of North Americans. But summer hours can be erratic.

Museum Street Café

CAFÉ

47 MUSEUM ST, WC1, 0171-405 3211

Mon.-Fri. 8am-6pm, Sat. 9am-6pm, Sun. 11.30am-6pm.

U: Tottenham Court Rd.

Bloomsbury's nicest restaurant—winning a toque in the last edition—has turned itself into an upmarket snack bar! But at least the new opening hours make it the ideal place on a visit to the British Museum. Chef/propietors Gail Koerber and Mark Nathan have run their restaurant here since 1989 so obviously know their customers. Gail's baking remains a highlight of the new, more casual menu. Her breads are a varied delight, and her savoury tarts (caramelised onion, or spinach and olive), and pizzas (as in pizzetta with grilled vegetables), make a tasty light lunch. Traditional English teas feature superb and unusual cakes there are very few places serving Valrhona chocolate cake, Earl Grey fruitcake or Cragganmore single-malt whisky cake. A broad choice of teas, infusions and coffees in a smoke-free environment refresh further forays to the Museum or relax with a discriminating and fairly priced selection of wines, many by the glass.

Wagamama

JAPANESE

4 STREATHAM ST, WC1, 0171-323 9223

Mon.-Sat. noon-11pm, Sun. 12.30pm-10pm.

U: Tottenham Court Rd.

Not everyone's cup of jasmine tea, but good food, trendy decor (as in minimal and noisy), young service and remarkably good value at this Japanese-style noodle bar which began in a basement restaurant near the British Museum and has now expanded into a second, larger branch in Soho. Noodles come pan-fried, in soup or with a sauce, otherwise there are rice dishes. Ramen, one of Japan's most popular fast foods comes with chicken, seafood, salmon or even chargrilled steak as well as seasonal greens and a whole lot more. Soba come pan-fried, again with a whole mixture of meat and vegetables. Main dishes are between £4.50 and £7. You can drink wine, or try their freshly squeezed fruit juices for 'energy, cleansing and digesting'. You eat at long communal tables which can be great or hell, depending on your neighbours, and invariably have to queue. **Also at 10A Lexington St, W1, 0171-292 0990.**

CAMDEN TOWN

Café Delancey

FRENCH

3 DELANCEY ST, NW1, 0171-387 1985

Daily 8am-11.30pm.

U: Camden Town/Mornington Crescent.

Bleary-eyed residents gulp down a cappuccino or a vegetarian breakfast in the mornings; from around 8pm onwards, it's favoured by ravers going on to any of Camden Town's many nightspots. In between they serve pretty well everything you expect from a French bistro. Wooden floors, those French bistro-type chairs and tables (small and uncomfortable), good atmosphere, great staff, blackboards listing daily specials and more put you in the mood for grilled lamb with ratatouille or just a filling croque monsieur to get you through the day or night. Great pit stop for weekend Camden Market visitors also.

Daphne

GREEK CYPRIOT

83 BAYHAM ST, NW1, 0171-267 7322

Lunch & Dinner Mon.-Sat.

U: Camden Town/Mornington Crescent.

A cut above the usual Camden Town Greek Cypriot places, it's still family run and it shows in the pretty decor with its checked tablecloths and small rooms (and there's a lovely roof terrace which is well worth checking out on sunny days) and imaginative cooking. Meze is always a good bet at £10.75 for the meat, or £15.75 for the fish version; otherwise it's worth going for the more ambitious dishes which they do so well, like their excellent xifias-marinated, char-grilled swordfish.

Marine Ices

ITALIAN/ICE CREAM PARLOUR
8 HAVERSTOCK HILL, NW3, 0171-485 3132.
Lunch & Dinner daily. U: Chalk Farm.

There's an Italian restaurant here too, but the main point is the ice cream. Since the 1940s the Mansi family have been filling cones and glasses with fresh fruit sorbets and ice creams with natural flavours along with those old staples, cassata and bombes. On a hot day after a trawl around any part of sprawling Camden Lock, this is a delightfully refreshing venue.

NW1

ITALIAN
30 HAWLEY CRESCENT, NW1, 0171-267 7755
Daily 11-midnight.
U: Camden Town/Chalk Farm.

Housed in a former garage which has been refurbished in high-tech style both inside and out (so the floor-to-ceiling glass wall at the front is impossible to see into), NW1 clearly owes something to the new-style Pizza Express chain. But NW1 holds its own in every respect and ventures further than pizzas, although these are one of the mainstays here. Pizzas are reasonably priced (from £3.95) and come on proper dough with well-tried fillings like the favourite Margherita. Pastas are imaginative, fresh and good value from £4.95, and there are other, more expensive fish dishes, salads and dishes like grilled vegetables. Great desserts, large range of coffees and teas and great cakes, so try teatime as well.

Nontas

GREEK CYPRIOT
14 CAMDEN HIGH ST, NW1, 0171-387 4579
Lunch & Dinner Mon.-Sat.
U: Mornington Crescent/Camden Town.

Nontas is looking rather shabby these days, and still sporting those '60s-style crocheted lampshades which shed a dim light over the interior, even though they've now got linen tablecloths. But this family-run restaurant with useful outside seating at the back for summer months, remains one of our favourites. Meze at £6.75 per person always brings out the best in everyone and comes in great waves of small plates, covering the gamut. Otherwise main dishes around £6 remain exactly the same—good marinated chicken kebabs, kleftiko, oven-cooked dishes. At the next door Ouzerie try incredibly sweet Greek pastries in the morning, or a simple lunch.

CHELSEA

Big Easy

AMERICAN
332-334 KING'S RD, SW3, 0171-352 4071
Daily noon-midnight. U: Sloane Sq.

'Dig In, get messy' the menu exhorts, and that's the way to do it at this large, bustling, wood-panelled joint half way down the King's Road, where portions are huge, tastes are robust and the staff is great. Big ribs, steaks, hamburgers, lots of southern fried seafood, all washed down with cocktails and beer (or not-bad Californian wine if you prefer). Great fun, noisy and very crowded.

Bluebird Café

CAFÉ
350 KING'S RD, SW3, 0171-559 1000
Mon.-Wed. 10am-8pm, Thurs., Fri. to 9pm, Sat. 9am-9pm, Sun. noon-6pm. U: Sloane Sq.

Part of Sir Terence Conran's Bluebird garage conversion into a restaurant, mega gourmet-food store and cookery shop. The café and the outside tables look onto the old forecourt, now a mini vegetable and fruit marketplace dramatically lit by flares in the evening. Invariably full of Chelsea Sloanes, complete with designer babes and babies, it's a great place (if you can get a table) for coffee and pastries and very good light meals.

Chelsea Ram

PUB/INTERNATIONAL
32 BURNABY ST, SW10, 0171-351 4008
Lunch & Dinner daily. U: None near by.

The Chelsea Ram has been gathering very positive comments from customers and critics alike recently. The pub is light and friendly, serving mainly locals and their friends. It's a bit off the main Chelsea drag—from one direction you have to walk past World's End to get there—but definitively worth the detour. A carefully selected wine list with 'wine of the moment' on the blackboard, and beers which fit nicely with the food, make the Chelsea Ram more a restaurant than a drinking pub. Choose the great Chelsea Ram salad (with chicken, bacon, avocado with sour cream and chives) or for something a little different, start with blinis followed by salt cod cakes.

The Garden Restaurant

CAFÉ
GENERAL TRADING COMPANY
144 SLOANE ST, SW1, 0171-730 2001
Mon.-Fri. 9.30am-6pm, Wed. to 7pm, Sat. to 5pm. U: Sloane Square.

The café of the General Trading Company is much loved by Chelsea's Sloane Rangers and well-heeled mothers up from the country. It's a delightful place in summer with a small patio garden at the back; inside it's usually cramped and crowded, but you can enjoy good food here—dishes like a plate of smoked salmon and mixed salad, savoury tart with salad or a hot dish like lamb casserole with apricot and thyme—while listening to the secrets of the smart Chelsea set (divorces, affairs, scandals are discussed at great length and great volume).

New Culture Revolution

CHINESE
305 KING'S RD, SW3, 0171-352 9281
Daily noon-11pm. U: Sloane Sq.

First Islington, then Camden Town, now the trendies of Chelsea are being treated to a New Culture Revolution with its minimalist decor and simple, cheap dishes. The craze that began with Wagamama carries on here with noodles, dumplings and rice (around £4-£6 a dish) done every-which-way, chow mein (wok-fried noodles) and tong mein (noodles in soup stock with seafood, vegetables or meat) at simple wooden tables. Great for a quick bite. **Also at 42 Duncan St, N1, 0171-833 9083; 43 Parkway, NW1, 0171-267 2700.**

Tiger Lil's

FAR EASTERN
500 KING'S RD, SW10, 0171-376 5003
Mon.-Fri. Dinner, Sat., Sun. noon-midnight. U: Sloane Sq.

Flaming woks here, offering £11 of unlimited helpings from a display of exotic vegetables like shaved carrot with Japanese seaweed, cloud-ear fungus with mushrooms, shooting pulses with corn nibs, all ready to add to pork, squid, beef, turkey, tofu or more. Mix and match gone mad. Alternatively the adventurous can do it themselves at the table in a steaming firepot. Waitresses bring you rice and noodles. Just to complete the street image, the decor makes good use of all sorts of generally unwanted materials, like odd reclaimed railway sleepers, old oil drums, telegraph poles and so on. **Also at 16 Clapham Common South Side, SW4, 0171-720 5433, 270 Upper St, N1, 0171-226 1118 (call for opening times).**

CHINATOWN

Joy King Lau

CHINESE
3 LEICESTER ST, WC2, 0171-437 1132/1133
Mon.-Sat. noon-11.30pm, Sun. 11am-10.30pm. U: Leicester Sq.

Somewhat institutional cream-and-green walls are relieved by large pictures and back windows overlooking a whitewashed courtyard. Cool service does not deter the Chinese and the few westerners who come for a reliable fairly priced dim sum lunch. Good ingredients are used, producing delicate, rather than striking, flavours in such favourites as roast pork 'lasagne'—known outside Italy as cheung fan; or appetisingly named yum croquettes, better known as 'yam'. Only the brave order 'duck weds with bean curd roll', the bird's pedal extremity (aka duck's web) wrapped in tofu skin, and grasping a giant prawn ball.

Poons & Co

CHINESE
27 LISLE ST, WC2, 0171-437 4549
Daily noon-11.30pm. U: Leicester Sq.

'Little Poons', the tiny single room which became a group, has quadrupled in size. There are now four small rooms, and the decor is ten times smarter than it was back in 1973. Yet it still offers top quality basic Cantonese food at amazingly low prices. Plates of rice or noodles with meat or fish from £3.30; meat dishes from £4; seafood and specialities up to £7. Menus from £7.50. Here London first tasted hot-pots and wind-dried foods. Don't miss them. With pleasant service you have an eating house which would be outstanding at double the price.

Tokyo Diner

JAPANESE

2 NEWPORT PL, WC, 0171-287 8777

Daily noon-midnight. U: Leicester Sq.

 *No booking.*

London's first cheap Japanese is still one of the best and cheapest. Donburi dishes on rice are from £3.90 (that is for Japanese omelette) and miso soup and fruit are included until 5.30pm. Bento (lunch boxes), start at £9.90. Tips are not accepted. At such prices something has to give, and dear reader it may be you—if you are long or large—for tables and chairs are minuscule. But they fit the authentic decor and the layout of this warren of tiny rooms on a Soho corner.

CHISWICK

Bedlington Café

THAI

24 FAUCONBERG RD, W4, 0181-994 1965

Lunch and Dinner daily. U: Chiswick Park/Turnham Green.

No cards

Still one of the jolliest Thai cafés around, packed in the evenings with locals who are quite different from the daily clientele when it serves a different menu as a greasy spoon café. Spicy, well cooked Thai dishes take in some specialities from Laos also, like a well chillied pork larb. Otherwise there's a good sprinkling of Chinese starters on the spring roll theme. Try the squid with garlic and peppers (£4.95); it's hot stuff. Bring your own wine.

THE CITY

Babe Ruth's

AMERICAN

172-176 THE HIGHWAY, NR TOWER BRIDGE, E1, 0171-481 8181

Lunch & Dinner daily. U: Tower Hill.

This large, purpose-built sports restaurant opened in April 1996 for some 700 fans, all granite, stone, stainless steel and glass just near Tower Bridge. A fifteen-foot square video wall overlooks the restaurant; sporting memorabilia is dotted around the place; and TV monitors feature live and recorded sporting moments from around the world. And you can actually chuck a basketball around a small court, or enjoy a spot of virtual reality entertainment in a games room which spells death to normal family life. The food is chargrilled wild mushrooms sautéed with spinach and mozzarella cheese on garlic toast, dips, generous salads, like sesame chicken and noodles. Salads are imaginative; there's a good range of sandwiches, pizzas and pastas. And naturally you can buy a Babe Ruth's memento. Expect to pay anything from £10 to £25 per person.

Café Naz

BANGLADESHI

46/48 BRICK LANE, E1, 0171-247 0234

Daily 6am-midnight. U: Aldgate East.

The most upmarket of Brick Lane curry houses, in a refreshingly flock-free, modern interior. While the slogan is Contemporary Bangladeshi Cuisine, it is more honest to call it properly prepared traditional Indian with Bengali touches like the ayre fish, floured with spices and fried with onion. Other starters are the standard assortment of chicken tikka, tandoori lamb chop and boti kebab, tandoori lamb with a spicy and slightly sweet marinade and sauce. Mains are better, like the aromatic gosht (lamb) kata masala and garlic-chilli chicken, or the Bangladeshi fish curry, rasum machli with onion, tomato and garlic. Good vegetables and breads. Starters are £2.50-£4; mains are £4-£6 and all are very good value for money.

Futures!

VEGETARIAN
2 EXCHANGE SQ, EC2, 0171-638 6341
Mon.-Fri. 7.30am-11pm, evening for drinks only. U: Liverpool St.

City traders, brought up, one believes, as rampant carnivores, flock to Futures! in the Broadgate Centre, partly for the excellent location and conservatory-style decor (particularly good in summer with delightful outside tables), and partly for its excellent vegetarian dishes, imaginative salads and daily hot pots or perhaps a moussaka bake, not forgetting an excellent breakfast which is particularly popular. It's also incredibly good value, another virtue City traders obviously appreciate. **Also at 8 Botolph Alley, EC3, 0171-623 4529.**

Lahore Kebab House

INDIAN
2 UMBERSTON ST, E1, 0171-481 9737
Daily noon-midnight. U: Aldgate East.
No cards.

Unprepossessing in the extreme from the outside, you have to know that this is one of the most famous inexpensive Indian restaurants in London or you'd walk right past. But clearly the locals know, and at lunchtime it's full of City types. The menu, written on a board on the wall, is limited—curries, tikkas and karahis of lamb and chicken—but pick well and you'll understand the popularity. Chicken karahi (£4.95) served at the table was well spiced; a lamb curry full of flavour with whole peppercorns. Most dishes are under £5; bring your own wine.

Moshi Moshi Sushi

JAPANESE/SUSHI BAR
UNIT 24, LIVERPOOL ST STATION, EC2, 0171-247 3227
Mon.-Fri. 11.30am-9pm. U: Liverpool St.

Certainly less glamorous than the Train Bleu restaurant at the Gare du Lyon in Paris, but here you actually see trains arriving and leaving. And London's first kaiten—conveyor-belt sushi bar—is not only cheaper than some newcomers (sushi portions from 90p, light meals from £4.90) but better too, because robots are not as clever as people at preparing rice. Good standard sushi, but avoid the lunch-time rush hour to enjoy such made-to-order epicurean luxuries as eel, fatty tuna, even gloriously rich sea urchin—which French gastronomes agree is amongst the finest and most recherché of sea-foods.

CLAPHAM

Eco Pizzeria

PIZZERIA
162 CLAPHAM HIGH ST, SW4, 0171-978 1108
Daily lunch & dinner. U: Clapham Common.

London is truly international these days, with this Italian pizzeria owned by Sami Wasif, an Egyptian who is also the chef, underlining the fact. If you want further proof, the ultra-modern minimalist decor was designed by the creator of the cement walls and the sneaking stainless steel pipes of Belgo (see Restaurant section) which also adds to the considerable hubbub. So what about the pizzas? Well, some are traditional with excellent bases (the chef knows his flours and doughs), covered by, for instance, the basic Margherita—spiced tomato sauce, mozzarella, olive oil, garlic and herbs; others are ambitious mixes using smoked salmon, seafood (the most expensive at £7.50). There are calzones and focaccio, as well as salads, oven-baked dishes like baked crab and spinach, and great desserts. The internationalisation of the pizza is definitely good news here.

Gastro

FRENCH
67 VENN ST, SW4, 0171-627 0222
Daily 8am-midnight. U: Clapham Common.
No cards. No booking.

Gastro and the Clapham Common Picture House (just opposite) have a synergistic relationship; one fills up, the other empties. So try and time your visit after the feature has started. It's a young, fun, sidle-up kind of bistro, where no credit cards or bookings are taken and the service is cheeky but good-natured. It looks like a caricature of what you will rarely find in France any more: zinc tops, large shared tables, witty and pretty Gallic detail, and a robust menu at affordable prices. The menu is written on a blackboard which is moved table-to-table: perhaps a soupe aux poissons followed by some nicely dressed chicken liver salad, or fresh oysters from the tiny seafood bar followed by andouillette (chitterlings sausage) in a mustard sauce. The wine selection is lamentable and pricey for the bottles on offer, but still the place packs out every evening with fun-loving Claphamites who go for the atmosphere and prices at around £16 per head.

Polygon Bar & Grill

INTERNATIONAL
4 THE POLYGON, SW4, 0171-622 1199,
FAX 0171-622 1166
Lunch & Dinner daily. U: Clapham Common

Highly minimal, highly fashionable, hugely busy, Polygon certainly makes a statement with its concrete bar, wooden tables, wild colours and real mixture of cooking styles. Trawl around the world with lemongrass and chillis and a lot of up-to-the-minute wasabi, salsa and aubergine chutney spicing up the meat dishes, much spice-rubbing, and good, honest char-grilling from the rotisserie. This is on the expensive side for a quick bite, but dishes like lamb with the ever fashionable couscous are worth the journey and the price. Expect to pay around £20 per person.

CLERKENWELL

Al's Café and Bar

CAFÉ
11-13 EXMOUTH MARKET, EC1, 0171-837 4821
Mon.-Tues. 8am-midnight, Wed.-Fri. 8am-2am, Sat. 10am-2am, Sun. 10am-10.30pm. U: Farringdon.

A curious mixture of clients in this corner café in Exmouth Market—young trendies from nearby up-and-coming Clerkenwell, a stash of local workers and the odd old bod who could be homeless but who fits in quite happily into the laid-back atmosphere. The menu is just about as mixed: breakfast from the solid English variety or a dainty croissant, and a large range of dishes from sandwiches to grills to nachos. Beers are good with a mix of British and Continental brews at less than West End pub prices. Or you can have, as the old guy next to us did, just a cup of strong tea. The decor—bare walls, low plastic-covered seats along the window and basic tables and chairs, along with the hippy air of the place—brings back New York cafés in the 80s. No bad thing.

Eagle

PUB/MEDITERRANEAN
159 FARRINGDON RD, EC1, 0171-837 1353
Mon.-Sat. noon-11pm. Lunch 12.30pm-2.30pm, dinner 6.30pm-10.30pm. U: Farringdon.
No cards.

This pioneer of what has become known as the 'gastro' pub continues to charm. But the result, both of its fame and of the consistent quality of the cooking, is a fight for a table, crowds and noise. Never mind, it's all very good-natured. The chargrill behind the bar provides most of the dishes which are chalked up on a large blackboard, so expect grilled Italian sausages with Puy lentils and salsa verde for £8.75 packed with gutsy flavours, or fish grilled to perfection with lightly cooked vegetables. The blackboard list of well priced wines (beginning at £8.50) offers all by the glass; beers are on tap or bottled. Portions are generous, service is rightly brisk, decor is basic. You won't feel shortchanged here.

Kolossi Grill

GREEK
56-60 ROSEBERRY AVE, EC1, 0171-278 5758
Lunch Mon.-Fri., Mon.-Sat. Dinner. U: Farringdon.

On the corner of Roseberry Avenue and Exmouth Market, this long-established family-run Greek place is a comfortable restaurant with linen napkins, carpets and well-uphostered chairs, and will soon be something of a rarity in this area which is rapidly becoming the place to be for the trend-setters. All the usuals are served here, from meze (£12 per person) to moussaka, a comforting place for the die-hard Greek food fan.

Medina's

ITALIAN
10 CLERKENWELL GREEN, EC1, 0171-580 4673
Mon.-Fri. 11.30am-11pm. U: Farringdon

Clerkenwell Green is being rapidly trendified, as businesses give way to restaurants like Medina's with their plate glass, stainless steel and large echoing rooms. This is not a put-down when it's done well, and it is here at this bustling Italian joint which offers good value pizzas and pastas at reasonable prices (around £6-£7) in a buzzing atmosphere.

Room 240

PUB/INTERNATIONAL

PEASANT 240 ST. JOHN ST, EC1, 0171-336 7726

Pub Mon.-Fri. noon-11pm, Sat. 6pm-11pm. Lunch & Dinner Mon.-Sat.. U: Angel.

This very hip, cutting-edge restaurant is upstairs from the pub. The interior is light and airy, bright with art on the walls and sculpture standing on the floors (too infrequently seen as restaurants are keen to utilise every square millimetre of space). The menu changes every two weeks, but the house style is Modern English/Mediterranean/Pacific Rim. This may sound like an awful mish-mash, but it all comes together well on the plate. Starters have included sweetcorn, chilli and coriander fritter with tomato and chilli jam; mussels with lemongrass, coriander and garlic in a white wine court bouillon; rosemary foccaccia with goats' curd and preserved quinces. Main courses might include a monkfish, salmon, squid and prawn kebab on a bed of tabbouleh; ham hock with mustard mash, Savoy cabbage and parsley sauce; fried potato cake with capers, leeks, poached egg and hollandaise sauce. Desserts do not let the side down either: roasted peaches with grappa and mascarpone; home-made vanilla ice cream with chilli syrup. A meal for two is around £40.

COVENT GARDEN

Browns Restaurant & Bar

BISTRO

82-84 ST. MARTIN'S LANE, WC2, 0171-497 5050

Open Mon.-Thurs. noon-midnight, Fri., Sat. to 12.30am, Sun. to 11.30pm. U: Leicester Sq.

A

Browns, sandwiched between the St. Martin's Lane Theatre and a new Pizza Express, certainly holds it own with its imposing façade and flaming torchères. It's part of the chain started by Jeremy Mogford in Oxford but now owned by one of the big brewing companies. The original owner's policy was to take over dramatic and historic premises such as a hospital (Cambridge), a former tailor's shop (Mayfair), and here it's the old Westminster Law Courts. It's pretty big inside, pretty noisy, pretty crowded and just plain pretty with lots of greenery everywhere (another trademark of Browns), cream walls, wooden floors, tables that are too small, and a buzz to make any restaurateur green with envy. Food is good, a rich bistro mix of almost everything from traditional fish soup to pasta, salads and main dishes of the chargrilled variety, not forgetting fish, hot sandwiches and a vast array of filling puddings. Pre- and post-theatre meals are two courses for £9.95; Sunday brunch is three courses at £12.95, and in true generous spirit which many might copy, children eat a special children's menu free with an adult ordering a main course. **Also at 47 Maddox St, W1, 0171-491 4565; 114 Draycott Ave, SW3, 0171-584 5359.**

Cranks

VEGETARIAN

1 THE MARKET, WC2, 0171-836 5226

Mon.-Fri. 9am-8pm, Sat. 9am-9pm, Sun. 10am-8pm. U: Covent Garden.

Cranks has changed since its early days. Now the decor is more 'designed' and the menu concentrates on lighter dishes, sushi and the like, rather than the rather stodgy salads and main courses it did before. Start the day with excellent meg muesli or apple filo; a light lasagne or energising pasta salad will keep you going at lunchtime; roasted fruits in ginger or lemon give you that sweet lift. There's a good balcony in the Covent Garden branch to look down from. **Branches throughout London.**

Food for Thought

VEGETARIAN

31 NEAL ST, WC2, 0171-836 0239

Breakfast, Lunch & Dinner Mon-Sat. Lunch Sun. U: Covent Garden.

No cards.

Excellent value, good self-service downstairs café and upstairs take-away in Covent Garden with everything freshly made runs the gamut from breakfast (their home baking makes this meal a must) to lunches and dinner with dishes like soup at £2.20, perhaps walnut or spicy tomato and peanut, mushroom pie, or Mediterranean roasted vegetables. Leave room for desserts. Bring your own wine. Alternatively come here for afternoon tea. It's pretty crowded downstairs at peak times, though two tables are available outside in the summer.

Monmouth Coffee House

CAFÉ

27 Monmouth St, WC2, 0171-836 5272

Mon.-Sat. 9am-6.pm, Sun. 11am-5pm.

U: Covent Garden/Tottenham Court Rd.

Lovely atmospheric old coffee house in Covent Garden selling some of the best and most varied coffees at the front, and offering tables for a taste at the back. Accompanied by great baking from Sally Clarke's bakery—croissants, pain au chocolat etc (which sell out early on a Saturday)—this makes a very pleasant stop.

Neal's Yard Beach Café

CAFÉ

13 Neal's Yard, Seven Dials, WC2,
0171-240 1168

Daily noon-6.30pm. U: Covent Garden.

No cards.

Particularly good in summer when the doors open onto the busy scene of Neal's Yard, this excellent café specialises in freshly prepared fruit and vegetable juices. On the menu, too, are some of the best sundaes in town which might mix banana and nuts, strawberry and melon, cream and honey or combinations you never dreamed of. First-class sandwiches on Mediterranean breads, soups and coffees fit the bill here.

Palms Pasta on the Piazza

MEDITERRANEAN

39 King St, WC2, 0171-240 2939

Daily noon-11.pm. U: Covent Garden.

A jolly would-be Italian scene painted on one wall puts you in the right frame of mind for a fairly predictable menu, weighted towards the Mediterranean, of starters like baby prawns sautéed with garlic and chilli, or deep-fried calamari and courgettes, pastas, and main courses of chargrilled chicken, steaks and Italian sausages. Coffee is good and with friendly opening hours, it's worth noting in an area with more than its fair share of poor restaurants.

PJ's Grill

AMERICAN

30 Wellington St, WC2, 0171-240 7529

Mon.- Sat. noon-midnight, Sun. noon-4pm.

U: Covent Garden.

A

Hugely successful, this long restaurant is furnished with much mahogany and brass, and polo sticks and sporting pictures on the walls, owner Brian Stein's other interests. The menu includes grilled meat (a lot of it), but also has specialities like roast suckling pig with braised red cabbage and honeyed apples, or honey-roast duck breast with shallot confit. Starters tend to the international—roast corn, snapper and mushroom chowder, asparagus risotto with rocket and goat's cheese; puddings move around the world. Service is terrific, and very friendly, which explains the large number of regular customers in what is a mainly tourist area. They have a special children's menu. Expect to pay around £18 per person without wine for a three-course meal. The 2-course pre-theatre menu (Mon.-Sat. 5.30pm-7.30pm) is £8.95 incuding coffee. **Also at 52 Fulham Rd, SW3, 0171-581 0025.**

The Poetry Place

CAFÉ

22 Betterton St, WC2, 0171-420 9880

Mon.-Fri. 11am-11pm, Sat. 6.30pm-11pm. U: Covent Garden.

No cards.

Small, rather esoteric licensed café belonging to the Poetry Society which publishes the Poetry Review and generally encourages, well...poetry. The café is simple and tiny, four or five tables on the ground floor, but the food is well cooked as in freshly baked leek tartlets coming with crisp vegetables and salads at £3.90, and there are good cakes to be had. Newspapers and the friendly atmosphere favour the single or the silent. Modern jazz helps you relax. Every Saturday from 7.30pm-11.30pm there are poetry readings, live jazz and jam sessions (£3 entry).

Punjab

INDIAN

80-82 Neal St, WC2, 0171-836 9787

Lunch & Dinner daily.

U: Tottenham Court Rd.

A

An old stager on the northernmost outskirts of Covent Garden, Punjab under Mr

Maan (grandson of the Mr Maan who originally opened here in 1951), is a delightful, deservedly popular restaurant with old prints and pictures on the walls in an old-fashioned décor. The cuisine sticks firmly in the Punjab, producing some excellent surprises, as in pumpkin on a puri, or the Punjabi baby pumpkin with spices. Tandoori cooking is a major attraction here, with the marinades working particularly well to produce definite tastes. Be guided by the waiters, as many of the French do who come here, encouraged by the Eurostar campaign in France which trumpets the virtues of the Punjab.

Sofra

MIDDLE EASTERN

36 TAVISTOCK ST, WC2, 0171-240 3773

Open daily noon-midnight. U: Covent Garden.

Owner Huseyin Ozer has created a mini empire with his Turkish restaurants and cafés. Here in Covent Garden, the décor is simple but effective: white-washed walls, lots of greenery and polished wood. The food is similarly impressive and genuine, as in a parsley salad, good falafal, manca (spinach in fresh yogurt with garlic), artichoke heart salad with beans, hummus and taramasalata as starters or part of the mezze. Here too, you'll find the tiny lahma, spicier ancestor of the pizza. Many of the main courses are grilled; otherwise go for one of the casseroles—incik (large knuckle of lamb cooked with its own sauce), or seafood. Desserts are sweet; service is charming. The wine list has a number of very good Turkish wines, though they are not cheap. And it all takes place in the house where Thomas de Quincy wrote *Confessions of an English Opium Eater*. The 'Healthy Lunch/Dinner' for two at £9.95 per person consists of eleven or so different hot and cold mixed mezes. **Also at 18 Shepherd St, W1, 0171-493 3320; 1 St. Christopher's Pl, W1, 0171-224 4080; 17 Charing Cross Rd, WC2, 0171-930 6090.**

EUSTON

Diwana Bhel Poori House

INDIAN VEGETARIAN

121 DRUMMOND ST, NW1, 0171-387 5556

Daily noon-11.30pm. U: Euston.

Adding to the choice in this area is this long-established popular vegetarian restaurant, specialists in south Indian dishes where the pooris are particularly good. Either order a selection of starters like bhel poori, samosas (excellent) and onion bhajis, or go for the full buffet lunch, at £3.95 for all you can eat, one of London's great bargains. Take your own alcohol.

Great Nepalese

INDIAN

48 EVERSHOLT ST, NW1, 0171-388 6737

Lunch & Dinner daily. U: Euston.

Another of the 'little India' restaurants, but this time the inspiration is Himalayan. Tandoori, chicken tikka, good mutton, fish masalas and curries are all on the menu, and there's a Nepalase section for the adventurous who want to savour a different emphasis. In fact, the Nepalese set meal at £10.95 is a great introduction and offers a new sensation for those brought up on the ubiquitous tandoori-cooked food.

FINCHLEY

Two Brothers Fish Restaurant

BRITISH

297-303 REGENT'S PARK RD, N3, 0181-346 0469

Lunch & Dinner Tues.-Sat.

U: Finchley Central.

The variety and freshness of the fish and its careful frying in batter (or matzo meal if preferred) make the journey to north London worthwhile. Add near-perfect chips, and the pilgrimage becomes compulsory for devotees of this great English institution. Superb white fish soup is English too; Arbroath smokies (a sort of cured haddock) in cream are Scottish; oysters are Irish, herbed sardines with garlic are . . . you get the idea. All this plus decent wines (including the owners' own from the Dordogne) in a large cheerful room. No booking but worth a short wait to eat like this for under £15.

GOLDERS GREEN

Laurent

MIDDLE EASTERN
428 FINCHLEY RD, NW2, 0171-794 3603
Lunch & Dinner Mon.-Sat. U: Golders Green.

Five different varieties of couscous only are on offer here from vegetarian at £6.60 to the royale at £10.25, which along with vegetables includes lamb chop, brochette and spicy merguez. Owner/chef Laurent Farrugia does a wonderful job of this well-known but frequently under-rated Middle Eastern dish, souped up with hot harissa. You can only start with brik à l'oeuf-a deep-fried wafer-thin sheet of pastry folded across an egg, and finish with crêpes Suzette or ices, but couscous is the star. Wash it down with a North African wine if feeling adventurous.

HACKNEY

Shanghai

CHINESE
41 KINGSLAND HIGH ST, E8, 0171-254 2878
Daily noon-11pm. BR: Dalston Kingsland.

A

Something of a surprise this, a Chinese restaurant in a former thoroughly British jellied eel-pie-and-mash restaurant, but it just goes to show the cosmopolitan nature of London's eating scene these days. After shopping or just looking in Ridley Road, one of the classic East End markets, a few dim sum, served throughout the day, or perhaps king prawns in hot bean sauce or deep fried shredded beef with chillis will hit the spot. Starters are around £2-£3, main courses £5-£6. And all served in the beautifully traditionally tiled interior of this former working man's restaurant.

HAMPSTEAD

Café des Arts

FRENCH
82 HAMPSTEAD HIGH ST, NW3, 0171-435 3608
Mon.-Sat. noon-11.30pm, Sun. to 11pm.
U: Hampstead.

A ☎

A good neighbourhood restaurant in an area curiously bereft of decent eating places, the Café des Arts is really a cosy set of two rooms, still wood-panelled and with changing displays of art for sale on the walls. Both the menu and the prices suit the local Hampstead clientele-starters from £3.75-£5.75, main dishes £8.75-£11.75 (though side orders around £3 to £4 are a bit steep), and desserts at £4.50. Surf the world with swordfish carpaccio with grilled aubergine salad and sesame-and-lemon dressing, or duck magret to start, then sautéed sea bream with potatoes mashed with olive oil and a stew of peppers, tomato, mint and lemon, or lamb and broad bean fricasée. Desserts run the safe route of mousse, tarts such as lemon and almond, or pears poached in red wine. A reasonably priced, reasonably thought-out wine list completes the picture. All in all, this is worth making a journey for.

Louis Pâtisserie

CAFÉ
32 HEATH ST, NW3, 0171-435 9908
Daily 9am-6pm. U: Hampstead.
No cards.

Wonderful continental atmosphere at this coffee shop with a tiny area in front of a window laden with cakes which serves as a shop, and a small number of tables in a little room behind. Coffee is good, pastries are first-rate, overheard conversation is invariably interesting.

ISLINGTON

Afghan Kitchen

AFGHAN
35 ISLINGTON GREEN, N1, 0171-359 8019
Lunch & Dinner Tues.-Sat. U: Angel.
No cards. ☎

This ethnic restaurant in Islington, minimally decorated with cream walls brings in the local trendies in droves. The limited menu means that the four meat dishes and four vegetable dishes for around £4.50 are freshly prepared; try lamb and spinach. All dishes come with rice or naan in large portions. Drink house wine or green tea. Service is brisk.

Japanese Canteen

JAPANESE
394 ST. JOHN ST, EC1, 0171-833 3222
Lunch Mon.-Sat., Dinner nightly. U:Angel

The minimalistic interior with benches and communal wooden tables fits the straightforward and inexpensive Japanese food served in this friendly canteen. You can get a Donburi lunchbox for £2.95, or eat sushi or tempura from the same price upwards. Noodle soup is £3.95 and all this can be washed down with Japanese beers like dark or light Asahi or hot sake. Above the Canteen is The World Café, where you can surf the Internet while having refreshments. **Also at 5 Thayer Street, W1, 0171 -487 5505; and 305 Portobello Road,. W10, 0181- 968 9988.**

Patisserie Bliss

CAFÉ

428 St John St, EC1, 0171-837 3720

Mon.-Fri. 8am-6pm, Sat., Sun. 9am-6pm. U: Angel.

No cards.

Just below the Angel and so a little out of the way for the visitor to Camden Passage, Bliss is a great local venue with a regular clientele. Islington residents thrive on mini quiches on excellent light pastry, cakes and coffee. When the chain restaurants along Upper Street fill up and you despair of a friendly face, this is the place to head for.

Upper Street Fish Shop

BRITISH

324 Upper St, N1, 0171-359 1401

Tues.-Sat. 11.30am-2.15pm, Mon.-Fri. 6pm-10.15pm. U: Angel.

No cards.

Definitely a fry above the rest, this family-run restaurant has been serving fish and chips for some 18 years now to those taking away and those eating in. In a wood-panelled interior with blackboards announcing daily specials, you eat tempting starters like fish soup or deep-fried mussels on a skewer, battered and deep-fried fresh cod, haddock or halibut, depending on the daily catch (from £7 to £10), and homemade desserts like crumbles or treacle tart. Take your own wine.

White Onion

FRENCH/MEDITERRANEAN

297 Upper St, N1, 0171-359 3533

Lunch Mon.-Sun., Dinner Mon.-Sat. U: Angel

The White Onion has joined the Green Olive and the Red Pepper (see Maida Vale) for a veritable Mediterranean mix, which is what, naturally, the place majors in. It's a simply decorated place, with good grills paving the way. Try dishes where the mix is rich and unusual, like foie gras, mozzarella and rocket salad, and if you can, don't miss the lamb which comes with a potato ravioli niçoise, as good and as interesting as it sounds. The wine list concentrates on France. Set lunch 2 courses £10.50, 3 courses £13.50.

KENSINGTON

The Orangery

CAFÉ

Kensington Palace, W8, 0171-376 0239

Oct-Mar: daily 10am-5.30pm, Apr-Sep: daily 10am-6pm. U: High St Kensington.

Just the place after a stroll through Kensington Gardens. Good home baking makes teas particularly tempting here and the blue-and-white china it's served on is delightful, just like your aunt might use. Otherwise it's a useful stop for a light lunch, and the setting is magnificent—a high-ceilinged, classical building that is part of Kensington Palace.

Sticky Fingers

AMERICAN

1a Phillimore Gdns, W8, 0171-938 5338

Mon.-Sat. noon-11.30pm, Sun. to 11pm. U: High St Kensington.

Owned by Bill Wyman, Sticky Fingers is covered with glorious memorabilia from the Stone's tours worldwide, from old instruments and record covers to Mr Wyman's own photographs of his ex-colleagues. It's a great hamburger joint, particularly good for families. The menu stretches to guacamole and tortilla chips, salads, specials like grilled fish of the day and puddings like Brown Sugar (of course), apple pie or ice cream. Drinks cover cocktails, sodas and juices. Friendly, young staff work hard and fast. Music isn't as overwhelming as in the Hard Rock or Planet Hollywood.

KILBURN

Organic Café

26 Lonsdale Rd, NW6, 0171-372 1232

Tues.- Sun. 9.30am-10.30pm, Mon. noon-10.30pm. U: Queen's Park

No cards.

It started small but it's become immensely popular with locals, who were presumably the only people who could find it, tucked away as it is in a Victorian mews building. With the current mania for all things pure, it had to arrive, but its popularity is really due to the fact that it's simple and good and organic. It runs from continental breakfast, or the fry-up variety to sandwiches and daily specials. Service is slow, so take something uplifting to read.

KNIGHTSBRIDGE

Chicago Rib Shack

AMERICAN

1 RAPHAEL ST, KNIGHTSBRIDGE GN, SW7, 0171-581 5595

Mon.-Sat. 11.45am-11.45pm, Sun. noon-11pm. U: Knightsbridge.

A

Just off Knightsbridge, this large American-style restaurant is popular with singles after work (happy hour 5.30pm-7.30pm, Monday to Saturday), and families at most other times. It's impeccably run, atmospheric and offers a good menu. Try the barbecued meat for which the restaurant is best known; it's grilled over apple wood in specially imported ovens. Barbecued beef sandwich is great; rack of baby back ribs is tenderer than the more usual spare ribs and rightly popular. Otherwise the Combination Platter offers ribs, chicken and barbecued beef. Every year around the end of February and beginning of March they showcase Britain's soul performers. But at all times, it's noisy, colourful and fun and the food is genuine.

The Fifth Floor Café

MODERN BRITISH

HARVEY NICHOLS, KNIGHTSBRIDGE, SW1, 0171-235 5250

Mon.-Sat. 11am-10.00pm, Sun. noon-6pm. U: Knightsbridge.

A ☎

Harvey Nichols's mouth-watering fifth floor is devoted to food—either consumed in the designer restaurant, bar or café, or taken home from the store in smart monochrome carrier bags. Customers are disgorged by lift or escalator into the bustling market place which can be deserted at night although bar and restaurant are always humming. You can't book a table at the café and may have to queue at peak times for light lunchtime dishes of, say, twice-baked goat's cheese soufflé, and salads suitable for lunching ladies, although heartier dishes like calf's liver with olive oil enriched mashed potato are more fattening than you might expect given the clientele. And the plate of chips is wonderful. Puds are good. Prices aren't insubstantial for a café, (although they're a snip compared to the restaurant). In the evenings it's quieter and atmospherically sky-lit. Either side of lunch it's also just the place for taking the weight off tired feet when there's morning refreshments and a splendid afternoon tea at £12.50.

Le Métro

MODERN BRITISH

28 BASIL ST, SW3, 0171-589 6286

Mon.-Sat. 7.30am-10.30pm. U: Knightsbridge.

A

Le Métro began as a wine bar, made famous because it was the first to offer very high quality wines by the glass. Then, with its top food, supervised by chef Philip Britten at The Capital Hotel (see Restaurant section), it became known equally as a small restaurant. It continues to uphold both traditions very well indeed, and this is still one of the best places for interesting, good wines, beautifully kept, 50 of them served by the glass. Used by L'Hôtel guests (see Hotel section), it kicks off the day with breakfast to 10.30am, then has a menu running from noon to 10.30pm. When the menu states 'A seriously good chicken liver paté', you'd better believe it, the chefs know what they're doing here. There's something for every taste, from a basic sausage and mash (£6.90) to more sophisticated chargrilled monkfish on white beans, garlic and tomato (£7.95). Desserts are to slim for; otherwise you can go for afternoon tea.

Minema Café

CAFÉ

43 KNIGHTSBRIDGE, SW1, 0171-235 6000

Mon.-Sat. 9am-9pm. U: Hyde Park Corner.

A

Try a filled baguette like a BLT with mayo, pastrami on rye with sauerkraut and Gruyère cheese, or oak-smoked salmon with lemon, capers, onion and crème fraîche, salad, or a wicked chocolate brownie with whipped cream in this friendly goldfish bowl of a café, next to the Minema cinema. Or stand at a table toying with a cake and sipping a cappuccino, watching the fashionable world go by. Prices are reasonable, particularly for this neck of the woods.

Pâtisserie Valerie

CAFÉ

215 OLD BROMPTON RD, SW3, 0171-823 9971

Open Mon.-Fri. 7.30am-7.30pm, Sat. 8am-7pm, Sun. 8.30am-6pm. U: Knightsbridge.

A

These excellent pâtisseries have expanded beyond their original Soho branch and long may they go on doing so. They began in 1926 with coffee and pastries, and it is these that many people come for. And so they should—wonderfully light millefeuilles, rich gâteaux and tarts dripping with fruit await you. Brompton Road is the largest of the Pâtisserie Valeries and offers breakfast, sandwiches through the day and hot dishes like warm goats' cheese salad (from £6-£8). **Also at 44 Old Compton St, W1, 0171-437 3466; 105 Marylebone High St, W1, 0171-935 6240 (the old Maison Sagne); the Royal Institute of British Architects (RIBA), 66 Portland Pl, W1, 0171-631 0467; 8 Russell St, WC2, 0171-240 0064.**

Pizza on the Park

PIZZERIA

11 KNIGHTSBRIDGE, SW1, 0171-235 5550

Daily 8am-midnight. U: Knightsbridge.

A

Two reasons to come here: first the range of pizzas served in the spacious, elegant restaurant looking out onto Knightsbridge traffic but sufficiently far away to feel superior rather than overwhelmed, and secondly the basement jazz room which offers some of the best music and acts in town. Pizzas range from Margherita to fresh prawns, mozzarella and tomato. It's also a first-rate place for breakfast, setting you up for a foray into the Knightsbridge shops. Downstairs is not just jazz; they often have cabaret style acts, too. Prices around £16 per person. Also great Sunday jazz brunch.

MAIDA VALE

Café Laville

CAFÉ

453 EDGWARE RD, W9, 0171-706 2620

Daily 10am-10.30pm. U: Edgware Rd/Warwick Ave.

Straddling the canal at Little Venice, there are wonderful views of the canal boats gently bobbing on the Regent's Park Canal from this modern, small café. It's a great place for a leisurely weekend breakfast; otherwise heartier evening meals follow the fashionable Mediterranean mode. Breakfasts are around £6-£7; main meals around £25-£30 for two.

The Green Olive

ITALIAN

5 WARWICK PL, W9, 0171-289 2469

Lunch Sun., Dinner nightly. U: Warwick Ave.

The perfect rustic chic neighbourhood restaurant—decor is cosy bare brick plus crisp linen—serving bold country-style Italian food. The new chef hails from Lombardy and is keen to experiment. A hugely generous bread basket including ultra-thin Sardinian unleavened bread and good olive oil is a great welcoming gesture. Carpaccio of tuna with lime and corinader oil was meltingly good, as was the tenderest quail wrapped in speck with roast red peppers. Good, hearty mains include roast cod with a startling squid ink polenta, saffron and mushroom soup, and lamb shank with aubergine caviar and oven-roasted tomatoes. Interesting Italian wines from small producers and enthusiastic staff.

The Red Pepper

ITALIAN

8 FORMOSA ST, W9, 0171-266 2708

Lunch Sun.-Fri., Dinner nightly. U: Warwick Ave.

Justifiably hugely popular (opt for the marginally less cramped upstairs when booking), for the superb ultra-thin crust pizzas baked in a wood-fired oven with gorgeous fresh tomato sauce and simple picante toppings—the basilico with masses of fresh basil and a good wedge of buffalo mozzarella is excellent.

Interesting anitpasti choices include octopus salad with French beans and roasted onions or cos lettuce with Parmesan sauce. Don't neglect the pasta dishes which are also carefully conceived: squid ink taglioni with scallops and saffron was a good choice. A sophisticated version of much-maligned tiramisù was well complemented with bitter expresso sauce. All served in a convivial dining room in minimal white and rust red.

MARYLEBONE

Back to Basics

FISH

21A FOLEY ST, W1, 0171-436 2181

Lunch & Dinner Mon.-Fri. U: Oxford Circus.

Small fish restaurant in a pleasant area growing in popularity—this is the rag trade section just north of Soho and bound to be prime fashionable territory soon. So 'discover' this excellent café-cum-restaurant which opened in 1997 and where fish is the order of the day. It's small and crowded inside with the 'Catch of the Day' chalked up on blackboards. Cod, skate, mami mami, plaice are regularly on offer here, with dishes such as bream with basil, chillies, garlic and olive oil at £12.95, and sea bass with spring onions and ginger at £13.50 the most expensive dishes on a menu which majors on freshly caught fish simply cooked.

R & K Stanley's

BRITISH

6 LITTLE PORTLAND ST, W1, 0171-462 0099

Mon.-Sat Lunch & Dinner. U: Oxford Circus.

Done out as a working man's café with red leather banquette seating and booths running down one side, aluminium chairs and tables down the middle, R & K Stanley's is, in fact, a very superior sausage restaurant which also celebrates British beers, overseen by Robert Gutteridge formerly at Alfred's who own this new venture (see Restaurant section). But sausages and mash like you've not eaten elsewhere. Tuck into game sausages with wine-scented cabbage, mash made pungent with mustard, glazed parsnips and crispy pancetta, or going a little mad here with fusion fever, try Thai sausages with Thai noodles. Every taste will be met in sausages which stretch the imagination. Great fun; long may it thrive.

Spighetta

ITALIAN

43 BLANDFORD ST, W1, 0171-486 7340

Lunch & Dinner daily. U: Baker St.

Behind Spighetta are some pretty good names, including Giorgio Locatelli, chef and part-owner of Zafferano (see Restaurant section). But there's a world of difference, for here the emphasis is on simple dishes, particularly great pizzas cooked in a wood-burning oven, which is now obligatory for anyone claiming authenticity. Spighetta has got it absolutely right. The basement dining room is warm and welcoming, with a gorgeous terracotta tiled floor, white walls with some interesting ceramic lights, wooden chairs and tables. Starters include classics like carpaccio of tuna and bresaola with rocket. If pizza is your thing, look no further. Here they come on thin, fragile pizza dough, with lightly cooked toppings that make good use of the conventional ingredients of mozzarella, tomatoes, hams and mushrooms. Those wanting something else can choose pasta, equally as well cooked as in linguine alle vongole.

Topkapi

TURKISH

25 MARYLEBONE HIGH ST, W1, 0171-486 1872

Daily noon-midnight. U: Baker St.

Reliable Turkish restaurant in Marylebone High Street, full of pictures and colourful artefacts. You go in past a cold counter where the hors d'oeuvres are prepared, to a narrow room (try to get a table at the back) with a wood-effect gas fire. We've been going for years and the only thing that seems to change is the waiting staff (and these not often). Mixed mezze remains an excellent bet with stuffed vine leaves, cacik, hummus, taramasalata and the like, all freshly prepared. Good chargrills follow: mainly lamb but chicken too. Accompaniments—rice, onions, tomatoes—are fresh and well cooked. Saslik kebab (thinly sliced lamb marinated and cooked with onions and green peppers) is still a favourite. Desserts are the usual very sweet, very sticky variety. Turkish coffee is the real thing.

MAYFAIR

Condotti

ITALIAN
4 MILL ST, W1, 0171-499 1308
Mon.-Sat. 11.30am-midnight, Sun. noon-11pm. U: Bond St.

A

Cool, modern design with good art on the walls and an open-plan kitchen at this useful pizzeria off Conduit Street. It serves traditional pizzas on a tomato and mozzarella base (Margherita, American hot etc) though there is the occasional flight of fancy (King Edward, a potato base and four cheeses which sinks anyone with less than a country appetite). Prices are reasonable, around £5 to £6 and there are some other dishes like Scottish smoked salmon, and salads. Service is friendly.

Sotheby's Café

MODERN BRITISH
34 NEW BOND ST, W1, 0171-408 5077
Mon.-Fri. 9.30am-5pm, Sun noon-4pm. U: Bond St.

A ☎

Definitely a croissant above the rest, Sotheby's Café scores for its cool decor in a cramped location on the ground floor of the great auction house. Banquette seating, black-and-white colours echoed in the glorious blown-up fashion photographs of Cecil Beaton, and a light menu suits the movers and shakers of the art world who gather here to discuss their purchases, as well as the ladies-who-lunch in from Bond Street's designer shops. It's not cheap, but would anything in Sotheby's be? Try spiced parsnip soup with yoghurt (£4.50), or char-grilled lamb with a warm salad of chickpeas, feta and mint (£12.95). And of course, there's the Lobster club sandwich so beloved of Sothebey's owner/chairman, Mr Alfred A Taubman (£10.50). Book for lunch. Great place for tea, also.

NOTTING HILL GATE

Books for Cooks

CAFÉ
4 BLENHEIM CRESCENT, W11, 0171-221 1992
Bookshop open Mon.-Sat. 9.30am-6pm. Café open for lunch Mon-Fri 12.30pm-3pm, Sat. for lunch and tea. U: Ladbroke Grove.

A ☎

Walk into this crammed book shop (around 8,000 titles in stock all relating to food and drink) and the smell of garlic or baking will take you to the back and a tiny café and test kitchen. Recipes come from books on the shelves and the idea was instigated by food writer, Annie Bell. You also have the pleasure of sitting in a tiny room that might double as someone's home with the odd customer leaning over you to take a book off the shelves. You'll pay around £10 for two courses and eat well. You must book. If there are any cakes left, they serve afternoon tea, but that's a bit hit and miss.

Café Med

MEDITERRANEAN
184A KENSINGTON PARK RD, W11, 0171-221 1150
Mon.-Sat. noon-11.30pm, Sun. to 10.30pm. U: Ladbroke Grove/Notting Hill Gate.

A

Café Med is spreading its exotic wings far and wide, but this, the original one, is still pulling in the customers with its would-be-North African decor and fun artefacts. Majoring in the open grill technique, best bets like lamb fillets with sharply marinated peppers or rib of beef with mustard aioli for two come with thin, crisp fries. Desserts are predictable, but nontheless good, like baked cheesecake with fresh fruit or the ubiquitous lemon tart with a dollop of crème fraîche. Expect to pay around £20 per person. **Also at 2 Hollywood Rd, SW10, 0171-823 3355; 320 Goldhawk Rd, W6, 0181-741 1994; 22-25 Dean St, W1, 0171-287 9007; The Blenheim, 21 Loudon Rd, NW8, 0171-625 1222.**

Calzone

ITALIAN
2A KENSINGTON PARK RD, W11, 0171-243 2003
Daily 10am-midnight. U: Notting Hill Gate.

VISA MasterCard ☎

Small, glass-fronted, fish-bowl-like pizzeria on the corner of Kensington Park Road and Pembridge Road handy for Portobello market. It's known for thin-based traditional pizzas, and fresh, well-seasoned ingredients at reasonable prices. Apart from the traditional, try Inferno (with chillis), or frutti di mare (with mussels, calamari and tuna), all on a tomato and mozzarella base. Starters include antipasti, or perhaps chilled grilled vegetables in olive oil, and there are pastas too. **Also at 35**

Upper St, N1, 0171-704 0111; 66 Heath St, NW3, 0171-794 6775; 335 Fulham Rd, SW10, 0171-352 9797 (this latest one is particularly stylish).

Costas Fish Restaurant

BRITISH/FISH AND CHIPS
18 HILLGATE ST, W8, 0171-727 4310
Tues.-Sat. noon-2pm & 5.30pm-10pm.
U: Notting Hill Gate.
No cards.

Highly rated fish-and-chip place with its related Greek restaurant, Costa's Grill, next door. They've been feeding locals for decades in this small room on lightly battered and fried fish and crisp chips, plus those wonderfully British green mushy peas. Due to the Greek influence, there are offerings like houmous, calamares and baklava. Reckon around £12 a head.

The Cow Pub

MODERN BRITISH
89 WESTBOURNE PARK RD, W2, 0171-221 0021
Lunch Sun., Dinner Tues.-Sun.
U: Westbourne Park..

Unfortunate name you might think, given the ban on British beef, but nobody is put off, judging from the buzz in this perennially popular simple dining room above the Cow Pub. It's an entirely separate venture from Tom Conran's Cow below, now with Francesca Melman at the helm. Her credentials include the River Café and Alastair Little Lancaster Road, so you know you're in good hands. The menu changes often, and is a mix of cultures. Try dishes like chicken and foie gras terrine with onion confit accompanied by toasted brioche, and a delightful belly of pork braised with pak choy, soy sauce and spring onions. Great puddings of the true British variety like gooseberry fool round off a thoroughly enjoyable experience.

Geales

BRITISH/FISH AND CHIPS
2 FARMER ST, W8, 0171-727 7969
Lunch & Dinner Tues.-Sat.
U: Notting Hill Gate.

In one of London's most fashionable areas, this die-hard fish-and-chip restaurant remains resolutely old-fashioned. Furnishings are cottagey, and superbly battered fish is fried the northern way in beef fat for a crunchier covering than usual (vegetarians take note). The pop star inhabitants of Holland Park, like Van Morrison are reputed to eat here, or so the photographs of the customers hanging on the walls suggest. Eccentricities such as the extra charge for a dollop of tartare sauce and 15p cover charge, are endearing or irritating depending on your disposition. Steady the buffs with time-honoured puds such as apple crumble and cream.

Lisboa Patisserie

CAFÉ
57 GOLBORNE RD, W10, 0181-968 5242
Daily 8am-8pm. U: Ladbroke Grove.
No cards

Great Portuguese deli complete with Portuguese maritime murals on the walls and a café serving excellent espresso and authentic pastries. Try the custard tart for a real treat, but avoid Saturdays if you can when it's crammed with visitors to Portobello Road market.

Prince Bonaparte

INTERNATIONAL
80 CHEPSTOW RD, W2, 0171-229 5912
Lunch Sat., Sun., Dinner nightly.
U: Notting Hill Gate.
No cards.

A large former pub built around a U-shaped bar, with terracotta-painted walls, tables beside the windows and at the back, people hanging out at the bar building up the temperature even further in this crowded, well-patronised place. One of that breed of pubs that became restaurants when an enthusiastic new young band of restaurateurs turned up, it can be noisy, but it's friendly and a good place to drink if you don't want to eat. Dishes are chalked up on the blackboard, but if you get there late you're likely to see a lot of blank spaces where they've run out. Everything is freshly prepared and modish ingredients like squid, and homemade pastas, are cooked imaginatively. Expect to pay around £20 per person.

The Westbourne

P MEDITERRANEAN
101 WESTBOURNE PARK VILLAS, W2,
0171-221 1332
Lunch & Dinner daily. U: Royal Oak.

The epitome of boho trustafarian West London gastro-pubs: incredibly laid-back with masses of comfy bohemian chic, huge leather chesterfields, roaring open fire, beat-up but interesting furniture and masses of old cookery books. Outside are burners and high stools so it's possible to pose nonchalantly even when the temperature is cool. Honest, simple food in generous portions keeps punters extremely content: roast pheasant with red cabbage and mash and a rich red wine jus, fish cassoulet with monkfish, mussels and lentils, plus an extraordinarily large and excellent lemon tart. Notable beer and wine list.

PICCADILLY CIRCUS

Fountain Restaurant

INTERNATIONAL
FORTNUM & MASON, 181 PICCADILLY, W1,
0171-973 4140
Mon.-Sat. 9am-6pm. U: Piccadilly Circus.

It's amazing the number of Londoners who don't know this restaurant at the back of Fortnum & Mason. The decor is pretty, with colonial scenes painted on the walls and the feeling of a summer pavilion with light wooden chairs and light colours. All day long it offers a huge menu, from sandwiches and ice creams to salads, and attracts well-heeled visitors laden down with items from Fortnum's food halls. Service is good.

Hard Rock Café

AMERICAN
50 OLD PARK LANE, W1, 0171-629 0382
Daily noon-1am. U: Hyde Park Corner.

What can one say about the Hard Rock Café? It must be one of the most famous names in the world, if the ever-present queues are anything to go by. Founded, according to legend and constant publicity, by two Americans who couldn't find a good burger in London, it manages to hold its rivals at bay. It's due to its top location just by Hyde Park Corner, the decor—great memorabilia on the walls—the buzz and noise, the absolutely necessary souvenir T-shirts and good hamburgers. They come as burger platters, all with french fries, lettuce, tomato, onion, pickle and coleslaw 'Our claim to fame', from HRC's country-charbroiled burger ('a recipe from the Old South') to the downhome double burger. Make sure you eat upstairs; downstairs is crowded and noisy and if you get a table near the kitchen, it's just too busy.

La Madeleine

CAFÉ
5 VIGO ST, W1, 0171-734 8353
Mon.-Sat. 8am-10pm. U: Piccadilly Circus.

This is a real local's spot, and much loved. But because it's in a small street running between Regent Street and Bond Street it is curiously overlooked by visitors. Seek it out; the pastries are some of the best in London, a tempting sight in the front windows. At the back more substantial food is served and it's wonderfully located for a shopper's lunch.

Planet Hollywood

AMERICAN
13 COVENTRY ST, W1, 0171-287 1000
Mon.-Sat. 11.30am-1am, Sun.11am-10.30pm.
U: Piccadilly Circus.

One of the stalwarts on the theme scene, but with owners of the likes of Arnold Schwarzenegger, Sylvester Stallone, Bruce Willis and Demi Moore, restaurateur Robert Earl and film producer Keith Barish, this restaurant could hardly fail. Imagine a huge space with the barrel of James Bond's gun on one side, a screen projecting film clips on another, a star-studded sky, palm trees of immense proportions and memorabilia that includes R2D2 and C3PO, Harrison Ford's whip from *Indiana Jones and the Last Crusade*, and Sylvester Stallone's motorbike from *Judge Dread*. Think big—and we mean big—portions of burger platters, chips, sandwiches, salads, garlic prawns, grilled platters, and pizzas, not to mention The Terminator, Goldfinger or Dirty Harry to drink and you'll see why. And that's before you decide to buy a souvenir.

Eating in Museums and Galleries

Things have improved in London's museums and galleries from the days when you were lucky to get a sandwich and a cup of tea in a small room tucked away behind the main museum spaces. Try the **Sainsbury Wing Brasserie** at the National Gallery, Trafalgar Sq, WC2, 0171-839 3321, and look out onto the Square. The small **Museum of Garden History**, housed in the old church of St. Mary-at-Lambeth, Lambeth Palace, Rd, SE1, 0171-261 1891, has a small café serving snacks. It's very attractive in summer when you can take your tea and cakes outside to the tiny churchyard with its seventeenth-century herb garden. **The Victoria & Albert Museum**, Cromwell Rd, SW7, 0171-938 8500, has a well-run restaurant.

The restaurant at the **Tate Gallery**, Millbank, SW1, 0171-887 8877, goes periodically in and out of favour and fashion. Whatever the state of the kitchen, it's a wonderful room with Rex Whistler's famous mural on one wall and a wine list which is becoming less legendary as time goes on, but is still well worth perusing. And finally, the excellent restaurant at the **Royal Academy of Arts**, Burlington House, Piccadilly, W1, 0171-287 0752, remains a favourite. At popular exhibitions it can get very crowded, but is somewhat relieved by a new, smaller coffee bar, serving tea, coffee, sandwiches and cakes.

Royal Academy Restaurant

BRITISH
ROYAL ACADEMY, BURLINGTON HOUSE, W1, 0171-439 7438
Daily 10am-5.30pm.
U: Green Park/Piccadilly Circus.

You'll find the café/restaurant at the back of the Royal Academy. Beloved by the RA's country members who 'make a day of it' by doing the exhibition and then sitting over lunch, it serves good food from a self-service area. There's always a homemade soup of the day with fresh bread and butter. Salads come with a quiche or a pie perhaps while hot dishes might include salmon escalope with saffron mayonaise, a pasta, and a casserole. Desserts attract people all day for a calorie blow-out and coffee. It's all very civilised in a large room decorated with murals by past members. Expect to pay around £15 for three courses, but in fact you can have as little or as much as you like.

The Wren at St. James's Church

VEGETARIAN
35 JERMYN ST, SW1, 0171-437 9419
Daily 9am-5pm. U: Green Park/Piccadilly Circus.
No cards.

This split-level, airy place works well for breakfast, while at lunch or for an early supper there's always a soup and casserole, perhaps with jacket potato or brown rice. It concentrates on organic food and is proud of it. Excellent cakes go with herbal teas. In the summer you can eat outside in the peaceful church courtyard. And if you're there at lunchtime, try to catch a concert in the church; they are first-rate and should be supported.

PIMLICO

Chimes

BRITISH
26 CHURTON ST, SW1, 0171-821 7456
Daily Lunch & Dinner. U: Victoria.

The decor is rather ad hoc—mis-matching wooden tables, odd old photographs on the walls, cider-making paraphernalia—but it works charmingly in this delightful, small wood-floored restaurant. And the food is a cut above average, too, well worth making a special journey for. The menu is rather coyly divided up into sections like The Larder—country mushroom crumbles (mushroom caps filled with savoury stuffing and served with chopped hazelnuts), or black pudding with creamy Stilton sauce; The Oven—individual pot pies and casseroles from traditional steak and mushroom to pheasant, orange and walnut cooked in port wine; The Garden which fooled us a little as it consists of dishes like oak-smoked chicken served with soured cream and chives, Chimes salad for vegetarians; The Cupboard which includes crunchy topped ratatouille, jacket potatoes and vegetables of the day. Never mind, their heart is definitely in the right place here. If you're feeling adventurous, try a flagon cider, but do take their advice on everything. They told us that dandelion and burdock was an acquired taste, and boy, were they right.

The Footstool Restaurant

MODERN BRITISH

ST. JOHN'S SMITH SQUARE, SW1, 0171-222 2779

Mon.-Fri. 11.30am-3pm & evenings when concerts are held. U: Westminster.

A

A little off the tourist's beaten track, this basement restaurant below St. John's Smith Square is a godsend to local office workers. Originally the church crypt, it has brick archways and walls usually covered with an art exhibition. There's a good lunchtime wine bar buffet with pies, salads and hot dishes. If you're going to one of the concerts here, then it's ideal for a meal before or after the event, and you'll probably be rubbing shoulders with the musicians you've just been listening to.

The Little Bay Bar and Eatery

BRITISH

147 LUPUS ST, SW1, 0171-233 9828

Lunch Mon.-Sun., Dinner Mon.-Sat. U: Pimlico.

A

Peter Ilic is the master of good inexpensive eating places, and this one is no exception. Located in mainly residential Pimlico, his fixed-price policy of all starters at £1.65, mains at £3.85 and desserts at £1.25 means you can dine off the likes of moules marinières or salmon mousse, cod with crusted topping and duck en croûte and apple pie for under a tenner. It's friendly and relaxed and though it's not gourmet cuisine, it's served in a bright setting with stained glass windows and jazz on Friday and Saturday nights.

PRIMROSE HILL

The Engineer

PUB/MEDITERRANEAN

65 GLOUCESTER AVE, NW1, 0171-722 0950

Lunch & Dinner daily. U: Chalk Farm.

Most successful bar and restaurant with a fresh and enthusiastic feel to it, though can become crowded thanks to its popularity. For those who want to eat away from a press of young drinkers, there's the advantage of a separate dining area, contiguous with the bar. Enjoyment of the tasty, trendy Mediterranean food is enhanced by white tablecloths, good lighting and world-wide wines (from nearby wine merchant Bibendum). A meal costs around £15 for a couple of courses and drinks. In the bar, simpler dishes such as bruschettas, tapas, potato skins and root vegetable crisps make excellent snacks.

The Lansdowne

PUB/MEDITERRANEAN

90 GLOUCESTER AVE, NW1, 0171-483 0409

Pub Mon. 6pm-11pm, Tues.-Sat. 11am-11pm, Sun. noon-3pm & 7pm-11pm. Lunch & Dinner daily. U: Chalk Farm.

This old pub in upmarket, pleasantly residential Primrose Hill has transformed itself into a very decent restaurant. Bare wooden boards on the floor, tables and chairs dotted around, and a blackboard with a chalked-up menu has become de rigueur these days, and The Lansdowne holds its own with such new eateries that are challenging the more established restaurants. A daily-changing short menu might include well-made pâtés, soups, and main dishes like fish cakes, steak or lamb. There is a good wine list.

Lemonia

GREEK
89 REGENT'S PARK RD, NW1, 0171-589 7454
Lunch Sun.-Fri., Dinner Mon.-Sat.
U: Chalk Farm.

This is a popular local place with reliably good food. One of what has almost become a family of Greek Cypriot restaurants (one of the waiters came from a restaurant that subsequently became Daphnes), the staff are always affable and pleased to see you, whether regular or newcomer. Sharp tasting olives come when you sit down in this airy, large restaurant with a conservatory-style area at the back full of plants. The menu doesn't stray off the traditional path but is none the worse for that. Freshly made dolmades, creamy tahini, grilled mushrooms to start, mainstays like stifado, kleftiko and charcoal grills to follow. The wine list is good, the atmosphere fun; book at peak times.

Limani

GREEK
154 REGENT'S PARK RD, NW1, 0171-483 4492
Lunch Sat., Dinner Tues.-Sun. U: Chalk Farm.

This younger and smaller cousin of Lemonia (see above), is pretty—a crowded, bustling place on three floors with brick walls and the ubiquitous wooden tables and chairs. The menu is very similar to Lemonia. A good bet here is the full meze, either meat or fish where plates of well cooked quails, chicken, lamb, keep appearing in a tide of generosity. Otherwise the classic dishes—tabbouleh, grilled haloumi, hummus, afelia, kebabs—are excellent.

Primrose Pâtisserie

CAFÉ
136 REGENT'S PARK RD, NW1, 0171-722 7848
Mon.-Sat. 8am-9pm, Sun. 9am-9pm.
U: Chalk Farm.
No cards

In a pretty room that feels more like a private dining room with a counter at the front, locals gather for top-class pâtisserie and coffee over newspapers or erudite Primrose Hill-type conversation. You queue at the counter for take-away which varies from those above mentioned superb cakes to salads and hot dishes (around £4). Service can be extraordinarily off-hand, but it doesn't seem to put off the locals, though the occasional visitor has been known to flounce out.

PUTNEY

Talad

THAI
320 UPPER RICHMOND RD, SW15, 0181-789 8084
Mon.-Sat. 9am-10pm, Sun. 10am-8pm.
U: East Putney.
No cards.

This gem in the gastro-wasteland that is Putney has metamorphosed from a supermarket with a restaurant attached into a fully-winged restaurant (the supermarket has moved next door). The owners import vast quantities and varieties of ingredients directly from Thailand and fresh vegetables and flowers are kept in a chilled room, so all is sparklingly fresh. The open kitchen turns out authentically prepared dishes, so timid palates should take note. Try the chicken wrapped in screwpine leaves, the green papaya salad, the long beans with minced pork and green curry with baby aubergines, kaffir lime leaves and basil. Good fun, fabulous food, excellent value at around £14 per person. Take your own wine; it's unlicensed.

ST. JOHN'S WOOD

Maison Blanc

CAFÉ
37 ST. JOHN'S WOOD HIGH ST, NW9,
0171-586 1982
Mon.-Sat. 8.30am-6.30pm, Sun. 9am-6pm.
U: St. John's Wood.

Being rich and residential, as well as close to the Saatchi Gallery, St. John's Wood has become quite a café area, so there's plenty of choice. But one of the best, to our minds, is Maison Blanc, a small café behind the main shop with its counter where you can choose whichever particular delicacy—sweet croissants, chocolate cakes or rich fruit tarts—catches your fancy. They also do light snacks which seem to hit the local spot-filled croissants, sandwiches and salade niçoise-from around £4 to £6. **Also at 102 Holland Park**

Ave, W11, 0171-221 2494; 11 Elystan St, SW3, 0171-584 6913; 62a Hampstead High St, NW3, 0171-431 0338.

Sea Shell Fish

BRITISH/FISH AND CHIPS
49-51 LISSON GROVE, NW1,
0171-723 8703/724 1063
Mon.-Sat. noon-10.30pm, Sun. noon-3pm.
U: Marylebone.

On one side a take-away (invariably busy), on the other a no-nonsense restaurant with tiled floor and wooden booths and tables attracts a complete cross section of Brits after one of the staples of traditional British cooking. Main course deep-fried fish gets top billing for light batter and satisfying chips, or you can go for grilled or poached halibut or fried plaice (on the bone), priced from around £8 to around £15. **Also at Gutter Lane, Gresham St, EC2, 0171-606 6961.**

SHEPHERD'S BUSH

Adam's Café

NORTH AFRICAN
77 ASKEW RD, W12, 0181-743 0572
Daily 7am-11pm. U: Shepherd's Bush.
No cards.

A café all day, a simple north African eating house in the evening. The Tunisian and Moroccan repertoire includes spicy soup; brik, 'samosas' filled with egg and tuna, vegetables or seafood; ojja-scrambled egg with spicy ratatouille and merguez or shrimps. Main dishes are Tunisian grills, Moroccan tajines of meat and fruit and couscous, (including fish with 48 hours notice.) Drink north African wine (rosés are outstanding); mint tea, with or without pine nuts, or Arabic coffee. A la carte is about £17 per person, set menus are £10 to £12.50.

Anglesea Arms

PUB/MODERN BRITISH
35 WINGATE RD, W6, 0181-749 1291
Lunch and dinner daily. U: Goldhawk Rd.

Dan Evans, the chef here, has a long respected pedigree and continues to pull in the local crowds as well as those from afar after a good meal. This serious, well-respected chef earned numerous accolades in his former establishments, beginning at Alastair Little, then moving on to Odette's, then to perennially fashionable 192 in Notting Hill Gate, (see Restaurant section), and finally to the Fire Station in Waterloo (see below). Here at this excellent pub-cum-restaurant, inviting with its old-fashioned bar, sofa and fire, he turns out serious food at keen prices—griddled squid with mango, ginger and coriander, breast of duck with cherries and celeriac, rabbit and polenta. Staff are helpful and cheery, prices are keen. Make the effort and go. Reckon on around £18 per head without wine for an excellent three-course meal.

Chez Marcelle

MIDDLE EASTERN
36 BLYTHE RD, W14, 0171-603 3241
Open noon-midnight daily.
U: Kensington (Olympia).

A

Middle eastern eating houses don't come simpler than this. The only hint of sophistication is the computerised bill—surprisingly small even with a main course grill or stew. Choose from 40 meze (some may be unavailable) for a feast of more flavours than you can name for £12 to £15. Try bazinjan rahib, grilled aubergines with garlic and lemon; kalaj, halloumi cheese 'croque madame'; fried chicken liver with lemon; and batata harra, cubed fried potatoes with aubergine, cauliflower, garlic and coriander. Habra nayah, spiced raw meat with onion and pickled cucumber is Lebanese lamb tartare.

SOHO

Andrew Edmunds

MODERN EUROPEAN
46 LEXINGTON ST, W1, 0171-437 5708
Lunch and dinner daily. U: Piccadilly Circus.

Thoroughly attractive, intimate spot much loved by locals, this noisy and cramped, candle-lit wine bar in a Georgian house next door to, and owned by, Andrew Edmunds, print dealer, serves imaginative modern food. The menu changes daily, advertised on handwritten menus or a blackboard; expect hearty, very well executed dishes like lamb cooked slowly and richly with onions and red peppers, grilled swordfish or magret of duck equally well done. Desserts are first-rate—leave room for a tiramisù or chocolate mousse cake. The wine list is excellent.

Bar Italia

CAFÉ
22 FRITH ST, W1, 0171-437 4520
Daily 24 hours except 6am-7am.
U: Leicester Sq/Tottenham Court Rd.
No cards.

A Soho institution this, cramped and friendly, with an outmoded decor featuring Formica (though with the fickle changes of fashion, that can be very modish). There's a huge television screen at the back and it's the place to go during a football match, particularly if Italy is playing. Some snacks, but this old Soho institution is the place for a pick-me-up dose of caffeine in the small hours after some heavy clubbing. It's invariably full of the trendiest people you've ever seen.

Café Mezzo

CAFÉ
100 WARDOUR ST, W1, 0171-314 4000
Open Mon.-Sat. 8am-11pm, Sun. 10am-9.30pm. U: Piccadilly Circus.

Part of the immensely successful (and crowded) Mezzo complex of Sir Terence Conran, this small but oh-so-fashionably minimalist café serves some of the best pastries and breads in town (it supplies the next door eatery as well), along with newspapers and magazines and news broadcasts on TV monitors.

Café Sofra

MIDDLE EASTERN
33 OLD COMPTON ST, W1, 0171-494 0222
Daily 8am-1.30am. U: Leicester Sq.
No cards.
Unlicensed.

Not a café so much in the sense of majoring in coffee and croissants European-style, but in the sense of a street-food snackery. The cafés are part of a Middle Eastern chain from the Sofra mini empire, dedicated to healthy food and healthy (that is 'good for you') prices. Try any of the mixed meze as well as hot pita bread sandwiches around £4 and sweet baklava. They open long hours, many from 8am to midnight daily, but telephone first to check each separate café; Fleet Street for instance is only open Mon-Fri. **Also at 10 Shepherd Market, W1, T 0171-495 3434; 63 Wigmore St, W1, T 0171-486 7788; 33 Old Compton St, W1, T 0171 494 0222; 1-3 New Oxford St, WC1, T 0171-430 0340; 15 Catherine St, WC2, T 0171-240 9991; 101 Fleet St, EC4, T 0171-583 6669; 5 Garrick St, WC2, T 0171-240 6688.**

Caffè Nero

CAFÉ
43 FRITH ST, W1, 0171-434 3887
Sun.-Thurs. 7am-2am, Fri.-Sat. to 4am.
U: Leicester Sq/Tottenham Court Rd.
No cards.

Two huge plate-glass windows on the corner let you sip a coffee and watch the world go by in relative comfort. Like much of Soho, they keep the clubbers happy in the small hours, serving great coffee, snacks—pizza slices are popular—and cakes. **Also at 66 Old Brompton Rd, SW7, 0171-589 1760; 29 Southampton St, WC2, 0171-240 3433; 1a Hampstead High St, NW3, T 0171-431 5958; 225 Regent St, W1, T 0171-491 0763.**

Canadian Muffin Company

CAFÉ
9 BREWER ST, W1, 0171-287 3555
Mon.-Fri. 8am-9m, Sat. to 10pm, Sun. to 8pm.
U: Piccadilly Circus.
No cards.

Good cappuccinos and of course a wide variety of muffins (50 different types) all from organic products. They also offer soups, filled jacket potatoes, frozen yoghurts, ice creams and good coffee. They taste good and the emphasis on organic, high fibre, low sugar gives you a warm intellectual glow, too. **Also at 5 King St, WC2, 0171-379 1525; 353 Fulham Rd, SW10, 0171-351 0015; 13 Islington High St, N1, 0171-833 5004; 19 Rotterdam Drive, E14, 0171-538 1667.**

Kettners

INTERNATIONAL
29 ROMILLY ST, W1, 0171-734 6112
Daily noon-midnight.
U: Leicester Sq/Tottenham Court Rd.

The decor is perfect turn-of-the-century with its glass-canopied entrance way, moulded ceilings, and gentle colour scheme and slightly incongruous as a pizza joint. Founded in 1867 by Auguste Kettner, Napoleon III's chef, it has a loyal clientele who come for pizzas, hamburgers, fish and the odd dish like smoked salmon and for the atmosphere. There's an excellent, friendly Champagne bar to one side to wait for a table in.

Maison Bertaux

CAFÉ

28 GREEK ST, W1, 0171-437 6007

Daily 9am-8pm.

U: Leicester Sq/Tottenham Court Rd.

No cards.

How long can this old-fashioned, charming, slow-moving place survive as hungry, ambitious restaurateurs look around for space in Soho? As long as possible, we hope, for it's delightful, serving excellent cakes, baked in the basement and displayed in the windows, as well as savoury snacks like stuffed croissants. It also operates a theatre (occasionally) in the upstairs room. Only old-fashioned café au lait; no fashionable cappuccinos here.

Mezzonine

INTERNATIONAL

100 WARDOUR ST, W1, 0171-314 4000

Lunch Sun.-Fri, Dinner nightly.

U: Tottenham Court Road.

A ☎

If you like noisy, crowded joints, you'll like Mezzonine, Sir Terence Conran's Soho eaterie where you can look down on the more serious diners in Mezzo or sideways at the glassed-in kitchen. This is a case of the design winning hands down over the food, particularly with some great black-and-white photographs on the walls. It's all mix and match or mismatch here, with plenty of Thai herbs, chillis and noodles appearing. You can snack on pork and prawn spring roll with sweet chilli and peanuts, or spiced pumpkin noodles with coconut and lime, or splash out on two-people dishes like whole steamed sea bass with ginger and spring onions, or roast duck with fierce Thai red curry and rice. There's a cute 7B47 menu—two dishes for £7 from 5.30pm to 7pm-and a set lunch menu. Otherwise expect to pay around £20 per head. Never one to miss a trick, you can buy *The Mezzo Cookbook* by John Torode (who's now gone on to rescue the fortunes of Bluebird).

Pizza Express

ITALIAN

10 DEAN ST, W1, 0171-437 9595

Daily 11.30am-midnight. U: Leicester Sq.

A

The Pizza Express expansion is phenominal, and so it should be when the interiors are always exciting, fresh and spacious and the pizzas some of the best in town. At Coptic Street (handy for the British Museum) you can see them making them—thin-based, fresh doughs piled up with good ingredients then banged into the vast oven. The menu never changes, the prices barely (£3.50 to £6.15 a pizza) and they still support Venice in Peril with a contribution from every Veneziana sold. Dean Street is special because of its live music. Down in the expanded basement Jazz Room you can hear the greats—Scott Hamilton, Herb Ellis, the not-so-well known, and the Pizza Express Modern Jazz Quintet. **Also at 30 Coptic St, WC1, 0171-636 3232, and branches throughout London.**

Soho Spice

INDIAN

124-126 WARDOUR ST, W1, 0171-434 0808

Daily 11.30am-3am.

U: Tottenham Court Rd/Leicester Sq.

A

This large 200-seat eatery from Amin Ali, owner of The Red Fort, is all vibrant sari colours—vivid purples, oranges and bright greens—both on the walls and in the kurtas worn by the waiting staff. The menu is brief as far as Indian restaurants go, with starters like spiced prawns or chaat (sliced chicken in a tangy, peppery sauce) ranging from £2.95 to £3.95 and main courses such as tandoori fish of the day or hot lamb curry from £6.95 to £8.50. All the latter are served with pulao rice, naan, dal and seasonal vegetables of the day which means that the trendy Soho crowd can concentrate on themselves rather than deciding what to have. A regional menu from Hyderabad has been added at £15.95 for three courses, with dishes like luqmi—a light flaky pastry patty stuffed with vegetables and served with a tamarind sauce, and achar gosht—chunks of lamb cooked with tomatoes and onions in a spiced pickled garlic and ginger paste with curry leaves and chillies. Open until 3am, it's a good place for a curry to keep you partying all night long. There's a basement bar for cocktails and bar snacks.

Spiga

PIZZA
84-86 WARDOUR ST, W1, 0171-734 3444
Daily noon-midnight. U: Leicester Sq.

A

Spiga is the big sister of Spighetta in Blandford Street, and is doing remarkably well after its March 1998 opening. Giorgio Locatelli, chef and co-owner of Zafferano, is once again overseeing the menu; pizza chef Nino Manni worked at Red Pepper in Maida Vale, and head chef, Michele Franzolin, was Giorgio's sous chef at Zafferano. The formula which does so well in Marylebone is adopted and adapted here, with pizzas still taking pride of place. Expect more excellent light pizza dough topped with unfamiliar ingredients like rocket salad, swordfish and herbs, or tuna, basil and aubergine, and dishes like char-grilled lamb which work less well. But this light, large restaurant with a good curved bar and ochre-coloured walls is a good place to hang out and a good addition to an already crowded restaurant area.

Yo! Sushi

SUSHI
52 POLAND ST, W1, 0171-287 0443
Daily noon-midnight. U: Oxford Circus.

A

Conveyor-belt sushi may be known in the USA but it's a relatively new phenomenon over here and is catching on fast. Light years away from expensive, formal Japanese restaurants, you sit around a central island where sushi chefs prepare fresh sushi (the best bet) and pile up those and prepared plates on the ever-moving belt. Pick off what you want (dishes are colour-coded for price, and you can run up a steep bill), then wait for the robot trolley to trundle around past you for drinks. The sushi can be pretty hit and miss here, but the customers don't seem to mind, or perhaps they don't know or care. It's fun and always crowded and Yo! Sushi has now set up in Harvey Nichols' Fifth Floor.

SOUTHALL

Brilliant

INDIAN
72-74 WESTERN RD, SOUTHALL, MIDDLESEX, 0181-574 1928
Lunch Tues.-Fri., Dinner Tues.-Sun. BR: Southall.

A ☎

Appropriately named, Brilliant is still an eating house despite the recent enlargement to 200 seats. The menu has been augmented with grills, kebabs and breads from newly installed tandoors. But the style remains basically Punjabi—via East Africa—so mogo (cassava chips) and tilapia are on the menu. The 'signature dishes,' both starters and 'special meals' for two to five persons, are semi-dry curries of chicken and lamb-jeera, butter or masaladar. Also conventional portions of curries, and specials on a blackboard. Service is usually friendly, occasionally disorganised. Three people should get change from a £50 note.

SOUTH BANK

Gourmet Pizza

PIZZA
GABRIEL'S WHARF, 56 UPPER GROUND, SE1, 0171-928 3188
Mon.-Sat. noon-11pm, Sun. to 10.30pm. U: Waterloo.

A

Well, if you want a cosmopolitan pizza, try English breakfast with Cumberland sausage, eggs, bacon, tomatoes, mozzarella and mushrooms. You can have a simple one, but why not take advantage of the squid and garlic or wild mushroom variety? Prices range from around £4.50 to £6.40 and they have salads, some pasta dishes and desserts. It's just by the river and though the decor is more like an office than a jolly pizzeria, it's got a wonderful view of London's opposite bank, and you can get an appetite from the wind coming off the river.

SOUTH KENSINGTON

Daquise

POLISH
20 THURLOE ST, SW7, 0171-589 6117
Mon.- Fri. 11.30am-11pm, Sat.-Sun.10am-11pm. U: South Kensington.

My God, it's still there! is most people's reaction to this institution that always seems under threat from surrounding improvements and redevelopments. A wonderful place with a decor that has changed not one jot over the years—all brown paint, wooden tables and chairs, a waiting staff that take everything with a world-weary air, and solid Polish fare, from beetroot soup to pierogis. Prices are low and there's a good, and as ever, filling set lunch at £6.80 for two courses and coffee.

Fileric

CAFÉ

57 OLD BROMPTON RD, SW7, 0171-584 2967

Mon.- Sat. 8am-8pm, Sun. 9am-8pm.

U: South Kensington.

Two fun pâtisseries with an unmistakeable Gallic whiff to them, particularly in the strong excellent coffees and the top pastries, plus that French staple of croque monsieur that keeps you going indefinitely. Cramped premises but a useful place in fashionable South Kensington. **Also at 12 Queenstown Rd, Battersea, SW8, 0171-720 4844.**

Francofill

FRENCH

1 OLD BROMPTON RD, SW7, 0171-584 0087

Daily 11am-11pm. U: South Kensington.

Cheerful, useful though not beautiful (it's on a corner site with large windows and has an office feel to it; it's best to sit at a window table looking at the beautiful people outside), Francofill serves honest reliable food at good prices, particularly in view of its superior location in South Kensington and near the museums. Lamb, steak frites, tart tatin are the order of the day here.

La Bouchée

FRENCH

56 OLD BROMPTON RD, SW7, 0171-589 1929

Mon.-Sat. 9am-11pm, Sun. 9am-10pm.

U: South Kensington.

Full-blooded French (i.e. fun and sometimes frantic) with staff buzzing around between packed tables in the ground-floor dining room, which is decked out in typical bistro style with a menu to match (steak frites et al). The French doors also open up to provide pavement tables, and there's always plenty to see 'en passant' on Brompton Road. The basement dining room is more spacious, but lacks the same action. There's a set menu (£9.95 for three courses before 8pm), and dishes like soupe de poisson, Lyonnais sausages and gigot d'agneau.

La Brasserie

FRENCH

272 BROMPTON RD, SW3, 0171-581 3089

Mon.-Sat. 8am-midnight, Sun. 9am-11.30pm.

U: South Kensington.

One of the first such French brasseries in London, and still going strong after a recent refurbishment, La Brasserie looks the part—large space, small tables, rushed waiters (at least when you want something) in traditional black and white, newspapers to browse over and a menu running the French gamut. Le chef vous propose dishes like duck confit. Coffee comes in cafetières. All very jolly in this well located restaurant in Brompton Cross just near the Michelin building.

The Oratory

FRENCH

232 BROMPTON RD, SW3, 0171-584 3493

Mon.-Sat 11am-11pm, Sun. 11am-4pm.

U: South Kensington.

Just near the Brompton Oratory and the Victoria & Albert Museum, this now expanded brasserie is a direct rival to Brasserie St Quentin (see Restaurant section), and La Brasserie (see above). The decor is different here, it's spacious and lit by some rather snazzy chandeliers, while the wrought-iron chairs and wall lamps give it a faintly gothic air, all in keeping with the name. The atmosphere is more Knightsbridge fashionable than the other two aforementioned French joints. A well-priced menu offers some fairly ordinary offerings—fish cakes, Caesar salad, much chargrilled meat. The wine list is mainly French and excellent and judging from the diners around us, one of the main reasons for coming here. It's a good place for families with children.

STOKE NEWINGTON

Istanbul Iskembecisi

TURKISH

9 STOKE NEWINGTON RD, N16, 0171-254 7291

Daily noon-5am. BR: Dalston.

This most upmarket (you might even spend £20) of many Turkish places in the area has decor redolent of distant times and places. Authenticity extends to being opening until 5 am-and to service, always willing, sometimes efficient. And to food which is often remarkably good and never less than acceptable. Offal is a speciality and tripe soup, bland at first tasting, is transformed by the addition of salt, pepper, chilli and both vinegar and lemon. The long mezze list may tempt to excess but enjoy superb lamb kebabs too. Decent Turkish wines, great Turkish coffee.

TOOTING

Kastoori

INDIAN VEGETARIAN
188 UPPER TOOTING RD, SW17, 0181-767 7027
Lunch Wed.-Sun, Dinner nightly.
U: Tooting Broadway

A ☎

One of the best of its type in London and certainly the best south of the river, run by the Thanki family, Brahmins from East Africa. And there's definitely a twist to the cooking which originates in the Katia Wahd region in Gujurat. This partly explains why the restaurant has no slow nights in the week, and why it draws celebrity diners like singer Annie Lennox. Even very basic dishes like onion bhajis (£2.10) are better and different-in this case they're small, light, sweet with banana and scented with the house masala. Mogo (cassava) bhajis (£2.10) with tamarind sauce are more addictive than chips and samosas (£1.80) which are delicate, but heavily scented. Tomato curry (all curries are £4.25) sounds more like a sauce, but meaty Egyptian or Canary tomatoes hold together, as does the baby aubergine curry. Desserts are all made at the restaurant and also a cut above: shrikhand (£2.95), saffroned yoghurt with nuts; gulab jamun (£2.25) which is a lot like baba au rum. And the physically purified sensation you get ought to be patented.

TOTTENHAM COURT ROAD

The Caspian

MODERN BRITISH
14 CHARLOTTE ST, W1, 0171-580 0850
Lunch and dinner daily. U: Goodge St.

Charlotte Street's newest and arguably smallest eaterie specialising in seafood and modern cuisine shows considerable promise. Andrew Rose-Taylor has been lured from the Café Royal and the quality of his ingredients and cooking skills belie the simplicity of the surroundings and erratically spelt short menu. Oven-roasted plum tomatoes, garlic and Parmesan crust had a delightful intensity of flavours, whilst an enjoyable supreme of Scottish salmon was baked with chilli and coriander. Puddings do not seem such a strong point so far. Downstairs is more comfortable than the couple of upstairs tables which have the feel of dining in the corner store.

Jamies

INTERNATIONAL
76 CHARLOTTE ST, W1, 0171-636 7556
Mon.-Fri. noon-11pm. U: Goodge St.

A

Go at lunchtime and you'll be crowded out by the young local media workers. Those in the know make for the back with armchairs and a more relaxed feel; otherwise there's the bar and tables and chairs dotted around the front window and along one wall. It's a friendly place, with a casual menu running from salads to good sandwiches with fashionable ingredients like crispy duck in a tangy hoisin sauce and chargrilled chicken taking pride of place, along with the more ordinary cheese and salad style. Service is friendly and not pushy. When we came in a lady of more mature years was happily sipping slowly at her wine and reading a tome of some serious nature at the next door table; when we left she was still there, the wine evaporating rather faster than it was being drunk. Jamies is part of a small chain of wine bars, mainly in the City. **Also at 50 Kingsway, WC2, 0171-405 9749, 155 Bishopsgate, EC2, 0171-256 7279; 54 Gresham St, EC2, 0171-606 1755.**

TRAFALGAR SQUARE

Café in the Crypt

INTERNATIONAL
ST.-MARTIN-IN-THE-FIELDS, DUNCANNON ST, WC2, 0171-839 4342
Mon.-Sat.10am-8pm, Sun. noon-8pm.
U: Charing Cross.
No cards.

Underneath St.-Martin-in-the-Fields, the restaurant and coffee bar is a cavernous brick room surrounded by an art gallery, brass rubbing centre, book shop and a little chapel for private prayer. Food in the restaurant area, served lunch and dinner from a series of counters, ranges from starters like soups to pastas and different specials—chicken with vegetables, poached salmon and a wide selection of desserts and cakes. The coffee bar is open all day, and it's a friendly and useful place, somewhere you can go by yourself while waiting for a concert or to meet a friend. Perhaps the welcoming, gentle atmosphere comes from the fact that St. Martin's is one of the most important centre for London's homeless, and the spirit of charity has permeated the place.

VAUXHALL

Hotstuff

INDIAN

19 WILCOX RD, SW8, 0171-720 1480

Mon.-Sat. noon-10pm. U: Vauxhall.

No cards. *Unlicensed.*

Great name and great atmosphere in this tiny little Pepto-Bismol-pink eaterie near Vauxhall. 'Like eating in someone's front room', is the most frequent comment. This is due to the warmth and genuine friendliness of the husband-and-wife owners, Abdul and Bele, who both come from East Africa. The food is also very much the real thing—Indian home cooking from a home where they know how to cook. Some dishes are more East African in flavour than others, like the Wednesday-Friday special fish curry. But everything is sparkling, fresh, a joy to eat: honest curries, brilliant vegetables and dhal, breads like only a mother can make. Prices are so cheap, you could take a taxi from and back to the West End and still come out ahead, especially as the restaurant is unlicensed. You'd have to stuff yourself to spend more than £7 to £8. A real gem.

VICTORIA

Ichi-Riki Sushi House

JAPANESE SUSHI

7B STRUTTON GROUND, SW1, 0171 -233 1701

Mon.-Fri. lunch and dinner. U: Victoria

No cards.

Classic sushi and sashimi at really low prices are doubly welcome in the gastronomic desert in and around Victoria Street—so book for lunch. Teishyoku menus—rice, soup, pickles and vegetables with yakitori chicken, teriyaki salmon or sashimi are £7.99. Sushi 'sets', with miso soup from £6.99; the one departure from authenticity is that wasabi 'horseradish' comes with, not in, the sushi. This clean, bright little dive with tiled floor and plain pine furniture could be in Tokyo. It is no surprise that the English owner, with his Japanese wife, ran one there for several years.

Jenny Lo's Tea House

CHINESE

14 ECCLESTON ST, SW1, 0171-259 0399

Lunch & Dinner Mon.-Sat. U: Victoria.

No cards

Jenny Lo's Tea House is a real find, a rather bare, but distinctly stylish place inspired by Jenny Lo, the late Ken Lo's daughter. Plenty of noodles here, from soup noodles like chilli-beef soup ho fun, large and full of noodles plus thinly sliced beef and spices, and wok-fried, similarly carefully prepared. Otherwise there are rice dishes like long cooked belly of pork with chestnuts. Good side dishes, plus special teas, which aid health, like long-life tea and others to cleanse, energise and generally help you live a long, healthy, and hopefully happy existence. Great fun.

Marché Mövenpick, The Freshtaurant

INTERNATIONAL

PORTLAND HOUSE, STAG PLACE, SE1, 0171-630 1733

Mon.-Sat. 11am-midnight, Sun.11am-10pm. U: Victoria.

A bit out of the way, but immensely useful, especially for families. Located in a basement near Victoria, it's run on a market stall system. You choose your kind of food—fresh pasta, grilled meat, fish, rösti, soups or whatever from different stands and they'll cook it to your specification. The cooking can be pretty hit and miss. The decor is extraordinary, a sort of theme park of different themes, but it's quite jolly and you can eat as much or as little as you like at any time of the day. Great for families as anyone can choose whatever they like.

Marmaris

TURKISH
45 WARWICK WAY, SW1, 0171-828 5940
Mon.-Sat. noon-midnight, Sun. 6pm-midnight. U: Victoria.

Murmurs of appreciation rise from discreet corners of this pleasant, but low-lit, café as customers enjoy the standard Turkish repertoire of mezze and kebabs. Mezze from £2.20 (or a set combination at £11.50) suit both carnivores and vegetarians. Yoghurt and fried or spring onions enliven many of them, including lambs' liver, meat balls, Turkish sausage, aubergine and artichoke and a notable yoghurt salad with flat parsley. Turkish beer and wines are unmemorable but acceptable at the price, and good Turkish coffee is accompanied by Turkish Delight.

WANDSWORTH

Brady's

BRITISH/FISH AND CHIPS
513 OLD YORK RD, SW18, 0181-877 9599
Dinner Mon.-Sat. BR: Wandsworth Town
No cards
No bookings.

Family run, this attractive restaurant with its wooden floor, seafaring models and friendly staff, does a good line in smoked cod roe paté, British staples like cod and plaice and more foreign offerings such as grilled tuna. Fish is well cooked, chips are crisp and puds are of the treacle tart type. Portions are generous.

WATERLOO

The Fire Station

MODERN BRITISH
150 WATERLOO RD, SE1, 0171-401 3267
Lunch & Dinner daily. U: Waterloo.

Crowded, noisy and with a decor that could be described as haphazard, The Fire Station doesn't seem to have suffered too much from the sad closure of the Old Vic opposite. But then, apart from Livebait, there's not a lot of choice in this area. You'll have to wait for a table, then choose from grilled fish, as in chargrilled squid with modish mango and garlic crisps, meat, perhaps with the inevitable couscous, and vegetables all simply cooked but well sourced.

WESTMINSTER

Politico's

CAFÉ
8 ARTILLERY ROW, SW1, 0171-828 0010
Open Mon.-Fri. 9am-.30pm, Sat. 10am-6pm, Sun. 11am-5pm. U: St. James's Park.

Iain Dale used to be a political lobbyist, now while running the hugely popular Politico's he's also writing books. He got the idea from a shop in Washington that sold political books, memorabilia and fine coffee and opened this one just before New Labour got in in 1997. Downstairs is a huge selection of political journals; upstairs take your coffee and watch the goings-on in the House of Commons on large-screen television as it happens. Oh, and keep your eyes open, you never know which politician you may be sitting next to.

IN-STORE RESTAURANTS

In-store restaurants vary from the casual to the ambitious, with some as serious destination restaurants in their own right. **Nicole's** at **Nicole Farhi**, 158 New Bond St, W1, 0171-287 8787, is such an example, as is the **Fifth Floor Restaurant** at **Harvey Nichols**, Knightsbridge, SW1, 0171-235 5250 (for both see Restaurant section). Also up here competing for a slice of the action is the **Fifth Floor Café**, another excellent watering hole and pit stop. Downstairs at this cutting-edge store is **The Foundation**, a great bar serving a modern menu. Smart ladies who shop still flock to **L'Express at Joseph**, 16 Sloane St, SW1, 0171-235 9869, or they might go to **Emporio Armani Express** at 191 Brompton Rd, SW3, 0171-823 8818, where the waiters are so smart it's hard to distinguish them from the punters. The **Fountain Restaurant** in **Fortnum & Mason**, 181 Piccadilly, W1, 0171-734 8040, is a useful address (see Quick Bites section). The St. James Restaurant on the fifth floor is old-fashioned and comforting and more formal.

Worth a stop while you're shopping for china is **Goodes**, the very smart and quite expensive restaurant where you dine off beautiful china from the parent store, Thomas Goode, 19 South Audley St, W1, 0171-499 2823. It's a great place for tea.

Of the department stores, **Premier** on the third floor of **Selfridges**, Oxford St, W1, 0171-318 3155, designed by Conran, operates as restaurant and bar. **Dickins & Jones**, 224 Regent St, W1, 0171-734 7070, now has the smart **224 Restaurant** with a mix of Mediterranean, English and Oriental influences. Harrods, being **Harrods**, has eighteen places to eat. Check them out, and the huge **Georgian Restaurant** (complete with Scottish piper each day at 1pm) at Knightsbridge, SW1, 0171-730 1234. **The Table Cafe at Habitat**, 196 Tottenham Court Rd, W1, 0171-631 3880, is good for vegetarians. **Café Sogo**, the small restaurant looking onto Picccadilly Circus and the Haymarket that belongs to the fashion department store **Sogo**, 28 Haymarket, SW1, 0171-333 9000, is excellent for sushi. Also check out **Café Plaza**, at 7a Hanover St, W1, 0171-409 0750, part of Plaza Igirisuya. **Mitsukoshi**, Dorland House, 14-20 Lower Regent St, SW1, 0171-930 0317, has a serious restaurant, with good food at top prices. **Liberty**, 210 Regent St, W1, 0171-734 1234, has, amongst its three cafés, a delightful small one on the second floor next to the book section. **Fenwick**, 63 New Bond St, W1, 0171-495 5402, has a **Joe's** restaurant where ladies from the nearby Vogue offices toy at lettuce leaves among the designer frocks.

Almost opposite Fenwicks, and definitely for the young and trendy, **Guess Café**, part of the **Guess?** store at 95 New Bond St, W1, 0171-629 8008, offers swift service for its snacks. Further along Bond Street, sit at the counter at ultra-trendy **DKNY**, 24 Old Bond St, W1, 0171-499 8089, and snack.

Down in Knightsbridge, one of the most elegant in-store diners is **Alberta's Café** at **Alberta Ferretti**, 205-206 Sloane St, SW1, T: 0171-838 9777. Expensive but tops. And finally, **The Garden Restaurant** at **the General Trading Company**, 144 Sloane St, SW1, 0171-730 0411 has an excellent small garden for summer days.

TEA TIME

Tea remains so much the quintessentially English drink that one imagines it to have been around forever. But as the diarist Samuel Pepys wrote 300 years ago: "I did send for a cup of tea (a China drink) of which I never had drunk before". Tea as an occasion in itself has come right back into fashion. Many London hotels, and other places, too, serve an elegant afternoon tea which, to qualify, should include thinly cut sandwiches (going beyond cucumber for the fillings), a selection of pastries, scones with clotted cream and jam and a wide choice of teas.

Many are the tales about the evolution of afternoon tea. Was it really invented by the seventh Duchess of Bedford who, finding herself peckish between an early lunch and a late dinner, invited her friends around for tea with light refreshments? And was the sandwich really invented by the Earl of that name who was so engrossed in a game of chance that he refused to get up from the table, preferring instead to slap a piece of beef between two slices of bread? Does it matter? It all adds to the rich history of afternoon tea in British life.

Tea is both a practical treat—if you're going to the theatre, a substantial tea will keep you going until after the show—and a positive pleasure. As soon as you sit down in front of a teapot, life slows down. Bookings are sometimes not taken for tea, but try to book if possible. If you cannot, arrive early as once settled in for a cuppa, the clientele does like to stay put. London's top hotels all do an excellent tea; here we recommend a few top favourites.

Brown's Hotel

30-34 ALBERMARLE ST, W1, 0171-493 7020
Daily 3.30pm-5.45pm. U: Green Park.

A ☎

One of the best and our favourite place to have tea, a drawing room with old glass in the windows, chintz-covered sofas and chairs, an open fire and wood panelling with waiters gliding around with pots of tea and trays of cakes. All very old-fashioned and all very satisfying. Large selection of teas include Browns Afternoon Blend. £17.95 per person.

Cannizaro House

WEST SIDE, WIMBLEDON COMMON, SW18, 0181-879 1464
Daily 4pm-5.30pm. BR: Wimbledon.

A ☎

Built in the early eighteenth century, Cannizaro House was patronised by Victorian figures like Lord Tennyson, Oscar Wilde and Henry James. In winter the full tea is taken in the restaurant (£12.50 per person); in good weather (Spring onwards), you sit on the terrace looking out over gardens and parkland with a lighter tea at a lighter price of £6.50.

And Also...

The Bakeries and Pâtisseries and Coffee & Tea in the Food section have more detailed descriptions of the following places for tea and coffee, which are adjuncts of the main shops rather than pâtisseries or coffee shops in their own right. They include: **The Beverly Hills Bakery**, 3 Egerton Terr, SW3, 0171-584 4401; **Clarke's**, 122 Kensington Church St, W8, 0171-229 2190; **De Gustibus**, 52 Blandford St, W1, 0171-486 6608; **H R Higgins**, 79 Duke St, W1, 0171-491 8819; **Jane Asher's Party Cakes and Tea Rooms**, 24 Cale St, SW3, 0171-584 6177.

Claridge's

BROOK ST, W1, 0171-629 8860
Daily 3pm-5.30pm. U: Bond St.

A ☎

Tea in The Reading Room really does take you back to the days of Mrs Claridge (who looks sternly down on you from a portrait hanging on the wall). But tea here is all grace and comfort. 'Lady' Claridge's Tea at £18.50, includes all the usuals, delicate smoked salmon or ham, egg and cress sandwiches, scones and cream and assorted pastries. Teas are selected by specialist tea supplier, Mariage Frères, though what a French company is doing in this most British of meals and most British of hotels, is beyond us, offering exotic perfumed teas like Eros (with hibiscus and mallow flowers), and Casablanca, Moroccan green tea perfumed with mint and bergamot.

College Farm

THE TEA HOUSE, 45 FITZALAN RD, N3, 0181-349 0690
Sun. 2.30pm-5.30pm. No U or BR nearby.
No cards.

College Farm, a small farm in the middle of urban north London, is an ecccentric place to find a delightful old dairy. Built in 1864, it became a tea house in 1925 and was restored a few years ago by the energetic Su Russell. There are blue-and-white Minton tiles on the walls of this octagonal building with windows looking out onto the farm and the fields, solid chairs and tables covered with lace tablecloths, proper tea pots and old-fashioned china, and if you take a child, a tray of toys for them to play with. Scones are homemade, fresh clotted cream comes with the proper hard crust, and they will refill your teapot as often as you like. On the first Sunday of the month the farm has an open day, so it can get pretty busy. Around £5 per person.

'The sooner the tea's out of the way
The sooner we can get out the gin, eh?'
Henry Reed, *Two Particular English Vices.*

Fortnum & Mason

PICCADILLY, W1, 0171-734 8040
Mon.-Sat. 3pm-5.15pm. U: Piccadilly Circus.

A ☎

Just the place to take your great aunt or grandmother to, the dignified fourth floor restaurant, complete with sofas at the entrance, feels more like someone's private drawing room than a shop. It's peaceful as surprisingly few people make their way up to this excellent time-warp. Motherly waitresses help, and you can buy the teas in the downstairs food hall afterwards. £13.50. Otherwise try the ice cream afternoon tea in the downstairs Fountain Restaurant at £13.95.

Four Seasons Hotel

HAMILTON PL, PARK LANE, W1, 0171-499 0888
Daily 3pm-6pm. U: Hyde Park Corner.

A ☎

The Four Seasons has really gone to town with its teas, introducing four seasonal afternoon teas a year. Eric Deblond and Sam Twining select seasonal teas and a seasonal menu to match. Not only are the fillings appropriate, what goes into the bread and cakes changes too. So spring brings spiced duck and kumquat sandwiches on orange-flavoured bread, summer grilled tuna and vegetables on basil bread and so on. Quite delicious. Throwing all caution to the winds, the Four Seasons also has the likes of scones with lemongrass, and French pastries with lavender and honey mousse. For spring, the recommended tea is Queen Mary, first brought out in 1911, which we imagine must have a very definite taste, the lady herself being a strong character. Accompanying the teas throughout the year is a sorbet served in a chocolate mini tea-cup. Take the great aunt; if she is of a modern turn of mind, she will be delighted. And the Chocolate Treat Tea features chocolate at every stage. Devonshire Tea £16; Seasonal tea £18.50; Chocolate Treat £21.50.

The Goring

17 BEESTON PL, GROSVENOR GDNS, SW1, 0171-396 9000

Daily 3pm-5pm. U: Victoria.

A ☎

Little has changed at this delightful hotel near Victoria, a haven for those up from the country for shopping and wanting to stretch the day out a little further, and a godsend for thirsty visitors who have just been round Buckingham Palace in the summer. Afternoon tea in the quiet drawing-room with its splendid ornate mantlepiece and a view over the gardens at the back is a special treat. The two fluffy sheep still guard the open fire and the waiters give a very good impression of family butlers. All in all, tea is a pleasure. £12.50 per person.

Hyatt Carlton Tower

2 CADOGAN PL, SW1, 0171-235 1234

Daily 3pm-6pm. U: Knightsbridge.

Sitting amongst the Chinese artefacts in the most pleasant Chinoiserie, with a harpist in the background, you can forget the worries of the world. Along with your traditional tea come nine regular teas including the exotic and not often seen gunpowder coreen tea, so full marks to their tea buyer. £14.50 per person.

'We will, however, forthwith treat on tea, the most popular of our beverages, the one which makes 'the cup that cheers but not inebriates'. The beverage called tea has now become almost a necessary of life.'

Mrs Beeton, *Book of Household Management*, 1861.

The Landmark Hotel London

222 MARYLEBONE RD, NW1, 0171-631 8000

Daily 3pm-6pm. U: Baker St.

A ☎

You're likely to get a crick in your neck in this magnificent setting. The Winter Garden where you have tea is in the middle of the eight-storey, palm-bedecked Atrium. Top marks to them, those old-fashioned Viennese bridge rolls are on the menu again here. They have gone thoroughly modern also with a Champagne tea which is exactly the same but with a glass of Champagne and strawberries. Good choice of teas, including herbal infusions and 'alternative' teas of the like of cinnamon, blackcurrant, passion fruit etc. Landmark traditional tea £15.50, Champagne tea £21.50 per person.

Lanesborough Hotel

1 LANESBOROUGH PL, SW1, 0171-259 5599

Daily 3.30pm-6pm. U: Hyde Park Corner.

A ☎

A truly superlative experience in this most gracious of hotels in the extravaganza of the Conservatory, quite the best setting for a tea which comes from the samovar. Good afternoon tea both set or à la carte (though it might be difficult to spend as little as the minimum charge of £9.50; this is a top London hotel), offers all the staples, plus a variety of teas which include seasonal speciality teas. So you can get the first flush of whatever is in season. Lanesborough Tea £18.50, Belgravia tea with Champagne and strawberries £23.

The Langham Hilton

PORTLAND PL, W1, 0171-636 1000
Daily 3pm-6pm. U: Oxford Circus.

A ☎

A pianist playing gently in the Palm Court sets the tone here. It's a good, rather stately spot with a tea which includes York ham on its sandwich menu and a variety of pastries. £14.95 per person.

'E. M. Forster never gets any further than warming the teapot. He's a rare fine hand at that. Feel this teapot. Is it not beautifully warm? Yes, but there ain't going to be no tea.'

Katherine Mansfield, *Journal*, May 1917.

Le Meridien

21 PICCADILLY, W1, 0171-734 8000
Daily 3pm-5.30pm. U: Piccadilly Circus.

A ☎

Afternoon tea seems to bring out the lyrical in afternoon—tea—menu writers. Here, in a splendid light panelled room, you are offered a 'quartet of tea sandwiches' along with the rest of the splendid rich repast. 35 blends of tea from gunpowder to China Oolong, with explanations beside each of the taste. And all to the strains of a harpist. £17.50 per person.

The Mandarin Oriental Hyde Park

66 KNIGHTSBRIDGE, SW1, 0171-235 2000
Daily 3pm-6.30pm. U: Knightsbridge.

A ☎

You look out over a small garden into the leafy expanses of Hyde Park where in summer, nannies still push prams along the paths, and at all times you're likely to see the army exercising its magnificent horses from the nearby Knightsbridge barracks. Sitting at tables with proper crisp white linen, a selection arrives of finger sandwiches and joy!—again think of those great aunts—Viennoise bridge rolls, which are soft and squashy and used to feed children on picnics but which went out of fashion for a while. There's a choice of twelve different teas. The Queen Mother used to bring the two little princesses for tea here. £18 per person.

The Montcalm

GT. CUMBERLAND PL, W1, 0171-402 4288
Daily 3pm-6pm. U: Marble Arch.

A

The Montcalm Hotel is a delightful place for tea, just north of Oxford Street near Marble Arch and set in a gracious crescent. Tea in the comfortable library bar, sitting in large sofas, offers the rather poshly named sandwich 'collection' plus all the usual trimmings. But, great for traditionalists, it includes brown bread and butter with preserves, a masterly touch designed to satisfy all great aunts. £13.95 per person.

Original Maids of Honour

KEW RD, KEW, SURREY, 0181-940 2752
Mon. 9.30am-1pm, Tues.-Sat. to 5.30pm. No booking. BR: Kew Gardens.

Bow-fronted windows look out onto Kew Gardens opposite, the perfect place for thoroughly English tea and cakes after admiring all those exotic foreign blooms. With cottage-style furniture and blue-and-white china, you could be in the country. The place is relaxed and friendly, the selection of cakes (which you can buy also on your way out) wide and the service excellent. Set tea £4.65.

The Ritz Palm Court

THE RITZ, PICCADILLY, W1, 0171-493 8181
Daily 3.30pm-5.30pm. U: Green Park.

A ☎

You may have to book weeks in advance—a sign of the overwhelming popularity of tea in the legendary Palm Court of the Ritz Hotel. The oval setting is beautiful, the gold and red chairs a little uncomfortable and the clientele mixed, but tea at the Ritz is something everyone should do once in a lifetime. Traditional sandwiches include cucumber and anchovy and the more unusual cottage cheese with carrot and hazelnut. Service is impeccable, the experience unforgettable. £23.50 per person.

The Savoy

STRAND, WC2, 0171-836 4343
Daily 3pm-5.30pm.
U: Embarkment/Charing Cross.

The Savoy afternoon tea menu is pretty, and informative enough to take away-they must lose a lot of them. A picture on the front shows a terrace with various elderly gentlemen entertaining various much younger ladies and bottles of Champagne on the table. Rather surprisingly, what look like Chinese junks sail up and down the Thames. Inside there's a little piece about the Thames Foyer, which is where you take tea, full of wonderful nuggets about the Savoy Orpheans, and the famous who came here. The actual menu seems rather meek compared to the rest, but the tea when it comes, borne by stately waiters to your armchair or sofa, is delicious. A tinkling pianist whiles away the time in this slightly fantastic setting. There's a choice of teas including The Savoy's own blend of China tea, Ceylon tea or coffee. £18.50 per person.

'There is nothing yet discovered which is a substitute for the English patient for his cup of tea; he can take it when he can take nothing else; and he often can't take anything else if he has it not.'

Florence Nightingale in the Crimea.

Thomas Goode

19 SOUTH AUDLEY ST, W1, 0171-409 7242
Mon.-Fri. 4pm-6pm. U: Marble Arch.

In this most posh china and glass shop, afternoon tea, taken in their small but elegant corner restaurant, is a delight. It's served off the best china, of course, Thomas Goode's own Carousel design, and offers all the right ingredients, including a mint and a mango infusion to drink, both of which are a little different. Served by waiters in rather startling waistcoats in a room decorated with more panache than you might expect, this is fun. Afternoon tea £16; Champagne tea £23.50.

The Waldorf Meridien

ALDWYCH, WC2, 0171-836 2400
Mon.-Fri. 3pm-5.30pm, Sat., Sun. Tea dance 3.30pm-6.30pm. U: Covent Garden.

There's a straightforward tea during the week (and an unlimited chocolate buffet on Fridays). At the weekends, trip the light fantastic with similarly inclined souls to the music of the band playing a selection from the 1920s and '30s. It all takes place in the fabulous Palm Court—all shining brass, colourful stained glass and marble floors. There's a strict dress code: jackets and ties for the gentlemen, smart dresses for the ladies. And quite right too. Traditional tea £17; Friday chocolate buffet £12.50; weekend tea dances £24 per person.

NIGHTLIFE

CONTENTS

BARS & WINE BARS

BELGRAVIA

Motcombs

5 HALKIN ARCADE, WEST HALKIN ST, SW1, 0171-235 5532
Daily noon-3.30pm, Mon.-Sat. 8pm-3am. U: Knightsbridge.

This friendly, pretty wine bar is a delightful find in Belgravia. Filled with art of all styles and virtues on the walls, the fiercely loyal local clientele (many of them Irish like the proprietors), give this place a clubby, though by no means exclusive, feel, except when there's a sporting event on television when it beomes downright partisan. Lunchtime dishes like Caesar salads, fish cakes and Irish oysters in season are on offer and there's a more expensive restaurant downstairs.

CAMDEN TOWN/CHALK FARM

Cotton's Rhum Shop Bar &Restaurant

55 CHALK FARM RD, NW1, 0171-482 1096
Daily noon-midnight. U: Chalk Farm.

Cotton's brings back memories of the Caribbean for those lucky enough to have been there. The interior radiates fun with sunny colours and good humour. They serve fruity cocktails and beers from Americas.

Odette's

130 REGENT PARK RD, NW1, 0171-722 5388
Daily 12.30pm-2.30pm, Mon.-Sat. 5.30pm-11pm. U: Chalk Farm.

Odette's is a real gem in Primrose Hill, located underneath Odette's restaurant—the best and most expensive establishment in the neighbourhood (see Restaurant section). The wine list is sectioned according to the style of wine which is practical when it comes to finding the right combination of food and wine. Geographically the list covers the world from California to Lebanon. And the food here is really good.

CHARING CROSS

Gordon's

47 VILLIER'S ST, WC2, 0171-930 1408
Mon.-Fri. 11am-11pm. U: Charing Cross/Embankment.

A dark, cosy cellar with apparently damp walls and an excellent atmosphere, Gordon's has a lived-in look, attracting a mixed audience of commuters, wine lovers and eccentrics. It's the sort of place where you might hear a monocled poet testing his latest masterpiece on the barman. When the building above was renovated, the owners of Gordon's were clever enough not to change a thing, except, according to the waiter, the age of the bar staff which had advanced slightly. On summer evenings the crowd spills out into a small garden at the back to sip their drinks and enjoy good, basic snacks. The wine list, which is usually chalked on the blackboard, is not the longest in London, but offers a good mix.

THE CITY

Balls Brothers

BISHOPSGATE, EC2, 0171-626 7919
Mon.-Fri. 11am-9pm. U: Liverpool St.

Balls Brothers have seen it all in the London wine business: the rise, decline and the new rise of wine bars. When they started some twenty-odd years ago, the customers often ordered the only plonk de plonk they knew. In the yuppie '80s wine bars became one of the symbols of the nouveaux riches and trendy. Today wine bars have settled down as a part of British life and can concentrate on what they are really here for: serving good wines. Balls Brothers ship their own wines and run several wine bars in London. The food is mainly snacks. **Various branches around London.**

BieRRex

2-3 CREED LANE, EC4, 0171-329 3118
Mon.-Fri. noon-11pm. U: Blackfriars.

This new bar in the City sells Belgian, Czech, German and Dutch beers. And the weekly changing guest beers may come from the Ukraine or Sweden if the product is good enough. Try the syrupy Czech Black Regent, the Belgian Kwak in its special glass or the Belgian abbey-brewed Grimbergen Dubbel.

BieRRex has a nicely mixed audience sporting everything from suits to jeans. Bar food is available. **Also at 22 Putney High St, SW15, 0181-785 0266.**

Bow Lane Wine Vaults

10 Bow Churchyard, EC4, 0171-248 1121
Mon.-Fri. noon-11pm. U: Mansion House.

The Bow Wine Vaults, situated in Bow Churchyard just opposite St. Paul's cathedral, has a strong local following. The wine list, with its good selection of bin ends, attracts well-heeled customers from all over London. Lunch on daily specials like smoked salmon and travel the world with different wines.

Corney & Barrow Champagne Bar

10 Broadgate Circle, EC2, 0171-628 1251
Mon., Tues. 11am-10pm, Wed.-Fri. to 10.30pm. U: Liverpool St.

Champagne days are here again in this City bar overlooking Broadgate Circle and next to Liverpool Street station. During the City boom this was the place for young barrow-boys-turned-stockbrokers to celebrate their megadeals with a jeroboam or two, and once again they stock a good selection of grandes marques. This is also a good place for a pre-theatre, concert or cinema glass of bubbly before heading for the Barbican Centre. **Branches throughout London.**

The Olde Wine Shades

6 Martin Lane, EC4, 0171-626 6303
Mon.-Wed.12.30pm-8.30pm, Thurs.-Fri. to 9pm. U: Monument.

This dark and friendly wine bar is part of the El Vino chain, so all the attributes are similar to their place on Fleet Street. El Vino seems to collect regular customers who enjoy the odd glass now and then with their colleagues and business partners. Maybe these wine bars are the last refuge for the old money City-types, who are being overtaken by more boisterous young traders.

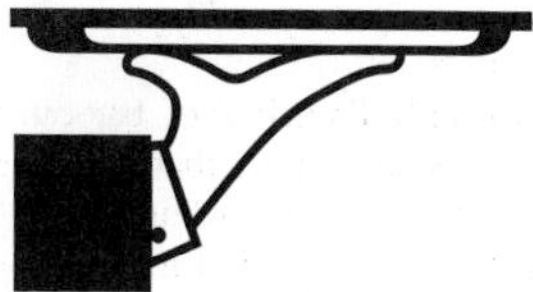

Oysters and Champagne

The fashion for the most fashionable pastime of sipping Champagne and downing oysters is growing in London. Oysters vary in price according to where you are, but reckon to pay from around £9 to £18 for a dozen. If you're in the City, try **Sweeting's**, 39 Victoria St, EC4, 0171-248 3062, which has been serving oysters since 1889. **Green's Restaurant and Oyster Bar**, 36 Duke St, SW1, 0171-930 4566, will see you sitting among a business-suited crowd (see Restaurant section), or you can eat at the splendid central bar. **Scott's**, 20 Mount St, W1, 0171-629 5284, is a favourite place for the edible mollusc (see Restaurant section). Also try **Wilton's**, 55 Jermyn St, SW1, 0171-629 9955, which remains one of the establishment's favourite venues, so expect captains of industry here (see Restaurant section). **Bibendum Oyster Bar**, 81 Fulham Rd, SW3, 0171-589 1480, is fashionable and good for people watching (see Restaurant section). Pretty, old-fashioned **Bentley's**, 11 Swallow St, W1. 0171-734 4756, is comfortable and often full at the casual downstairs bar and the upstairs restaurant which caters to the serious fish eater. For something a little different, try the small bar in the famous meat and fish hall of **Harrods**, Knightsbridge, SW1, 0171-730 1234.

CLERKENWELL

East One

177 St John Street, EC1, 0171-566 0088
Open Mon.-Fri. noon-11pm, Sat. 5pm-11pm.
U: Farringdon

This is one of those modern, steely interiors that actually works. One corner of the restaurant is dedicated to the stir-fries, which are unlimited. You choose what you want and the meal is cooked in front of your eyes. On the other side of spacious East One is a cool, crescent-shaped bar with stools.

COVENT GARDEN

Bar des Amis du Vin

11-14 Hanover Pl (off Long Acre), WC2, 0171-379 3444
Mon.-Sat. 11.30am-11pm. U: Covent Garden.

This long-established Covent Garden wine bar has been refurbished and extended. The wine list remains predominantely European but now includes more from the New World, and many more wines by the glass. Still on offer is that famous 'Les Routiers Award Winning' cheese board, along with classics like steak frites and moules served throughout the day. Upstairs the Cafe des Amis du Vin has a new, cool look with a small glass-canopied terrace, and offers brunch on Saturdays and Sundays.

Christopher's Bar

18 Wellington St, WC2, 0171-240 4222
Mon.-Sat. 11am-midnight. U: Covent Garden.

You'll find this discreet and stylish American bar in the heart of theatreland on the ground floor below Christopher's restaurant (see Restaurant section). A large mural depicts the financiers backing the establishment, and behind the bar a television offers the latest from CNN news network. This is the place to sit down with your *International Herald Tribune.* The Champagne cocktails are deceivingly strong, but the smartly dressed crowd knows how to behave.

Crusting Pipe

27 The Market, WC2, 0171-836 1415
Mon.-Sat. 11.30am-11pm, Sun. noon to 6pm.
U: Covent Garden.

This sawdust-on-the-floor-style of wine bar, part of the splendid and large Davy's chain which names all its wine bars after a wine-making term, is found on the lower level of the Covent Garden market building. It's a good place, where you can sit outside listening to classical music played by young performers or find a little table in a dark quiet corner of the vaults. The Crusting Pipe is very popular with both tourists and shoppers, has a good selection of wines, and offers a substantial menu. **Branches throughout London.**

Detroit

35 Earlham St, WC2, 0171-240 2662
Mon.- Sat. 5pm- midnight,
Sun. is gay club night. U: Covent Garden.

Seriously stylish Detroit announces its existence to the outside world with a metal relief above the front door. Downstairs, the walls are plastered in a warm yellowish brown reminding you more of New Mexico than Motor City. There's a long steel bar to sit at for top cocktails. Try a shot or shooter like a B 52 (kahlua, Baileys and grand marnier, layered), or hazard your all on a house speciality, a Carol Channing perhaps? To quote: 'A devastating mix of framboise eau de vie, framboise liqueur and Champagne'. Detroit became popular soon after it opened and has kept its reputation with clubbers and trendies. It's worth a visit even if you don't feel like raving the night away.

Garrick Wine Bar

10 Garrick St, WC2, 0171-240 7649
Mon.-Wed. noon-midnight,
Thurs.-Sat. to 11pm.
U: Leicester Sq/Covent Garden.

Tiny describes this friendly bar in the heart of Covent Garden. The ground-floor room and slightly larger cellar is all there is. The Garrick Wine Bar serves food and is a good place for a glass or a bottle with a friend at any time of the day.

Le Beaujolais

25 Litchfield St, WC2, 0171-836 2277
Mon.-Fri. noon-3pm, 7pm-11pm.
U: Leicester Sq.

This seriously French wine bar can squeeze in about 50 people. After that it's time to use your elbows to get to the counter, full of people who want to drink good but inexpensive wines. The food is described by some as being like a

'French picnic', which is a complimentary remark about the tasty snacks and pies on offer here. The sparse interior is decorated with about 100 ties hanging from the ceiling, though only specialists in the English class system can recognise prominent regiments and public schools from the ties of lesser institutions.

FLEET STREET

El Vino

47 FLEET ST, EC4, 0171-353 7541
Bar: Mon.-Wed. 11.30am-8pm, Thurs.-Fri. to 9pm, Restaurant: 12.15pm-3pm.
U: Temple/Blackfriars.

El Vino is an honestly old-fashioned wine bar with dark panelling, stacked shelves of bottles and a quiet, genteel charm. They announce their dress code politely outside the front door: jacket and tie, no jeans or trainers, and for female customers: suitable attire. El Vino has an excellent wine list, with clarets particularly well represented. The bar on the ground floor serves sandwiches; the tables at the back behind the partition are suitable for discreet talk about business or legal matters, and the cellar is taken over by a small restaurant. El Vino is also a wine merchant with various branches in the City and a delivery service throughout Britain.

FULHAM

Jim Thompson's

617 KING'S RD, SW6, 0171-731 0999
Mon.-Sat. noon-midnight, Sun. to 10.30pm.
U: Fulham Broadway.

Walk in here and you feel part of the great Silk Route. But then it's named after the American who introduced Thai silk to the West after World War II, and then mysteriously and romantically went missing in Malaysia. Brightly coloured silks hang around the place, there are wooden bowls and wooden figures dotted here and there, all for sale (and not expensive either), and there's an inexpensive Thai restaurant behind. Otherwise this is an excellent, fun place to drink in, full of Fulham and Chelsea young trendies to whom they serve a wide variety of drinks and Tiger beer.

Po Na Na Souk Bar

617 KING'S ROAD, SW3, 0171- 352 7127
Open: U: Sloane Square, Fulham Broadway

A Northern African/Middle Eastern watering hole for the young and fashion-concious in Fulham and Chelsea. Harem drapes and fake animal skin sofas, intimate corners and cocktails to relax while dancing to the DJs. A reasonably nice cellar oasis. **Also at 408 Upper Richmond Rd, SW15, 0181-788 3737.**

HOLBORN

Bleeding Heart Wine Bar

BLEEDING HEART YARD, GREVILLE ST, EC2, 0171-242 8238
Mon.-Fri. noon-3pm, 6pm-10.30pm.
U: Farringdon.

This well-hidden wine bar and restaurant can be found at the end of the intriguingly named Bleeding Heart Yard, mentioned in Charles Dickens' *Little Dorrit*. It's a small yard off Greville Street and definitely worth searching out. The mainly French menu in the bar and restaurant changes continuously. Staff are sometimes more fluent in French than English, which is not necesseraly a negative comment. The wine list covers a good geographical range and is sensibly priced.

HOLLAND PARK

Julie's Bar

137 PORTLAND RD, W11, 0171-727 7985
Mon.-Sat. 10am-midnight, Sun. to 10pm.
U: Holland Park.

On a warm summer day, Julie's is a place to sit outside and watch the world go by. Rather expensive wines and generous portions of food are the attractive ingredients in this charming West London bar. Julie's is a delightful place to relax, if you like the stuffed birds in their cages and Gothic interiors—and most people do.

ISLINGTON

Finca

96-98 PENTONVILLE RD, N1, 0171-837 5387
Daily noon-midnight, Sat. to 2.30am.
U: Angel/King's Cross.

Finca is a lively tapas bar serving decent food with occasional live music. The real catch is the first-floor El Tiempo, the Latin night club where people come to dance. And they do it the Latin way!

Minogue's Bar

80 Liverpool Rd, N1, 0171-354 4440
Mon.-Sat. noon-11pm, Sun. to 10.30pm.
U: Angel.

The place to have a few pints of Guinness or enjoy the Irish whiskies. Minogue's is also serious about its hearty Irish food which is reasonably priced and excellent value for money. Live music adds to the general jollity. A place for a good night out.

KNIGHTSBRIDGE

Fifth Floor Bar

Harvey Nichols, Knightsbridge, SW1, 0171-584 0011
Mon.-Fri. noon-3pm, weekends to 3.30pm, Mon.-Sat. 6.30pm-11pm. U: Knightsbridge.

Even when you get in (expect to queue at peak times, which is bizarre for a bar), it's a zoo—very noisy and a favourite singles place, full of people pretending to be someone else. Part of the Fifth Floor food emporium, it's slightly off to one side, has great views, a wide range of drinks, and some 'Australian'-sized sandwiches at lunch.

Le Shaker/Nam Long

159 Old Brompton Rd, SW3, 0171-373 1926
Mon.-Fri. lunch 12.30pm-2.30pm, Mon.-Sat. dinner 6.30pm-11.30pm. U: South Kensington.

The cocktail bar ruled by Marc Boccard-Schuster also serves Vietnamese food, but the best value is found at the bar. Mr Boccard-Schuster has won almost every cocktail mixing award and is happy to share his art with his customers. Marcolor (gin, apricot and Champagne) is dedicated to the master, Blue Frozen margarita adds colour with cointreau. For those living permanently in the fast lane, there's Formula One that will keep you going in all-night race, and Flaming Ferrari which will burn your wallet as well as the real thing would. This concoction of green chartreuse, grand marnier and 100 percent rum should inflame the evening!

LEICESTER SQUARE

Cork and Bottle

44-46 Cranbourn St, WC2, 0171-734 7807
Mon.-Sat. 11am-11.30pm, Sun. 11am-10pm.
U: Leicester Sq.

The accent is on Californian and Australian wines in this cosy bar situated next door to a Soho sex shop. This one is the more enjoyable alternative. They have about 150 different wines from all over the world in stock. The Cork and Bottle has kept its enthusiasm for wine over the years, and the food is good, too.

LONDON BRIDGE

Skinkers

42-46 Tooley St, SE2, 0171-407 9189
Mon.-Fri. 11.30am-9pm. U: London Bridge.

A Dickensian, atmospheric bar: dark ceilings, black beams, candles, and a ghost or two in the vaults. Situated in a converted warehouse underneath railway arches by London Bridge, Skinkers gives a pretty passable impression of a good London spot for mysterious dealings and secret plotting. And to keep your stamina up, they serve a proper lunch of the order of game pies and fish. The wine list is long and interesting.

MAYFAIR

Dover Street Wine Bar

8-9 Dover St, W1, 0171-629 9813, 0171-491 7509
Mon.-Fri. noon-3pm, 5.30pm-3am, Fri.-Sun. 7.30pm-3am. Cover charge for music £3-£8, entrance free in the early evening. Fri. & Sat. diners only before 10 pm. U: Green Park.

They boast that it's 'More than just a restaurant, more than just a wine bar', and who are we to disagree? The Dover Street Wine Bar offers live music both at lunchtime and in the evening and has even published a CD of its best-loved artists. The menu is directed at both beefeaters and vegetarians, while the wine list will delight thirsty readers. The Dover Street Wine Bar is one of the best bars in London. Dress code smart/casual (no jeans or trainers).

NOTTING HILL GATE

Beach Blanket Babylon

45 Ledbury Rd, W11, 0171-229 2907
Mon.-Sat. noon-midnight, Sun. to 11pm.
U: Notting Hill Gate.

How do they do it? BBB has kept its charm over the years. Lavish in a decadent

Hollywood style, as strange and charming as the Barcelona cathedral, a post-apocalyptic bar for new bohemians...the list of varied descriptions goes on and on. BBB used to be a pub, but then Tony Weller and Carmel Azzobardi turned it into something else, and the same recepe was subsequently applied to the Cross Keys in Chelsea. Beach Blanket Babylon feels still exotic and fun for all ages, a kind of New Age inn. Beer, cocktails, wines and reasonably priced food make it worth a visit.

Jac's

48 LONSDALE RD, W11, 0171-792 2838
Mon.-Fri. 5pm-11pm, Sat. from noon, Sun. to 10.30pm.
U: Ladbroke Grove/Notting Hill Gate.

Jac's used to be called Boom Boom and at the time it felt like stepping inside a spaceship. Now the interior is slightly toned down with painted walls and softer seating, but the round bar is still the centre piece of action in this popular haunt for Notting Hill's youngish locals.

Market Bar

240A PORTOBELLO RD, W11, 0171-229 6472
Mon.-Sat. noon-11pm, Sun. noon-10.30pm.
Live jazz Sunday lunchtime.
U: Ladbroke Grove.

Notting Hill attracts new bohemians from near and far and they like to drink in style. The eccentric Market Bar is just the place to stop while browsing through Portobello Market. Interiors are baroque in their richness, with an extravagant, slightly decadent feeling. The upstairs restaurant is a logical next stop if you enjoy the Gothic athmosphere.

PICCADILLY

Sports Café

80 HAYMARKET, SW1, 0171-839 8300
Mon.-Thurs. noon to 2am, Fri., Sat. to 3am, Sun. to 11.30pm. U: Piccadilly Circus.

Huge theme bar with two floors and dozens of video screens to watch sport from all over the world. The interior designer has had a field day collecting items varying from a formula one racing car (a real one) to slightly smaller objects. The first floor tables are dedicated to diners only. With big games on you have to book or use your elbows—in a sporty manner.

SOHO

Alphabet Bar

61-62 BEAK STREET,W1, 0171-439 2190
Mon.-Sat. 11am-11pm.
U: Tottenham Court Rd.

One of the most celebrated new bars in Soho and a place for those who are-or like to think they are-cool. This said, it has a nice mix of clientele and a relaxed feeling, a good place for a quick drink standing at the bar area. They also serve food, but drinking is the main attraction. The downstairs floor has the London map painted on it, maybe to help you get home if you get lost in this crowded bar.

Mezzonine Bar

100 WARDOUR ST, W1, 0171-314 4000
Mon.-Sat. 11am-1am, Sun. to 10.30pm.
U: Piccadilly Circus/Tottenham Court Rd.

The lounge of the eating and feeding machine known as Mezzo. A stylish place to have a glass of wine or a bottled beer while waiting for a table, or an easy place to find when meeting someone. Definitively worth seeing, though with the crowd here, you may think only once.

Shampers

4 KINGLY ST, W1, 0171-437 1692
Mon.-Sat. 11am-11pm. U: Oxford Circus.

Shampers is hidden in a narrow alley between Regent Street and that fading artery of 'Swinging London' called Carnaby Street. The name suggests bubbly, but the wine list covers almost 200 different wines and over twenty Champagnes. This buzzing bar is a branch of the Cork and Bottle chain and deserves the same compliments. Reserve a table for meals: a light bite upstairs or the full agenda downstairs in the basement.

VICTORIA

Carriages

43 BUCKINGHAM PALACE RD, SW1, 0171-834 0119
Mon.-Fri. noon-11pm. U: Victoria.

Carriages is located between Buckingham Palace and Victoria Station and tends to stop people from going where they were originally intending to go. It's an inviting place for a drink: Champagne if you feel rich, otherwise try the cocktails. The bar with alcoves on the ground floor invites you to stay, and Charlie's cellar bar get particularly busy at lunchtime and after office hours. They offer a lunchtime 'menu express', a selection of bar food, afternoon teas and pre- theatre suppers.

WATERLOO

Archduke Wine Bar

CONCERT HALL APPROACH, SE1, 0171-928 9370
Mon.-Fri. 11am-11pm, Sat. 5pm-11pm., Sun. noon-7.30pm. Restaurant: Lunch and Dinner Mon.-Sat. U: Waterloo.

The Archduke has wooden floors and brick vaults and you can feel the trains passing overhead in and out of Waterloo station. But it is handily situated just behind the South Bank Centre and a few hundred steps from the station, and gets busy with both commuters and the theatre and arts crowd. Its food is excellent and well worth making a special visit for. They also have live jazz regularly.

Babushka

173 BLACKFRIARS RD, SE1, 0171-928 3693
Mon.-Sat.noon-midnight. U: Waterloo.

Babushka means grandmother in Russian, but there's nothing traditional about this bar unless your granny has a good head for vodka! Babushka has become a chain with branches across London, but the bars vary in their success of re-creating the original formula.

HOTEL BARS

American Bar

THE SAVOY, STRAND, WC2, 0171-836 4343
Mon.-Sat. 11am-11pm, Sun. noon-3pm.
U: Charing Cross/Temple.

This very professional, very traditional and very expensive piano bar is an absolute must for cocktail aficionados. The bar staff take pride in their mixing abilities and year after year, they introduce innovative, instant classic new drinks on the bar list. The Champagne cocktails seem to taste better here than elsewhere.

Dorchester Hotel Bar

53 PARK LANE, W1, 0171-629 8888
Mon.-Sat. 11am-11pm, Sun. noon-10.30pm.
U: Hyde Park Corner.

The wonderful Promenade is a delightful environment for a quiet drink or a place to meet a friend. The actual Dorchester bar is covered with tiles and mirrors; it's your slightly old-fashioned, glitzy cocktail bar where you can listen-you guessed it-to cocktail jazz played either by a pianist on Liberace's old instrument, or a trio. The menu has dishes from northern Italy: pastas, seafood and meats. The Promenade is also great for afternoon teas.

The Heights

ST. GEORGE'S HOTEL, LANGHAM PL, W1, 0171-636 1939
Mon.-Sat. 9am-11pm, Sun. from 11pm.
U: Oxford Circus.

Great views from the 15th floor of St. George's Hotel, especially when the sun sinks slowly. Only a one-minute walk-yes, really!-north of Oxford Circus and you can enjoy comfortable armchair seating in a refurbished bar, good wines and excellent snacks.You can have breakfast here to 11am and afternoon tea between 3pm and 6pm.

Library Bar

LANESBOROUGH HOTEL, 1 LANESBOROUGH PLACE, HYDE PARK CORNER, SW1, 0171- 259 5599
Mon.-Sat. 11am-11pm, Sun. noon-10.30 pm.
U: Hyde Park Corner.

The bar walls are suitably covered with bookshelves and the atmosphere is quietly serene. This is one of London's seriously charming bars, and the world seems pleasantly far away as you sit with a glass of Champagne and very good little bar snacks listening to an entertaining pianist.

The Ritz

150 PICCADILLY, W1, 0171-493 8181
Mon.-Sat. 11am-11pm, Sun. to 6pm.
U: Green Park.

The bar is a place for an enjoyable glass of Ritz Champagne where for a long and wonderful moment you can forget all life's little and big worries. A friendly and not at all snooty place with a long list of Champagne cocktails like Marie Antoinette (with strawberry liqueur, cointreau, calvados and lemon juice) and Ritz Fizz (with amaretto, blue curaçao and lemon juice). The staff do all the classic mixes and there is a short wine list.

The Stafford

16 ST JAMES'S PLACE,SW1, 0171- 493 0111
Mon.-Sat.11.30am-3pm, 5.30pm-midnight, Sun. noon-2.30pm and 6.30pm-10.30 pm. U: Green Park

One of the nicest and cosiest bars in London is situated on a quiet back street away from the buzz of Piccadilly. The small bar is covered with ties, American football helmets, caps and whatever else fits the atmosphere. When the bar was renovated a couple of years ago, the setting was photographed to secure the same chaotic order that has taken years to assemble. Pop in early to secure a good start for an evening. A real find.

The Tenth

ROYAL GARDEN HOTEL, 24 KENSINGTON HIGH STREET, W8, 0171-937 8000 EXT. 1799
Daily noon-2.30pm, 5.30pm-11pm. U: High Street Kensington

The bar and adjoining restaurant have a slightly '30s look with clear, clean lines and colours. The windows overlook Kensington Gardens towards the West End and the City and the night horizon of London is a beautiful background for a drink. You can dance the night away on a Saturday to the soft live music supplied by the talented students of the nearby Royal College of Music.

Trader Vic's

LONDON HILTON ON PARK LANE, 22 PARK LANE, W1, 0171-208 4113
Mon.-Sat. 5pm-12.30am, Restaurant 6pm-12.30am, Sun. 6pm-10.30pm. U: Hyde Park Corner.

Trader Vic's is decorated as in a set for an amateur production of South Pacific, but very professionally run. Good-value, old-fashioned cocktails with the emphasis on straws, parasols and fruit in big glasses, plus waitresses in South Sea outfits make Trader Vic's a warm, welcoming and fun bar to visit. The menu consists of Oriental dishes cooked either on the grill, wok or the Chinese wood-fired oven-a method that dates back to the Han Dynasty which pre-dates the Christian era. Dress code is smart/casual.

Tsar's

THE LANGHAM HILTON, PORTLAND PL, W1, 0171-636 1000
Mon.-Thurs. noon-midnight, Fri., Sat. to 1am, Sun. 6pm-1am. U: Oxford Circus.

Tsar's offers a vast selection of flavoured vodkas, which seems to have become the fashionable drink in London these days. There is also live music with Russian overtones, although on our visit the accordionist probably was born nearer to Marylebone than Moscow. The menu expands the Russian theme. Great fun.

Windows Roof Bar

LONDON HILTON ON PARK LANE, PARK LANE, W1, 0171-493 8000
Mon.-Sat. noon-3pm, 5.30pm-2am Sun. noon-3pm. U: Hyde Park Corner.

The spectacular views from the 28th floor of the Hilton embrace both central London way beyond Hyde Park and all the way to Chelsea and the City. The scenery is at its best on a dark evening, when the city lights bring the metropolis to life. Drinks can be taken with a short bar menu or try a top, in every sense, full meal at Windows Restaurant (see Restaurant section). This is a seriously good bar, and well worth a special visit.

The Winter Garden

THE LANDMARK LONDON, 222 MARYLEBONE RD, NW1, 0171-631 8000.
Mon.-Fri. 7am-1am, Sat., Sun. 8am -2am. U: Marylebone.

The atrium full of palm trees is about six floors high and has a nicely calming atmosphere. You can eat breakfast here or light snacks, served noon to midnight. It's a relaxing place to meet friends and enjoy a drink with unintimidating piano music in the background.

PUBS

BELGRAVIA

Antelope

22 Eaton Terr, SW1, 0171-730 7781
Mon.-Sat. 11.30am-11pm, Sun. noon-3pm & 7pm-10.30pm. U: Sloane Sq.

This 200 year-old pub is a pretty, quiet and relaxing place for a good lunch. The restaurant upstairs has dark paneling and the menu on the chalk board is varied and hearty. The wine list includes over 30 decently priced labels. Downstairs, the bar has a good selection of ales and bitters and provides meals and snacks.

Grenadier

18 Wilton Row, SW1, 0171-235 3074
Mon.-Sat. noon-11pm, Sun. noon-10.30pm. U: Hyde Park Corner.

This pub is a haven of peace and quiet, covered with vines and tucked down a cobbled mews away from the noise of nearby Hyde Park Corner. Despite the story about the ghost of a Guardsman caught cheating at cards and beaten to death who, it is said, haunts the pub, the Grenadier has a friendly atmosphere. The rather expensive restaurant becomes crowded in the evenings so book a table in advance.

Star Tavern

6 Belgrave Mews West, SW1, 0171-235 3019
Mon.-Sat. 11.30am -11pm, Sun. noon-3pm, 7pm-10.30pm.
U: Hyde Park Corner/Knightsbridge.

This is an old-fashioned pub in the best sense of the word with real coal fires, upholstered seats, mahogany tables and thankfully, no piped music or slot machines. In warm weather the outside tables in the cobbled mews, overshadowed by hanging flower baskets, get crowded. The Great Train Robbery was allegedly planned here in the 1960s, but nowadays the customers are much more respectable.

The Talbot

1 Little Chester St, SW1, 0171-235 1639
Mon.-Fri. 11am-11pm. U: Hyde Park Corner.

This is a friendly, old-fashioned pub with welcoming Irish landlords offering hearty fare like fish and chips, homemade pies and treacle sponge. It's an excellent, traditionally furnished place, and a welcome find after trawling around Buckingham Palace in the summer, and there's a small outside seating area for sunny days and mild evenings.

BERMONDSEY

Angel

101 Bermondsey Wall East, SE16, 0171-237 3608
Open Mon.-Sat.11am-11pm, Sun. noon-10.30pm. Restaurant: Mon.-Sat. Lunch & Dinner, Sun. Lunch. U: Rotherhithe.

The Angel is one of the nicest pubs in London, but it suffers from being in a shabby neighbourhood. The clientele is an interesting mix: in the downstairs bar locals talk about soccer or greyhounds, while others are deep in discussion about the latest insider dealings in the City. The upstairs restaurant—looking over the river towards Tower Bridge and Docklands—serves a typically British menu with dishes like Scottish salmon, the Earl of Ronaldshay's sausages and English cheeses. Lunchtime customers usually wear pinstripes.

BLOOMSBURY

Lamb

94 Lamb's Conduit St, WC1, 0171-405 0713
Mon.-Sat. 11am-11pm, Sun. noon-4pm, 7pm-10.30pm. U: Russell Sq.

This friendly local near the Russell Square hotel area has its walls covered with old photographs and prints. The original snob screens—cut-glass panels above the bar—can still be twisted to protect those who want to drink privately from general view. Once providing liquid inspiration for the local writers of Bloomsbury, today the Lamb has a strong local following and an international clientele. You can enjoy games of chess, cribbage and dominoes with your pint and home-cooked bar food. There is a non-smoking room at the back and a few wooden seats outside.

Real Ale

The English are particular about their beer. They usually have their own firm favourites— either ale or bitters. This type of beer is almost organic and has a shortish life span compared to lager, which took its name from a German word meaning 'to store'. Take note, a visitor usually needs some time to learn to appreciate traditional bitter, but after a while, courage pays off.

In the 1970s the big British breweries tried to kill off this fine tradition of ales for economic reasons—it's easier to manufacture and distribute rather tasteless lager. However, the fearless beer lovers of the United Kingdom united and formed **CAMRA - Campaign for Real Ale** - to turn the tide. The association is now over a quarter of a century old and runs its own beer festivals and information services for ale enthusiasts. CAMRA can be contacted at 34 Alma Rd, St. Albans, Herts AL1 3BW, 01727-867 201.

CHALK FARM

The Enterprise

2 Haverstock Hill, NW3, 0171-485 2659
Mon.-Sat.11am-11.30pm, Sun. noon-11.30pm.
U: Chalk Farm Rd.

The first thing you notice about The Enterprise is the brightly coloured, stripy exterior. It invites you into this Irish literary themed pub with wooden floors and almost rural furniture. The bookshelves and posters tell about famous authors and the function room provides a venue for up-and-coming writers to read their work at regular literary events.

CHARING CROSS

Sherlock Holmes

10 Northumberland St, W1, 0171-930 2644
Mon.-Sat. 11am-11pm, Sun. noon-10.30pm.
Restaurant: Lunch & Dinner daily.
U: Charing Cross.

An elementary pub for friends of Mr Holmes, but if you want to avoid tourists, stay away! This pub is filled with Holmes' memorabilia and is a shrine to all admirers of the great detective. Sir Arthur Conan-Doyle popped in now and then in his time and mentioned the pub—then The Northumberland Arms—in *The Hound of the Baskervilles.* The upstairs restaurant serves a menu with dishes named after different Sherlock Holmes' cases and his study, complete with various artefacts, is re-created on the first floor.

CHELSEA

The Cross Keys

1 Lawrence Street, SW3, 0171-349 9111
Mon.-Sat. noon-11pm, Sun. to 10.30pm.
Restaurant Lunch and Dinner daily.
U: Sloane Sq.

This nicely open pub conversion has a spacious two-floor gallery to give room for conversation. At the back the light-filled conservatory is dedicated to diners. Modern art adorns the place which now only has the name to remind of the past. The interior design is by the very same people who made the wonderfully strange Beach Blanket Babylon into a modern bar classic.

King's Head & Eight Bells

50 Cheyne Walk, SW3, 0171-352 1820
Mon.-Sat. 11am-11pm, Sun. noon-10.30pm.
Food Mon.-Sat. noon-10pm, Sun. 12.30pm-4pm, 7pm-10pm. U: Sloane Sq.

In the past, eight bells were rung to warn the locals to behave as the monarch sailed past on the river—hence the intriguing name. Today this 400 year-old pub has a limited view of the Thames but you can just see barges going by across the busy Embankment. You can play traditional games like Shut the Box, Crib or Shoveha' penny, even Monopoly and Scrabble. Apart from the entertainment value, there's a wide selection of beer, wine and malt whisky available as well as food throughout the day, and a traditional roast on Sunday.

Sporting Page

6 CAMERA PL, SW10, 0171-376 3694
Mon.-Sat. 11am-11pm, Sun. noon-10.30pm. Lunch and dinner daily. U: South Kensington.

This pub looks more like a restaurant and feels better for eating than for drinking in. Food varies from sandwiches to more ambitious dishes at both lunchtime and in the evening. Its sister pub—The Front Page, at 35 Old Church St (0171-352 0648)—is more traditionally decorated with pews, wooden tables and huge old gas lamps lighting the hanging flower baskets outside. They serve lunchtime bar snacks only.

THE CITY

Blackfriar

174 QUEEN VICTORIA ST, EC4, 0171-236 5650
Mon.-Fri. 11.30am-11pm, Sat., Sun. noon-4pm. U: Blackfriars.

The Blackfriar is a delightful collection of curiosities. The listed building has an Art Nouveau interior with bronze reliefs and marble mosaics depicting happy monks at work, and getting happily intoxicated. The side chapel is even more interesting with mosaics and aphorisms on the walls like 'Seize the occasion', 'Finery is foolery' and 'Wisdom is rare'. A note of reality is introduced from the noise of trains rumbling over Blackfriars Bridge. Bar snacks are available throughout the day.

The Cock Tavern

THE POULTRY MARKET, CENTRAL MARKETS, EC1, 0171-248 2918
Mon.-Fri. 6am-4pm. U: Farringdon/Barbican.

The licence of this market traders' pub allows it to cheer its customers up with breakfast and a pint in the early hours of the day. The early birds are usually from Smithfield Market which is literally above this cellar establishment, and the food is fry-ups and meat from the market. A breakfast here keeps you going for the day but if you need more energy, come back for a bargain lunch.

The Fox and Anchor

115 CHARTERHOUSE ST, EC1, 0171-253 4838
Mon.-Fri. 7am-11pm. U: Farringdon/Barbican.

The place not to take vegetarian friends to, as it's bang next door to Smithfield Meat Market. The Fox and Anchor opens its doors at 7am to serve breakfast to both market traders and the City business community. The large English breakfast is so popular that it is advisable to book a table for 7am! The market, part of which is being developed as offices, may be on a downslide, but the pub is doing fine.

Ye Olde Mitre

1 ELY CRT, ELY PL, EC1, 0171-405 4751
Mon.-Fri. 11am-11pm. U: Chancery Lane/Farringdon.

An area with a fascinating history and full of quirky facts. For instance, as a sign claims at the gate, the police can only come into Ely Court if invited by the residents. Not surprisingly, this eighteenth-century pub is justifiably proud of its history and there's even a printed copy of it for interested patrons. The panels are dark and the furniture simply comfortable. Small tables outside between the pub and St. Ethelreda's church give extra space for customers to enjoy good bar snacks.

CLERKENWELL

The Crown Tavern

CLERKENWELL GREEN, EC1, 0171-250 0757
Mon.-Fri.11am-11pm. U: Farringdon.

At the beginning of the century, this was a place for musical entertainment and theatrical performances. Now it's a busy, large tavern serving the office staff from the trendy agencies and production companies blooming in fashionable Clerkenwell and nearby Farringdon. The food is simple and hearty.

Jerusalem Tavern

55 BRITTON RD, EC1, 0171-490 4281
Mon.-Fri. 11am-11pm. U: Farringdon.

This wonderfully rambling old tavern is named after the Priory of St John of Jerusalem which was founded in 1140. Only St John's gate is left of the priory, but the site at the pub can be traced back to the 14th century. The current building is from the 1700s and was originally a merchant's house. This was then turned into workshops for watch and clock craftsmen like escapment-makers and fusee-cutters. The biblical theme reaches the pub's beer selection, where St Peter's Brewery's products are prominent. A gem.

O'Hanlon's

8 Tysoe St, EC1, 0171-837 4112
Mon.-Sat. noon-11pm, Sun. 6pm-10.30pm.
U: Farringdon.

What can an Irishman do when running a pub in London? Not turn it into a mock-Oirish drinking den, but produce a quality corner pub. A friendly welcome, a good beer on the tap and hearthy Irish stew in the pot—these are some of the ingredients in O'Hanlon's success. A happy start with the pub led to the founding of O'Hanlon's Brewery, which supplies this and over twenty other free houses in London with delicacies like Dry Stout, Malster's Weiss and Myrica Ale. It's no use explaining them, let your taste-buds do the work.

COVENT GARDEN

The Cross Keys

31 Endell St, WC2, 0171-836 5185
Mon.-Sat. 11am-11pm, Sun. noon-10.30pm.
U: Covent Garden.

One of the real 'locals' in the centre of Covent Garden. The front of the pub is covered with plants and flower baskets; the inside is full of copper pans and Beatles memorabilia. Pub grub is available and there is more room upstairs if the bar gets too crowded.

Lamb & Flag

33 Rose St, WC2, 0171-497 9504
Mon.-Sat.11am-11pm, Sun. noon-10.30pm.
U: Covent Garden/Leicester Sq.

This busy old pub just off Garrick Street used to be called the 'Bucket of Blood' from the barefist boxing bouts once popular on the premises. Now the pleasure is in good beer and food, especially British cheeses. An open fire, low ceilings and dark panels make the Lamb & Flag one of the most attractive pubs in central London. In the summer the crowd spills out into the alley to enjoy the warm evenings.

The Maple Leaf

41 Maiden Lane, WC2, 0171-240 2843
Mon.-Sat.11am-11pm, Sun. noon-10.30pm.
U: Covent Garden.

This Canadian pub in London serves lagers from over there, and ice hockey fans over here with NHL Satellite broadcasts. The sporty theme is underlined in the decor with ice hockey jerseys and flags.

Nell of Old Drury

29 Catherine St, WC1, 0171-836 5328
Mon.-Sat. 11am-11pm, Sun. noon-3pm.
U: Covent Garden.

Nell of Old Drury is named after Nell Gwynne, King Charles II's mistress who performed at the nearby Drury Lane Theatre. Hardly surprisingly, the interior of this small, busy pub in the heart of theatreland is covered with thespian posters. And you can order interval drinks from the upstairs Theatre Bar which is a good way to beat the rush at the theatre. Downstairs, bar food like leek and mushroom pie is served all day, and upstairs at lunchtime and during the evening.

The Roundhouse

1 Garrick St, WC2, 0171-836 9738
Mon.-Fri. noon-11pm.
U: Covent Garden/Leicester Sq.

A good place to stop for a refresher while exploring Covent Garden, the Roundhouse is a small pub with a wide selection of real ale and foreign beers. The pub is part of a chain called London's Famous Pubs which combines pub tradition and sound business sense with a good pint and and delicious pies. It gets crowded after office hours and patrons often spill outside, weather permitting.

Salisbury

90 St. Martin's Lane, WC2, 0171-836 5863
Mon.-Sat. 11am-11pm, Sun. to 10.30pm.
U: Leicester Sq.

Cut-glass glittering mirrors and brass fittings in a red velvet interior make this one-bar pub near theatreland an attractive haunt for a good mixture of customers. One corner is dedicated to diners and there is a welcoming gas fire at the back. The Salisbury is one of the prettiest pubs in the West End.

FLEET STREET

The Old Bank of England

194 Fleet St, EC4, 0171-430 2255
Mon.-Fri. 11am-11pm. Food noon-8pm.
U: Temple.

It's always good to see a bank turned into a pub, especially one as handsome and decorative as this one. The Old Bank of England is a welcome addition to Fleet Street and is now one of the prettiest pubs in London. In the early evening it fills up with City types and lawyers from the neighbouring Old Bailey, but the audience is nicely mixed and friendly. Fuller's brewery has started a clever chain of upmarket pubs under the title of 'Ale & Pie House'. They are situated in handsome buildings converted from banks or offices back to more humane use. The menu offers dishes like The Sweeney Todd, 'Scotland's finest beef cooked with England's finest ale—Fullers ESB', and The Banker's Lunch which, like its rural equivalent, the Ploughman's lunch, consists of Cheddar cheese with French bread, salad, pickles and chutney. Spotted dick is a favourite pudding.

Punch Tavern

99 Fleet St, EC4, 0171-353 6658
Mon.-Fri.11am-11pm, Sat.11am-6pm, Sun. noon-6pm. U: Blackfriars.

The walls are covered with old cartoons from Punch, the satirical and humourous magazine that faded away within living memory after being a symbol of English humour for a century. The newly resurrected version of Punch has not caught the nation's imagination in the same way. The Punch Tavern used to be one of the great journalists' haunts when Fleet Street was at its peak; today the customers are tourists and City suits at lunchtime.

Ye Olde Cheshire Cheese

145 Fleet St, EC4, 0171-353 6170
Mon.-Fri. 11.30am-11pm, Sat. 11am-3pm & 5.30pm-11pm, Sun. noon-4pm. Restaurant: Mon.-Fri. Lunch & Dinner. Chop Room: Mon.-Fri. noon-9.30pm, Sat. Lunch & Dinner, Sun. Lunch. U: Temple.

The Cheese bustles in spite of losing customers when the Fleet Street newspapers and printing offices moved down to Docklands several years ago. But some of the journalists and printers still do a pilgrimage back to their old haunt. As one of the bar men pointed out, there has been a pub here for 700 years and there will be one here for another 700 years, whatever happens to the rest of the world. The pub was rebuilt after the Great Fire in 1666 and has been doing brisk business ever since. Sawdust scattered on the floors in the small rooms, staircases and narrow passages takes you back to the days when Dr. Samuel Johnson drank here with his literary companions. The restaurant food is traditionally British, and the bar does a good range of snacks.

FULHAM

The Imperial Arms

577 King's Rd, SW6, 0171-736 9179
Open Mon.-Sat. 11am-11pm, Sun. noon-5pm. U: Sloane Sq.

The Imperial is now under new management and was recently given a face-lift. Now it boasts orange and blue walls, wooden floors and a candle-lit atmosphere. The tastebuds are tempted with oysters and quality pub food and drinkers can enjoy the pub's own beer, brewed in Haggard Bros' brewery south of the river.

GREENWICH

The Trafalgar Tavern

Park Row, SE10, 0181-858 2437, Restaurant 0181-293 3337
Mon.-Sat. 11am-11pm, Sun. noon-10.30pm. Lunch and dinner daily. BR: Maze Hill.

This imposing tavern is situated literally only five minutes away from the Cutty Sark clipper, but there's a park between Greenwich's hubbub and this peaceful corner where you can enjoy your drink. This does not mean that The Trafalgar Tavern is quiet and empty—it is just large. Downstairs there is a row of bars; upstairs the magnificent Nelson Room with classical mouldings has a splendid view over the river Thames. Famous for over a century for its dinners of whitebail which originally came from the Thames, this piece of history has returned, and they are once again doing whitebait dinners. The building dates back to 1830s when it was built in classical Regency style and it shows.

HAMMERSMITH

Blue Anchor

13 Lower Mall, W6, 0181-748 5774
Mon.-Sat. 11.30am-11pm, Sun. noon-11pm. U: Hammersmith/Ravenscourt Park.

This charming riverside pub which was first licensed under this name in the 1700s is a pleasant place to stop on your walk by the river Thames and Hammersmith Bridge. On summer evenings the light turns the river view into an Impressionist painting—a good place to share the experience with someone.

Dove

19 UPPER MALL, W6, 0181-748 5405
Mon.-Sat. 11am-11pm, Sun. noon-10.30pm.
U: Hammersmith/Ravenscourt Park.

The 300 year-old Dove has contributed more than its fair share to British culture and history. King Charles II is reputed to have drunk here with his mistress Nell Gwynne, and the otherwise obscure James Thompson composed *Rule Britannia* in the bar. Appetites and thirsts—well catered for at the bar—are generally sharpened by the sight of keen oarsmen and oarswomen strenuously rowing their boats past on the river.

Rutland

15 LOWER MALL, W6, 0181-748 5586
Mon.-Sat. 11am-11pm, Sun. noon-10.30pm.
U: Hammersmith/Ravenscourt Park.

On a warm summer evening, take your pint, lean against the river wall and reflect on life overlooking the Thames. The London scene can be surprisingly quiet around you, while the more gregarious can chat to the patrons at the next door pub, the Blue Anchor.

HAMPSTEAD

Freemasons Arms

32 DOWNSHIRE HILL, NW3, 0171- 433 6811
Mon.-Sat. 11am-11pm, Sun. noon-10.30pm.
U: Hampstead.

This large pub with a pretty garden bordering Hampstead Heath serves filling pub food to Hampstead types and visitors. In good weather it's a real pleasure to eat outside. Traditional English Sunday roast beef, a skittle alley and lawn billiards add to the charm. A good place to stop after, during, or before a walk on the Heath.

Holly Bush

22 HOLLY MOUNT, NW3, 0171-435 2892
Please phone for opening times. U: Hampstead.

Refurbished as we go to press, just arriving through the lanes at this picturesque village-style pub in the middle of Hampstead gives pleasure. The outside is covered with a vine; inside you'll find Edwardian lamps, old prints and posters and little corners and alcoves with etched glass partitions that ensure privacy.

Jack Straw's Castle

NORTH END WAY, NW3, 0171-435 8885
Mon.-Sat. 11am-11pm, Sun. noon-10.30pm.
U: Hampstead.

The inn was built as a coaching inn in 1721 and named after the second-in-command of Wat Tyler's 1381 Peasant Revolt against King Richard II. Poor Jack Straw hid in a house on the site, but was caught and executed by the King's men. The inn was later patronised by the Victorian writers Wilkie Collins, Thackeray and Charles Dickens, but was damaged during World War II and the spacious weatherboarded inn you see today dates only from the 1960s.

King William IV

77 HAMPSTEAD HIGH ST, NW3, 0171-435 5747
Mon.-Sat. noon-11pm, Sun. to 10.30pm.
U: Hampstead.

A cosy, well-known and long-running gay pub with dark panelling and cottage-style curtains. The predominantly male clientele enjoys hearty snacks and piped music in this seriously nice local. There's a beer garden at the back and an excellent van selling crèpes just outside.

Spaniard's Inn

HAMPSTEAD RD, NW3, 0181-455 3276
Mon.-Sat. 11am-11pm, Sun. noon-10.30pm.
U: Hampstead.

The pub is named after the Spanish ambassador to the court of James I who lived here; another historical anecdote concerns the infamous highwayman Dick Turpin who preyed on his victims from the upstairs windows. Now the upstairs bar is ideal for a meditative drink while downstairs you can enjoy your pint and bar food in antique settles or by an open fire. The pretty garden has an aviary and roses. A nice pub for a break away from Hampstead's busy streets.

HIGHGATE

Flask

77 HIGHGATE WEST HILL, N6, 0181-340 7260
Mon.-Sat. 11am-11pm, Sun. noon-10.30pm.
U: none nearby.

The Flask takes its name from the bottles people used to buy here to fill with water from the Hampstead wells. It has enjoyed its fair share of notoriety—the local hero, Dick Turpin, once hid in the cellars; William

Hogarth used to draw here, and slightly more recently, Karl Marx, buried in nearby Highgate Cemetery, patronised the place. Maybe this charming pub with its sash windows and low-beamed bars is worth a visit just for inspiration? A large front patio has about a dozen tables for outside drinking.

HOLBORN

Cittie of Yorke

22 HIGH HOLBORN, WC1, 0171-242 7670
Mon.-Sat. 11.30am-11pm. U: Chancery Lane.

This huge pub has one of the longest bars in London. Dark, with an extremely high ceiling and small cubicles, it's the place where lawyers and judges gossip about cases over their pub lunches and real ale in comparative privacy. To help the historical atmosphere, the entrance hall is decorated with medieval-style paintings. The Cittie of Yorke is easy to find—there's a large metal sign and an imposing clock hanging outside.

Princess Louise

208 HIGH HOLBORN, WC1, 0171-405 8816
Mon.-Sat. 11am-11pm. U: Holborn.

The big horseshoe-shaped bar is usually crowded with lovers of real ale as the Princess Louise is well known for its own selection of beers as well as the many different ales from around Britain that it stocks. Fast, friendly staff work between the stone columns and etched mirrors in this old gin palace. Locals also know the Princess Louise for its food, served upstairs at lunchtime.

ISLINGTON

The Crown

116 CLOUDESLEY RD, N1, 0171-837 7107
Mon.-Sat. noon-11pm, Sun. noon-10.30pm.
U: Angel

A bit away from the buzz of Islington's Upper Street, but definitely worth the walk. Stripped wooden floors, a leather sofa in one corner and cut-glass windows and partitions make The Crown a pleasant place to ponder the world. The tables outside offer an al fresco alternative to eat and drink. They take their food seriously without fussing, and the short, inexpensive wine list covers the globe from France to Argentina.

KENSINGTON

Churchill Arms

119 KENSINGTON CHURCH ST, W8, 0171-727 4242
Mon.-Sat. 11am-11pm, Sun. noon-10.30pm.
Restaurant: Lunch daily, Mon.-Sat. Dinner.
U: High St Kensington/Notting Hill Gate.

On one side the wall is covered with pictures of Sir Winston, on the other side with US presidents. A huge collection of jugs and jars hangs from the ceiling and the back of the pub is taken up by a conservatory dining room serving Thai food. This may sound like a hodgepodge, but in fact it's a very successful formula. The Churchill Arms is a popular pub whose regular customers know each other well and it even boasts its own cricket club. The Thai food, only available in the evenings, is authentic; good regional dishes are well cooked by the resident chefs. At lunchtime the pub also serves a traditional British ploughman's lunch.

KENTISH TOWN

The Bull & Last

68 HIGHGATE RD, NW5, 0171-267 3641
Mon.-Sat. 11.30am-11pm, Sun. noon-10.30pm.
Lunch and Dinner daily. U: Kentish Town

The Bull & Last is one of the modern breed of pubs: as comfortable and safe as your own living room; it's welcoming to women and children, and throws in excellent food as an extra bait. At lunch there are usually more female customers than men, people on their lunch break from nearby offices, mothers with babies, and locals enjoying their daily pint—a sure sign that the times are changing—even in pubs. Tables outside overlook Parliament Hill across the road. There is also a separate room for parties.

MARYLEBONE

O'Conor Don

88 MARYLEBONE LANE, W1, 0171-935 9311
Mon.-Fri 11am-11pm, Sat. noon-10.30pm.
Food noon-10pm, Dining room Lunch and dinner Mon.-Sat. U: Bond St.

At a time when fake Irish pubs are suddenly appearing in the strangest corners of London, it's nice to meet the real thing. The

O'Conor Don in Marylebone takes its name from the title of an ancient Connacht prince. It covers three floors: a small pub where they also serve snacks on the ground floor, a brick-vaulted bar and a more stylish dining room. A suitable choice for a meal might be buttered oysters, traditional lamb stew and a selection of Irish cheeses. The set menu gives half-a-dozen choices for each course, two courses including coffee is £16.50, and three courses £19.

PIMLICO

Orange Brewery

37 PIMLICO RD, SW1, 0171-730 5984
Mon.-Sat. 11am-11pm, Sun. noon-10.30pm.
U: Sloane Sq.

This pub serves its own in-house brewed ales: SW1 for beginners, stronger SW2 for the initiated, Pimlico Porter which is very rich, and a Victoria lager brewed according to old German purity laws—no chemicals! The Orange Brewery produces over four thousand pints of beer per week, and has a cellar below to mature the product for the right length of time before it's pumped up for the thirsty customers. The curious can book a visit to the cellars. The Pie and Ale Shop next door serves good home-cooked food that is delicious washed down with the Orange Brewery's products. In summer, tables outside facing a little green are very popular.

ROTHERHITHE

Mayflower

117 ROTHERHITHE ST, SE16, 0171-237 4088
Mon.-Sat. 11.30am-11pm, Sun. noon-10.30pm.
U: Rotherhithe.

It was from Rotherhithe that the Pilgrim Fathers set sail for America in 1611 and this seventeenth-century inn celebrates them with a model of The Mayflower and other marine memorabilia. To emphasise the ties between the Old and the New World, the Mayflower is the only pub in Britain licensed as a post office and selling both British and American stamps, although when we asked the stock was rather low on stamps. In summer you can brave the windy Thames with a pint on the jetty, and in winter stand by an open fire in the beamed bar.

ST. JOHN'S WOOD

The Clifton

96 CLIFTON HILL, NW8, 0171-624 5233
Mon.-Sat.11am-11pm, Sun. noon-10.30, daily lunch, dinner Mon.-Sat.
U: St. John's Wood/Maida Vale.

This is a pub worth even a long walk through the pleasant streets of St. John's Wood. It is reasonably handy after a pilgrimage to Abbey Road studios, where the Beatles did most of their best work, or it could be visited after a visit to Saatchi Gallery's modern art exhibitions. We walked a mile on a sunny spring afternoon to get there specially and were delighted with the real fire, pine panels and a good pint. They do food in the conservatory at the back and there are tables outside at the leafy front. The Clifton also has its own royal legend: Edward VII is said to have met his mistress Lily Langtry here when he was still the Prince of Wales.

Crocker's Folly

24 ABERDEEN PLACE, NW8, 0171-286 6608
Mon.-Sat. 11am-11pm, Sun noon-10.30pm.
U: Warwick Avenue/Edgware Rd.

Frank Crocker died an unhappy man in 1899, jumping from the top of this handsome, huge Victorian pub. He had inside information that the new Marylebone Station would be built just next door and so he invested heavily in this magnificent building. In the end, the station missed the pub by two miles and Mr Crocker took the jump. What we have now is a much above-average giant pub in the middle of a residental area. Have a pint as a 'thank you' to poor Mr. Crocker.

SOHO

De Hems

11 MACCLESFIELD ST, W1, 0171-437 2494
Mon.-Sat. noon-midnight, Sun. noon-10.30pm.
U: Leicester Sq/Piccadilly Circus.

Soho has always been the most international of London's 'villages', the place where immigrants from all over the world settled and started to build their lives anew. This large, spacious Dutch pub attracts both tourists and Londoners. There's live jazz downstairs and comedy club Oranje Boom-Boom upstairs about once a week.

French House

49 DEAN ST, W1, 0171-437 2799
Mon.-Sat. noon-11pm, Sun. to 10.30pm.
U: Leicester Sq.

The French House is deeply rooted in history: during World War II General de Gaulle, leader of the Free French in exile, met his compatriots here. In the 50s and 60s well-known artists, writers and musicians drank here and the walls are covered with photographs of old and new bohemian regulars. Two things make the French House a unique pub: it only serves half-pints and its customers probably drink more wine than beer. The upstairs dining room has a good reputation (see Restaurant section).

Waxy O'Connor's

14-16 RUPERT ST, W1, 0171-287 0255
Mon.-Sat. 11am-11pm, Sun. noon-10.30pm.
U: Piccadilly Circus.

A little bit of London that will from now onwards be forever Irish. Waxy O'Connor's is a vast pub with four separate bars and five inter-connecting rooms. The centre piece of the pub is a huge beech tree reaching two floors up. There is also a pulpit and a confession box—just in case you feel the need for them while happily drinking. The whole lot is imported, including the friendly 'blarney'. The menu offers oysters, mussels and other Irish dishes.

SOUTHWARK

Anchor

34 PARK ST, BANKSIDE, SE1, 0171-407 1577
Mon.-Sat. 11.30am-11pm, Sun. noon-10.30pm.
Restaurant: Lunch & Dinner daily.
U: London Bridge.

In one of London's most historic area—near the sites of the Globe Theatre and the original Clink Prison on Clink Street (hence the good old English expression 'in the clink' meaning in prison)—this wonderfully rambling pub has a restaurant as well as delightful intimate bars like the Financial Times Bar and the Thrale Bar. The Anchor attracts tourists for obvious reasons: the scenic river view from the terrace, good food and the atmospheric, dark-panelled interior. The original pub on this site was destroyed in the Great Fire of London in 1666; it is rumoured that the diarist Samuel Pepys stood here watching the old wooden city burn.

George Inn

77 BOROUGH HIGH ST, SE1, 0171-407 2056
Mon.-Sat.11am-11pm, Sun. noon-10.30pm.
Restaurant: Lunch Mon.-Fri.,
Dinner Wed.-Fri. U: London Bridge.

Southwark, sprawling around this beautiful old coaching inn, has changed over the centuries, but the inn itself is still luckily the same. Mentioned first in 1590, the George Inn—one of the last galleried inns in England—was rebuilt after the Great Fire of 1666. Upstairs there is a restaurant; downstairs you can have a meal in the old-fashioned rooms or in the wine bar. Outside tables face the courtyard where they used to perform plays by the local hero, a man by the name of William Shakespeare.

SWISS COTTAGE

Ye Olde Swiss Cottage

98 FINCHLEY RD, NW3, 0171-722 3487
Mon.-Sat. 11am-11pm, Sun. noon-3pm &
7pm-10.30pm. U: Swiss Cottage.

It's not often that a pub gives a name to the neighbourhood, but that is exactly what happened when Finchley Road was built in the 1840s. The Swiss chalet was the most stylish thing the Victorians knew and someone got the idea of building a pub in the same mode. This wonderfully silly building is still going strong, and the four bars and a private billiard club are doing brisk business. But the fumes from the busy traffic around the big junction affect the use of the balcony and the outdoor tables.

WIMBLEDON

The Crooked Billet

14 CROOKED BILLET, SW19, 0181-946 4942
Mon.-Sat. 11am-11pm, Sun. noon-10.30pm.
U: Wimbledon.

This pub was first mentioned in official documents about 500 years ago and it has been steadily rebuilt and added to ever since. The proximity of Wimbledon Common and the stylishness of the building have made this place a firm favourite among locals and visitors. The green Common turns into a natural beer garden in the summer.

Fox & Grapes

CAMP RD, SW19, 0181-946 5599
Mon.-Sat 11am-11pm, Sun. noon-10.30pm, food daily noon-9.30pm. U/BR: Wimbledon.

Take a walk across Wimbledon Common, pass Cannizaro House and a few yards along Camp Road you'll find this friendly pub with two bars. Caesar's Bar takes it name from the emperor who built a Roman camp nearby. The other end of the building used to be a stable, but now serves diners and lunchers. The room has a high ceiling and wooden beams. Very popular with common-walkers, golfers, tourists and shoppers from Wimbledon village.

MUSIC CLUBS

London is full of live music every night. You can choose from acoustic folk in a quiet pub to hardhitting heavy rock in a noisy club or stylish jazz in a cosy dive. Telephone the venue first for artist and opening times.

Borderline

ORANGE YARD, OFF MANETTE ST, W1, 0171-734 2095
U: Tottenham Court Rd.

A small and intimate place for music.

Bottom Line

SHEPHERD'S BUSH GREEN, W12, 0181-740 1304
U: Shepherd's Bush.

A mid-size rock venue in West London.

The Forum

9-17 HIGHGATE RD, NW5, 0171-344 0044
U: Kentish Town.

The Forum books established names in rock music to fill this 1,000-seater in north London.

The Jazz Café

5 PARKWAY, NW1, 0171-916 6060
U: Camden Town.

This serves the Camden Town trendies and serious music lovers with a daily doze of varied rhythm-orientated music.

The Mean Fiddler

28A HIGH ST, NW10, 0181-963 0940
BR: Willesden Junction.

The Mean Fiddler in Harlesden is a bit out of central London but definitely worth a visit. It is at its best with well-known Irish artists playing for the London Irish community.

The 100 Club

100 OXFORD ST, W1, 0171-636 0993
U: Tottenham Court Rd.

A long-established venue for blues and its more rhythmic relations.

Ronnie Scotts

47 FRITH ST, W1, 0171-439 0747
U: Leicester Sq/Tottenham Court Rd.

Ronnie Scotts is a British institution. Though owner-saxophonist Ronnie Scott died some years ago, it is still as popular as ever. The club invariably books internationally known artists, and people go there to listen to the music rather than talk to friends.

The 606 Club

90 LOTS RD, SW10, 0171-352 5953
U: Fulham Broadway

A a real musicians' club, a cool cellar dive for the jazz-minded.

The 12 Bar Club

DENMARK PL, WC2, 0171-916 6989
U: Tottenham Court Rd.

This is a small club for acoustic music, just off the musicians' place of pilgrimage-Denmark Street.

COMEDY CLUBS

The British are famous for their sense of humour, but when it comes to describing this humour, opinions vary. It might be gentle P G Wodehouse; it could be the 1960s with Monty Python's Flying Circus or it could be the 90s stand-up comic type in pubs and clubs. For a visitor live comedy is a two-edged affair: lots of the verbal fireworks are comprehensible even to a foreigner, but many jokes and gags are based on current affairs in Britain. An essential part of club behaviour is heckling the comedian, but beware the wrath of the artist. You'd better be witty if you open your mouth; nothing is more embarrassing or recieved with such contempt as a boring heckler. The audience is a legitimate target for the artists and the verbal whipping can sometimes be extremely rude. Telephone to get information on artists and times.

Comedy Store

HAYMARKET HOUSE, OXENDON ST, SW12, 0171-344 4444
U: Piccadilly Circus.

Comedy Store offers a staple diet of improvised comedy. The performers are supposed to make up a show from a given theme or style, or from famous names.

Jongleurs

THE CORNET, 49 LAVENDER GARDENS, SW11, 0171-228 3744. *BR: Clapham Junction.*
DINGWALLS BUILDING, MIDDLE YARD, CAMDEN LOCK, CHALK FARM RD, NW1, 0171-267 1999.
U: Camden Town.

Jongleurs has built up a steady following in both its venues. Well-known names from the club circuit perform here.

SHOPPING

CONTENTS

ANTIQUES

ANTIQUE CENTRES

Alfie's

13-25 CHURCH ST, NW8, 0171-723 6066
Open Tues.-Sat. 10am-6pm.

This sprawling maze of almost 200 dealers occupies a large building, formerly a Victorian department store, at one end of Church Street. An open-air fruit and vegetable market adds to the bustle. Alfie's was established in 1974 and sells everything under the sun from large pieces of furniture to small items of jewelry, from advertising memorabilia to Art Deco metalware, Clarice Cliff and Shelley ware; tins, Bakelite products, children's games and commemorative ware.

Antiquarius

131-141 KING'S RD, SW3, 0171-351 5353
Open Mon.-Sat.10am-6pm.

Around 120 dealers sell china, glass, antiquarian books and paintings with a good choice of specialists selling clocks, watches, porcelain, and silver. Search out the X.S. Baggage Co for antique leather suitcases and bags, and if you're interested in clocks, Gerald Mathias has fine Victorian and Edwardian longcase clocks and a large assortment of lapdesks and writing boxes.

Bond Street

124 NEW BOND ST, W1, 0171-351 5353
Open Mon.-Fri.10am-5.45pm.

This small centre with 30 dealers has a good reputation for portrait miniatures, Oriental antiques and silver as well as unusual jewelry from dealers like N. Bloom & Son who have a range from fine pieces of estate jewelry to pre-1920 Rolex watches. PMR Antiques specialises in ladies' Art Deco diamond watches and other jewelry of the period up to 1950.

Gray's Antique Market

58 DAVIES ST, W1, 0171-629 7034
Open Mon.-Fri. 10am-6pm.

An excellent antique market in central London, just by Bond and South Molton Streets with some interesting dealers. Britannia has commemorative mugs and plates, especially of royal coronations and anniversaries, while about 95 percent of the top china and pottery wares sold by Solveig and Anita Gray are Oriental ceramics—Chinese, Japanese and Korean—with pieces from 2,000 BC up to eighteenth- and occasional nineteenth-century Imperial ware. The quality is high at this centre, though there's a more informal atmosphere downstairs where you'll find the Thimble Society of London. At the entrance, Paul Lesbirel at Abacus specialises in a wide range of good, inexpensive silver jewelry.

Gray's Mews

1-7 DAVIES MEWS, W1, 0171-629 7034
Open Mon.-Fri. 10am-6pm.

An off-shoot of the main market, the mews has a smart air with a good selection of Art Deco furniture, scientific instruments, paintings, Oriental china, militaria, fine glassware and jewelry.

The Mall Antiques Arcade

CAMDEN PASSAGE, N1, 0171-351 5353
Open Wed. 7.30am-5pm, Sat. 9am-6pm. Some shops open Tues.-Fri. 10am-5pm.

Dealers here offer mainly china, along with posters, prints and decorative objects as well as Bakelite products, including radios. Some dealers keep to their own opening days and hours rather than the Mall's.

ANTIQUE MARKETS

Bermondsey (New Caledonian) Market

LONG LANE AND BERMONDSEY ST, SE1
Open Fri. 5am-2pm.

Long before dawn breaks, sharp-eyed dealers and bleary-eyed tourists rub elbows as they try to spot the bargain of the moment among a large and motley selection of basic stalls. The serious buyers, even some high-powered dealers, get there when it opens. Tourists are more likely to be bewildered at the vast array of second-hand bric-a-brac, which includes an eccentric mix of gas masks, old radios, old-fashioned telephones and lots of jewelry, china and glass.

Off the Beaten Track

A pedestrianised two-street shopping expedition can easily be devised just off busy Oxford Street. First head for South Molton Street, a wide pedestrianised road lined with designer fashion shops of all sorts including the famous **Browns** at the Oxford Street end. Just opposite, to the north of Oxford Street, a pretty old-fashioned sign will direct you into **St. Christopher's Place**. This is a quiet, narrow passageway starting with little Gees Court which has quality and fun fashion and gift shops. Running just off it is **James Street**, also well worth a browse. There are also plenty of small restaurants.

Camden Passage Market

OFF UPPER ST, N1, 0171-359 9969

Open Tues.-Sat. 10am-5pm, market days are Wed. & Sat. 8am-4pm.

A pedestrianised path cuts through one of the country's biggest concentration of antiques businesses, with 200 shops in the arcades and side streets. A few are open during the week. On market days, there are 150 stalls and a cheerful ambience, enhanced by little cafés and restaurants. It makes good browsing territory for engravings, prints, jewelry and lots of collectibles. Explore side passages such as Pierrrepoint Row. Human nature being what it is, you come away feeling anything and everything is a potential collectors' item. There is a second-hand and antiquarian book market, Thurs. 9.30am-3.30pm.

Greenwich Market

COLLEGE APPROACH, SE10

Open Sat. & Sun. 9am-6pm.

Tables are piled high with a motley collection of second-hand books, medals, jewelry and china tea cups. It's more a bric-a-brac than serious market, but no less fun for that, and you can find some bargains. Nearby, the covered crafts market is good for handmade children's clothes, wooden toys and jewelry.

Portobello Road Market

PORTOBELLO RD, W11, 0171-371 6960

Open Sat. 6am-4pm.

London's best known street market for antiques, bric-a-brac and collectables gets very crowded on Saturdays as visitors jostle one another to look at the coins, jugs, rugs, inkstands, silverware and second-hand clothes on display at stalls and in side arcades. Treasures and junk lie side by side. An Information Booth at the junction of Portobello Road and Westbourne Grove gives out a free comprehensive brochure on the stall holders and galleries, and directs visitors to specialist dealers whose wares include African art and jewelry, glass domes and paperweights, jelly moulds, Russian icons and woodwork tools. It changes its personality as you walk along the street. The Notting Hill end has the finer choice of shops and stalls, then there is a fruit and vegetable market, and it all ends with a scruffy selection of stands selling cheap clothes and bric-a-brac. Note also that there are some 90 antique dealers and art shops usually (though not always) open on Wednesdays and some during the week when the market is closed. A free shuttle bus runs from points around Hyde Park (like the Sheraton Park Tower and the De Vere Park Hotel) to the market on Saturdays.

ART DECO & ART NOUVEAU

Editions Graphiques Gallery

3 CLIFFORD ST, W1, 0171-734 3944

Open Mon.-Fri.10am-6pm, Sat. to 2pm.

Established in 1966, this gallery shows off the decorative flair of the Art Nouveau and Art Deco eras. From the sculptures in the window to the interior's wide array of paintings, lamps, books and ceramics, Erté posters, Lalique vases and collectible artefacts, such as decanters and ice-coolers, this is a wide-ranging showplace.

Crafts Fair

The south side of the Thames is changing, an off-the-beaten track area getting livelier all the time thanks to the rise of some interesting shopping and eating enclaves. A little east of the South Bank Centre and on the river, is the **Oxo Tower**, Bargehouse Street, SE1, 0171-401 3610, a converted warehouse building with a restaurant at the top (see Restaurant section), a big bar/brasserie on the second floor and many small units. Many of the artist/craftspeople originally came from Gabriel's Wharf - a collection of brightly painted, small craft shops which is due to be redeveloped. The shops often double as studios so you can see the artists at work. There are knitwear designers, silk painters, ceramic artists and jewellers among them. There are also restaurants in this small area. **Gabriel's Wharf**, 56 Upper Ground, Waterloo, SE1, 0171-401 3610.

Gordon Watson

50 Fulham Rd, SW3, 0171-589 3108
Open Mon.-Sat. 11am-6pm.

This shop stays essentially as it was when first founded, specialising in Art Deco, with some magnificent examples of 1930's metal furniture, Daum glass, Puiforcat silver and signed 1940's jewelry by Van Cleef, Cartier and other famous names.

Haslam and Whiteway

105 Kensington Church St, W8, 0171-229 1145
Open Mon.-Fri.10am-6pm, Sat. to 2pm.

Founded in 1972, this firm has two floors specialising in the periods from the Victorian Gothic Revival to the Arts and Crafts era. The furniture is designed by architects of that time who often decorated the houses they built. There is always a good choice of William Morris tiles. Other finds have included stained glass by Henry Holliday and the only known painted furniture by Bruce Talbert.

John Jesse

160 Kensington Church St, W8, 0171-229 0312
Open Mon.-Fri. 10am-5.30pm, Sat. 11am-3pm.

Lalique, Liberty, Tiffany, Daum, Galle—all the famous names are found at this shop specialising in Art Nouveau and Art Deco objets d'art, jewelry and all the decorative arts from 1880 to 1950 though there are also some fine pieces up to 1980. Good finds here include names like Cartier and Omar Ramsden as well as others in the Arts and Crafts style.

AUCTION HOUSES

The quality daily newspapers give details of auctions; otherwise telephone to enquire which particular sales are coming up. Apart from the serious business of buying, previews of sales offer wonderful opportunities to look at antiques before they disappear back into private hands.

Academy Auctioneers & Valuers

Northcote Ave, Ealing, 0181-579 7466, Fax 0181-579 0511

Monthly, two day auctions of antiques and fine arts, as well as some specialist auctions.

Bonhams

Montpelier St, SW7, 0171-393 3900, Fax 0171-393 3906
Open Mon.-Fri. 9am-5pm, Sun. 11am-4pm.

Bonhams Chelsea

65-69 Lots Rd, SW10, 0171-393 3900, Fax 0171-393 3906
Open Mon.-Fri. 9am-5pm, Sun. 11am-4pm.

Going under the hammer at the Knightsbridge auctioneers are wide-ranging categories including modern and antique guns, arms, armour and militaria, sporting memorabilia, vintage fountain pens, old masterpieces, nineteenth-century paintings as well as modern British and continental pictures, furniture, clocks and watches, ceramics, books and many other antiquities. Rather more informal than the main branch, and less expensive, the Lot's Road galleries hold regular sales of paintings, furniture, prints, silver, jewelry, ceramics and collectibles.

Brooks Specialist (Cars and Motorcycles) Auctioneers

81 Clapham Common, West Side, SW4, 0171-228 8000, Fax 0171-585 0830

Specialists in vintage, veteran and classic cars and motorcycles, they hold irregular auctions in different venues. Tel for information.

Christie's

8 King St, SW1, 0171-839 9060, Fax 0171-839 1611

Open Mon.-Fri. 9am-4.30pm. During a sale, viewing is Tues. 9am-8pm, Sun. 2pm-5pm.

Christie's South Kensington

85 Old Brompton Rd, SW7, 0171-581 7611, Fax 0171-321 3321

Open Mon. 9am-7.30pm, Tues.-Fri. 9am-5pm. During a sale viewing on Sun. 10am-1pm.

A household name associated with the sale of fine paintings, this firm was established in 1766. It quickly became known for its sales of artists' studio works, starting with Gainsborough and continuing with Reynolds, Landseer, Rossetti, Burne-Jones, Leighton, Sargent and others. The smart galleries on King Street hold sales of important works of art and Old Master paintings although the range includes anything which collectors covet, from fine wines (for which they have made a name for themselves), to English furniture and decorative art objects. Christie's publishes more than 1,200 different catalogues annually from eleven showrooms world-wide. The Brompton Road branch has a smaller display area and is less pricey but has an equally wide range of sale themes, often connected with seasonal subjects such as Valentine cards. Miniature aircraft, fans, dolls and teddy bears, posters, and everything up to large Oriental carpets are sold here.

Criterion Auction Rooms

53-55 Essex Rd, Islington, N1, 0171-359 5707, Fax 0171-354 9843

Open Fri. 4pm-8pm, Sat. & Sun. 11am-3pm. Auctions every Mon.

A good, less expensive auction house where you can really pick up the odd bargain. They concentrate on furniture, but have a good range of unusual accessories and small furnishings. On the first Monday of every month there's an auction of higher quality items.

Lots Road Galleries

71 Lots Rd, SW10, 0171-351 7771
Fax 0171-376 8349

Open for viewing Thurs 5pm-7pm, Fri, Sat, Sun 10am-4pm. Auctions every Monday.

A great place for some good deals at this slightly off-the-beaten-track auction house which covers a vast range of items.

Phillips

101 New Bond St, W1, 0171-629 6602
Fax 0171-629 8876

Open Mon.-Fri. 8.30am-5pm, Sun. 2pm-5pm.

10 Salem Rd, W2, 0171-229 9090
Fax 0171-792 9201

Open Mon.-Fri. 8.30am-5pm, Sun. 2pm-5pm.

Established in 1796, Phillips has salesrooms throughout Britain, all staffed by specialists and experienced valuers who can advise on all aspects of buying and selling at auction. The Bond Street saleroom specialises in fine furniture, paintings, ceramics, jewelry, silver clocks, watches, Oriental works of art, textiles, books, musical instruments, stamps, medals and decorative arts.

Sotheby's

34 New Bond St, W1, 0171-493 8080
Fax 0171-409 3100

Open Mon.-Fri. 9am-4.30pm, Sun. noon-4pm.

Founded in 1744, these huge galleries, extending beyond the small entrance back to St. George Street and Conduit Street, have a tranquil air. Sotheby's is a traditional setting for the modern bustle of viewing days and the excitement of the crowds on sales days, when the atmosphere can heighten as lots are sold at the rate of two a minute for thousands of pounds. Like Christie's, Sotheby's offers an excellent advice and valuation service. The busy shop up-front sells its own range of catalogues, and also beautifully illustrated books on art and the decorative arts, including specialist subjects such as *The Royal Palaces of India* and *The Jewels of the Duchess of Windsor*. They also have an excellent café (see Bargain Bites).

BOOKS & MANUSCRIPTS

We have included Fax numbers for the antiquarian booksellers for requests for their catalogues and information.

Bernard Quaritch

5-8 LOWER JOHN ST, W1, 0171-734 2983
FAX 0171-437 0967
Open Mon.-Fri. 9.30am-5.30pm.

Dating back to the 1840s, this, the oldest and largest antique book shop in London, can be rather intimidating, catering to serious customers in a formal atmosphere. Each department, from the arts to Islamic culture, is run by its own director. Look out for the illustrated medieval manuscripts, called 'leaves' in the trade, usually in a display case by the entrance.

Bertram Rota

31 LONG ACRE, WC2, 0171-836 0723
FAX 0171-497 9058
Open Mon.-Fri .9.30am-5.30pm.

Now run by Anthony Rota, this book shop has a strong literary background. It has the interesting approach of frequently pursuing themes, such as collecting the books of both English and American authors published by a particular firm. Special short-run editions on special paper, signed by contemporary authors, like Margaret Atwood, are an interesting sideline.

Bloomsbury Workshop

12 GALEN PL, OFF BURY PL, WC1, 0171-405 0632
Open Mon.-Fri. 10am-5.30pm.

Virginia Woolf and her literary and artistic cronies in the Bloomsbury Group—Duncan Grant, Lytton Strachey, Clive Bell, and her sister, Vanessa—are the star attractions of this little shop tucked in an enclave near the British Museum and stocking many first editions by Bloomsbury writers. There are changing exhibitions of art by their off-spring and others connected with the famous group.

G Heywood Hill

10 CURZON ST, W1, 0171-629 0647, FAX 0171-408 0286
Open Mon.-Fri. 9am-5.30pm, Sat. to 12.30pm.

Strewn with books and manned by charming staff, this shop is a delight, selling both new and second-hand books and with a specialist children's book section downstairs. The last of the carriage trade booksellers, they also specialise in antiquarian natural history, illustrated books and volumes on architecture.

Henry Sotheran

2-5 SACKVILLE ST, W1, 0171-734 1150, FAX 0171-434 2019
Open Mon.-Fri. 9.30am-6pm, Sat. 10am-4pm.

This large wood-panelled shop looks exactly how a fine vintage bookseller's should. The fine books might include a bible of 1767 bound in a lavishly tooled design of flowers and thistles, a first edition of Lewis Carroll's Through the Looking Glass complete with misprints, or a first trade edition of T E Lawrence's Pillars of Wisdom. The shop is strong on literature, modern first editions, children's and illustrated books, travel, exploration and natural history. Look out for the remaindered table by the door. There is also a print department specialising in John Gould bird prints and some travel and architectural engravings. In the basement the gallery of The Folio Society sells reprinted good books with contemporary illustrations and fine hard-back bindings.

Jarndyce Antiquarian Booksellers

46 GREAT RUSSELL ST, WC1, 0171-631 4220, FAX 0171-436 6544
Open Mon.-Fri. 9.30am-5pm.

Brian Lake has become the leading specialist in Dickens (including first editions) as well as in eighteenth- and nineteenth-century books, with a strong emphasis on English literature. The catalogues are full of gems and good ideas, like women's literature, and are amusingly illustrated. The recently opened ground floor has a range of interesting, less expensive books; the upper floor is for the serious collector who should make an appointment.

Maggs Brothers

50 BERKELEY SQ, W1, 0171-493 7160, FAX 0171-499 2007

Open Mon.-Fri. 9.15am-5pm.

The very reassuring atmosphere of a long-established library sets the tone for this grand shop overlooking Berkeley Square where it is advisable to know what you are interested in beforehand. Maggs are one of the oldest and most respected antiquarian book businesses. Early travel books and modern first editions, including foreign language books, are a good theme to explore. This is the place to buy famous autographs, with an excellent choice from the famous and infamous to royalty.

Pickering and Chatto

36 GEORGE ST, SW1, 0171-491 2656, FAX: 0171-491 9161

Open Mon.-Fri. 9.30am-5.30pm.

This much-renowned bookseller has comprehensive stocks of English literature, economics, medicine and science. Books might include the first publication about the theory of evolution by Charles Darwin, and a first edition of Jonathan Swift's Gulliver's Travels.

Robert Frew

106 GREAT RUSSELL ST, WC1, 0171-580 2311, FAX 0171-580 2313

Open Mon.-Fri. 10am-6pm, Sat. to 2pm.

Prints by Thomas Rowlandson, Arthur Rackham and David Roberts catch the eye in this handsome shop where books on travel and illustrated books on English literature are stocked. It also carries a good range of maps and atlases.

Sam Fogg

35 ST. GEORGE ST, W1, 0171-495 2333, FAX 0171-409 3326

Open Mon.-Fri. 9.30am-6pm.

Sam Fogg sells wonderful, luminous medieval and Renaissance illuminated manuscripts from all over the world, with an emphasis on European works and a big collection of Ethiopian origin. Established in 1971, this firm does not sell books, but is the major manuscript dealer in the country, including a wide choice of miniatures, from Armenian to Indonesian to Slavonic.

Simon Finch Rare Books

10 NEW BOND ST, W1, 0171-499 0974, FAX 0171-499 0799

Open Mon.-Fri. 10am-6pm, Sat. 11am-5pm.

A rarity amid the fashion and jewelry shops of this most prestigious of London streets, the shop is found up the stairs of the premises and has a sitting-room atmosphere. It specialises in books from the fifteenth to the nineteenth century as well as prints and artefacts.

Sims Reed

43A DUKE ST, SW1, 0171-493 5660, FAX 0171-493 8468

Open Mon.-Fri. 9am-6pm.

The dark wood shelves of this antiquarian book shop display rare, out-of-print, and new reference books on fine and applied art from architecture to contemporary design. The shop is probably London's biggest dealer in decorative books with original prints.

Thomas Heneage

42 DUKE ST, SW1, 0171-930 9223, FAX 0171-839 9223

Open Mon.-Fri. 9.30am-6pm.

Based in St. James's, this leading supplier of fine-art books sells both newly published works and secondhand books for art collectors and dealers.

Ulysses

40 MUSEUM ST, WC1, 0171-831 1600, FAX 0171-419 0070

Open Mon.-Sat.10.30am-6pm, Sun. noon-6pm.

There's a comfortable atmosphere in the downstairs level of this shop, where neatly arranged shelves of collectors' items of modern first editions are a delight for browsers.

CONTINENTAL & ENGLISH FURNITURE

Anton Chenevière

27 BRUTON ST, W1, 0171-491 1007

Open Mon.-Fri. 10am-5.30pm, Sat. by appointment.

These impressive showrooms are devoted to ornately designed eighteenth- and nineteenth-century Russian, Austrian, German and Italian furniture along with many objets d'art. Among the display you might find a Russian mosaic-malachite tazza of c. 1820, or an

Italian-made rosewood and kingwood Italian-made table, c. 1780.

Carlton Hobbs

46A PIMLICO RD, SW1, 0171-730 3640

Open Mon.-Fri. 9am-6pm, Sat. 10am-5pm.

This firm, established more than 20 years ago, is a leading dealer in seventeenth-, eighteenth- and early nineteenth-century English and continental furniture, objets d'art, paintings and tapestries. Displayed in the dramatically lit showroom, each piece has been researched before going for sale. Important historical discoveries have included the Hope Weir Cabinet, an extraordinary 18th-century cabinet inset with Florentine pietra dura panels.

G Sarti

55 JERMYN ST, W1, 0171-491 0449

Open Mon.-Fri. 10am-6pm.

Only the sixteenth to the eighteenth centuries are represented in the Italian furniture for which this showy gallery is known, like a rare ornately decorated Arte Povera cabinet of 1750. The gallery also specialises in thirtheenth- to fifteenth-century paintings.

Jeremy

29 LOWNDES ST, SW1, 0171-823 2923

Open Mon.-Fri. 8.30am-6pm, Sat. 9am-5pm.

Brothers Michael and John Hill carry on the family tradition of selling high-quality English and continental furniture from the eighteenth and early nineteenth centuries in their smart premises on a quiet Knightsbridge street. They have outstanding examples of French, Russian and English decorative art; the Getty Museum in California has bought from them.

Jonathan Harris

54 KENSINGTON CHURCH ST, W8, 0171-937 3133

Open Mon.-Fri. 9.30am-6pm.

In these large show rooms are important English, continental and Oriental furniture and works of art, with rare finds for collectors such as a pair of gilded Sèvres vases which Napoleon presented to Josephine in 1807.

O F Wilson

3-6 QUEENS ELM PARADE, OLD CHURCH ST, SW3, 0171-352 9554

Open Mon.-Fri. 9.30am-5.30pm, Sat.10.30am-1pm.

The shop has a wide choice of eighteenth- and early nineteenth-century English and continental furniture. Here you might see a pair of Venetian armchairs from the mid-eighteenth century, Roman gilt wood console tables from around 1750 and Italian statuary marble lions from the nineteenth century. Marble mantelpieces and architectural items are a speciality.

Partridge Fine Arts

144-146 NEW BOND ST, W1, 0171-629 0834

Open Mon.-Fri. 9am-5.30pm.

This large antiques firm is housed in an impressive building with a grand staircase and marble pillars, built in 1913 as showrooms for Colnaghi, the art dealers. It is the only custom-built gallery of that era still used for the original purpose of showing off masterpieces, now in the form of English and French furniture, silver, paintings of the English and Italian school and hundreds of related artefacts.

Pelham Galleries

24-25 MOUNT ST, W1, 0171-629 0905

Open Mon.-Fri. 9am-5.30pm.

The emphasis here is on decorative arts and furniture displayed in well laid-out, stylish galleries. Unusual forms of painted and lacquered decoration are well represented, such as a large pair of Imperial Wanli lacquer wardrobes, c. 1600, and a pair of Chinese export lacquer coffers decorated with landscapes, c. 1780. Exceptional craftsmanship and interesting historical associations are appealing features of many pieces.

EIGHTEENTH- & NINETEENTH CENTURY ENGLISH FURNITURE

Apter-Fredericks

265-267 FULHAM RD, SW3, 0171-352 2188

Open Mon.-Fri. 9.30am-5.30pm, Sat. by appointment.

The large windows of Apter-Fredericks, a firm which goes back five generations, display some of the fine eighteenth-century English furniture of this leading dealer. Researching with meticulous care, they know the provenance of most of this grand furniture that illustrates the tastes of a past, more gracious age. They have helped form major public collections and furnished the odd royal residence.

Brian Rolleston Antiques

104A KENSINGTON CHURCH ST, W8, 0171-229 5892

Open Mon.-Fri. 10am-1pm & 2.30pm-5.30pm.

Eighteenth-century English furniture fills the three large showrooms here, pieces of museum quality like a Queen Anne double-domed bureau cabinet in figured walnut, c. 1710.

David Pettifer

219 KING'S RD, SW3, 0171-352 3088

Open Mon.-Fri. 9.30am-5.30pm.

For the last 30 years, David Pettifer has been perfecting his own particular eclectic approach to presenting attractive and unusual items together, with everything from decorative biscuit tins to Georgian marble busts and Regency mahogany English-made library armchairs from the 1820s. In keeping with the contemporary wish to see objects in context, he holds themed exhibitions.

H Blairman and Sons

119 MOUNT ST, W1, 0171-493 0444

Open Mon.-Fri. 9am-6pm.

These discreet premises of a firm founded in 1884 are full of surprises. Blairman's specialises in eighteenth- and early nineteenth-century English furniture and later English architect-designed furniture. To complement the furniture, you'll find related objects in the three showrooms.

Hotspur

14 LOWNDES ST, SW1, 0171-235 1918

Open Mon.-Fri. 8am-6pm, Sat. 9am to 1pm.

Robin and Brian Kern, the third generation of their family firm, specialise in fine eighteenth-century English furniture and works of art, trading from a delightful Regency townhouse which retains its original character. Established in 1924, Hotspur presents carefully selected rare and fine furniture such as a George III lacquer secretary made by Thomas Chippendale for Harewood House in 1773 for £23.

John Bly

27 BURY ST, SW1, 0171-930 1292

Open Mon.-Fri. 9.30am-5pm, Sat. by appointment.

Comfortably laid out with eighteenth-century tables, desks and chairs, this firm was founded in 1891 by the grandfather of the present proprietor, John Bly. The present expert owner is something of a celebrity among the antique fraternity because of his television appearances on the BBC's excellent Antiques Roadshow and his Daily Telegraph Saturday column. This small, well-stocked shop has many stylish objets d'art to co-ordinate with the furniture. Knowledgeable and enthusiastic, he is one of the more forward-looking dealers. The firm has its own restoration workshop in Tring, Hertfordshire.

Mallett and Son

141 NEW BOND ST, W1, 0171-499 7411

Open Mon.-Fri.9am-6pm, Sat. 11am-4pm.

Mallett at Bourdon House

2 DAVIES ST, W1, 0171-629 2444

Open Mon.-Fri. 9.30am-5.30pm, Sat. by appointment.

Established in 1865, Mallet in Bond Street has five floors arranged into rooms, with richly coloured walls to show English furniture, paintings and decorative objects delightfully laid out as they would be in a fine home. One room is devoted to the later nineteenth and early twentieth centuries including interesting examples of Victorian Gothic Revival and the Arts and Crafts movement. The large antique glass department in the basement displays museum-standard pieces such as air-twist candlesticks from 1745 and Dutch wine glasses, 1790, by David Wolff. There is also the Christopher Wood Gallery on the first floor with eighteenth-, nineteenth- and early twentieth-century paintings and watercolours as well as some contemporary works and changing exhibitions. At Mallett's charming Bourdon House premises, until 1953 the townhouse of the second Duke of Westminster, a more eclectic display of paintings, sculpture, objets d'art and garden statuary is on display.

Norman Adams

8-10 HANS RD, SW3, 0171-589 5266

Open Mon.-Fri. 9am-5.30pm.

Opposite the west side of Harrods, this firm, established in 1923, has eighteenth-century English furniture and a wide choice of chandeliers, mirrors and barometers as well as objets d'art from England and France, many by well-known makers and with a history attached.

Richard Courtney

112-114 FULHAM RD, SW3, 0171-370 4020

Open Mon.-Fri. 9.30am-6pm.

One of the leading dealers in eighteenth-century furniture, the shop also specialises in fine Queen Anne walnut furniture. There are also beautiful choices in George III pieces, such as carved walnut library chairs, c. 1760, or satinwood and marquetry inlaid tea tables, c. 1780.

Stair & Company

14 MOUNT ST, W1, 0171-499 1784

Open Mon.-Fri. 9.30am-5.30pm, Sat. by appointment.

Established in 1911, this firm has a huge stock of eighteenth-century English furniture and art, and is the place where you might find a fine set of dining chairs, a mahogany bookcase or a carved George II wood and gilt geso mirror, c. 1740. Everything from chandeliers to huge dining room tables gleam importantly in this showroom.

GLASS

Jeanette Hayhurst

32A KENSINGTON CHURCH ST, W8, 0171-938 1539

Open Mon.-Fri. 10am-5pm, Sat. noon-5pm.

A friendly and enthusiastic proprietor, Jeanette Hayhurst features eighteenth- to twentieth-century glassware, all British-made, for collecting or for using. There is a wide choice of Georgian decanters and Victorian sundae dishes and wine goblets. Modern glass work is represented in a range of light fixtures, chandeliers and table ornaments.

ICONS

Maria Andipa Icon Gallery

162 WALTON ST, SW3, 0171-589 2371

Open Mon.-Sat. 11am-6pm.

The golden glow of a medieval altar panel depicting saintly figures with haloes sets the atmosphere of the window display and the exotic interior of this gallery which has become one of Europe's largest collections of fourteenth- to nineteenth-century icons from Russia, Greece, the Balkans, eastern Europe and Ethiopia. Celebrating nearly 30 years of her fascination with these evocative treasures, Maria Andipa was one of the first dealers to open a gallery specialising in Byzantine objects.

The Temple Gallery

6 CLARENDON CROSS, W11, 0171-727 3809

Open Mon.-Fri. 9am-6pm by appointment.

From small, gold-leafed altar pieces of saints to large painted church doors, the collection of Greek and Russian icons and objects here dates from the twelfth to sixteenth centuries. Established in 1960, Richard Temple's little gallery is well established with collectors who head for this quiet residential corner, dotted with some interesting shops, to appreciate Byzantine art at its finest. He has written several books about icons.

MAPS & PRINTS

Henry Sotheran

80 PIMLICO RD, SW1, 0171-730 8756

Open Mon.-Fri. 10am-6pm, Sat. to 4pm.

Sotheran was established in 1815 by Thomas Sotheran, whose family firm of booksellers had been founded in York in 1761 and is still a centre for booksellers today. This branch carries a huge range of topographical and architectural prints by artists such as Piranese, Roberts and Daniells and it welcomes browsers. The print department at 2-5 Sackville Street, W1, 0171-439 6151, concentrates mainly on original ornithological prints, especially by John Gould, although this latter branch is principally a book shop.

Japanese Gallery

66D KENSINGTON CHURCH ST, W8, 0171-229 2934

Open Mon.-Sat. 10am-6pm.

Every inch of the walls in this small gallery is covered with colourful wood-block prints, mainly from the nineteenth century though there are earlier artists too. Birds and flowers jostle with portraits of beautiful women from masters like Utamaro. In the many cases dotted around, Satsuma medicine 'inros', incense burners and tea ceremony pots compete for your attention, plus Noh masks.

Jonathan Potter

125 New Bond St, W1, 0171-491 3520
Open Mon.-Fri. 10am-6pm.

Ring the bell to gain entry to an upstairs gallery of early maps covering all parts of the known world—including maps of the North American Great Lakes with the original Indian names. Jonathan Potter is one of the most important map dealers and has a huge selection and range of prices.

London Cartoon Gallery

44 Museum St, WC1, 0171-242 5335
Open Mon-Sat 10am-6pm.

Gosh Partnership took over the former Jack Duncan Cartoons & Books and have continued to delight the world with work from eminent cartoonists for Private Eye, The Guardian, Oldie and more. Each month one artist is highlighted. They stock a wide range of interesting playing cards plus some ceramics alongside a changing stock of prints.

The Map House

54 Beauchamp Pl, SW3, 0171-589 4325
Open Mon.-Fri. 9.45am-5.45pm, Sat. 10.30am-5pm.

Besides antique maps, atlases and globes, the five galleries here offer reference books on the subject of maps and map-making, reproductions and prints, and decorative engravings, all beautifully presented and most published between 1600 and 1900. Despite its size, it has a congenial atmosphere.

The O'Shea Gallery

120A Mount St, SW1, 0171-629 1122
Open Mon.-Fri. 9.30am-6pm, Sat. to 1pm.

A must for any map enthusiast—there are thousands of examples contained in the plan chests. O'Shea's is a specialist dealer in fifteenth- to nineteenth-century prints and maps; the stock can be viewed by county, country or by continent. Prints cover topographical, decorative, natural history, sporting and marine subjects.

The Parker Gallery

28 Pimlico Rd, SW1, 0171-730 6768
Open Mon.-Fri. 9.30am-5.30pm, Sat. by appointment.

There is always a wide range here of antique prints and engravings with the emphasis on marine, nautical and military sciences, and personalities. They also stock prints on the more light-hearted side of life: games, pastimes and sports.

The Schuster Gallery

14 Maddox St, W1, 0171-491 2208
Open Mon.-Fri. 10am-5.30pm, Sat. by appointment.

Illuminated manuscripts and interesting prints of London or botanical subjects are the specialist wares in this no-nonsense shop. There are also books illustrated with the same themes.

METALWARE

Jack Casimir

23 Pembridge Rd, W11, 0171-727 8643
Open Mon.-Sat. 10am-5.30pm.

From fireplaces to candle snuffers, Ray and Michael Casimir carry on a third-generation family business in this well-stocked shop, specialising in the sixteenth to nineteenth centuries. The shelves are filled with British and European pewter tankards, copper pots, brass door-knobs and occasional rare items, such as fifteenth-century German braziers in either brass or bronze.

ORIENTAL ART

Barry Davies Oriental Art

1 Davies St, W1, 0171-408 0207
Open Mon.-Fri. 10am-6pm.

Japanese works of art are the speciality of this smart gallery which has some furniture and rare samurai armour. Behind small screens, shelves display fine netsuke, cloisonné, ivory and lacquer ware, such as a three-compartment inro after a print by Utamaro. The firm meticulously classifies individual artists and schools. To encourage modern craftsmen in the old traditions, the shop features contemporary lacquer work, especially by Unryuan whose work is predicted to rival the old masters.

Eskenazi

10 Clifford St, W1, 0171-493 5464
Open Mon.-Fri. 9am-6pm.

More like a museum than a shop, this establishment's dramatically lit showcases display Ming porcelain, Tang figures, jade objets d'art and bronze pieces, many with BC dates. Museums and learned institutions refer to Eskenazi's expertise in Chinese antiquities. Its netsuke collection is considered to be the best in Europe, with prices ranging from £1,000 to the sky.

John Eskenazi

15 OLD BOND ST, W1, 0171-409 3001

Open Mon.-Fri. 9am-6pm, by appointment.

Previously with a Milan base, this gallery on the second floor of the building has a wide-ranging collection of artefacts from south-east Asia and the Himalayas including Buddhist and Tibetan sculptures, rugs, carpets and textiles and, on occasion, Chinese hangings.

Michael Goedhuis

116 MOUNT ST, W1, 0171-629 2228

Open Mon.-Fri. 9.30am-6pm.

Amid the Oriental works of art are such fine pieces as a gilt copper rakan, signed Kado from the eighteenth-century Edo period, and a pair of bronze candelabra from the sixteenth-century Ming dynasty. Michael Goedhuis has a wide choice of sculptures, bronzes and ceramics from Japan and China.

Robert Hall

15C CLIFFORD ST, W1, 0171-734 4008

Open Mon.-Fri. 10am-5.30pm.

Established in 1976 and now probably the world's leading dealer in antique Chinese snuff bottles, Robert Hall recently opened this shop to show off hundreds of pieces, which can be made of glass, agate, jade, enamel or porcelain, and range in price from £200 to £400,000. They were originally made for the emperors of the Qing dynasty, becoming extremely popular in the mid-nineteenth century. The equivalent of the European snuff box, the bottle would have a stopper and a little spoon for scooping out the snuff. Robert Hall has written and published books, on sale at the shop, on the subject of collecting snuff bottles.

Rossi & Rossi

91C JERMYN ST, SW1, 0171-321 0208

Open Mon.-Fri.10.30am-5.30pm, Sat. by appointment.

The friendly proprietors at this second-floor gallery specialise in top south Asian and Himalayan art, from the second century BC to the seventeenth century. Sculptures include bronze, stone and terracotta pieces; they also stock textiles and paintings.

S Marchant & Son

120 KENSINGTON CHURCH ST, W8, 0171-229 5319

Open Mon.-Fri. 10am-6pm.

Sydney Marchant founded the firm in 1925 and it's still mainly family owned and run. There are three floors of Chinese pottery and porcelain including a 'blue-and-white room', jade pieces, works of art and Chinese furniture and Japanese art, porcelain and ivory ware. And what a priceless collection it is. From the 1400s, a fine Chinese early Ming dynasty dish in blue-and-white porcelain painted with flower-heads and scrolling foliage, and a rare Ming blue-and-white vase decorated with birds, ducks and flowering branches and trees from the late 1500s. There are annual exhibitions on such themes as Qing mark and period wares, monochrome and two-coloured, and marked imperial pieces.

Sydney L Moss

51 BROOK ST, W1, 0171-629 4670

Open Mon.-Fri.10am-5.30pm

At the large, sedate showrooms of this respected dealer are Chinese paintings, calligraphy and literati works, as well as bronzes, jades and furniture. There are also Japanese paintings, calligraphy, netsuke, sculpture and lacquerware.

POTTERY & PORCELAIN

Alistair Sampson Antiques

120 MOUNT ST, W1, 0171-409 1789

Open Mon.-Fri. 9.30am-5.30pm, Sat. by appointment.

English pottery from the seventeenth and eighteenth centuries is the speciality of this shop which has other decorative and interesting items from that period, such as English naive painting, needlework and brass ware. It also specialises in eighteenth-century English furniture.

Brian Haughton Antiques

3B BURLINGTON GDNS, W1, 0171-734 5491

Open Mon.-Fri.10am-5pm.

The company, housed in a small, smart showroom, specialises in English and continental ceramics and offers a wide range of objects from all factories like Chelsea 'Hans Sloane' plates with the red anchor mark, 1755-6. Other dramatic displays might include Sèvres parcel-biscuit gilt baskets and stands. Brian Haughton is a ceramic specialist who organises the International Ceramics Fair and Seminar each June.

Constance Stobo

31 HOLLAND ST, W8, 0171-937 6282

Open Mon.-Fri.11am-5pm, Sat 10am-2pm.

Sunderland lustre figures depicting autumn and winter, and Staffordshire pottery spaniel jugs from around 1850, might be found among the large choice of mantel dogs, Staffordshire cow creamers and other pieces of eighteenth- and nineteenth-century pottery at this corner shop in a quiet enclave near Kensington High Street. Regular collectors are kept informed about unusual items to add to their shelves, with Sunderland lustre plates decorated with ships and biblical sayings being very popular.

Jonathan Horne

66B & 66C KENSINGTON CHURCH ST, W8, 0171-221 5658

Open Mon.-Fri. 9.30am-5.15pm.

From medieval pots and early English pottery up to the Arts and Crafts era, this firm founded in 1968, has many rarities. The two showrooms display Staffordshire cow creamers, Delft ware and many tin-glazed tiles. Exhibitions about aspects of the collection are held every March.

Klaber and Klaber

P O BOX 9445, NW3, 0171-435 6537

By appointment only.

Specialists in fine eighteenth-century and continental porcelain, this firm exhibits at the Grosvenor House Antiques Fair each June.

London Curiosity Shop

66E KENSINGTON CHURCH ST, W8, 0171-229 2934

Open Mon.-Sat. 10am-6pm.

Designed to look like a traditional 'Cabinet of Curiosities', this shop displays British china and Meissen cups and saucers as well as figures. It also specialises in French bisque dolls.

RUGS & TAPESTRIES

C John (Rare Rugs)

70 SOUTH AUDLEY ST, W1, 0171-493 5288

Open Mon.-Fri. 9.30am-5pm.

Established in 1947, this firm excels in its choice of French Aubusson and Savonnerie carpets from the eighteenth and nineteenth centuries. A mid-eighteenth-century French Beauvais tapestry, finely woven in silk and wool, and a mid-Victorian English floral needlework carpet are typical of the finds among the collection which includes hand-made carpets, rugs, textiles and tapestries from Persia, Turkey, India, China, Spain, Italy, France, Portugal, Russia, the Caucuses and England.

David Black Oriental Carpets

96 PORTLAND RD, W11, 0171-727 2566

Open Mon.-Fri.10am-6pm, Sat.11am-5.30pm.

Decorative carpets from Delhi to Donegal are displayed—or stand in rolled-up abundance—at this cheerful, informal shop. Here you see vintage carpets from Turkey, India, Persia, plus modern carpets brightly coloured with vegetable dyes, thanks to the Dobag project which the shop started. Local craftsmen in Turkey are encouraged to use traditional handcraft methods in making carpets. Prices are excellent, and restoration work is undertaken.

Linda Wrigglesworth

34 BROOK ST, W1, 0171-408 0177

Open Mon.-Fri. 10am-6pm.

Specialising in Chinese costumes and textiles, this gallery and shop is arrayed with vibrantly coloured robes from the eighteeth and early nineteenth centuries, including a multi-hued wedding skirt, decorative panels and fans, as well as other accessories, such as hats and footwear worn by attendants to the court. Linda established her business in 1978, intrigued by the symbolism, workmanship and colours of early Chinese costume. She has a special interest in the Qing period, 1644-1911.

The Textile Gallery

12 QUEEN ST, W1, 0171-499 7979

Open Mon.-Fri. by appointment.

Behind the blue door of this corner Georgian house are comfortable rooms where the owner shows antique textiles from before 1800 as well as carpets, mostly from Persia, India, China and Turkey. The gallery, founded in the late 1960s, also has antique embroideries, needle-work pieces and wall-hangings.

Victor Franses Gallery

57 Jermyn St, SW1, 0171-493 6284
Open Mon.-Fri. 10am-5pm.

The contrast of nineteenth-century bronze animal sculptures against the rich background of hanging carpets from the Far East gives drama to these showy galleries. The carpets come from all over the world, including Russia, Persia, China and Turkestan; the animal sculptures are from France.

SCIENTIFIC INSTRUMENTS, CLOCKS & WATCHES

Arthur Middleton

12 New Row, WC2, 0171-838 7042
Open Mon.-Fri. 10am-6pm, Sat. by appt.

Step back in time in this fascinating, old-fashioned shop where antique globes, including beautifully illustrated celestial varieties that depict constellations, are stocked, alongside compasses, telescopes, sextants and other scientific and navigational instruments of the past. Globes range from several hundred pounds for early twentieth-century models, to many thousands for eighteenth-century examples. Only serious enquiries are welcome; ring the bell for entry.

Asprey

165-169 New Bond St, W1, 0171-493 6767
Open Mon.-Fri. 9.30am-5.30pm, Sat. 10am-5pm.

Amid its comprehensive antique furniture selection, this famous store has a workshop for clock and watchmakers who undertake the restoration of timepieces and marine chronometers.

Camerer Cuss & Co

17 Ryder St, SW1, 0171-939 1940
Open Mon.-Fri. 9.45am-5pm, or by appointment.

Sharing the same neat premises in the heart of St. James's are two experts. John Carlton-Smith specialises in longcase clocks, particularly up to 1830, and carriage clocks up to 1900, in addition to vintage barometers. Terence Cameron Cuss concentrates on watches, mostly up to 1910, as well as clocks.

Harriet Wynter

50 Redcliffe Rd, SW10, 0171-352 6494
By appointment.

Harriet Wynter was one of the first dealers in the specialised world of astrolabes, globes, lode-stones, microscopes and telescopes, plus wonderful theodolites. She now operates from her house, only seeing serious collectors, and also deals in pictures.

John Carlton-Smith

17 Ryder St, SW1, 0171-930 6622

Pendulum of Mayfair

51 Maddox St, W1, 0171-629 6606
Open Mon.-Fri. 10am-6pm, Sat. 10am-5pm.

This is a good place to come for a vast selection of longcase and bracket clocks as well as a wealth of advice and information from the knowledgeable and helpful staff. All the clocks are authenticated and none have been restored to more than 5 percent of the original works.

Raffety

34 Kensington Church St, W8, 0171-938 1100
Open Mon.-Fri. 11am-5pm, Sat. by appointment.

A George III mahogany longcase by Edward Pistor, London, is one of the fine showpieces you might find in this shop. Even the doorway has a large clock face over it. The firm deals in English-made clocks, mostly from 1670 to 1860, and scientific instruments and barometers, in addition to exquisite examples of eighteenth-century English furniture.

Trevor Philip & Sons

75a Jermyn St, SW1, 0171-930 2954
Open Mon.-Fri. 10am-6pm, Sat. 10.30-3.30pm and by appointment.

Fine old clocks and some unusual objets d'art are displayed here along with scientific instruments, especially navigational varieties, which can date back to 1450. Vintage globes are a speciality, particularly from the eighteenth century.

SILVER

Asprey and Garrard

165-169 New Bond St, W1, 0171-493 6767
Open Mon.-Fri. 9.30am-5.30pm, Sat. 10am-5pm.

With a large silver 'factory' on the premises, Asprey offers its own designs of modern silverware and exquisite antique silver, especially from the Georgian era, such as sugar baskets and candlesticks. With its antique glass and furniture and its own workshops, Asprey can comfortably be listed under every shopping category, from leather goods to fine jewelry.

J H Bourdon-Smith

24 Mason's Yard, SW1, 0171-839 4714
Open Mon.-Fri. 9.30am-6pm.

In business for almost 50 years, John Bourdon-Smith believes antique silver should be bought 'for the love of the article and its useful purpose', and it also makes a good long-term investment. In a secluded corner of St. James's, this family-run shop gleams with coffee pots, platters, tankards, candlesticks, caskets, coasters, tureens, tea sets, snuff boxes and cutlery, mostly from the Georgian era.

London Silver Vaults

Chancery House, 53-65 Chancery Lane, WC2, 0171-242 3844
Open Mon.-Fri. 9am-5.30pm (last entry 5.20pm), Sat. 9am-1pm.

Going through the thick and heavy door, visitors feel they are stepping into a giant underground safe, which turns out to house a series of little rooms where some 40 dealers show fine silver in a no-nonsense fashion. The Vaults have the reputation of offering well-priced Sheffield plate and sterling silver.

Silver Galleries

111-112 New Bond St, W1, 0171-493 6180
Open Mon.-Fri. 9am-5pm.

It may be a bit intimidating to climb the steps up to the clutch of serious-looking silver dealers but the exercise is worthwhile. For that special wedding present, head for A and B Bloomstein's large selection of silver and silver plate candelabras, tureens, teapots and platters. Tucked away on the top floor is Brian Bett, open by appointment only (0171-437 4975), who has silver wine accessories and specialises in unusual silver objects.

SILVER & JEWELRY

Bentley and Co

8 New Bond St, W1, 0171-629 0651
Open Mon.-Sat. 10am-5.30pm.

This family-run business, established in 1934, has two floors to show off its antique silverware from the eighteenth century onwards, including complete canteens of English-made cutlery, and a very large choice of English period jewelry plus pieces from Cartier and Fabergé.

D S Lavender

26 Conduit St, W1, 0171-629 1782
Open Mon.-Fri. 9.30am-5.30pm.

The walls are bedecked with framed miniatures, a speciality of this firm established in 1945. It has good antique jewelry and objets d'art like a Queen Anne snuff box, 1710, and a pair of eighteenth-century lorgnettes.

Ermitage

14 Hay Hill, W1, 0171-731 1810
Open Mon.-Fri. 10.30am-5pm

Russian works of art, objets de vertu, continental silver and Fabergé pieces are among the enticing stock at this little gallery. Fabergé's enamel boxes, clocks, frames, Easter eggs and floral pieces were so well documented in London sales ledgers that their previous ownership enhances their appeal.

Hancocks

1 Burlington Gdns, W1, 0171-493 8904
Open Mon.-Fri. 9.30am-5pm, Sat. 10-4pm.

Like many of the specialist silver dealers, this shop, established in 1849, also has a wide array of jewelry from the Victorian, Edwardian and Art Deco eras. The silverware ranges from £100 to £150,000.

Harvey and Gore

41 Duke St, St. James's, SW1, 0171-839 4033
Open Mon.-Fri. 9.45am-4.45pm.

A small, bright shop whose stock of silver and old Sheffield plate is the backbone of a firm founded in 1723. Its jewelry displays have included such choice items as a bracelet from the Imperial Russian collection, reported to have been worn by Catherine the Great. Also a good collection of fine modern pieces.

Mappin and Webb

170 Regent St, W1, 0171-734 3801
Open Mon., Tues., Wed., Fri. 9.30am-6pm, Thurs. 9.30am-7pm.

First registered in 1774, the Mappin hallmark is renowned for high quality, well designed silverware and gifts. Among the beautiful jewelry, clocks, watches, cufflinks, desk accessories and tableware, you'll find exquisite christening gifts and Lalique porcelain. Also worth seeking out are the antique and second-hand silver pieces. The company also operates a bridal service and a firm called Carrington & Co on the first floor, which specialises in regimental silver and sporting trophies. **Also at 65 Brompton Rd, SW3, 0171-584 9361.**

Moira

23 New Bond St, W1, 0171 629 0160
Open Mon.-Fri. 9am-6pm, Sat. 9am-5pm.

Established in 1985, this showy, sleek shop always has eye-catching, high-quality antique jewelry, with novelty charm bracelets, chunky Art Deco earrings and signet rings and stylised floral art nouveau pieces. The well known designers Van Cleef & Arpels, Tiffany and Cartier are well represented alongside stylish 'cocktail jewelry'.

N Bloom and Son

124 New Bond St, W1, 0171-629 5060
Open Mon.-Fri. 10.30am-5.30pm, Sat. 11.30am-5.30pm.

Proprietor Ian Harris, a celebrity expert who appears in the BBC Antiques Road Shows, prides himself on unusual pieces. The jewelry is mostly from 1860 to 1960, ranging from approximately £200 to £30,000, with some Georgian and Victorian silver. Located at these premises within the Bond Street Antiques Centre for several years, the firm has been welcoming connoisseurs since 1912, when it was founded by Ian Harris's maternal grandfather, Nathan Bloom.

S J Phillips

139 New Bond St, W1, 0171-629 6261
Open Mon.-Fri. 10am-5pm.

Nothing seems to change at this old shop, founded in 1869, with its wide choice of fine silver on display in traditional glass-fronted showcases. Run by the Norton family, it has antique necklaces, brooches, rings and a host of other exquisite pieces.

Sandra Cronan

18 Burlington Arcade, W1, 0171-491 4851
Open Mon.-Fri. 9.30am-5pm.

A polo player herself, Sandra Cronan usually has silver-plated polo trophies and related artefacts in her tiny arcade boutique, but her speciality is high quality, rare antique jewelry. She stages interesting exhibitions such as cufflinks through the ages and faux gems.

Tessier's

26 New Bond St, W1, 0171-629 0458
Open Mon.-Fri. 10am-5pm, Sat. 10.30am-4pm.

There are coronets and tiaras in the window of this charming old shop where the silver tankards, tureens and candlesticks are of superb quality. There is a wide-ranging jewelry collection and many objets d'art, including Fabergé pieces.

Wartski

14 Grafton St, W1, 0171-493 1141
Open Mon.-Fri. 9.15am-5pm.

Flower studies, snuff boxes and trinkets, including the famous eggs made with charm and humour by the legendary jeweller, Fabergé, make this shop a little retrospective museum of his work. Emmanuel Snowman, the father of the current chairman, A. Kenneth Snowman, made the first forays into post-Revolutionary Russia to save imperial works of art so Wartski has an historic interest in maintaining its worldwide reputation as keepers of the Fabergé archives and remaining a centre for the study of Russian art. At the front, amid shelves of antique silver, the work of talented modern craftsmen is displayed.

SPORTING ANTIQUES

Sean Arnold Sporting Antiques

21-22 Chepstow Corner, Westbourne Grove, W2, 0171-221 2267
Open Mon.-Sat. 10am-6pm.

Two floors now for this dealer in sporting items who moved from Grays Market. Everything you could possibly imagine people needing for tennis, polo, golf, boating, yachting, shooting, hunting—in fact all the traditional English country pursuits—is here. It's a fascinating shop and they also have a big library stocking books.

TEXTILES & CLOTHING

Gallery of Antique Costumes and Textiles

2 CHURCH ST, NW8, 0171-723 9981
Open Mon.-Sat. 10am-5.30pm.

Lovers of lavish fabrics and costumes delight at this treasure trove of a shop stocking exquisite quilts, antique velvets, brocades, silks and textiles dating back to the nineteenth century. Although the stock is international, there is a strong emphasis on English and French items, plus examples of Chinese, Indian, Russian and Turkish textiles. Cushions are covered in a riot of colours and flowers of the fields, and chintzes hang beside antique tassles and swags. This is a wonderful place to pick up a shawl or a piece of antique material. Prices start from £400-£3,000 for a shawls, £200 for a small piece of antique fabric.

Lunn Antiques

22 CUCUMBER ALLEY, THOMAS NEAL'S, SHORTS GDNS, WC2, 0171-379 1974
Open Mon.-Sat. 10am-6.30m.

Antique lace, textiles, clothing and costumes from the nineteenth century to the early 1960s are decked out in this little shop. Especially interesting are the beaded dresses from the 1920s. Another branch of Lunn Antiques can be found at 86 New King's Rd, SW6, 0171-736 4638; here you will find linen, unusual bed covers and quilts plus reproduction Victorian nightdresses from £18 and children's smocks from £15.

Steinberg & Tolkien

193 KING'S RD, SW3, 0171-376 3660
Open Mon.-Sat. 10.30am-7pm, Sun. noon-6.30pm.

If you're after the best vintage fashion labels, look no further than Steinberg & Tolkien. Everything from Chanel and Schiaparelli jewelry to immaculate ensembles from Chanel and Pucci are always to be found here (that is if the fashion press don't pick them up first). A good place for inspiration as well as a great place to shop.

WALKING STICKS

Michael German

38B KENSINGTON CHURCH ST, W8, 0171-937 2771
Open Mon.-Fri. 10am-5pm, Sat. 10am-2pm.

A walking stick was once a prestige decorative item shown off at court by royalty, then it became a necessary fashion accessory for gentlemen in the Victorian era. Today it is a collector's item. Here you'll find hundreds of walking sticks, from 1650 to 1920, mostly with curiously carved handles. Prices start at £60 to £200, going up to thousands of pounds for rare varieties. Collectors are very particular in their tastes; one customer collects only dogs'-head handled sticks. Also stockist of vintage guns.

AT YOUR SERVICE

CAR CLEAN

The London Valet Company

31 BEDFORD SQ, WC1, 0171-299 4215/0171-314 1516

Offering everything from a basic wash and hoover to a full hand polish and interior upholstery shampoo, owner Declan Barry says he will do his utmost to bring your car back to showroom condition. Special rates available for weekly service.

CHAUFFEURS

Limousines of London

MILTON HOUSE, 2 FERNSHAW RD, SW10, 0171-351 7408

When you're out to impress, why not sit back and let someone else do the driving? Whether you choose a super-stretch limo or a low-key, four-door saloon, all cars from Limousines of London come equipped with mobile phones and air-conditioning. Bodyguards and translators available at extra cost.

CLOTHING REPAIRS

British Invisible Mending Service

32 THAYER ST, W1, 0171-487 4292
Open Mon.-Fri. 8.30am-5.45pm, Sat. 10am-1pm.

If you have something special you need mended, this is the place for specialist invisible work that involves taking threads individually from a hem and reweaving them in elsewhere, changing buttonhole sizes and anything else required to make your clothes look as good as new. Items take approximately one week. Prices from £30 + VAT.

First Tailored Alterations

85 Lower Sloane St, SW1, 0171-730 1400
Open Mon.-Sat. 9am-6pm.

Specialising in leather and suede, although all fabrics are more than adequately catered for, this useful place can alter waistbands or re-shape coats. Items take about one week.

DRY CLEANERS

Buckingham Dry Cleaners

83 Duke St, W1, 0171-499 1253
Open Mon.-Fri. 8am-6pm, Sat. 9.30am-12.30pm.

Particularly noted for cleaning the ball-gowns of the smart Mayfair set, they also clean waxed jackets and run a men's shirt service.

De-Luxe Cleaners

30 Brewer St, W1, 0171-437 1187
Open Mon.-Fri. 8.30am-6pm.

De-Luxe are used by local fashion houses, partly because they can clean so fast (1-2 hours). They also undertake alterations, repairs and invisible mending.

Jeeves of Belgravia

8-10 Pont St, SW1, 0171-235 1101
Open Mon.-Fri. 8.30am-6.30pm, Sat. 8.30am-5pm.

For items that you truly treasure, take them to Jeeves, which has built an enviable reputation for great care and impeccable cleaning—and packaging everything in tissue paper for collection. They also re-proof raincoats and skiwear, clean and vacuum-pack wedding dresses, launder household linens including duvets, and carry out shoe repairs and essential repairs for briefcases. Free collection/delivery. Prices for men's two-piece suit, £17.85, blazers £9.95 and trousers, £8.45. Branches throughout London.

HIRE

...An Evening Dress

The Merchant of Europe

232 Portobello Rd, W11, 0171-221 4203
Open Mon.-Sat. 11am-6pm, Sun. noon-5pm.

Whether you fancy yourself as a flirtatious flapper or a 1950s Hollywood diva, you'll find the original outfits and accessories you need to bring your fantasy to life. The helpful staff advise on hairstyles and make-up for a truly authentic look.

One Night Stand

44 Pimlico Rd, SW1, 0171-730 8708
Open Mon.-Fri. 10am-6.30pm, Sat. 10am-5pm. Appointments preferred.

For a really special occasion, this shop has cocktail dresses, ball gowns and all the accessories from evening wraps to handbags—everything, in fact, except shoes. Hire is £70-£90 for a short dress, £90-£140 for a long one.

...A Formal Gentleman's Outfit

Austin Reed

103-113 Regent St, W1, 0171-437 2140
Open Mon., Tues. & Fri. 9.30am-6pm, Wed. 10am-6pm, Thurs. 9.30am-7pm, Sat. to 6.30pm.

Formal wear for hire ranges from dinner jackets to morning suits for all special occasions. Evening suits £22.95-£46.95, morning suits £39.95 for weekend hire (Thurs.-Mon.).

Moss Bros

27 King St, WC2, 0171-497 9354
Open Mon.-Fri. 9am-5.30pm, Thurs. to 6.30pm.

The name in formal hire for men, Moss Bros has been kitting out gents for decades. A dinner jacket with all the trimmings will cost approximately £49. Last fitting is half-an-hour before the shop closes, and the length of time you can keep the suit is usually three days.

Tom Gilbey

2 New Burlington Pl, Savile Row, W1, 0171-734 4877
Open Mon.-Fri. 10am-6pm, Thurs. to 7pm, Sat. to 5.30pm

Forget traditional morning dress; this designer, renowned for his opulent-looking waistcoats and flamboyant couture suits, has a hire service of suits and accessories for men who temporarily want to look like dandies. Choose your velvet suits, some with embroidered collars and pockets, and accessories; a complete outfit is £295 for four-day hire. It is a great way to look sumptuous without buying elaborate clothes you may not want to wear again.

...A Theatrical Costume

Angels and Bermans

119 SHAFTESBURY AVE, WC2, 0171-836 5678
Open Mon.-Fri. 9am-4.30pm for costume hire, to 5.30pm for returns.

When you want to make an impression at a fancy dress party, call into Angels and Bermans for your costume. Maybe you fancy yourself as an authentic flapper or perhaps you want to step back in time to the medieval era—whatever the occasion or your particular preference, you're likely to find it here. Many outfits have been used in films and it is possible to hire one of the costumes Madonna wore in *Evita* or Kate Winslett wore in *Titanic*. Prices from £60 + VAT for 7 day hire.

HIRED HANDS

Childminders

6 NOTTINGHAM ST, W1, 0171-935 3000
Open Mon.-Fri. 8.45am-5.45pm.

With over 1,000 babysitters on their register, Childminders aim to provide the ideal childcare. All references are checked and most of the staff are off-duty nurses, nannies and primary school teachers with specific childcare experience.

Koala Nannies

22 CRAVEN TERR, SW10, 0171-402 4224
Open Mon.-Fri. 10.30am-5pm.

Originally started to provide Australian and New Zealand nannies and mother's helps, this agency finds childcarers, cooks, companions and housekeepers.

Nannies Incorporated

317 THE LINEN HALL, 162-168 REGENT ST, W1, 0171-437 1312
Open Mon.-Fri. 9am-6pm.

This firm provides qualified maternity nurses, baby nurses and British nannies with experience and verified references. Worldwide placements.

Pippa Pop-ins

430 FULHAM RD, SW6, 0171-385 2457

London's only children's hotel also acts as creche and nursery school for children aged 2 to 12. The list of services on offer is staggering, covering everything from creche workshops where participating children can learn to make exciting things like ice sculptures and pottery, or try out trampolining, either for a few hours (£30 from 9am-2pm; £25 from 2pm-6pm) or a whole day (£34 from 9am-6pm). During school holidays the creche workshop provides extra activities such as pony riding, trips to Euro Disney, the theatre or Thorpe Park at the regular workshop prices, plus the price of admission. The hotel offers meals, activities and accommodation during the week for £40 per night (from 6pm-9am), at weekends for £50 per night (from 5pm-10am), or a full weekend (from Fri. 6pm-Sun. 6pm) at £145. The friendly company also extends to school runs and nanny service.

Top Notch Nannies & Brilliant Babysitters

22A CAMPDEN GROVE, W8, 0171-938 2006
Mon.-Fri. 9am-5.30pm. Appointment essential.

A brilliant, as they claim, service for harassed parents. Jean Birtles will help you find a fully-vetted nanny, mother's help, or childminder with equal parts humour and sympathy.

Universal Aunts

P O BOX 304, SW4, 0171-738 8937

Established in 1921, Universal Aunts is famous for providing almost everything you need, from daily attendance at an embassy if you're after a visa, to escorting you wherever you want to go. They also act as an employment agency for staff, providing the grand with butlers for parties and the harrassed with a mother's help. They are best known for escorting unaccompanied children.

HOME DELIVERY

Food Ferry

0171-498 0827

With its claim to be the fastest home delivery service in London, Food Ferry aims to deliver orders for fresh, frozen and packaged foods, plus household good and pet foods placed by 10.30am the same day. £3 day delivery, £4 evening. Catalogue of over 2,500 lines.

Nappy Express

0181-368 0132 (24-HOUR ANSWERPHONE/FAX ORDERLINE)

Providing a nappy laundry service, baby products and household delivery service. Specify whether you require boy or girl nappies.

Room Service

0171-431 5555

Customers have a booklet listing a good selection of restaurants like Chutney Mary (in our restaurant section), which offer special take-away meals. You select your meal, phone your order and await your delivery (within the hour unless it is very large). With some advance notice, you can have a whole restaurant meal for a dinner party.

PROPERTY MAINTENANCE

N D Management

41 BROXASH RD, SW11, TEL & FAX 0171-738 0151, MOBILE 0836-767009

Like all the companies recommended here, the two young directors, Nicky Gill and Di Robertson, have an efficient and enthusiastic team of helpers. This first-rate company undertakes everything to do with property. They will maintain your apartment or house while you're at home or away, clean, shop, garden, decorate and repair, as well as make travel bookings and theatre reservations. They will even start your Bentley once a week while it is sitting in the garage!

SHIPPERS

Trans Euro World Wide Movers

DRURY WAY, BRENT PARK, NW10 0JN, 0181-784 0100

This company efficiently moves furniture all over the world and also has a helpful antiques and fine art division.

SHOE REPAIRS

The Complete Cobbler

26 TOTTENHAM ST, W1, 0171-636 9040

Open Mon.-Fri. 8am-6.30pm, Sat. 9.30am-1pm.

At this family business, which includes an extensive dry cleaning service, George Zorlakkis specialises in trade repairs for big names like Gucci and Charles Jourdan, and mends leather handbags and luggage. He can do repairs on the spot and also makes riding boots (he is on the premises Thurs. & Fri. from 5pm onwards). They will also re-stitch, replace trims and re-cover scuffed heels. Prices: £4.50 ladies heels, £7.80 mens; half leather sole £13.50 ladies, £17.50 mens.

Krantz & Son

180 DRURY LANE, WC2, 0171-405 0609

Open Mon.-Fri. 9am-4.30pm.

This company, established in 1905, is one of the few London shoe repairers still using traditional stitching machines. Prices for heels, men's £8.50, ladies, £4.50; leather half-sole and heels, £25 men, £15 ladies.

K G Shoes

253 EVERSHOLT ST, NW1, 0171-387 2234

Open Mon.-Fri. 8am-5.30pm, Sat. 9am-2pm.

With a client list including Gucci, Selfridges and Harrods, this family firm has built up a great reputation for quality repairs. Also popular for adjusting the 'bag factor' in women's boots.

BEAUTY AND HAIR

ALTERNATIVE THERAPIES

Alternative Medicine Centre

56 HARLEY HOUSE, MARYLEBONE RD, NW1, 0171-486 8087

Open Mon.-Thurs.10am-7pm, Fri. to 8pm, Sat. to 1pm.

A wide range of alternative therapies are offered in this 30-year old practice. Using everything from aromatherapy to zoning massage, hypnotherapy to reflexology, Bach flower remedies to stress reduction, the female therapists combat a variety of problems. They specialise in treating scarring, particularly with African, Asian and Oriental skins.

The Hale Clinic

7 PARK CRESCENT, W1, 0171-631 0156; NEW PATIENT ENQUIRY LINE: 01923 775 666

Open Mon.-Fri. 8.30am-9pm, Sat. 8.45am-4.30pm.

Thankfully, the clinic operates a new patient enquiry line to guide clients through the plethora of treatments and 100 or so private practitioners available at this popular clinic They cover everything from some things you may have heard of like aromatherapy, physiotherapy, chiropody and allergy testing, through to more unusual therapies such as polarity therapy, buteyko and kinesiology. If that list doesn't appeal, try out shyness counselling, colonic irrigation, Marma massage and a whole lot more. Prices vary according to the practitioner, call for details.

Natureworks

16 BALDERTON STREET, W1, 0171-355 4036

Open Mon.-Fri. 10am-6pm.

If you want the more alternative alternative treatments, spend an hour or two at Natureworks. Try out rebirthing, rejuvenessence, McTimoney chiropractic, kriyas or zero balancing; otherwise succumb to an Indian head massage, shiatsu massage or Thai massage.

BEAUTY SALONS & SPAS

Aveda Concept Salon

4TH FLOOR, HARVEY NICHOLS, 67 BROMPTON RD, SW3, 0171-201 8610

Open Mon.-Fri. 10am-9pm, Sat. 8am-7pm, Sun. noon-6pm.

An air of harmony prevails in this tailor-made, Feng Shui-designed beauty salon, devised to take the stress out of urban living. All treatments are based on the principles of Ayurveda, an ancient Indian healing philosophy.

The Dorchester Spa

THE DORCHESTER, PARK LANE, W1, 0171-495 7335

Open Mon.-Sun. 7am-9.30pm.

As you'd expect from a beauty salon located in one of London's top hotels, The Dorchester Spa is the epitome of luxury. From the moment you walk into the lavish cream-and-gold spa area on the lower ground floor, all stresses and strains are left behind, freeing your mind to enjoy the hedonistic treats on offer. Choose from half a dozen or so facials, manicures, pedicures, body treatments including Detoxifying Algae Wrap, £60 or Holistic Aromatherapy Total Body care, £90, reflexology, waxing and special packages like the Dorchester Spa Day which costs £230 for six-hour top-to-toe pampering. Men are adequately catered for with specially tailored programmes and individual treatments including the Gentlemen's Spa Day, five hours of grooming for £180, including light lunch.

Elizabeth Arden Red Door Hair & Beauty Spa

29 DAVIES ST, W1, 0171-629 4488

Open Mon., Tues., Fri., Sat. 9am-6pm, Wed. & Thurs. to 8pm.

Back in 1921 when the original salon opened, this was the place where all the beautiful people came to make themselves even more beautiful. The famous lacquer red door closed its London premises in 1981 but re-opened again in May 1997 in its new premises, a former bank spread over two floors on the corner of Grosvenor and Davies Streets. Treatments include Salt Glow £30, to smooth away dry skin, Body Wraps to detoxify and tone, Hot Mud foot treatment, £15 and a complete range of hair and make-up services to meet individual needs. The Arden Spa Packages such as Spa Body Retreat, £100, and Visible Difference Day, £130, are justifiably popular.

The Sanctuary

12 FLORAL ST, WC2, 0171-420 5151

Open Mon. & Tues. 10am-6pm, Wed.-Fri. to 10pm, Sat. & Sun. to 6pm.

As the name implies, this women-only pampering-zone is a haven in the centre of London. Entry is by membership which is £49.50 day or £29.50 evening (from 5pm-10pm on Wed.-Fri. only) and includes use of sauna, steam room, jacuzzi, meditation suite with massage chairs and the tropical swimming pool, complete with tinkling waterfall. The vast range of treatments available at extra cost include reflexology, body treatments, facials, manicures, pedicures, heat treatments, tanning sessions, waxing and make-up lessons.

Sher System Studio

30 New Bond St, W1, 0171-499 4022

Open Mon.-Fri. 10am-6pm.

Helen Sher and daughter Glenda have developed their own unique beauty treatment, based on an easy warm water therapy: just splash the face regularly in tap water specially treated with Sher crystals. A kit with toner, emollient and other requirements comes in travel-pack form with lightweight plastic bottles. Despite the cost, enthusiastic clients with rejuvenated faces keep rushing back for more.

COSMETICS

Cosmetics à la Carte

19b Motcombe St, SW1, 0171-235 0596

Open Mon.-Sat. 10am-6pm.

Christina Stewart and Lynne Sanders produce hypo-allergenic products from their own factory for use in the make-up diagnosis and lessons which take place at the shop. Price for a half-hour Express make-up is £30, rising to £100 for a full make-up lesson. For information about other branches or to order the mail order catalogue, call 0171-622 2318.

Dickins & Jones

Regent St, W1, 0171-734 7070

Open Mon., Tues., Fri., Sat. 10am-6.30pm, Wed. to 7pm, Thurs. to 8pm, Sun. 11am-5pm.

Since undergoing a £3.5 million facelift, Dickins & Jones has expanded and updated its cosmetics hall, making it one of the most spacious and unrivalled in town. Alongside the cosmetic giants such as Clarins, Estée Lauder, Christian Dior and Chanel, you'll find newer and fresher faces such as Bobbi Brown, Jurlique and Aveda. Exclusive lines include LeClerc and Make Up For Ever. Also home to John Gustafsson and his team of experts in the Personal Beauty Studios (women on second floor, men on the lower-ground floor) where they offer unbiased, impartial advice on the best cosmetics to suit your skintype, lifestyle and budget. The service is complimentary and operates on an appointment basis. Call 0171-287 4947.

Joan Price's Face Place

33 Cadogan St, SW3, 0171-589 9062

Open Mon.-Fri. 10am-6pm, Tues. to 8pm, Sat. to 5pm.

From model to beauty editor, Joan Price opened the first salon in 1967 to offer make-up sessions as one-to-one lessons rather that just applications of cosmetics. A one-hour lesson is £35. The salon stocks twenty brands in all price ranges. Clients can buy at the salon and as the staff are not on commission, recommendations are genuine. An informal, welcoming approach attracts everyone from teenagers to the over-50s. Joan Price did the make-up for Mrs Thatcher's TV appearances.

Liberty Perfumery

210-220 Regent St, W1, 0171-734 1234

Open Mon.-Sat. 10am-6.30pm, Thurs. to 7.30pm, Sun. noon-6pm.

No bouffant-haired, overly made-up consultants here, just a team of friendly and helpful staff who are passionate about their products. The cosmetics area is small, but still manages to create an illusion of light and space, thanks to careful design and the natural light streaming in from Great Marlborough Street. Representation veers towards the new and natural rather than old-fashioned and established, with skincare companies such as E'Spa, Kiehls, Aveda, Aesop and Philosophy and colour cosmetics from Shu Uemura and Face Stockholm.

MAC

109 King's Rd, SW3, 0171- 349 0601

Open Mon.-Sat. 10.30am-6.30pm, Sun. 11.30am-5.30pm.

Devised and formulated by a professional make-up artist and used by a host of Supermodels, the two London MAC outlets and their area in Harvey Nichols, are very much in vogue with Kate Moss-wannabes and make-up artists. The company, who are part of the giant Estée Lauder umbrella, operates a recycling service whereby tokens are issued for each returned container—when you have collected six tokens, you receive a free product. **Also at 28 Foubert's Pl, W1, 0171-439 0501.**

Mary Quant

3 Ives St, SW3, 0171-581 1811

Open Mon.-Sat. 10am-6pm.

A great place to shop for funky make-up colours which include 101 lipsticks in shades ranging from white to deepest violet, 80 nail colours and 120 eye shadows which can be handpicked then housed in the daisy print compacts. Reasonable prices make this a popular range with teenagers, the wild and wacky colours appeal to fashionable types.

Screenface

24 Powis Terrace, W11, 0171-221 8289
Open Mon.-Sat. 9.30am-6pm.

The place where those who make beauty their business stock up on the tools for their trade. Make-up artists and famous faces like Cher, supermodels Helena Christensen and Linda Evangelista are among those in the know seeking out professional plastic eyelash curlers, illuminiser foundation and make-up palettes and containers. Also at 48 Monmouth St, WC2, 0171-836 3955 for less focus on professional compacts and products.

Space NK

45-47 Brook St, W1, 0171-355 1727
Open Mon.-Sat. 10am-6pm.

Founder Nicola Kinnaird makes frequent trips abroad to source new and exciting cosmetic brands to add to the Space NK counters. Labels include François Nars, Stila, E'Spa, Antonia's Flowers, Laura Mercier and Eve Lom. The colour cosmetics are arranged in customer-friendly 'play stations' where shoppers can test out the ranges without obligation or intimidation. The helpful staff, who do not work on a commission basis, are trained make-up artists knowledgeable on all the ranges. Mail order service available for customers outside London, while those within central London can take advantage of the to-your-desk courier service. **Also at 7 Bishopsgate Arcade, 135 Bishopsgate, EC2, 0171-256 2303; 307 Kings Rd, SW3, 0171-351 7209.**

HAIR SALONS

Cadogan Club

18 Lowndes St, SW1, 0171-235 3814
Open Mon.-Fri. 9am-6pm.

This pleasant Mayfair salon for men and women has always been popular with the fashionable set, with a cut and blow-dry from £48.50.

Charles Worthington

12 Charlotte Pl, W1, 0171-631 1370
Open Mon.-Thurs. 8am-8.15pm, Fri. 8am-7.15pm, Sat. 9.15am-5.15pm.

An award-winning stylist, Charles Worthington's salons are every bit as glitzy as his ever-increasing celebrity client roster. Worthington himself is at the salon one day a week but the waiting list for an appointment is several weeks. **Also at The Dorchester, 0171-629 8888. Other branches at 34 Great Queen St, WC2, 0171-831 5303, and 1 Exchange Pl, The Broadgate Club, EC2, 0171-838 0802.**

Cool Cuts

First Floor, Kings Walk Mall, 122 King's Rd, SW3, 0171-591 0400
Open Mon.-Sat. 10am-7pm, Sun. noon-6pm.

The prices are very reasonable at this trendy salon. For either men or women, a shampoo is £3, a cut from £9.95 and re-style £12.95, with a blow-dry from £7 depending on the style. Children welcome; there are soft drinks and children's videos to entertain them. No appointment necessary but advisable at busy times.

Gene Bagley

58 Upper Mon.tagu St, W1, 0171 723 4576
Open Tues. & Wed. 9am-6pm, Thurs. to 8pm, Fri. to 7pm, Sat. to 5pm.

Natural and organic products only—even for colouring and perming—are used in this environmentally-friendly salon. All tints are ammonia free so are kinder to hair; grey hair can also be totally coloured with organic tints. Free consultations without obligation are available. A cut and blow-dry with Gene Bagley, the salon's top stylist, is £43. **Also at 12 Ridgway, Wimbledon Village, SW19, 0181-946 4789.**

Jo Hansford

19 Mount St, W1, 0171-495 7774
Open Tues.-Sat. 9am-6pm.

One of London's top colourists, Jo Hansford is held in high-esteem by the fashion press and her list of glitzy clients which includes Lauren Hutton, Patsy Kensit and Melanie Griffiths. Colour with Jo from £125 for half-head, £175 full-head; highlights from £95.

John Frieda

75 New Cavendish St, W1, 0171-636 1401
Open Mon.-Sat. 9am-5pm.

One of the top names in hairdressing and erstwhile spouse of pop singer Lulu, John

Frieda no longer cuts hair himself but has an expert team of stylists. A cut and blow-dry for ladies is from £20 to £50. **Also in Claridges hotel, 0171-499 3617, and at 4 Aldford St, W1; 0171-491 0840.**

Mahogany

17 ST. GEORGE ST, OFF HANOVER SQ, W1, 0171-629 3121

Open Mon., Tues., Fri. 10am-6.15pm, Wed. & Thurs. to 7.45pm, Sat. to 4.45pm.

Already well-established in Bath and Oxford, this hairdressing firm has branched out onto the London scene and is fast establishing a reputation for stylish haircuts and a welcoming approach. A ladies' cut is £36-£49.50; a restyle is £39.50-£54.50. The name is derived from the handsome mahogany timber floors and fittings.

Neville Daniel

162B SLOANE ST, SW1, 0171-245 6151

Open Mon.-Sat. 9am-6pm, Wed. to 8pm.

This luxurious, air-conditioned salon purports to be one of the largest in London and dresses the hair of a galaxy of stars like Pierce Brosnan and Joanna Lumley. But rest assured—you'll be given a haircut that suits you rather than what is currently in fashion. As well as full hairdressing facilities, there is also a Thalgo spa institute, offering a full range of beauty treatments. Cut and finish starts from £20 with a junior stylist to £70 for women and from £18-£40 for men.

Nicky Clarke

130 MOUNT ST, W1, 0171-491 4700

Open Mon.-Sat. 9am-6pm.

A celebrity in his own right, Nicky Clarke—of the shoulder-length mane and figure-hugging leather trousers—has cut Fergie's hair as well as tending to the tresses of, amongst others, Cindy Crawford, Greta Scaatchi, Paloma Picasso and Queen Noor of Jordan. A ladies' cut and blow-dry for a first time visit with Nicky is a staggering £300, with subsequent visits at £200. For men, the initial visit is £220, then £175. Otherwise, try an appointment with one of the senior stylists at £120 for ladies and £80 for men. Arezoo, the beauty therapist, offers excellent Cathiodermie facials, manicures and pedicures, with lots of TLC.

Vidal Sassoon

130 SLOANE ST, SW1, 0171-730 7288

Open Mon.-Sat. 9am-last appt 6pm, Wed. & Thurs. last appt 6.45pm.

The reputation of this internationally known hairdresser is based on the Sassoon philosophy of cutting hair to suit the bone structure of the face and the commercial success of the sixties 'bob'. Prices range from £41 to £62 for a cut and finish. Manicures and pedicures are available. **Salons throughout London.**

Vidal Sassoon For Men

56 BROOK ST, W1, 0171-318 5222

Open Tues.-Sat. 9am-6.45pm.

Formerly for men only, this salon added three new stylists for women. Prices range for a cut and finish from £41 to £62, blow dry £30. Manicures and hand massages are available.

SCENTS, SOAPS & TOILETRIES

L'Artisan Parfumeur

17 CALE ST, SW3, 0171-352 4196

Open Mon.-Fri. 10am-1pm, 2pm-6pm, Sat. to 5.30pm.

There are several branches of this delightful perfumery in France but only one in Britain. L'Artisan sniffs out the scent to suit you. It's a little boutique where the art of fragrance is taken seriously and in addition to romantic potions, pot pourri and scented Gris Gris, you'll be tempted by modern versions such as the French Dressing bath set including Bath Salts, Vinegar Tonic and Bath Oil. Surprisingly, the precious bottles cost no more than a brand name—a 50 ml. bottle is £33.50.

The Body Shop

268 OXFORD ST, W1, 0171-629 9365

Open Mon. Fri. 9.30am-7.30pm, Thurs. to 8.30pm, Sun. 11am-6pm.

Responsible for bringing affordable, environmentally friendly beauty products to the masses, this nationwide chain, devised and set up by Anita Roddick, now has a prime position in most High Streets. The shops are filled with everyone from teenagers seeking out the latest shade of lipstick, to grandmothers stocking up on jojoba shampoo, and young men buying skincare and shaving products from the hugely successful Mostly Men range. Besides a wide range of scents, cosmetics and grooming products, the Endangered Species range comprising brightly coloured animal-shaped soaps is aimed at children. Basket assortments are popular presents. **Branches throughout London.**

Crabtree & Evelyn

30 James St, WC2, 0171-379 0964

Open Mon.-Sat. 10am-8pm, Sun. noon-6pm.

Prettily packaged hand and body lotions, soaps and bath products are the main attraction of these well-known shops, which also offer preserves, vinegars and teas. Best seller is the Evelyn range, based on a fragrance from the essence of living roses called Evelyn, which was specially created for the shops by the rose expert David Austin. **Branches throughout London.**

The Crown Perfumery

51 Burlington Arcade, W1, 0171-408 0088

Open Mon.-Sat. 9.30am-5.30pm.

After extensive research, Barry Gibson has recreated the perfumes which British and European society enjoyed at the turn of the century and has also revived the name of the firm which made the scents which include Sandringham and Tanglewood Bouquet. Prices start from £30, although the Marechale brand, bottled in limited edition Baccarat crystal bottle, will set you back £480. Soaps are modestly priced at £7.50-£13.50.

Culpeper

21 Bruton St, W1, 0171-629 4559

Open Mon.-Fri. 9.30am-6pm, Sat. 10am-5pm.

Aromatic food products add extra interest to these herbalist shops which have followed a 'green policy' since the company was founded in 1927. Sachets of curry powder, jars of ginger and spicy Major Grey's mango chutney tempt the palate, and aromatherapy oils boxed in an attractive starter set, lift the soul. There are also books, herb-filled pillows, prettily covered hot water bottles, 'make your own' potpourri, scented candles and aroma oil burners to enhance the home, and nutmeg graters, honey and ginger juice cordial and mulled wine spices to liven up the larder. **Also at 8 The Market, Covent Garden, WC2, 0171-379 6698.**

Czech & Speake

39c Jermyn St, W1, 0171-439 0216

Open Mon.-Fri. 9.30am-6pm, Tues. 10am-6pm, Sat. to 5pm.

Besides exotic bath oils of frankincense and myrrh, bathroom fittings designed to make even lavatory roll and brush holders look elegant are the showpieces of these smart little shops. A wall-mounted ivory-coloured porcelain lavatory-brush and holder with a chrome finish costs around £195 + VAT. **Also at 125 Fulham Rd, SW3, 0171-225 3667.**

D R Harris & Co

29 St. James's St, SW1, 0171-930 3915

Open Mon.-Fri. 8.30am-6pm, Sat. 9.30am-5pm.

The original 'Pick-Me-Up' specially devised by Victorian proprietor, Daniel Rotely Harris, is still sold, from £5.95. No doubt it always did well here located near the gentlemen's clubs. This small shop offers diverse ranges, such as cucumber and rose cream for facial care, the Arlington line of men's cologne and shaving creams and soaps, plus Bewitch silky bath essence. It is a chemist shop where prescriptions can be filled and thus adheres to the original purpose of the shop which was co-founded in 1790 by a surgeon and one of the first pharmaceutical chemists.

Floris

89 Jermyn St, SW1, 0171-930 2885

Open Mon.-Fri. 9.30am-5.30pm, Sat. 10am-5pm.

Commissions to blend fragrances for the Queen and the Prince of Wales are all in a day's work for the Bodenham family, perfumiers for eight generations and direct descendants of a Spaniard, Juan Famenias Floris, who first set out his sign here in 1730. Now known for their English flower scents, such as rose and lily of the valley, the shop sells old-fashioned perfume bottles with silk bulbs and tassels as well as crystal and cut-glass potpourri bowls, alabaster soap dishes and tortoiseshell combs.

Jo Malone

154 Walton St, SW3, 0171-581 1101

Open Mon.-Sat. 10am-6pm.

Jo Malone is considered to be a guru amongst skincare aficinados. The lucky few actually have their faces tended to by Malone's skillful hands (even the waiting list is closed), and the rest of us have to contend with the delightful skincare and fragrance ranges which line the pristine shelves and counters in the relaxing cream-coloured shop. 'Sent a Scent' delivery service is also available.

Les Senteurs Specialist Perfumery

227 EBURY ST, SW1, 0171-730 2322

Open Mon.-Sat. 10am-6pm.

VIP treatment is the norm at this sensually bedecked shop which stocks imported, independent French and Italian brands. The proprietor, Karin Hawksley, takes time matching fragrances to a client's skin, which entails trying fragrances, whether flowery or pungent, onto sample cards first. There are also lovely room fragrances and bath and beauty solutions. Prices for Eau de Toilette start from £15.95.

Lush

11 THE MARKET, THE PIAZZA, COVENT GARDEN, WC2, 0171-240 4570

Open Mon.-Sat. 10am-7pm, Sun. noon-6pm.

At first glance Lush appears to be a thriving delicatessen. Look a little closer at the packages in the chill cabinets and you'll find that they are in fact natural beauty products with edible-sounding names like Aroma Bread face mask, made from brown bread and garlic. Soaps can be bought by the chunk, similar to cheese, where you can buy as much or as little as you want. Customers serve themselves, scooping up the lotions and potions stored in the fridge into little tubs. Just like a deli, most products are labelled with a sell-by date as the company use virtually no preservatives.

Neal's Yard Remedies

2 NEAL'S YARD, WC2, 0171-379 7222

Open Mon. 10am-6pm, Tues.-Fri. to 7pm, Sat. to 5.30pm, Sun. 11am-5pm.

The striking deep-blue glass bottles, filled with shampoos, bath oils and ready-made lotions, gleam on the shelves in the subdued lighting of this popular shop where the staff are kept busy measuring out herbs, seeds, powders and leaves from giant glass jars for aficionados of natural remedies. To help decide what preparations can be used to cure which ailments, there is a shelf of relevant books to consult. Information about courses and talks about herbalism, essential oils and homeopathy are on display.

Penhaligons

41 WELLINGTON ST, WC2, 0171-836 2150

Open Mon.-Sat. 10am-6pm.

These prettily outfitted shops, whether the Victorian-style interior of the Covent Garden premises or the tiny glass-roofed Mayfair shop, are a step into a recreated turn-of-the-century past. Fragrances are hand-blended to rediscovered recipes of William Penhaligon, court barber and perfumier extraordinaire in Queen Victoria's reign. The oldest, Hamman Bouquet, was created in 1872, its exotic name and scent—including jasmine, lavender, rose and sandalwood—inspired by the Turkish baths situated next to his original shop. Antique perfume bottles and silver table accessories add to Penhaligon's charm. **Also at 20a Brook St, W1, 0171-493 0002; 16 Burlington Arcade, Piccadilly, W1, 0171-629 1416; Royal Exchange, Cornhill, EC3, 0171-283 0711.**

Trumpers

9 CURZON ST, W1, 0171-499 1850

Open Mon.-Fri. 8.30am-5.30pm, Sat. to 1pm.

The Curzon Street shop opened in 1875 is lovingly maintained with dark wood panelling and display cases of their fragrances for men and shaving requisites, reflecting the fact that the founder, George Trumper, ran one of the first exclusive barbershops in London and was court hairdresser. Both shops still provide a barber's service in a soothing and pampering ambience, with face massage and moustache-curling on offer. Additionally, men who require advice on shaving can book up for a lesson with one of the experts, costing £35 for an hour. Colognes and after shaves include Wellington, with rosemary and neroli among the ingredients, Astor, with sandalwood and caraway base notes, and Wild Fern, featuring oak moss and basil. Besides razors, soaps, shampoos, loofahs and sponges, there is a superior range of leather gifts including flasks and cup sets, plus clothes and bathroom brushes. Hair cuts from £24. **Also at 20 Jermyn St, SW1, 0171-734 1370.**

Virgin Vie

242 OXFORD ST, W1, 0171-629 9862

Open Mon.-Sat. 9.30am-7pm, Thurs. to 8pm, Sun. noon-6pm.

The latest venture from entrepreneur Richard Branson brings a calm yet contemporary outlet to Oxford Street. Water falls down acid-etched glass panels into pools of water with engraved stones, reminiscent of a Japanese garden, reflecting the fact that many of the products are concerned with the rituals of bathing. Designed to reflect a fresh sunny day, the shop has good value products for face, hair and body. The special Consultation Zone screen features a sofa shaped like ruby red lips.

Zarvis

4 PORTOBELLO GREEN, W10, 0181-968 5435

Open Wed. & Sat. 11am-5pm. Occasionally Thurs. & Fri. Call to check.

Beautiful place to seek out over 120 medicinal cosmetic herbs sold by the ounce and a popular range of bath herbs and oils.

BOOKS

ARTS

A Zwemmer Arts Bookshop

24 LICHFIELD ST, WC2, 0171-240 4158

Open Mon.-Fri. 10am-6.30pm, Sat. to 6pm.

Three floors are filled with books on artists and every facet of the visual arts with in-depth coverage of medieval, Oriental, twentieth-century art and art history. In the basement, shelves are packed with books on architecture and the decorative arts such as ceramics, fashion, textiles and other crafts. The sister shop in Charing Cross Road specialises in media arts, stocking books on film, photography and graphic design. **Also at 80 Charing Cross Rd, WC2, 0171-240 41570.**

Atrium

5 CORK ST, W1, 0171-495 0073

Open Mon.-Fri. 10am-6pm, Sat. to 4pm.

This welcoming art book shop has a press book of current reviews to browse through on the new publications table. The shelves hold a comprehensive selection of books on photography, architecture, textiles and costume, sculpture, gardens, old masters, stained glass, Islamic and Indian art, Latin American arts, travel, interior design, icons and many other subjects. There are foreign language editions and many exhibition catalogues, and the staff take a genuine interest in tracking books down. Events, festivals, readings and other events on the subject of literature and books take place regularly.

BBC Shop

BROADCASTING HOUSE, PORTLAND PL, W1, 0171-765 0025

Open Mon.-Sun. 9.30am-6pm.

An outlet for all the BBC publications, tapes, videos and books, cards and posters, this is smaller than the spacious BBC World Service Shop but jam-packed with the corporation's products which include coffee-table books on some of the popular series and historical programmes.

BBC World Service Shop

BUSH HOUSE, STRAND, WC2, 0171-257 2576

Open Mon.-Fri. 10am-6pm, Sat. to 5.30pm.

Shows which have been broadcast on the 'Beeb', as it is sometimes affectionately called, whether radio or TV, often produce publications about the programme, the cast, or compilations of favourite scripts. The shop started as an information centre for its million of listeners worldwide. There are videos, cassettes and CDs about some nostalgically remembered shows and current popular programmes, as well as short wave radios.

Cinema Bookshop

13-14 GT. RUSSELL ST, WC2, 0171-637 0206

Open Mon.-Sat. 10.30am-5.30pm.

The largest book shop in Britain on the subject of cinema covers all aspects, catering for everyone from established cinematographers to students. They have biographies and technical books plus a good stock of ephemera, posters and photos, and they carry a good out-of-print section.

Dance Books

15 CECIL CT, WC2, 0171-836 2314

Open Mon.-Sat. 11am-7pm.

Founded by a former Ballet Rambert dancer, this shop has books on all types of dance and human movement, plus videos, posters and prints, some of which decorate the walls.

Dillons Arts Bookshop

8 Long Acre, WC2, 0171-836 1359

Open Mon.-Sat. 9.30am-10pm, Sat. noon-7pm.

Housing a wonderful collection of art books and a huge range of fashion and art magazines, this shop is always busy.

French's Theatre Bookshop

52 Fitzroy St, W1, 0171-387 9373

Open Mon.-Fri. 9.30am-5.30pm, Sat. 11am-5pm.

This firm, which has published plays since 1830, stocks more than 4,000 play titles in well-assembled order. There are reading and acting versions of plays. It has a reference collection of sound effects, and dialect recordings to help producers, playwrights and actors. There are also a couple of thousand books on the theatre.

National Portrait Gallery Shop

St. Martin's Pl, WC2, 0171-306 0055

Open Mon.-Sat. 10am-6pm, Sun. noon-6pm.

Attached to the National Portrait Gallery, the shop also boasts an extensive book shop, which is strong not only on books about art and related subjects, but also on biographies and critical appraisals of the people depicted in the gallery. Books by authors and painters are also included.

Royal Institute of British Architects

66 Portland Pl, W1, 0171-580 5533

Open Mon.-Fri. 9.30am-5.30pm, Sat. 10am-5pm.

The RIBA, as it is known, has an excellent specialist book shop which includes foreign publications (0171-251 0791) for anyone interested in architecture and (serious) landscape gardening in the context of architecture. If you're in the building, take in the exhibitions which are often on show. There is also an excellent Pâtisserie Valerie café located here.

Victoria and Albert Museum Shop

Cromwell Rd, SW7, 0171-938 8500

Open Tues.-Sun. 10am-5.45pm, Mon. noon-5.45pm.

Appealing range of art books in the V&A shop. Subjects include architecture, fashion design, pottery and general crafts.

CHILDREN

Children's Book Centre

237 Kensington High St, W8, 0171-937 7497

Open Mon.-Sat. 9.30am-6.30pm, Sun. noon-6pm.

This bright, well-organised shop with over 12,000 books thoughtfully arranged by age and subject, is usually full of children, sometimes sprawled on the floor, perusing a book or watching the latest video. They stock a wide choice of fiction and educational books for young children as well as cuddly bears and toys by Galt, Fisher Price and Lego. From babies to teenagers.

Daisy & Tom

181 King's Rd, SW3, 0171-352 5000

Open Mon.-Sat. 10am-6pm, Wed. to 7pm, Sun. noon-6pm.

The spacious galleried bookshop is the ideal environment to shop for children's books with or without the kids. The atmosphere is calming, the selection of books is extensive and also includes a good selection of reference and audio material.

COMICS

Forbidden Planet

71 New Oxford St, WC1, 0171-836 4179

Open Mon.-Wed. & Sat. 10am-6pm, Thurs. & Fri. to 7pm.

One of London's largest stockists of comics and cartoons. Nobody has counted the selection, but the description is 'two full floors'. Forbidden Planet also sells novels and spin-offs from popular comics: models, T-shirts and memorabilia. There is a wide selection of videos.

COOKING & FOOD

Books for Cooks

4 Bleinheim Crescent, W11, 0171-221 1992

Open Mon.-Sat. 9.30am-6pm.

There is a little café at the back of the shop. Cooking demonstrations by cooks/authors take place upstairs in the evening, £20, including a meal. Booking is essential. The shop is notable for its exhaustive selection of food and wine books and is one of the best in the country. From simple cook books to exotic cuisine, this shop is a must for anyone interested in the art of food.

CRIME

Murder One

71-73 Charing Cross Rd, WC2, 0171-734 3483
Open Mon.-Wed. 10am-7pm, Thurs.-Sat. to 8pm.

A vast stock of books covers only three topics: crime and mystery, romantic fiction and science fiction, but within those categories there is a huge number of books published in Britain and many books imported from the USA.

ECONOMICS

The Economist Shop

5 Regent St, SW1, 0171-839 1937
Open Mon.-Fri. 10am-6pm, Sat. to 5pm.

Behind the handsome façade of its premises, this efficiently run shop stocks books on important issues in world affairs, especially in the economic, political and social fields. Countries and continents are divided into their own sections. Its own range of publications include titles such as the Economist Dictionary of International Finance.

ESOTERICA

Mysteries New Age Centre

9-11 Monmouth St, WC2, 0171-240 3688
Open Mon.-Sat. 10am-6pm.

A mystical purple façade sets the off-beat mood of this pyschic and New Age book shop which sells tarot cards, crystal balls, incense, pendulums and other devices for exploring the secrets of the universe. Tarot readings available from £20.

Skoob Two

17 Sicilian Ave, WC1, 0171-405 0030
Open Mon.-Sat. 10.30am-6.30pm.

Part of Skoob, this shop specialises in New Age books, books on the occult and subjects like Greek and Latin, archeology and ancient religions.

Watkins Books

19 Cecil Ct, WC2, 0171-836 2182
Open Mon.-Wed. & Fri. 10am-6pm, Thurs. to 8pm, Sat. 10.30am-6pm.

In this large modern shop you'll find the widest range of books on esoteric themes to do with New Age philosophies: holistic health, Eastern religions, and subjects connected with natural health therapies.

FASHION

R D Franks

Kent House, Market Pl, W1, 0171-636 1244
Open Mon.-Fri. 9am-5pm.

This well-stocked bookshop is ideally located for designers in the rag trade and students at the nearby London College of Fashion and Central St. Martin's School of Art. The shelves are packed with books on everything to do with the fashion industry, including designer biographies, encyclopedias, fashion illustration and specialist subjects. All of the major international fashion magazines such as Harper's Bazaar, Allure, Donna and every issue of Vogue are represented here along with the bumper seasonal fabric and trend reports from all the fashion capitals.

FEMINIST

Silver Moon Women's Bookshop

68 Charing Cross Rd, WC2, 0171-836 7906
Open Mon.-Sat. 10am-6.30pm, Sun. 2pm-6pm.

All Virago's titles are stocked here, along with books relating to women's issues from women's rights to giving birth. They hold regular readings; consult the listings magazines or telephone for details.

GAY

Gay's the Word

66 Marchmont St, WC1, 0171-278 7654
Open Mon.-Sat. 10am-6.30pm, Sun. 2pm-6pm.

A well-stocked shop covering all aspects of gay life, including sexuality, living with AIDS and general information and advice. Occasional author readings are held here, telephone for details.

GENERAL INTEREST

Blackwell's

100 Charing Cross Rd, WC2, 0171-292 5100
Open Mon.-Sat. 9.30am-8.30pm, Sun. noon-6pm.

Originally set up in Oxford, this renowned company has now moved to London's famous book-shop street. The large premises stock 50,000 titles and although Blackwell's is strong on academic subjects such as economics, history, computing, social science, psychology, architecture, archeology and business, it does have a general interest section for fiction, biographies and travel. **Branches throughout London.**

Books etc

120 CHARING CROSS RD, WC2, 0171-379 6838
Open Mon.-Fri. 9.30am-8pm, Tues. 10am-8pm, Sun. noon-6pm.

Bright, well-stocked and well-organised, these premises, complete with an in-house Aroma coffee shop, are the flagship of this popular chain which was founded in 1981 and now boasts **17 branches throughout London.** There is an excellent choice of paperback and hardback fiction.

Borders Books and Music

203 OXFORD ST., W1,0171-292 1600
Mon.-Sat. 8am-11pm, Sun. noon-6pm.
U: Oxford Circus

Great new spacious book shop and café on four floors originally started in the U.S., offering a huge range of 150,000 books, 50,000 CD's and tapes, 5,000 videos, 2,000 magazines and newspapers and stationery. All topics covered here and many discounted titles in an environment which encourages browsing. Also very good for children's books.

Dillons The Bookshop

82 GOWER ST, WC1, 0171-636 1577
Open Mon.-Fri. 9am-7pm, Tues. 9.30am-7pm, Sat. to 6pm, Sun. noon-6pm.

This flagship store of a large chain, which has very well stocked and organised shops, is huge. As it is located in the midst of London University, it has a strong academic section. It is housed in a Victorian building with an unmistakeable, fantastically decorated façade. Some of the branches specialise in one or more subjects, like Dillons Arts Bookshops (see Arts).

Hatchards

187 PICCADILLY, W1, 0171-439 9921
Open Mon., Wed.-Fri.9 am-6pm, Tues. & Sat. 9.30am-6pm, Sun. noon-6pm.

Now part of the Dillons chain, Hatchards is still the book shop with cachet. This is the place where discerning readers while away their time browsing in the genteel, carpeted rooms. It has three Royal Warrants on display and traditionally sends a selection of books for royal summer holiday reading. There are five floors of books on general subjects with the latest hardbacks by the entrance.

John Sandoe

10 BLACKLANDS TERR, SW3, 0171-589 9473
Open Mon.-Sat. 9.30am-5pm, Wed. to 7.30pm.

Locals speak with real affection about this shop, just off the King's Road near Sloane Square. Sandoe's is particularly strong on literature and the arts but also stocks lots of paperbacks of fiction, poetry and classics along with the latest hardbacks.

Pan Bookshop

158 FULHAM RD, SW10, 0171-373 4997
Mon.-Fri. 9.30am-9.30pm, Sat. 10am-10pm, Sun. 11am-9pm. U: Gloucester Rd.

One of those very helpful, knowledgeable bookshops which have sprung up in spite of the big chains. Very wide selection of titles, plus expert staff make this a great favorite with locals. Good for browsing, and especially known for its signed copies by well known authors.

Talking Bookshop

11 WIGMORE ST, W1, 0171-491 4117
Open Mon.-Sat. 9.30am-5.30pm.

This smart, modern shop covering everything from Shakespeare to Dame Edna Everage's 'memoirs', stocks Britain's largest selection of spoken-word CDs and cassettes, including unabridged versions of fiction, biography and drama. There is also a small selection in French.

W & G Foyle

113-119 CHARING CROSS RD, WC2,
0171-437 5660
Open Mon.-Sat. 9am-6pm, Thurs. to 7pm.

This giant, old-fashioned shop with its countless corridors and heavily laden shelves and tabletops is probably London's most famous bookseller, an old-fashioned place, constantly bustling with browsers overwhelmed with choice. Fiction is displayed by publisher. It has become a running joke that Foyles definately has the book you want somewhere—but can't necessarily locate it.

W H Smith & Son

36 SLOANE SQ, SW1, 0171-730 0351
Open Mon.-Sat. 8.45am-6.30pm, Sun. 10am-5pm.

One of the longest-established newsagents and booksellers in Britain, W H Smith & Son continue to act as good general bookshops, with an emphasis on fiction and travel. Many of their shops concentrate on stationery or computer supplies, but they remain one of the most reliable sources of newspapers and magazines as well as books. **Branches throughout London**, and well-represented at mainline train stations and airports.

Waterstone's

121-125 CHARING CROSS RD, WC2, 0171-434 4291

Open Mon.-Sat. 9.30am-8pm, Sun. noon-6pm.

Readings, book launches and signings by authors regularly take place at the lively Waterstone branches which have made a name for themselves for their literary strength. A welcome sight in many High Streets in London, each shop has its own character whilst remaining true to the orginal Waterstone's concept. The Charing Cross shop is in a rambling array of rooms and is actually housed in two premises almost next door to each other (129-131 Charing Cross Rd). All branches have an excellent and extensive selection of books packed on the shelves, displayed invitingly on tables and sometimes stacked on the floor. **Also at 193 Kensington High St, W8, 0171-937 8432. Branches throughout London.**

Waterstone's at Harrods

HARRODS, KNIGHTSBRIDGE, SW1, 0171-730 1234

Open Mon., Tues., Sat. 10am-6pm, Wed.-Fri. to 7pm.

As expected in a department store of such calibre, Harrods has a well-stocked book shop, managed by Waterstone's with the same keen enthusiasm which characterises this chain's many branches nationwide. There is a strong emphasis on literary book launches and a good selection of finely bound and printed books. The department occupies about an eighth of the second floor, with a well-stocked magazine and periodicals area next to it.

LANGUAGES

European Bookshop

5 WARWICK ST, W1, 0171-734 5259

Open Mon.-Sat. 9.30am-6pm.

Specialising in European books, the emphasis is on French, German, Spanish, Italian, Portuguese and Scandinavian books, plus books on English as a foreign language. You also find an extensive selection of language course books and learning materials.

Grant & Cutler

55-57 GREAT MARLBOROUGH ST, W1, 0171-734 2012

Open Mon.-Sat. 9am-5.30pm, Thurs. to 7pm.

This impressively stocked language bookshop has publications in languages you may never even have heard of, ranging fr Afrikaans and Albanian to Yoruba and Zul. For mainstream languages, there are learn-at-your-leisure language cassettes and videos, as well as handy tourist travel packs of essential phrases. You can also find literature, drama and poetry in the original languages and sometimes in English translation. There are some videos of popular cinema releases in foreign languages.

SECOND-HAND

Skoob Books

11A-17 SICILIAN AVE, SOUTHAMPTON ROW, WC1, 0171-404 3063

Open Mon.-Sat. 10.30am-6.30pm.

The largest second-hand book shop in London, with around 50,000 titles always in stock. Although essentially a second-hand book shop, Skoob specialises in up-to-date academic books and is the only specialist in scientific and technical titles. There is also a small antiquarian department and a host of other titles. Although slightly shabby, this is a great shop for browsing in a truly serendipious manner.

SPORTS

Sportspages

CAXTON WALK, 94-96 CHARING CROSS RD, WC2, 0171-240 9604

Open Mon.-Sat. 9.30am-7pm.

'The book shop that takes sport seriously' runs the slogan for this specialist shop with a selection of 8,000 worldwide titles. If it's not here, it isn't a recognised sport, as this shop has books, magazines and videos for all sport enthusiast (with the exception of chess, board and card games). Titles cover all aspects from training to tactics, from biographies to medical studies.

TRAVEL

Daunt Books for Travellers

83 MARYLEBONE HIGH ST, W1, 0171-224 2295

Open Mon.-Sat. 9am-7.30pm.

This delightful, airy shop laid out on two floors carries a vast and varied stock of 25,000 travel books. Upstairs is devoted to the British Isles while the ground floor concentrates on Europe; for books on the rest of the world, look no further than the downstairs floor.

According to James Daunt, the owner, they file books the way people read them, so sitting alongside the Cuban shelves you'll find the latest book on Caribbean communism and Graham Greene's *Our Man in Havana*. They also have large stockrooms, so if you're after a particular title that is not displayed on the shelves, the chances are it might be stacked away, so do check.

Stanford

12-14 LONG ACRE, WC2, 0171-836 1321
Open Mon. 10am-6pm, Tues.-Fri. 9am-7pm, Sat. 10am-7pm.

A travel specialist, this shop has a large ground floor devoted to books and guides to worldwide destinations. Downstairs are books on Britain and a well-organised department of maps, including the Ordnance Survey series, for which this shop is justly famous. **Also at 52 Grosvenor Gdns, SW1, 0171-730 1314, and in the British Airways Shop, 156 Regent St, W1, 0171-434 4744.**

The Travel Book Shop

13 BLEINHEIM CRESCENT, W11, 0171-229 5260
Open Mon.-Sat. 10am-6pm.

The shelves of this small, interesting shop are jam-packed with travel books to take your mind off the British weather. They stock the usual quota of guides, plus some rare books kept under locked cabinets. For a small fee, the staff will try to trace any title. A real enthusiasts shop.

CLOTHES & SHOES

CHILDREN'S CLOTHES & SHOES

Some womenswear chains like Next, Monsoon, Jigsaw, Laura Ashley and French Connection also stock very good children's ranges.

Anthea Moore Eade

16 VICTORIA GROVE, SW3, 0171-584 8826
Open Mon.-Sat. 10am-6pm.

If you yearn for your child to resemble a Kate Greenaway drawing, this is the place to head for. Featuring hand-smocked dresses, white taffeta and velvet party wear, crisp cotton nightgowns, tweed coats and traditional boys' shirts, the Anthea Moore Eade label represents the best in classic childrenswear.

Buckle-My-Shoe

19 ST. CHRISTOPHER'S PL, W1, 0171-935 5589
Open Mon.-Sat. 10am-6pm, Thurs. to 7pm.

Bright and fashionable shoes, boots, sandals and trendy trainers, rather than the sports variety, are sold in this busy shop which caters for children up to ten years old. Even the most particular child (and parent) should find something from the 85 different styles of shoes, boots and slippers in 300 colourways both from well-known designers and their own range.

Children's Pavilion

7 PAVILION RD, SW1, 0171-235 6513
Open Mon.-Sat. 10am-6pm.

No shoes or outerwear from this smart childrens shop selling French and Italian clothes for boys and girls up to twelve. Styles range from very dressy to casual play clothes.

Createx

27 HARRINGTON RD, SW7, 0171-589 8306
Open Mon.-Sat. 10am-6pm.

A very well-stocked shop, including footwear, with high-fashion French and Italian clothes for infants through to fourteen year-olds. Brand names include Catimini, David Charles, Simonetta and Baby Bottle.

The Disney Store

140-141 REGENT ST, W1, 0171-287 6558
Open Mon.-Sat. 10am-8pm, Sun. noon-6pm.

Expect to see all the Disney characters from Winnie-the-Pooh to Pocohontas and 101 Dalmations depicted on casual clothes including T-shirts, baseball caps, sweaters, jackets, trousers and underwear. The dressing-up costumes are fun as are the hair accessories and jewelry. A favourite with children.

Instep

45 ST. JOHN'S WOOD HIGH ST, NW8, 0171-722 7634
Open Mon.-Sat. 9.30am-5.30pm.

Trained, delightful staff help take those headaches out of shopping for children's shoes. Are they fitting right? Can the child be persuaded to like them? Ranges go from those sensible Start-Rites to Doc Martens, and there's a play area set aside for entertainment. Branches throughout London.

Joanna's Tent

289B KING'S RD, SW3, 0171-352 1151

Open Mon.-Sat. 9.45am-6pm, Wed. to 7pm.

The childrenswear department in the basement is very well stocked and includes a wide range of accessories such as gloves, belts, bags and hats. Designer names include NoNo, Hakka Kids, Paul Smith, DKNY, Junior Armani, Blu Kids, Les Enfants and Joanna's Tent own collection.

La Cigogna

6A SLOANE ST, SW1, 0171-235 3845

Open Mon.-Sat. 9.30am-6pm, Wed. to 7pm.

A useful one-stop shop selling designer clothes and accessories for babies and children up to sixteen and mothers-to-be. A strong Italian presence, with designs from the likes of Giorgio Armani.

Oilily

9 SLOANE ST, SW1, 0171-823 2505

Open Mon.-Sat. 10am-6pm, Wed. to 7pm.

Colourful stripes, bold florals and bright patterns are the trademarks of this Dutch company specialising in fun and funky yet traditional clothes for children up to the age of twelve. The vast range includes pretty dresses, smocks, dungarees, casual beach wear, jackets, coats and accessories. Also stocks a range of ladies clothing following the same casual and colourful styling.

Osh Kosh B'Gosh

17 KING'S RD, SW3, 0171-730 1341

Open Mon. & Tues. Thurs.-Sat. 9.30am-6pm, Wed. 10am-7pm, Sun. noon-5pm.

For hard-wearing childrens playclothes, Osh Kosh B' Gosh is hard to beat. Most of the styles are denim or pinstriped, with a few corduroys and bright plain colours thrown in to ring the changes.

Patrizia Wigan

19 WALTON ST, SW3, 0171-823 7080

Open Mon.-Fri. 10am-6pm, Sat. to 5.30pm.

Special clothes in pretty styles and fabrics. Patrizia Wigan's designer clothes, which include casual wear and intricate dressy garments, are known on the international circuit for their quintessential English look. **Also at 72 New King's Rd, SW6, 0171-736 3336.**

Tartine et Chocolat

66 SOUTH MOLTON ST, W1, 0171-629 7233

Open Mon.-Sat. 10am-6pm.

French flair is evident in the clothes and accessories sold at this shop which features designs by Parisian designer, Catherine Painvin. The range is for babies to twelve-year olds, and includes coats, dressy outfits and play clothes.

Trotters

34 KING'S RD, SW3, 0171-259 9620

Open Mon.-Sat. 9am-6.30pm, Wed. to 7pm, Sun. 10am-6pm.

An ideal one-stop shop for parents and children alike. Parents can take their time choosing from the clothes, shoes, toys, videos, books and games, whilst children are distracted as they have their hair cut near the goldfish swimming in the tanks.

Young England

47 ELIZABETH ST, SW1, 0171-259 9003

Open Mon.-Fri. 10am-5.30pm, Sat. to 3pm.

Hand-smocked and formal dresses, tailored coats, swimwear, nightdresses and dressing gowns, all with a traditional appeal, are sold in this well-stocked shop catering to children seven and younger. Natural fabrics such as taffeta, wool and cotton are favoured. Everything is well made with well thought-out touches like generous hem allowances, linings on wool products, net petticoats with party dresses and matching accessories. Wool coat-dresses and sailor-look outfits are popular.

Warner Brothers Studio Store

178-182 REGENT ST, W1, 0171-434 3334

Open Mon.-Sat. 10am-7pm, Thurs. to 8pm, Sun. noon-6pm.

Head for the first floor to find children's clothes (the larger ground floor is reserved for grown-ups with a penchant for baseball caps, jackets and quirky T-shirts). Kid's clothes include pinafore dresses, T-shirts, dressing gowns, underwear, baseball caps and fringed leather jackets. Sylvester the Cat and Tweetie Pie are popular motifs along with Bugs Bunny, Daffy Duck and Taz, the Tazmanian Devil.

DESIGNER LABELS FOR MEN & WOMEN

For more designer-fashion shops, see separate Menswear and Womenswear sections.

Agnès b.

35-36 FLORAL ST, WC2, 0171-379 1992

Open Mon.-Sat. 10.30am-6.30pm, Thurs. 10am-7pm, Sun. noon-5pm.

The Agnès b label is synonymous with understated elegance—think Jean Seberg and Audrey Hepburn and you've got the idea. The range of mix and match separates and suitings, all impeccably designed and finished, work just as well in the boardroom as they do for a casual weekend stroll. Agnès b, the label's designer and creator, has never been influenced by fashion trends, hence the clothes are bought to be worn (and reworn) not to gather dust in the closet. Signature styles include best in T-shirts, simple knitwear, slim-fitting suits and leather coats and jackets, for men and women, plus a range for children and teenagers. While you're there, stock up on the cosmetics and fragrance lines. **Also at 111 Fulham Rd, SW3, 0171-225 3477; 235 Westbourne Grove, W11, 0171-792 1947; 58-62 Heath St, NW3, 0171-431 1995.**

Browns

23-27 SOUTH MOLTON ST, W1, 0171-491 7833

Open Mon.-Sat. 10am-6pm, Thurs. to 7pm.

You don't need to have confidence to walk through the number of doors leading into this stalwart among the favourite places to find top designer looks, but it certainly helps. At first glance, the sales assistants are haughty but once you've managed to overcome their sleek, almost superior appearance, they are friendly and extremely helpful. Walk through the interconnecting rooms for the world's most desirable labels such as Jil Sander, Shirin Guild, Anna Sui, Dries van Noten, Alexander McQueen, Prada, Missoni and Helmut Lang, in fact all of the designers with that 'must-have' appeal. They also stock a capsule collection Dosa clothing and home accessories. **Also at 6c Sloane Street, SW1, 0171-493 4232.**

CK Calvin Klein

53-55 NEW BOND ST, W1, OPEN MON.-SAT. 10AM-6PM.

King of American Cool, Calvin Klein opened his first London store last year. Although a diffusion line aimed at a younger audience, his famous clean lines as modelled by Carolyne Bassette-Kennedy, are prevalent. Expect lots of earthy tones such as stone, graphite and putty, put together to create a sleek, sporty style.

The Changing Room

THOMAS NEAL'S CENTRE, EARLHAM ST, WC2, 0171-379 4158

Open Mon.-Fri. 11am-7pm, Sat. 10.30am-7pm, Sun. 12.30pm-5.30pm.

A butcher's block and a large wood-framed mirror provide a simple backdrop for designs from Lezley George, Betty Jackson, Sara Sturgeon, John Rocha, Pleats Please by Issey Miyake, Tehen and half-a-dozen or so more. **Also at 10a Gees Court, W1, 0171-408 1596.**

Comme des Garçons

59 BROOK ST, W1, 0171-493 1258

Open Mon.-Fri. 10am-6pm, Thurs. to 7pm, Sat. to 5pm.

Minimalist to the point that you feel your presence upsets the balance, this small shop tucked off South Molton Street appeals to confident fashion types. The mere fact that you have to ring the bell for entry is enough to send the unitiated running in the opposite direction, and that's before they catch sight of the price tags. Designs look as though they are incomplete, so expect lots of frayed hems, exposed seams and complicated, conceptual designs.

DKNY

27 OLD BOND ST, W1, 0171-499 8089

Open Mon.-Wed. & Fri. 10am-7pm, Thurs. to 7pm, Sat. to 6.30pm.

If you want to buy into the Donna Karan lifestyle without paying for the hugely expensive 'black label' clothes from the designer's mainline collection further along the street, this is the place to come. The audience is younger, the atmosphere is noisier and the prices are marginally cheaper for the sportswear-influenced and diffusion-line designer clothes. There's a juice bar and video banks to add to the busy floorspace, plus a heavy security-guard presence.

Dolce & Gabbana

175 Sloane St, SW1, 0171-235 0335

Open Mon.-Fri. 10am-6pm, Sat. 10.30am-6pm.

Always producing collections that send fashion editors into a flutter, Domenico Dolce and Stephano Gabbana make the most of manipulating the female form, having fun and producing dynamic clothes at the same time. Leopard-print and Mafiosa-style trouser suits usually make an appearance. Sun glasses, beautiful bags, T-shirts and more recently, a range of cushions, gives more affordable access to the D&G club.

Donna Karan

19 New Bond St, W1, 0171-495 3100

Open Mon.-Sat. 10am-6pm, Thurs. to 7pm.

In sharp contrast to the DKNY store, Donna Karan is sleek, serene and for the seriously moneyed. The clothes are beautiful—well-cut suits and separates in the menswear department in the basement and Oscar-winning evening dresses and power dressing for women spread over two floors.

Emporio Armani

57-59 Long Acre, WC2, 0171-917 6882

Open Mon.-Wed. & Fri. 10am-6.30pm, Thurs. to 7.30pm, Sun. 11.30am-5.30pm.

Understated, classic and elegant, the Armani label oozes the smooth taste of Italy like melted mozzarella. Men's and women's styles work just as well on the young as they do on the old, and the colour choice is suited to all but the wildly eccentric. Includes jeans, underwear, childrenswear plus desirable accessories.

Etro

14 Old Bond St, W1, 0171-495 5767

Open Mon.-Sat. 10am-6pm.

This family-run business is steeped in tradition and Milanese style. Well-thought out touches like the inclusion of paintings and furniture from the Etro family's antique collection make customers feel they are entering the home of an affluent friend. Famous for their gloriously mis-matched and paisley velvets for men and women, and exotic fragrances and candles.

Gianni Versace

34-36 Old Bond St, W1, 0171-499 1862

Open Mon.-Sat. 10am-6pm.

Three things spring to mind when Versace's name is mentioned. Firstly, there is the designer himself; then there is his friend, Diana, Princess of Wales, both of whom died tragically last year. Lastly, there is Elizabeth Hurley, who made the headlines of every tabloid when she stepped out nearly wearing 'that dress' at the première of Four Weddings and a Funeral. The label is mostly known for excess and brash colours (largely due to the Liz Hurley exposure), less for the classic and tasteful designs favoured by Diana.

Gucci

17-18 Sloane St, SW1, 0171-235 6707

Open Mon., Tues., Thurs., Fri. 9.30am-6pm, Wed. 10am-7pm, Sat. to 6pm.

After a metamorphosis by Texan designer, Tom Ford, the Gucci label is the epitome of clothes and stylish accessories with attitude. The globally recognised snaffle loafers are still present, along with gravity-defying stilettoes and a variety of classic and modern styles. The men's collection borders on the sleek, modern-day playboy, while the women's clothes encompass everything from chic executive to disco diva. **Also at 32-33 Old Bond St, W1, 0171-629 2716.**

Guess?

171-175 Brompton Rd, SW3, 0171-823 8008

Open Mon.-Sat. 10am-6pm, Wed. to 7pm.

A store for bright young things to stock up on their Guess? jeans, dresses, seperates, shoes and accessories. For an experience only for the strong of heart, pop into the changing rooms which come complete with self-positioning cameras to allow you to see yourself from every angle. The Guess? light, health-conscious menu on the lower ground floor at the Bond Street branch serves fresh fruit juices, smoothies and salads that won't break the bank, nor will the healthy meals add extra inches for you to gawp at in those mirrors. **Also at 95-96 New Bond St, W1, 0171-629 8008.**

Hermès

179 Sloane St, SW1, 0171-823 1014

Open Mon.-Sat. 10am-6pm.

A coveted label since 1837, the Hermès insignia, brandished on clothes, fragrances, scarves and accessories, is the stamp of international style. Grace Kelly popularised the 'Kelly' bag during her pregnancy. Since then, Elle 'The Body' MacPherson has had her name immortalised in the 'Elle' bag, with handy, supermodel compartments for make-up and accessories.

Issey Miyake

270 Brompton Rd, SW3, 0171-581 3760

Open Mon.-Sat. 10am-6pm.

Origami as clothing, an original concept and a hugely profitable one for this successful Japanese designer. Clients include architects, artists, actresses and members of the fashion fraternity. The perma-pleats are perfect for travelling which, apart from the stylish look, may be the reason for the huge success.

Jean Paul Gaultier

Galerie Gaultier, 171-175 Draycott Ave, SW3, 0171-584 4648

Open Mon.-Sat. 10am-6pm, Wed. to 7pm.

Before Paris took on John Galliano, it had its own enfant terrible, Jean Paul Gaultier, a designer who always cited London as being the source of his inspiration. Designed to resemble a Parisian courtyard, his shop holds his bold, bright and exotic creations for men and women, including the JPG and jeans ranges, as well as his successful range of fragranced products encased in an hourglass female form.

Joseph

77 Fulham Rd, SW3, 0171-823 9500

Open Mon.-Fri. 10am-6.30pm, Wed. to 7pm, Sat. 10am-6pm, Sun. noon-5pm.

When it comes to striking the right fashion note, Moroccan-born Joseph Ettedgui hits it perfectly every time. For the past ten years, he has carved out a niche for delivering cool, classic and contemporary clothes in a fashionable but friendly environment. Both men and women can slip into the designer's own label products, or eye up the ranges from Martin Margiela, Prada and Helmut Lang. The first exclusively menswear store in the Joseph stable includes Gucci and Jil Sander in a minimal, arty setting. **Men's store at 74 Sloane Ave, SW3, 0171-590 6200. Branches throughout London.**

Moschino

28-29 Conduit St, W, 0171-318 0555

Open Mon.-Sat. 10am-6pm, Thurs. to 7pm.

London's first Moschino store offers Couture!, Cheap and Chic, Moschino Jeans and accessories in the funky store filled with oversize buttons, exclamation marks and cutlery used as door handles. The clothes are bright—almost garish—in the gimmicky style which has become symbolic of the label.

Nicole Farhi

158 New Bond St, W1, 0171-499 8368

Open Mon.-Sat. 10am-6pm, Thurs. to 7pm.

Thanks to designers like Nicole Farhi, the British fashion industry is booming. She might not produce the headline-grabbing collections or send her models down the catwalks with outrageous accessories, but she consistently manages to create clothes that men and women buy and will wear forever. This ultra-sleek flagship store is in keeping with the luxurious but minimalist interiors of the international names who have found their way to Bond Street. Take time to admire the clothes and Farhi's new homeware collection, then book yourself a table in her wonderful restaurant Nicole's (see Restaurant section).

Paul Smith

40-44 Floral St, WC2, 0171-379 7133

Open Mon.-Sat. 10.30am-6.30pm, Thurs. to 7.30pm.

Approaching this small, cobbled street from the Piazza end, it seems as if the whole of Floral Street belongs to British designer Paul Smith. The four connecting shops are home to his dapper line in menswear, the more recent womenswear collections, children's clothing, stylish accessories and novelty gadgets.

Polo Ralph Lauren

143 New Bond St, W1, 0171-491 4967

Open Mon.-Sat. 10am-6pm, Thurs. to 7pm.

Ralph Lauren serves up an Americanised version of British style to his loyal customer base. There's the mainline Ralph Lauren collection, the Ralph Lauren Cruise collection, Polo Sport featuring shirts and sporty items, the Ralph collection which is aimed at a younger audience, and the Polo and Golf collections. The styling of the shop is homely, in a ramshackley but expensive way, and it is always busy with an appreciative public.

Prada

44-45 SLOANE ST, SW1, 0171-235 0008
Open Mon.-Sat. 10am-6pm, Wed. to 7pm.

Head here for the so-trendy-it-hurts nylon rucksacks, gorgeous leather shoes and some of the most influential designs of the past decade. The calming green interior allows even the most anti-fashion person to appreciate the precision detailing of Miuccia Prada's collections of cool utility-chic clothing.

Vivienne Westwood

6 DAVIES ST, W1, 0171-629 3757
Open Mon.-Sat. 10am-6pm, Thurs. to 7pm.

In the days when London's fashion designers were regarded as experimentalists of little substance, only one was making headlines for clothes which combined wit, wisdom and wearabilty. People may have mocked Vivienne Westwood for her seemingly outrageous creations, but they could never deny the fact that she was—and still is—one of Britain's hottest fashion exports. Her collections always have some historical references and feature smartly tailored tweeds, clingy dresses and endless suits with neat little nipped-in waists and leg-o-mutton sleeves. You will find the demi-couture 'Gold Label' at Davies Street, the funkier 'Red Label' at Conduit Street, and a selection of Westwood classics in the shop where it all started in World's End. **Also at 43 Conduit St, W1, 0171-439 1109, World's End, 430 King's Rd, SW10, 0171-352 6551.**

Voyage

115 & 177 FULHAM RD, SW3, 0171-823 9581
Open Mon.-Fri. 10.30am-6.30pm, Wed. to 7pm, Sat. to 6pm.

A hippy-chic label for the ultra-hip and super-chic. Fans of the bohemian, ancient velvet trim and creased silk creations of Tiziano and Louise Mazzilli, former designers at Valentino, include Jemima Khan, Nicole Kidman, Emma Thompson, Melanie Griffith and any self-respecting fashion editor. Entry is selective and operates on a ring-the-doorbell policy. If they like your face, the staff will let you in to admire the colourful garments hanging from the bamboo rails and wooden shelves. Don't take it too personally if you're not admitted—refusees extend to fashion editors and major celebrities. Prices are high, from £400 for a shirt, approx. £350 for a waistcoat. The recently opened men's store down the road at 177 Fulham Rd offers the same flamboyant styles for men.

Yohji Yamamoto

14-15 CONDUIT ST, W1, 0171-491 4129
Open Mon.-Sat. 10am-6pm, Thurs. to 7pm.

Purity and elegance are two words that spring to mind when describing the mainly monochromatic collections Yohji Yamamoto produces for men and women. The styling is ingenious yet comes across as being deceptively simple. It is wonderful that the designer now has his first outlet in London.

Yves Saint Laurent Rive Gauche

135-137 NEW BOND ST, W1, 0171-493 1800
Open Mon.-Fri. 9.30am-6pm, Thurs. to 7pm, Sat. 10am-6pm.

That old adage, "if it ain't broke, why fix it?" springs to mind when describing Yves Saint Laurent's collections, as he sees no harm in giving his customers variations of the same theme they buy year after year. The YSL staple is the classic, black Le Smoking, the perfect trouser suit which he first introduced to an appreciative public in 1966. His skirt-suits, coats, jackets, dresses and shirts are finished to perfection and allow any woman to look and feel like a star.

GENERAL FASHION FOR MEN & WOMEN

All the major department stores carry very good ranges of all kinds of clothes for both sexes, from designers to general labels. Here we recommend some top British clothing companies.

Aquascutum

100 REGENT ST, W1, 0171-734 6090
Open Mon.-Sat. 9.30am-6pm, Thurs. to 7pm, Sun. noon-6pm.

Traditional clothes from this now-refurbished store which offers a good range of all clothing, including some top new accessories. **Also at 9-13 Brompton Rd, SW1, 0171-581 4444.**

Austin Reed

103-113 REGENT ST, W1, 0171-734 6789
Open Mon.-Sat. 9.30am-6pm, Thurs. to7pm.

Mostly catering to men, this shop is a four-floor delight of moderately conservative, but well designed and made clothes. They do cater for women, again with well-cut and well-designed clothes. They are particularly good for countrywear. They stock Laurel, KL as well as their own range. **Branches throughout Britain.**

Burberrys

18-22 HAYMARKET, W1, 0171-930 3343
Open Mon.-Wed. & Fri. 10am-6pm, Thurs. to 7pm, Sun. noon-6pm.

That distinctive check is seen all over the world, most famously on its outerwear. They stock good women's woollens, and a lot of new accessories. The new Thomas Burberry range is aimed at a younger audience. Find bargain- priced seconds at the factory shop tucked away in the East End at 29-53 Chatham Pl, E9, 0181-985 3344. **Also at 165 Regent St, W1, 0171-734 4060.**

Jaeger

200-206 REGENT ST, W1, 0171-200 4000
Open Mon.-Sat 9.30am-6pm, Thurs. to 7pm.

Jaeger is a byword in conservative women's dressing. This store has undergone a refurbishment so that it glitters on Regent Street. But the clothes remain much in the style of before, and they do stock Jean Muir which stays forever classically well designed and cut. Men's clothes are also on the very conservative side. But search through if you're after something less conventional; there are occasional beautiful designs to be found.

Simpson

203 PICCADILLY, W1, 0171-734 2002
Open Mon.-Fri. 10am-7pm, Sat. 9.30am-6pm.

Makers and stockists of the ever-popular Daks label, Simpson also stocks designers like Armani. There's a good tailoring service and a barber shop. Clothes are well designed and well made and the classic styles suit every City gent and working lady.

MENSWEAR

The area in and around Jermyn Street is a good starting point for any man wanting to cut a dash in the best of British style.

Men's Designer Wear

Jones

13 & 15 FLORAL ST, WC2, 0171-240 8312
Open Mon.-Sat. 10am-6.30pm, Sun. 1pm-5pm.

For men looking for a good cross-section of the hottest designer names, Jones is a great starting point. The Activewear shop at Number 13 houses the latest sporty fashion styles; the designer shop at Number 15 is given over to labels like Dries Van Noten, Issey Miyake, Helmut Lang, Alexander McQueen and Dirk Bikkembergs.

The Library

268 BROMPTON RD, SW3, 0171-589 6569
Open Mon.-Sat. 10am-6pm, Wed. to 7pm.

Fashion-conscious males are well served in this shop which gets its name from the back-drop of books on show. Seek out the latest collections from designers such as Alexander McQueen, Dirk Bikkembergs, Martin Kidman, Dries van Noten and YMC.

Men's Hats

Bates

21A JERMYN ST, SW1, 0171-734 2722
Open Mon.-Fri. 9am-5.13pm, Sat. 9.30am-4pm.

Established in 1902, Bates knows a thing or two when it comes to the art of making splendid hats. The company offers a wide range of styles including top hats, felt trilbys and the largest selection of tweed flat caps, selling from £35. Good mail order catalogue available.

Herbert Johnson

10 OLD BOND ST, W1, 0171-408 1174
Open Mon.-Sat. 10am-5pm.

Jack Nicholson in *Batman*, Harrison Ford in *Raiders of the Lost Ark*, Rex Harrison in *My Fair Lady* and Peter Sellars in *Inspector Clouseau*—what do they all have in common? They all wear hats made by this traditional hatters that has catered to high society and the military since 1899. This family business has an in-house design team for such interesting cinematic projects as well as your ordinary trilby. Alongside hundreds of styles of hats always on display, are accessories like fancy waistcoats, scarves and silk dressing gowns.

James Lock & Co

6 St. James's St, SW1, 0171-930 5849
Open Mon.-Fri. 9am-5.30pm, Sat. 10am-5.30pm.

A legendary hat-maker established in 1676 to kit out the nearby court of St. James, this shop became famous for the 'coke', or the 'bowler' hat as it is more commonly known. It was made for William Coke in 1850 and was transported to America to become the 'Derby'. Hats have made a come-back and this is the place to come to find anything from a cap for country pursuits to a straw boater for watching cricket. Although a venerable institution, Lock's has friendly and helpful staff. They also include a range of women's hats.

Men's Large Sizes

High & Mighty

83 Knightsbridge, SW1, 0171-589 7454
Open Mon. 10am-6pm, Tues.-Sat. 9am-6pm.

The ready-to-wear suits and separates here are designed for men who are over six foot three inches, or whose chest sizes are from 40 to 60 inches. **Also at The Plaza, 120 Oxford St, W1, 0171-436 4861; 145-147 Edgware Rd, W2, 0171-723 8754.**

Rochester Big and Tall

90 Brompton Rd, SW3, 0171-838 0018
Open Mon.-Sat. 9.30am-6pm, Wed. to 7pm.

This firm, well-known in America, has a popular shop here that caters to men who are more than six feet tall and shorter men with chest sizes from 44 to 64 inches. Among their famous brands are Burberry, Gieves and Hawkes, Ermenegildo Zegna and Jhane Barnes.

Bond Street High Fashion

Bond Street is one of the two premier prestige shopping streets in London (the other one is Sloane Street). Old Bond Street, dating from 1686 starts at Piccadilly and runs to Clifford Street, where the name changes to New Bond Street, laid out in the early eighteenth century. International and British fashion designers vie for attention and many have their flagship stores here. There are also top quality jewellers, antique shops, linen shops, art galleries and Sotheby's the auctioneers. Names include **Anna Molinari Blumarine** (11a Old Bond St, 0171-493 4872), **Calvin Klein** (53-55 New Bond St, 0171-491 9696), **Cerruti 1881** (106 New Bond St, 0171-495 5880), **Chanel** (26 Old Bond St, 0171-493 5040), **Christian Lacroix** (29 Old Bond St, 0171-409 1994), **Donna Karan** (19 New Bond St, 0171-495 3100), **DKNY** (27 Old Bond St, 0171-499 8089), **Emporio Armani** (112a New Bond St, 0171-499 8080), **Gianni Versace** (34-36 Old Bond St, 0171-499 1862), **Gucci** (32-33 Old Bond St, 0171-629 2716), **Guess?** (95 New Bond St, 0171-629 8008), **Hermès** (155 New Bond St, 0171-499 8856), **Joan & David** (150 New Bond St, 0171-499 7506), **Karl Lagerfeld** (173 New Bond St, 0171-493 6277), **Loewe** (130 New Bond St, 0171-493 3914), **Louis Vuitton** (149 New Bond St, 0171-493 3688), **MaxMara** (153 New Bond St, 0171-491 4748), **Nicole Farhi** (158 New Bond St,0171-499 8368), **Polo Ralph Lauren** (143 New Bond St, 0171-491 4967), **Yves Saint Laurent** (137 New Bond St, 0171-493 1800).

Men's Shirts and Ties

Harvie & Hudon

77 & 97 JERMYN ST, SW1
Mon.-Fri. 9am-5.30pm, Sat. to 5.15pm.

Rolls of striped, checked and plain blue, navy or pink cotton poplin line the back of Number 97, ready for measurement here to be made up at the workshop at Number 77. Thomas Harvey and George Hudson set up business three generations ago and their shirt-making expertise is maintained by their direct descendants to this day. Keeping to a very traditional look, the company's own designers come up with the large range of classic stripes and solid colours in the finest two-fold poplins, Oxfords, batistes and voiles. A range of ties complement your chosen shade to perfection. Shirts can be made to measure or bought from stock in sizes fourteen and a half to eighteen and a half collar, in link- or button-cuff styles. A range of blazers also available. **Also at 55 Knightsbridge, SW1, 0171-235 2651.**

Hilditch & Key

37 JERMYN ST, SW1, 0171-734 4707
Open Mon.-Fri. 9.30am-6pm, Sat. to 5pm.

The classic white shirt is still the favourite at this company, in business since 1899. The ready-to-wear range is excellently made, with hand-cutting using two-fold poplin in a variety of stripes and plain colours. Famous for a distinctively shaped collar, the shirts have fine single-needle stitching, extra body length and are finished with real mother-of-pearl buttons. The handmade-to-order shirts are cut and made at Number 73. This shop also sells hand-slipped ties, plus fine quality pyjamas and dressing gowns. Both shop sell ladies' cotton shirts. **Also at 88 Jermyn St, SW1, 0171-930 2329.**

T M Lewin

106 JERMYN ST, SW1, 0171-930 4291
Open Mon.-Sat.9.30am-6.30pm, Thurs. to 7pm.

Established more than 100 years ago, this firm makes classic shirts from the finest two-fold poplin or pin-point Oxford cotton, and the colours match up perfectly with the ties and quality cufflinks on offer. There are also striped and check shirts, plus dress shirts. Accessories can be fun, with teddy bear images on braces and novelty cufflinks in the shape of sink taps, scissors, knife and fork, pewter pigs or with dollar and pound symbols for those on the trading floor. There is a large ladies' wear shop next door.

Thomas Pink

85 JERMYN ST, SW1, 0171-930 6364
Open Mon.-Fri. 9.30am-6pm, Thurs. to 7pm, Sun. noon-5pm.

Quality, a certain cachet and reasonable prices make this shop a must for young city types. Appropriately enough, there are two outlet in the City of London, both of which sell the best-selling pure cotton poplin shirts. Little silk knot cufflinks which punctuate the cuffs with clever twists of colour are also available here. **Branches throughout London.**

Turnbull & Asser

71-72 JERMYN ST, SW1, 0171-930 0502
Open Mon.-Sat. 9am-6pm.

James Bond was always partial to a Turnbull & Asser shirt or two, so too have been Katharine Hepburn, Naomi Campbell and Winston Churchill. It's the impeccable quality and fine details such as hand-stitching, bone collar stays and shell buttons which bring customers through the door, along with the attentive after-sales service which includes replacement collars and cuffs. The minimum order is six shirts, which will last for years. There is a large ready-to-wear selection and the firm holds a Royal Warrant as shirtmaker for the Prince or Wales. **Also at 23 Bury St, SW1, 0171-930 0502.**

Jermyn Street Cachet

Just off Piccadilly Circus, sedate Jermyn Street—dating back to 1680—is lined with traditional shops still offering traditionally made goods, mostly for men, such as handmade shirts and shoes. The street boasts entrances to Simpson, Fortnum & Mason and Alfred Dunhill and leads into St. James's Street and its surrounding streets offering antiques, paintings, jewelry and clothes.

Men's Suits, Sportswear and General

Alfred Dunhill

48 Jermyn St, SW1, 0171-290 8600
Open Mon.-Fri. 9.30am-6pm, Sat. 10am-6pm.

You could easily spend the whole day in this wonderfully light and airy store which was founded in 1893 and recently underwent a total transformation. Firstly, the clothes are excellent, appealing to the most conservative dresser through to those looking for casual but elegant sportswear. If you don't trust your own taste, simply enlist the help of one of the personal dressing stylists who will happily advise on cut and colour to suit your style and budget. The jewelry range is first-rate, as are the briefcases and luggage on offer. Other treats within the store include a tie-loan service, complimetary jewelry polishing, tailoring service (available on items bought in the store only), and a fine humidor with complimentary whisky tastings. The company has also installed a fax and you can catch up on the latest share prices. In the basement you can marvel at the archive products in the Alfred Dunhill Museum. One of the best mens' shops around.

Hackett

85 Jermyn St, SW1, 0171-930 1300
Open Mon.-Sat. 9.30am-6pm.

For a while the description 'young fogey' was bandied about to describe that conservative look reminiscent of previous decades. This firm started to make its own garmets in 1984, borrowing details from the vintage clothing the founders came across on market stalls. The firm now sells brushed cotton shirts, tweed sports jackets, hand-knit sweaters, plus-fours and all manner of clothing for everything from attending events like polo and race meetings to looking well-turned out at the office. **Also at 137-138 Sloane St, SW1, 0171-730 3331; 165 New King's Rd, SW6, 0171-371 7964.**

Joseph

74 Sloane Ave, SW3, 0171-590 6200
Open Mon.-Sat. 10am-6.30pm, Wed. to 7.30pm, Sun. noon-6pm.

For the fashionable man around town, this, the first of Joseph Ettedgui's exclusively menswear stores, provides myriad dressing options. Label addicts will be drawn to the collections from Jil Sander, Prada and Gucci as well as the sleek lines from Joseph himself. Accessories include J. P. Tod, Granello and Duchamp.

Kent & Curwen

30 St. James's St, SW1, 0171-409 1955
Open Mon.-Sat. 9.30am-6pm.

A jaunty air prevails in this shop in its premier location, thanks to the brightly striped blazers and caps, usually worn at sporting events like Henley Regatta. Many of these are official colours to be worn strictly by the members of a particular club, regiment or school, but there are also adaptations of the striped look. The jackets are sometimes bought by overseas visitors for occasions when an English look is de rigueur. Chunky cricket sweaters with their bold stripe trims are popular for men and women.

Moss Bros

27 King St, WC2, 0171-497 9354
Open Mon.-Fri. 9am-5.30pm, Thurs. to 6.30pm

Moses Moses started selling second-hand suits in 1860; his sons, under a new company name, Moss Bros, found themselves lending a formal suit to an unsuccessful stockbroker just once too often and started charging him for the loans in 1897. Thus, suit hire was born. Still outfitting men for formal occasions, this Covent Garden shop has dark panelled walls stretching back to rooms which include a traditional barber shop. Among the many racks of men's clothes on sale are Hugo Boss, Pierre Cardin and Chester Barrie ranges of suits and cashmere coats. **Also at 88 Regent St, W1, 0171-494 0666; 33 Eastcheap, EC3, 0171-626 4247.**

Men's Tailors

Anderson & Sheppard

30 Savile Row, W1, 0171-734 1420
Open Mon.-Fri. 8.30am-5pm.

In this brash world of aggressive advertising it makes a refreshing change to come across an industry where quality and expertise are allowed to speak for themselves. Anderson & Sheppard, established in 1906, is held in high esteem and is considered to be the tops in the tailoring network. British maverick designer, Alexander McQueen, sharpened his cutting skills here and the results of his training can be witnessed in his impeccable tailoring. If you are recommended by someone, the team at A&S will match the cutter your friend had to achieve a similar look or feel. Prince Charles has his double-breasted suits made here.

Blades of Savile Row

8 Burlington Gdns, W1, 0171-734 8911
Open Mon.-Sat. 9.30am-5.30pm.

A lovely shop, furnished like a posh gentlemen's club, this smart men's tailor offers a wide selection of made-to-measure suits, made with computer technology. There's also a handmade, bespoke tailoring service. Customers may find this shop less formidable than some of the more austere tailoring establishments in Savile Row itself.

Dege

10 Savile Row, W1, 0171-287 2941
Open Mon.-Fri. 9.15am-5.15pm, Sat. 9.30am-12.30pm.

Founded in 1856, the firm holds three Royal Warrants including one from the Sultan of Oman, and makes bespoke suits, shirts and military uniforms. Its styles are influenced by its equestrian, military and sporting background. Representatives regularly visit Europe, the Gulf, USA and Japan.

Gieves & Hawkes

1-2 Savile Row, W1, 0171-434 2001
Open Mon.-Sat. 9am-6pm.

A large shop with a genteel ambience featuring wood-panelling and Schooner prints, the firm sells mostly ready-to-wear suits and shirts using the latest computer technology. Past clients included Admiral Nelson and the Duke of Wellington. It is well stocked with scarves, belts, shirts and accessories and has a casual range of clothing in the shop next door. **Also at 18 Lime St, EC3, 0171-283 4914.**

H Huntsman and Sons

11 Savile Row, W1, 0171-734 7441
Open Mon.-Fri. 9am-1pm; 2pm-5.30pm.

One of the venerable names of Savile Row, this firm has been making top-of-the-range menswear since the 1920s. It has a distinctive range of well-fitted jackets and blazers and offers a bespoke service where customers are fitted four times before walking off with their suit. Like many other Savile Row tailors, Huntsman sends staff to the USA twice a year to fit customers.

Henry Poole

15 Savile Row, W1, 0171-734 5985
Open Mon.-Fri. 9am-5.15pm.

In typically discreet Savile Row style, this firm has been going since 1806 and has occupied the present building since 1887, being the first tailor to open a showroom on Savile Row. It received its first Royal Warrant from Queen Victoria, an honour bestowed today by Queen Elizabeth.

Savile Row Style

Savile Row is associated with the best of British quality, with tailoring establishments that have been here for generations, as well as a few newcomers on the scene.

Hogg Sons & J B Johnstone

19 Clifford St, W1, 0171-734 5915
Open Mon.-Fri. 8.45am-4.4.5pm.

Two tailoring establishments share these traditional-looking premises. The cutting room is on the ground floor where customers can catch a glimpse of the meticulous attention to detail. The front shop stocks some ready-to-wear trousers, shirts, waistcoats and ties. Sara Haydon is the only female proprietor in Savile Row and the shop also makes suits for women.

Kilgour, French & Stanbury

8 Savile Row, W1, 0171-734 6905
Open Mon.-Fri. 9am-5.30pm, Sat. 10am-4pm.

There are some 5,000 fabrics to choose from at this traditional tailors where everything is made by hand from beginning to end. The company shares the premises with another famous tailor, the equestrian specialist Bernard Weatherill, which is why a saddle prop is on hand to ensure measurements are absolutely right. This is sent to Buckingham Palace when the Queen orders new riding wear.

Maurice Sedwell

19 Savile Row, W1, 0171-734 0824
Open Mon.-Fri. 9am-5.30pm, Sat. 9am-1pm.

Maurice Sedwell died in 1991 but his tradition lives on. About 90 percent of the company's bespoke suits are made from British worsted cloth, involve a three-stage fitting process and some 60 hours of highly skilled hand-stitching until the final fitting. There is an in-house shirtmaker, and a bespoke shoemaker visits the shop by appointment. Accessories include silk ties, antique cufflinks, cummerbunds, braces and handkerchiefs.

Richard James

31 Savile Row, W1, 0171-434 0605

Open Mon.-Fri. 10am-6pm, Sat. 11am-5pm.

One of the newest tailors on the block, Richard James brings with him a more modern approach to tailoring. The genial and good-humoured James has both ready-to-wear and bespoke suits, following the tradition of Savile Row, and boasts a glitzy client list that includes Liam and Patsy Gallagher, Elton John, Jarvis Cocker, Viscount Linley and Christian Lacroix. A two-piece suit (men's or women's) takes between six to eight weeks to make. There are also sharp-looking off-the-peg jackets, shirts and knitwear.

Tom Gilbey

2 New Burlington Pl, W1, 0171-734 4877

Open Mon.-Fri. 10am-6pm, Thurs. to 7pm, Sat. to 5.30pm.

From wildly flamboyant to traditional Savile Row, this designer's made-to-measure suits always have a distinctive flair and the fabrics used include silks, velvets and brocades as well as wools.

Men's Waistcoats

Favourbrook

9-21 Piccadilly Arcade, Jermyn St, SW1, 0171-491 2337

Open Mon. & Tues. 9am-6pm, Wed.-Thurs. to 7pm, Sat. 10am-6pm.

A wealth of luxurious fabrics are employed in the fabulous-looking waistcoats, smoking jackets, frock coats and tasselled, fez-style hats bearing the Favourbrook label. It makes for a unique, dandified look, as famously portrayed in the film Four Weddings and a Funeral, where one of the characters wore a hand-painted waistcoat festooned with angels from this store. The ladies' wear includes the same English-meets-Oriental style with a full range of waistcoats, beautifully tailored Nehru jackets and coats.

Tom Gilbey

2 New Burlington Pl, W1, 0171-734 4877

Open Mon.-Fri. 10am-6pm, Thurs. to 7pm, Sat. to 5.30pm.

Waistcoats are the main selling point of Tom Gilbey's business. His designs are often likened to works of art due to the decorative processes and fine materials employed. His distinctive waistcoats are popular with the pop and film set.

Knightsbridge

A couple of streets to the west of Harrods, Beauchamp Place is a pretty shopping street which has a real neighbourhood air, with little restaurants, Bar Min, a bespoke cobbler's (Deliss) plus fashion designers, jewelry, woollen and china shops. It ends at Walton Street, which is even more charming, starting with a residential area and finishing up with boutiques offering jewelry, antiques, stationery and home accessories.

OUTERWEAR FOR MEN & WOMEN

For specific sporting outerwear, see the Sporting Goods section.

Aquascutum

100 Regent St, W1, 0171-734 6090

Open Mon.-Sat. 9.30am-6pm, Thurs. to 7pm, Sun. noon-6pm.

The first Aquascutum showerproof coat went on sale in 1851, the year of the Victorian Great Exhibition held to show off the best British inventions. Some things have not changed. Today, the Aquascutum name is still highly regarded and the distinctive 'club check' in khaki and red appears in numerous guises. They have even extended the range to include slim tailoring and nylon coats aimed at a younger audience with an eye for quality. **Also at 9-13 Brompton Rd, SW1, 0171-581 4444.**

Burberrys

18-22 Haymarket, W1, 0171-930 3343
Open Mon.-Wed. & Fri. 10am-6pm, Thurs. to 7pm, Sun. noon-6pm.

The distinctive Burberry check appears as a lining on solid trench coats, which have earned a worldwide reputation for being quintessential rainwear. It was created by Thomas Burberry in 1870s, and fast gained the reputation of being untearable, rain-proof yet cool and comfortable. Meryl Streep wore one in Kramer vs. Kramer, Michael Douglas in Wall Street and Warren Beatty in Dick Tracy. A wool-lined trench coat is £635, unlined is £525. Find bargain priced seconds at the factory shop tucked away in the East End at 29-53 Chatham Pl, E9, 0181-985 3344. **Also at 165 Regent St, W1, 0171-734 4060.**

Cordings

19 Piccadilly, W1, 0171-734 0830
Open Mon.-Fri. 9.30am-6pm, Sat. 10am-6pm.

John Charles Cordings went into business in 1839 to provide classic country clothes for the hunting, shooting and fishing fraternity. Occasional adventurers included Sir Henry Morton Stanley, who was kitted out in 1871 with Cordings' apparel for his expedition to find Dr. Livingstone in Africa. The recently refurbished shop has been at this site since 1890. It is known for using materials such as moleskin, corduroy and traditional tweeds in colours inspired by the Scottish moors like lichen green, bracken and heather. It has a made-to-order service. Cordings has the appeal of one-stop shopping for all-weather coats, jackets and boots as well as shirts, knitwear, ties, shoes, socks, luggage and accessories.

Farlow's

5 Pall Mall, SW1, 0171-839 2423
Open Mon.-Fri. 9am-6pm, Sat. 9am-4pm.

Besides stocking a comprehensive range of fishing tackle, this shop has separate premises devoted to country clothes, including an adjoining shop for women. Farlow's probably has the largest selection of Barbour waxed clothing in London as well as other well-known brands and footwear.

The General Leather Company

56 Chiltern St. W1, 0171-935 1041
Open Mon.-Fri. 10am-6pm, Sat. to 5pm.

In business since 1970, this shop is a good place for finding that perfect leather jacket, as they design as well as manufacture leather, suede and sheepskin garments. Styles are popular with people who prefer made-to-measure clothes, which are often a must where leather and suede are concerned. They will also alter old models and do repairs.

The Highlands

48 Brompton Rd, SW3, 0171-581 5814
Open Mon.-Sat. 11am-7pm.

Stocking all the major country clothing brands such as Henri Lloyd, Driza-Bone and Barbour among the huge selection for men and women. **Also at 73 Regent St, W1, 0171-434 0881.**

R M Williams

223 Regent St, W1, 0171-629 6222
Open Mon.-Wed. & Fri. 10am-6.30pm, Thurs. to 7.30pm, Sun. noon-6pm.

The classic Akruba bushwhacker hats that Prince Charles wears during his Australian visits are one of the best-selling items here, along with Australian-made moleskin trousers, oilskin jackets and hand-crafted boots. The racks are full of cotton, denim and linen shirts and jeans, trousers and shirts for men and women, with a line of sturdy skirts for ladies, too. Established more than 60 years ago, this Aussie firm pays attention to detail, with only the best-quality buttons, zips and rivets. The overall great outdoors look is devastingly romantic à la Indiana Jones.

SHOES FOR MEN & WOMEN

Audley

96 Mount St, W1, 0171-491 3441
Mon.-Fri. 9.30am-5.30pm, Sat. to 5pm.

A glorious new shoe shop with a difference, combining bespoke and ready-to-wear in a very clever way. Each season they produce a collection in a standard range of leather, from £80 for women and £100 for men. But also on offer are ranges of leather in different colours—and for a mere £50 you can get a pair made to your choice. Going the whole bespoke route costs from £500, which is much less than most such services.

Bertie

36 SOUTH MOLTON ST, W1, 0171-493 5033
Open Mon.-Sat. 10am-7pm, Thurs. to 8pm, Sun. noon-6pm.

This shop caters to the demand in fashion trends with a wide choice of reasonably comfortable shoes for women, mostly in varying shades of brown and black. However, more delicate dressy shoes in lighter colours have been making an appearance, no doubt to 'lift' the uniform of black, grey and brown outfits which continue to dominate the nation's wardrobes.

Church's

58-59 BURLINGTON ARCADE, W1, 0171-493 8307
Open Mon.-Sat. 9.30am-6pm.

This shop is one of the branches of a famous Northampton-based manufacturer. A pair of Oxford brogues or Penny loafers is £185. All styles, many in the timeless English classic mode, are well-made, in narrow and wide fittings, and tend to last forever. Some of the women's shoes look like clones of men's styles, sensible and comfortable with old-fashioned chic, but there are many surprises in store and they have started a range of high-fashion designs. **Branches throughout London** and through big department stores. Women's shoes are available only at the following branches: **143 Brompton Rd, SW3, 0171-589 9136; 133 New Bond St, W1, 0171-493 1474; 201 Regent St, W1, 0171-734 2438.**

D L Lord

70 BURLINGTON ARCADE, W1, 0171-493 5808
Open Mon.-Fri. 9.30am-6pm.

The classic shoe styles have made this shop a must for people who appreciate quality. It has a bespoke service for men's shoes, run by the Grenson firm, shoemakers since 1866. A Grenson consultant is available by appointment and it takes eight to ten weeks and several fittings to make the shoes. The shop stocks traditional, ready-to-wear shoes for men starting at £99, with a smaller selection for women starting at £79, including a range of smart boots, buckle and elasticated styles and lace-ups.

Deliss

15 ST. ALBAN'S GROVE, W8, 0171-938 2255
Open Mon.-Fri. 9.30am-5.30pm, Sat. 10am-2pm.

In the village atmosphere of this richly endowed shopping street, it seems fitting to find a working cobbler's shop with customers being measured for handmade shoes in full view of the window frontage. Lizard, crocodile, elephant and ostrich skin are among the shoe and boot coverings available. Other handmade products include matching bags and belts. Men's shoes start from £470 + VAT; women's shoes are from £390 + VAT. They can be made within three or four days but the usual time is two to three weeks.

Edward Green

12-13 BURLINGTON ARCADE, W1, 0171-499 6377
Open Mon.-Sat. 9am-5.30pm

Smart men's shoes are available from stock or made to order, from £350, boots from £375; however, they do not have a made-to-measure service.

Emma Hope

33 AMWELL ST, EC1, 0171-833 2367
Open Mon.-Sat. 10am-6pm, Thurs. to 7pm.

Emma Hope makes beautiful women's shoes with a hint of the baroque. Her designs are elegant and timeless, coming in choice leathers such as nappa, suede, morroco and snakeskin, and fabrics such as silk velvet and satin, often with delightful bows and distinctive decoration. She also produces a collection of bridal shoes, which can be made up in the fabric of the chosen dress. **Also at 12 Symons St, SW3, 0171-259 9566.**

Gina Shoes

189 SLOANE ST, SW1, 0171-235 2932
Open Mon.-Sat. 10am-6pm, Wed. to 7pm.

Gina Shoes have been around for years now, but this is their first retail venture under their own name. An English, in fact London-based firm, their women's shoes are highly individual and stylish. They stock a particularly good and popular line in high-heeled glamour shoes that attracts a host of celebrity customers.

Hobbs

UNIT 17, THE PIAZZA, COVENT GDN, WC2, 0171-836 9168
Open Mon.-Sat. 10.30am-7pm, Thurs. to 7.30pm, Sun. noon-5pm.

Well known for its fashionable but functional women's shoes in conservative colours, Hobbs also makes women's clothes and accessories, thus creating a totally co-ordinated look.

Jimmy Choo

20 MOTCOMB ST, SW1, 0171-235 6608
Open Mon.-Sat. 10am-6pm.

Previously, the Malaysian designer produced his custom-made, delicate satin women's shoes in a workshop in Hackney. His well-heeled client list must be thanking their lucky stars that Jimmy is now located so much nearer their homes. The shop has been designed according to Feng Shui principles to improve mental, physical and financial well-being. It must be doing the trick, because his classic ready-to-wear shoes literally walk out of the door.

Joan & David

150 NEW BOND ST, W1
0171-499 7506
Open Mon.-Sat. 10am-6pm, Thurs. to 7pm.

This sophisticated store fits well into Bond Street, offering expensive American designed footwear to both men and women in a minimalist setting.

John Lobb

88 JERMYN ST, SW1, 0171-930 8089
Open Mon.-Sat 9.30am-5.30pm, Sat. to 4.30pm.

Not to be confused with the bootmakers below, this shop is now owned by Hermès, Paris. The firm makes beautiful classically styled pret-à-porter shoes for men, from £225-£425. They also offer a service for clients in hotels, who can arrange for a representative to call with different styles. They also make classic women's shoes.

John Lobb Bootmaker

9 ST. JAMES'S ST, SW1, 0171-930 3664
Open Mon.-Sat 10am-6pm, Thurs. to 7pm.

Possibly one of the most famous shoemakers in the world, set in a delightfully old-fashioned shop. Here you'll be fitted for life, the lasts, stretching back to figures like the Duke of Wellington, kept downstairs in labeled boxes. Handmade to the highest specification and of the finest leathers, the shoes here are incredibly expensive but last a lifetime.

Joseph Azagury

73 KNIGHTSBRIDGE, SW1, 0171-259 6887
Open Mon.-Sat. 10am-6pm, Wed. to 7pm.

Designer Azagury comes up with beautiful delicate designs for women always right up to the minute, whether the fashion is high-steppin' strappy sandals, or low-heeled town shoes for the sophisticated shopper.

Kurt Geiger

49 NEW BOND ST, W1, 0171-491 8562
Open Mon.-Sat. 9.30am-6pm, Thurs. to 7pm.

Part of the Ferragamo and Bruno Magli group of companies, Kurt Geiger sells women's and men's shoes from around £80 to £350. The shop features mostly Continental designers but some styles come from their American suppliers in US sizes.

Manolo Blahnik

49-51 OLD CHURCH ST, SW3, 0171-352 3863
Open Mon.-Fri. 10am-6pm, Sat. 10.30am-5pm.

Sexy, flamboyant, totally irresistable—and very expensive—are the words that sum up Manolo Blahnik's shoes for women. They may be impossible to walk in, but women will bear the pain just to experience the glamour of the impossibly high heels which are made in limited edition batches of fifteen. They are on display in this minimalist shop in a charmingly quiet residential corner of Chelsea.

New & Lingwood

53 JERMYN ST, SW1, 0171-493 9621
Open Mon.-Fri. 9am-5.30pm, Sat. 10am-5.30pm

Best known for their excellent range of shirts, this shop has wonderfully woody brown shades in its classic men's shoes. You can buy them made-to-measure or ready-to-wear. Velvet slippers are around £100, but are more expensive with a hand-embroidered monogram or crest and take three months to make. There are many other accessories to complete a gentleman's wardrobe. Old Etonians continue to shop here, having been introduced to the firm's branch near the famous school as boys.

Patrick Cox

8 SYMONS ST, SW3, 0171-730 6504
Open Mon.-Sat. 10am-6pm, Wed. to 7pm.

It all started with a loafer that everyone just had to have, and Patrick Cox's status was confirmed. His original store is a mixture of coveted shoes and equally desirable furniture which both do a brisk trade for this Canadian designer. The Wannabe range is available at **129 Sloane St, SW1, 0171-730 8886.**

Small & Tall Shoe Shop

71 York St, W1, 0171-723 5321

Open Mon.-Sat. 10am-5pm, Thurs. to 7pm.

As the name suggests, this shop caters to those who have difficulty finding the right size, either because their feet are bigger or smaller than the average size. Shoes range from thirteen to two-and-a-half in small sizes (American one to four-and-a-half, European 31 to 34) and large English sizes eight-and-a-half to eleven (American ten-and-a-half to thirteen, European 42 to 46). The shoes are stylish and foreign made. They also specialise in special occasion and party shoes for all sizes. A useful find.

Tricker's

67 Jermyn St, SW1, 0171-930 6395

Open Mon.-Fri. 9.30am-5.30pm, Sat. to 5pm.

The all-leather shoes for men are made in Northampton, the historic centre of the English footwear industry. This old-fashioned shop offers a made-to-measure service where classic brogues and tasselled penny loafers are popular styles. The walls are lined with wooden lockers, adding to the olde-world charm.

SWEATERS & WOOLLENS FOR MEN & WOMEN

Assets

29 Floral St, WC2, 0171-240 7835

Open Mon.-Sat. 10.30am-6.30pm.

In the architecturally minimalist interior, the designer knitwear for men and women is in muted colours and comfortable shapes in 100 percent wool, angora, alpaca or cotton and Lycra mix. The garments are designed and made in the firm's factory in Newcastle-upon-Tyne.

Berk

46 Burlington Arcade, W1, 0171-493 0028

Open Mon.-Sat. 9.30am-5.30pm.

A small shop stocked with neatly folded piles of cashmere sweaters, Berk has its own label and also stocks 'the world's largest selection of Ballantyne products'. Within Burlington Arcade are two other Berk branches: at Number 6 (0171-493 1430), there is more women's knitwear, including throws; at Number 20 (0171-493 6558), there are assorted designer labels, includi and Burberry accessories for men **Also at 61 Brompton Rd, SW3 8000.**

N Peal

192 Piccadilly, W1, 0171-437 0106

Open Mon.-Fri. 10am-6.30pm, Sat. to 6pm.

This roomy branch in Piccadilly stocks a wide selection of famous cashmere goods from N Peal, the company that was one of the first to redesign the ordinary cardigan or twinset and turn it into a high-fashion item. At the corner of Burlington Gardens, you find the original N Peal store at **Number 37 (0171-493 9220)**, displaying elegant cashmere separates in fashionable colours for men and women. At the other (Piccadilly) end of the arcade at **Number 71 (0171-493 0912)**, the cashmere sweaters are for men only.

Scotia

Ivory House, St Katharine's Dock, E1, 0171-481 2556

Open daily 10am-6pm.

Near the Tower of London, this is both a tartan and knitwear shop for men and women, stocking tartan kilts, capes, blankets and clothes for children as well as knitwear in cotton and wool. There is a wide choice of Burberry and Pringle products.

The Scotch House

2 Brompton Rd, SW1, 0171-581 2151

Open Mon.-Sat. 9am-6pm, Wed. 10am-7pm.

Located in Scotch Corner, the Scotch House has a wonderful collection of cashmere, lambswool and Shetland knits for men and women. Most are traditional in style and colouring, but a younger audience is catching on to the classic shapes and well-made knits (particularly the Barrie knitwear Tartan Rose twinsets, combining bold rose prints against a tartan backdrop) which look contemporary when worn with jeans. The store also has an extensive selection of pure new wool tartans as well as a tartan room, where you can seek out your clan's tartan. **Also at 84-86 Regent St, W1, 0171-734 0203; 165 Regent St, W1, 0171-734 4816.**

Shirin Cashmere

11 BEAUCHAMP PL, SW3, 0171-581 1936
Open Mon.-Fri. 10am-6pm, Wed. to 7pm, Sat. 10.30am-6pm.

Founded in 1982, this family business designs and makes in its own factory, glamorous but wearable dresses, coats, jackets, separates and legwear for women, all in cashmere, or in silk knits. Each season brings its own new clever motif in the patterns of some garments. The styles are timeless. Upstairs a useful cashmere clinic will wash and redress any cashmere garments to make them look like new; also some classic cashmere sweaters for men.

Westaway & Westaway

65 GREAT RUSSELL ST, WC1, 0171-405 4479
Open Mon.-Sat. 9am-5.30pm, Sun. 11am-5.30pm.

There is something reassuring about shops like this one, where shelves are lined with sweaters and the tables are laden with tartan scarves which match the sensible skirts hanging on the rack. A wonderful place for traditional woollens for men and women at reasonable prices and particularly favoured by young Italian and Spanish visitors. A sister shop down the street at Number 92 (0171-636 1718), also has a wide choice with some distinctively patterned sweaters still hand-made by crofters in the Fair Isles of Scotland. **Also at 26 Henrietta St, WC2, 0171-497 5060.**

UMBRELLAS

James Smith & Sons

3 NEW OXFORD ST, WC1
0171-836 4731
Open Mon.-Fri. 9.30am-5.30pm, Sat. 10am-5.30pm.

Although very traditional, with umbrellas still made on the premises, this large shop is fun and pleasant to visit, thanks to its vast array of styles including frilly parasols. There are wonderful colours, too, plus walking sticks in various lengths. The handsome façade, with its Victorian letterhead, is worth a photograph: it has been here since 1857 and the shop itself was established in 1830.

Swaine Adeney

54 ST. JAMES'S ST, SW1, 0171-409 7277
Open Mon.-Sat. 10am-6pm.

Long-time fans of this fine riding and country-clothes shop remember when 'Briggs' was part of the store name. The firm still holds the Royal Warrant as the umbrella maker to the Queen Mother and the quality Briggs umbrellas are still an important accessory and sold in a variety of styles. There are golf umbrellas from £45 to £64, the famous, collapsible 'stubby' is from £45 to £55. The new address for this store now only focuses on menswear. Womenswear is available from the factory shop at **Nursery Rd, Saffron Waldon**, Gt. Chesterford, Essex, 01799 530521 only.

WOMENSWEAR

Women's Affordable Chic

Episode

172 REGENT ST, W1, 0171-439 3561
Open Mon., Tues. 10am-6.30pm, Wed., Fri. to 7pm, Thurs. to 8pm, Sat. 9.30-7pm, Sun. noon-6pm.

It's easy to pull together a co-ordinated look from the smart collections on offer in staple colours such as beige, red and black. Episode is good for the classic working wardrobe as they concentrate on strong and elegant knits, simple dresses and neatly tailored trouser suits in fabrics such as wool, silk and cashmere. **Also at 53 Brompton Rd, SW3, 0171-589 5274; Bishopsgate Arcade, Liverpool St. Station, EC2, 0171-628 8691.**

Esprit

38 LONG ACRE, WC2, 0171-497 0620
Open Mon.-Sat. 10am-7pm, Thurs. to 8pm, Sun. noon-6pm.

Although American, this company's brand of stylish casual wear is mostly made in Germany and Hong Kong. They offer jeans and a wide range of sweaters, shirts, trousers, skirts and T-shirts in neutral colours, plus coordinating gloves, hats, scarves and belts. **Also at 165-167 Kensington High St, W8, 0171-376 0012; 82 King's Rd, SW3, 0171-589 7211. Other branches throughout London.**

French Connection

249 REGENT ST, W1, 0171-5493 3124
Open Mon.-Wed. 10am-6.30pm, Thurs. to 8pm, Fri. & Sat. 10am-7pm, Sun. noon-6pm.

This firm, winner of such fashion awards as More Dash than Cash, and High Street

Retailer of the Year, offers well-made directional clothes at reasonable prices. Branches throughout London.

Hobbs

84 King's Rd, SW3, 0171-581 2914
Open Mon.-Sat. 10am-6.30pm, Wed. to 7pm, Sun. noon-5pm.

Linen-mix suits, cashmere-blend coats and a good range of lean knitwear make this shop a popular choice with career women with more dash than cash. The own-label shoes, boots and bags complete the look. **Branches throughout London.**

Jane & Dada

20 St. Christopher's Pl, W1, 0171-486 0977
Open Mon.-Sat. 9.30am-6pm, Thurs. to 7pm.

For around 20 years, this shop has been offering womenswear at affordable prices. Ranges include Fenn, Wright & Manson, In Wear, Marina Rinaldi and Jackpot. **Also at 59 Hampstead High St, NW3, 0171-431 0708.**

Jigsaw

126-127 New Bond St, W1, 0171-491 4484
Open Mon.-Sat. 10am-6.30pm, Thurs. to 7pm.

Created by the minimalist interior designer, John Pawson, this flagship Jigsaw store hosts regular exhibitions amidst the well-designed contemporary clothing collections. Don't let that put you off because the prices are surprisingly realistic (particularly for a store on this street), ranging from £30-£250. Four branches are exclusively menswear; some branches feature clothes for both men and women. **Branches throughout London.**

Karen Millen

46 South Molton St, W1, 0171-495 5297
Open Mon.-Wed. 10am-7pm, Thurs. to 8pm, Sat. to 6.30pm, Sun. noon-6pm.

Since opening her first store at the age of 21, this designer has become known for her combination of fine tailoring and directional cuts There is a good line of understated separates in neutral colours, with jackets from £150, skirts from £60 and dresses from £90. She also uses strong colours in her more off-beat styles which appeal to a younger audience. **Branches throughout London.**

Monsoon

264 Oxford St, W1, 0171-499 2578
Open Mon.-Sat. 9.30am-6.30pm, Thurs. to 8pm, Sun. noon-6pm.

Look beyond the tie-dye prints and sundresses and you'll find beautiful Nehru-collared jackets with appliqué detailing, structured coats, slim-fitting trousers and waistcoats and some of the best eveningwear on the high street. **Branches throughout London.**

Phase Eight

28A Kensington Church St, W8, 0171-937 5498
Open Mon.-Sat. 9.30am-6pm, Thurs. to 7pm.

A well co-ordinated shop selling clothes for casual/smart occasions. Ranges on offer include Fenn Wright & Manson, Sasperilla and the Patsy Seddon Collection. It's a good place for everything from a dress or linen separates for a summery event, to tailored clothes and stylish wedding outfits. They also offer a wide range of soft casual silks, knitwear and accessories. **Branches throughout London.**

Pied a Terre

19 South Molton St, W1, 0171-629 1362
Open Mon.-Sat 10am-6.30pm, Thurs. to 7pm.

The shop name means shoes to many customers but there are several branches, including the one in South Molton Street, which incorporate 'Basics for Woman' clothes, made to complement the shoes. The garments are designed in-house using the latest catwalk trends as inspiration, with separates and dresses retailing between £75 and £115. **Branches throughout London.**

Whistles

12 St. Christopher's Pl, W1, 0171-487 4484
Open Mon.-Wed. 10am-6pm, Thurs. to 7pm, Fri., Sat. to 6.30pm.

With up to 50 new lines a season, the shop's philosophy is to spot up-and-coming designers before they hit the big time. Owner Lucille Lewin's success has been built on her foresight to bridge the gap between High Street and high design. **Branches throughout London.**

Women's Designer Wear

À la Mode

36 HANS CRESCENT, SW1, 0171- 584 2133
Open Mon.-Sat. 10am-6pm, Wed. to 7pm.

A good source for avant-garde as well as established designers. Run by husband-and-wife team Peter and Josephine Turner who are blessed with the eye and gut instinct for what is going to be 'the next big thing', they were the first to stock Julien MacDonald's cobwebbed knits, and the acid bright creations from Britain's latest fashion genius, Matthew Williamson. Other designers carried include the Americans Richard Tyler, Marc Jacobs and Isaac Mizrahi, figure-hugging dresses from Hervé Leger and breathtaking evening wear from John Galliano. Free alterations and overseas delivery.

Alberta Ferretti

205-206 SLOANE ST, SW1, 0171-235 2349
Open Mon.-Sat. 10am-6pm, Wed. 10am-7pm.

London showcase for the first lady of Italian fashion. With her state-of-the-art manufacturing company, Aeffe, producing collections for the likes of Jean Paul Gaultier, Moschino and Narcisco Rodriguez, high-quality workmanship is assured. Ferretti designs beautiful, feminine clothes for real women with trademarks such as lace, chiffon and appliqué detail. The first-floor restaurant is popular with ladies who make an art of lunching without eating.

Amanda Wakeley

80 FULHAM RD, SW3, 0171-584 4009
Open Mon. Sat. 10am-6pm, Wed. to 7pm.

This young, very successful British designer has won the coveted Glamour Designer of the Year twice in a row. She sells ready-to-wear clothes for women but also continues her couture business, by appointment only, at the same premises. Understated and elegant, the dresses, suits, knitwear and separates make a striking impact, matched up with shoes and accessories, but evening wear is her forte.

Anna Molinari Blumarine

11A OLD BOND ST, W1, 0171-493 4872
Open Mon.-Fri. 10am-6pm, Sat. 10.30am-6pm.

Not for the shy retiring types, Anna Molinari designs for women who like showing off their assets. Colours are bright, fabrics are mostly clingy and the effect is sheer drama.

Betty Jackson

311 BROMPTON RD, SW3, 0171-589 7884
Open Mon.-Fri. 10.30am-6.30pm, Sat. to 6pm, Sun. noon-5pm.

Always managing to keep a finger on the pulse of fashion, Betty Jackson, MBE, has built up a loyal customer base who update their wardrobes with her simple but elegant designs. Her knitwear is always worth seeking out, as are her flattering separates and coats.

Catherine Walker

65 SYDNEY ST, SW3, 0171-352 4626
Open Mon.-Sat. 10am-6pm.

French-born designer Catherine Walker produces simple but elegant clothes for the rich and famous. Her clients include the Duchess of Kent, Shakira Caine, the ballerina Darcey Bussell and one of Britain's most favoured style icons, the late Diana, Princess of Wales. **She also has a bridal shop at 46 Fulham Rd, SW3, 0171-581 8811.**

Caroline Charles

56-57 BEAUCHAMP PL, SW3, 0171-589 5850
Open Mon.-Sat. 10am-6pm, Wed. to 6.30pm.

Well established with the town-and-country set, Caroline Charles is one of Britain's most successful designers. Her clothes are aimed at business women who want to put together a look that is classic, practical and easy, not for those who want to make bold fashion statements.

Chanel

26 OLD BOND ST, W1, 0171-493 5040
Open Mon.-Fri. 9.30am-5.30pm, Sat. 10am-4pm.

The Chanel label needs no introduction. Those interlocking 'Cs' embossed on everything from the cap of the best-selling No. 5 fragrance and shiny black powder compacts through to quilted leather bags and the lining of the chicest tweeds suit are coveted the world over. This particular boutique reopened in 1996 after a remodelling process to reflect the style of the famous Parisian store. Amidst the black lacquer fittings, beige carpeting and sumptuous suede furniture, you'll find the latest mix of traditional and sometimes quirky offerings from Chanel designer Karl Lagerfeld as well as cosmetics, watches and accessories. **Also at 31 Sloane Street, SW1, 0171-235 6631.**

Christian Dior

22 SLOANE ST, SW1, 0171-235 1357

Open Mon.-Fri. 10am-6pm, Sat. 10.30am-6pm.

Since British designer John Galliano took the helm at Dior, the sensible suits and wonderfully crafted but 'safe' dresses associated with 'the House' are a distant memory. As a tribute to the late, great designer, Galliano has created a collection in keeping with the 'New Look' Dior collection which caused a revolution in 1947. Nipped-in jackets and dresses emphasise the bust and waistline as before, but hot colours like fuschia, silver and acqua add a modern flavour—particularly when worn with the bold accessories like the chunky chokers and net hats also available in the store. All in a shop reflecting Galliano's flamboyant style.

Christian Lacroix

8A SLOANE ST, SW1, 0171- 235 2400

Open Mon.-Fri. 10am-6.30pm, Sat. 10am-6pm.

Clash, dash and a lot of cash are believed to be the only criteria required for wearing Christian Lacroix's designs. In fact, his unique blend of mis-matching is a distinct art form and some of his plainer garments like trouser suits or the stunning taffeta ball gowns are truly inspirational.

Egg

36 KINNERTON ST, SW1, 0171-235 9315

Open Tues.-Sat. 10am-6pm.

This smart shop with its regular exhibits of ceramics and paintings, has a wonderful range of spiritual-looking clothes, including reasonably priced Khadi cotton basic designs made in India, from £70-£200. More intricate designs can cost up to £2,000 and feature the djellabah style popularised by Jemima Khan.

Ghost

13 HINDE ST, W1, 0171- 486 0239

Open Mon.-Sat. 10am-6pm, Thurs. to 7pm.

Hugely popular for their luscious velvets and distinctive floral viscose dresses which cover up a multitude of sins, the shop has introduced the newer, directional pieces including simple shapes with dramatic slashes of colour. They also carry handmade knitwear by Marion Foale in silk, cotton and wool yarns.

Liza Bruce

9 PONT ST, SW1, 0171-235 8423

Open Mon.-Fri. 11am-6pm, Sat. to 5.30pm.

When it comes to bravado, designer Liza Bruce has it in spades. Not just in the cut of her second-skin skirts, tops, swimwear and PVC coats, but in her determination to rebuild her business after an unsuccessful and costly legal case against retail giants Marks & Spencer a few years ago. Her latest venue in a light interior will appeal to body-conscious clubby types with credit limits to match their attitudes. Trousers from £200.

Margaret Howell

29 BEAUCHAMP PL, SW3, 0171-584 2462

Open Mon.-Sat. 10am-6pm.

Mannish, beautifully tailored clothes are Margaret Howell's hallmarks. The shop is pristine yet homely, and similarly, the clothes, often featuring linens and crisp cottons, are smart whilst still possessing a relaxed air. Look out for the recently introduced homeware collection with pyjamas, bathrobes and washbags. **Also at 24 Brook St, W1, 0171-495 4888, and in Liberty.**

Paul Costelloe

156 BROMPTON RD, SW3, 0171-589 9480

Open Mon.-Sat. 10am-6pm, Wed. to 7pm.

One of the best known of the new breed of Irish designers who enjoy designing in natural fabrics, particularly in Irish linen. His collection includes everything from jeans to eveningwear. The Dressage Collection includes separates for daywear plus dress suits.

Tomasz Starzewski

177-178 SLOANE ST, SW1, 0171-235 4526

Open Mon.-Sat. 10am-6pm.

London-born but of Polish heritage, Tomasz Starzewski combines fun and elegance in his daywear, short sexy cocktail dresses and dramatic evening gowns. His designs are favourite with the high society set and past clients include Diana, Princess of Wales. His shop encompasses three floors of ready-to-wear, including his Gold Label range which is exclusive to the shop, couture garments and a bridal collection.

Valentino

174 SLOANE ST, SW1, 0171-235 4526
Open Mon.-Fri. 10am-6pm, Sat. 10.30am-6pm.

A glamorous shop filled with glamorous clothes. The spiral staircase leads you up to the women's collections which include sumptuous evening wear such as long column dresses and sophisticated daywear. Downstairs is devoted to menswear with suits, shirts and sweaters for the elegant man-around-town.

Wardrobe

42 CONDUIT ST, W1, 0171-494 1131
Open Mon.-Sat. 10am-6pm, Thurs. to 7pm.

Since 1973, Susie Faux has been fairy godmother to busy, high-powered women who come to her shop for overall advice on a complete look—everything from hosiery to make-up. Waving her magic wand, Susie and her team prescribe clothes from her stock of mainly Italian, French and German designers including Erruno, Mani, Strenesse, Jil Sander and Antonio Fusco. The staff are attentive, advising on cut, colour and styles to suit individuals, and records are kept for regular customers so new purchases will be in keeping with the co-ordinated wardrobe. This also helps dutiful partners to buy the appropriate gift without making a costly mistake. There is also a beauty treatment salon in store

Women's Evening & Special Occasion

Anouska Hempel

2 POND PL, SW3, 0171-589 4191
Open Mon.-Fri. 9am-6pm by appointment.

When she isn't tending to the design details at the Hempel or Blakes hotels, Lady Weinberg—or Anouska Hempel as she is more commonly known—is designing gorgeous frocks for her equally enchanting clientele. Exquisite details and precision cutting put her couture garments in the £2,000+ bracket. Clothes to die for.

Basia Zarzycka

135 KING'S RD, SW1, 0171-351 7276
Open Mon.-Sat. 11am-7pm by appointment.

Stunning evening wear and bridal gowns, and all the appropriate accessories, are the mainstay of this pretty shop, decked out with beautiful hats and beaded shoes, handbags and jewelry. Basia's custom-made, special occasion clothes in velvets, laces and silks are one-offs; most are intricately decorated. Handbags are often a combination of antique frames and lavish fabrics. There are approximately 500 tiara-style headdresses for brides (there is a choice of about a hundred, including antique models dating to 1790, for hire). Basia has also designed waistcoats and posh slippers for celebrities. This is a friendly shop and customers are welcome even if they they want to buy a silk flower or merely to browse. Overseas shipping available.

Bellville Sassoon

18 CULFORD GDNS, SW3, 0171-581 3500
Open Mon.-Fri. 9.30am-5.30pm.

This large, highly stylised showroom has racks of breathtaking evening gowns, cocktail dresses and special occasion clothes, all in jewel colours and designed and made in Britain under the Bellville Sassoon/Lorcan Mullany label.

Droopy & Browns

99 ST. MARTIN'S LANE, WC2, 0171-379 4514
Open Mon.-Wed. 10.30am-6.30pm, Thurs. to 7.30pm, Fri. to 7pm, Sat. 9.30am-5.30pm.

Founded in York in 1972, Angela Holmes's company is strong on wedding dresses (best to make an appointment for these), evening wear and smart day suits and dresses. All fabrics are coloured, dyed and woven to Angela's specifications to complement her designs. The dress racks are always brimming with romantic clothes and matching hats. It is an informal, fun place to browse for ready-to-wear special occasion clothes. **Also at 16-17 St. Christopher's Pl, W1, 0171-486 6458.**

Elizabeth Emanuel

49 DORSET ST, W1, 0171-224 4522
Open Mon.-Sat. 9.30am-5.30pm.

Best known for the fairy tale wedding dress she and erstwhile partner, David Emanuel, created for Diana, Princes of Wales's wedding, it should come as no suprise that Elizabeth Emanuel specialises in glamorous dresses for glamorous occasions. The shop, situated off Baker Street, is like a seductive dressing-up box, filled with sensuous dresses, immaculate tailoring and tactile fabrics. There is also a collection of wedding outfits from elegant suits through to formal outfits. For a total wedding package, Emanuel can link the bride up with top names such as florist Kenneth Turner, and jewellers Butler & Wilson.

Tatters

74 Fulham Rd, SW3, 0171-584 1532
Open Mon.-Fri. 10am-6pm, Sat. to 5pm.

For funky thirteen year-old girls or 70 year-old matrons, this shop is the place to go for off-the-peg evening wear including frothy little dresses, regal ballgowns and a mélange of velvet and satin garments.

Zandra Rhodes

79-85 Bermondsey St, SE1, 0171-403 5333
Open by appointment.

A riot of colour and patterns describes Zandra Rhodes and the clothes she creates. After fitting, one of her chiffon or organza dresses will take between 6-8 weeks for completion. Highly individual and guaranteed to make you stand out in a crowd. Plans for a museum of fashion and textiles of British designers is under way.

Women's Hats

The British Hatter

36b Kensington Church St, W8, 0171-361 0000
Open Tues.-Sat. 1015am-5.30pm.

A good source for the mother-of-the-bride and the kind of frothy confections favoured by traditional Ascot-goers. In addition to the swathes of silk, owner Pamela Bromley stocks a selection of big, bold and brash hats guaranteed to stop the traffic.

Fred Bare

118 Columbia Rd, E2, 0171-739 4612
Open Sun. 10am-2pm only.

The eclectic hat collections in the shop are ideal for the myriad visitors to Columbia Road market. Men can choose from trilbys, straw pork pie hats and puffa hats while younger women will veer towards the colourful hats, floral caps, woolly or fluffy hats. For granny, there are even nylon sou'westers. A wonderful shop for tantalising tifters. A warehouse sale is held twice a year in the studio at **134-136 Curtain Rd, EC2, 0171-739 4612.**

The Hat Shop

14 Lamb St, Spitalfields, E1, 0171-247 1120
Open Tues.-Fri. 10.30am-6.30pm, Thurs. to 7pm, Sat., Sun. 11am-5pm.

When you're looking for a hat, this should be your first stop. You'll find everything from plain berets at approximately £5 and woolly caps through to grand designs costing up to £250. Somewhere in the middle, there are men's bowlers, trilbies and top hats, plus a few hats for children. The shop will also spruce up a tired hat to fit in with the new season's fads.

Herald & Heart

131 St. Philip St, SW8, 0171-627 2414
Open Mon.-Fri. 10am-6pm, Sat. 9.30am-5pm.

With screen credits such as *Four Weddings and a Funeral* and *101 Dalmations* under their belts, Herald & Heart are reaping the rewards they deserve. The team produces two dramatic collections each year, mostly using felt and straw as the basis with individual touches such as embroidery and beaded feathers adding the necessary flair.

Herbert Johnson

30 New Bond St, W1, 0171-408 1174
Open Mon.-Sat. 10am-6pm.

Founded in 1899, this family business can boast a millinery department for women and an in-house design team. Dozens of styles are on display, including some famous headgear from films such as *Batman*, *My Fair Lady* and *Raiders of the Lost Ark*.

James Lock & Co

6 St. James's St, SW1, 0171-930 5849
Open Mon.-Fri. 9am-5.30pm, Sat. 10am-5.30pm.

This shop sees more women entering its hallowed portals since it opened a millinery department with four milliners, two on the premises, to offer pretty hats for occasions like Ascot and garden parties. Prices are £105 for a man's felt hat, a tweed cap is £59; ladies ready-to-wear start from £39 to £149.

Philip Treacy

69 Elizabeth St, SW1, 0171-259 9605
Open Mon.-Fri. 10am-6pm.

Philip Treacy's hats are works of art. That's why designers like Karl Lagerfeld seek him out to create the dream toppings for their creations. His own catwalk shows are among the hottest tickets in London Fashion Week, and each time you think he has surely run out of ways to twist, bend and shape a hat, the unassuming, soft-spoken Irish designer comes back with an even stronger collection. His salon in Belgravia is the epitome of elegance. The striking designs are displayed on milky-coloured mannequins, the perfect foil to show off the often gravity-defying shapes and imaginative use of colour. He also designs a small handbag collection which includes satin paisley shapes with tassles and simple suede clutch bags.

Stephen Jones

36 GT. QUEEN ST, WC2, 0171-242 0770
Open Tues.-Fri. noon-7pm, Sat. 11am-5pm.

Another of the great British modern milliners, Stephen Jones has created hats for designers such as John Galliano, Claude Montana, Antonio Berardi and Vivienne Westwood. His shapes are sharp and often witty, featuring nifty little flowerpots, mini bowlers and flirty feathery concoctions. In his lilac boutique, customers can buy ready-to-wear and custom-made hats. The latter may involve two or three fittings as well as discussions on fabric and colour. A diffusion line, Miss Jones, is available from major stores including Harvey Nichols.

Women's Large Sizes

Also try Selfridges for their large-size collections and Hennes for the Big & Beautiful range. Designs by Shirin Guild, even though expensive, are well worth saving up for as they are stylish and cover a multitude of sins. Available from Browns and Liberty.

Base

55 MONMOUTH ST, WC2, 0171-240 8914
Open Mon.-Sat. 10am-6pm.

Rushka Murganovic designs a range of separates for her shop which specialises in sizes 16-28. There are also clothes from Scandinavia, Germany, America and Israel.

Sloane Street

Sloane Street is a remarkable shopping street running from Knightsbridge to Sloane Square and the beginning of the King's Road. You'll find many of the big international designer names, who frequently also have stores in Bond Street.

Alberta Ferretti (25-26 Sloane St, 00171-235 2349); **Chanel** (31 Soane St, 0171-235 1357); **Christian Lacroix** (8a Sloane St, 0171-235 2400); **Dolce e Gabbana** (175 Sloane St, 0171-235 0335); **Emmanuel Ungaro** (36 Sloane St, 0171-259 8089); **Giorgio Armani** (178 Sloane St, 0171-235 6232); **Gucci** (17 Sloane St, 0171-235 6707); **Hermès** (179 Sloane St, 0171-823 1014); **Kenzo** (15 Sloane St, 0171-235 4021); **Louis Vuitton** (198 Sloane St, 0171-235 3356); **MaxMara** (32 Sloane St, 0171-235 7941); **Prada** (43-45 Sloane St, 0171-235 0008); **Valentino** (174 Sloane St, 0171-235 5855); **Yves Saint Laurent** (33 Sloane St, 0171-235 6706).

At the Sloane Square end there is a more neighbourhood feel thanks to the church and small shops like the dry cleaner's. In addition there are some excellent interior designer shops, like the **General Trading Company** (144 Sloane St, 0171-730 0411); **Lady Daphne** (145 Sloane St, 0171-1131), **India Jane** (140 Sloane St, 0171-730 1070; and **Jane Churchill** (151 Sloane St, 0171-730 9847. The well-bred, well-heeled young laides who live and shop around here were dubbed 'Sloane Rangers' in the late 1970s, a nickname that has stuck, They are likely ot have their wedding lists held at the General Trading Company and at Peter Jones department store on Sloane Square.

Long Tall Sally

21 CHILTERN ST, W1, 0171-487 3370

Open Mon.-Sat. 9.30am-5.30pm, Thurs. 10am-7pm.

One of twenty outlets nationwide, this popular shop commissions manufacturers who supply the High Street fashion stores, to re-proportion the current styles to fit women from five foot nine and up. From teenage to any age, the range of clothes includes casual wear, business suits and special occasion dresses.

1647

69 GLOUCESTER AVE, NW1, 0171-483 0733

Open Mon.-Sat. 10am-6pm.

Set up by comedienne Dawn French and ex-architect Helen Teague, this company produce a range of casual and stylish clothes for big women. The name has a double meaning; firstly it refers to the fact that 47 percent of British women are size 16 or over; secondly it states their sizing which goes from a modest 16 to a more generous 47. They produce two main collections a year in fabrics like linen, jersey and silk. Prices are very reasonable, starting at around £40. Styles are deliberately loose and are made in their own workshops.

Women's Lingerie

Agent Provocateur

6 BROADWICK ST, W1, 0171-439 0229

Open Mon.-Sat. 11am-7pm.

Vivienne Westwood's son Joe Corre runs this salon-like, specialist lingerie shop with his partner Serena. Both of them believe in the appeal of seductively beautiful underwear and have spread their gospel to the masses. Decked out like a boudoir with ornate chairs, ostrich-feather fans and swansdown powder puffs, the shop displays hour-glass corsets, delicate slips, negligées and matching bras and knickers—even belly chains and decorative nipple clamps. Not for the fainthearted.

Bradleys

57 KNIGHTSBRIDGE, SW1, 0171-235 2902

Open Mon.-Fri. 9.30am-6pm, Sat. 10am-6pm.

The lingerie ranges from hot and spicy French briefs, baby doll nightdresses and saucy bras through to cocoa-and-slipper snug cotton nightgowns, sensible pyjamas and slippers. Top designers from all over the world are represented here including Christian Dior, Nina Ricci, Aubade and Cotton Club.

Femme Fatale

64 HIGH ST, WIMBLEDON VILLAGE, SW19, 0181-947 8588

Open Mon.-Sat. 10am-6pm, Sun. 11am-5pm.

When you have a penchant for the finest lingerie and you can't find anything where you live, it makes sense to open your own shop. That's what model Tamzin Greenhill did three years ago. Judging by the number of locals who seem to be big on their smalls, it seems like she hit the proverbial nail right on the head. There's nothing overtly sexual here; the draped ceilings and chaises longues create a more romantic feel and provide the perfect backdrop for delicious lingerie, swimwear, nightwear and hosiery from Cotton Club, Gottex, Hanro, Huit and Marie Jo.

Fogal

36 NEW BOND ST, W1, 0171-493 0900

Open Mon.-Sat. 9.30am-6pm.

Luxury hosiery is the main product in this shop which has pantyhose in the window for up to £165. Inside prices start from £12. It is the quality of the fibres and the finishing techniques which make some of the products so pricey. One style has 1000 crystals sewn up the side. Fogal also stocks the popular body, with a cotton style at £99. Bodies in cashmere, silk and velvet are also available, depending on the season. **Also at 31 Sloane St, SW1, 0171-235 3115.**

Janet Reger

2 BEAUCHAMP PL, SW3, 0171-584 9360

Open Mon.-Sat. 10am-6pm.

Janet Reger was responsible for putting the 'oomph' back into lingerie when she draped Joan Collins in glamorous satin in the film, The Bitch. In her elegant white-wash-walled shop, skimpy knickers hang importantly and incongrously, each pair on its own little hanger.

Rigby & Peller

2 HANS RD, SW3, 0171-589 9293

Open Mon.-Fri. 9am-6pm, Wed. to 7pm, Sat. 9.30am-6pm.

As corset-maker to the Queen and Queen Mother, this firm displays two Royal Warrants and offers a discreet, unrivalled made-to-measure service for underwear which has been operating for more then fifty years. As well as their own label, designed by June Kenton, the shop sells ranges from Lejaby, Primadonna and Marie Jo, and offers a wide choice of swimwear. The demand for its expert fittings has led to a further shop at **22a Conduit St, W1, 0171-491 2200.**

Women's Maternity

NITYFormes

33 BROOK ST, W1, 0171-493 2783
Open Mon.-Sat. 10am-6pm, Thurs. to 7pm.

Pregnant women have no need to feel frumpy in the clever designs dreamed up by Daniel Boudon. Styles include adjustable cropped jackets with nipped-in waists, day dresses, trousers and flamboyant evening wear, all in flattering shapes and fabrics. **Also at 313 Brompton Rd, SW3, 0171-584 3337; 28 Henrietta St, WC2, 0171-240 4777.**

Night Owls & Great Expectations

78 FULHAM RD, SW3, 0171-584 2451
Open Mon.-Sat. 10am-6pm, Wed. to 7pm.

Everything from stretchy jeans to formal evening wear can be found in this shop, which carries labels including Pertesi, Pringle and Neuf Lune.

La Cicogna

6A SLOANE ST, SW1, 0171-235 3845
Open Mon.-Sat. 9.30am-6pm.

Very stylish designers such as Giorgio Armani are found in the Italian-made maternity fashions in this large shop which also sells stylish, mostly continental children's fashions.

Maman Deux

79 WALTON ST, SW3, 0171-589 8414
Open Mon.-Sat. 9.30am-6pm.

A curious little shop which sells unusual gifts such as pillows with slogans like 'Never complain, never explain', also has clothes for pregant women who don't want to look dull. The stock includes jeans, smart suits, dresses and bathing suits.

Women's Petite Sizes

Next

160 REGENT ST, W1, 0171-434 2515
Open Mon.-Wed. 10.30am-7pm, Thurs. to 8pm, Fri., Sat. 10am-7pm, Sun. noon-6pm.

In the 1980s this chain of unisex fashion shops began delivering co-ordinated high-street fashions at affordable prices. Next introduced a welcome range of well-proportioned petite sizes for women, five foot three and under, in sizes 6 to 14. Clothes tend to be polyester-mix and can be found at the chain's larger branches.

Principles

149 OXFORD ST, W1, 0171-493 5371
Open Mon.-Sat 10am-7pm, Thurs. to 8pm, Sun. noon-6pm.

Another popular chain of reasonably priced, fashionable clothes for men and women. The collection includes a range for women under five foot, three inches tall, in sizes six to 16. The fit is very good and liked by the fashion press.

Women's Scarves

Georgina von Etzdorf

50 BURLINGTON ARCADE, W1, 0171-409 7789
Open Mon.-Sat. 10am-6pm.

For an instant, opulent lift to any outfit, Georgina von Etzdorf's beautiful scarves, shawls and stoles are unbeatable. The colour blends are superb, the fabrics which include plain and elaborate devoré velvet, organza devoré linens, lace and silks, are truly magical. Velvet devoré scarves start from £115 and velvet devoré stoles up to £195. A lace shawl is £150.

Young & Trendy Street Fashion

Amazon

7A KENSINGTON CHURCH ST, W8
NO TELEPHONE NUMBER.
Open Mon-Sat 10am-6pm.

Amazon started as one small shop and has proceeded to take over its neighbours, now stretching over five premises in fashionable Kensington Church Street at 1, 3, 7a, 7b, 19 to 22. The company buys up seconds and discontinued lines from a variety of sources and offers labels such as Ralph Lauren, Nicole Farhi, Katharine Hamnett Jeans and Jasper Conran at up to 60% off. Expect even greater reductions on mid-range items from French Connection and In Wear. The stock changes rapidly, so if you see something you like, buy it—it may be gone the next day.

American Classics

398 & 400 KING'S RD, SW10, 0171-352 2853/352 3248

Open Mon.-Sat. 11am-7pm.

These shops sell new and secondhand clothing, styled on the classic American 1950s look. Think James Dean or Marlon Brando in On the Waterfront and you've got the idea. Popular items include monogrammed satin baseball jackets, flying jackets, checked cotton shirts and original, red label Levi 501's. **Also at 20 Endell St, WC2, 0171-831 1210.**

American Retro

35 OLD COMPTON ST, W1, 0171-734 3477

Open Mon.-Sat. 10.15am-7pm.

High-style American clothes and accessories made in the styles of the past. The stock is varied and fast-moving and includes mens fashions from W<, Ben Sherman and John Smedley, plus lingerie, underwear, sun glasses, cigarette lighters and books. Their own-label motorcycle bags are exremely popular.

Biba

15 SHORTS GARDENS, WC2, 0171-240 6694

Open Mon.-Sat. 10.30am-6.30pm, Thurs. to 7pm, Sun. noon-6pm.

In the '60s, this distinctive black and gold label was the epitome of cool. In its new guise, the focus on rich colours and fabrics like velvets and brocades is still there, but sadly, the magic of the past will never be recaptured.

Bond

10 NEWBURGH ST, W1, 0171-437 0079

Open Mon.-Sat. 10.30am-6pm.

Sportswear is very much in vogue and this cheerful shop is aimed at skateboarders. Labels carried include Stussy, Pervert and Fuct plus all the latest trainers. Bond also stock a range of sports magazines and hip-hop tapes. Catalogue available.

Boxfresh

UNIT 6, THOMAS NEAL'S, EARLHAM ST, WC2, 0171-240 4742

Open Mon.-Sat. 11am-6.30pm.

Stockist of British and American urban sportswear labels, such as Carhartt, Penfield, G Star, DSSIS, Dickies and Yak Pak Boys. Also stocks their own exclusive collection which is designed and produced in Los Angeles four times a year.

Browns Focus

38-39 SOUTH MOLTON ST, W1, 0171-629 0666

Open Mon.-Sat. 10am-6pm, Thurs. to 7pm.

Younger, funkier sister to the exclusive Browns store further along the street. Prices are still, well, pricey but the collections are geared more towards the street-smart who want to keep one step ahead of the fashion-pack. Many designs, such as the oversized Phat pants are imported and devotees think nothing of parting with their cash to get their hands on the latest styles. Along with Hysteric Glamour T-shirts, Orla Kiely bags, there are diffusion lines from designers such as Helmut Lang, Dolce & Gabbana, Lilly Pulitzer and Vivienne Westwood. Other treats are the modern-art installations and window displays created by young artists. A great place to immerse yourself in emerging trends before they hit the high street.

Diesel

43 EARLHAM ST, WC2, 0171-497 5543

Open Mon.-Sat. 10.30am-7pm, Thurs. to 8pm, Sun. noon-6pm.

A perfect hanging-out place for the young and impressionable. The interior is fun and funky, with an in-your-face glass stairway, fish-headed mannequins and almost cheesy 1970s decor grabbing the attention. The clothes veer towards 1950s trailer park trash, with around 140 styles of jeans including skinny and 'Wanker' pants, retro shirts and children's socks.

Dr Martens Dept Store

1-4 KING ST, WC2, 0171-497 1460

Open Mon.-Sat. 10am-7pm, Thurs. to 8pm, Sun. noon-6pm.

The minimalist factory look of this shop is an apt background for the sturdy range of clothes for men, women and children, all of which complement the Dr. Marten range of chunky footwear. There is also a hairdresser's and a café.

Duffer of St George

29 Shorts Gdns, WC2, 0171-379 4660
Open Mon.-Fri. 10.30am-7pm, Sat. to 6.30pm, Sun. 1pm-5pm.

Women can now buy into the successful street-smart Duffer style with neat suedette jackets and hipsters to match their boyfriend's ultra-smooth Duffer button-down shirts, flat-front hipsters and Gloverall duffle coats. The company's own label products include anything from knitwear to denim while imports run from Blue Martin, Ku USA and John Bull jeans.

High Jinks Clothing

Unit 25, Thomas Neal's, Earlham St, WC2, 0171-240 5580
Open Mon.-Sat. 10am-7pm, Sun. noon-6pm.

Specialising in club, street and skate wear for young, hip men and women. Labels include Technics, Arc, One World, Komodo and Custard Shop.

Hype DF

48-52 Kensington High St, W8, 0171-938 4343
Open Mon.-Fri. 10am-6pm, Wed. to 8pm, Sat. to 6.30pm, Sun. noon-6pm.

Once there was Hyper Hyper, then it grew up and became Hype DF. Thankfully. This new incarnation is airier than its overcrowded, ramshackle appearance of old. You'll find outlets from Red or Dead, Ally Capellino, Biba, Dexter Wong and Armand Basi plus accessories, Nails to Go and a restaurant/bar spread over the three floors.

Mambo

Units 2 & 3 Thomas Neal's, Earlham St, WC2, 0171-379 6066
Open Mon.-Sat. 10am-7pm, Sun. noon to 6pm.

We may not have the climate or facilities for it, but surfwear is proving popular in London. Mambo, originating in that surfing country Australia, provides some of the best up-to-the-minute styles for active surfers as well as those who only want to make waves. **Also at 26-27 Carnaby Street, W1, 0171-434 2404.**

Mash

73 Oxford St, W1, 0171-434 9609
Open Mon.-Sat. 10am-7pm, Thurs. to 8pm, Sun. 11am-6pm.

Favourite Saturday-afternoon haunt for clubbers searching for the perfect outfit for the weekend. The dance music is loud and appeals to the crowd looking out for the latest hip-hop sportswear labels to wear on the dance floor later in the evening.

O'Neill

11 Neal St, WC2, 0171-836 7686
Open Mon.-Sat. 10am-7pm, Sun. noon-5pm.

When Californian surfer Jack O'Neill invented the first wetsuit in 1952, little did he know he was starting a trend which would become fashionable on the street as well as in the water. The first London outlet is spread over three floors and each has its own individual characteristics. The ground floor and basement is modern and urban, featuring simplistic steel interiors. The mezzanine has traditional wooden fixtures with authentic memorabilia. The store holds all of O'Neill's four clothing lines, Boardcore, O'52, Main line and Boardbabes, as well as a year-round supply of swimwear and wetsuits.

Red or Dead

1 Sloane St, SW1, 0171-235 1335
Open Mon.-Sat. 10am-6.30pm.

As with Red or Dead's designs, the Sloane Street location is an injection of humour into the often too serious world of fashion. The designs are bold, often brash, sometimes tasteful but never boring. Owner Wayne Hemingway and his wife Geraldine have a tongue-in-cheek approach to their collections; however, their efforts have earned them the British Street Designer of the Year award on a fairly regular basis. **Also at Thomas Neal's Centre, Earlham St, WC2, 0171-240 5576; 33 Neal St, WC2, 0171-379 7571 (shoes only).**

Shop

4 Brewer St, W1, 0171-437 1259
Open Mon.-Sat. 10am-6pm.

A babe's delight—all girly pink, upbeat and doll-like with a range of well-sourced clothes to put the fun back into shopping. Expect lots of T-shirts and dresses with attitude with labels like Anna Sui, Hysteric Glamour, Stussy Sister and Fiorucci. At the higher end of the price range you'll find gorgeous Tocca dresses and a few pieces from Sofia Ford Coppola's Milk Fed range.

Young & Trendy Street-Fashion Shoes

Buffalo

47-49 NEAL ST, WC2, 0171 379 1051

Open Mon.-Sat. 10.30am-7pm, Sun. 2pm-6pm.

From the outset of their career, Buffalo shoes have had the Spice Girls' stamp of approval, which probably explains the mass appeal of these over-sized, built-up trainers and shoes. No matter that Baby Spice made the front pages of the tabloids when she took a tumble from her colossal wedges, Buffalo have become the fashionable way to walk tall.

Dr Martens Dept Store

1-4 KING ST, WC2, 0171-497 1460

Open Mon.-Sat. 10am-7pm, Thurs. to 8pm, Sun. noon-6pm.

As the name suggests, shoppers find more than shoes here—clothes, jeans, accessories, gifts, a café and a hairdresser's for men and women—but there certainly are lots of styles of this famous brand name which are both practical and fashionable. Some of the chunky boots and shoes come in zany patterns and colours; others come with laminated sequins. There are also myriad dressing options for the kids, including floral patterns to soften the look of those tough leather boots. The fourth floor has an exhibition on the company's history.

Office

57 NEAL ST, WC2, 0171-379 1896

Open Mon.-Sat. 10am-7pm, Sun. noon to 6pm.

Their own range features good value, high-fashion shoes that look straight to the catwalk for inspiration—from a distance you'd never know the difference. Elsewhere in the shop, there are collections from footwear designers like Robert Clergerie, Maud Frizon and Nicholas Deakins which appeal to a much broader audience. Branches throughout London.

Red or Dead Shoes

33 NEAL ST, WC2, 0171-379 7571

Open Mon.-Fri. 10.30am-7pm, Sat. 10am-6.30pm, Sun. noon-5pm.

Red or Dead make shoes which are a far cry from the slim and elegant Italian classics. These shoes for men and women evoke memories of the extremes of the 1970s platform days and some are clearly inspired by Frankenstein's monster. More fun than most shoe shops!

Shellys

266-270 REGENT ST, W1, 0171-287 0939

Open Mon.-Sat. 9.30am-6.30pm, Thurs. to 7.30pm.

The three-storey shop is always busy with men, women and children on the look out for fashionable shoes without exorbitant price tags. There's the Shellys own range which features everything from clumpy platforms to toe-crunching stilettos, plus trainers styles and boots. They also sell a good range of Dr Marten products and shoes from Kickers, No Box and LA Gear.

DEPARTMENT STORES

Dickins & Jones

222-224 REGENT ST, W1, 0171-734 7070

Open Mon., Tues., Fri. 10am-6.30pm, Wed. to 7pm, Thurs. to 8pm, Sun. 11am-5pm.

This department store is mainly devoted to fashion and beauty, from the perfume and cosmetics on the ground floor to the extensive designer ranges on offer on the upper floors. All the top, classic designer names are here—Karl Lagerfeld, MaxMara, Escada, Calvin Klein, George Rech—plus their own label (House of Fraser). In addition, it has contemporary fashions from Whistles, Hobbs, Monix and Betty Jackson. The stylish 'At Home' department on the fourth floor is residence for exclusive gifts, including soaps from Marseilles to contemporary or reproduction silverware, and individual, elegant pieces for the home. There are beauty and hair salons, personal shopping services for men and women, cafés and restaurants.

Fenwick

63 New Bond St, W1, 0171-629 9161

Open Mon.-Sun. 9am-6pm, Thurs. to 7pm

Founded in 1891 in its present corner location on prestigious Bond Street, Fenwick is one of the less hectic department stores in the locale. The ground floor is given over to high- fashion accessories such as quality bags by Bill Amberg and Hervé Chapelier, belts by Sally Gissing, hats by Philip Treacy, plus scarves, gloves and a good range of jewelry. Concessions include Maison de la Fausse Fourrure dedicated to fake fur clothing, accessories and home furnishings. On the upper floors you find designers you can rely on to pull together a good working wardrobe like Paul Costelloe, English Eccentrics, Caroline Charles, Joseph, and Jasper Conran. Menswear, located on the lower ground floor with gifts, is also well stocked. The lingerie department is worth seeking out for excellent labels like Valentino, Dolce e Gabbana, Emporio Armani and Wolford. Round off your shopping trip with refreshment from Joe's Restaurant Bar on the second floor.

Fortnum & Mason

181 Piccadilly, W1, 0171-734 8040

Open Mon.-Sat. 9am-6pm

Fortnum & Mason stays in an agreeable time warp with its glittering chandeliers, opulent packaging and the world-famous array of luxury food and wine, though it has expanded next door. And though prices have changed from the early eighteenth-century days when a baronet in Berkeley Square paid a mere £5 for six dozen bottles of the finest claret, this very traditional department store is a monument to the elegance of a bygone era—the assistants in the food hall still wear tail coats. The exterior is famous for its clock—the figures of Mr Fortnum and Mr Mason greet each other as the hour is struck. The original duo founded this remarkable store in 1707 to cater for the aristocracy of St. James's. Mr Fortnum was a footman in the Royal Household who knew the exact grocery requirements of the royal family, and Mr Mason supplied the delivery wagons. However, there is life beyond the food hall; upstairs a further four floors provide women's fashions, millinery, lingerie, jewelry, accessories, menswear, stationery and gifts, plus a china and glass department on the lower ground floor. Also, restaurants and a Champagne and smoked salmon bar.

Harrods

Knightsbridge, SW1, 0171-730 1234

Open Mon., Tues., Sat. 10am-6pm, Wed., Thurs., Fri. to 7pm.

Harrods is so vast—it occupies a 4.5 acre block—and so famous that it has become a tourist attraction in its own right. And justifiably so, with its magnificent exterior and equally impressive departments inside which include, on the ground floor alone, the Egyptian Hall for gifts, a glittering perfumery hall and the renowned food hall—well known for its Edwardian picture-tiles and daily changing displays of fish. Harrods began as a small Victorian grocery store, but from its humble beginnings was always in the forefront of fashion. It was the first London shop to install an escalator—because the manager hated lifts. This 1898 novelty proved such an excitement for the first clients that an attendant had to be stationed at the top to hand out brandy or sal-volatile as appropriate to the gentlemen and ladies overcome by the experience. These days the list of its departments and services goes on and on, and includes a bank, theatre ticket services and safe-deposit boxes, justifying its claim to sell anything and everything. There are 18 restaurants and bars. The January sale, opened by a celebrity, always starts on the first Wednesday of the year and brings Knightsbridge to a halt.

Harvey Nichols

109-125 Knightsbridge, SW1, 0171-235 5000

Open Mon.-Sat. 10am-7pm, Wed. to 8pm, Sun. 12pm-6pm.

If Harrods is the grande dame of Knightsbridge shopping, then Harvey Nichols is the funkier sister. Harvey Nicks, as it is known in fashion circles, is a shiny, streamlined temple for label addicts wishing to get their fix on the latest international designer looks. From the most coveted cosmetic brands to the hottest fashion labels, scrumptious food to enjoy on the premises or the most desirable ingredients to rustle something gorgeous up at home. At a price of course. The ground floor is hallowed ground for make-up and fragrance, with many companies signing deals to launch their products exclusively in the store; the first floor is given over to Contemporary Collections and big name International Designers. Further up on two you find the successful Personal Shopping suites and more Designer Collections from the likes of Nicole

Farhi and Joan & David. Three is the place for casual wear and lingerie, whilst four houses the luxurious Aveda Concept salon and five is dedicated to the finest food, to eat in the ultra-fashionable Fifth Floor restaurant or to buy from the equally fashionable food supermarket.

Liberty

214-220 REGENT ST, W1, 0171-734 1234
Open Mon.-Sat. 10am-6pm, Thurs. to 7.30pm, Sun. noon-6pm.

There are two faces to Liberty. One is romantic, from the mock-Tudor, half-timbered façade and quaint, rambling departments, many of which are filled with the famous Liberty print fabrics, Oriental departments and gifts; the other is cutting edge. Founded in 1875 at the height of the Aesthetic Movement, Liberty has become one of the best London stockists of contemporary designers with global representation from Alexander McQueen flying the flag for Britain to Yohji Yamamoto representing Japan. The light, airy cosmetics hall, although small in comparison to some of London's other department stores, is gaining a reputation as being one of the best places to shop, thanks to new and exciting ranges like E'Spa, Philosophy, François Nars and Face Stockholm and the beauty bonus of being swathed in natural daylight. Elsewhere you'll find a good selection of Oriental rugs, furnishings and accessories, exotic jewelry, a good range of furnishing and dress fabrics, plus the excellent basement Bath Shop.

Marks & Spencer

458 OXFORD ST, W1, 0171-935 7954
Open Mon.-Fri. 9am-8pm, Sat. to 7pm, Sun. noon-6pm.

Whether it's a packet of briefs from the underwear department or a three-seater sofa from furnishings, there's something for everyone at Marks & Spencer. The M&S logo has become synonymous with quality and value worldwide. The company, which began life in1884 as a penny-stall business, seeks out the design skills of the leaders in their field and employs them in everything from the clothing (Tania Sarne at Ghost), to leading make-up artist Charlie Green for the colour cosmetics and a team of chefs to develop new flavours for its phenomenally successful ready meals.

Peter Jones

SLOANE SQUARE, SW1, 0171-730 3434
Open Mon.-Sat. 9.30am-6pm, Wed. to 7pm.

Chelsea's only department store holds the wedding lists for the well-born, well-heeled and well-connected town and country set. It's the ideal place for distinctive fabrics, linens, china, glass, antiques and fashionable gifts as well as clothes and accessories. A bonus here is that both its coffee shop and licenced restaurant have views over London's roof tops.

Selfridges

400 OXFORD ST, W1, 0171-629 1234
Open Mon., Tues. 10am-7pm, Wed., Thurs., Fri. to 8pm, Sat. 9.30am-7pm, Sun. noon-6pm.

Having recently undergone major cosmetic surgery, Selfridges is back in the running with the other big-league department stores. Although undeniably one of the biggest and busiest stores in Oxford Street, it was beginning to look a little ragged around the edges, but under the direction of Vittoro Radice who previously spruced up Habitat, it has doubled its turnover in three years, and Selfridges' future is looking bright. A central atrium houses new glass-encased escalators and a sculpture of Josephine Baker by Sir Eduardo Paolozzi has pride of place.

Sogo

PICCADILLY CIRCUS, SW1, 0171-333 9000
Open Mon.-Sat. 10.30am-7pm, Sun. 11am-5pm.

The biggest department store in Japan chose a very central London location for its premises, which features some very British fashion names, such as Alfred Dunhill, Aquascutum, Burberry, DAKS and Paul Smith. International labels are well represented with Etienne Aigner, Hanae Mori, Iceberg, Maxmara, Versace jeans and Moschino Jeans. Stocking china, crystal, leather accessories, make-up, modern and antique jewelry and Japanese-made giftware in the Fuji boutique, and boasting a travel agency, this compact, two-floor department store is understandably popular with Japanese visitors, who also appreciate the adjoining Sogo Café which even has 'sushi for children' on the menu.

FLOWERS AND PLANTS

FLOWER SHOPS

Cameron Shaw

279 New King's Rd, SW6, 0171-371 8175

Open Mon.-Fri. 9am-6pm, Sat. 10am-5pm.

Dried-flower sculptures are created with wit and humour by Kerry Longmuir. The final effect might be a moss-covered bicycle or the corner of a wheat field. The shop also supplies top furnishing stores.

Edward Goodyear

45 Brook St, W1, 0171- 629 1508

Open Mon.-Fri. 8.30am-5.30pm.

Located inside Claridge's Hotel, this long-established florist has been arranging country flowers for high society since 1880 and holds four Royal Warrants—the most you can get.

Fast Flowers

339 Fulham Rd, SW10, 0171-352 8618

Open Mon.-Fri. 10am-6pm, Sat. 10.30am-4pm.

This turquoise-fronted shop has eye-catching displays and the pretty jugs of flowers look picturesque against the red-tiled floor. A small bunch costs £20 + delivery charge **Also at 609 Fulham Rd, SW6, 0171-381 6422.**

Felton & Sons

220 Brompton Rd, SW3, 0171-589 4433

Open Mon.-Fri. 9am-5.30pm, Sat. to 11am.

From its large corner shop in the heart of fashionable Kensington, Felton's—lit by a chandelier—offers a good service to a regular clientele who appreciate their traditional arrangements.

Jane Packer Floral Design

56 James St, W1, 0171-935 2673

Open Mon.-Sat. 9am-6pm.

Strong, wonderful arrangements using unusual combinations catch the eye from this artist in flower design. Flower arranging courses give you the chance to try it yourself. **Also at 101 Allitsen Rd, NW8, 0171-586 2766.**

Kenneth Turner

125 Mount St, W1, 0171-355 3880

Open Mon.-Fri. 9.30am-5.30pm, Sat. 10am-4pm.

Quite simply, the best designer of dried-flower arrangements in Britain, possibly in the world. Kenneth Turner creates the most fabulous decorations for private homes, weddings, clubs and hotels and flies around the world for clients. In the sweetly scented shop, you can be inspired by wonderful aromatic candles, dried arrangements, and a good selection of candlesticks and holders.

McQueens

126 St John St, EC1, 0171-251 5505

Open Mon.-Fri. 8.30am-6pm, Sat. 9am-3pm.

Maybe it's a coincidence but McQueen's, like British fashion's hottest export of the same name, produces some of the best floral designs around. The window display is minimal and modernist with the kind of artistic displays that stop you dead in your tracks.

Moyses Steven

157-158 Sloane St, SW1, 0171-259 9303

Open Mon.-Fri. 8.30am-5.30pm, Sat. to 4.30pm.

Masses of seasonal flowers and a selection of garden ornaments greet discerning customers at this top florist with imaginative designs.

Parterre

8 Marylebone Passage, W1, 0171-323 1623

Open Mon.-Fri. 9am-5.30pm.

The stunning impact of this shop is due to the well-laden baskets of fabulous flowers, including exotic varieties. There is a dried flower room and a floristry school, all run by the talented owners, Jane Durbridge and Nigel Wooller.

Paula Pryke Flowers

20 Penton St, N1, 0171-837 7336

Open Mon. 8.30am-5pm, Tues.-Fri. to 6.30pm, Sat. to 5.30pm.

Exotic is the name of the game here, with bright hot colours and some unusual plants. Paula Pryke is much in demand for her arrangements, working in some of London's top restaurants.

Pulbrook & Gould

127 Sloane St, SW1, 0171-730 0030
Open Mon.-Fri. 9am-5.30pm, Sat. 10am-2pm.

A large, glamorous showplace, established more than 30 years ago by Lady Susan Pulbrook and Rosamund Gould, the eponymous shop became known for its innovative, natural approach to flower arranging, and for its use of masses of white flowers. They also sell their own range of reviving lotions such as herbal hand cream, hand scrub gel and herbal products as well as scented candles. The Lady Pulbrook Flower School passes on its techniques in one-day sessions. They cost £160 and include flowers and lunch.

Wild at Heart

Turquoise Island, 222 Westbourne Grove, W11, 0171-727 3095
Open Mon.-Sat. 8.30am-7pm, Sun. 10am-2pm.

If you know the Portobello Road market and that area generally, the chances are that you've seen this gorgeous oasis of lilies, roses, greenery or whatever is in season in what used to be a public loo.

FLOWER MARKET

Columbia Road Market

Columbia Rd, E2, Open Sun. 7am-3pm.

There's a wonderful atmosphere at this busy Sunday market. Pick up bargain bedding plants by the tray, house plants, plus bunches of fresh and dried flowers. The shops in this picturesque Victorian street cater to the gardening fan and are full of delightful ceramics, urns, garden furniture, vases and accessories. Even if you don't want to buy plants you can still enjoy the bustling environment and take in a bagel, bun or tea in the number of good small cafés in the locale.

GARDENING

Avant Garden

77 Ledbury Rd, W11, 0171-229 4408
Open Mon.-Sat. 10am-5pm.

Joan Clifton runs this delightful shop that's an inspiration to the aspiring indoor and outdoor gardener. You'll find original candelabra, amphorae and pot stands, as well as gardening tools like her 'Monet' watering cans, buckets and jugs. Wire work is a speciality and comes in various shapes to use as topiary frames. Also a good range of English-made terracotta plant pots.

The Chelsea Gardener

125 Sydney St, SW3, 0171-352 5656
Open Mon.-Sat. 10am-6pm, Sun. noon-6pm.

Being located in trendy Chelsea means this garden centre is always up-to-date with the latest fashion in gardening plants. The various plots are well labelled, helpfully pointing out which plants are suitable for shady or sunny spots. Inside, there is a wide choice of unusual house plants, cacti and dried and silk flowers.

Clifton Nurseries

5a Clifton Villas, W9, 0171-289 6851
Open summer Mon.-Sat 8.30am-6pm, Sun. 10.30am-4.30pm, in winter they close half an hour earlier.

Popular, well-tended centre which caters for the patio gardeners through to those fortunate enough to have a larger plot, with plants, trees, shrubs, and some pretty wonderful and expensive garden ornaments, from furniture to urns. Staff are extremely friendly and helpful; the selection is one of the best in London and gives you great inspiration.

FOOD

Anyone even moderately interested in food should visit the food halls of the big department stores. The 'Big Four' are Harrods, Fortnum & Mason, Selfridges and Harvey Nichols. We have also included here several smaller shops that nonetheless cover the whole spectrum of gastronomic endeavours.

BAKERIES

& Clarke's

124 Kensington Church St, W8, 0171-229 2190
Open Mon.-Fri. 8am-8pm, Sat. 9am-4pm.

Proprietor Sally Clarke opened the shop as an offshoot of Clarke's, her next-door restaurant. Clarke's breads (delicious creations like Parmesan bread, apricot bread, rye bread with poppy seeds, black olive bread, and walnut bread) first gained the adulation of Londoners in the restaurant; you can buy them here along with the assortment of English cheeses from Neal's Yard, homemade ginger-nut and gingerbread-man cookies, rhododendron honey and Whittard's teas and Monmouth's coffees which you can savour in the shop.

Bagatelle Boutique

44 HARRINGTON RD, SW7, 0171-581 1551
Open Mon.-Sat. 8am-8pm, Sun. 8am-6pm.

Bagatelle is a traditional French pâtisserie and traiteur, a little piece of Paris in London, producing a wide range of pastries, breads like baguettes, old-fashioned white, walnut, and raisin (all made with French flour), and caters for small and large parties. Jacky Lesellier's family mill in France provides the flour, hence the genuine 'French' flavour of the bread. There are hams, terrines, pâtés and quiches, and mouth-watering ready-made dishes to take away, fresh foie gras in season and a selection of gourmet dishes for those at-home parties.

Baker & Spice

46 WALTON ST, SW3, 0171-589 4734
Open Mon.-Sat. 7am-7pm, Tues. to 6pm, Sun. 8.30am-2pm.

The aroma of freshly baked bread of all kinds, from sour dough (particularly good) to brioche and croissants, overwhelms you even on the street. They also make pastries, cakes, pains au chocolat, tartes tatin and some take-away dishes, as well as Chelsea buns. The outside catering service includes sandwiches, canapés and wedding cakes.

Beverly Hills Bakery

3 EGERTON TERR, SW3, 0171-584 4401
Open Mon.-Sat. 7.30am-6.30pm, Sun. 8am-6pm.

Homesick Americans and USA-style muffin fans head for this bakery and tea room, which serves mini-sized and hefty-sized muffins in wonderful flavours such as blueberry, carrot, double chocolate and, around Thanksgiving Day, pumpkin. They also make cookies, cakes and pies including key lime and pecan and make up gift baskets of their products.

Café Mezzo

100 WARDOUR ST, W1, 0171-314 4000
Open Mon.-Sat. 8.30am-11pm, Sun. to 10.30pm.

This is also a bakery and pâtisserie and bar, serving the adjoining Mezzo restaurants, Sir Terence Conran's huge Soho establishment, so expect gourmet standards in the range of speciality breads and pastries, from poppyseed rolls to lemon tart, and minamalist chic in the surroundings. It also sells sandwiches and hot dishes to take away or eat-in. To pass the time, there are racks of British and international newspapers for sale and news broadcasts on TV monitors.

Carmelli Bakeries

126-128 GOLDERS GREEN RD, NW11, 0181-455 2074
Open Mon.-Thurs. & Sun. 7am-1am, Fri. 7am-until one hour before sunset, Sat. one hour after sunset.

A north London institution, Carmelli supplies the locals and the whole of the north London Jewish community with breads like cholla, bulka, plain, sesame and poppy seed bagels and an assortment of cakes. The shop is always packed with people buying huge amounts of bread and cakes which are baked practically around the clock. They also produce bagels with smoked salmon and cream cheese, tuna, and egg and onion to take out.

De Gustibus

53 BLANDFORD ST, W1, 0171-486 6608
Open Mon.-Fri. 7.30am-4.30pm, Sat. 9am-2pm.

De Gustibus, still based in Thame, Oxfordshire, has this small London outlet. Dan Schickentanz bakes in a traditional matter, producing all kinds of international breads, like Six Day Sour, Old Milwaukee Rye, ciabattas, Italian olive bread, muffins, brownies and carrot cakes. There are also ranges of olive oils, pastas, and a good take-away section with hot food. You can also eat sandwiches and drink tea or coffee in the miniscule shop.

Jane Asher Party Cakes

24 CALE ST, SW3, 0171-584 6177
Open Mon.-Sat. 9.30am-5.30pm.

Run by actress Jane Asher, this shop supplies customers with some wonderfully designed cakes. In addition to the huge numbers of designs on offer in its brochure, you can design your own cake, as many people do, and the shop will make it up for you to your specifications—castle, golf course or whatever you fancy. The small, delightful tea room serves morning coffee, set afternoon tea, and light lunches.

Louis Pâtisserie

32 HEATH ST, NW3, 0171-435 9908

Open daily 9am-6pm.

Hampstead locals come to chat, read the papers—and after a walk on the Heath—to treat themselves to the fabulous cakes including lots of Hungarian specialities. This bakery also makes croissants, cheesecakes, poppyseed rolls and chocolatey-creamy concoctions.

Maison Blanc

102 HOLLAND PARK AVE, W11, 0171-221 2494

Open Mon.-Tues. 8am-7pm, Wed.-Fri. 8am-7.30pm, Sat. 7.30am-7pm, Sun. 8.30am-6pm.

Maison Blanc was such a roaring success in Oxford they opened in London and though ownership has changed, they continue to go from strength to strength serving top French-style patisserie. Gâteaux are worth going a long way for. **Also at 11 Elystan St, SW3, 0171-584 691; 62a Hampstead High St, NW3, 0171-431 8338; 37 St. John's Wood High St, NW9, 0171-586 1982.**

Neal's Yard Bakery

6 NEAL'S YARD, WC2, 0171-836 5199

Open Mon.-Sat.10.30am-4.30pm.

This little co-operative bakery in the heart of Neal's Yard produces unusual artisan-style breads. Each day they bake large and small whole-wheat, three-seed, sunflower-seed, cheese-and-herb, olive-and-garlic, fruit-and-malt, and sourdough loaves.

Pâtisserie Valerie

44 OLD COMPTON ST, W1, 0171-437 3466

Open Mon.-Fri. 8am-8pm, Sat. to 7pm, Sun.9.30am-6pm.

Pâtisserie Valerie has expanded, but this, the original, is our favourite. It's small with panelled wooden walls and crowded with locals and tourists alike. The gâteaux are a treat to the eye, and the profiteroles to die for. **Also at 215 Old Brompton Rd, SW3, 0171-823 9971; 105 Marylebone High St, W1, 0171-935 6240; 8 Russell St, WC2, 0171-240 0064; RIBA, 66 Portland St, W1, 0171-631 0467.**

CHEESE

Barstow & Barr Fine Cheeses

24 LIVERPOOL RD, N1, 0171-359 4222

Open Mon.-Fri. 10am-8pm, Sat. to 6pm, Sun. 11am-4pm.

Known for its British unpasteurised cheeses, this tiny shop is piled high with names like Colston Bassett Stilton, the hard ewes' milk cheese Tyning, cheeses from the Isle of Mull, Gubbeen and more, as well as biscuits, olives and chutneys. In the Earl's Court branch they also stock Sally Clarke's breads. **Also at 32 Earl's Court Rd, W8, 0171-937 8004.**

Cheeses

13 FORTIS GREEN RD, N10, 0181-444 9141

Open Tues.-Fri. 10am-6pm, Sat. 9.30-5.30pm.

You could easily miss this tiny shop in Muswell Hill, but seek it out for the vast array of around 150 cheeses in stock. Mainly from France and Britain, the cheeses include unusual types like goat's milk from the Canary Islands, as well as cheeses made from ewe's milk. Farm-made cheeses, where the milk is produced and the cheeses made in the same place, are their speciality.

International Cheese Centre

21 GOODGE ST, WC2, 0171-631 4191

Open Mon.-Sat. 9.30am-6.30pm.

With anything from 350-400 cheeses from ten countries available at any given time, the International Cheese Centre offers an impressive range. English cheeses, mostly farmhouse cheeses, are best represented, with France not far behind. A good proportion are made with unpasteurised milk, and—helpful for strict vegetarians—the list shows which cheeses are made using vegetarian rennet. Also a good selection of biscuits, jams, sauces, and mustards made by small suppliers. Mail order. **Also at 53 Charing Cross Rd, WC2, 0171-494 0794; The Parade, Victoria Station, SW1, 0171-828 2886; Liverpool St Station, EC2, 0171-628 2343.**

Jeroboam's

51 ELIZABETH ST, SW1, 0171-823 5623
Open Mon.-Fri. 9am-6pm, Sat. 9am-5pm.

This is one of the best known and most popular cheese shops in London, concentrating on French and British farmhouse cheeses. Cheeses are properly looked after here, and staff are friendly and knowledgeable. Wines, pasta, oils, vinegars and other staples of the good life are also on sale here. You can join the monthly cheese club here; you'll learn a lot. Mail order. **Also at 24 Bute St, SW7, 0171-225 2232; 6 Clarendon Rd, W11, 0171-727 9359.**

La Fromagerie

30 HIGHBURY PARK, N5, 0171-359 7440
Open Mon.-Fri. 9.30am-7.30pm, Sat., Sun.10am-5pm.

A great shop for French and Italian cheeses, from Tomme Val d'Isère to the Pecorino Foglie di Noce, matured in walnut leaves and shells. Patricia Michelson is keen you should taste her unusual cheeses, so you're likely to come away with something entirely new to you. She also sells home-made tarts, pastas, Poilane bread delivered weekly from Paris as well as breads from Sally Clarke and chocolates.

Neal's Yard Dairy

17 SHORTS GDNS, WC2, 0171-379 7646
Open Mon.-Sat. 9am-7pm, Sun. 10am-5pm.

It is probably true to say that Randolph Hodgson has single-handedly saved true British and Irish cheeses from virtual extinction. The shop opened in 1979 with Hodgson making and selling his own cheese. Now the business has expanded to include farm-produced cheeses from throughout Britain and Ireland. Every cheese in this shop has been hand-made by a real person using real milk from real animals, properly 'brought up' on the premises. The cheeses are turned by hand and aged to perfection. Hodgson puts the maker's name on the cheese he or she produces. The vast majority are made from unpasteurised cow's, sheep's and goat's milk. Also yogurt, olives and chutneys and breads from Sally Clarke. Mail order.

Paxton & Whitfield

93 JERMYN ST, SW1, 0171-930 0259
Open Mon.-Fri.. 9.30am-6pm, Sat. to 5.30pm.

Paxton & Whitfield is now in new hands and a delightful refurbishment has taken place, giving more room and better display space to this busy shop in Jermyn Street which has been selling cheeses to the cognoscenti since 1797. There are around 200 varieties in stock, from Britain and throughout Europe. There's also a good selection of hams, meats and hand-raised pies, as well as chutneys and pickles and they offer an excellent mail order service. There's a cheese society you can join and they hold tutored tasting.

CHOCOLATE & CONFECTIONERY

Charbonnel et Walker

ONE THE ROYAL ARCADE, 28 OLD BOND ST, W1, 0171-491 0939
Open Mon.-Fri. 9am-6pm, Sat. 9.30am-5.30pm.

Founded over 120 years ago when the Prince of Wales persuaded Madame Charbonnel to come to London to found a confectionary establishment with a Mrs Walker, Charbonnel et Walker continue to sell fabulous chocolates, made in oh-so-British Tunbridge Wells. They hold a Royal Warrant and from their miniscule premises sell English-style chocolates like rose and violet fondants. Seasonal chocolates are a big thing—in February for Valentine's Day and of course at Christmas. They'll courier chocolates the same day to addresses within London and they have a good mail order.

Godiva

247 REGENT ST, W1, 0171-495 2845
Open Mon.-Sat. 9.30am-6pm, Thurs. 9.30am-7pm.

Fabulous displays of luxury Belgian chocolates are imported weekly from Belgium to this always crowded small shop, and there are always new ideas on tastes and shapes. Their gift wrapping makes everything look special, and they offer mail order.

Rococo

321 KING'S RD, SW3, 0171-352 5857
Open Mon.-Sat. 9am-7pm, Sun. noon-5pm.

If you have a genuine passion for real chocolate, visit this shop, set up in 1983 by Chantal Coady, who, while working part-time at Harrods to finance her art degree, worked at Harrods chocolate counter. She became hooked and after a great deal of research, opened up shop, wrote the authoritative book Chocolate: Food of the Gods and more recently, The Chocolate Companion, and founded the Chocolate Society. Here you will find bars of 'cru' chocolate—each type coming from specific beans from specific plantations. There are three Grand Cru bars made by the French Valrhona firm of which the No.1 is made from the rare Criollo cocoa bean produced on an island in the Indian Ocean. Grand Cru Manjari Pure Criollo 64 percent has a fruity flavour and a velvety, quick-to-melt feeling in the mouth. She also stocks handmade English truffles. Try to get there as early in the day as possible, chocolates arrive daily and they might run out of your particular favourite. The shop has a great sense of fun: some of the gourmet chocolate is wrapped in painted silver to resemble brightly coloured fishes; there are scary looking chocolate dinosaurs and seasonal delights like snowballs and holly berries at Christmas.

COFFEE & TEA

Algerian Coffee Stores

52 OLD COMPTON ST, W1, 0171-437 2480

Open Mon.-Sat. 9am-7pm.

This is the shop to come to for great coffee and advice; they've been in business since 1887 and supply many smaller stores and cafés. You can't miss it—the delicious aroma of freshly ground coffee wafts into the street. Coffees and teas from around the world, their own specials such as Lebanese beans with cardomoms and Maragogype, the largest coffee bean in the world, fruit-flavoured and herbal teas, spices and a whole array of coffee making equipment are on sale. World-wide mail order service.

Angelucci Coffee Merchants

23B FRITH ST, W1, 0171-437 5889

Open Mon.-Sat. 9am-5pm, Thurs. to 1pm.

This tiny corner shop, still run by the Angelucci family, has stood in the same place for its entire 70-year history. Very little, it appears, has changed in that time, and the shop has a wonderful, old-fashioned atmosphere. Choose from 35 coffees from around the world—Puerto Rico, Angola, Kenya and Haiti, make up your own blend or go for their 'secret blend' Mokital coffee.

Drury Tea & Coffee Co

3 NEW ROW, WC2, 0171-836 1960

Open Mon.-Fri. 8.30am-6pm, Sat. 11am-5pm.

This well-known company has been in London for more than 50 years and has a very comprehensive list The shop is bright, friendly and traditional. Teas are from Sri Lanka, India, China, Formosa, and Africa, and there are flavoured teas as well. Try China Rose Tippy Golden Darjeeling, or one of Drury's traditional blends, like English Breakfast. You can buy infusers, teapots and accessories here. **Also at 37 Drury Lane, WC2, 0171-836 1960; 1-3 Mepham St, SE1, 0171-928 0144.**

H R Higgins

79 DUKE ST, W1, 0171-491 8819

Open Mon.-Wed. 8.45am-5.30pm, Thurs., Fri. to 6pm, Sat. 10am-5pm.

The company was founded in 1942 by Mr H R Higgins, who wanted to become the coffee man in London and it's still in family hands. The coffees come from everywhere, from Colombia, India, Sumatra, Costa Rica, Mexico, Tanzania, Jamaica, Guatemala, Ethiopa, Brazil, and Java. The company now sells tea as well as coffee, and gift packs of both coffee and tea. The people at Higgins are helpful, and in a small tea room downstairs you can sit and enjoy a good cuppa.

Java Java

26 RUPERT ST, W1, 0171-734 5821

Open Mon.-Thurs. 10am to 10pm, Sat. to 11pm, Sun. 1pm-8pm.

A tiny, rather hippy hang-out which mainly serves as a café, but also sells take-out coffee beans and a huge range of teas from first-flush Darjeeling Leaf at £4.75 for 125 grams to herbal infusions of all kinds, including 'Mental Clarity', 'Serenity' and 'Digestibility'. Their ranges of syrups to flavour coffee or sodas is over 60 strong.

L Fern & Co

27 RATHBONE PL, W1, 0171-636 2237

Open Mon.-Fri. 9am-5.30pm, Sat. 9am-2pm.

Originally a Covent Garden coffeehouse founded in 1863, the company later moved to this address but retains the feeling of the past with its old wooden dressers and glass-fronted desk. They stock a number of coffees and loose fruit teas as well as own-brand packaged teas, Twining and Jacksons.

Monmouth Coffee Company

27 MONMOUTH ST, WC2, 0171-836 5272
Open daily 9am-6.30pm.

Probably the best place to buy coffee in London. In addition to being retailers, the Monmouth Coffee Company imports its own Arabica beans from Colombia, Kenya, Nicaragua, Costa Rica and Papua New Guinea and roasts them on the premises six days a week; each is available in medium and dark roasts. You can sit and sample the varieties at the back of the shop. You can even buy green (unroasted) coffee beans and roast them yourself (instructions provided).

The Tea House

15 NEAL ST, WC2, 0171-240 7539
Open Mon.-Sat. 10am-7pm, Sun. noon-6pm.

In keeping with this particular patch of Neal Street, The Tea House has a distinctly Oriental air, and if loose tea in a myriad flavours is your bag, stop in. The Tea House stocks teas from China, India, Japan, Sri Lanka, Taiwan, Kenya, Russia, Turkey and South Africa, and has a huge assortment of fruit, flower, and flavoured teas like mango, caramel, coconut, honey, passion fruit and vanilla. Upstairs, there is a wide assortment of unusual teapot shapes including a dragon, elephant and Sherlock Holmes.

Twinings

216 STRAND, WC2, 0171-353 3511
Open Mon.-Fri. 9.30am-4.30pm.

Tea lovers shouldn't miss this wonderful, rather eccentric shop. Not only can you find a wide selection of all Twinings' varieties as well as tea towels, tea pots and infusers, there's also a little museum at the back which traces the family firm's long history (it was founded in 1706). The present Sam Twining is still involved in the tea business.

Whittards

43 CARNABY ST, W1, 0171-437 1107
Open Mon.-Sat. 10am-7pm, Sun. noon-5pm.

Whittards was established in Chelsea in the 1860s. Coffee and tea are pretty much on an equal par here, and all their speciality teas and Arabica coffees are imported specially for them. Darjeeling First Flush, a true tea-lover's brew, is available here and there are fruit teas and commercial blends as well. A range of wacky teapots rounds out the goods on offer. **More than 70 branches throughout London.**

FISH & GAME

The Caviar House

161 PICCADILLY, W1, 0171-409 0445
Open Mon.-Sat.10am-10pm.

The Danish-owned Caviar House, operating internationally since 1950, incorporates a restaurant, La Cave, and sets out to show that caviar is not just a luxury product. On offer is Iranian Sevruga, Oscietre, Beluga, Imperial, Royal Black, and Classic Grey caviars. Caviar is packed daily, fresh from the tins imported from the Caspian; containers come in many sizes, are attractive and designed for long distance travel. Knowledgeable staff answer any questions you might have about caviar, and there are complementary goods, such as wine, smoked wild Norwegian salmon, vodka and chocolates.

Jefferson's Seafood

17 CLIFTON RD, W9, 0171-266 0811
Open Mon.-Sat. 9am-6pm.

Amid the cluster of interesting food shops in this street, this fishmonger displays not only Dover sole, sea bass, turbot, brill, John Dory and swordfish, but also prepares its own gravadlax, sashimi and sushi. Besides its local clientele, they supply some 30 quality restaurants all over London from Daphne's to Zafferano.

John Blagden

65 PADDINGTON ST, W1, 0171-935 8321
Open Mon. 7.30am-4.30pm, Tues.-Fri. to 5.30pm, Sat. to 1pm.

A really pretty shop, with glazed blue bricks, where the family staff are helpful and knowledgeable, guiding you through the displays of sea bass, red mullet, wild Scottish salmon, Scottish lobsters and native oysters. They are also noted for their game, for Aylesbury and Barbary ducks, teal and grey-legged partridge all hung and plucked on the premises.

R H Jarvis & Sons

56 COOMBE RD, KINGSTON-UPON-THAMES, SURREY, 0181-546 0989
Open Mon. 8am-3pm, Tues., Thurs.-Sat. to 5pm, Wed. to 4pm.

Easily one of the best fishmongers in the London area, they stock flappingly fresh fish, and the staff are very knowledgeable. It is one of the few places where you can get first-rate sushi and sashimi cuts as well as delights like sea urchin, so Japanese Londoners travel miles to buy here. For the more traditional British taste, there are Devon smoked sprats and usually jellied eels on offer. In the autumn, this is the place for game—wild duck, pheasant, quail, grouse, venison and hare.

Steve Hatt

88-90 Essex Rd, N1, 0171-226 3963

Open Tues.-Sat. 7am-5pm.

This fourth-generation fishmonger sells only prime-quality fresh fish and smokes its own haddock, trout and mackerel on the premises. From Dover sole to Devon squid, everything is amazingly fresh, and there is an enormous range. They stock all the prime fish such as brill, turbot, John Dory, halibut and sea bass. Fish flown in fresh include tuna, swordfish, snapper and doranda as well as fresh raw king prawns. Of course, there is also a wide array of cod, plaice, haddock, herrings, mackerel, trout, salmon (wild and farmed), sea bream, monk fish, skate, whiting and red mullet. Most importantly, they are happy to advise and provide on-the-spot processing of cuts required for recipes.

GOURMET SHOPS & EMPORIUMS

Bluebird

350 King's Rd, SW3, 0171-559 1141

Open Mon.-Wed. 10am-8pm, Thurs., Fri. 10am-9pm, Sat. 9am-9pm, Sun. noon-6pm.

Conran's newest emporium, housed in the old Bluebird garage, is pretty impressive. Where the petrol pumps once were, there's now a long stand of fruit and vegetables, lit at night by magnificent flares at each end and protected somewhat by a glass canopy. The whole of the ground floor, with the exception of a café, is taken up by a food, wine and cook shop. The selection is admirable; excellent Bresse chickens, exceptional cheeses, all the speciality foreign labels in sauces and preserves, biscuits and pastas, and Conran's own label, too, which come in Conran's own style packaging. Prices are high, but so is quality.

Fortnum & Mason

188 Piccadilly, W1, 0171-734 8040

Open Mon.-Sat. 9am-6pm, Thurs. to 7pm.

Fortnum & Mason, established in 1707, is definitely one of the 'must see' sights for food lovers. The food hall is very grand and very traditional. Most of the myriad goods on display here are own label, and range from condiments to jams. Then, of course, there are wines, a range of fresh fruits and vegetables and an excellent selection of cigars. Around 200 cheeses are on offer at any one time, as well as sausages, smoked fish, pâtés, hams, fresh pasta, traditional English pies, and freshly ground coffee. For sweet lovers there are mouth-watering pastries and a large chocolate counter. The tea section is always busy, with visitors buying phenomenal amounts. In summer and at Christmas, their food hampers are amongst the most sought-after in the world.

Harrods Food Hall

Knightsbridge, SW1, 0171-730 1234

Open Mon., Tues., Sat. 10am-6pm, Wed.-Fri. to 7pm.

Harrods is one of London's greatest tourist musts, particularly just before Christmas when the crowds thicken to a real throng. Harrods has a reputation as a supreme retailer of quality, and the food halls are justly famous. The most traditional British fare sits beside continental and eastern delicacies. There are Harrods wines, as well as native oysters, in fact almost anything you can think of in stunning decorations.

Harvey Nichols Food Hall

109-125 Knightsbridge, SW1, 0171-235 5000

Open Mon.-Sat. 10am-7pm, Wed. to 8pm, Sun. noon-6pm.

Harvey Nicks, as it is affectionately known to Londoners, is now almost as famous for its food hall as for its fashion. The whole of the fifth floor is devoted to food and drink in one form or another, there's a bar, café and famous restaurant. It's all very high-tech and stainless-steel gleams as does polished wood. There are great cheeses, fruit and vegetables in barrow displays, meats and fish and a good traiteur selection. Fashion-conscious foodies go for the packaging as much as for the contents, those tins look great on your shelves at home. Designer olive oils are much in evidence. The wine shop is first-rate.

Le Pont de la Tour Food Store

36 SHAD THAMES, SE1, 0171-403 4030
Open Mon.-Fri. 9am-8.30pm, Sat., Sun. 10am-6pm.

Part of Sir Terence Conran's Thameside 'Gastrodome', as opposed to his Chelsea gourmet emporium, Bluebird. The Oil and Spice shop offers a wide array of around 90 spices, all ground on the premises; there are vinegars and a selection of olive oils open for tasting (0171-403 3434); the Food Store stocks cooked meats, Neal's Yard cheeses and jams, and splendid breads baked at the gastrodome by Stuart Powell, products from France, Italy, Spain and Britain (0171-403 4030); and finally at the Smoked Fish and Crustacea shop you can choose from a fairly comprehensive display (0171-403 7573).

Partridges

132 SLOANE ST, SW1, 0171-730 0651
Open daily 8am-10pm.

Just off Sloane Square, Partridges, established in 1972 and holding a Royal Warrant to Her Majesty, is just as posh as its surroundings. You'll find everything in this relatively small but packed space: exotic fruits and vegetables, wine, freshly baked breads, ground-to-order coffees, and an assortment of ready-made dishes each day. Also a good selection of cold meats and salamis, caviar, biscuits, and wine. They roast their own free-range chickens, Barbary ducks and gammon knuckles daily; this is a good place to buy an impromptu meal. They also prepare picnic hampers and have a good mail order.

The Real Food Store

14 CLIFTON RD, LITTLE VENICE, W9, 0171-266 1162
Open Mon-Fri. 8am-8pm, Sat. 8.30am-7pm, Sun. 11am-4.30pm.

The Real Food Store is 'a healthy grocers', an apt description, for the shop is a cross between a health food and a gourmet food shop, combining the best of both worlds. Amongst the vitamins, smoked tofu and organically grown vegetables, you'll find carefully chosen products from 50 to 60 countries around the world. Lavender honey from Provence, organically grown almonds from Spain, Iranian dried apricots, olives flown in weekly from Provence with a selection available for tasting, Neal's Yard cheeses, olive oils and the shop's own label products like pesto sauces and mincemeat. You won't find anything with refined sugar, artificial colours or flavours, MSG, or E-numbers—but the owner finds that suppliers are eager to provide him with goods up to his standards, often with special recipe dishes. A demonstration kitchen, headed by chef Sam Davies, makes dishes for the shop and also for their catering service.

Selfridges Food Hall

400 OXFORD ST, W1, 0171-629 1234
Open Mon., Tues. 10am-7pm, Wed.-Fri. to 8pm, Sat. 9.30am-7pm, Sun. noon-6pm.

Unlike the quintessentially English Harrods and Fortnum & Mason, Selfridges is international. Here you can taste food from around the world, running from ranges of British meats, cheeses, biscuits, mustards and condiments to Lebanese sweets made with almonds, pistachios, pastry and honey; Indian curries to take out; Far Eastern and Mediterranean foods. There are usually small titbits on offer to taste before buying.

GOURMET SPECIALISTS, ETHNIC FOODS & TAKE-AWAY

Carluccio's

30 NEAL ST, WC2, 0171-240 1487
Open Mon.-Thurs. 11am-7pm, Fri. 10am-7pm, Sat.10am-6pm.

Owners Antonio and Priscilla Carluccio have done much to elevate Italian cuisine to cult status in the UK. In their Italian shop you can find the new gastronomic treats they search out on their annual 'hunting trips' to Italy. Delicacies might include fresh cuttlefish pasta, white Alba truffles in brine and marinated aubergines. Olive oils from all over Italy, a wide selection of Italian cheeses and salamis, cooked pasta dishes and antipasti are available and they sell some of the best Tuscan wild-boar and pork sausages (salsiccia di cinghiale).The lazy cook can choose from set-price, ready-prepared meals which they can deliver. Antonio Carluccio is a mushroom fiend so you'll find a wonderful assortment of hand-picked fungi, gathered from secret sources around the suburban London area (there is a wider choice in September and October) as well as truffles flown over fresh from Italy.

Drones The Grocer

3 PONT ST, SW1, 0171-259 6188
Open Mon.-Fri. 8.30am-10pm, Sat., Sun. 9.30am-10pm.

This small shop is next door to Drones restaurant and is stocked with all kinds of goodies like olive oils, relishes and sauces as well as daily antipasti, cheeses and all the dishes served in the next-door café. Most usefully, they offer complete meals for the harrassed host or hostess.

Finns

4 ELYSTAN ST, SW3, 0171-225 0733
Open Mon.-Fri. 8am-7pm, Sat. 8am-2pm.

Finns specialises in food you can take home to eat—always two or three soups, prepared meat, vegetables, and fish dishes, and always seasonally driven. In addition there is a range of jams (made in Yorkshire), flavoured olive oils and vinegars, chutneys and flavoured mustards made on the premises. If it's a party you have in mind, Finns can organise that too.

Fratelli Camisa

1A BERWICK ST, W1, 0171-437 7120
Open Mon.-Sat. 9am-6pm.

One of the delis that make this area such an attractive place to shop; an old-fashioned shop stocking all the staples like hams hanging from the ceiling, ground coffe, home-made pastas truffles in brine, oils, of course, and antipasti. **Also at 53 Charlotte St, W1, 0171-255 1240.**

Hédiard

239 BROMPTON RD. SW3, 0171-581 4403
Open Mon.-Sat 6a.m-7pm.

The famous Parisian food name is providing for South Kensington residents and those from further afield with their relatively new store, stocking 80 percent of all they have in Paris. All the goodies are here, and they also have a delicatessen section for hams and French sausages. All packaging is in that distinctive black and red, so you can always pretend you've crossed the Channel for the chocolates you take to a dinner party.

The Hive

53 WEBBS RD, SW11, 0171-924 6233
Open Mon.-Sat. 10am-6pm, closed lunchtime 1pm-2pm.

A third-generation beekeeper, Californian James Hamill specialises in honeys made from individual flower species rather than blends, so expect to find flavours like pure apple or cherry blossom, linden lime tree or blackberry—some 250 types of honey and honey products altogether.

I Camisa & Son

61 OLD COMPTON ST, W1, 0171-437 7610
Open Mon.-Sat. 9am-6pm.

It is difficult to see how I Camisa crams so many Italian specialities into such a small area. Inside the shop you could be in Italy, and many of the customers are as fluent in Italian as the owners. Both fresh (different varieties made daily) and dried pasta, and an excellent array of salamis are specialities along with a good range of own-brand olive oils from Tuscany and Liguria, breads and fresh white truffles when in season. The shop is very busy so you might have to queue, giving a good opportunity to sniff and browse.

Limoncello

402 ST. JOHN ST, EC1, 0171-713 1678
Open Mon.-Fri. 8.30am-7pm, Sat. 9.30am-2.30pm.

This cheerful, brightly painted traiteur and deli has a wide range of ready-to-go food and sandwiches, all made in its own kitchen which also offers outside catering. Their specialities include couscous, pot-roast boned leg of lamb and more. There is a range of goods such as organic flour, dry-cured bacon, farmhouse cheeses, dried fruits and pulses, free-range eggs and speciality breads, wine, fresh fruit and vegetables and excellent olive oils.

Lina Stores

18 BREWER ST, W1, 0171-437 6482
Open Mon.-Fri. 7am-5.45pm, Sat. 7am-5pm.

A neighbourhood Italian delicatessen with a warm atmosphere, the shop is full of the scents of fresh basil, sage, parsley and tarragon. They stock De Cecco dried pasta, fresh pasta, home-made ravioli, Italian cheeses and meats, and sacks of various rices for risotto and semolina for polenta. You can have your coffee freshly ground to order.

Mauro's

229 MUSWELL HILL BROADWAY, N10, 0181-883 2848

Open Tues.-Sat. 10am-7pm, Sun. 11am-4pm.

The front window is bright with Mauro's multi-coloured fresh pastas—green, yellow, red, black and white, made with spinach, saffron, beetroot and squid's ink in various shapes, lengths, and sizes. Mauro also makes dried pasta in unusual flavours, like wild mushroom, carrot, anchovy, and bitter chocolate. To complement them are ten to fifteen different home-made sauces available daily, and home-made sausages, marinated grilled aubergines and more.

Mr Christian's

11 ELGIN CRES, W11, 0171-229 0501

Open Mon.-Fri. 6am-7pm, Sat. 5.30am-6pm, Sun. 7am-4pm.

This bustling deli, the first in the area, has its own chef and kitchen to prepare their wide range of take-away food including roast chickens, risotto, salads and daily specials. It has wines, champagne, its own-brand chocolates, pastries, chutneys, 60 kinds of bread, cheeses from everywhere and 35 salamis. It's a friendly place which gets even more bustling on Saturday when the Portobello Market is in full swing and a tempting display of their produce is laid out on a table outside the shop.

Mortimer & Bennett

33 TURNHAM GRN, W4, 0181-995 4145

Open Mon.-Fri. 8.30am-6.30pm, Sat. 8.30am-5.30pm.

They import directly from artisan producers all over Europe, with many products exclusive to this shop. There is a wide range of gourmet goods, including Mauro's pasta sauces, cheeses from France, Italy, Spain and Britain (you can taste before you buy), smoked salmon, pâtés, fresh pasta and agnolotti, coffee, tea, olive oil and 12 varieties of olives including the trendy new pumpkin seed oils, plus different breads from Sally Clarke.

R Garcia & Sons

248-256 PORTOBELLO RD, W11, 0171-221 6119

Open Tues.-Sat. 8.30am-6pm.

Notting Hill's large Spanish community flock to this family-run shop which has been in Portobello Road, and in the same family, since its opening. Manager Raphael Garcia is happy to assist with any questions customers have. This mini supermarket stocks all things Spanish—matured hams which swing from the ceiling, chorizo, top quality canned fish products, paella rice, Spanish biscuits and turrón (a Spanish confectionery), plus a wide selection of Spanish and Italian olive oils, cheeses like Manchego and olives.

The Rosslyn Delicatessen

56 ROSSLYN HILL, NW3, 0171-794 9210

Open Mon.-Sat 8am-8.30pm, Sun 8am-8pm.

Unusual items include marinated baby figs, cranberry and raspberry relish, flavoured mustards, oils, vinegars, teas and coffees. There is a large selection for homesick Americans. Service is friendly and knowledgeable, and you can taste any of the 100 to 120 cheeses in stock before buying. This shop is famous for its freshly baked croissants and pastries as well as its wide choice of cheese and charcuterie. The lazy gourmet can enjoy prepared salads and several cooked dishes on offer daily, such as chicken roulade and beef Wellington. Christmas hampers are a speciality. Catalogue available.

The Spice Shop

1 BLENHEIM CRESCENT, W11, 0171-221 4448

Open Mon.-Sat. 9.30am-6.30pm.

What an aroma greets you as you enter this small Notting Hill Gate shop, where over 1,700 spices jostle for attention and space. Run by Birgit Erath who learned about herbs from her grandmother, she had a market stall for years before putting all that knowledge to good use here. You see only small displays of the spices, which keeps them fresh. The mixes are tantalising; the possibilities of new tastes endless.

Tom's

226 WESTBOURNE GROVE, W11, 0171-221 8818

Open Mon.-Fri. 8am-7pm, Sat. to 6pm, Sun. 10am-4pm.

'Tom', who is Tom Conran, son of restaurateur Sir Terence Conran and nephew by marriage of Antonio Carluccio, shows that good taste runs in the family. This busy little aqua-and-blue west London market packs a lot into a small space. The influence is largely Italian, with a selection of single-estate Italian olive oils, but France is not left out with a French cheese selection that includes

ROEDERER
the
Silky Seduction
of
Brut Premier

Reblochon and Epoisses. There is a selection of ready-prepared dishes to take out (lemon and parsley gnocchi, chargrilled vegetables with Herbes de Provence and olive oil), and arguably the best gourmet sandwiches in town made with ciabatta which you can have with a coffee at the coffee counter. There is also a café for their own ready-made dishes.

Traiteur Pagnol

170 Regent's Park Rd, NW1, 0171-586 6988
Open Mon.-Fri. 9.30am-8pm, Sat. to 6pm.

A vast range of the most delicious looking and tasting goods are laid out here, from pan-fried scallops to poussin with rosemary, fresh soups to terrines, roast whole aubergines to pasta, all prepared on the premises. You'll also find Sally Clarke breads, cheeses, home-made jams and pickles and an array of desserts to die for.

Villandry

170 Gt Portland St, W1, 0171-631 3131
Open Mon.-Sat. 8.30am-8pm.

Jean-Charles Carrarini has upped sticks from Marylebone High Street, leaving the premises to the excellent Ibla (see Restaurant section), and moved to a much larger and very impressive place in Great Portland Street. He has the same idea as before, i.e. to supply top gourmet foods (at high prices), all beautifully packaged and arranged. It's an easy shop to move around, selling little known cheeses from France as well as top British varieties, fresh vegetables, freshly baked bread, hams, pâtés and a delicious range of charcuterie. There's a restaurant at the back (see Restaurant section).

HEALTH FOODS

Neal's Yard Wholefoods Ltd

21-23 Shorts Gdns, WC2, 0171-836 5151
Open Mon.-Fri. 9am-7pm, Sat. 9am-6pm.

Health food of the best sort is found in this spacious, friendly shop, which displays just about everything healthy under one roof. You'll find all sorts of untreated dried fruits and nuts, herbal teas, bags of spices from around the world (very good value), and organic rice, as well as vegeburgers, tofu and vegetarian pies and doorstop loaves of wholemeal bread.

Planet Organic

42 Westbourne Gr, W2, 0171-221 7171
Open Mon.-Sat. 9am-8pm, Sun. 11am-5pm.

This is an entire supermarket devoted to natural and organic foods, both fresh and packaged, as well as environmentally friendly household cleaners, body-care ranges and vitamins. The large, bright modern premises have a bakery, delicatessen, wine department, butcher's and a fishmonger's. The lamb, pork, beef and turkeys all have certificates from the appropriate authorised organisations attesting to the conditions under which they are reared. Organic sausages (free Saturday tastings) include the Arbroath fish sausage with smokey-flavoured fish blended with lemon grass and herbs. 'Health-conscious customers can shop without having to read every label because each product conforms to our high standards,' say the innovative owners Jonathan Dwek and Rene Elliott, who went to California to look at similar enterprises there. There's a coffee bar and a qualified nutritionist to give advice.

Wholefood Ltd

24 Paddington St, W1, 0171-935 3924
Open Mon. 8.45am-6pm, Tues.-Fri. to 6.30pm, Sat. 9am-1pm.

Part of the same company as Wholefood Butchers, Wholefood echoes the belief in products without artificial colourings, flavours, or chemical additives. Seasonal organically grown vegetables are available, as are dried fruits from California, France and Israel, and there are breads, preserves, honeys, free-range eggs, fruit juices, pasta, cheeses and yogurt and a selection of organic wine. They also stock a good range of books and health care products.

Wild Oats

210 Westbourne Grove, W11, 0171-229 1063
Open Mon.-Fri. 9am-7pm, Sat. to 6pm, Sun. 10am-5pm.

Wild Oats is a three-storey emporium selling everything for the whole food enthusiast including around twenty-five different types of bread and twenty-two breakfast cereals. They have organic baby food and products for people with food allergies, and a large range of grains and beans. Staff are expert and enthusiastic.

Covent Garden

The former fruit and vegetable market, immortalised in Shaw's *Pygmalion* and later the *My Fair Lady* movie, is now a covered shopping enclave called The Piazza. Its success with shops of every kind - food, fashion, gifts - has inspired the streets around to become a lively shopping and restaurant quarter. Don't miss pedestrianised **Neal Street** which also has the enclosed shopping mall, Thomas Neal's.

MEAT & GAME

A Dove & Son

71 NORTHCOTE RD, SW11, 0171-223 5191
Open Mon. 8am-1pm, Tues.-Sat. 8am-5.30pm.

The shop was opened in 1889—and has the document on the wall to prove it. Now third generation, this family butcher offers excellent quality meats, mostly free-range. The lamb comes from Wales, the beef from Aberdeen, and in season, a wide array of game is available. Home-cooked hams and a good range of cheeses from France and England, all from small suppliers who don't supply supermarkets, add to the attraction. They make their own great pies, too, like steak and mushroom, using their own meat.

Allen & Co

117 MOUNT ST, W1, 0171-499 5831
Open Mon.-Fri. 4am-4pm, Sat. 5am-12.30pm.

Established in Mayfair for more than two hundred years, and here for one hundred and forty years, this is one of the best butchers in town. The shop is traditional, the meat is first-class. It comes as no surprise to learn that Allen's supplies some of the best kitchens in London. They are equally good with the general public, and will produce any kind of cut needed. Long may they remain on a prime site in the middle of Mayfair, providing the kind of service any community would love.

Biggles

66 MARYLEBONE LANE, W1, 0171-224 5937
Open Mon.-Sat. 9.30am-6pm, Mon., Sat. to 4.30pm.

London's second dedicated sausage maker (O'Hagan's of Greenwich claimed the victory), this ten-year old business produces over 60 different varieties, all handmade daily on the premises. With a minimum of 85 percent meat, when you taste them you realise why there has been such a huge revival in the popularity of the British banger recently. Alongside well known Toulouse and Cumberland, try Swedish potato or Beaujolais Nouveau.

Curnick

170 FULHAM RD, SW10, 0171-370 1191
Open Mon.-Fri. 8am-5.30pm, Sat. to 4pm.

The meat on display here—crown roast of lamb, larded pheasants and more, is top quality and expertly butchered. The beef is of particular interest as it comes from free-range, organically fed cattle on Curnick's own farm . This very obliging butcher will prepare any cut of meat you like.

The Highgate Butchers

76 HIGHGATE HIGH ST, N6, 0181-340 9817
Open Tues.-Sat. 7.30am-5.45pm, Mon., Sat. 7am-5pm.

Highgate residents are lucky in their top-notch local butcher. This is a small shop, tucked into a row of small shops in Highgate village's picturesque High Street. The meat is all very good quality, and the butcher can handle special requests for customers, such as crown roast of lamb, boned saddle of lamb and Dutch veal. A list of sixteen different speciality sausages is on offer, including the traditional English favourites of Cumberland, alongside the more adventurous lamb and mint, and beef and Guiness, to name a few—all freshly made on the premises.

The House of Albert Roux

229 EBURY ST, SW1, 0171-730 3037
Open Mon.-Fri. 7.30am-8.30pm, Sat.-Sun. 8am-4pm.

With its baskets of fresh vegetables, herbs and wild mushrooms (in season), this shop has everything to please the eye and the palate. The famous British-based chef, Albert Roux, is the inspiration behind this very French traiteur. Cheeses come in from Paris, as does the flour for the breads which are baked in their Wandsworth kitchens. At the butcher's counter you can buy prepared and tied meats to order, plus genuine boudin blanc and boudin noir sausages. Try any of the seasonally inspired, prepared dishes to take away, like roulade of salmon or stuffed quails. The pâtisserie also pleases.

Lidgate's of Holland Park

110 Holland Park Ave, W11, 0171-727 8243
Open Mon.-Fri. 7.30am-6pm, Sat. 8am-5pm.

Lidgate's, established in 1850, is one of the best butchers/charcutiers in the country, and possibly the best in London. The panelled walls, piled high with goodies, are festooned with myriad awards that Lidgate's has earned throughout its 146-year history. All the beef, lamb, pork, chicken and eggs are organic or free range, and proprietor David Lidgate keeps in touch with the farmers who rear the animals that end up at Lidgate's. Prince Charles' Highgrove Farm is one of the suppliers. Exotic products include marinated wild boar cutlets (in season), bison, kangaroo and ostrich. Not to be missed are Lidgate's famous pies—lamb and leek, steak and kidney, cottage, game, and coq au vin. They have a wide selection of English and French cheeses and preserves.

O'Hagan's Sausage Shop

192 Trafalgar Rd, SE10, 0181-858 2833
Open Mon.-Fri. 9am-5pm, Sat. 8.30am-4pm.

The first specialist sausage shop supplies the whole of this area with their British staple. Bill O'Hagan makes endless varieties—over 50 in fact, running from pork with apricot and cognac to Welsh leek and not forgetting the ever popular O'Hagan's Specials!

Portwine

24 Earlham St, WC2, 0171-836 2353
Open Mon., Sat. 7.30am-2pm, Tues.-Fri. to 5.30pm.

Graham Portwine has become a bit of a local celebrity thanks to his appearances on a TV food series with cookery writer, Sophie Grigson. He is very helpful and cheerfully advises on cuts for recipe requirements. He has additive-free meat, free-range poultry, seasonal game, ducks' eggs and Scottish products including haggis from MacSween's.

Richardson's of Ealing

88 Northfield Ave, W13, 0181-567 1064
Open Mon.-Thurs. 8am-5.30pm, Fri. to 6pm, Sat. to 4pm.

A gold-medal winner no less for his sausages, which include the Knightsbridge and Old Speckled Hen made with Morland's Old Speckled Hen beer. He also sells organically fed beef, free-range lamb, home-cured bacon and more at this site and in the refurbished South Ealing shop. **Also at 110 South Ealing Rd, W5, 0181-567 4405.**

Simply Sausages

341 Central Markets, EC1, 0171-329 3227
Open Mon.-Fri. 8am-6pm, Sat. 9.30am-1.30pm.

Just the place to come for sausages, being 'bangers' next to Smithfield, the range is good, with 35 different types on offer as well as seven types of vegetarian ones, though whether mulligatawny makes a good flavoured-sausage is a matter of opinion. **Also at 93 Berwick St, W1, 0171-287 3482.**

South Kensington Butchers

19 Bute St, SW7, 0171-581 0210
Open Mon.-Fri .7.30am-5.30pm, Sat. to 5pm.

A top-class butcher that caters for the choosy tastes of the large local French community with Scotch beef, Dutch veal, English lamb, game, and free-range poultry. French cuts of meat are always possible and they stock a selection of French tinned goods such as cassoulet.

Stenton

55 Aldensley Rd, W6, 0181-748 6121
Open Tues.-Fri. 7.30am-6.30pm, Thurs. to 1pm, Sat. to 5.30pm.

When the beef-on-the-bone ban came into effect, there was a flurry of articles about local butcher's shops. One national newspaper featured broadcaster John Humphrys' local where John Stenton only deals in certified organic and free-range meat, as well as home-made sausages and burgers. It's a delightful place, and still family run.

Wholefood Butchers

31 PADDINGTON ST, W1, 0171-486 1390
Open Mon.-Thurs. 8.30am-6pm, Fri. to 6.30pm, Sat. to 1pm.

All the meat sold in this small shop is organically produced, which means that it comes from animals that have been allowed to grow, feed, and develop naturally without artificial growth stimulants or hormones; the ground on which they graze must also adhere to strict requirements. The meat is all of the best quality, and in season there is plentiful game as well as duck, goose, and turkey eggs.

WINES & SPIRITS

A visit to any of the main wine shop chains (liquor stores are known as 'off-licences') will reveal an excellent selection of wines from around the world—from California, New Zealand, and South Africa as well as those from France and Italy, Romania and Chile. The best wine shop chains are Oddbins with a very wide choice and its own selections and Nicolas which not surprisingly given its name, offers some top French wines (look in the telephone directory for your local branch), but for the avid wine fan, the following independent shops are recommended.

Berry Bros & Rudd

3 ST. JAMES'S ST, SW1, 0171-396 9600
Open Mon.-Fri. 9am-5.30pm.

Few wine merchants in London have such an 'olde worlde' feel as this excellent shop with its polished wood-panelled interior. And that's because Berry Bros & Rudd has stood in this spot since the mid-eighteenth century, and very little in the shop has changed—apart from the wines. In addition to traditional red Bordeaux and Vintage Port, on which Berry Bros is very strong, there is a good selection of wines from California, Australia and New Zealand. They stock an array of single-malt Scotch whiskies, and a fairly large selection of half bottles, too. They have also recently branched out into coffees and some exclusive liqueurs. They have a shop at **Terminal 3, Heathrow Airport**. Mail order.

Bibendum

113 REGENT'S PARK RD, NW1, 0171-722 5577
Open Mon.-Thurs.10am-6.30pm, Fri. to 8pm, Sat. 9.30am-5.30pm.

Housed in a large warehouse in Chalk Farm, this is a top wine merchant used by many of London's best restaurants for its knowledge and expertise in sourcing unusual names. They go beyond Europe, naturally, finding some of the great full-bodied Australian, New Zealand, North American and now South American wines. They hold regular tastings and are very helpful. Mail order.

Corney & Barrow

194 KENSINGTON PARK RD, W11, 0171-221 5122
Open Mon.-Sat. 10.30am-9pm.

With its main office in the ultra-conservative City, London's financial district, and a shop in the eternally arty Portobello area, Corney & Barrow attracts wine lovers from a large spectrum with a wide range of top-quality wine. For the pin-striped City gent all the Bordeaux first growths and top-name Burgundies, while for the bohemian crowd there is a well-chosen list of house wines and wines from the New World. They have recently increased their emphasis on fine and rare wines as well as older vintages. **Many other branches.**

Justerini & Brooks

61 ST. JAMES'S ST, SW1, 0171-493 8721
Open Mon.-Fri. 9am-5.30pm.

Justly proud of its great Bordeaux, this old-established wine merchants (almost 250 years) in St. James's also has some serious Burgundy and Rhône wines as well as venturing further afield to the rest of Europe and the New World. Friendly and helpful, don't be put off by the address, you'll also find cheaper wines here too. Mail order.

La Vigneronne

105 OLD BROMPTON RD, SW7, 0171-589 6113
Open Mon.-Fri. 10am-8pm, Sat. to 6pm.

Master of Wine Liz Berry, the 'vigneronne' herself, is the genius behind this well-stocked little shop. Liz makes frequent travels to the Continent, particularly France, and knows all of the producers' wines—and most of the producers themselves on a first-name basis. This being the only La Vigneronne, Liz is not confined by size, so if there's something good, but not much of it, she is happy to stock it. There are wines here that you won't find elsewhere. Speciality areas are Alsace and the Languedoc-Rousillon region in southern France, about which Liz has written a book.

GIFTS

Upmarket gifts are available at many of the shops listed under sections such as china, leather, jewelry and department stores but this list features some small or specialist shops worthy of a visit. In keeping with the times, museum shops have greatly improved beyond the well-stocked postcard counter and we have noted our favourites here. Now most museum shops are first-rate, so if you have a specialist interest, check in the museum section for more.

Animation Art Gallery

13-14 GREAT CASTLE ST, W1, 0171-255 1456
Open Mon.-Fri. 10am-7pm, Sat. 10am-6pm, Sun. noon-4pm.

Disney characters are the stars at this unusual gallery specialising in drawings made on celluloid (called 'cels') of cartoon characters such as Bugs Bunny, Peanuts or characters in movies such as Snow White and The 101 Dalmations. A video shows you exactly which frame of the final film you have purchased. Some original drawings are also on sale, plus a few limited editions.

Annabel Jones

52 BEAUCHAMP PL, SW3, 0171-589 3215
Open Mon.-Fri. 10am-5.30pm, Sat. 10.30am-5.30pm.

The ground floor has delightful jewelry (look for the star and flower ranges), giftware, which includes glass globes in blue, green and yellow. Among the silverware are heart-shaped clocks, dice-shaped paperweight clocks, egg-timers, cigar tubes, champagne coolers, novelty pepper mills, and many other objects including picture frames, pens and enamel cufflinks.

Asprey and Gerrard

165-169 NEW BOND ST, W1, 0171-493 6767
Open Mon.-Fri. 9.30am-5.30pm, Sat. 10am-5pm.

'It can be done' is the motto of the resident artists, so expect to see an extravagant showpiece on display by the entrance. From the filigreed white wrought-iron trim and arches around the outside to the fifth floor, this is the ultimate gift shop with both tradition and a sense of frivolity. Look for the leather-bound photograph albums and agendas, playing cards, roulette wheels and dice on the ground floor.

Barclay & Bodie

7-9 BLEINHEIM TERR, NW8, 0171-372 5705
Open Mon.-Sat. 9.30am-5.30pm.

A wonderful source of ideas for gifts, and some delightful boxes to put them into in this elegant shop in St. John's Wood. Practical as well as pretty, their French Provençal oven-to-tableware consists of hand-painted dishes designed to come straight from the oven or microwave to sit neatly in pretty woven baskets. They stock all sorts of goodies like bags, pewter boxes, initialled ladies handkerchiefs and something irresistible—miniature tea pots in the shape of garlic heads, cabbages and cauliflower. Just the thing for a collector.

British Museum

GREAT RUSSELL ST. WC1, 0171-636 1555
Open Mon.-Sat. 10am-5pm, Sun. 2.30pm-6pm.

There is a book shop, a children's shop and a gift shop which sells very good reproductions of hundred of items from the museum's impressive collection, from Roman earrings to an Egyptian cat.

Cologne and Cotton

791 FULHAM RD, SW6, 0171-736 9261
Open Mon.-Sat. 9.30am-7pm.

The cotton part of the title comes from the ranges of crisp cotton products—from bedlinen and embroidered night dresses to baby clothes and accessories. The cologne part comes into play with the ranges of eau de toilette and pure vegetable soaps which are made specially for the company. **Also at 39 Kensington Church St, W8, 0171-376 0324.**

Contemporary Applied Arts

2 PERCY ST, W1, 0171-436 2344
Open Mon.-Sat. 10.30am-5.30pm.

A light, bright and airy art gallery, filled with original, high-quality artefacts. Beautifully crafted and designed vases, pitchers and bowls are always on show along with changing displays of basketwork, ceramics, textiles, glassware, metal, wood work and more. Although you can buy the exhibits from the upstairs gallery, you can't take them away until the end of each exhibition, which runs for approximately six weeks. If you do want something you can walk away with, stick to the jewelry and crafts in the gallery shop downstairs.

The Conran Shop

MICHELIN HOUSE, 81 FULHAM RD, SW3, 0171-589 7401

Open Mon. & Tues. 10am-6pm, Wed. & Thurs. to 7pm, Fri. to 6pm, Sat. to 6.30pm, Sun. noon-6pm.

The shopping list is endless and the products are irrestistible at Sir Terence Conran's stylish emporium. There's china, stationery, toys, kitchenware, glassware, candles and candle holders, posh gardening tools, Indian textiles and a small range of wonderful baby clothes. It would be virtually impossible not to find something for anyone in this wonderful store. **Also at 55 Marylebone High St, NW1.**

The Cross

141 PORTLAND RD, W11, 0171-727 6760

Open Mon.-Sat. 10.30am-6pm.

The area around Notting Hill Gate and Portobello Road seems to have cornered the market for stylish independent boutiques selling a variety of covetable products. The Cross is one such place, frequented by people seeking out beautiful home accessories and clothes including delightful Irish candles, hand-painted glass, woven baskets, picture frames and mirrors. Well worth seeking out.

Equinox

28 NEAL ST, WC2, 0171-497 1001

Open Mon.-Sat. 9am-7pm, Thurs. to 8pm, Sun. 11am-7pm.

This astrology shop has the sun, moon and stars as well as star signs printed on mugs, glassware, aprons, keyrings, candle holders, cards and a wide selection of giftware. There are lots of posters of the sky at night and an extensive range of astrology books. Why not make a gift of an astrology or compatibility chart which can be compiled while you wait?

Eximious

10 WEST HALKIN ST, SW1, 0171-235 7828

Open Mon.-Fri. 9.30am-5.30pm, Sat. 10am-4pm.

This beautiful shop looking like an elegant private drawing room contains a first-class collection of gifts and accessories for the home. By appointment to the Prince of Wales, they sell a wide range from lacquered wooden planters to architectural bookends. They can monogram items for you, and will also produce personalised enamel boxes with your house, favourite animal or just a message as decoration on it. Their mail order catalogue is a delight to browse through.

Fitch's Ark

6 CLIFTON RD, W9, 0171-266 0202

Open Mon.-Sat. 11am-7pm, cal for Sun. opening times as they vary.

Rightly subtitled 'The Animal Gallery', this shop displays handcrafted objects based on images of animals and birds. Created by top designers such as David Mach whose work has been displayed at the Tate Gallery, the products are of superior quality. There are no paintings, just three-dimensional objects ranging in price from £1 to £15,000. There are animal-head doorknobs (cats, rams, frogs) in reconstituted marble as well as wall plaques, mosaic panels, jewelry and sculptures including wooden cats and dogs and a fibreglass iguana. The owner, Susan Fellows, a former actress, stages six exhibitions a year and donates a contribution from each sale to the Born Free Foundation to help animal conservation.

Gallery Shop

CRAFTS COUNCIL, 44A PENTONVILLE RD, N1, 0171-278 7700

Open Tues.-Sat. 11am-6pm, Sun. 2pm-6pm.

Well away from the city centre, this shop has a constantly changing range of contemporary crafts created by artists who make sculptures, design scarves, carve wood and produce ceramics, pottery and glass. The handmade jewelry is wonderful but it is possible to buy handmade automata too. It is part of the National Centre for the Crafts and houses a reference centre, exhibition space and café. The Crafts Council also produces booklets and information on working in the crafts and runs regular workshops and offers advice on funding, awards and bursaries. Some items are sold at the Victoria and Albert Museum shop.

Graham & Green

4, 7 & 10 ELGIN CRESCENT, W11, 0171-727 4594

Open Mon.-Sat. 10am-6pm.

Eye-catching windows in the middle of the Portobello district attract passers-by into this shop. Crammed full of original items such as planters, exotic candle sticks, ornate mirrors, glassware, rustic earthenware plates, linens and many intricate wrought-iron decorative items, you'll find kitchen and garden utensils in the basement and the remainder of the desirable stock on the ground floor. Cross the road for more of the same at Number 4 and Number 10 for clothing. **Also at 164 Regents Park Rd, NW1, 0171-586 2960.**

Halcyon Days

14 Brook St, W1, 0171-629 8811

Open Mon.-Sat. 9.15am-5.30pm.

Charming enamel boxes are decorated with themes like Victorian flowers from the Victoria and Albert Museum archives or specific designs made for anniversaries or celebrations. Some have messages like 'Thank You'; other display sporting pursuits. There is always a Christmas, New Year and Valentine's Day box to commemorate the day. The enamel is fired onto copper in Bilston, West Midlands, and each box has a certificate of authenticity. Antique enamel boxes and other antique and collectable objects such as pot-pourri baskets, mirrors, spill vases and photo frames fill the shelves and cabinets. **Also at 4 Royal Exchange, EC3, 0171-626 1120.**

Idonia van der Bijl

25A Museum St, WC1, 0171-636 4650

Open Mon.-Fri. 10am-6pm, Sat. 10.30am-6pm.

Certainly a favourite with visitors in small hotels around here and those going to the British Museum, this small shop is stocked with a pretty wide range of, well anything, from pottery to desk objects, jewelry to scarves. It's a great hunting ground for unusual items.

Irish Shop

14 King St, WC2, 0171-379 3625

Open Mon.-Thurs. 11am-7pm, Fri., Sat. to 10.30pm, Sun. noon-6pm.

Quality products from Ireland include fine Waterford, Galway and Tyrone crystal, Belleek and Royal Tara china, hand-knit Aran sweaters and a wide range of capes, jackets and outerwear.

For the Left-Handed

This is a wonderful and eccentric shop and a delight to visit. Their best selling range is scissors, but they also sell items such as a left-handed sickle. Oh yes, and their catalogue opens back to front, that is from the back, or rather the wrong way to a right-handed person... If you see what we mean! **Anything Left-Handed**, 57 Brewer St, W1—0171-437 3910, open Mon.-Fri. 9.30am-5pm, Sat. from 10am.

Just Fish

14A, Thomas Neal's Centre, Earlham St, WC2, 0171-240 6277

Open Mon.-Sat 11am-7pm, Sun. noon-6pm.

The largest variety of gifts based on worldwide fish and marine life in the UK, ranging from fishy salt and pepper shakers to pewter figurines and embroidered polo and sweat shirts.

Lady Daphne

145 Sloane St, SW1, 0171-235 2905

Open Mon.-Sat 9.30am-6.30pm, Wed. to 7pm.

Hand-painted artefacts and decorative bits and pieces for the home have been designed by Lady Daphne Bailey using motifs such as the fleur de lys, flowers and butterflies. They include waste paper baskets, table lamps, cache-pots, umbrella stands and silk cushions.

London Transport Museum

33 Earlham St, WC2, 0171-379 6344

Open daily 10am-6pm, Fri. 11am-6pm.

The London Underground map is the most popular selling item, but reproductions of the best transport posters of previous decades make great souvenirs—works of art commissioned regularly to promote the destinations along the route from opulent Art Deco styles of the twenties and thirties through to today's modern graphics. Also worth looking out for are the T-shirts and boxer shorts aimed at a younger, fashionable audience. They include logos such as Hold Tight, Push Once and All Zones on the skinny-fit T-shirts and Open Flap for ventilation, Emergency Exit and Fire Extinguisher on the boxer shorts.

Museum Store

37 THE MARKET, THE PIAZZA, COVENT GARDEN, WC2, 0171-240 5760

Open Mon.-Sat. 10.30am-6.30pm, Sun. 11am-5pm.

Museums from all over the world have some of their products on sale at this first-floor shop making its collection of gifts very eclectic; they even have Michaelangelo's David as a refrigerator magnet. **Also at 50 Beauchamp Pl, SW3, 0171-581 9255, and 4a-5a Perrins Ct, NW3, 0171-431 7156.**

National Gallery Shop

TRAFALGAR SQ, WC2, 0171-839 3321

Open Mon.-Sat 10am-6pm, Sun. noon-6pm.

A major revamp has made this into a spectacular shop, with a large range of art books, many published by National Gallery Publications, prints, gifts and of course postcards and posters of many of the exhibitions.

National Portrait Gallery Shop

ST. MARTIN'S PL, WC2, 0171-306 0055

Open Mon.-Sat. 10am-6pm, Sun. noon-6pm.

A wonderful selection of postcards with the famous, historic and infamous faces of people featured in the gallery await the collector, along with giftware such as paperweights, bookmarks, fine art calendears, address and art books.

National Trust

BLEWCOAT SCHOOL, 23 CAXTON ST, SW1, 0171-222 2877

Open Mon.-Fri. 10am-5.30pm, Thurs. to 7pm.

Inside this early-1800s building, an historic attraction in its own right, are products designed and produced for the National Trust, the powerful charity that maintains stately homes, country houses and much of the English countryside. The building was once a school for poor children: look for the little figure of a boy and girl on the back outside wall. The designs on the aprons, tea towels, tea cosies, diaries, china and paper products are based on authentic patterns from National Trust properties like palatial Ickworth in Suffolk, or are specially commissioned.

Neal Street East

5 NEAL ST, WC2, 0171-240 0135

Open Mon.-Wed. 11am-7pm, Tues.-Sat. 10am-7pm, Sun. noon-6pm.

More like a bazaar than a shop, covering all things Oriental, from cards and notebooks to kimonos, folk craft, brightly coloured bed coverings, cloth bags, scarves, I Ching books and sculptures of Buddha.

Obsessions

30 MONMOUTH ST, WC2, 0171-379 1740

Open Mon.-Wed. 10.30am-6.30pm, Thurs.-Sat. 11am-7pm, Sun. 1pm-5pm.

Call in for a good range of silver-plated clocks, bottle openers, corkscrews, photograph frames and glassware. **Also at 18 Blomfield St, EC2, 0171-638 7491; 151 Cheapside, EC2, 0171-600 7410; 2 Hay's Galleria, SE1, 0171-403 2374; 23 Old Brompton Rd, SW7, 0171-589 0071.**

Oggetti

135 FULHAM RD, SW3, 0171-581 8088

Open Mon.-Sat. 9.30am-6pm, Sun. noon-5pm.

A temple for hi-tech and the unusual. Expect the unexpected: domino sets composed of a variety of woods, a letter opener inlaid with pear, cherry, apple and other fruit woods, and beautiful coloured glass tumblers. A branch a few doors away at **143 Fulham Rd, SW3, 0171-584 9808**, stocks ultra-smart Alessi kitchenware, including their distinctively shaped kettles.

Past Times

146 BROMPTON RD, SW3, 0171-581 7616

Open Mon.-Sat. 9am-6pm, Sun. 11am-5pm.

The theme behind this shop's products is that all eras of history are represented, whether it is a medieval manuscript jigsaw puzzle or a CD of Georgian chants. Laid out in chronological order, the varied giftware includes tapestry kits, jewelry, card games, calendars, candles and cards. Mail order catalogue. **Also at 179 Kensington High St, W8, 0171-795 6344; 102 King's Rd, SW3, 0171-591 0068; 155 Regent St, W1, 0171-734 3728.**

Royal Academy of Arts

BURLINGTON HOUSE, PICCADILLY, W1, 0171-300 5722

Open Mon.-Thurs. 10am-6pm, Fri. 10am-5.30pm.

You'll find finely designed gifts here, like china, clothes, glass and paper products, most of them unique to the Royal Academy. They commission work in connection with their exhibitions and also stock a very good range of designs from Royal Academicians. Their ceramic plates and bowls are exquisite.

Tate Gallery Shop

MILLBANK, SW1, 0171-887 8000

Open daily 10.30am-5.30pm.

From a 20p bookmark to gorgeous coffee table books, this spacious shop has wonderful art publications and fun art T-shirts.

Tiffany & Co

25 OLD BOND ST, W1, 0171-409 2790

Open Mon.-Fri. 10am-5.30pm, Sat. to 6pm.

What could be nicer than a gift presented in a Tiffany-blue box and tied with a simple white ribbon? Surprisingly, it is possible to buy a present from this smartly turned-out store without breaking the bank. Teenagers will either love or appreciate the 'Teenage Book of Manners' at £10, while it would be hard to offend anyone with a gift of a smart key-ring. Christening gifts are also a forte here with a christening rattle starting from around £50. Of course it is the jewelry which has earned Tiffany its impeccable reputation and you will find Tiffany cross pendants in 18-carat gold at £1,425. Spend time browsing around the three-storey shop, as you'll find leather and silver gifts, scarves, picture frames, clocks, cutlery, china and crystal, plus the wonderful jewelry collections by Elsa Perretti and Paloma Picasso.

The Tintin Shop

34 FLORAL ST, WC2, 0171-836 1131

Open Mon.-Sat. 10am-6pm.

The Belgian cartoon character has inspired a range of gifts including stationery, jigsaws, T-shirts, watches, badges, books, videos and audio cassettes.

Victoria & Albert Museum Shop

CROMWELL RD, SW7, 0171-938 8500

Open Mon. 2pm-5.30pm, Tues.-Sun. 10am-5.30pm.

With its spacious room and its constantly evolving stock, this is a good gift-hunting ground, especially for exclusive items made to coincide with exhibitions as well as limited edition products matching up with the newer galleries. There are excellent books on decorative arts and a Crafts Council shop with a range of beautifully designed products—ceramics, glassware, textiles and jewelry.

HOME

CHILDREN'S FURNITURE

Dragons

23 WALTON ST, SW3, 0171-589 3795

Open Mon.-Fri. 10am-5.30pm, Sat. to 6pm.

A white four-poster bed has pride of place in the back of this long shop which stocks miniature armchairs, tables, desks and hand-painted furniture by several artists, including one who specialises in Beatrix Potter animals. All decorative techniques feature on the designs and are demonstrated for pretty children's rooms, including sponging, gilding and lacquering. The shop stocks everything from rag dolls to handsome, hand-crafted rocking horses to take pride of place in any nursery.

The Nursery Window

83 WALTON ST, SW3, 0171-581 3358

Open Mon.-Sat. 10am-5.30pm.

Fabrics and wallcoverings for the smartest nurseries are in abundance at this shop which also stocks a wide choice of changing mats and bags, cot and pram quilts, hooded towels, lampshades and blankets.

CHINA & GLASS

Bridgewater

739 FULHAM RD, SW6, 0171-371 9033

Open Mon.-Fri. 10am-5.30pm, Sat. to 5pm.

Emma Bridgewater has revived the old-fashioned spongewear technique of decorating pottery, and the process lends itself well to her quintessentially English china. Everything is included in her collections, from delightful children's mugs to large pasta and salad dishes in a variety of colours. You can have items personalised with your choice of name, or order specially commission pieces. She also sells a few designs at Harrods and the General Trading Company; Harvey Nichols houses a Bridgewater shop with the complete range. Check out the shop in January and the summer when there are good sales of seconds. They also now have a Pottery studio where you can try your own, and a café, where you can sit and plan your decorations.

Chinacraft

71 REGENT ST, W1, 0171-734 4915
Open Mon.-Wed. 9am-6pm, Thurs. to 7.30pm, Fri., Sat. 9am-6pm, Sun. 11am-5pm.

Chinacraft makes a wide range of dinner service and crystalware which is stocked in a variety of large London shops. For novelty and souvenir items ranging from life-sized china dogs to the Lilliput Lane range of houses, try their main shop. **Branches throughout London.**

Contemporary Ceramics

7 MARSHALL ST, W1, 0171-437 7605
Open Mon.-Sat. 10am-5.30pm, Thurs. to 7pm.

Since 1960, the members of the Craft Potters Association have had a large, bright gallery in which to sell their distinctive, highly original pieces. The pottery on sale ranges from simple yet stunning everyday domestic ware to collectable statuary, pots and vases and a small collection of jewelry. There are changing exhibitions and a large stock of books and magazines on ceramics, plus a selection of tools for the trade. The whole wide-ranging display makes for excellent browsing.

Cosmo Place Studio

11 COSMO PL, WC1, 0171-278 3374
Open Mon.-Sat. 10am-6pm.

The contemporary, hand-painted bone china on offer at Cosmo Place Studio makes a truly original gift. Sourcing English china from factories in Stoke-on-Trent, the tream of designers on site also produce a number of one-off pieces for individual commissions which can be personalised with messages for special occasions. Prices start from £5 for egg cups to £100 for large vases. Inscriptions cost approx. £5 extra.

Famous Names

6 AND 7 COLONNADE WALK, 123 BUCKINGHAM PALACE RD, SW1, 0171-233 9313
Open Mon.-Sat. 9am-6pm.

This is primarily a china shop with many ranges of English-made tableware but also carries the Swarovski jewelry and charm ranges.

The Glasshouse

21 ST. ALBAN'S PL, N1, 0171-359 8162
Open Mon.-Fri. 10am-5pm.

Four of Britain's top contemporary designers—Annette Meech, David Taylor, Fleur Tookey and Chris Williams—produce stunning original glass which is sold from the premises. You will find repeated designs like glass card holders at £4.50 to the most stylish one-off pieces. You can watch them blowing the glass (except Saturday), and they also undertake restoration work. Some glassblowing courses are run throughout the year; call for details.

Hugh Johnson Collection

68 ST. JAMES'S ST, SW1, 0171-491 4912
Open Mon.-Fri. 9am-5pm.

Wine critic Hugh Johnson has gathered an elegant array of wine accessories, including fine decanters and glasses, some antique, plus magnificent corkscrews—in fact everything for the wine connoisseur (except the wine).

Lalique

162 NEW BOND ST, W1, 0171-499 8228
Open Mon.-Fri. 10am-6pm, Sat. to 5pm.

The trademark crystal created in 1913 sits in fine company with scarves, handbags, fragrances, jewelry and a limited edition range of children's crockery. Following the tradition set by the Art Deco craftsman, René Lalique, the fine crystal sculptures still captivate. The shop displays glow in the illuminated interior where the crystalware is beautifully offset by Limoges porcelain pieces and Christofle silverware. **Also at 201 Sloane St, SW1, 0171-245 9090.**

Portobello China and Woollens

89 PORTOBELLO RD, W11, 0171-727 3857
Open Mon.-Sat 10am-5pm.

Choc-a-bloc with tableware from all over Britain and Ireland, with many discontinued lines, this shop also sells knitwear including scarves, shawls, Aran sweaters and lambswool ranges at very reasonable prices. Lambswool from £19.95, cashmere from £65.

The Reject China Shop at Chinacraft

134 Regent St, W1, 0171-434 2502

Open Mon.-Sat. 9am-6pm.

When this company started up more than 35 years ago, an abundance of 'seconds' were being released by the china manufacturers, so a shop in Beauchamp Place seemed like a good idea for bargain hunters. Today, although the company trades under the same name, their shops stock mostly high quality china, though still retaining a seconds area, clearly distinguished by labels and a more cluttered display. **Also at 183 Brompton Rd (corner of Beauchamp Pl), 0171-581 0739; 34 Beauchamp Pl, SW3, 0171-581 0737.**

Rosenthal Studio House

137 Regent St, W1, 0171-734 3076

Open Mon.-Sat. 9.30am-6pm, Thurs. to 7pm.

Art on your everyday table was the intention of the original Philipp Rosenthal in 1900, an ideal still pursued by the firm which submits designs to a jury of independent judges before making delightful pieces with amazing motifs like The Voyage of Marco Polo or Medusa, plus limited editions.

Royal Doulton

167 Piccadilly, W1, 0171-493 9121

Open Mon.-Sat. 9.30am-6pm, Thurs. to 7pm, Sun. noon-6pm.

This is the main shop for this famous china company with a huge display of their tableware including famous brands such as Royal Albert, all displayed with the company's glassware. **Also at 154 Regent St, W1, 0171-734 3184.**

The Tea House

15 Neal St, WC2, 0171-240 7539

Open Mon.-Sat. 10am-7pm, Sun. noon-6pm

Astonishingly shaped teapots on the upper level attract visitors as much as the wide variety of tea on the ground floor. Sherlock Holmes looking for a clue, a couple dancing, a snowman, a cottage—any subject can inspire a teapot maker. Brightly coloured, plain-shaped teapots make an appearance as do teacups for fortune telling, plus a range of books.

Thomas Goode

19 South Audley St, W1, 0171-499 2823

Open Mon.-Sat 10am-6pm.

Not only does the exterior look like a grand townhouse, the interior feels like one as well. The elegant appearance reflects Thomas Goode's status as an institution for gentrified shopping since 1845. There is a flamboyance along with tradition and unexpected nooks to explore in the various rooms, several with tables lavishly decked out with a wide array of coloured glassware. Designer Peter Ting has recently introduced a modern touch to the china and glass. This is an exclusive shop; look for the Wall of China in the basement which depicts various designs over the decades, and for the little museum on the ground floor. There is a very stylish restaurant decked out with its own expensive china, crystal and silver.

Villeroy & Boch

267 Merton Rd, SW18, 0181-870 4168

Open Mon.-Sat. 10am-5pm, Sun. 11am-5pm.

This is the factory shop for the famous brand name of fine tableware. Rich colours used within distinctive designs have been the trademark of this firm's tableware since its formation in 1748. It stocks ends of lines and special offers, with sales taking place twice a year.

Waterford Wedgwood

158 Regent St, W1, 0171-734 7262

Open Mon.-Wed., Fri. 10am-6.30pm, Thurs. to 7.30pm, Sat. 9.30am-6.30pm.

The shop stocks all the ranges produced by these two famous manufacturers. At Christmas, its trees are magnificently decorated. You'll find inspiration in the elegant tables laid out for different occasions, like a formal dinner party or summer picnic.

FABRICS

Ian Mankin

109 Regent's Park Rd, NW1, 0171-722 0997

Open Mon.-Fri. 10am-5.30pm, Sat. to 4pm.

A small shop specialising in all those tickings, muslins, canvases and more in stripes, checks and tartans that give a wonderfully clean, uncluttered feel to a room and that have recently become the height of fashion. **Also at 271 Wandsworth Bridge Rd, SW6, 0171-371 8825.**

Material World

6 PARKWAY, NW1, 0171-482 2548
Open Mon.-Sat. 9.30am-5.30pm, Sun. 10am-5pm.

This busy and useful shop buys up and sells designer clearance fabrics including fake fur, PVC, velvet, silks and has a small range of uphostery materials. **Also at 650 Holloway Rd, NI, 0171-272 0819.**

Pierre Frey

251-253 FULHAM RD, SW3, 0171-376 5599
Open Mon-.Fri 9.30am-6pm, Sat. 10am-5pm.

If you're after that delightful French and Provençal look, then go no further than this delightful shop where colours like vibrant yellow on all kinds of fabrics will provide the Francophile with a fix. Also accessories.

Thomas Dare

341 KING'S RD, SW3, 0171-351 7991
Open Mon.-Sat. 9.30am-5.30pm.

Specialists in 100 percent cotton furnishing fabrics, though they do have a wonderful silk collection, their fresh designs appeal to people across the spectrum of tastes. They also produce matching trimmings, ropes, cords, tassels and tiebacks. Prices start at £15 per metre.

Timney Fowler

388 KING'S RD, SW3, 0171-351 6562
Open Mon.-Fri. 9.30am-6pm, Sat. 10am-6pm.

Definately not for shrinking violets, the bold, mainly monochrome prints inspired by dramatic images such as medieval stained glass, rococo panache or even the crown jewels, make a dramatic statement. Colour has been introduced to the range of fabrics, cushions, wraps, scarves and boxes to equally breathtaking effect. Devotees of their signature range of Roman emperors' head and mythological scenes will be pleased to know that these are still available. The shop now offers an extensive range of home accessories such as picture frames and mirrors which co-ordinate with their fabrics.

FURNISHINGS, FABRICS & INTERIOR DESIGN

The English Style

Before World War II, Paris and New York were the most important centres for interior decoration. But for the last few years, it has been London that people look to for inspiration. In 1972 Mrs Munro (see below) helped organise an exhibition in Paris called Le Style Anglais, which consolidated the English approach to interior design. Unlike much European design which is often very formal, it is based both on practical consideration and on the eternally beautiful English style as epitomised by the chintzes and antiques found in English country houses. From being an exclusive look, it can now be seen everywhere, a move helped by the early popularity of the Laura Ashley shops. But English design is not all chintz and grand country houses and we have included shops with a very different style. Many of the shops we recommend here undertake commissions and offer an interior decorating service; others may just sell wallpapers and fabrics.

Andrew Martin

200 WALTON ST, SW3, 0171-584 4290
Mon.-Fri. 9.30am-5.30pm, Sat. 10.30am-4pm.

Classy, well designed and always in the forefront of designer home fashion, Andrew Martin stocks a wonderful range of exotic fabrics (expensive but worth the price), as well as modern furniture and some accessories.

Barkers

63 KENSINGTON HIGH ST, W8, 0171-937 5432
Open Mon.-Sat. 9.30am-6pm.

Reopened in Spring 1998, this old favourite has been brought thoroughly up to the minute by House of Fraser and brings a huge new homewares floor of goodies to this shopping-mad area of Kensington. Barkers now offers everything from the best home design (currently a British obsession), with names like Designers Guild china, Boda Nova, Alessi and Bodum, flooring and rugs.

Cath Kidson

8 Clarendon Cross, W11, 0171-221 4000
Open Mon.-Fri. 10.30am-6pm, Sat. 11am-6pm.

Cath Kidson's interior style achieves an unfussy, bright look, based on her own taste for unusual fabrics, wallpaper designs and a love for 1950s simplicity. She opened this fun shop in a villagey corner of posh Holland Park to sell renovated tables, chairs and dressers from her favourite era, as well as interesting fabrics and artefacts from her visits to antique and bric-a-brac markets. Some of these finds are still sold but Cath has now branched out to design her own stationery and a range of fabrics.

Colefax & Fowler

39 Brook St, W1, 0171-493 2231
Open Mon.-Fri. 9.30am-5.30pm.

When the firm started in the 1930s, John Fowler took the romantic spirit of late eighteenth-century decoration as his inspiration. Now the famous Colefax and Fowler firm is located in an authentic Georgian house in Mayfair which shows off the great swags of fabrics, floral wallpapers and antique furniture to perfection. The firm is famous for creating that certain English style so characteristic of the grand English country houses.

Designers Guild

267-271 and 277 King's Rd, SW3, 0171-243 7300
Open Mon., Tues. 9.30am-5.30pm, Wed., Thurs. to 6pm, Fri., Sat. 10am-6pm, Sun. noon-5pm.

Tricia Guild's innovative firm has sold fabrics, wall coverings, upholstery and accessories since the 1970s. Every decorative device combined with stunning, often dramatic wallpapers and curtain fabrics make these inspiring showrooms to visit. Number 277 King's Road offers the exclusive Designers Guild fabric and wallpaper ranges, including printed floral, geometric patterns, woven plain, checks and stripes, silks, velvets, jacquards and children's designs. The two-storey sister shop sells furniture, kelims, one-off crafts, jewelry, unusual garden accessories and brightly coloured stationery. Woven and embroidered cotton bed linen, wool blankets, rugs, cushions, tableware and even gourmet food —Italian and French olive oils, English jams and chutney—is also sold. They offer a complete design service.

Jane Churchill

151 Sloane St, SW3, 0171-730 9847
Open Mon.-Sat. 10am-6pm, Wed. to 7pm.

A good source for innovative and stylish wallpapers and fabrics which are matched up with a co-ordinated range of lampshades, towels, bedlinens and accessories.

Joanna Wood

48A Pimlico Rd, SW3, 0171-730 5064
Open Mon.-Fri. 10am-6pm, Sat. 10am-4pm.

Another shop offering the quintessential English look. Go for the large, distinctive furniture and fabrics, or add an instant stately feel to your home with prettily finished objects such as hat boxes, stationery and desk accessories, lampshades, miniature china boxes, visitor books, freeze-dried rose heads with pungent aromas, and cushion covers.

Laura Ashley

256 Regent St, W1, 0171-437 9760
Open Mon.-Tues. 10am-6.30pm, Wed. to 7pm, Thurs. to 8pm, Sat. 9.30am-7pm, Sun. noon-6pm.

These days the company have extended their collections to include funkier cushions and accessories with a broader appeal although their main style is still pretty and chintzy. Only the larger womenswear shops have a home furnishings department and a curtain and blind making service as well as an interior styling service (the direct line to the stylist at this shop is 0171-434 1343; also try 9 Harriet St, SW1, 0171-823 2287). Branches throughout London include three Homebase shops which stock home furnishings only, such as 193 Warwick Rd, W14, 0171-603 2285.

Mary Fox Linton

4 Hewlett House, Havelock Terr, SW8, 0171-622 0920
Open by appointment.

There are two sides to this firm. Under the Mary Fox Linton banner, they sell decorative objects and fabrics in ranges exclusive to them such as Dedar and Gland, Jim Thompson, Thai Silks and Fabergé, all of which can be seen at her two showrooms at Chelsea Harbour (0171-351 9908), along with contemporary furniture for the home and office. Fox Linton Associates, established in 1962, is the design practice side of the business and is called on to decorate house and corporate buildings all over the world, whether it's a Georgian-style house in Tokyo or modern-looking flats with the emphasis on interesting uses of space for which the designer, Mary Fox Linton, has become well-known.

Mrs Munro Ltd

16 MOTCOMB ST, SW1, 0171-235 0326

Open Mon.-Thurs. 9.30am-5.30pm, Fri. to 5pm.

Set up in 1926 by Geraldine Munro, the company is now run by her daughter, Jean, whose particular passion is the eighteenth-century style. You can see her work at Number 1 Royal Crescent, Bath. But mostly Jean Munro and director John Lusk work privately, creating delightful replicas of the English country style all over the world. Although primarily an interior design firm, they also stock a range of chintzes, the designs for which have been researched and discovered in old books and houses. They then have them made up either for private clients or their showroom.

Osborne & Little

304-308 KING'S RD, SW3, 0171-352 1456

Open Mon.-Fri. 9.30am-6pm, Sat. 10am-5.30pm.

Although mainly regarded for its take on the English look, which includes a strongly traditional range of floral and striped wallpapers, it is worth noting that Osborne & Little include a good range of modern looks from designers such as Nina Campbell.

Sanderson

112-120 BROMPTON RD, SW3, 0171-584 3344

Open Mon.-Sat. 10am-6pm.

The Sanderson name is famous for quality fabrics and wallpapers. You'll find florals, checks, stripes and plains at fairly competitive prices here. The shop is on two floors and also stocks rugs, accessories and furniture.

The Shaker Shop

322 KING'S RD, SW3, 0171-352 3918

Open Mon.-Sat. 10am-6pm.

Admiration of the simple and practical style of the furniture of the Shakers in America—a religious group who broke away from the Quakers in the late 1700s—led Liz Shirley and Tim Lamb to open their first shop selling chairs, tables and other products made at the Shaker Workshops in Massachussetts. The unusual and definitely non-English sight of chairs hung from peg rails on the wall first brought customers into the shop out of curiosity; the superior craftsmanship of the products enticed them to buy. The pure lines and first-rate woods employed in the trestle and candle tables, wall cupboards, pegrails and Shaker boxes is breathtaking. **Also at 25 Harcourt St, W1, 0171-724 7672.**

Simon Horn Furniture

117-121 WANDSWORTH BRIDGE RD, SW6, 0171-731 1279

Open Mon.-Sat. 9.30am-5.30pm.

Europe's leading specialist in French and classical wooden beds, Simon Horn offers 60 traditional designs from the Lit Bateau to splendid four posters. His antique replicas are made from solid woods such as rosewood and cherrywood and clients can also specify their preferred stain or patina. For children's rooms, the Simon Horn Cot is a real treat since the design, based on the classic French Lit Bateau, serves first as cot, then child's bed and finally becomes a sofa.

Viaduct

1-10 SUMMER'S ST, EC1, 0171-278 8456

Open Mon.-Fri. 9.30am-6pm, Sat. 10.30am-4pm.

Former archictect, James Mair, stocks cutting-edge designed furniture in his showroom on the ground floor of an old print warehouse in Clerkenwell. In the huge well-lit space he sells minimalist contemporary furniture, lighting and accessories from top European designers such as Maarten van Saveren, Martin Ryan and Hannes Wettstein.

FURNISHING ACCESSORIES

Aero

96 WESTBOURNE GROVE, W2, 0171-221 1950

Open Mon.-Fri. 10am-6.30pm, Sat. to 6pm, Sun. noon-5pm.

A treat for those seeking a company who manufacture, retail and promote modern furniture, lighting and accessories. Stocking everything from animal-shaped CD holders to stainless steel wall panels to hang kitchen equipment on, this shop sells designer products which stylishly solve practical problems in the home. Lamps, ultra-modern tables and chairs for home and office all have a minimalist flair.

After Noah

121 UPPER ST, N1, 0171-359 4281
Open Mon.-Sat 10am-6pm, Sun. noon-5pm.

Rambling stylish recyclers of old objects which can be put to suprising uses if you think hard enough. They stock items from old toys to cabinets, candlesticks to bedlinen, alongside stylish new designs. Just like anyone's home, in fact. **Also at 261 King's Rd, SW3, 0171-351 2610.**

Barclay & Bodie

7-9 BLEINHEIM TERR, NW8, 0171-372 5705
Open Mon.-Sat. 9.30am-5.30pm.

You could actually be stepping into somebody's drawing room in this shop. They stock a fair amount of Victorian antiques but this is mainly a shop for well-designed accessories for the home, with items ranging from a Parisian navy gingham cotton frame for photographs to candle sconces, padded hangers and rugs. Look out for unusual items like sepia-coloured ironing board emlazoned with the image of a male nude.

Ciel Decor

187 NEW KING'S RD, SW6, 0171-731 0444
Open Mon.-Sat. 10am-5.30pm.

Besides its own range of fabrics, this shop stocks the sunny Provençal fabrics produced by the Les Olivades company, made up into accessories such as table mats, lamp shades, wash bags and towels.

The Conran Shop

MICHELIN HOUSE, 81 FULHAM RD, SW3, 0171-589 7401
Open Mon. & Thurs.-Fri. 9.30am-6pm, Tues. 10am-6pm, Wed. 9.30am-7.30pm, Sat. 10am-6.30pm, Sun. noon-5.30pm.

Inside the fantastic Art Nouveau building that was once the headquarters of the Michelin tyre company, this is one of the most exciting shops in London. It's impossible to miss, with its motoring-motif tiled murals and stained glass windows. The shop's buyers travel extensively to source new and unusual products so there are antiques and artefacts from all over the world. As Conran works with contemporary designers and manufacturers, much of the furniture collection is exclusive to the store. They also stock more than 200 fabric designs, exclusive bed linens, garden furniture, a small but wonderful range of children's toys and clothes, lovely accessories and gifts. **Also at 55 Marylebone High St, NW1, 0171-723 2223.**

And Also...

One of those shops where you walk in and say, 'Why hasn't anyone done this before?' V V Rouleaux aka Annabel Lewis has searched through the shops of Paris and New York to come up with the greatest selection of ribbons, trimmings and braidings you are ever likely to see. It is a veritable treasure-house for designers, milliners, stylists and ordinary members of the public. **V V Rouleaux**, 10 Symons St, SW3, 0171-730 3125, open Mon.-Sat. 9.30am-6pm. If you thought stencilling was hard, then make your way to **The Stencil Store**, 91 Lower Sloane Street, SW1, 0171-730 0728, open Mon.-Sat. 10am-5.30pm, Wed. to 6.30pm. You'll be inspired to put paint to stencil and convert your room into an architectural haven or perhaps an English garden. Chests of drawers can be transformed very quickly. Here they sell stencil designs, paints and sticks, books, sponging kits and special paint effects. They also run stencilling courses. Branches throughout London.

Crucial Trading

79 WESTBOURNE PARK RD, W2, 0171-221 9000
Open Tues.-Sat. 10am-6pm.

As specialists in supplying natural floor coverings, this shop has a choice of 120 designs in materials such as sisal, seagrass, jute and wool. **Also at 4 Barnabas St, SW1, 0171-730 0075; 174 Tower Bridge Rd, SE1, 0171-234 0000.**

David Linley Furniture

60 Pimlico Rd, SW1, 0171-730 7300

Open Mon.-Fri. 9.30am-6pm, Sat. 10am-5pm.

David Linley is a remarkably talented designer, and his furniture and accessories are commissioned from clients all over the world, as well as for instance, the Savoy Hotel in London which has a marquetry screen in the River Room Restaurant. Beautifully made out of fine woods, the wonderfully turned candlesticks or boxes in the style of Italian villas, are in the nature of an investment, and priced to match.

The Dining Room Shop

62-64 White Hart Lane, Barnes, SW13, 0181-878 1020

Open Mon.-Fri. 10am-5.30pm, Sat. 10.15am-5.30pm.

The name lives up to its promise of supplying everything for the dining room. You'll find furniture including antique tables and chairs, plus the necessary accoutrements for a well-dressed table such as china, linen, glass, lace and cutlery.

Elephant

94 Tottenham Court Rd, W1, 0171-813 2092

Open Mon.-Fri. 10am-6pm, Sat. 10am-6pm.

Good selection of diverse items on the inexpensive side but which look chic, from candlesticks to some excellent East European glassware. They also stock sofas, candles, wastepaper bins, throws and more—a great asset in a street which is famous for interior design shops.

The General Trading Company

144 Sloane St, SW1, 0171-730 0411

Open Mon.-Sat. 9.30am-6pm, Wed. to 7pm.

A place where you can find every kind of household object from a candlestick to a library pole holder with antiqued hide covering. This is an institution among the local 'Sloane Ranger' set and still one of the top places for a traditional wedding list for young brides. All the departments—antiques, upholstery and furniture, Oriental, garden, stationery, kitchen, linen, cutlery, china, glass—cater for shoppers with an appreciation of good design. The shop holds all four Royal Warrants, and is only one of six other companies in the country to share the honour.

Habitat

196 Tottenham Court Rd, W1, 0171-631 3880

Open Mon.-Fri. 10am-6pm, Thurs. to 8pm, Sat. 9.30am-6.30pm, Sun. noon-6pm.

After having lost direction slightly, Habitat is back delivering well-designed furniture and accessories for the style-conscious with more dash than cash. A good all-round place for ready-made or custom-made curtains, bold cushion covers, basic furniture including ranges for children's bedrooms, plain or bright bed linen, glass, china, lamps and cutlery. **Other branches include 206 King's Rd, SW3, 0171-351 1211.**

Heal's

196 Tottenham Court Rd, W1, 0171-636 1666

Open Mon.-Wed. 10am-6pm, Thurs. to 8pm, Fri. to 6.30pm, Sat. 9.30am-6.30pm.

Heal's is a must for anyone who appreciates good craftsmanship and design. With three floors of stylish, modern furniture and a wide range of imaginative and exciting accessories to choose from, it's almost impossible to leave empty-handed (unless your budget gets the better of you). The company began as a bed-maker and its handmade beds are still sought after. Heal's reputation for being a forerunner in the 1920s is maintained today: it is a good place for exclusive designs and bursting with new ideas. **Also at 234 King's Rd, SW3, 0171-349 8411.**

The Holding Company

345 King's Rd, SW3, 0171-352 1600

Open Mon.-Sat. 10am-7pm, Sun. noon-6pm.

Sometimes the best business ideas are the most obvious ones, and this was certainly the case for American Donna Walter who set up her thriving business when she moved to London and wanted storage solutions in her London flat. The company offer every kind of object to organise your home and office life: wicker baskets, hessian or plastic containers, card drawer dividers (to keep socks and knickers tidy) and more. Many ranges are in bright colours and unusual patterns or natural fabrics to blend in with currently modish minimalist surroundings.

India Jane

140 Sloane St, SW1, 0171-730 1070

Open Mon.-Sat. 10am-6pm, Sun. noon-5pm.

Everything here (with the very odd exception) is imported from India, hence the name.

It's a good collection of colourful and very fashionable furniture and small objects, linens, rugs, planters and china.

Jerry's Home Store

163-167 FULHAM RD, SW3, 0171-225 2246
Open Mon.-Sat. 10am-6pm, Sun. 11.30am-5.30pm.

The stylish simplicity of American homes appealed to Jeremy Sacher so much he decided to introduce the look to London. The airy store is filled with novelty items such as popcorn makers and functional products like cookie jars, brightly coloured crockery and extensive kitchen ware and equipment. The large room downstairs has a New England feel, from the expensive sofas, handsome wooden tables, gleaming lamps and accessories. Much of the merchandise is made in America. **Also at Harvey Nichols; 57 Heath St, NW3, 0171-794 8622; Bentall Centre, Kingston-upon-Thames, Surrey, 0181-549 5393.**

Maryse Boxer & Carolyn Quartermaine Chez Joseph

26 SLOANE ST, SW1, 0171-245 9493
Open Mon.-Fri. 10am-6.30pm, Wed. to 7pm, Sat. 9.30am-6pm.

Underneath the Joseph shop in Sloane Street you'll find a treasure trove of a shop with items designed or sourced by these two remarkably talented designers. Ceramics and glassware, items like silk sleeping bags for the sophisticated, but possibly intrepid traveller, cutlery and more. Expensive and collectable. Mail order.

Mulberry Home

219 KING'S RD, SW3, 0171-352 1937
Open Mon.-Sat. 10am-6pm, Wed. to 7pm.

Walking into the Mulberry Home store is like walking into a lavish film set. The look, inspired by romantic and medieval themes, is rich and warming with harmonious blues, reds and golds creating an inviting homely environment The furniture consists of Chesterfield sofas covered in beautiful brocades, handsome wooden chests and Ottomans, accessories include imposing wooden candlesticks, throws, suede and brocade cushions and refined crockery. The shop also offers a complete interior design service.

Nina Campbell

9 WALTON ST, SW3, 0171-225 10
Open Mon.-Fri. 9.30am-5.30pm
4pm.

A delightful shop well worth a visit for its mixture of goods, many of which you will be tempted to buy for your own home as well as for gifts. Items include beeswax bamboo-shaped candles, a variety of lamps and shades, lustrous flower pots, traditional and unusual photograph frames, cut cystal and silver dressing table bottle, hand-painted coffee cup and saucer sets, and glamorous Fortuny silk vases.

Purves & Purves

80-81, 83 TOTTENHAM COURT RD, W1, 0171-580 8223
Open Mon.-Sat. 9.30am-6pm, Thurs. to 7.30pm.

Whatever your taste, it's virtually impossible to walk past the Purves & Purves stores without glancing at their eye-catching furniture and accessories. Like a beacon, the jewel-bright colours, flamboyant shapes and unique designs capture the imagination, enticing you into the light-hearted and unfussy store to take a closer look at the plethora of wonderful creations. The furniture may be a bit on the pricey side, but you can always brighten up your washing line with funky flying fish clothes pegs or add a bit of character to your kitchen with the quirky, but well-designed Garbo waste basket.

The Source

26 KENSINGTON HIGH ST, W8, 0171-937 2626
Open Mon.-Sat 10am-7pm, Sun. noon-6pm.

Large shop stocking most things for the home in different themed sections at remarkably low prices. Trendy, up-to-the-minute, they pile them high and sell.

KITCHENWARE

David Mellor

4 SLOANE SQ, SW1, 0171-730 4259
Open Mon.-Sat. 9.30am-6pm.

Devoted to the well-appointed kichen featured in interior magazines, the ground floor stocks glassware from Poland, Finland and Spain as well as English Dartington. Downstairs are clay cooking pots, bright blue earthenware, corkscrews, aluminium moulds and many other products designed to make

[co]oking easy, enjoyable and stylish. The shop also stocks bottles of special olive oils and jars of sauces, aromatic olives, olive pesto and sun-dried tomatoes.

Divertimenti

45-47 Wigmore St, W1, 0171-935 0689

Open Mon.-Fri. 9.30am-6pm, Sat. 10am-6pm.

This is what the kitchen in foodie heaven must look like—all gleaming surfaces and shiny utensils. The shop is always busy with people looking for the perfect kitchen accessory—whether it be the best pot to cook in, pretty ochre-toned earthenware, the right coffee pot or white net coverings for storing food; and this atmospheric shop delivers the goods. It is perfect for browsing, with two floors devoted to pots, plates, cookery books and culinary miscellania. **Also at 139-141 Fulham Rd, SW3, 0171-581 8065.**

Elizabeth David Cook Shop

3 North Row, The Market, Covent Garden, WC2, 0171-836 9167

Open Mon.-Fri. 10.30am-6.30pm, Sat. 10am-7pm, Sun. noon-5pm.

A rainbow of Le Creuset pots and pans are displayed in abundance on the small ground floor. Up the wooden stairs, you'll also find them keeping company with all the cooking accessories like coffee makers, jelly moulds, icing equipment and kitchen necessities, plus a selection of cookbooks, incuding, of course, those by the influential cook herself.

Richard Dare

93 Regent's Park Rd, NW1, 0171-722 9428

Open Mon.-Fri. 9.30am-6pm, Sat. 10am-6pm.

This kitchenware shop may seem small fry but it carries a very good, professional range of kitchenware, suspended from the ceiling, piled high on shelves and stacked on the floor. Good earthenware pottery includes Quimper faience crockery alongside fish kettles, pots and pans and more.

Summerill & Bishop

100 Portland Rd, W11, 0171-221 4566

Open Mon.-Sat. 10am-6pm.

A truly delightful and inspiring kitchen shop that mixes the old and the new, French and British in such a way that you imagine yourself in a Provençal farm or on a patio in the South of France. Plenty of items here make this a good inspirational place.

LIGHTING

Besselink & Jones

99 Walton St, SW3, 0171-584 0343

Open Mon.-Fri. 10am-5.30pm, Sat. to 4.30pm.

From antique to modern, big or small, Besselink & Jones offers a dazzling selection of lamps and many handmade lampshades designed in traditional style. The firm also sells in Harvey Nichols, although specialist vintage lamps are mostly found in this jam-packed shop.

Christopher Wray Lighting

600 King's Rd, SW6, 0171-736 8434

Open Mon.-Sat. 9.30am-6pm.

Christopher Wray stocks a dazzling array of one-off and Tiffany-style lamps. Prices vary, depending on whether you go for a reproduction or an original item to light up your life. **Also at 199 Shaftesbury Ave, WC2, 0171-437 6199.**

London Lighting Company

135 Fulham Rd, SW3, 0171-589 3612

Open Mon.-Sat. 9.30am-6pm, Sun. noon-5pm.

Almost 80 manufacturers from all over Europe are represented in this huge gallery devoted to contemporary lighting. One of their suppliers has the rights to the Bauhaus designs and makes lamps based on the original styles. There is also a wide choice of lights to illuminate paintings.

LINEN

Cologne & Cotton

791 Fulham Rd, SW6, 0171-736 9261

Open Mon.-Sat. 9.30am-7pm.

Delightful shop selling beautiful crisp matching bed linen in pretty designs which you can buy in sets or separately. Plus a good range of toiletries. **Also at 39 Kensington Church St, W8, 0171-376 0324.**

Descamps

197 Sloane St, SW1, 0171-235 6957

Open Mon.-Sat. 10am-6.30pm, Wed. to 7.30pm.

Pyjamas in classic styles plus a selection of fun designs to ring the changes, this bright shop has a large selection of French ranges which include bedlinen, towels, bathrobes, and baby accessories.

Frette

98 NEW BOND ST, W1, 0171-629 5517

Open Mon.-Sat. 10am-6pm, Thurs. to 7pm.

The colour choice of Frette's cool, crisp Italian linens, sink-into towels and Hollywood-style bathrobes span the spectrum, and the quality is unrivalled. All of the items on sale in the long galleried room can be matched or fully co-ordinated.

The Irish Linen Company

35 BURLINGTON ARCADE, W1, 0171-493 8949

Open Mon.-Thurs. 11am-7pm, Fri. & Sat. 10.30am-7pm, Sun. noon-6pm.

A wonder in white is how this little corner shop looks with all its stock draped around, but there are colour ranges should you wish to add a little variety. The linen is Irish and very good and they have a range running from small napkins to huge tablecloths for a palatial dining room.

The Linen Merchant

11 MONTPELIER ST, SW7, 0171-584 3654

Open Mon.-Sat. 9.30am-6pm.

A charming shop full of reasonably priced and beautiful linens. Their range of Belgian linen cushions and tablecloths in both bold and pastel colours is particularly eye-catching. They also have a good range of embroidered Madeiran cotton. All items can be gift-wrapped.

The Monogrammed Linen Shop

168 WALTON ST, SW1, 0171-589 4033

Open Mon.-Fri. 10am-6pm, Sat. to 5pm.

Choc-full of bed linen, towels and children's clothing, this pretty white-fronted shop can personalise almost any item in a week.

The White House

40-41 CONDUIT ST, W1, 0171-629 3521

Open Mon.-Sat. 10am-6pm.

The most famous of London's linen shops is expensive, but the stock should last you a lifetime. A delicate pink cotton voile sheet set, which includes an embroidered top sheet, plain bottom sheet and two pillow cases costs around £2,000, while a silk-satin nightgown and jacket cost more than £1,000. They sell towels with daintily scalloped edges, dressing gowns, exquisitely made lingerie and many matching accessories, a range of tablecloths and hand-embroidered dining room linen. The shop will undertake commissions to custom-make one-off designs of all of the above. Its own W H Collections label includes bed linen, towels, table linen, throws and other accessories. Like a traditional department store, the White House has a children's designer clothes section; check out the hand-smocked dresses for babies up to 2 year olds—from £79 to £200.

IMAGE & SOUND

MUSICAL INSTRUMENTS

Blanks

273 KILBURN HIGH RD, NW6, 0171-624 7777

Open Mon.-Sat. 10am-5.30pm.

A large department store of musical ideas from guitars and sheet music to brass and traditional Irish folk instruments.

Foote's

10 GOLDEN SQ, W1, 0171-734 1822 FOR PERCUSSION, 0171-437 1811 FOR ORCHESTRAL INSTRUMENTS

Open Mon.-Fri. 9am-6pm, Sat. to 5pm.

Anything from educational percussion to orchestral brass, strings and accessories. Chas E Foote's short-term hire is very practical for those impractical musicians who leave their Stradivarius on a train on the day of a Royal gala performance. Good rental service for schools and parents who want their child to learn on a good instrument.

London Rock Shop

26 CHALK FARM RD, NW1, 0171- 267 5381

Open Tues.-Sat. 10am-6pm.

Three floors with amps, guitars and keyboards for rock musicians of all ages and styles. Anything from a busker's amplification to hi-tech sampling stations can be found here.

Rose Morris

11 Denmark St, WC2, 0171-836 0991 for equipment, 0171-836 4766 for printed music.
Open Mon.-Sat. 10am-6.30pm, Thurs. to 7pm.

Six floors of instruments, amplification, software, tutorial videos and accessories. The basement is full of electric guitars, the ground floor has a selection of printed music, the first floor is packed with professional keyboards, the second with digital pianos, acoustic guitars are stored on the third floor and recording equipment is up on the fourth.

Denmark Street

Denmark Street is an oasis for every budding musician. It's full of music shops offering everything that can be banged, plucked, hit, rattled, programmed, blown or otherwise used to make any kind of noise. The dozen or so shops serve customers from young beginners to seasoned professionals. The price range is very wide and you can find anything from a child's practise drum kit to a complicated sampling station.

SPECIALISTS

Accordions of London

365a Kilburn High Rd (corner of Loveridge Rd), NW6, 0171-624 9001
Open Mon.-Sat. 10.30am-6pm, Sun.11am-4pm.

A specialist shop with a range from beginners' instruments to concert accordions and related instruments and a repair, estimate and spare parts service. The shop even has accordions made specially for them in Italy, one of the very few countries where they are still manufactured.

All Flutes Plus

5 Dorset St (off Baker St), W1, 0171-935 3339
Open Mon.-Fri. 10am-6pm, Sat. 10am-4.30pm.

The name gives it all away: sales, repairs and rentals of quality flutes with an odd recorder and saxophone thrown in. New and second-hand instruments and accessories.

Andy's

27 Denmark St, WC2, 0171-916 5080
Open Mon.-Sat. 10am-7pm, Sun. 12.30pm-6.30pm.

Andy's is one of those shops where they really love what they are doing. And that is vintage guitars (but they are also good at selling them!). The ground floor is dedicated to electric instruments, guitars and basses of all shapes and ages, the first floor to beautiful acoustic instruments. Prices are sensible and service is expert. This is a serious shop; Bob Dylan has been spotted browsing through the vintage selection. The shop's repair service is used by super professionals like Brian May of Queen. The workshop also makes guitars and has a 'finder service' for those who want a particular instrument.

Bill Levington

144 Shaftesbury Ave, WC2, 0171-240 0584
Open Mon.-Sat. 9.15am-5.30pm.

Bill Levington specialises in brass and woodwind instruments, so the shop has anything from trumpets to sousaphones. Other things to blow or to breathe through are bagpipes, recorders and top grade flutes. Get your brass band equipped here!

J & A Beare

7 Broadwick St, W1, 0171-437 1449
Open Mon.-Fri.9am-12.15pm & 1.30pm-5pm.

These violins are almost for virtuosi for Beare's quietly elegant shop is not for time-wasters. J & A Beare has a long tradition as violin makers, repairers and retailers. It is necessary to book an appointment if you want to see their antique instruments. Here quality goes before quantity.

Macari's

92-94 Charing Cross Rd, WC2, 0171-836 2856
Open Mon.-Sat. 10.30am-5.30pm.

An excellent shop for guitars, amplifiers and accessories, they have a good selection of vintage guitars from a 1930s lap steel to twelve-string Stratocasters and more conventional instruments.

Professional Percussion

205 Kentish Town Rd, NW5, 0171-485 0822

Open Mon.-Sat. 10am-6pm.

A large selection of drum sets and ethnic percussion instruments from different corners of the world and a repair and hire service.

Ray Man

9 Monmouth St, WC2, 0171-240 1776

Open Mon.-Sat. 10.30am-6pm.

Ray Man specialises in Eastern and African instruments from gongs and flutes to the most complicated stringed things you've ever seen. And most of them are playable as well as beautiful.

Spanish Guitar Centre

36 Cranbourne St, WC2, 0171-240 0754

Open seven days a week 10.30am-6pm.

A selection of acoustic guitars from £60 beginners models to £10,000 virtuoso instruments. More than just a shop, you can learn to play by having lessons at the centre.

Synthesiser Service Centre

6 Erskine Rd, NW3, 0171-586 0357

Open Mon.-Fri. 8.30am-6.30pm.

Not a shop but a place to get your keyboards and amplifiers repaired. The centre is used by some famous people and service is efficient and friendly. Expect to wait about two weeks to get your machinery back from their workshop.

T W Howarth

31-35 Chiltern St, W1, 0171-935 2407

Open Mon.-Fri .10am-5.30pm, Sat. to 3pm.

London's premier woodwind shop gets larger every time you pass them. Now they occupy three shops: Number 31 has oboes and bassoons, Number 33 saxophones and Number 35 clarinets. T W Howarth is a full-service shop for woodwind players and their instruments.

PHOTOGRAPHY

Fox Talbot

154 Tottenham Ct Rd, W1, 0171-387 7001

Open Mon.-Fri. 9am-6pm, Thurs. to 7pm, Sat, to 5.30pm.

Specialising in second-hand cameras, Fox Talbot stock names like Leica, Canon, Minolta and Nikon but they can get any make of camera. The Strand shop is popular with professionals and has the most up-to-the-minute equipment. **Also at 443 Strand, WC2, 0171-379 6522.**

Jessop Photo Centre

67 New Oxford St, WC1, 0171-240 6077

Open Mon.-Sat. 9am-6pm, Thurs. to 8pm, Fri. to 7pm, Sun.11am-5pm.

There are so many camera shops in London that it can be most confusing. But Jessop's is one of the best for amateur equipment and their staff are friendly and helpful. They carry a large stock of everything the amateur might need.

Joe's Basement

113 Wardour St, W1, 0171-434 9313

Open 24 hours.

Used by amateurs and especially by professionals needing to process film in the small hours of the night for the next day, this is a friendly fast place with a small trade counter for films, batteries etc. **Also at 82 Clerkenwell Rd, EC1, 0171-253 3210; 247 Euston Rd, NW1, 0171-388 3210; 111 Hammersmith Rd, W14, 0171-371 3210.**

Keith Johnson & Pelling

93 Drummond St, NW1, 0171-380 1144

Open Mon.-Fri. 9am-5.30pm, rental 8.30am-6.30pm .

This is the biggest photographic company in Europe, a real professional's place with a superb range of equipment including Hasselblads and film. They also have a comprehensive hire section. Book well in advance, as serious equipment is sometimes difficult to come by. There is also a first-class repair service.

Silverprint

12b Valentine Pl, SE1, 0171-620 0844

Open Mon.-Fri. 9.30am-5.30pm.

The place to come to for special papers imported from India and Japan (among other places) that you will not get elsewhere. No cameras on sale here; they are in the business of supplying processing, developing and printing materials and very special chemicals. So expert and specialised are they that they have been known to export an order to Malaysia—of paper from Japan! They have a first-rate catalogue and mail-order service.

RECORDINGS

Classical, Pop Easy Listening

The Coliseum Shop

31 St. Martin's Lane, WC2, 0171-240 0270
Open Mon.-Sat. 10am-7.30pm, if there is no performance on Mon. closes at 6pm.

Next to the English National Opera, the Coliseum shop is dedicated to opera from its beginnings to today. They also sell a wide selection of opera videos.

Dress Circle

57-59 Monmouth St, WC2, 0171-240 2227
Open Mon.-Sat. 10am-7pm.

Recordings and videos of musicals, soundtracks, celebrity nostalgia and memorabilia. For those who love musical entertainment.

HMV

150 Oxford St, W1, 0171-631 3423
Open Mon.-Sat. 9.30am-7.30 pm, Thurs., Fri. to 8pm, Sun. noon-6pm.

HMV's megastore is a bit difficult to find your way around. The ground floor covers the mainstream in pop, rock, reggae and soul. No big surprises here, but things get better a floor down. Jazz, folk and world music from all over the globe are well represented with Indian music from films, country from America, Latin pop songs and Ethiopian jazz. The classic section is also excellent.

Intoxica

231 Portobello Rd, W11, 0171-229 8010
Open Mon.-Sat. 10.30am-6.30pm, Sun. noon-4pm.

A mini-megastore on two floors. Dance music from swing-beats to rare grooves is situated in what they coyly call the 'bassment'. Upstairs it's indie, trash, noise and hardcore. Intoxica has everything from collectable reggae to classic soul and 60s psychedelia, and a good second-hand department.

Tower Records

1 Piccadilly Circus, W1, 0171-439 2500
Open Mon.-Sat. 9am-midnight, Sun. noon-6pm.

If you have a severe need to buy a CD of, say, Fauré's Requiem or Miles Davis's Sketches of Spain late at night, then go to Tower Records, the second megastore in the area. The ground floor has a vast selection of pop and rock and imports. The first floor has a huge collection of classical and contemporary music, jazz, country and world music. Their free monthly magazine called Top tells you about new releases and forthcoming concerts. **Also at 162 Camden High Street, NW1, 0171-424 2810.**

Virgin Megastore

14-30 Oxford St, W1, 0171-631 1234
Open Mon.-Sat. 9.30am-8pm, Thurs. 10am-8pm, Sun. noon-6pm.

The original megastore still has a wide selection of music from every area. But Virgin also sells videos, T-shirts, books, magazines, notes, cartoons, games and concert and aeroplane tickets. It is purely a matter of taste which of the megastores you prefer, but Virgin is well organised with good listening facilities.

Specialists

Beanos

7 Middle St, Croydon, Surrey, 0181-680 1202
Open Mon.-Fri. 10am-6 pm, Sat. 9am-6pm.

This is the largest second-hand record store in Europe and is reasonably priced for normal records and hugely expensive for collectors' items. Beanos offer also a mail order service.

Black Market

5 D'Arblay St, W1, 0171-437 0478
Open Mon.-Sat. 10am-7pm.

Noisy and buzzing with house, hip hop and rap, but no rock, hard core or reaggae. Black Market also sells merchandise like baseball caps.

Cheapo Cheapo Records

53 Rupert St, W1, 0171-437 8272
Open Mon.-Sat. noon-10pm.

A huge selection of music from folk to psychedelia, from classical to children's songs.

Daddy Kool Music

9 Berwick St, W1, 0171-437 3535
Open Mon.-Sat. 11am-6.30pm.

Reggae, ska and generally Jamaican music from the last few decades is stocked at the intriguingly named Daddy Kool which also sells second-hand records and rarities.

Hobgoblin Music

24 Rathbourne Place, W1, 0171-323 9040
Open Mon.-Sat.10am-6pm

What used to be The Folk Shop in Cecil Sharpe House has moved into a more central location between Oxford Street and Tottenham Court Road. A wide selection of instruments needed in the English folk music and a sturdy stock of folk music from all over the world.

Mole Jazz

311 Pentonville Rd, N1, 0171-278 8623
Open Mon.-Sat. 10am-6pm, Fri. to 8pm.

Just around the corner from King's Cross Station, this shop is always packed with enthusiasts. Records, cassettes, books and posters are well organised and you can listen to the music before buying. They also have a special collector's section with rarities.

Ray's Jazz

180 Shaftesbury Ave, WC2, 0171-240 3969
Open Mon.-Sat. 10am-6.30pm.

Small, but packed with wonderful recordings from Dixieland to avant-garde and with good listening facilities. The friendly staff know their stuff and are honest in their comments. They have a good selection of second-hand albums. There is a silent auction for rare records: they are put on display and customers put in their bids within a given time. Downstairs is an excellent selection of roots music from all over the world: from the Lappish joiku to the country yodel.

Rough Trade

16 Neal's Yard, WC2, 0171-240 0105
Open Mon.-Sat. 10am-6.30pm.

This indie specialist stocks all the unknown independent record companies you can imagine (and some more, too) from around the world, and a good selection of fanzines. **Also at 130 Talbot Rd, W11, 0171-229 8541.**

Sounds of China

Gerrard St, W1, 0171-734 1970
Open daily noon-8pm.

The shop, which stocks both classical and popular Chinese music, also sells books and magazines.

Stern's African Record Centre

116 Whitfield St, W1, 0171-388 2756
Open Mon.-Sat. 10.30am-6.30pm.

Good selection of African, Caribbean and Latin music at reasonable prices and an information point for world music concerts in London.

SHEET MUSIC

Argent's Music

20 Denmark St, WC2, 0171-379 3398
Open Mon.-Fri. 9am-6pm, Sat. 10am-6pm.

A wide collection of sheet music for the classical players and hard rockers. The shop also sells instruments to make the notes come alive from the print.

Boosey & Hawkes

295 Regent St, W1, 0171-580 2060
Open Mon.-Fri. 9am-6pm, Sat. 10am-4pm.

This shop which includes publisher Peters Edition's special department, celebrates printed music by covering everything from educational music to classical, opera, jazz and pop.

Foyle's

119 Charing Cross Rd, WC1, 0171-437 5660
Open Mon.-Sat. 9am-6pm, Thurs. to 7pm.

One floor of this massive book shop is dedicated to sheet music and music books.

Schott

48 Great Marlborough St, W1, 0171-287 2854
Open Mon.-Fri. 9am-5.30pm.

All classical printed music from early times to contemporary, and miniature scores for orchestras or solo pieces for recorder, educational music and books.

JEWELRY

CONTEMPORARY DESIGNERS

Crazy Pig Designs

38 SHORTS GDNS, WC2, 0171-240 4305
Open Mon.-Sat. 10.30am-6.30pm.

The chunky silver jewelry made on the premises of Crazy Pig Designs appeals to rock and rollers like Ozzie Osbourne and The Rolling Stones. Little wonder really as the styles include skull motifs, heavy identity bracelets and Batman logos which work as well in photographic sessions as they do on the stage. Semi-precious stones feature in some of the work. Customers' own designs can be made up in either silver or gold.

Dinny Hall

200 WESTBOURNE GROVE, W11, 0171-792 3913
Open Mon.-Fri. 11am-7pm, Sat. 10am-6pm.

A former British Accessory Designer of the Year, Dinny Hall is known for her fine, delicate jewelry, mostly in silver, from which hand-cut, semi-precious stones are suspended. She also creates pieces in 18-carat gold and precious stones and will undertake commissions. Her range now includes a small collection of bath oils, with floral or spicy notes, housed in 'gold' and 'silver' aluminium cans by the designer herself. Exhibitions of other designers' work are held at her other shop at **44 Fulham Rd, SW3, 0171-589 9192.**

Electrum Gallery

21 SOUTH MOLTON ST, W1, 0171-629 6325
Open Mon.-Fri. 10am-6pm, Sat. to 2pm.

Barbara Cartlidge's small but comprehensive showcase for contemporary jewelry by more than 80 worldwide designers still looks fresh despite being founded over 20 years ago. There is usually an exhibition following a theme or promoting a new artist; Vicki Ambery-Smith, for instance, produces architecturally inspired jewelry, such as Shakespeare's Globe. Wendy Ramshaw, who creates distinctive ring sets, and who received an OBE honour for her contribution to the art, is represented here.

The Great Frog

51 CARNABY ST, W1, 0171-734 1900
Open Mon.-Sat. 10.30am-6.30pm.

You need a big personality and it helps if you have a penchant for black leathers and Harley Davidsons to fully appreciate the wide range of jewelry available at this shop. Carol and Pat Reilly's creations have attracted rock star attention for over twenty years, and there are photographs of groups wearing wild-faced belt buckles and articulated rings on show to prove it. Skull motifs are popular themes as is the spooky enamelled 'eyeballs'. **Also at 10 Ganton St, W1, 0171-439 9357.**

Janet Fitch

25 OLD COMPTON ST, W1, 0171-287 3789
Open Mon.-Sat. 11am-7pm, Sun. 1pm-6pm.

An exciting showcase for British craftsmen. The work of some of the country's most talented jewelry designers is displayed in the stylish contemporary setting where prices run from approximately £14 to £400. For aspiring jewellers, Janet Fitch has compiled the ultimate book called The Art and Craft of Jewelry. **Also at 37 Neal St, WC2 0171-240 6332; 188a King's Rd, SW3, 0171-352 4401.**

Burlington Bertie

Burlington Arcade is a delightful enclave, where every shop is a must, whether it stocks woollens, scent, jewelry, leathergoods, shoes, linen or fashion accessories.

Jess James

3 NEWBURGH ST, W1, 0171-437 0199
Open Mon.-Fri. 11am-6.30pm, Tues. noon-6.30pm, Thurs. 11am-7pm, Sat. to 6pm.

Among the innovative designs of jewelry on display, Jess James has a range of diamond navel jewels and nipple rings made in platinum with diamonds. This shop is a showcase for top international designers such as Jacqueline Rabun, Wright & Teague, Dinny Hall, plus Jess James' own range.

Kiki McDonough

77 Walton St, SW3, 0171-581 1777

Open Mon.-Fri. 9.30am-5.30pm, Sat. 10am-1pm.

A favourite with the Chelsea set, Kiki McDonough designs and produces delightful jewelry, drawing on inspiration from all ages and from all over the world. Using precious metals and stones, a gold, pearl and diamond choker or an eighteen carat gold, diamond and sapphire eternity ring at £1,900 is a worth-while investment. She creates a range of understated earrings for day wear in both nine and eighteen-carat gold, for approximately £425, plus a range of cufflinks for women. Catalogue available.

Lesley Craze Gallery

34 Clerkenwell Gn, EC1, 0171-608 0393

Open Mon.-Sat. 10am-5.30pm.

A showcase for some of the best contemporary designers located in a thriving neighbourhood of creativity. It is made up of two gallery spaces, one area displaying work in precious metals while Craze 2 sells jewelry made from a variety of non-precious metals including brightly coloured acrylic, papier-maché and tin. There are always works on display and regular exhibitions. Lezley Craze is keen to promote commissions for her stable of jewellers, and some of the exhibitions include technical drawings which add to the interest.

Merola

178 Walton St, SW3, 0171-589 0365

Open Mon.-Sat. 10am-6pm.

Imaginative designs by Maria Merola include novelties such as cherub earrings and a wide range of decorative crosses. This jewel of a shop glitters with vintage costume pieces from the Twenties to the Fifties sourced by Maria up and down the country, particularly by the designer Miriam Haskell. A good spot for pieces in crystal, jet beads, dazzling wedding tiaras and the cutest vintage handbags.

Solange Azagury-Partridge

171 Westbourne Grove, W2, 0171-792 0197

Open Mon.-Sat. 11am-6pm.

Big, bold jewelry is made by Solange for people who like unconventional designs. She chooses striking gemstones like rose quartz, aquamarine, citrine and peridot. Her informal and friendly shop is as striking as the jewelry she creates—with a purple velvet sofa, orange walls and jewelry designed by Tom Dixon. It also stocks her other interests such as 1960s vases by Vallauris, modern chandeliers by Droog, sculptures by Roger Partridge and leather goods by William Wallace.

Theo Fennell

169 Fulham Rd, SW3, 0171-591 5000

Open Mon.-Thurs. 10am-6pm, Fri.-Sat. to 5pm.

Theo Fennell designs, makes and sells his witty, highly stylish pieces in this smart three-storey shop. In addition to the beautiful traditional jewelry, Fennell offers a range of hugely popular quirky items such as a silver and gold tub for placing your Hagen Daaz ice-cream in, silverscrew lid tops for jars of Marmite and a cleaning lady. His 'London charms' with miniature London icons such as traditional telephone booths and post boxes are also on sale at Harrods.

COSTUME JEWELRY

The Amber Centre

24 St. Christopher's Pl, W1, 0171-224 2953

Open Mon.-Sat. 10am-6pm, Thurs. to 7pm.

If you like amber, you'll love this shop devoted entirely to Baltic amber jewelry. The items, which run into the hundreds, include chunky and delicate earrings, pendants, bracelets, necklaces and objets d'art. Prices range from £20 to £1,000. They can also re-polish your own amber.

Butler & Wilson

20 South Molton St, W1, 0171-409 2955

Open Mon.-Sat. 10am-6pm, Thurs. to 7pm.

Owners Nicky Butler and Simon Wilson were originally antique jewellers and still display some Victorian and Art Deco pieces in their stores. They are more popular for their ranges of costume jewelry which includes jet, diamanté and silver baubles.

Ciro

9 New Bond St, W1, 0171-491 7219

Open Mon.-Fri. 9.15am-5.30pm, Sat. 10am-5pm.

This firm, in business since 1917, has built its reputation on all manner of pearls. Whether cultured, oyster shell or artificial, this is the place to come for the finest examples, plus expert knowledge, jewelry repair service, pearl re-stringing and special orders. **Also at 61a Brompton Rd, SW3, 0171-489 5584.**

Cobra & Bellamy

149 Sloane St, SW1, 0171-730 2823

Open Mon.-Fri. 10.30am-5.30pm, Sat. to 5pm.

Tania Hunter and Veronica Manussis set their own distinctive designs, including amber and jet, at their little black-and-white boutique. Look out for silver pieces and objets d'art. They also sell exclusive jewelry made by Italian designer Barbara Bertagnolli in applied 24-carat gold with gem stones and a range of watches.

Fior

31 New Bond St, W1, 0171-493 0101

Open Mon.-Fri. 9.30am-6pm, Sat. to 5.30pm.

A shimmering array of bejewelled evening bags, silk, satin or handmade gold and silver-plated, are specialities here. Styles come in scrunchy as well as square, round, oval and novelty shapes. Their costume jewelry is celebrated for its styling which rivals the designs in the fine jewelry world. Discreetly displayed inside the shop the Royal Warrant, 'By appointment to HRH the Prince of Netherlands' proves you're in good company wearing Fior. **Also at 27 Brompton Rd, SW3, 0171-589 0053.**

Van Peterson Designs

194 Walton St, SW3, 0171-584 1101

Open Mon.-Sat. 10am-6pm, Wed. to 7pm.

Run by a husband-and-wife team who design fashionable statement jewelry mostly in silver and gold. The shop sells elegant designs by other vogueish designer including Ericsson Beamon and Linda Levinson. **Also in Liberty.**

FINE JEWELRY

Adler

13 New Bond St, W1, 0171-409 2337

Open Mon.-Fri. 9.30am-5.30pm, Sat. 10am-5pm.

The third generation of the Adler family keeps the opulent influence of the Ottoman civilisation in striking pieces influenced by the designs of their grandfather, Jacques Adler, who started in a workshop in Constantinople in 1910. Look for the Seraglio multiple ring with gold hoops linked by a bar and studded with diamonds, set off by round sapphires, rubies and emeralds. In-house designer, Dominque Bott, will undertake commissions or redesign old jewelry.

Asprey and Gerrard

165-169 New Bond St, W1, 0171-493 6767

Open Mon.-Fri. 9.30am-5.30pm, Sat. 10am-5pm.

An institution, full of beautiful pieces, including its own designs. This is also a place to come for antique jewelry, plus a range of Art Deco pieces.

Boodle & Dunthorne

128-130 Regent St, W1, 0171-437 5050

Open Mon.-Sat. 9am-6pm.

Established in 1798, this family business started in Liverpool and its three London showrooms pride themselves on offering something for everyone. It has its own in-house designers and commissions and also offers good-value jewelry and watches by top international designers. Its specialist shop in Harrods features pieces by goldsmith Leo de Vroomen. **Also at 58a Brompton Rd, SW3, 0171-584 6363; 1 Sloane Sq, SW1, 0171-235 0111.**

Cartier

175 New Bond St, W1, 0171-493 6962

Open Mon.-Fri. 10am-6pm, Sat. to 5pm.

The name speaks for itself but if you need verification of their appeal—Richard Burton showered Elizabeth Taylor with a Cartier 69-carat diamond for a birthday present. Synonymous with classic French design since it opened in 1909, the London branch sells its own range of watches. Gift items include a monogrammed inkwell. The shop has a showcase of vintage Cartier pieces on sale and sometimes advertises its search for Cartier objects, jewels and watches made before 1970.

Collingwood

171 New Bond St, W1, 0171-734 2656

Open Mon.-Fri. 10am-5pm, Sat. to 4.30pm.

Collingwood, in existence for two hundred years and holding Royal Warrants from the Queen and the Queen Mother, stocks watches and classic jewelry including some vintage pieces. They also undertake commissions.

David Morris

25 Conduit St, W1, 0171-499 2200
Open Mon.-Fri. 10am-5.30pm, Sat. 10.30am-4.30pm.

This small shop carries a range of David Morris's distinctive designs, making him one of Europe's foremost jewellers. There is a 'boutique range' of signature pieces. He will undertake commissions and is especially popular for jewelry set with pink and yellow diamonds.

Elizabeth Gage

20 Albemarle St, W1, 0171-499 2879
Open Mon.-Fri. 10am-5.30pm.

One of the top designers whose inspiration comes from many different sources, such as nature, to suit the mood of the end of the 1990s. Floral twists and turns appear on her pieces which she designs around some of the most beautiful stones. She also has a particular love for nineteenth-century intaglios and baroque pearls, while classical artefacts also appear.

Heller Pearls

84 York St, W1, 0171-723 6111
Open Mon.-Sat. 10am-5.30pm.

Beautiful strings of lapis lazuli, turquoise, jade and other semi-precious stones adorn the window along with the cultured pearls which were once Naomi Heller's trademark. She now considers coral jewelry her speciality. You can design your own with guidance from the owner.

Hennell

12 New Bond St, W1, 0171-629 6888
Open Mon.-Fri. 9.30am-5.30pm, Sat. 10am-4.30pm.

The gold and platinum jewelry on sale here is dazzling. Established in 1736, the firm has design books dating back to the 1850s, so adapts many traditional, classic features in its necklaces, rings bracelets and brooches. The gift selection which includes silver pencils, glassware, inkwells and blotters, is equally stylish and very popular. Their Committment range is one of the great success stories of the decade.

Ilias Lalaounis

5 Sloane St, SW1, 0171-235 9253
Open Mon.-Sat. 10am-6pm.

At their Athens workshops, the four daughters of the family are the sixth generation to carry on the tradition of producing high quality, opulent-looking gold jewelry, inspired by Greek tradition and Byzantine influences.

Longmire

12 Bury St, SW1, 0171-930 8720
Open Mon.-Fri. 9.30am-5.30pm.

This small, handsome shop has three Royal Warrants and the world's largest selection of cufflinks. Designs include traditional, modern, estate or custom-made to include a monogram, crest or the image of your choice. Prices from approximately £240.

Philip Antrobus

11 New Bond St, W1, 0171-493 4557
Open Mon.-Sat. 9.30am-5pm.

This venerable firm founded in 1815 made the engagement ring given to the Queen by HRH Prince Philip. It carries a good range of antique and Victorian pieces plus a selection of modern jewelry. It is known for its workshop which makes up specially commissioned pieces.

Richard Ogden

28 Burlington Arcade, W1, 0171-493 9136
Open Mon.-Fri. 9.30am-5.15pm, Sat. to 5pm.

Well-known for fine antique and traditional jewelry, all British hand-crafted, this family-run firm, established in 1948, has a wide selection of engagement and wedding rings, from £200 to £15,000.

Tiffany & Co

25 Old Bond St, W1, 0171-409 2790
Open Mon.-Sat. 10am-5.30pm.

Understated surroundings for some of the world's most famous jewelry which includes designer rings, brooches and necklaces in organic shapes from Paloma Picasso and Elsa Perretti. Their silver range is very reasonable and rightly popular.

The Watch Gallery

129 FULHAM RD, SW3, 0171-930 9488

Open Mon.-Sat.10.30am-6pm.

With their traditional and popular Swiss watch brands like Breitling, Jaeger-Le Coultre and Audermars Piguet, through to the more unusual such as Ulysée Nardin, Girard-Perragaux and IWC, customers take their time while considering a purchase from the myriad timepieces at this excellent shop. They specialise in selling and repairing vintage watches and are often supplied with the first of a limited edition piece, making the shop the ideal hunting ground for serious watch collectors.

Watches of Switzerland

16 NEW BOND ST, W1, 0171-493 2716

Open Mon.-Fri. 9.30am-5.30pm, Tues. & Sat. 10am-5.30pm.

There are many branches of this company, selling a wide range of watches, but in this corner of New Bond Street are such specialist showrooms as the Rolex centre and a Patek Phillipe salon. **Branches throughout London.**

LEATHER & LUGGAGE

Anya Hindmarch

15-17 PONT ST, SW3, 0171-838 9177

Open Mon.-Sat. 10am-6pm.

The chicest bags in a variety of shapes and sizes from one of Britain's foremost handbag designers. The new shop in Pont Street is the ideal location for those who have just had a shopping bonanza in Sloane Street and need the perfect beaded or shiny leather bag to complete their outfit. The shop also offers a good range of agendas and accessories—very stylish and equally desirable. **Also at first floor, 91 Walton St, SW3, 0171-584 7644.**

Asprey

165-169 NEW BOND ST, W1, 0171-493 6767

Open Mon.-Fri. 9.30am-5.30pm, Sat. 10am-5pm.

Still a family business, Asprey dates back to the 1780s when an ancestor of Huguenot descent worked as a silk printer and craftsman of fitted dressing cases. His son, Charles, went on to make more portable cases in leather and moved in 1848 to the present premises where luggage is still hand-stitched and gold-tooled.

Barrow & Hepburn

25 BURY ST, ST. JAMES'S, SW1, 0171-925 2578

Open Mon.-Fri. 10am-5pm.

This company, founded in 1780, at one time was an exclusive business making fine leather goods for gentlemen, the Royal Maundy purses and Ministerial despatch boxes. Nowadays they stock a delightful and impressive range of leather goods, including luggage and Gladstone bags, briefcases and small hand-crafted leather items like stud boxes.

Bill Amberg

10 CHEPSTOW RD, W2, 0171-727 3560

Open Mon., Tues. & Fri., Sat. 10am-6pm, Wed. & Thurs. to 7pm, Sun. noon-5pm.

The modern British name to tote on your fashionable handbag. At this, his first independent outlet, you will find his beautiful bags, briefcases and luggage. Commissions are undertaken for luggage, furniture and leather flooring.

The Bridge

53 BEAUCHAMP PL, SW3, 0171-589 8055

Open Mon.-Sat. 10am-6pm, Wed. to 7pm.

For leather so soft you could melt in it, The Bridge offers the best of Florentine flair. The range includes suitcases and carriers, travel bags, briefcases, holdalls, Filofaxes and accessories, all designed by Fernando Biagioni and produced in Italy. Prices start from around £20 for a keyring.

Coach

8 SLOANE ST, SW1, 0171-235 1507

Open Mon.-Fri. 10am-6pm, Wed. to 7pm.

The American company Coach has been making high-quality, durable, classic handbags and small leather goods since 1941. Their handsome designs, hand-crafted in the finest leather might be on the expensive side—from £75 to £390—but the bags last forever and improve with age.

Connolly

32 GROSVENOR CRESCENT MEWS, SW1, 0171-235 3883

Open Mon.-Sat. 10am-6pm.

You can trust the people who make the sleek leather interiors for Rolls Royce, Aston

Martin and Jaguar to deliver something a little bit special when it comes to leather bags and accessories. The luggage has a smooth walnut frame, the credit card holders, agendas and road maps are encased in melt-in-your-mouth, buttersoft leather.

Goldpfeil

5 OLD BOND ST, W1, 0171-499 8611
Open Mon.-Sat. 9.30am-6pm.

Named after 'The Golden Arrow', one of the glamorous Pullman trains of the 1920s, Goldpfeil offers chic bags, classic cases and elegant accessories in a variety of shapes, sizes and colours. **Also at the Fine Leather Room in Harrods.**

Gucci

32-33 OLD BOND ST, W1, 0171-629 2716
Open Mon.-Fri. 9.30am-6pm, Sat. to 5.30pm.

Gucci bags inspire as many rip-offs as they do sales from their beautiful store. Their bamboo- handled shoulder bags spawned a bamboo-fest on the high street with nearly every major retailer following the inspiration of designer Tom Ford. However, despite or perhaps because of, the price tag, only a real Gucci carries the necessary panache. **Also at 17 Sloane St, SW1, 0171-235 6707.**

Hermès

155 NEW BOND ST, W1, 0171-499 8856
Open Mon.-Sat. 10am-6pm.

Grace Kelly sparked off the worldwide love affair with Hermès bags. The waiting list for a 'Kelly' bag is at least a couple of years. Those who do not have the patience can console themselves with the recently introduced range of shoes, belts and horse motif scarves. **Also at 179 Sloane St, SW1, 0171-823 1014.**

J & M Davidson

62 LEDBURY RD, W11, 0171-243 2089
Open Mon.-Sat. 10am-6pm.

Although John and Monique Davidson have extended their talents to include knitwear, outerwear and bed linen, the husband-and-wife team are best known for their luscious leathers. Their delicious, quality luggage, belts and wallets are classic yet contemporary and have been 'finishing off' the smartest outfits for the past 13 years. **Also at 60 Sloane Ave, SW3, 0171-584 1779.**

Loewe

130 NEW BOND ST, W1, 0171-493 3914
Open Mon.-Sat. 9.30am-6pm.

From luxurious suede suits to leather and suede luggage, the elegant products from Narcisco Roderiguez, formerly of Cerruti, include handbags, purses and briefcases, embellished with a logo that is one of the most prestigious among leatherware shops.

Louis Vuitton

17-18 NEW BOND ST, W1, 0171-399 4050
Open Mon.-Sat. 9.30am-6pm.

Marc Jacobs has taken over the helm at Louis Vuitton. The new global flagship store, the second largest in the world, opened in Spring 1998 amid a blaze of publicity. In addition to the luxurious trunks, suitcases, travelling bags, handbags, travel journals and accessories, the new London flagship store carries the long awaited Prêt-a-Porter and shoe collections by Marc Jacobs.

Mulberry

41-42 NEW BOND ST, W1, 0171-491 3900
Open Mon.-Sat. 10am-6pm, Thurs. to 7pm.

For that perfect English country look, this large shop is the place to find everything form satchels to chic little handbags, from laptop cases to belts, sturdy Filofaxes to nifty little manicure cases and key rings. The range on display on the first floor includes suitcases and overnight bags. **Also at 11-12 Gees Ct, St. Christopher's Pl, W1, 0171-493 2546; 185 Brompton Rd, SW1, 0171-225 0313.**

Osprey

11 ST. CHRISTOPHER'S PL, W1, 0171-935 2824
Open Mon.-Sat. 10am-6pm, Thurs. to 7pm.

The Osprey firm produces fashionable, smart hand-made leather handbags and accessories, including genuine looking Kelly bags you might not be able to find at Hermès. They have expanded their range to include luggage, gloves, handsewn suede and leather-bound folios, diaries and photo frames. **Also at 42 Beauchamp Pl, SW3, 0171-823 8338, and major department stores.**

Pickett Fine Leather

41 Burlington Arcade, W1, 0171-493 8939
Open Mon.-Sat. 9am-6pm.

One person makes a crowd in this cupboard of a shop, but what a tempting cupboard, packed with hundreds of wallets, handbags and briefcases in a variety of colours. **Also at 149 Sloane St, SW1, 0171-823 5638.**

Revelation

170 Piccadilly, W1, 0171-493 4138
Open Mon.-Sat. 9.30am-6pm, Sun. 11am-5pm.

A good choice of prices and labels from this leather and luggage specialist. For the young and street-conscious, there's Hervé Chapelier, Le Sac and Sequoia, while the more classically minded can choose from Mulberry and The Bridge, amongst others. **Also at 184a King's Rd, SW3, 0171-352 9351.**

W&H Gidden

15 Clifford St, W1, 0171-734 2788.
Open Mon.-Sat. 9am-6pm.

The smart wallets, purses, handbags, document holders and briefcases have the Gidden logo, which is famous for its equestrian products, also available within the store.

SPORTING GOODS

CLOTHING & EQUIPMENT

Lillywhites

Piccadilly Circus, SW1, 0171-930 3181
Open Mon.-Fri. 9.30am-7pm, Sat. 9.30am-6pm, Sun. 11am-5pm.

This six-storey department store has the widest choice of sportswear and equipment in town. There are departments devoted to baseball, hockey, squash, golf, tennis, badminton, darts, football—in fact, this is the place to find everything you need for any sport ranging from ski clothing and equipment to Wimbledon products. There is also an entire floor dedicated to footwear for over 30 sports and a comprehensive book and video section. It may be a little daunting finding your way around this rambling series of rooms and departments, but the staff are helpful.

Sam de Téran

151 Fulham Rd, SW7, 0171-584 0902
Open Mon.-Fri. 10am-6.30pm, Sat. to 7pm, Sun. noon to 6pm.

When you take your annual snow in Klosters and soak up the sun in Mustique, the only place to buy your sportswear is from Sam de Téran. Since she created her first swimwear collection in 1992, this designer has gone on to produce the most coveted tennis, gym, swim and ski-wear, appealing to the jet set. The clothes are displayed on a perspex table and glass shelving spanning the length of the shop, while the spacious dressing rooms are made ultra-luxurious by the inclusion of sofas.

Soccer Scene

30 Gt. Marlborough St, W1, 0171-439 0778
Open Mon.-Sat. 9.30am-7pm, Sun. 11am-5pm.

The best place to kit yourself out in the home and away strips of all the British teams, plus some foreign teams. They also carry other sporting gear. Sizes from infants to adults.

YHA Adventure Shop

14 Southampton St, WC2, 0171-836 8541
Open Mon.-Wed. 10am-6pm, Thurs., Fri. to 7pm, Sat. 9am-6.30-pm, Sun. 11am-5pm.

The arctic explorer, Sir Ranulph Fiennes, and mountaineer, Sir Chris Bonnington, use YHA cooking and camping equipment on their adventures, and the author Michael Palin drops by to stock up for his travels—which speaks volumes for the excellent stock and durability of the products. The staggering selection of parkas, knapsacks, sleeping bags and all the necessary equipment for camping and mountain climbing is further verification that this shop is serious about its business. Even in winter when the ski equipment takes up valuable floor space, there is a geodesic dome tent set up and the staff talk customers through the intricacies of its maintenance. Once part of the Youth Hostel Association, the company is now privately owned but there is a membership department (0171-836 1036), at the shop for people who wish to join and want to make bookings at a hostel. The company also runs the Campus Travel Agency (0171-836 3343). **Also at 174 Kensington High St, W8, 0171-938 2948; 52 Grosvenor Gdns, SW1, 0171-823 4739.**

FISHING

Farlow's

5 PALL MALL, SW1, 0171-839 2423
Open Mon.-Fri 9am-6pm, Sat. to 4pm.

Established in 1840 and sheltering under a banner at the corner of the Royal Opera Arcade, this neat row of three delightful shops is home to everything connected with angling. Farlow's, London's oldest fishing tackle shop, specialises in trout and salmon fishing but has departments for coarse, sea, big game and salt water enthusiasts. Among its stock of leading manufacturers' products, it carries the entire House of Hardy range of rods, reels and accessories (which is now the parent company). You'll also find multi-pocketed fishing bags, fishing glasses, books and all manner of fishing paraphenalia, plus windstopper sweaters, furlined hats and boots. The firm offer an invaluable fishing rod repair service and sells game guns and shooting accessories.

House of Hardy

61 PALL MALL, SW1, 0171-830 5515
Open Mon.-Fri. 9am-6pm, Sat. to 5pm.

A distinguished name in angling circles and a rival to Farlow's, Hardy's stocks all the best quality fishing requisites in a neatly arranged modern shop. These include cane rods, special salmon flies, its own brand of safety vest, Barbour garments, unusual carved walking sticks, videos on angling, hand warmers and sporting prints. It has a computerised service for booking services like salmon fishing on the Tweed.

HUNTING & SHOOTING

Asprey

165-169 NEW BOND ST, W1, 0171-493 6767
Open Mon.-Fri. 9.30am-5.30pm, Sat. 10am-5pm.

In 1990, this luxury store started producing hand-made English shotguns, bolt and double rifles, all bearing the distinguished Asprey hallmark. It also has a wide selection of quality second-hand guns from other famous gun-makers such as Holland & Holland, Purdey and Boss. Its handsome Gun Room has everything from cartridge holders to cufflinks with sporting motifs in addition to weatherproof clothing and well-tailored tweed and whipcord garments.

Boss & Co

13 DOVER ST, W1, 0171-493 1127
Open Mon.-Fri. 10am-5pm.

There is nothing grand about this Dickensian-looking shop, but this is the specialist maker of Boss single trigger guns, including the famous Boss Over and Under in 410 inch, 12, 20 and 28 gauge. The firm, now under the expert eye of managing director Tim Robertson, the great-grandson of the founder, still hand-makes 'Best Guns Only' to the original specifications which includes side-by-side Express Double rifles. All firearms are made to order, taking from eighteen months to three-and-a half years to complete.

Holland & Holland

31-33 BRUTON ST, W1, 0171-499 4411
Open Mon.-Sat. 9.30am-6pm.

Established in 1835, this famous gunmaker holds the Royal Warrant of the Duke of Edinburgh for rifles, and the Prince of Wales for shotguns, country clothing and accessories. In its Gun Room, customers have preliminary fittings for bespoke weapons or choose from antique, second-hand or imported makes. Their top range of 'Best London' guns includes 'Royal models' with the highest standard of hand craftsmanship and technical excellence. The shop has an extensive range of practical country shoes and accessories for men and women as well as books and gifts. Its art gallery has sporting and wildlife pictures and sculptures and its Sporting Agency can tailor-make sporting tours in almost any country.

James Purdey & Sons

57 SOUTH AUDLEY ST, W1, 0171-499 1801
Open Mon.-Fri. 9.30am-5.30pm, Sat. 10am-5pm.

Old Royal Warrants remain painted on the window frontage of this top people's gunmaker, obscuring the interior except for the mounted big game heads. Inside there is an established-for-decades feel, where guns and rifles, all hand-made, are works of art and collector's items. They are displayed and sold in the corner shop which has an adjoining, more modern shop on Mount Street for accessories and a range of first-class outdoor clothing and footwear ranging from woollen shawls for ladies to tweed hats for men.

William Evans

67A ST. JAMES'S ST, SW1, 0171-493 0415
Open Mon.-Fri. 9.30am-5.30pm, Sat. 10am-4pm (shop only on Sat., not gun room).

Smart apparel for the country, including leather-lined wellington boots and Barbour waxed coats, plus cartridge bags, belts and framed shooting caricatures. An order for a pair of guns, which can cost over £54,000, takes about two years to complete. Besides new Sidelock and Boxlock game guns and rifles, there is a wide range of secondhand guns, both William Evans' own brand and other well-known makes.

I-Spy

For James Bond wannabes or more serious surveillance equipment, spy shops are big business. The best in London include **Spymaster**, 3 Portman Sq, W1, 0171-486 3995 & 38 Park Lane, W1, 0171-493 6633; **Queensway Spy Shop**, 56A Queensway, W2, 0171-221 9029; **Lorraine Electronics Surveillance**, 59 South Audley St, W1, 0171-493 4007 and **The Counter Spy Shop**, 62 South Audley St, W1, 0171-408 0287. Check them out for everything from concealed TV cameras and microphones to bugging and de-bugging devices.

RIDING

Swaine Adeney

54 ST. JAMES'S ST, SW1, 0171-409 7277
Open Mon.-Sat. 10am-6pm.

A new address for this firm whose illustrious history dates back to 1750 when Captain John Ross got the initial carriage whip business off the ground. It was sold to James Swaine and his son and son-in-law 48 years later and has become one of the brand leaders in the whips, canes and leather goods world. Its fashions for men have classic style and the store is well-stocked with outdoor clothing such as Klondike waxed jackets with leather trim. Swaine Adeney holds three Royal Warrants including umbrella makers to the Queen Mother. The factory shop at **Nursery Rd, Saffron Waldon, Gt. Chesterford, Essex, 01799 530521**, sells women's clothes.

W&H Gidden

15D CLIFFORD ST, W1—0171-734 2788
Open Mon.-Fri. 9am-6pm, Sat. 10am-5pm.

In business since 1806 and holder of the Queen's Royal Warrant for saddlery, this is the only shop in London entirely devoted to the requirements of the rider. Its three well-stocked floors attract both novices and the world's leading competitors. A video screen on the ground floor might recall the highlights of the Badminton horse trials while customers take their pick from merchandise which includes sweatshirts and scarves with horsey motifs. Mail order catalogue available.

SAILING

Arthur Beale

194 SHAFTESBURY AVE, WC2, 0171-836 9034
Open Mon.-Fri. 9am-6pm, Sat. 9.30am-1pm.

This shop's history goes back some 400 years to a rope chandler's business. It stocks marine hardware, fixtures and fittings and has some bright weatherproof clothing and boots. Because of its location, in fashionable Covent Garden, its wares are often bought to add a twist to shop window displays, fashion photographic shoots and artistic sculptures as well as providing necessary support for barrier ropes at restaurants and nightclubs.

Captain O M Watts

5-7 DOVER ST, W1, 0171-493 4633
Open Mon.-Fri. 9am-6pm, Sat. to 5pm.

Walk into this specialist sailing suppliers and you can almost smell the sea. They stock everything for the dinghy and keelboat sailor, including charts and yachting clothing labels like Henri Lloyd and Musto. The knowledgable staff offer expert advice when needed.

SKIING & MOUNTAINEERING

Black's

176 KENSINGTON HIGH ST, W8, 0171-938 1911
Open Mon.-Wed. 10am-6pm, Thurs. to 7pm, Sat. 9.30am-6pm, Sun. noon-6pm.

In winter, colourful ski-wear and a wide range of equipment are in abundance; in summer, camping and climbing gear takes its place. However, there is always a choice of country clothes and walking boots on offer. **Also at 10 Holborn, EC1, 0171-404 5681; 53 Rathbone Pl, W1, 0171-636 6645.**

Ellis Brigham Mountain Sports

30-32 SOUTHAMPTON ST, WC2, 0171-240 9577
Open Mon.-Wed., Fri. 10am-7pm, Thurs. to 7.30pm, Sat. 9.30am-6.30pm, Sun. 11.30am-5.30pm.

You know things are serious when even the door handles are ski-shaped! This specialist shop sells snowboards along with Raichle and Solomon ski boots and also has a good choice of back-up products for winter and summer sports.

Snow & Rock

188 KENSINGTON HIGH ST, W8, 0171-937 0872
Open Mon.-Sat. 10am-6pm, Thurs. to 7pm, Sat. 9am-6pm, Sun. 11am-5pm.

The name says it all succinctly and this large shop stocks skiwear and trekking gear in a good range of styles at reasonable prices. It has a climbing wall for customers to try out boots on; in summer, there's a good choice of tents and camping equipment. The range of essentials is wide, from thermal silk underwear to hand-and-finger exercise gadgets.

STATIONERY & PENS

Alastair Lockhart

97 WALTON ST, SW3, 0171-581 8289
Open Mon.-Fri. 10am-6pm, Sat. to 5pm.

As you'd expect from any establishment in this delightful street, Alastair Lockhart specialises in some of the most beautiful writing papers which are almost too good to write on. The tiny shops stocks Crane's 100 percent cotton paper in a host of colours and takes orders for engraving and printing.

Blade Rubber Stamps

2 NEAL'S YARD, WC2, 0171-379 7391
Open Mon.-Sat. 10.30am-6pm, Sun. 11.30am-5pm.

Design your own stationery or get into stamp design art at this little shop which stocks hundreds of rubber stamps and pads in a variety of designs. Children's kits are also available.

Bureau

10 GT NEWPORT ST, WC2, 0171-379 7898
Open Mon.-Fri. 10am-7.45pm, Sat. to 7pm, Sun. 1pm-6pm.

A rainbow of colours greets you as you walk into this modern stationery shop which stocks pens, papers, notebooks and accessories to brighten up the dullest office. No decorative process is left unexplored, with notepaper taking cover in fake leopard skin, dalmation hide, acid-bright prints and glitter.

Filofax

69 NEAL ST, WC2, 0171-836 1977
Open Mon.-Fri. 9.30am-6pm, Sat. 10.30am-6.30pm.

The whole range of Filofax and Lefax products are on display as well as many top name pens. **Also at 21 Conduit St, W1, 0171-499 0457.**

Just Fax

43 BROADWICK ST, W1, 0171-734 5034
Open Mon.-Fri. 9am-6pm, Sat. 10am-5.30pm.

All the big names in loose-leaf diary or organisers are neatly arranged in this small shop which also sells pens and pencils from prestige companies.

Paperchase

213 TOTTENHAM COURT RD, W1, 0171-580 8496
Open Mon.-Sat. 9.30am-6.30pm, Thurs. to 7.30pm, Sun. 11am-5pm.

One of the best stationery stores in town. Paperchase is always packed with bright, exciting stationery-based products for the office and home, and the flagship store here is filled with cards, wrapping paper, pens and pencils, photograph albums and frames, gift ideas and a wide selection of storage boxes. This branch has a good selection of art materials and, in season, a Christmas speciality room (September to January) with stylish decorations. **Branches throughout London.**

Papyrus

48 FULHAM RD, SW3, 0171-584 8022
Open Mon.-Sat. 9.30am-6pm.

This shop has two sides to its services. In true cottage-industry style, a team of craftsmen carry out their own designs, book-binding and marbling to produce photo albums and all manner of desk accessories, including leather book jackets. The second arm is a design and print business, specialising in letterheads, invitations and personalised stationery.

Penfriend

BUSH HOUSE, STRAND, WC2, 0171-836 9809
Open Mon.-Fri. 9.30am-5.30pm.

You could describe this shop as a little museum devoted to the craft of writing utensils and curios like Georgian skirt-lifters, lorgnettes and early pencil sharpeners. The shop has a genial proprietor, Peter Woolf, who is invariably on hand when visitors come to browse in the shop located in an off-beat arcade that includes the BBC World Service Shop. Mr Woolfe sells fully restored vintage pens such as Mentmore, Conway Stewart, Parker and Swan, which he often supplies for films and photographic shoots. The shop also includes a huge range of modern pens and the workshop will repair pens. **Also at 34 Burlington Arcade, W1, 0171-499 6337.**

Scribbler

39 NEAL ST, WC2, 0171-240 6221
Open Mon.-Sat 10am-8pm, Sun. 12.30pm-6pm.

For a wide choice of greetings cards, brightly coloured stationery and related products, including T-shirts, this popular corner shop has a varied and fun range. **Also at 173 Kensington High St, W8, 0171-938 1861.**

Smythson

44 NEW BOND ST, W1, 0171-629 8558
Open Mon.-Fri. 9.15am-5.30pm, Sat. 10am-5.30pm.

As stationers to the Queen, Smythson wear the paper products crown. The store offers some of the most beautiful diaries, notebooks, pocket books, organisers and quality papers to be found anywhere in London. There is hand-bordered, water-marked stationery at £17 for 25 sheets and matching envelopes, wine connoisseur's notebooks, handsome atlases and the smartest leather-bound photograph albums. Among the elegant stock for sale are novelties such as American edition diaries. Some of the more extravagant items include a deluxe leather picnic case for two, with china plates and cups at approximately £995. If you want to create a good impression, Smythson offer a hand engraving and printing service. **Also at 35 Sloane St, SW1, 0171-730 5520.**

The Stationery Department

181 NEW KING'S RD, SW6, 0171-384 1871
Open Mon.-Sat. 10am-6pm.

For an excellent choice of high-quality writing paper and envelopes in a colour palette that spans the spectrum, plus printing of invitations.

TOBACCONISTS

Alfred Dunhill

48 JERMYN ST, SW1, 0171-290 8600
Open Mon.-Fri. 9.30am-6pm, Sat. 10am-6pm.

On the first floor of this men's fashion department store is a large, specially set aside area which is a walk-in humidor room with an extensive choice of cigars from Cuba and the Dominican islands. Sitting pride of place is a magnificient humidor specially commissioned from David Linley. Regular customers store their cigars in 306 lockers, all original cedar cabinets dating to the store's origins as a tobacconist shop founded by Alfred Dunhill in 1907. Aromatic loose tobacco is sold, including Alfred's own and Blenders' Own. Customers can also enjoy a complimentary whisky in this calm oasis.

Astley's

16 PICCADILLY ARCADE, SW1, 0171-499 9950
Open Mon.-Sat. 10am-6pm.

Moving to these premises from its Jermyn Street location has meant that the firm, established in 1862, no longer stocks tobacco. However, it is still one of the best places to visit for an extensive choice choice of own-brand pipes, including its specialities, the fine Briar and Meerschaum ranges. The shop also stocks a few pipe accessories.

Benson & Hedges

13 OLD BOND ST, W1, 0171-493 1825
Open Mon.-Fri. 9am-5.30pm, Sat. 10am-5pm.

The cool, clean-cut, efficient look of the shop belies its historic tradition of selling tobacco products, pipes and cigarettes since 1870. There is also a range of small leather gifts.

Davidoff

35 St. James's St, SW1, 0171-930 3079
Open Mon.-Fri. 9am-5.45pm, Sat. 9.30am-5.45pm.

A showy, spacious store with one of the best selections of Havana cigars in town. Davidoff has its own humidor and sells all of the smoking requisites like cognac, lighters and top-quality accessories.

Desmond Sauter

106 Mount St, W1, 0171-499 4866
Open Mon.-Fri. 9am-6pm, Sat. to 4.30pm.

The antique smoking memorabilia is one of the attractions in this old square-shaped shop with its glass walk-in humidor standing priding of place among the wooden fixtures. They specialise in Cuban cigars and also sell hall-marked silver boxes and decorative pipes.

G Smith and Sons

74 Charing Cross Rd, WC2, 0171-836 7422
Open Mon.-Fri. 9am-6pm, Sat. 9.30am-5.30pm.

A specialist in hand-blended snuff, which is available in some 50 aromatic varieties, this small shop stocks its own brand of tobacco as well as antique snuffboxes and little spoons for taking snuff.

Inderwicks

45 Carnaby St, W1, 0171-734 6574
Open Mon.-Sat 10.30am-6.45pm.

Incongruous among the off-beat fashion shops on the street, this little shop has an amazing array of pipes for sale. Subtle differences such as stem length and size are taken into account by serious smokers and Inderwicks delight in catering to them with their made-to-measure pipes. They also sell lighters, snuff boxes and a variety of tobaccos.

James J Fox & Robert Lewis

19 St. James's St, SW1, 0171-493 9009
Open Mon.-Sat. 9am-5.30pm.

The sign says James J Fox but this little shop is home to two well-known cigar merchants. It is devoted to cigars made with care and attention to detail from all over the world. James Fox also runs the tobacco department at Harrods and Selfridges.

Shervington

337-338 High Holborn, WC1, 0171-405 2929
Open Mon.-Fri. 9am-6pm.

Established in 1864, this shop is set in a half-timbered building which dates back to 1845. Not surprisingly, there is a specialist atmosphere to savour while perusing the full range of pipes, tobaccos and smoking products.

TOYS, GAMES & BOOKS

Benjamin Pollock's Toy Shop

44 The Market, Covent Garden, WC2, 0171-379 7866
Open Mon.-Sat. 10.30am-6pm, Sun. noon-5pm.

Model theatres and intricate cardboard cut-outs of old-fashioned theatres with all the accoutrements are the delightful wares at this shop, which has puppets, traditional toys and teddy bears.

Daisy & Tom

181 King's Rd, SW3, 0171-352 5000
Open Mon.-Sat. 10am-6pm, Wed. to 7pm, Sun. noon-6pm.

Offering everything for children under one roof. The fairground carousel is one of the attractions, along with the bright and cheerful soda bar. There is also a children's hairdressing salon, galleried book department and the best in toys, games, clothes and shoes. Regular events, activities, competitions and author visits take place within this busy and popular store.

The Disney Store

140-141 Regent St, W1, 0171-287 6558
Open Mon.-Sat. 10am-8pm, Sun. noon-6pm.

Mickey Mouse and all the other Walt Disney characters are represented on mugs, toys, games and various products throughout the store where adults and children can be seen singing along with the characters on the multi-screen video. There are two floors, with the lower level filled with stuffed toys and its own travel centre which arranges trips to the various Disneyland destinations.

Early Learning Centre

36 KING'S RD, SW3, 0171-581 5764

Open Mon.-Sat. 9am-6pm, Wed. to 7pm, Sun. 11am-5pm.

Always very busy, this welcoming shop geared to children, has a wide selection of games, books, puzzles and other cheerful products aimed to make learning fun. There is a special area where kids are usually found erecting giant building blocks or trying their hand at the latest game. **Also at 225 Kensington High St, W8, 0171-937 0419, and other branches.**

Hamleys

188 REGENT ST, W1, 0171-734 3161

Open Mon., Tues., Wed. 10am-7pm, Thurs. & Fri. to 8pm, Sun. noon-6pm.

A huge, five-storey department store entirely devoted to toys and games for children. It's always heaving with children looking at toys ranging from the cheap and cheerful pocket money varieties to top-of-the-range computer games. Adults are just as likely as children to find entertaining toys, but beware, prices can be higher than in other toy shops.

Just Games

71 BREWER ST, W1, 0171-734 6124

Open Mon.-Sat. 10am-6pm, Thurs. to 7pm.

From the obscure to the obvious, the trivial to the important games like chess and Mah Jong, this shop stocks everything that a board game enthusiast could want, including books on the subject.

The Kite Store

48 NEAL ST, WC2, 0171-836 1666

Open Mon.-Wed. & Fri. 10am-6pm, Thurs. to 7pm, Sat. 10.30am-6pm.

The cheerful window display of brightly coloured kites says it all. Inside there are high-powered designer kites in every shape imaginable.

London Dolls House Co.

29 COVENT GARDEN MARKET, WC2, 0171-240 8681

Open Mon-Sat 10am-7pm, Sun. noon-5pm.

A small shop with houses from Victorian and Georgian up to more modern versions, plus kits, accessories and furniture, mostly aimed at children rather than specialist collectors.

The Singing Tree

69 NEW KING'S RD, SW6, 0171-736 4527

Open Mon.-Sat. 10am-5.30pm.

Everything you could possibly want for a dolls' house is available here plus houses in either kit form or made up. Much of the furniture, perfectly scaled-down and spanning all kinds of eras and styles, is made by quality craftsmen so these are perfect replicas. But be warned, prices are justifiably high. This fascinating shop is as much, if not more, for adult collectors and enthusiasts as it is for children.

Tridias

25 BUTE ST, SW1, 0171-684 2330

Open Mon.-Fri. 9.30am-6pm, Sat. 10am-6pm.

Small shop stuffed full of excellent toys spanning the range from science to dressing up. Well-made toys, many in wood, please all ages and they have good party bag and stocking fillers. Mail order catalogue. **Also at 6 Lichfield Terrace, Richmond, Surrey, 0181-948 3459.**

Warner Brothers Studio Store

178-182 REGENT ST, W1, 0171-434 3334

Open Mon.-Wed. & Fri. 10am-7pm, Thurs. & Sat. to 8pm, Sun. noon-6pm.

Kid's toys, stuffed animals and videos take up the first floor. There are hands-on activities to try, incuding computer colouring-by-numbers, and a video screen showing cartoons or action scenes from shows like the Adventures of New Superman. Naturally the company's animated characters are emblazoned on mugs, watches and all manner of accessories. There is a large animation art gallery for adults, selling original hand-painted drawings on celluloid, some signed by the company's famous cartoonists, and ranging in price from about £150 to £1,000.

WHERE TO ENTERTAIN CHILDREN

The Little Angel Marionette Theatre

14 DAGMAR PASSAGE, CROSS ST, N1, 0171-226 1787

The Ugly Duckling, Sleeping Beauty, Christmas opera and much more, all expressed with delightful marionettes have been captivating children for years at this tucked-away theatre in Islington.

Polka Theatre for Children

240 THE BROADWAY, WIMBLEDON, SW19, 0181-543 4888

Well worth making the trek to Wimbledon for the wonderful performances at the Polka Theatre. Arrive early and enjoy a meal in the railway restaurant; children like sitting in the brightly coloured carriages after making their choice from a menu featuring favourites such as baked potatoes, toasted sandwiches, fish fingers and freshly baked cakes. If it's sunny, the children can run about in the garden, complete with climbing frames and a large wooden play house.

Unicorn Theatre for Children

6-7 GT. NEWPORT ST, WC2, 0171-836 3334

Year-round professional entertainments for children from old favourites like Pinocchio to commissioned new works. Children's parties catered for.

Arts & Leisure

CONTENTS

ART GALLERIES

CONTEMPORARY

The Bond Street area has long been acknowledged as the heart of the established art scene, but in recent years it is less of an indicator of a gallery's status. Two alternative groups of galleries are now well established to the west and to the east of central London, often showing slightly more 'advanced' art, with mostly the real avant-garde being shown in quite isolated galleries in the East End. Check on all opening times before making a visit if it is out of the way as some galleries are only open when an exhibition is on show.

Two free publications—***Galleries*** and ***New Exhibitions of Contemporary Art***—are available from most major galleries.

Alan Cristea

31 CORK ST, W1, 0171-439 1866
Open Mon-Fri 10am-5.30pm, Sat 10am-1pm. U: Piccadilly Circus.

When Alan Cristea took over the premises of Waddington Graphics in 1995, he continued the role of the gallery as the major print venue in Cork Street. Here are prime examples of contemporary and master prints from artists like Picasso and Matisse, alongside changing exhibitions of recent printed editions by artists such as Jim Dine, Antoni Tapies and Mick Moon and new names like Lisa Milroy.

Annely Juda Fine Art

23 DERING ST, W1, 0171-629 7578
Open Mon-Fri 10am-6pm, Sat 10am-1pm. U: Oxford Circus.

Founded in 1960 by Annely Juda, this gallery is known world-wide for its exhibitions of Constructivism, Dada, Russian Avant-Garden, Bauhaus and de Stijl. Some of the best international contemporary artists like Ackling, Edwina Leapman, Nash, Anthony Caro and Christo now join such classics as Kandinsky, Mondrian, Rodchenko, Schwitters and Chillida.

Anthony d'Offay Gallery

20 DERING ST, W1, 0171-499 4100
Open Mon-Fri 10am-5.30pm, Sat 10am-1pm. U: Oxford Circus.

Anthony d'Offay started his gallery in the tiniest of spaces, developing spectacularly into one of the most important international venues when, in 1980, a Joseph Beuys installation opened the first of several museum-like galleries. A real galaxy of celebrated artists, including Andre, Gilbert & George, de Kooning, Morley, Richter, Turrell, Warhol and Long, demonstrate the breadth of d'Offay's interests. The catalogues should not be missed.

Art Space Gallery

84 ST. PETER'S ST, N1, 0171-359 7002
Open Tues-Sat 11am-7pm. U: Angel.

Michael Richardson's gallery in Islington is a delight, showing new names like Andrea McLean and Nigel Massey and top contemporary artists like Anthony Whishaw and George Rowlett, with prices from £500 to £40,000.

Association of Photographers

9-10 DOMINGO ST, EC1, 0171-608 1445
Open Mon-Fri 9.30am-6pm, Sat noon-4pm. U: Barbican/Old St.

The gallery of the Association of Photographers shows work from professional photographers in a series of themed exhibition, which might cover 'The Dog', or a geographical area such as East and South Asia.

BCA Boukamel Gallery

9 CORK ST, W1, 0171-734 6444
Open Mon-Fri 10am-6pm, Sat to 2pm. U: Piccadilly Circus.

The fact that this was originally a German gallery is reflected in the work it shows: Hídicke, Fetting, Eugene Leroy and other major contemporary painters introduced to London from Raab Berlin. The established department of photographic art has a distinct international feel with works by Sherman, Serrano, Lagerfeld and Skogland and Rainer Fetting.

Beardsmore Gallery

22 PRINCE OF WALES RD, NW5, 0171-485 0923
Open Tues-Fri 10am-6pm, Sat noon-6pm, or by appointment. U: Kentish Town.

Small, excellent gallery of architect Brian Beardsmore and his wife in part of their architectural offices. Seek this gallery out; the Beardsmores' selection is highly regarded.

They have about 20 regular artists in stock with changing one-man and group exhibitions of paintings, works on paper, ceramics and sculpture from artists like Royal Academician Lisa Wright, Stathis Logoudakis, Michael Druks, and Henry Moore Fellow, sculptor Oliver Barratt.

Bernard Jacobson Gallery

14A CLIFFORD ST, W1, 0171-495 8575
Open Mon-Fri 10am-6pm, Sat 10am-1pm.
U: Oxford Circus.

The sign above the door "Modern English Masters" is no false declaration. The results of Bernard Jacobson's decades of dealing in this area are on the walls, from Bomberg, Abrahams, Rauschenberg, Nicholson and Weight, to the new additions of Glynn Williams and Maggi Hambling. Comprehensive gallery publications sometimes include conversations with the artists and provide a personal insight into the work.

Blains

BRUTON ST, W1, 0171-495 5050
Open Mon-Fri 10am-6pm, Sat to 5pm.
U: Bond St.

Young dealers Harry Blain and Charles Phillips established themselves five years ago, then launched an exciting gallery at the end of December 1997 in Mayfair's many-galleried Bruton Street. At 5,000 square ft, this, the largest privately owned commercial gallery in the West End, became an instant draw. They cater to a young, wealthy, distinctly non-establishment clientele with artists like Degas, Giacometti, Henry Moore, Matisse and Warhol.

Curwen Gallery

4 WINDMILL ST, W1, 0171-636 1459
Open Mon-Fri 10am-6pm, Sat 11am-5pm.
U: Goodge St.

Set up to act as a showcase for the prints made at the Curwen Studio, the gallery now promotes artists working in all media. British masters such as Ben Nicholson, William Scott and Henry Moore are still dealt with but the overall emphasis in the monthly exhibitions is the introduction of new work, including Paul Neagu and Martin McGinn. This said, the company is still actively involved in the publishing of limited edition prints.

England & Co

14 NEEDHAM RD, W11, 0171-221 0417
Open Tues-Sat 11am-6pm. U: Notting Hill Gate.

Australian Jane England specialises in retrospective exhibitions of overlooked British artists of the 1940s, '50s and '60s. Ralph Rumney, William Green, Robert Hardy and Paule Vézelay are among those rediscovered thanks to her efforts. As well as producing these scholarly reassessments she organises annual thematic shows. The gallery expands to nearby Westbourne Grove at the end of 1998; the telephone number remains the same.

Flowers East

199-205 & 282 RICHMOND RD, E8, 0181-985 3333.
Open Tues-Sun 10am-6pm. U: Dalston/Kingsland.

Angela Flowers and her son, Matthew, made a brave move to the East End, into what is now a complex of spaces, which has enabled the showing of large-scale sculpture and painting, plus the initiation of a separate graphics/print department. The enormous warehouse space means there is always plenty of work on show, from such varied artists as Patrick Hughes, John Loker, Nicola Hick, Trevor Sutton, and Kevin Sinott.

Frith Street Gallery

60 FRITH ST, W1, 0171-494 1550
Open Tues-Fri 10am-6pm, Sat 11am-4pm.
U: Leicester Sq.

Jane Hamlyn has united two houses to create a haven of calm in the middle of bustling Soho. The spaces are interconnected on several levels and the spare style of the architecture is reflected in the careful selection of contemporary art from the most innovative artists of the international scene.

Gimpel Fils

30 DAVIES ST, W1, 0171-493 2488
Open Mon-Fri 10am-5.30pm, Sat 10am-1pm.
U: Bond St.

The Gimpel family has built on their long association with established artists but are not trapped by their 50 years' history. In fact they are one of the few galleries to take on 'difficult' new art in the West End giving many young artists a chance alongside top established international names.

Hamiltons

13 CARLOS PL, W1, 0171-499 9493.
Open Tues-Sat 10am-6pm. U: Bond St.

A treasure trove of a photographic gallery. On entering, the line of framed work stretching the length of the gallery may appear daunting. However for the persevering photo fan there are some real classics here, including Richard Avedon, David Bailey, Helmut Newton, Imre Kinzki and Ansel Adams. Exhibitions of new work from contemporaries such as Linda McCartney, Irving Penn and Herb Ritts are mounted with panache.

Jason & Rhodes Gallery

4 NEW BURLINGTON PL, W1, 0171-434 1768
Open Mon-Fri 10am-6pm, Sat 10.30am-1pm. U: Oxford Circus.

This is an understated gallery with a very English feel about it. It is committed to searching out new art but within a traditional arena. They have a wide scope with an adventurous feel and show photographs, videos and paintings from artists like Robert Davies and Paul Storey.

Jay Jopling/White Cube

2ND FLOOR, 44 DUKE ST, ST. JAMES'S, SW1, 0171-930 5373
Open Fri & Sat 10am-6pm; other times by appointment. U: Green Park.

For the 'hottest' work in town, this is the place to go. Discreetly hidden in a small room in St. James's, the new stars of the British art world show their latest works. Mona Hartoum, Damien Hirst, Tracey Emin, Gary Hume, Carroll Dunham and Sam Taylor-Wood are just some of those exhibited in the (necessarily) one-person shows.

London's Crafts Markets

There are plenty of open-air craft markets in London—try the stalls in the middle of **Covent Garden** for interesting handmade items by young designers, the daily market at the church of **St. Martin-in-the-Fields** and on Fridays and Saturdays the collection of stalls at **St. James's Church**, Piccadilly. On Sunday the **Brixton Market** offers bric-a-brac; and **Greenwich** is also a very good hunting ground at weekends.

Jill George Gallery

38 LEXINGTON ST, W1, 0171-439 7343
Open Mon-Fri 10am-6pm, Thurs to 8pm, Sat 11am-5pm. U: Tottenham Court Rd.

A lively spot hinting at its one-time genesis as a graphics and print gallery. Limited edition and monoprints are usually on show downstairs, paintings upstairs. Jill George who has been established over 11 years here, has a policy of showing younger artists and believes in working with architects and interior designers often on commissions. Her 'stable' of 20 or so regular artists like Scottish figure painter, David Hosie, and Alison Lambert, are joined in different shows by new artists, and she occasionally has reciprocal exhibitions like one with three Dublin-based artists.

Lisson Gallery

BELL ST & 67 LISSON ST, NW1, 0171-724 2739
Open Mon-Fri 10am-6pm, Sat to 5pm. U: Edgware Rd.

Geographically isolated but right at the centre of the art world, Lisson promotes artists in Britain and abroad. Nicholas Logsdail has been based in the Bell Street area for over 30 years but it is in this present purpose-built gallery that museum-like shows from artists such as Dan Graham, Anish Kapoor, Tony Cragg and Juan Munoz have made the gallery's reputation unassailable. The architect Tony Fretton designed both the gallery and its addition, and the dextrous use of space makes a visit worthwhile. As an example of architecture designed for art it is an unusual, if not unique, opportunity in London.

Marlborough Fine Art

6 ALBERMARLE ST, W1, 0171-629 5161
Open Mon-Fri 10am-5.30pm, Sat to 12.30pm. U: Green Park.

This is one of the most important galleries for twentieth-century works. Behind the scenes the estates of Francis Bacon, Barbara Hepworth, Kurt Schwitters and Graham Sutherland are dealt with, while in the gallery careful exhibitions of paintings and sculpture from gallery artists such as R B Kitaj, Paul Rego, Steven Campbell, Christopher Le Brun and Frank Auerbach are usually presented as one-person shows. The gallery also has a department of contemporary graphics.

Paton Gallery

FIRST FLOOR ABOVE ANGELA FOWERS GALLERY, 282 RICHMOND RD, E8, 0181-986 3409
Open Tues-Sat 11am-6pm, Sun noon-6pm. U: Dalston/Kingsland.

One of the few platforms for emerging talent from the post-graduate art schools in London. Graham Paton moved to this gallery complex from Covent Garden but continues his interest in new painting with vigour. Both abstract and figurative works from the crème-de-la-crème of the Royal College of Art, Royal Academy, Slade and Chelsea Schools of Art are not only shown but also sold to major collections world-wide.

The Photographer's Gallery

5 & 8 GREAT NEWPORT ST, WC2, 0171-831 1772
Open Mon-Sat 11am-6pm. U: Leicester Square.

This was the first independent gallery in Britain devoted to photography, and since its foundation in 1971 by Sue Davies OBE, it has maintained its reputation as the venue for contemporary photographic work. It has always shown innovative work alongside classic images, playing a major role in establishing such key names as Irving Penn, Andre Kertesz and Lartigue. Housed in two buildings, it holds exhibitions in several gallery spaces, the largest of which is in Number 8 Newport Street, along with the excellent bookshop. The print sales room and library are in Number 5 over another extensive showing area.

Rebecca Hossack Gallery

35 WINDMILL ST, W1, 0171-436 4899
Open Mon-Sat 10am-6pm. U: Goodge St.

This gallery has two areas of specialisation, showing a selection of contemporary British art and art from a non-European tradition from names like Alisdair Wallace, Jan Williams and Abigail McLellan. Several specialised shows each year feature work by Australian Aboriginal artists and contemporary African artists.

Redfern Gallery

20 CORK ST, W1, 0171-734 0578
Open Mon-Fri 10am-5.30pm, Sat to 1pm. U: Piccadilly Circus.

From its beginning in 1936, Redfern's gave one-man exhibitions to young painters, printmakers and sculptors, and the inclusion of young artists in mixed shows and as published print editions has never changed. Famous for its stock of works by well-known artists, ranging from paintings by Gauguin, van Gogh, Matisse and Monet to Hockney, Bacon and Tapies, and for artists established in the 1950s and '60s, it remains true to the tradition of Proctor, Tindle and Neiland.

Special Photographers Company

21 KENSINGTON PARK RD, W11, 0171-221 3489
Open Mon-Fri 10am-6pm, Fri to 5.30pm, Sat 11am-5pm. U: Ladbroke Grove.

This is a fine art photography gallery and agency which introduces unknown and internationally recognised photographers, such as Herman Leonard, Edward Sheriff Curtis, Joyce Tennison, Holly Warburton and Laura Wilson, in both group and one-person shows. There is always plenty to see on the two floors of this small gallery and it is all very well presented.

Timothy Taylor Gallery

1 BRUTON PL, W1, 0171-409 3344
Open Mon-Fri 10am-6pm, Sat 11am-2pm. U: Bond St.

An exciting, relatively new gallery in a small but dramatic space just off Bruton Street finds Timothy Taylor representing major artists like Schnabel, Miquel Barcel and Jonathan Lasker.

Victoria Miro Gallery

21 CORK ST, W1, 0171-734 5082
Open Mon-Fri 10am-5.30pm, Sat 11am-1pm. U: Piccadilly Circus.

Victoria Miro picks her artists with care and presents precise exhibitions in her equally precise space, re-designed by Claudio Silberstrin in 1990. The mood of the gallery suits works by Alan Charlton, Ian Hamilton Finlay and Richard Tuttle, although some may find the austerity a little severe.

Waddington Galleries

11/12 & 34 CORK ST, W1, 0171-437 8611
Open Mon-Fri 10am-5.30pm, Sat 10am-1pm. U: Piccadilly Circus.

Cork Street is truly Leslie Waddington's territory, with separate galleries all within a few yards of each other. At the newly renovated Corner Gallery (no. 34), 'Modern British' artists like Peter Black and Patrick Heron, John Piper, Stanley Spencer, Graham Sutherland, Ben Nicholson and Henry Moore are shown. Other established masters of 20th century art, British and international contemporary artists—names like Mondrian, Carl Andre, Piet Mondrian, Picasso, Dubuffet, de Kooning, Matisse, Picabia and Gris—are in stock at 11 and 12 Cork Street; the gallery is now the world-wide representative of the estate of Josef Albers.

Zelda Cheatle Gallery

99 Mount St, WI, 0171-408 4448
Open Mon by appointment, Tues-Fri 10am-6pm, Sat 11am-4.30pm. U: Bond St.

An impressive variety of photographic work in a gem of a gallery. It was started in 1989 (the year photography was 150 years old) by Zelda Cheatle, whose previous experience running the Print Room at the Photographers Gallery shows in the sure choice of stock. The range from Magnum professionals like Sebastiao Salgado to contemporary art photographers such as Hannah Collins is not only comprehensive but purposeful in its selection of examples.

EIGHTEENTH-, NINETEENTH- & TWENTIETH-CENTURY ART

As London's dealers in eighteenth- and nineteenth-century art are amongst the best in the world, many of them exhibit at the international fairs and may be closed during these times. So please check in advance.

Agnew's

43 Old Bond St, W0171-629 6176
Open Mon-Fri 9.30am-5pm, Thurs to 6.30pm. U: Green Park.

Established in 1867 and situated in a sumptuous 1870s building, this family firm is the thoroughbred of painting and print dealers. Behind a modest exterior lies a luscious array of paintings from the English eighteenth and nineteenth centuries, prints from artists of the French tradition—Vuillard, Redon, Bonnard, Picasso, Lautrec—alongside, interestingly, sculpture from British contemporary artists including Dame Elisabeth Frink.

Chris Beetles

8 & 10 Ryder St, SW1, 0171-839 7551
Open Mon-Sat 10am-5.30pm. U: Green Park.

Chris Beetles deals mainly in Victorian and contemporary watercolours and illustrations. The great variety of the stock means there is always a wide range of work on view from the likes of Arthur Rackham, Albert Goodwin and Helen Allingham. Each Christmas he issues a catalogue describing his voluminous stock, featuring more than 100 artists from 1780 to the present day.

The Fine Art Society

148 New Bond St, W1, 0171-629 5116
Open Mon-Fri 9.30am-5.30pm, Sat 10am-1pm. U: Piccadilly Circus.

The Fine Art Society is one of the most distinguished in London. Founded in 1876, it quickly established a rapport with such nineteenth-century luminaries as Ruskin, Whistler and Millais. This is still the area it excels in, and in more recent years it has pioneered the revival of interest in late nineteenth- and early twentieth-century British painting, most particularly the (original) Glasgow boys—Guthrie, Lavery, Melville and Crawhall—as well as the founder members of the New English Art Club.

Frost & Reed

2 King St, St. James's, SW1, 0171-839 4645
Open Mon-Fri 9am-5.30pm. U: Green Park.

Although Frost & Reed can trace its history back through 186 years of fine art dealing, don't get the idea that this is a dusty archive. The gallery, which is in a large space in St. James's, has six shows a year of really good eighteenth-, nineteenth- and twentieth-century sporting pictures, including Stubbs and Munnings, as well as important Impressionist and Post-Impressionist watercolours and drawings. The gallery also has a policy of showing living artists.

The Lefevre Gallery

30 Bruton St, W1, 0171-493 2107
Open Mon-Fri 10am-5pm. U: Bond St.

The choicest examples of French Impressionist paintings are shown in this long-established family business. Once in a while they also feature work outside that tradition, but only of twentieth-century greats like

Picasso or Georgia O'Keefe. The selection of catalogues, spanning many past years, is impressive in displaying the works that have gone through the gallery.

The Maas Gallery

15A CLIFFORD ST, W1, 0171-734 2302
Open Mon-Fri 10am-5.30pm. U: Piccadilly Circus.

On entering the gallery it feels as if you are in someone's sitting room—the fire is lit on cold days and the scale of the rooms is domestic. The Maas Gallery specialises in Victorian and Pre-Raphaelite drawings, paintings and watercolours, and here you will see the works of Burne-Jones and Alma-Tadema among others of that period in a correct setting. Five exhibitions of British contemporary art are held each year in addition to the stock work on show.

The Mallet Gallery

141 NEW BOND ST, W1, 0171-499 7411
Open Mon-Fri 9.30am-5.30pm, Sat 11am-4pm. U: Piccadilly Circus.

One of the foremost specialists in fine Victorian, Edwardian and Pre-Raphaelite pictures and works of art, showing nineteenth- and twentieth-century English and European paintings, as well as sculpture, ceramics, nineteenth-century gothic furniture and works of art. One gallery is devoted to eighteenth- and nineteenth-century watercolours and drawings.

Mathof Gallery

24 MOTCOMB ST, SW1, 0171-235 0010
Open Mon-Fri 9.30am-5.30pm. U: Knightsbridge.

Brian MacDermot founded the Mathof Gallery in 1975, when *The World of Islam Festival* was held in London. He concentrates on the paintings of Arabia and the Orientalist movement (not to be confused with oriental art), many depicting the customs of the Arab peoples. These works, although created by Europeans, can claim a place in the history of the Arab nations. Aside from this they are stunning, especially as presented here, in beautiful hand-carved frames covered in gold leaf.

Noortman

40-41 OLD BOND ST, W1, 0171-491 72484
Open Mon-Fri 9.30am-5.30pm. U: Green Park.

With its Dutch connection in Maastricht, this is one of the galleries specialising in nineteenth-century European paintings as well as Impressionist and Post-Impressionist. However, they are also well known for Old Masters, dealing with museum-quality pieces only.

Peter Nahum at the Leicester Galleries

3-5 RYDER ST, ST. JAMES'S, SW1, 0171-930 6059
Open Mon-Fri 10am-6pm. U: Green Park.

Peter Nahum left Sotheby's in 1984 to open his gallery in St. James specialising in paintings, drawings and sculpture of the highest quality from the nineteenth and twentieth centuries. Since that time he has handled the majority of important Victorian painting coming onto the market, including works by Burne-Jones, Millais, Tissot, Denis, Alma-Tadema and Watts. As he is a television personality, academic, lecturer and author in addition to being an advisor to many official departments of art, one can only envy the energy and enthusiasm for his chosen subject which results in the stock of sublime works.

Pyms Gallery

9 MOUNT ST, W1, 0171-629 2020
Open Mon-Fri 9.30am-5.30pm. U: Bond St.

A very wide range of work is on display here, with an interesting emphasis on the Irish eighteenth, nineteenth, and twentieth centuries, including work by Lavery and Orpen. French Naturalism as represented by the Barbizon School along with some British late nineteenth and early twentieth century—from Sickert to Nicholson—makes for a real mix of European flavours.

Richard Green

44 DOVER ST, W1, 0171-493 3939
Open Mon-Fri 10am-6pm Sat 10am-12.30pm. U: Piccadilly Circus.

A specialist dealer covering British, sporting and marine paintings, Victorian and European paintings, and fine Old Master paintings. With a collection which includes works by Pieter Brueghal, Canaletto, James Seymour, Barend Cornelis Koek-koek, Alfred Sisley, Boudin and Sir Alfred Munnings, it is one of the most comprehensive to be seen outside a museum.

Richard Philp

59 LEDBURY RD, W11, 0171-727 7915

Open Mon-Sat 10am-6pm (but check opening times before visiting). U: Ladbroke Grove/Notting Hill Gate.

On two floors of an elegant building just off Portobello Road, Richard Philp has a stock which spans centuries. Roman and Greek sculpture occupy the same space as Old Master drawings alongside early Elizabethan or Jacobean portraits. However, this is no casual selection—there is a genuine delight in the works of art here.

Spink & Son

5-7 KING ST, SW1, 0171-930 7888

Open Mon-Fri 9am-5.30pm. U: Green Park.

Rather like the British Empire, Spink's feels as if it has known better days of glory, and the kernel of an illustrious past is ever present. Not surprising when one considers Spink's was established in 1666 and grew to be one of the largest and most all-encompassing antiques establishments in England. Each room is relatively small and contains a selection of artefacts, most particularly Indian, south-east Asian and Islamic art. The Fine Art section usually researches and displays nineteenth-and twentieth-century art, and some exceptional works are exhibited.

Thomas Gibson Fine Art

44 OLD BOND ST, W1, 0171-499 8572

Open Mon-Fri 10am-5pm. U: Green Park.

The delightful interior, very stylishly decorated for English tastes—all minty and mossy greens—displays classic works both upstairs and in the small basement. It is refreshing to see works as disparate as those by Craigie Aitchieson and Giacometti on show at the same time.

OLD MASTER SPECIALISTS

Derek Johns

12 DUKE ST, ST. JAMES, SW1, 0171-839 7671

Open Mon-Fri 9.30am-5.30pm. U: Green Park.

As a specialist in Old Masters, Derek Johns has achieved international acclaim for discovering lost masterpieces and showing rare works never previously exhibited. In addition, annual shows present displays of European painting and sculpture.

John Mitchell & Son

160 NEW BOND ST, W1, 0171-493 7567

Open Mon-Fri 9.30am-5.30pm, Sat by appointment. U: Bond St.

This independent family firm was established in 1930 and is a well-known specialist in flower paintings. They offer a small, rigorously selected stock of paintings, watercolours and drawings from the seventeenth to nineteenth century.

Lane Fine Art

123 NEW BOND ST, W1, 0171-499 5020

By appointment only. U: Bond St.

This is one of many galleries in the Bond Street area that were built specially to exhibit paintings, and it shows. Top-lit, the red-and-green interior displays to their best advantage British paintings from the sixteenth to early nineteenth century, the gallery's specialty—most particularly early English portraits and marine and sporting pictures from masters such as John Knox and George Stubbs.

Leger

13 OLD BOND ST, W1, 0171-629 3538

Open Mon-Fri 9am-5.30pm. U: Green Park.

Based in this building since the 1930s, Leger has made quality an underlying aim, and the quality of each work, whatever its price, is assured. The best of British oils and watercolour paintings from 1720 to 1850 can and should be seen here in this very accessible atmosphere—Gainsborough, Turner, Girton, Adam, Payne—alongside lesser-known but equally respected artists.

P & D Colnaghi & Co

14 OLD BOND ST, W1, 0171-491 7408

Open Mon-Fri 9.30am-6pm. U: Green Park.

A reverential hush pervades the interior, hinting at the impeccable provenance of Colnaghi's. The company goes all the way back to 1760, and whilst concentrating on Italian and French schools up to the early 1800s, also has carefully selected Old Master paintings on view, including English paintings. The plush surroundings complement the works, which are allowed ample viewing space—as befits the quality of paintings destined for major collections in the world.

Raphael Valls

11 DUKE ST, ST. JAMES'S, SW1, 0171-930 1144
Open Mon-Fri 10am-6pm and by appointment. U: Green Park.

In a bustling, rather faded, atmosphere are paintings, drawings and watercolours (mostly) from the Dutch and Flemish tradition. European Old Masters such as Ruisdael, Arellano and Van Goyen are dealt with, and not behind the scenes. Relax and browse through the hubbub—it's well worth it.

Simon Dickinson Ltd

58 JERMYN ST, SW1, 0171-493 0340
By appointment. U: Green Park.

Whilst it is possible for the casual visitor to see the selection of Old Master and British paintings on show, the strength of this organisation is in finding important pictures from private collections.

Van Haeften Gallery

13 DUKE ST, SW1, 0171-930 3062
Open Mon-Fri 10am-6pm. U: Green Park.

Here, on green baize-lined walls, are real gems of seventeenth-century Dutch and Flemish Old Masters. Johnny Van Haeften has extended family in Holland, but is not Dutch; however, it is hard to imagine anyone more in tune with Dutch painting. These are works to be enjoyed and marvelled over in a small gallery before they are whisked off to some lucky museum.

Waterhouse & Dodd

110 NEW BOND ST, W1, 0171-491 9293
Open Mon-Fri 9.30am-6pm. U: Bond St.

Specialising in British and European paintings under £25,000, this gallery has a stock of French, Belgian and British artists working between 1870 and 1930. The essentially decorative paintings are by followers, rather than the important artists, but Belle Epoque artists like Paul-César Helley and French Academicians, such as Gérme, are lovingly presented.

Whitfield Fine Art

180 NEW BOND ST, W1, 0171-499 3592
By appointment. U: Bond St.

Clovis Whitfield is one of the most important and charismatic dealers in Old Master Italian paintings from the sixteenth to late eighteenth century. Drawings are also shown, along with Florentine and Venetian frames from the same period.

Wildenstein & Co

147 NEW BOND ST, W1, 0171-629 0602
By appointment. U: Bond St.

A venerable institution which deals in Impressionist and Old Master paintings. Shimmering silver-grey crushed velvet walls and period furniture set the scene for the occasional Van Gogh or Leonardo da Vinci sketch. Handy for the auction rooms and perfect for those dreaming of owning a masterpiece.

ART MUSEUMS

Barbican Gallery

BARBICAN CENTRE, SILK ST, EC2, 0171-638 4141
Open Mon-Sat 9am-11pm, Sun, public hols noon-11pm. U: Barbican.

The art gallery which holds some first-rate exhibitions is housed on Level 3 of this product of 1960s city planning. The residential, commercial and arts complex was built on a site destroyed during World War II and opened to the public in the 1980s. To many people it's a nightmare to navigate, but persist, as it contains two theatres, a concert hall, cinemas, library and a conservatory on the roof. It's always a lively place to visit, and the exhibitions are of major importance.

Courtauld Institute

SOMERSET HOUSE, STRAND, WC2, 0171-872 0220
Open Mon-Sat 10am-6pm, Sun 2-6pm. U: Temple.

Housed in grandiose Somerset House (1776-86), the Courtauld Institute Galleries is opening Autumn, 1998. It contains one of the best collections of Impressionist and Post-Impressionist paintings outside France. Apart from such masterpieces as Manet's *Bar at the Folies-Bergères* and Van Gogh's *Self-Portrait*—part of the original gift of textile magnate, Samuel Courtauld (1865-1947)—you can feast your eyes on paintings by Rubens, Tiepolo and Van Dyck, as well as British paintings, Roger Fry's pictures, art works by the early twentieth-century London Bloomsbury Group and the Omega Workshops, drawings and more. It's an important collection housed in impressive surroundings and there's a good book shop attached. The Witt Library, open to art historians and dealers by private application, contains the most complete catalogue of Western paintings in the world.

Crafts Council Gallery

44A PENTONVILLE RD, N1, 0171-278 7700
Open Tues-Sat 11am-6pm, Sun 2-6pm. Admission free. U: King's Cross/Angel.

The national centre for crafts shows work by Britain's foremost crafts-people. Britain has always had a reputation for producing first-rate craft items, and this gallery endorses that view. There's always something new and interesting to see in frequently changing exhibitions of silver, jewellery, wood-carvings, pottery and more. The shop is an excellent source of good, one-off items and presents you won't find elsewhere.

Dulwich Picture Gallery

COLLEGE RD, SE21, 0181-693 5254
Open Tues-Fri 10am-5pm; Sat 11am-5pm, Sun 2pm-5pm. BR: West Dulwich.

England's oldest public art gallery was designed by Sir John Soane (see the John Soane Museum) and opened in 1814. His use of skylights, which gave the rooms natural light, made it the model for subsequent art galleries. The twelve galleries and mausoleum contain a splendid collection of Old Master paintings belonging to Dulwich College, and some excellent exhibitions are mounted throughout the year.

Estorick Collection of Modern Italian Art

NORTHAMPTON LODGE, 39A CANONBURY SQUARE, N1, 0171 704 9522
Open Tues-Sat 11am-6pm.
U: Highbury & Islington.

A hugely important collection of early 20th century artists of the avant-garde Futurist movement, opened as a gallery early 1998. Boccioni, Severini and Russolo are just three of the many artists on show, from the original private collection of American sociologist, dealer, collector and writer, Eric Estorick (1913-1993).

Hayward Gallery

SOUTH BANK CENTRE, SE1, 0171-928 3144
Open for exhibitions only Tues-Wed 10am-8pm, Thurs-Mon 10am-6pm. U: Waterloo.

Part of the South Bank complex, this is one of London's main venues for major exhibitions of international importance.

Institute of Contemporary Arts

CARLTON HOUSE TERRACE, SW1, 0171-930 6393 (RECORDED INFORMATION)
Open (galleries) daily noon-7.30pm; Fri to 9.30pm. U: Charing Cross.

Established in 1947 by art critics Herbert Read and Roland Penrose to help British artists in the way American artists were by the Museum of Modern Art in New York, the Institute holds a lively and continual series of exhibitions, films, theatre and talks.

Friends

If you're in London for any length of time, consider becoming a Friend of one of your favourite museums. Although the main purpose of these organisations is to raise much-needed funds, becoming a Friend is rather like joining a club. You pay a yearly membership and receive news about the museum, free admission to exhibitions as well as the possibility of enjoying specially arranged holidays. Many of them also organise evening viewings which are only open to Friends. The Friends of the Royal Academy can take guests to private views for free, and use the special club room which is one of the best in London.

National Gallery

TRAFALGAR SQUARE, WC2, 0171-839 3321
Open Mon-Sat 10am-6pm (Weds to 8pm), Sun 2-6pm. Admission free. U: Charing Cross.

The National Gallery opened in 1824, much later than other national galleries in

Europe, when King George IV persuaded a philistine government to buy 38 major paintings, including works by Raphael and Rembrandt. Today this large and comprehensive collection, housed in the neo-classical William Wilkins building of the 1830s, and in the new Sainsbury Wing, provides a first-class panorama of European painting from Giotto to the French Impressionists. (Modern and British paintings are housed in the Tate Gallery.) The masterpieces here are well known: the Leonard da Vinci cartoon, Velazquez's Rokeby *Venus*, *The Baptism of Christ* by Pierro dell Francesca, Van Eyck's *Arnolfini Marriage* and *The Hawaiian* by John Constable. Divided into sections covering Early Renaissance (1260-1510) in the Sainsbury Wing, High Renaissance (1520-1600), English, French and German Painting (1800-1900) and more, the galleries are compact and easy to wander through.

National Portrait Gallery

ST. MARTIN'S PL, WC2, 0171-306 0055
Open Mon-Sat 10am-6pm, Sun 2pm-6pm. Admission free. U: Leicester Sq.

If you want to know what a favourite, famous or infamous British writer, King, Queen, Prince or Princess, poet, artist or villain looked like, go to the National Portrait Gallery which shows British history through its people. Covering five centuries of portraiture, the earliest portraits include a Hans Holbein cartoon of King Henry VIII, while the newest galleries display photographs, sculptures and pictures of contemporary figures. The latter is a difficult section; who will be considered important enough to be preserved in years to come? As the collection concentrates on the sitter rather than the artist, it is a mixture with works by some of the world's great artists hanging alongside more mundane efforts. The collection, arranged chronologically, gives an insight into different age's ideals of beauty, from the sloping shoulders and long noses in the eighteenth century, to the gamin waif-like looks in the 1990s.

Percival David Foundation of Chinese Art

53 GORDON SQUARE, WC1, 0171-387 3909
Open Mon-Fri 10.30am-5pm. Admission free. U: Euston Sq.

If you're at all interested in Chinese porcelain, you must see this important and relatively unknown collection of beautiful Chinese ceramics made between the tenth and eighteenth centuries. Percival David (1892-1964) was a Governor of the School of Oriental and African Studies and gave his collection to London University. It is exquisite; many of the pieces were once owned by Chinese emperors.

Queen's Gallery

BUCKINGHAM PALACE RD, SW1, 0171-799 2331
Open daily 9.30am-4.30pm. U: Victoria.

This small gallery has top quality exhibits, mostly from the Queen's collection of paintings and furniture—one of the finest and most valuable in the world. (Sir Anthony Blunt, for 30 years her art adviser until exposed as the 'third man' and a Soviet spy in 1979 and stripped of his knighthood, was a noted world expert.) The well-stocked shop sells all kinds of high-quality royal 'souvenirs' and other good gifts.

Royal Academy of Arts

BURLINGTON HOUSE, PICCADILLY, W1, 0171-300 8000
Open daily 10am-6pm. U: Green Park.

A splendid institution housed in the equally splendid Burlington House, Piccadilly, the Royal Academy of Arts was founded in 1768 by Sir Joshua Reynolds with King George III as patron. Although most widely known for its Annual Summer Exhibition (held for over 200 years), the Royal Academy has some of the best exhibitions in London and shows of major individual artists. The light, airy Sackler Galleries were designed by English architect, Norman Foster. Each elected Academician (a roster of names which includes every major British artist including Alan Jones, David Hockney and Elisabeth Frink and architects Richard Rogers and Norman Foster) has to give a piece of work before receiving a Diploma signed by the Sovereign. Along with bequests, gifts and purchases, this makes for an impressive collection of British Art over the past 217 years. Some is on show, some can be seen by appointment, and much is on loan to other institutions and exhibitions.

Courses & Lectures

Most of the big museums offer all kinds of lectures, tours and courses, frequently on the subject of their current exhibitions. Ring each museum separately for details.

Saatchi Gallery

98A BOUNDARY RD, NW8, 0171-624 8299

Open Thurs-Sun noon-6pm. U: St. John's Wood.

This spectacular space, converted by architect Max Gordon from an old paint factory for Charles Saatchi in 1985, is one of the few venues for viewing large-scale contemporary work in its correct setting. The private Saatchi Collection of International Contemporary Art is displayed in changing exhibitions.

Serpentine Gallery

KENSINGTON GDNS, W2, 0171-402 6075

Open daily 10am-6pm. Admission free. U: South Kensington.

Devoted to modern art, the gallery is now refurbished but continues its reputation for showing some of the most controversial artists of the day, like Damian Hirst, in a series of highly publicised exhibitions.

Tate Gallery

MILLBANK, SW1, 0171-887 8000.

Open Mon-Sat 10am-5.50pm, Sun 2pm-5.50pm. Admission free but charge for major exhibitions. U: Pimlico.

The Tate Gallery, which has space to show only a small part of its vast holdings, contains two major national collections: British art from the sixteenth century to 1900 and international modern art from the Impressionists to today. Under Nicholas Serota, it's become a gallery often at the centre of controversy. It was originally built through the generosity of sugar millionaire Sir Henry Tate, who also gave his own collection. The Clore Gallery, designed by Sir James Stirling and an architectural sight in its own right, houses the extensive collection of JMW Turner's works.

Wallace Collection

HERTFORD HOUSE, MANCHESTER SQUARE, W1, 0171-935 0687

Open Mon-Sat 10am-5pm, Sun 2pm-5pm. Admission free. U: Bond St.

Originally built for the Duke of Manchester, it was bought by the Marquess of Hertford in 1797. The family were great patrons of the arts and collectors, and what you see is one of the finest private collections of French art, including porcelain and sculpture as well as an eclectic mix of arms and armour and furniture in a peaceful, delightful setting that gives you a feeling of an aristocratic family's tastes and lifestyle.

Whitechapel Art Gallery

80 WHITECHAPEL HIGH ST, E1, 0171-522 7878

Open Tues-Sun 11am-5pm (Wed to 8pm). Admission free but charge U: Aldgate East.

Founded at the end of the nineteenth century to bring the West End to the East End, and housed in a splendid Art Nouveau building, this has been the Mecca of innovative art under a series of high profile directors since the 1960s. Two elegant main galleries, the upper one totally top-lit, are used for one-person contemporary shows and retrospectives.

ATTRACTIONS

We have noted where admission is free; otherwise, there is an admission charge. If you are in London over a public holiday, please check opening times.

Banqueting House

WHITEHALL, WC2, 0171-930 4179

Open Mon-Sat 10am-5pm (last admission 4pm). U: Westminster.

All that is left of the old Westminster Palace is the magnificent Banqueting House with its double cube room built by Inigo Jones from 1619 to 1622. The Rubens ceiling is magnificent, painted in 1634-6 for Charles 1 to honour his father, James I of England. Charles I was beheaded on a scaffold erected outside here; his son, Charles II, celebrated his restoration to the throne here.

Changing the Guard

BUCKINGHAM PALACE/HORSE GUARDS, WHITEHALL, SW1, 0839-123411 (24-HR INFORMATION)

Apr-July/August daily 11.30am; rest of the year even or odd dates depending on the month. Tel. for details. U: St. James's Park/Westminster.

The Foot Guards of the Household Division of the Cavalry, the Queen's personal guards leave Wellington Barracks at 11.27am precisely and march along Bird Cage Walk to the Palace. There's usually a band playing, but the ceremony is scaled down when the Queen is not at home (look for the Royal Standard flying from Buckingham Palace when she is there), and can be cancelled if the weather is very bad. In crowded summer months get to the palace by at least 10.30am. The mounted guard changing ceremony by the Household Cavalry in Whitehall takes place daily at 11am, Sun 10am.

Commonwealth Experience

COMMONWEALTH INSTITUTE, KENSINGTON HIGH ST, W8, 0171-603 4535

Open 10am-5pm. U: High St Kensington.

Housed in a remarkable 1960s building, with a hyperboloid roof of Zambian copper, visitors take a fun-packed adventure around the different Commonwealth countries. Also art exhibitions from the different countries.

Events and Exhibitions

There are two useful free publications giving information about contemporary exhibitions in London: **Galleries** and **New Exhibitions of Contemporary Art**. Both are available from most major galleries. It is worth looking out for special events organised by groups of galleries as street events, most particularly the Cork Street weekend. At the beginning of each year an art fair is held at **The Business Design Centre**, Islington, which presents the best of contemporary art in a market-stall atmosphere. An excellent way to see the galleries in a relaxed mood.

Cutty Sark

KING WILLIAM WALK, SE10, 0181-858 3445

Open Mon-Sat 10am-6pm, Sun noon-6pm; (Oct-May to 5pm). BR: Greenwich.

This absurdly small vessel now permanently marooned in Greenwich, was built at Dumbarton, Scotland in 1869 as one of the fast clippers that raced across the Atlantic and Pacific Oceans in the nineteenth century carrying first tea, then wool. In 1871 she won the annual China to London clipper race taking a mere 107 days. The brave clipper's last sea voyage was in 1938; she became a museum in 1957. On board you see the complex rigging and masts characteristic of the great days of sail; below deck the cramped quarters of the seamen are full of prints, instruments, odd personal artefacts and a collection of wooden figureheads.

Guildhall

GUILDHALL YARD, GRESHAM ST, EC2, 0171-606 3030

Open Mon-Sat May-Sept 10am-5pm, Oct-Apr 10am-5pm. U: Bank/St. Paul's

The seat of the City of London's municipal government since 1192, it's a beautiful old building, though very little of the original remains. The great hall is the scene of the Lord Mayor's annual banquet and other important occasions.

HMS Belfast

MORGAN'S LANE, TOOLEY ST, SE1, 0171-407 6434.

Open daily end-Mar-Oct 31: 10am-6pm; Nov 1-mid Mar: 10am-5pm. U: London Bridge.

The cruiser HMS Belfast, the Royal Navy's last big-gun ship, became a museum in 1971. During World War II, this floating city with 800 men on board had the unenviable task of guarding Russian convoys and in 1943 helped sink the greatest single danger to the Russian life-line, the German battle cruiser *Scharnhorst*. Part of the ship has been left as it was; the rest relates to the history of the Royal Navy. In these days of nuclear weapons the whole ship has a strange, outdated feel; was war really like this?

Houses of Parliament

PARLIAMENT SQUARE, SW1, 0171-219 4272.
See text for free admission times.
U: Westminster.

More correctly the Palace of Westminster, this splendid, flamboyant and rather pompous building was designed by Sir Charles Barry and built from 1837-1858 when the problematical Clock Tower housing 'Big Ben' was finished. The site is ancient, bound up with British history from the start, as the first Palace was built for Edward the Confessor before 1066. There is a very good exterior view from the river and from Westminster or Lambeth bridges. To go inside you either have to arrange it through your MP or as a visitor turn up when the House is sitting after 2.30pm (Mon to Thurs) and queue to get into the Stranger's Gallery which looks over the Chamber of the Commons and seats 100 to 150 people. Friday is Private Members' Bill day when the House sits 9.30am to 3pm. Get there early, but check first: no bills means the House doesn't sit.

London Aquarium

COUNTY HALL, RIVERSIDE BUILDING, WESTMINSTER BRIDGE RD, SE1, 0171-967 8000
Open daily 10am-6pm. U: Waterloo.

Huge aquarium beside the Thames in the former County Hall Building, showing a wide variety of different fish and sea life from around the world. Sharks are a great attraction, as is the pool where visitors can touch some of the fish.

London Balloon

SPRING GARDENS, VAUXHALL BRIDGE, SE11, 0345 023 842
Open daily 10am-9pm; Fri., Sat., Sun. to midnight. U: Vauxhall

Look at London below you from a balloon up several hundred feet (tethered, not free). Spectacular views give you an idea of how vast the metropolis is. The balloon carries up to 30 people and the ride takes 15 minutes. If it's winter, or very bad weather, check first. £12 per person.

London Dungeon

28-34 TOOLEY ST, SE1, 0171-403 7221
Open daily Apr-Sept: 10am-6.30pm; Oct-Mar: 10am-5.30pm. U: London Bridge.

The sort of ghoulish place children love and parents shudder at, full of the more bloodthirsty parts of British history and naturally accompanied by shrieks and groans. Even the entrance is fun: you enter a dark and different world, lit by candles. Their most popular exhibit? *The Jack the Ripper Experience*, they will cheerfully tell you.

London Zoo

REGENT'S PARK, NW1, 0171-722 3333.
Open daily Mar-Oct 10am-5.30pm, Nov-Feb 10am-4pm. U: Baker St/Camden Town.

Though relatively small, the zoo in Regent's Park is a delightful family destination, with a good children's zoo, an emphasis on conservation, a penguin pool, large animals and more.

Walks Around London

There are a lot of excellent companies taking you on walks through every part of London, concentrating on the fascinating and frequently disreputable side of London's history. Many of them also have historic pub walks, which is an excellent way to meet people. You can get information on the following by telephoning direct or from London Tourist Board offices: **Architectural Dialogue** (0181-341 1371); **Historical Walks of London** (0181-668 4019); **The Londoner Pub Walks** (0181-883 2656); **The London Walking Forum** (0199-271 7711); **The Original London Walks** (0171-624 3978); **Pied Piper Walks** (0171-435 4782; **Stepping Out Guided Walking Tours** (0181-881 2933).

Lord's Cricket Ground Tours & Museum

ST. JOHN'S WOOD, NW8, 0171-289 1611, TOURS: 0171-432 1033/266 3825
Open daily for tours (which include a visit to the museum) noon and 2pm, except for match days during the season (late April to September). U: St. John's Wood.

A visit to the Cricket Museum will not give you a huge insight into the rules and conventions of the game many find so distressingly obscure, but it will provide you with a bit of amusement (if such a thing can be allowed with such a revered pastime). It was not, it turns out, such a gentleman's game: the first rules state the width of the bat as early cads were making bats wider than the wicket behind them. There are paintings and objects, a talking head of WG Grace and eccentric objects like the stuffed sparrow killed by a cricket ball in play. And you do see the famous and very beautiful rooms and grounds. Telephone ahead for details and booking.

Madame Tussaud's Waxworks and The Planetarium

MARYLEBONE RD, NW1, 0171-935 6861.
Open Mon-Fri 9.30am-5.30pm; Sat & Sun 9.30am-5.30pm. Planetarium shows Mon-Fri 12.20pm-5pm every 40 minutes. U: Baker St.

One of London's greatest tourist attractions which you should try to avoid at peak times like school holidays, Madame Tussaud's began as a museum in 1835 when the redoubtable lady stopped touring England with her waxworks—originally death masks of many of the best-known victims of the French Revolution—and made a permanent exhibition. The scope is endless and international: from King Henry VIII to Nelson Mandela and is continually being added to. In the 'Garden Party' section you mingle with life-like models of celebrities. Man's gruesome side is displayed with a grim catalogue of torture and punishment in the ever-popular 'Chamber of Horrors'; a high-tech replica London taxi cab journey takes you through London's history in 'The Spirit of London'. The **London Planetarium** next door shows the mysteries of the planets and the solar system, and a separate Space Trail exhibition. Compared to similar exhibitions in France or the USA, it is limited, but nonetheless worth seeing.

Monument

MONUMENT ST, EC2, 0171-626 2717
Open Mon-Fri 10am-5.40pm, Sat, Sun 2pm-5.40pm (telephone in advance to check weekend times). U: Monument.

Built by Sir Christopher Wren to commemorate the Great Fire of London in 1666, it's 202 feet high, the distance from the start of the conflagration in a baker's shop in Pudding Lane.

Royal Mews

BUCKINGHAM PALACE RD, SW1, 0171-799 2331
Open winter: Wed noon-4pm; end Mar-Oct: Tues-Thurs noon-4pm. U: Victoria.

This collection of royal vehicles is housed in the old stables and coach houses of the Palace which were built by John Nash in 1825. Of major interest is the 1761 gold state coach of George III weighing a massive four tons and pulled at walking pace by eight horses. Don't miss the glass coach used for royal weddings or the splendid royal cars. The harnesses are among the finest in the world, and some of the magnificent heavy horses are stabled here.

St. Pauls' Cathedral

ST. PAUL'S CHURCHYARD, EC4, 0171-236 4128
Open Mon-Sat 8.30am-4pm, Sun for services only. U: St. Paul's.

Apparently on the site of a Roman temple dedicated to the goddess Diana, the present cathedral was designed by Sir Christopher Wren after the Great Fire of London in 1666. Taking 35 years to build, Wren went every week to superintend the work. Towards the end, he was hoisted up to the lantern in a basket, and appropriately he was one of the first of many distinguished people to be buried in the crypt. You can climb the 627 steps into the dome for a fabulous, if windy, view of London, via the Whispering, Stone and Golden Galleries.

Shakespeare Globe

NEW GLOBE WALK, BANKSIDE, SE1, 0171-902 1400
Open daily 10am-5pm. U: London Bridge

Shakespeare's Globe Theatre on the old Bankside site is a reconstruction of Shakespeare's original 'O'. Elizabethan-style, the thatched roof only partially covers the audience; the main auditorium is open to the elements, though the stage is also covered. It's a glorious experience to sit in this remarkably small space and the audience tends to react as an Elizabethan one, hissing or cheering according to whether villain or hero is on stage. There's a separate museum and shop, and tours of the site, which will include a second, covered, theatre and a much bigger exhibition space.

Tower Bridge Museum

TOWER BRIDGE, SE1, 0171-403 3761
Open daily Apr 1-Oct 31: 10am-5.15pm (last tickets); Nov 1-Mar 31: 9.30am-5.15pm (last tickets). U: Tower Hill.

Tower Bridge (1886-94) was one of London's wonders with its ability to open 135 feet high for ships to steam through. The museum has been rebuilt and now has all sorts of animatronic characters and special effects which create the past. It's also a good place to go for the spectacular views and, cleverly, there are pictures of the same views through the ages, showing just how much London has changed. The Bridge is not only for show; it is still raised an average of ten times a week to allow tall ships to pass.

Tower of London

TOWER HILL, EC3, 0171-709 0765
Open Mon-Sat 9am-5pm, Sun 10am-5pm. U: Tower Hill.

The finest medieval fortress in Britain, the Tower was begun by William 1 after 1066 to keep the subjects subdued, and added to through the ages. It's been a palace, prison and place of execution; it housed the Royal armouries, the Mint, the Royal Observatory, the Royal Zoo, the Public Records and still houses the Crown Jewels, one of the major attractions of the Tower. Yeomen Warders, the 'Beefeaters' who live in the 'casements' will regale you with stories of blood-thirsty happenings in the small towers that dot the walls—ripping good yarns and great fun.

Drinking Fountains

In 1859 the **Metropolitan Free Drinking Fountain Association** was established to supply drinking water to combat the dreadful water shortages, cholera and intemperance rife in London's poorer areas. By 1886 they had established 594 though few remain today.

Wembley Stadium Tours

WEMBLEY STADIUM, MIDDLESEX, 0181-902 8833
Open daily winter: 10am-3pm (except event days; tel first to check), summer 10am-4pm. U: Wembley Park.

Take a behind-the-scenes tour to see the pitch, the player's changing rooms, and the most impressive control room. Also the Royal Box where the FA cup is presented. Tours last around 45 minutes and take place continuously.

Westminster Abbey

BROAD SANCTUARY, SW1, 0171-222 5152
Open Mon-Fri 9.20am-3.45pm, Sat 9am-1.45pm & 3.45pm-5pm, Sun services only. U: Westminster.

Probably best known for its spectacular Royal occasions of marriages, coronations and funerals, it has served for hundreds of years as the focal point of Westminster and is full of treasures. The Royal chapels are magnificent, the Henry VII chapel awe-inspiring with its fabulous roof and colourful banners. The scope runs from tombs and memorials of the famous, high-born, infamous and plain odd (like Jonas Hanway, founder of the Marine Society, but being British better known for being the first man in London to carry an umbrella) to architectural details like the tiled floor of the Chapter House and the quiet oasis of the cloisters. Try to spend some time here—when it is not too crowded.

Westminster Cathedral

FRANCIS ST, SW1, 0171-798 9055
Open Sun-Fri 7am-7pm, Sat 8am-7pm. U: Victoria.

This Roman Catholic cathedral is a magnificent piece of Victorian Byzantine architecture, full of mosaics and ornamented with more than 100 different kinds of marble from all over the world. The tombs and memorials are no less interesting; the view from the tower (when open) is wonderful. If you have the chance, attend a concert here.

HOBBIES & SPORTS

ART COURSES

London's local authorities run large numbers of courses on every subject under the sun. Floodlight from any book store, is a useful booklet published annually and listing every possible course with full details from butterfly spotting to macramé. For private courses, try Sotheby's and Christie's. They both run a variety of courses, some lasting a year and leading to an academic qualification, others lasting anything from a day to a month and aimed at the person with a general interest in the subject. ***Time to Learn***, published by the National Institute of Adult Continuing Education, 21 De Montfort St, Leicester LE1 7GE, tel: 0116 2044200, gives details of learning holidays throughout Britain.

Christie's Education

63 Old Brompton Rd, SW7, 0171-581 3933, Fax 0171-589 0383

Evening courses cover fine and decorative arts and music (there's a very good opera course, for instance) and wine courses (see below), plus a professional course.

Sotheby's Institute

30 Oxford St, W1, 0171-323 5775, Fax 0171-580 8160

Apart from offering Master Degrees in fine and decorative arts, the Institute runs a large number of excellent specialised courses throughout the year, as well as evening study courses, day and weekend courses in fine arts, ceramics, furniture and wine (see below).

Art Supplies

Brodie & Middleton

68 Drury Lane, WC2, 0171 836-3280/9, Fax 0171-497 8425

Open Mon-Fri 8.30am-5pm.

A major shop for stage design and theatrical make-up since 1840 in the heart of London's theatre world, Brodie and Middleton sell everything for thespians from stage dyes and blood capsules to special brushes and paints for theatre sets.

Falkiner Fine Papers

76 Southampton Row, WC1, 0171-831 1151, Fax 0171-430 1248

Open Mon-Sat 9.30am-6pm (closed 1pm-2pm Sat only).

Falkiner stock a wide range of good and rare international hand-made papers for watercolours, drawings and printmaking such as kozo (oriental mulberry paper), vellum, parchment and beautiful hand-marbled papers in both large and small quantities.

Green & Stone

259 King's Rd, SW3, 0171-352 0837, Fax 0171-351 1098

Open Mon-Sat 9am-6pm, Wed 9.30am-7pm, Sun noon-5pm.

Near the Chelsea College of Art, Green and Stone sell almost everything for the artist. This is also the place to go if you want gilding materials such as real or fake gold, glazes for special effects and varnishes that will give a surface the aged or cracked look of an instant antique.

L Cornelissen & Son

105 Gt Russell St, WC1, 0171-636 1045, Fax 0171-636 3655

Open Mon-Fri 9.30am-5.30pm, Sat 9.30am-5pm.

We love the old-fashioned chests of drawers and displays in this 'Artists' Colourmen' specialists, established in 1855. You'll find unusual items here like lapis lazuli paints, as well as an extensive range of the best brushes, painting knives, glues and pastels, gilding materials and papers.

Rowney

12 Percy St, W1, 0171-636 8241, Fax 0171-580 7534

Open Mon-Fri 9am-5.30pm, Sat 10am-5pm.

Established in 1789 as a perfumery selling paints and pigments for cosmetics, Rowney's is now the largest UK manufacturer of artists' paints. As you can imagine, their shop contains the widest possible range of paints.

T N Lawrence & Son

117-119 Clerkenwell Rd, EC1, 0171-242 3534, Fax 0171-430 2234

Open Mon-Fri 9am-5pm, Sat 10am-4pm.

Founded in 1859 in Bleeding Heart Yard, this shop has moved and expanded. Apart from being the only place for wood-engraving materials, they also specialise in tools for all kinds of engraving, You'll find 'Golden' acrylics from the USA, materials for etching and ranges of paints and paper for book binders. In fact if it's paper you're after, Lawrence is world-famous for their wide range of rare supplies.

Tiranti

27 Warren St, W1, Tel and Fax: 0171-636 8565
Open Mon-Fri 9am-5.30pm, Sat 9.30am-1pm.

Tiranti's has been supplying materials for sculptors for over 100 years. But added to the mallets and chisels for stone sculpting and clays for modelling in the past, they now also supply dental plaster (apparently good for modelling), silicon rubber resins and more for the contemporary artists.

Winsor & Newton

51 & 52 Rathbone Pl, W1, 0171-636 4231
Open Mon-Fri 9.30am-5.30pm, Sat 9.30am-5pm.

In business for 150 years, they produce a very wide range of paper and paints and are particularly useful in supplying oil paints in small sizes, which are normally only available in large quantities.

BICYCLING

Bicycling in London, as in any city, can be hazardous and should be undertaken with caution. The following shops carry a wide range of accessories including protective helmets which you should wear. Deposits on hiring vary, but reckon on anything from £40 to £50 for a week's deposit.

On Your Bike

52-54 Tooley St, SE1, 0171-357 6958
Open Mon-Fri 9am-6pm, Sat 9.30am-5pm.

Major stockists of mountain bikes, touring and racing bikes, they hire by the day, week, month or longer. Daily rates begin at £12, and they have a special weekend rate.

Yellow Jersey Cycles

44 Chalk Farm Rd, NW1, 0171-485 8090
Open Mon-Fri 8.30am-7pm, Sat 9am-6pm, Sun 11am-5pm.

Open seven days a week, this friendly shop specialises in mountain bikes and hybrids (town-type mountain bikes). No hire service.

BRASS RUBBING

This peculiarly English hobby has many devotees. You'll find a lot of them carefully rubbing the impressions of knights and ladies, dogs and coats-of-arms at the two main brass rubbing centres.

London Brass Rubbing Centre

St. Martin-in-the-Fields Church, Trafalgar Square, WC2, 0171-930 9306
Open Mon-Sat 10am-6pm, Sun from noon.

Westminster Abbey Brass Rubbing Centre

North Cloister, Westminster Abbey, SW1, 0171-222 4589
Open Mon-Sat 9.30am-5pm.

COOKING

Le Cordon Bleu

14 Marylebone Lane, W1M 6HH
0171-935 3503, Fax 0171-935 7621

Attracting professionals and amateurs, Le Cordon Bleu offers a wide range of courses in the culinary arts from specialised short courses, demonstrations and daytime courses in classic cuisine, to guest-chef lecturers, tastings and advanced pâtisserie training. Unashamedly French, it issues certificates and diplomas on the professional courses, and has an arrangement with the Paris Cordon Bleu school whereby students on the 10-week classic cuisine course can transfer between the two. Facilities are excellent and the school offers restaurant-like conditions for the aspiring chef.

Leith's School of Food & Wine

21 St. Alban's Grove, W8 5BP, 0171-229 0177, Fax 0171-937 5257

If you want to learn about restaurant management, wine—or how to plan a sophisticated dinner party menu in one easy Saturday morning lesson—this is the place to come. But Leith's is also one of the most important schools for people who want to go into catering as a career, from cooking in a restaurant to cooking for directors. Courses run for different lengths of time and many lead to professional qualifications recognised the world over for their high standards.

The Mosimann Academy

Studio 5, The William Blake House, The Lanterns, Bridge Lane, SW11 3AD, 0171-924 1111; Fax 0171-924 7187

Seminars and demonstrations from chefs and teachers for both professional companies and corporations like British Airways, and for the amateur wanting to know everything about creating the proper dinner party, inspired and under the direction of top chef Anton Mosimann.

DANCE

Dance Works

16 BALDERTON ST, W1, 0171-629 6183, FAX 0171-499 9087

Open Mon-Fri 8am-10pm, Sat & Sun 9am-6pm.

Dance Works offers over 100 classes, including Russian classical ballet, contemporary, salsa and tap, all taken by experts. They also teach martial arts, hold aerobics classes, have various fitness studios and a rehearsal space.

Pineapple Covent Garden

7 LANGLEY ST, WC2, 0171-836 4004, FAX 0171-836 0806

Open Mon-Fri 9am-9pm, Sat to 6.30pm.

Seven studios offer 180 classes a week in every kind of dance from contemporary to jazz. They also have a hydra gym.

GARDENING

The English Gardening School

66 ROYAL HOSPITAL RD, SW3, 0171-352 4347, FAX 0171-376 3936

Established in 1983, the school which is for both professionals and amateurs, offers various options from one-day workshops on general subjects such as the English cottage garden tradition, roses and plant groupings to one-year courses in subjects like 'Garden Design' and 'Botanical Illustration' which lead to a professional qualification.

The Royal Horticultural Society

80 VINCENT SQUARE, SW1, 0171-834 4333

The RHS as it's popularly known, runs the famous Chelsea Flower Show. But they also have monthly flower shows in their splendid halls in Vincent Square. Like a mini-Chelsea but entirely indoors, each show concentrates on a theme or species from dahlias and rhododendrons to their Great Autumn Show. Telephone for details, and also for details of admission to their comprehensive library.

GOLF

Richmond Park

ROEHAMPTON GATE, RICHMOND PARK, SW15, 0181-876 3205

Two beautiful eighteen-hole golf courses to play on from only £13 a day Monday to Friday, or £16 Saturday or Sunday (the rate lowers each hour and starts at 11.30am. To get in a full round, you need to start by 1pm). They hire out golf clubs but you must have your own golf shoes. Playing times are governed by the Park opening times and can be eccentric (no playing during deer culls for instance), so get all the details on the telephone first.

FITNESS & SPORTS CLUBS

There are a number of good health and fitness clubs in London. Although the most economical way to enjoy them is to take out a year's membership, many of them have shorter memberships of one month, one week or just one day. In addition, many offer special days which include use of the facilities and special offers on beauty treatments. All clubs try to be flexible and you need to make an appointment or speak to the membership secretary to see what you can arrange. Most also offer beauty treatments and it is not necessary to take out membership for those.

Champneys The London Club

LE MERIDIEN, 21 PICCADILLY, W1, 0171-255 8000, FAX 0171-494 0876

Open Mon-Fri 7am-11pm, Sat, Sun 8am-9pm.

A swimming pool, fully-equipped gym, cardiovascular room, dance studio and squash courts are some of the many facilities this luxurious club offers. They have a Health and Fitness Day for £95 and a Top to Toe day for £175. The club's facilities are free to hotel guests. Short term and annual membership available.

Crystal Palace National Sports Centre

NORWOOD, SE19, 0181-778 0131

Open Mon-Fri 8am-10pm, Sat to 8pm, Sun to 6pm.

This huge and impressive complex is the premier sports centre in Britain. While it holds leading competitions on both the international and national circuit (frequently televised), it is also open to the public. Facilities are superb and include an Olympic-size pool, a diving pool, football pitches as well as six floodlit all-weather courts and ten squash courts.

The Dorchester Spa

THE DORCHESTER, PARK LANE, W1
0171-495 7335, FAX 0171-495 7351

Open daily 7am-9.30pm.

The place to come to for pampering, the Spa offers everything from eyelash tinting to assorted body wraps, massage, waxing and any treatment you can think of. There is also a fully-equipped gym and work-out studio, solarium and whirlpool bath. Hotel guests have free use of the club.

The Harbour Club

WATERMEADOW LANE, SW6, 0171-371 7700, FAX 0171-371 7770

Open daily 6.30am-11.30pm.

This spectacular £7 million development which opened in 1993 is impressive. Spread over four levels, it never feels crowded. There's a 25-metre ozone pool, crèche, ten indoor and four outdoor tennis courts plus the unique feature of the Real Tennis court (originally the game of royalty). Membership is expensive, and you are likely to run into international celebrities at this ultra-fashionable club.

Holmes Place Health Club

188A FULHAM RD, SW10, 0171-352 9452, FAX 0171-376 3517

Open Mon-Thurs 7am-11pm, Fri to 10pm, Sat & Sun 9am-9pm.

This is the place for celebrity-spotting, but those famous faces (and bodies) look quite different when working out on the state-of-the-art machines or trying to keep up with the aerobics, dance, step classes and yoga. Annual and monthly membership, plus other deals available.

Jubilee Hall

30 THE PIAZZA, WC2, 0171-379 0008, FAX 0171-379 8503

Open Mon-Fri 7am-10pm, Sat & Sun 10am-5pm.

In Covent Garden's former Flower Market, this popular club offers membership and is also open to non-members. Huge number of classes include contemporary jazz, cardio plus and something called 'fat-attack' workout which is surprisingly popular. The gym is large and light and they also have martial arts classes and a treatment centre. Prices are very good: classes are only £5.30 (gym £6.30) each for non-members and the membership rates are equally reasonable, and variable according to whether you want to include use of the gym or just go for the classes.

Jubilee Sports Centre

CAIRO ST, W10, 0181-960 9629, FAX 0181-960 9661

Mon-Fri 7am-10pm, Sat & Sun 8am-8pm.

A 30-metre pool, sports hall, squash courts, sun beds and multi-gym are just a few of the facilities at this excellent centre. To use the gym you have to take out membership for 13 months for £341; other facilities like squash courts you pay for when you use.

London Central YMCA

112 GREAT RUSSELL ST, WC1, 0171-637 8131, FAX 0171-631 5101

Open Mon-Fri 7am-10.30pm, Sat, Sun 10am-9pm.

Accessible to the general public, they offer a swimming pool, fitness classes, weight training, badminton, basketball and gymnastics. You can join as a member or just turn up and take temporary membership for the day. Rates are good: the weekly membership is £32; three months and yearly vary according to times used and age group.

Mecklenburgh Health Club

MECKLENBURGH PL, WC1, 0171-813 0555, FAX 0171-813 7757

Open Mon-Fri 6.30am-10.30pm, Sat & Sun 9am-9pm.

Excellent facilities at all these health clubs, which also offer good-value days. A one-day use of the gym, swimming pool, steam room and spa costs £25 for the whole day. The subterranean Mecklenburgh Health Club has a restaurant overlooking the pool and a huge gym with the kinds of machines that are used in American Olympic training centres. Monthly and annual membership.

The Peak

THE HYATT CARLTON TOWER, CADOGAN PLACE, SW1, 0171-858 7008, FAX 0171-245 6570

Open Mon-Fri 6.30am-10pm, Sat & Sun 7.30am-9pm.

On the ninth floor of the hotel, the Peak offers a great day of pampering for £100 which includes a personal health counsellor, a recommended exercise regime on top equipment, a buffet lunch, Clarins body treatment and more from 9am-5pm daily. They have various memberships from an overseas membership of 20 visits and 6 months duration at £550 to an annual membership.

The Sanctuary

11 FLORAL ST, WC2, 0171-420 5151, FAX 0171-497 0410

Open (health spa) Wed-Fri 10am-10m, all other days 10am-6pm.

A great place in the middle of Covent Garden for women only. Housed in an old banana warehouse, it's one of our favourite locations for swimming, sunbeds and aromatherapy. Membership is annual and varies according to times. The daily rate is £49.50; after 5pm it's £29.50. They have other memberships from 1 to 6 months. If you book treatments, you don't need membership.

HOT AIR BALLOONING

Balloon Safaris

15-17 CHURCH ST, STAINES, MIDDLESEX, 01784-451007, FAX 01784-440200

For a truly different view of England, try going up in the skies in a hot-air balloon for £120. If two or more book, it's £115. The company flies from March to Oct or Nov, depending on the weather, from different venues in the south-east. The balloons can take up to sixteen people, and yes, you do have a pilot on board.

ICE SKATING

Broadgate Ice Rink

BROADGATE CIRCLE, EC2, 0171-505 4068

Open Oct-Apr: Mon-Fri noon-2.30pm & 3.30pm-6.30pm, Fri also 7pm-10pm, Sat, Sun 11am-1pm, 2pm-4pm, also Sat 5pm-8.30pm, Sun 5pm-7pm.

Britain's only open-air ice rink and consequently operating only in wintertime, it's a pretty place in the middle of the impressive new Broadgate development in the City. You can hire skates, buy equipment and book skating lessons.

Queen's Ice Skating Rink

17 QUEENSWAY, W2, 0171-229 0172

Open daily 10am-10pm in 2- or 3-hour sessions, charged variously.

You can hire skates at this renovated ice ring.

NEEDLEWORK

Courses

The Embroiderers' Guild

APT 41, HAMPTON CT PALACE, EAST MOLESEY, SURREY, KT8 9AU, 0181-943 1229, FAX 0181-977 9882

Exhibitions, classes, a library, shop and study schemes are all run by this crafts-based organisation. They have thousands of members in the UK and overseas who receive a Newsletter giving news of the Guild's activities.

Royal School of Needlework

APT 12A, HAMPTON COURT PALACE, EAST MOLESEY, SURREY, KT8 9AU, 0181-943 1432, FAX 0181-943 4910

The School was founded in 1872 by a daughter of Queen Victoria and friends, with the purpose of showing the beauty of handcrafted needlework and of finding suitable employment for ladies of gentle birth in strained circumstances. Today the School designs and makes banners for the military, undertakes all kinds of commissions, does smocking, and stretches customers' own work—everything in fact to do with the gentle art of needlework. They also hold open days, exhibitions, classes and private lessons throughout the year.

Suppliers

Ehrman
28A LANCER SQUARE, KENSINGTON CHURCH ST, W8, 0171-937 8123

Open Mon-Fri 9.30am-5.30pm, Sat 11am-4pm.

A treasure trove for needlework enthusiasts, Ehrmans stocks Kaffee Fassett, Annabel Nellist, Candace Bahouth and other designers. You can see everything made up before you buy the kit or appropriate materials (though sadly one's own efforts never quite look as good). They also sell loose canvases, tapestry wools and stationery.

Liberty
210-220 REGENT ST, W1, 0171-734 1234

Open Mon-Sat 10am-6.30pm, Thurs to 7.30pm.

This department store has an excellent needlework department staffed by people who are themselves experts.

Tapisserie
54 WALTON ST, SW3, 0171-581 2715

Open Mon-Fri 10am-5.30pm, Sat to 4pm.

If you're after one-off traditional English and Continental designs, make your way to this small but well-stocked shop. Antique themes are designed by their own team and you can get a picture of your own adapted to a canvas. All their canvases come with wools.

WHI Tapestry Shop
85 PIMLICO RD, SW1, 0171-730 5366

Open Mon.-Fri. 9.30am-5pm.

Good specialist supplier with all the best yarns and canvases on offer. They can also make up a set to your own design.

RIDING

Riding horses in Hyde Park is one of London's singular pleasures. Book in advance at any of the following stables for every day except Mondays. Prices are around £25 per hour and they can lend you hats if necessary. If you want to go further afield, **Richmond Park** is delightful. **Trent Park Equestrian Centre** is cheaper and very good for children.

Hyde Park Stables
63 BATHURST MEWS, W2, 0171-723 2813

Ross Nye
8 BATHURST MEWS, W2, 0171-262 3791

Roehampton Gate Stables
PRIORY LANE, SW15, 0181-876 7089

Trent Park Equestrian Centre
BRAMLEY RD, SOUTHGATE, N14, 0181-363 8630. CLOSED MON

Wimbledon Village Stables
24 A/B HIGH ST, WIMBLEDON VILLAGE, SW19, 0181-946 8579

SHOOTING

Holland & Holland
DUCKS HILL RD, NORTHWOOD, MIDDLSEX, HA6 2SS, 01923-825 349, FAX 01923-836 266

The famous gunmakers Holland and Holland have a shooting school 50 minutes by underground from central London where for £50 (cartridges and clay extra), you can clay-pigeon shoot for an hour.

For Outdoor Swimming

Try **Highgate** (men) and **Kenwood** (women), both off Millfield Lane, N6, or **Hampstead** (mixed bathing at the Hampstead Ponds, off East Heath Rd, NW3. For all venues tel: 0171-485 4491.

SWIMMING

Apart from pools attached to health clubs (see above), there are a number of good central London pools. Local authorities all have swimming pools and have lists available at local libraries. Also for indoor swimming try:

Chelsea Sports Centre

CHELSEA MANOR ST, SW3, 0171-352 6985

Porchester Centre

QUEENSWAY, W2, 0171-792 2919

Crystal Palace National Sports Centre

NORWOOD, SE19, 0181-778 0131

TENNIS & SQUASH

Squash is very difficult to play on a casual basis in London. You have either to be a member of a club, or book a local authority court. **The Jubilee Sports Centre**, **Porchester Centre** and **Crystal Palace Centre** are good bets to try. **The Squash Rackets Association**, Westpoint, 33-35 Warple Way, W3 ORG (0181-746 1616) can supply lists of clubs if you send a stamped addressed envelope with your request.

The top tennis tournament is, of course, the **All England Lawn Tennis Championships (Wimbledon)** first held in 1877. (All England Lawn Tennis and Croquet Club, Church Rd, Wimbledon SW19, 0181-946 2244). It's difficult to get tickets for this world-class event, but if you want to pay a premium, ticket agencies can often supply tickets—look in the classified section of major national newspapers. The enthusiastic can try queuing for return tickets after lunch on the day; it's fun, cheap and you often get to see a good four hours or so of tennis.

An equally enjoyable event (though less prestigious), played on grass courts in a club small enough to see the players properly, is the **Stella Artois Tournament at Queen's Club** (the run-up to Wimbledon). For information on this championship, call Stella Artois Information, 0171-581 4554.

For information on tennis and where to play in London, contact the **Lawn Tennis Association**, 0171-381 7000, Fax 0171-381 6050, at Queen's Club, Barons Court, W14, 0171-385 3421. There are few indoor tennis courts in London. For private clubs, try:

The Carlton Tennis & Health Club

ALFRED RD, WESTBOURNE GREEN, W2, 0171-286 1985, FAX 0171-940 7141

Open daily 7am-11pm (Sun from 8am).

Three indoor courts with well-laid Escotennis carpet surfaces and good lighting. Fitness studio, and more facilities. No temporary membership; though off-peak and full membership available. Gym membership is separate.

The Vanderbilt Racquet Club

31 STERNE ST, W12, 0181-743 9816/9822, FAX 0181-740 0440

Open daily 7am-11pm.

This club offers eight indoor tennis courts and one show court with good spectator facilities, stretch and fitness classes, a beautician, bar and restaurant and special treatment centre for sports injuries and general conditions such as stress, spinal pain and migraine. Yearly membership and temporary membership for overseas residents.

WATER SPORTS

Within London, water sports centres are concentrated in **Docklands**. Getting out on one of the old docks is an exhilarating experience. Hours vary according to the time of year and amount of daylight.

Docklands Water Sports Club

TEREZA JOANNE, KING GEORGE V DOCK, GATE 14, WOOLWICH MANOR WAY, E14, 0171-511 7000, FAX 0171-511 9000

Open Summer: daily; Winter: Thurs-Sun

This is the club to go to for wet-biking and jet-skiing. You can either bring your own craft or hire from the centre.

Docklands Sailing and Watersports Centre

WEST FERRY RD, MILLWALL DOCKS, E14, 0171-537 2626, FAX 0171-537 7774.

Open Summer: daily; Winter: times vary.

A session fee means you can windsurf by the day, or sail, canoe and go dragon-boating—where you sit in a canoe with 22 people accompanied by a dragon and a gong. All very Hong Kong, they will tell you.

WINE COURSES

Christie's Education

63 OLD BROMPTON RD, SW7 3JS, 0171-581 3933, FAX 0171-589 0383

Christie's auction some of the world's greatest wine. They also run top wine courses, an introductory evening course on five consecutive Tuesday evenings, and a special master class course which takes a closer look at classic wines and vintages.

Sotheby's Educational Studies

30 OXFORD ST, W1R 1RE, 0171-323 5775, FAX 0171-580 8160

Both varietal and regional courses on offer here throughout the year, covering tastings of Cabernet Sauvignon and Merlot, New World wines and more.

Wine Wise

107 CULFORD RD, N1, 0171-254 9734

This is an excellent company, run by wine expert and author Michael Schuster who holds tastings (some with food) with wines ranging from the everyday drinking wines to the world's great vintages. The beginner's course takes six evenings and covers wines from all over the world, as well as related subjects like the right kind of glasses to use, decanting etc.

HOUSES TO VISIT

Londoners are particularly proud of their famous residents; walk around any area and you'll see blue plaques galore on the outside of houses telling you who lived where and when. Even more enjoyable, given our intense curiosity about how other people live, is going inside what were once private homes. Happily London has more than its fair share, from the Queen's official residence to Dr. Johnson's small house in the City.

Buckingham Palace

SW1, 0171-9799 2331

State rooms open Aug-Oct: daily 9.15am-4.15pm. U: Victoria.

Buckingham Palace opened to the general public for the first time in August 1993 to help fund the restoration of parts of Windsor Castle after a hugely damaging fire. Imposing? Yes. Comfortable, beautiful, homely? No. But what everyone agreed on was the quality of the art, much of which was purchased by the (thankfully) spendthrift George IV. It's a huge place, functioning as both office and home and used for ceremonial state occasions like banquets for visiting heads of state. What the visitor sees are the Throne Room, Picture Gallery, Drawing Rooms, Grand Staircase and other impressive State rooms. The general opinion is that this is a place for the art lover, rather than royal watchers, though you do see the door through which the Royal family makes a sudden and dramatic entrance before formal dinners, and pass through the Music Room where the late Princess Diana used to tap dance. You can purchase souvenirs on your way out, each year based on a different room in the palace.

Charles Dickens House Museum

48 DOUGHTY ST, WC1, 0171-405 2127

Open Mon-Sat 10am-5pm. U: Russell Sq.

Many of the rooms are laid out exactly as they were when Dickens sat at his desk and wrote *Oliver Twist* and *Nicholas Nickelby*, and finished *Pickwick Papers*. The only one of Dickens's London homes to survive (he lived here from 1837 to 1839), it was bought by the Dickens Fellowship in the 1920s and has enough mementoes to satisfy the most enthusiastic fan: first editions, portraits, his terrible colour schemes and carpet, his desk and chair and such personal items as marked-up prompt copies for his lucrative public readings.

Dr Johnson's House

17 GOUGH SQUARE, EC4, 0171-353 3745

Open Mon-Sat May-Sep: 11am-5.30pm; Oct-Apr: 11am-5pm. U: Aldwych/Chancery Lane.

Dive into Hind Court off Fleet Street and then into Gough Square for a glimpse of eighteenth-century life. Dr Samuel Johnson (1709-84) lived here from 1749 to 1759, compiling his great dictionary in the attic, surrounded by six assistants and scribes who stood at high desks, industriously scratching away with their quill pens. But go for the atmosphere and the sense of peace in this hectic part of the City of London. As the day comes to an end, it's easy to imagine the good Doctor putting down his pen, snuffing out his candle, and walking out for ale and good company at one of the nearby taverns.

Fenton House

20 HAMPSTEAD GROVE, NW3, 0171-435 3471
Open Mar: Sat & Sun 2pm-5pm; Apr-1 Nov: Wed-Fri 2pm-5pm, Sat, Sun & Bank hol Mons. 11am-5pm. National Trust. U: Hampstead.

This pretty, gracious William and Mary house, built in 1693, is full of early keyboard instruments (kept in full working order and used for concerts here), fine eighteenth-century furniture and a magnificent collection of porcelain. The formal garden is a delight on a sunny day and as the house is surrounded by other old Hampstead mansions, the sense of the past is palpable.

Who Lived Where

Walking around London's streets you'll notice **blue plaques** on the sides of houses telling you which famous personage lived there and when. You'll be surprised—an Indian poet in the Vale of Health on Hampstead Heath, **Mozart** in Ebury Street, **Handel** in Brook Street. There are some surprising finds as well as some obscure ones. To qualify a candidate must have been dead for at least twenty years and born more than one hundred years ago and to have made some positive and important contribution to human welfare or happiness.

Freud Museum

20 MARESFIELD GDNS, NW3, 0171-435 2002
Open Wed-Sun noon-5pm. U: Hampstead.

In 1938 Sigmund Freud (1856-1939), the founder of psychoanalysis, escaped war-time Vienna and arrived in leafy Hampstead. Until his death here a year later, he worked surrounded by his possessions in what was a replica of his Vienna consulting rooms. His collection of antiquities, his working library and papers and the famous desk and couch are all on display. On his death in 1939, his daughter Anna kept the house as it was; it opened as a museum in 1986.

Ham House

HAM ST, RICHMOND, 0181-940 1950
Open Mar-1 Nov: Sat-Wed 1pm-5pm, gardens Sat-Wed 10.30am-6pm. National Trust. U: Richmond.

Standing by the River Thames, Ham House was built in 1610 but came into its own with the redoubtable Countess of Dysart (c1626-98) and her second husband, the Duke of Lauderdale. In an age that valued comfort and elegance, the Duchess spared no expense. The house passed to the Duchess's son by her first marriage, a man as miserly as his mother was prodigal, and declined. But as a result the house remained in its original form and now appears locked in the past. The grand rooms contain wonderful furniture and fabrics while the kitchens are full of roasting spits, scrubbed wooden tables and even a seventeenth-century mouse trap.

John Wesley's House & Chapel

49 CITY RD, EC1, 0171-253 2262
Open Mon-Sat 10am-4pm, Sun noon-2pm. U: Old St.

John Wesley, the founder of the Methodist church, laid the chapel's foundation stone in 1777 and lived in the house next door in the last years of his life. Five storeys high but only two rooms deep, it's rightly plain with bare wooden floors and little furniture. The chapel where Baroness Thatcher was married is also austere, with columns made from ships' masts.

Kensington Palace

KENSINGTON GARDENS, W8, 0171-937 9561
Open daily 9.30am-4.30pm (last admission). U: High St Kensington.

Built in 1605 and beautifully sited in Kensington Gardens with some delightful grounds of its own, the palace is an architectural delight as well as the private home of various members of the Royal Family, particularly the late Princess Diana. The King's Gallery is spectacular but all has been beautifully restored. The Dress Collection, which is guided only, is arranged in different settings, all around the theme of presentation at court. You go through a tailor's workshop, a gentlemen's outfitters and more, complete with sound effects and special fibre optics displays.

Kenwood House

KENWOOD HOUSE, HAMPSTEAD LANE, NW3, 0181-348 1286
Open daily Apr-Sep: 10am-6pm or dusk; Oct-Mar: 10am-4pm. Wed, Fri open 10.30am. Admission free. U: Hampstead.

A magnificent mansion remodelled by Robert Adam in 1764, this neo-classical house set high on Hampstead Heath in landscaped gardens was rescued by Edward Cecil Guinness, 1st Earl of Iveagh, in 1925, and given to London. The library is the architectural highlight, but the real glory of the house is its collection of treasures: paintings many national galleries covet and the very finest English eighteenth-century furniture. It's beloved by locals—children and dogs play in the grounds, families picnic beside the lake. Now administered by English Heritage, it holds a series of highly popular open-air summertime concerts by the lake. (Look in national newspapers for details).

Leighton House

12 HOLLAND PARK RD, W14, 0171-602 3316
Open Mon-Sat 11am-5.30pm. Admission free. U: High St Kensington.

The flamboyant, purpose-built studio and house of Pre-Raphaelite artist Lord Leighton is a rare sight in fashionable Kensington. Built in 1866 at the height of the Victorian Aesthetic movement for the wildly fashionable portrait painter, the high point is the Arab Hall added in 1879 to accommodate the Islamic tiles he acquired on his travels, and Walter Crane's gilt mosaic frieze. Paintings by Leighton and his contemporaries hang in the richly decorated rooms.

Linley Sambourne House

18 STAFFORD TERR, W8, 0171-937 0663.
Open 1 Mar-Oct: Wed 10am-4pm, Sun 2-5pm. U: High St Kensington.

Built in the 1870s, Number 18 was the home from 1874 to 1910 of Linley Sambourne, book illustrator and political cartoonist for the satirical magazine *Punch*. As you enter the cluttered, olive-green hall with its small fireplace, dinner gong and heavy curtains to keep dangerous draughts at bay, and wander through the rooms, the years slip away. The house is a perfect, almost totally intact example of a late Victorian, early Edwardian home.

Queen's House

ROMNEY RD, SE10, 0181-858 4422
Open daily 10am-5pm. BR: Greenwich

Designed by Inigo Jones and finished in 1637, this charming small palace became home to various of England's queens. Recently restored and furnished to be as perfect a replica of a seventeenth-century house as possible, it is bright, almost garish in its decorations. The 'tulip staircase' is a famous architectural feature. Flickering candles give extra atmosphere.

Sir John Soane Museum

14 LINCOLN'S INN FIELDS, WC2, 0171-430 0175
Open Tues-Sat 10am-5pm. First Tues of each month 6pm-9pm. Admission free. U: Holborn.

The son of a brick-layer, John Soane (1753-1837) rose to become one of Britain's leading architects. He designed the Bank of England, Dulwich Picture Gallery and more, and as an art patron accumulated and commissioned a wide variety of works. The astonishing result is an eclectic collection remaining much as he left it, and both the house and the collection are full of surprises. The already crowded walls of the picture gallery unfold to reveal yet more paintings (such as William Hogarth's *Rake's Progress* series which cost £570 in 1802); the Monk's Parlour is full of grotesque Gothic casts; a vast sarcophagus stands in the crypt. Seek out the design for his wife's tombstone: it inspired Britain's old-style red telephone boxes.

Southside House

WIMBLEDON COMMON, SW19, 0181-946 7643
Open Oct-May Tues, Thurs, Sat & Bank hol Mons. Guided tours only every hour 2pm-4pm. Tel. to book and check times. U: Wimbledon.

This is a house where the phrase 'entering a time warp' has real meaning. Lived in continuously by the same family since it was built in 1687, this small red-brick mansion which has been left mercifully unrestored, is full of odd family treasures—the pearls worn by Marie Antoinette at her execution and the cuff links given by King Edward VII to Axel Munthe, the doctor who became famous for his work with the poor in southern Italy and who wrote the best-seller *The Villa of San Michele* in the 1920s. To the surprise of the fashionable world, Axel Munthe wooed and married the society beauty Hilda Pennington, whose family owned the house...but that's another story. Visit this atmospheric home, so full of ghosts. Each time you enter a room you feel that the occupants of the past have just closed the far door quietly behind them, leaving you to enjoy their house for a few minutes before they return.

Spencer House

27 St. James's Pl, SW1, 0171-499 8620

Open every Sun except in Jan & Aug. Guided tours only 10.30am-4.45pm. Timed tickets available from 10.30am on the day of the tour. U: Green Park.

Spencer House was built in the mid-eighteenth century for John, first Earl of Spencer, in fashionable St. James's, conveniently close to the monarch at St. James's Palace. The former London home of the late Princess of Wales's family, it has been sumptuously and correctly restored by Lord Rothschild, who currently leases the house, one of the very few examples surviving of an eighteenth-century townhouse. The Spencer family was noted for its art collection and legendary and lavish entertaining, and for a few thousand pounds, you too can hire the house and dine in the gilded surroundings.

Sutton House

2 & 4 Homerton High St, E9, 0181-986 2264

Open Feb-Nov Wed, Sun & bank hols: 11.30am-5.30pm, Sat 2pm-5.30pm. National Trust. BR: Homerton.

Built for a Tudor politician in 1535 when Hackney was a country village, this is the oldest surviving domestic building in East London. It has been beautifully restored to give a real idea of the period.

Thomas Carlyle's House

24 Cheyne Row, SW3, 0171-352 7087

Open Apr-Nov: Wed-Sun, Bank hol Mon. 11am-5pm. National Trust. U: Sloane Sq.

'A most massive, roomy, sufficient old house... Rent £35'. So wrote Thomas Carlyle in 1834 of his new lodging in fashionable Chelsea. Left as he and his wife Jane had it, it's a modest house where he wrote some of his greatest books like *The French Revolution*, and *Frederick the Great*. Personal touches—his hat hanging by the garden door, a screen his wife decorated—bring this little house to life.

Two Willow Road

2 Willow Rd, NW3, 0171-435 6166

Open Apr-31 Oct: Thurs, Fri, Sat noon-5pm, entry by timed ticket only. National Trust. U: Hampstead.

Great 20th century architect, Erno Goldfinger, designed and built 2 Willow Road for himself in 1939. The house is one of Britain's best examples of modernist architecture. The rooms contain furniture Goldfinger designed, and works by contemporary artists like Henry Moore.

IN SEARCH OF THE UNUSUAL

Cabaret Mechanical Theatre

Covent Garden Market, WC2, 0171-379 7961

Open Mon-Fri 10am-6.30pm, Sat to 7pm, Sun 11am-6.30pm. U: Covent Garden.

Fun collection of automata where old-fashioned, hand-built mainly wooden machines go through some extraordinary routines. Great for parents and children.

Cabinet War Rooms

Clive Steps, King Charles St, SW1, 0171-930 6961

Open daily 10am-6pm (last admission 5.15pm). U: St. James's Park.

The underground war rooms from where Sir Winston Churchill and his cabinet directed the war, it's a fascinating place, full of old equipment, radios and resounding to the sounds of war.

Clockmakers' Company Collection

Guildhall Library, Aldermanbury, EC2, 0171-606 3030

Open Mon-Fri 9.30am-4.40pm. Admission free. U: Moorgate/St. Pauls.

It's a good thing to try to go to the museum in the morning when this large collection (some 600 watches and 30 clocks dating from the sixteenth to the nineteenth centuries) chimes, bongs and tinkles the hours. But at any time, the collection holds surprises. The oldest surviving clocks date from the 1300s; by 1675 English watches using hair-springs could run to within an accurate two minutes a day; in 1752 the world's first watch to compensate against the effects of heat and cold was made; by 1785 there were self-winding watches. You come away wondering where our need for accurate timing will lead.

Dennis Severs' House

18 FOLGATE ST, E1, 0171 247 4013
Open 1st Sun of each month 2pm-5pm & next day Mon 6pm-9pm for candle-lit viewing. U: Liverpool St.

American Dennis Severs was one of the first enthusiasts to buy a house in Spitalfields and save it from destruction. In line with many of the people in the street, the house has been restored correctly to 200 years ago. In fact, so correctly, that a tour of the house gives an idea of what life really was like in the past. Telephone first to book.

Fawcett Library

LONDON GUILDHALL UNIVERSITY, OLD CASTLE ST, E1, 0171-320 1189
Open term time: Mon 9am-8.30pm, Thurs, Fri 9am-5pm. U: Aldgate East.

Britain's main reference collection on women is the direct descendant of the London Society for Women's Suffrage, founded in 1867. It holds over 50,000 books, pamphlets and leaflets, periodicals, boxes of papers on relevant organisations, newspaper cuttings and photographs, autographed letters and posters. The library is part of the university, but non-members can use it on a daily basis for a small fee. Dedicated feminists as well as those with a general interest in the women's movement will find it invaluable.

Museum of Rugby

RUGBY FOOTBALL UNION, RUGBY RD, TWICKENHAM, 0181-892 2000
Open Tues-Sat 10.30am-5pm. Sun 2pm-5pm. BR: Twickenham.

One of the great sports has finally got a museum worthy of it, though it's a museum for the aficionado rather than the casual visitor. Beneath Twickenham's famous stand, the Museum comes, if you like, as part of the package of the Twickenham Experience, where visitors take a guided tour of the stadium and see behind the scenes. The museum itself which can be visited separately, has caps and kits from past heroes, paintings, prints, trophies as well as ceramics, silver and bronze.

The Old Operating Theatre, Museum & Herb Garret

9A ST. THOMAS' ST, SE1, 0171-955 4791
Open daily 10am-4pm. U: London Bridge.

The oldest surviving operating theatre in the country was built in 1822 from part of the herb garret. With its banked seats for students to watch as surgeons performed their grisly tasks before the days of anaesthetics and antiseptic surgery it is just like a theatre. The herb garret, used by the Apothecary of nearby St. Thomas's, has objects like instruments for the ancient art of cupping and trepanning. With such reminders of the crude medicine of the past, you emerge doubly grateful for being born in the twentieth century. They hold lectures at 2.30pm on the first Sunday of every month on the history of Old St. Thomas's Hospital and Guy's and the history of health care, as well as frequent events, so check in advance.

Ragged School Museum

46-48 COPPERFIELD RD, E3, 0181 980 6405
Open Wed & Thurs 10am-5pm, 1st Sun of each month 2pm-5pm. Admission free. U: Mile End.

The philanthropist Dr Barnardo converted these Victorian warehouses beside the canal a century ago for orphans. East End local history is on display here in a reconstructed Victorian schoolroom. Enough to inspire today's school children that theirs is a happier lot than they give credit for. They regularly hold excellent activities for children, so check in advance.

Royal College of Music Museum of Instruments

PRINCE CONSORT RD, SW7, 0171-589 3643
Open Wed in term time: 2pm-4pm. U: South Kensington.

Housed in the prestigious Royal College of Music which has had as pupils Benjamin Britten, Ralph Vaughan Williams and other leading British musicians, this valuable collection of around 500 instruments must be on your list if you have an interest in music and the means of making it.

Winston Churchill's Britain at War

64-65 TOOLEY ST, SE1, 0171-403 3171
Open daily 10am-4.30pm. U: London Bridge.

Make your way through civilian London life in World War II—from air raids to rationing. Good shop also.

MUSEUMS

London has some of the best museums in the world, both large and small, so we have included in this section major museums and those we think you should see for their specialist interest or idiosyncratic nature. We have noted where admission is free; otherwise there is an admission charge. If you are in London over a public holiday, please check opening times.

Tourist/Visitor Passes

The English Heritage Overseas Visitors Pass, £12 for adults, £22 for two adults and £26 for a family gives 7 days free admission to more than 120 English Heritage castles, abbeys, houses and monuments as well as events in London and the countryside. A two-week Pass costs £16 for adults, £30 for two adults and £35 for a family. Available at all English Heritage properties. Tel for information: 0171-973 3434. **The London White Card** gives access to 15 major museums and galleries for £15 for 3 days, £25 for 7 days. Tel for information: 0171-434 4629. **The National Art Collection Fund's** membership (£25 per person, family membership £45, plus £12 postage outside the EC) gives free admission to many UK galleries, special exhibition discounts and more. Tel for information: 0171-225 4800.

Apsley House

149 PICCADILLY, HYDE PARK CORNER, W1, 0171-499 5676.

Open Tues-Sun 11am-5pm.
U: Hyde Park Corner.

Originally built by Robert Adam between 1771 and 1778 as just one part of a spectacular neo-classical terrace, Apsley House was lived in by the Duke of Wellington, or the 'Iron Duke' as he was familiarly known after he won the Battle of Waterloo in 1817. Known as 'Number One, London' because it was the first building you saw on entering London from the west, it is now full of a priceless collection of furnishing, fabrics, china and mementoes.

BBC Experience

BROADCASTING HOUSE, PORTLAND PLACE, W1, 0870 603 0304

Open daily 9.30am-5.30pm. U: Oxford Circus.

Down in the basement of Broadcasting House, 'Auntie' has revealed some great archival footage and secrets of her 75-year history. It's an interactive performance where you enter a series of small cinemas and listen to the voices of the past while images add to the effect, and you can take part in a studio radio performance (if you so wish). A great show.

Bank of England Museum

BANK OF ENGLAND, BARTHOLOMEW LANE, EC2, 0171-601 5545

Open Mon-Fri 10am-5pm, except Bank hols.
U: Bank.

'The Old Lady of Threadneedle Street' (as the bank was named by the playwright and politician Sheridan) was set up in 1694 to raise money for foreign wars, came under government control in 1766 and was nationalised in 1946. The museum tells the story of the 'banker's bank' (and a surprisingly exciting one it is), and the story of the development of the financial system, with displays from glittering gold bars to dealing desks.

Bethnal Green Museum of Childhood

CAMBRIDGE HEATH RD, E2, 0181-983 5200

Open Mon-Thurs & Sat 10am-5.50pm, Sun 2.30pm-5.30pm. Admission free.
U: Bethnal Green.

This delightful treasure house in the East End of London is housed in one of the temporary train-shed buildings put up for the original Victoria and Albert Museum (which it is still part of) in South Kensington. Re-erected piece-by-piece in 1872, the cast-iron building now contains the nation's toy box. Walk inside and you're magically transported back in time through your own childhood to the seventeenth century. What delights and reassures is the fact that children's pleasures have changed so little. Dolls' houses from three centuries still attract crowds of small children pointing out miniature pianos, plates and furniture; others put money into the machine that makes the model trains go around their eternal circle. It's a wonderful mix of toys and games, dolls and magic lantern shows, model railways and board games from all over Europe. They hold special children's workshops every Saturday.

Bramah Tea & Coffee Museum

THE CLOVE BLDG, MAGUIRE ST, BUTLERS WHARF, SE1, 0171-378 0222

Open daily 10am-6pm. U: London Bridge.

This museum, devoted to the history of the much-loved beverages, tea and coffee, is housed down by the warehouses where cargoes were brought ashore. It's the brain-child of Edward Bramah, former tea merchant and taster, whose huge and comprehensive collection of teapots, coffee pots and general tea and coffee making machinery forms the main bulk of the museum. And do have a cup of tea or coffee in the café—the taste (particularly of the tea) will remind you of the past glories of the drink before the almost universal use of the dreaded tea-bag.

British Museum

GREAT RUSSELL ST, WC1, 0171-636 1555

Open Mon-Sat 10am-5pm, Sun 2.30pm-6pm. Admission free. (Special evening opening: first Tues of the month 6pm-9pm, admission £5, free for members of the Friends of the British Museum).

U: Tottenham Court Rd.

The British Museum, one of the world's greatest museums, was started by the physician Sir Hans Sloane (1660-1753) who suggested in his will that the government buy his private collection. This they did and in 1753 passed the British Museum Act for London's (and the world's) first public museum. Benefactors gave generously and the collection rapidly outgrew the original location in Montagu House, Bloomsbury. George II bequeathed the Royal Library of 10,500 volumes (1757), Sir William Hamilton gave his antique vase collection (1772), the famous Greek Marbles from the Parthenon and Erechtheum from Greece were bought from Lord Elgin in 1816 and George III donated his library of 120,800 books in 1823. The present neo-classical building (1823-38) designed by Robert Smirke now houses some four million objects, divided between different departments (Greek and Roman, Egyptian, Ethnography, Prehistory and Roman Britain, Oriental, Coins and Medals, Medieval and Later Antiquities, Prints and Drawings, Western Asiatic and Japanese Antiquities). There are so many treasures—Egyptian mummies, the Portland Vase, the glorious Lindisfarne gospels, the Sutton Hoo ship burial, the magnificent Chinese art—it is impossible to see them all in one visit. The best way to explore the museum is to pick up a map in the front hall and choose one or two particular topics or galleries to wander around. And then come back for your favourites.

Cuming Museum

155-157 WALWORTH RD, SE17, 0171-701 1342

Open Tues-Sat 10am-5pm.

U: Elephant & Castle.

A wonderful collection and the museum of Southwark's history, full of artefacts relating to the life of Londoners.

Design Museum

BUTLERS WHARF, SHAD THAMES, SE1, 0171-403 6933

Open Mon-Fri 11.30am-6pm, Sat & Sun from noon. U: London Bridge.

This museum, the brain-child of Sir Terence Conran, is devoted to the design of mass-produced everyday objects from chairs to cars, lemon squeezers to radios. International design is displayed in temporary exhibitions with different themes, and there's an exciting interactive section where you can research details on the history and design of every object you can think of. You want to know about chairs? Legs of chairs? History? Famous designers? Just follow the instructions on the screen.

Fan Museum

12 CROOMS HILL, GREENWICH, SE10, 0181-305 1441

Open Tues-Sat 11am-4.30pm. BR: Greenwich.

Fans may seem at first an unlikely subject for a museum, but this one is full of surprises. The museum shows fans in themed exhibitions like those decorated with children or flowers; there is a permanent display on the history and materials used in fan making, and a craft workshop which holds fan-making classes and undertakes conservation and restoration.

Florence Nightingale Museum

ST. THOMAS'S HOSPITAL, LAMBETH PALACE RD, SE1, 0171-620 0374

Open Tues-Sun 10am-5pm. U: Waterloo.

Florence Nightingale, born into a well-to-do Victorian family, became a nurse (not a profession for a lady) and was sent to the Crimean War. Her reorganisation of Scutari Hospital and fame as 'the lady with the lamp' (she sat at the deathbeds of 2,000 men, believing no-one should die alone), turned out to be only a small part of her achievements. On her return home she became a tireless campaigner for hospital reform and set the standards of nursing care and training we know today. The museum tells the story of this formidable lady's remarkable life with room sets, pictures, and personal memorabilia.

Geffrye Museum

KINGSLAND RD, E2, 0171-739 9893

Open Tues-Sat 10am-5pm, Sun, Mon & public hols 2pm-5pm. U: Liverpool St.

This delightful museum is housed in a charming collection of alms-houses which were built for the poor in 1715. In the centre of the former furniture-making area in the East End, it became a museum in 1911. The interior is arranged as a series of room settings taking you through the story of English furnishings and decorative tastes, from a 1600 panelled Elizabethan room through the elegance of the Georgians to the 1950s. Outside there's a walled herb garden. It's a charming place and especially good to visit around Christmas for their special displays.

Guards Museum

WELLINGTON BARRACKS, BIRDCAGE WALK, SW1, 0171-930 4466

Open Mon-Thurs, Sat, Sun 10am-4pm.
U: St. James's Park.

If you're a military enthusiast, this is a must, full of tableaux, weapons, uniforms, models and dioramas to illustrate the battles that the five famous Guards regiments have taken part in.

Horniman Museum

100 LONDON RD, FOREST HILL, SE23, 0181-699 1872

Open Mon-Sat 10.30am-5.30pm, Sun 2pm-5.30pm. BR: Forest Hill.

The tea merchant, Frederick Horniman, clearly a man with a tremendous curiosity about his fellow human beings, had this Art Nouveau museum built in 1901 to house all the odd objects he had collected on his travels—everything from Navajo paintings to objects you'd be hard put to name if there wasn't a handy description nearby. Most famous is the collection of 1,500 musical instruments from all over the world. Displayed in the music room, you can hear, through headphones, hundreds of different instruments. The museum is set in 16 acres of gardens with extensive views over London.

Imperial War Museum

LAMBETH RD, SE1, 0171-416 5320

Open daily 10am-6pm. U: Lambeth North.

Perhaps it is appropriate that the Imperial War Museum, dedicated to the paraphernalia and story of twentieth-century war, should be housed in the former Bethlehem Hospital for the Insane ('Bedlam') built in 1811. The museum, with its huge guns outside and the machinery of war inside, is impressive. So, too, is the story of the social effects of war: the deprivation, food rationing, air raid precautions and censorship. Extracts from wartime films, radio programmes and literature, paintings and photographs are on display as are strange artefacts like Montgomery's caravan office and the German straw overboots for protection against Russia's cold. The museum is kept up-to-date: the most recent exhibits relate to the Gulf War of 1991.

The Jewish Museum

RAYMOND BURTON HOUSE, 129-131 ALBERT ST, CAMDEN TOWN, NW1, 0171-284 1997;
& 80 EAST END RD, FINCHLEY, N3, 0181-349 1143

Open Camden Town: Sun-Thurs 10am-4pm; Finchley: Mon-Thurs 10.30am-5pm, Sun to 4.30pm. Tel. first to check opening times on Jewish Festivals. Camden Town: U: Camden Town; Finchley U: Finchley Central

With one of the world's finest collection of Jewish ceremonial art, it also shows the lives of British Jews. Finchley houses the social history collections including an Oral History Archive, a Photographic Archive and many documents. There are also frequently changing exhibition.

Kew Bridge Steam Museum

GREEN DRAGON LANE, BRENTFORD, MIDDLESEX, 0181-568 4757

Open daily 11am-5pm. U: Gunnersbury/Kew Gardens.

In an unmistakable, extraordinary nineteenth-century pumping station next to Kew Bridge, this fascinating and idiosyncratic museum illustrates how steam engines pumped west London's water supply. New award-winning Water for Life gallery is interactive; telephone in advance for information on the days when the engines are in steam.

London Canal Museum

12-13 New Wharf Rd, N1, 0171-713 0836

Open Tues-Sun 10am-4.30pm. U: King's Cross.

In a former mid-19th century warehouse that held imported ice from Norway, it tells how London's canals were built and developed with many models on show.

London Toy and Model Museum

21/23 Craven Hill, W1, 0171-402 5222

Open daily 9am-5.40pm. U: Paddington.

With over 7,000 toys and models, this is a super museum for both parents and children. Originally a private collection, it has been renovated and now has 20 themed galleries each telling a different story with interactive displays. There's a delightful model railway in the garden and a good shop and café.

London Transport Museum

The Piazza, Covent Garden, WC2, 0171-379 6344

Open daily 10am-6pm, Fri from 11am.
U: Covent Garden.

Don't pass this one by thinking it's just full of old vehicles. It's a lively place, with lots of hands-on exhibits for children, and yes, lots of old but interesting vehicles from the original horse-bus of 1829 to trams and tube trains. The art collection fascinates, too: London Transport has always commissioned first-rate artists for their posters, including Graham Sutherland and Paul Nash.

Museum of Garden History

Lambeth Palace Rd, SE1, 0171-261 1891

Open 1st Sun in Mar-2nd Sun in Dec: Mon-Fri 10.30am-4pm, Sun 10.30am-5pm.
U: Lambeth North.

This was started as a labour of love by Rosemary Nicholson in what was the shut and decaying church of St. Mary-at-Lambeth, beside the Archbishop of Canterbury's London home, Lambeth Palace. With the help of dedicated gardeners, who included Lady Salisbury of Hatfield House and the Queen Mother, the church opened as a museum in 1979, dedicated to the history of gardening in Britain. It's officially the Tradescant Trust, called after the Tradescants, father and son, who were gardeners to seventeenth-century monarchs, and dedicated plant hunters in Russia, Europe and particularly the Americas. They were also the Salisbury family's gardeners. The museum has good changing exhibitions, and the churchyard, which has a knot garden planted with seventeenth-century plants, is a delightful place on a summer afternoon. The Tradescants are buried in the churchyard, alongside Captain Bligh of Bounty fame.

Museum of London

150 London Wall, EC2, 0171-600 3699.

Open Tues-Sat 10am-5.50pm; public hols, Sun noon-5.50pm. U: Barbican/Moorgate.

Arranged chronologically, the museum tells the story of London in an intriguing way with each section providing a vivid idea of what living in London was like throughout the ages. You pass through the newly reconstructed Roman section complete with Roman kitchen, see the Cheapside Hoard of jewellery cascading down a chimney just as it was found, walk past eighteenth-century prisons, grocers' shops, through elegant Regency London to the city of the Suffragettes, the Blitz and the Swinging Sixties. One of the high points is the cinematic experience of watching the Great Fire of London: Samuel Pepys' contemporary account is read with suitable solemnity while the model of London appears to burn and crash to the ground in front of your eyes. The museum offers a delightful visual experience, holds frequent exhibitions and in the cinema shows a changing programme of classic British movies from the days when Britain had a movie industry.

Museum of the Moving Image

South Bank Centre, SE1, 0171-401 2636.

Open daily 10am-6pm. U: Waterloo.

A fascinating journey through the history of moving pictures from the earliest flickering experiments with zeotropes and magic lanterns to holograms and beyond. Exhibits come in all sorts of guises; the section on Charlie Chaplin (born in nearby Kennington) is illustrated with clips from his films and artefacts from his life like his indispensable cane. Actors dressed in appropriate costumes invite you into a cinema to watch a silent movie, aboard a 1919 Lenin Agitprop train for a piece of early Russian propaganda, or to try for a part in an early Hollywood film. The amazing technology allows the artistic to draw their own cartoons and the ambitious to watch themselves reading the news.

National Army Museum

ROYAL HOSPITAL RD, SW3, 0171-730 0717
Open daily 10am-5.30pm. Admission free. U: Sloane Sq.

The museum records five centuries of the British Army from 1485 to the present day with weapons, paintings, tableaux, dioramas and film clips. Students of military history should write or telephone for a reader's ticket to the comprehensive, rare collection of manuscripts, books, maps, drawings and more.

National Maritime Museum

ROMNEY RD, GREENWICH, SE10, 0181-858 4422
Open daily 10am-5pm. BR: Greenwich.

This large museum, founded in 1934, is devoted to Britain's great maritime history. The superb collections include models of ships from all ages and of all types, the finest collection of globes in the world, early charts and instruments. An interactive gallery occupies an entire wing. The 'All Hands' centre concentrates on the lives of people connected with the sea. Each year there are major long-running exhibitions. The museum gives a wonderful insight into the importance of maritime developments to this island race, and goes a long way to helping understand British pride in past exploits and successes around the world.

Natural History & Geological Museum

CROMWELL RD, SW7, 0171-938 9123
Open Mon-Sat 10am-5.50pm, Sun 11am-5.50pm. Admission charge but free 4.30pm-5.50pm. U: South Kensington.

More than 65 million species make up one of the world's largest collections of animals, plants, fossils and minerals which was founded originally on the private collection of the celebrated physician Sir Hans Sloane whose collection also helped found the main British Museum. Traditional displays alongside interactive techniques prompt questions about ecology and evolution, the origin of the species and how human beings have developed. It has some spectacular new exhibits including the popular permanent Dinosaur Exhibition and one on insects (Creepy-Crawlies), both of which display life-like models. The building is worth a visit in itself: a huge cathedral-like space designed by Alfred Waterhouse using revolutionary Victorian building techniques and covered outside with a stone facade of a veritable zoo of animals as well as plants. The museum incorporates the former Geological Museum which tells the story of the Earth in a spectacular way. The Earth Galleries explore our planet and its natural resources; the gemstone collection draws students of gemology from all over the world who come to see the unique fibrolite, the orange sapphire, tourmalines and other priceless gems.

Old Royal Observatory

GREENWICH PARK, SE10, 0181-858 4422
Open daily 10am-5pm. BR: Greenwich.

Flamsteed House, originally built for the Flamsteed, the first Astronomer Royal and appointed by King Charles II, was the official government observatory from 1675 to 1948 when London's lights became too bright to see the heavens and it moved to Sussex. Today it is full of astronomical instruments, clocks and chronometers, but is perhaps best known as the place of the meridian (0 longitude) dividing the eastern and western hemispheres. The Observatory is part of the National Maritime Museum.

Royal Air Force Museum

GRAHAM PARK WAY, NW9, 0181-205 2266
Open daily 10am-6pm. BR: Mill Hill Broadway.

A must for anyone interested in the history of aviation and the story of the Royal Air Force with aircraft displayed in a vast hall. The museum has three separate sections: the RAF Museum, the Battle of Britain Museum and the Bomber Command Museum. There are also effective exhibits of room settings, air raid shelters and command posts which convey a very real atmosphere.

Science Museum

EXHIBITION RD, SW7, 0171-938 8000

Open daily 10am-6pm. Admission charge but free 4.30pm-6pm. U: South Kensington.

The Science Museum will thrill even the most unscientific-minded. Leaving aside the Space Exploration Galleries and Launch Pad, (a first-class hands-on exhibition for children), the museum, with its five floors of exhibits, brings such varied subjects as medical history, the art of navigation, the weather, computers and transport to life. Exhibits range from a magnificent collection of scientific instruments and apparatus originally belonging to King George III in the eighteenth century, Puffing Billy, the earliest surviving locomotive (1813), to Apollo 10. How scientific discoveries and progress have transformed our lives plays an equally important part, and there are enough interactive displays to satisfy the most avid seeker after scientific discovery, from age three upwards.

Sherlock Holmes Museum

221B BAKER ST, NW1, 0171-935 8866

Open daily 9.30am-6pm. U: Baker St.

A faithful reconstruction of Holmes' rooms at 221b Baker Street, this small museum with its memorabilia of the world's most famous sleuth is a must for Holmes' fans.

Sovereign Gallery

THE ROYAL MINT, 7 GROSVENOR GARDENS, SW1, 0171-931 7977

Open Mon-Fri 10am-4pm. U: Victoria.

Run by The Royal Mint, it tells the story of the sovereign, the gold coin King Henry VII introduced. Also all the new issues are on show (and many are on sale) here.

Theatre Museum

RUSSELL ST, WC2, 0171-836 2330

Open Tues-Sun 11am-7pm. U: Covent Garden.

There's a fascinating collection of theatrical memorabilia- from death masks, to playbills, costumes to make-up boxes, a model of Shakespeare's Globe to a jumpsuit of Mick Jagger's here. They hold different exhibitions throughout the year, and have on display the important Somerset Maugham collection of theatrical paintings, brought here from the Royal National Theatre. If you love the theatre it's worth a visit.

Victoria & Albert Museum

CROMWELL RD, SW7, 0171-938 8500. 24-HR INFORMATION LINE 0171-938 8441

Open Tues-Sun 10am-5.50pm, Mon from noon. Late viewing Wed 6.30pm-9.30pm. Donation suggested. U: South Kensington.

The V and A as it is popularly known, officially the National Museum of Art and Design, is the largest decorative arts museum in the world, covering a mind-boggling seven miles of galleries. Opened in 1857 with the accent on design and craft in commerce, it was the brainchild of Prince Albert and civil servant Sir Henry Cole (who, incidentally, sent the first Christmas card in 1843). The massive, comprehensive museum is arranged in a unique way. It is divided into galleries devoted to art and design to express the style of an age (such as Europe from 1600 to 1800), and into study collections which concentrate on materials and techniques. The Dress collection, the Historic Musical Instruments Collection, the Indian Gallery (which contains the greatest collection of Indian Art outside India, a legacy of the British Empire), the Chinese Gallery, the Japanese Toshiba Gallery, the Glass Galleries, the Silver Galleries, the Raphael Cartoons, and the Jewellery Gallery all merit visits. Unless you have a specific purpose in mind, the best way to enjoy the museum is to wander through at random. That way you discover sections like the vast metalwork department, full of snuff-boxes, arms and armour, watches, clocks, locks and salt cellars, or the extraordinary Cast Courts which turn out to be two galleries containing Victorian plaster casts of Europe's great sculptures and masonry originally made as teaching aids. As so much of Europe's art is eroding with pollution, this was not such a crazy idea.

Wimbledon Lawn Tennis Museum

CHURCH RD, WIMBLEDON, SW19, 0181-946 6131

Open Tues-Sat 10.30am-5pm, Sun 2-5pm. (Open during Wimbledon fortnight for ticket holders). U: Southfields.

Lawn tennis grew out of Real Tennis in the 1870s; in 1875 one croquet lawn at the All England Croquet Club was transformed into a tennis court and the new game became all the rage. The museum is both great fun (lots of good exhibits often displayed in appropriate room settings) and informative. Did you know that Bunny Austin was the first man to wear shorts on the Centre Court (1933), that each racket uses 33 feet of animal gut and that 33,000 bath buns and eighteen tons of strawberries are consumed every Wimbledon fortnight?

PARKS & GARDENS

Battersea Park

ALBERT BRIDGE RD, SW11

Open daily dawn-dusk. BR: Battersea Park.

London's second large park created for Londoners (the first being Victoria Park in the East End) was opened on marshy fields beside the river by Queen Victoria in 1853. Its delightful ornamental lake, Old English Garden and carriage drives made it an instant success with the Victorians, who used it almost exclusively for the great new craze of bicycling which was forbidden in royal Hyde Park. In 1985 the Peace Pagoda, one of more than 70 built around the world, was opened. Today the park contains a botanical garden, deer park, the Festival Pleasure Gardens (part of the 1951 Festival of Britain), tennis courts, boating lake and a children's zoo with monkeys, snakes, deer, otters and a reptile house.

Chelsea Physic Garden

SWAN WALK, SW3, 0171-352 5646

Open Apr-Oct: Wed noon-5pm, Sun 2pm-6pm. Open in February for special days. Tel in advance to check. U: Sloane Square.

Tucked away in a peaceful corner of Chelsea, this delightful garden was founded by the Worshipful Society of Apothecaries in 1673 to grow plants for medical study, following Pisa (1543) and Oxford (1621). Internationally important, the garden conducted a two-way traffic: plants were sent from all over the known world to be cultivated and studied here, while the first cotton seeds were packed up and sent from Chelsea down the Thames and on to the new colony of Georgia. Today it is a small, pretty four-acre garden of herbs, flowers, trees, and medicinal plants grown in a newly-established area. Pharmaceutical companies around the world are once again researching the uses of natural drugs from plants grown in Chelsea—the garden has come full circle, it seems. It's a wonderful place for a summer afternoon. To the sound of birdsong and the distant hum of traffic on the Chelsea Embankment, you can stroll around the ancient trees, historical walks and the first rock garden in this country, in 1772.

Chiswick House

BURLINGTON LANE, W4, 0181-995 0508

Open Apr-Sep: daily 10am-6pm, Nov-Mar: Wed-Sun 10am-4pm. BR: Chiswick.

Though called Chiswick House, it is really the gardens that people come to see. The house, modelled on a Palladian villa, was never intended to be lived in, but was built in 1725-1729 by the third Earl of Burlington, specifically to show off his works of art and as a place to entertain his friends. The gardens, full of delightful eighteenth-century temples and grottoes, were the first to move away from the formal Dutch style of gardens so popular up to then and epitomised by those at Hampton Court Palace. Only one or two of the little buildings remain, but the garden makes a delightful informal park and people come from miles around to see the camellias housed in the early nineteenth-century conservatory.

Crystal Palace Park

SYDENHAM, SE19,

Open daily dawn-dusk. BR: Crystal Palace.

This park where Joseph Paxton's great glass house was re-erected after the Great Exhibition in 1851, was formally opened in 1854 by Queen Victoria and became one of the showplaces of Victorian London. Fires in the vulnerable glass 'Crystal Palace' however took their toll and the park's importance and attraction gradually declined. The last and most disastrous fire was in 1936 when the flames were visible from Brighton, 60 miles away. Today it is best known for the Victorian prehistoric stone monsters; there's also a boating lake, a children's zoo and the Crystal Palace National Sports Centre.

Green Park

PICCADILLY, SW1,

Open daily 5am-dusk.
U: Green Park/Hyde Park Corner.

Full of daffodils in springtime, this small 53-acre park was once part of Henry VIII's hunting ground. Charles II made it into a royal park, and being a monarch who liked his pleasures built a snow-house in the middle of it to keep his wines cool in summertime (you can still see the mound). During the eighteenth century it was a known haunt for duelling, highwaymen, ballooning and for grand fireworks displays which reached their height in 1748 at the celebration of the end of the War of the Austrian Succession. Today it's a good place to hire a deck chair on a summer afternoon, or just to stroll around, away from the hustle and bustle.

Greenwich Park

GREENWICH, SE10,

Open daily 6am-dusk. BR: Greenwich.

Greenwich enjoyed its best days under the Tudors. Henry VIII was born here and retained a particular fondness for the park where he hunted deer and jousted. The park was first enclosed in 1433, but what we see today was created later by Louis XIV's gardener, Le NÙtre, who designed the gardens at Versailles and was invited by Charles II to do a similar job for him. The park is magnificent, rising from river level gently to the Queen's House and up to the top of the hill and the Royal Observatory. It's worth the climb to the top, though the wonderful symmetry of the original design is marred today by towering Canary Wharf.

Hampstead Heath

HAMPSTEAD, NW3,

Open daily 24 hours.

BR: Gospel Oak/Hampstead Heath.

U: Hampstead.

Some 790 acres of rolling hills, meadows, woods, ponds and lakes, this is one of London's wonders, an area of open spaces and great vistas which through legislation will be kept in perpetuity for the people's enjoyment. Lying between the hilltop villages of Hampstead and Highgate, it's a collection of properties added to the Heath over the years. Parliament Hill became part of the Heath in 1889, Golders Hill Park in 1898 and Kenwood in the 1920s. Further small areas were added subsequently (such as the delightful, secret Hill Garden signposted off the road beyond Jack Straw's Castle) and today it constitutes a 'green lung' for Londoners. At weekends it's full of people flying kites, jogging, having picnics and exercising their dogs. On the three main holiday weekends of Easter, May and late summer there's a popular funfair at South End Green.

Keeping Out of Step

If you're crossing **Albert Bridge** in Chelsea, look for the sign that demands that troops break step while marching over it. The vibrations, it was felt, might cause it to collapse.

Highgate Cemetery

SWAIN'S LANE, N6, 0181-340 1834

Eastern Cemetery open daily 10am-4pm. Western Cemetery Apr-Oct: guided tours only Mon-Fri noon, 2pm, 4pm; Sat & Sun 11am-4pm; Nov-Mar: Sat & Sun 11am-4pm on the hour. U: Archway.

The most fascinating of all London's Victorian cemeteries, Highgate opened its western part in 1839. A perfect example of exotic High Victorian taste with an Egyptian Avenue, a street of family vaults and the Circle of Lebanon, famous names which lie peacefully here include Tom Sayers (last of the bare-fisted fighters), scientist Michael Faraday, the poetess Christina Rossetti and writer Mary Ann Evans (George Eliot). Many have elaborate tombstone, with dogs, angels and other figures watching beside them. Rescued by the Friends of Highgate Cemetery, it is being sensitively restored and remains one of London's great nature reserves. In the newer Eastern Cemetery, the most famous tomb is (still) that of Karl Marx.

Holland Park

ABBOTSBURY RD, W14,

Open daily Apr-late Oct: 7.30am-10pm (can vary); late Oct-Mar: 7.30am-4.30pm (can vary). U: Holland Park.

A relatively late addition to London's parks, this small, intimate place full of wooded areas, rhododendrons and azaleas as well as the odd peacock the visitor comes across unexpectedly, was made into a public park in 1950. It stands in the former grounds of Holland House, a splendid mansion bombed during the war. Holland House, now a student hostel, forms the backdrop for the annual outdoor Holland Park Theatre which performs mainly opera (for details call the Central Library, 0171-937 2542). The former Garden Ballroom is now The Belvedere Restaurant.

Hyde Park

HYDE PARK, W2

Open daily 5am-midnight. U: Hyde Park Corner/Marble Arch/Lancaster Gate/Knightsbridge/High St Kensington.

This huge 619-acre park, made up of Hyde Park and Kensington Gardens, has been a royal park since 1536 when King Henry VIII seized the lands of Westminster Abbey at the Dissolution of the Monasteries. The monk's loss is our gain; it was turned from a hunting and hawking park for the indefatigable Henry VIII into a public park by Charles I. Protector Cromwell sold it off; Charles II took it back again and created the road which became the place for polite society to see and be seen. When William and Mary came to live in Kensington Palace they had 300 lamps hung from the trees along the route du roi (or Rotten Row as it became anglicised as). However even this eminently sensible precaution did nothing to deter the gangs of notorious highwaymen who, along with the duellists, continued to haunt the park. The Serpentine was created by damming the Westbourne river in the 1730 and during the 1814 celebrations for the defeat of Napoleon the complete Battle of Trafalgar was re-enacted on the lake. The park continues to be a place for entertainment today: both Mick Jagger and Luciano Pavarotti have each held a concert here and Speaker's Corner (by Marble Arch) provides a platform for anyone with a cause and a loud voice.

Regent's Park

REGENT'S PARK, NW1

Open daily 5am-dusk. U: Baker St/Regent's Park.

Another acquisition by Henry VIII, it became part of the town plans of the Prince Regent who commissioned John Nash in the early nineteenth century to design an extremely grand 'garden city' for his aristocratic friends within the park. Fifty-six villas in a variety of classical styles were planned though only eight were finally built. It's a beautiful and gracious park with Nash's terraces around the edge and Queen Mary's Rose Garden in the centre. In the summer, the Open Air Theatre puts on a season of plays while the boating lake is famous for its wide variety of water birds. The future of London Zoo, which has been in Regent's Park since 1830, is in doubt, as it is considered too small for the animals which roar, glide, slide and trot inside it.

Richmond Park

KINGSTON VALE, SW15

Open daily 7.30am-dusk. U: Richmond.

King Charles I first enclosed this huge park of 2,470 acres in 1637 with an eight-mile wall to form a hunting park. Today herds of deer still wander through these relatively wild areas of woods and bracken-covered heath. Big enough to absorb five cricket pitches, two golf courses and twenty-four football grounds without the public being aware of them, the park has two eighteenth-century lakes, beloved by anglers, and the Isabella Plantation, full of rhododendrons.

Royal Botanical Gardens

KEW, RICHMOND, SURREY, 0181-940 1171

Gardens open daily in daylight hours. Telephone first for seasonal house and museum opening hours. U: Kew Gardens.

First planted in 1759 by George III's mother, this 288-acre garden is the most complete public garden in the world. Sir Joseph Banks (1743-1820) who went round the world with Captain Cook established the garden as an international plant centre, sending gardeners and plant-hunters off to every known continent to collect specimens for the magnificent collection. The gardens contain glorious Victorian heated palm houses (wonderful to dash into on a cold winter's day), trees, flowers, formal and informal gardens as well as royal buildings like tiny Kew Palace, the Orangery and much more.

THEATRE & MUSIC

No city in the world has a richer or more varied theatrical life than London. Always the capital of English-speaking theatre, as well as a melting-pot of international talents, in the last couple of decades Andrew Lloyd Webber and a small group of British directors and designers have made London a serious competitor to New York for the musical crown as well. Only in opera and dance is London outshone by a few other centres of excellence boasting of stronger traditions and deeper purses.

THEATRE

Musicals

On any given night in the West End, more people are watching musicals than all the other forms of theatre put together. The names of many of the between fifteen and twenty or more shows will be familiar since the musical is international. Many of the current crop of musicals have come from Andrew Lloyd Webber and have been occupying the same theatres for years. But there are good reasons for seeing such familiar works in London—this is where many originated and the eagle eye of the original director ensures standards are maintained; competition to take over leading roles is intense, and many of the theatres they occupy are among the West End's most beautiful.

The West End

The **West End** is London's equivalent of Broadway—a relatively small area bounded by Shaftesbury Avenue and the Strand which for 300 years or so has been the heart of theatreland. Most theatres in this area were built between 80 and 110 years ago. Beautiful gilded interiors, a sense of history, and occasional discomfort can help or hinder your enjoyment, so choose carefully. London has too many theatres producing too many different plays to mention more than a few, and to give some guide lines as to what to expect. But if you are uncertain what to see, check ***Time Out*** (weekly), ***Where London*** (monthly and free in 4 and 5 star hotels), or ***Hot Tickets***, a Thursday supplement to the ***Evening Standard***. The weekend quality national newspapers publish helpful summaries of all the main plays and performances.

Drury Lane Theatre Royal

CATHERINE ST, WC2, 0171-494 5060,
U: COVENT GARDEN.

This is one of the most magnificent of London theatres and the oldest site in continuous use (since 1663). It deserves its royal title; it was here that Nell Gwynne delighted King Charles II and both King George I and George III survived assassination attempts. On a more artistic plane, David Garrick played in the eighteenth century as did the mighty Edmund Kean in the nineteenth. The present vast edifice (it seats 2,237), with its classical exterior, cupola-topped entrance and twin staircases leading to the Grand Salon Bar, was designed by Benjamin Wyatt in 1812. Since 1989, director Nicholas Hytner's acclaimed production of *Miss Saigon* has filled every seat.

Her Majesty's

HAYMARKET, SW1, 0171-494 5400, U:
PICCADILLY CIRCUS.

Phantom of the Opera is one of Andrew Lloyd Webber's most popular shows and opened eight years ago at this attractive 1896 theatre, which changes its gender to Her or His Majesty's according to who is on the British throne at the time.

London Palladium

ARGYLL ST, W1, 0171-494 5020,
U: Oxford Circus.

Another huge theatre (capacity 2,298), the Palladium was for many years the home of variety shows and 'to play the Palladium' was the ambition of every singer and comedian on both sides of the Atlantic. For the past few years these lavish acts have been replaced by musicals.

New London

167 DRURY LANE, WC2, 0171-405 0072,
U: Covent Garden.

Designed in 1973 by theatre designer Sean Kenny, the New London has been home to *Cats* since Trevor Nunn's first production opened here in 1981. Be warned 'latecomers are not admitted while the auditorium is in motion'!

Palace

CAMBRIDGE CIRCUS, W1, 0171-434 0909,
U: Leicester Square.

Owned by Andrew Lloyd Webber, this magnificent former opera house, dating from 1891, is one of the few West End theatres not hosting one of his works. Beautifully refurbished inside and out, it became home to director Trevor Nunn's production of *Les Misérables* in 1985.

Subsidised Theatre

One of the reasons London retains its pre-eminence in the English-speaking theatre is because of state subsidy. The subsidised theatres not only offer some of the best productions of a range of plays from the classic to the contemporary, they are also a training ground for Britain's best actors, directors and designers, as well as first stops for productions headed to the commercial West End. The two main companies are the **Royal National Theatre** and the **Royal Shakespeare Company**, both of whom occupy permanent purpose-built London homes.

Royal National Theatre

SOUTH BANK, SE1, 0171-452 3000,
U: Waterloo.

Opened in 1976, Sir Denys Lasdun's Royal National Theatre is a modernist concrete and glass building beside the Thames. It offers three contrasting theatre spaces and includes areas to relax with a drink and a snack, admire the sunset over the river, or enjoy a free informal concert or exhibition. It teems with life before or after the show and is always a pleasure to visit. The public foyers were enlarged, a road separating the theatre from the river removed, and backstage facilities enhanced with Lottery funding during 1997. Remarkably not one performance was missed during these works!

In 1997 Sir Trevor Nunn took over the artistic directorship from Sir Richard Eyre, whose 10-year reign had been the finest and most varied in the National's history. Nunn is maintaining this excellence and vitality and is a worthy heir to Lord Olivier, Sir Peter Hall, and Eyre. He continues to pursue a deliberately eclectic policy using directors from other companies around the country and top British stage and screen actors in conjunction with a dedicated ensemble permanently attached to the company. This marriage of the established with the new offers constant surprises and revelations and is reflected also in the breadth of works presented —native and foreign, originals and translations. Nunn is himself one of the finest theatrical directors of the century. It was Nunn whose long reign at the rival Royal Shakespeare Company made it the finest company in the English speaking world in the 1970s and 80s. It is ironic that at a time when the National is strengthening an already supreme position in London, its only rival, the RSC, has chosen to abandon its main London venue, the Barbican, for the six months of summer (see below).

The three auditoria offer distinct theatrical experiences. The largest, the **Olivier**, seats 1,100 in an amphitheatre facing a large, open stage equipped with magical mechanical devices for spectacles in large-scale works. The most conventional is the proscenium-arched **Lyttleton** which seats 900. The experimental **Cottesloe** seats up to 400, has flexible seating and offers everything from theatre-in-the-round to more conventional layouts. Despite the greater comfort and luxury of the two larger theatres, the Cottesloe can often be the most thrilling of the three because it offers wonderful intimacy with the actors. Many of the National's finest productions sell out completely. But don't despair—a limited number of seats for each production are sold on the day of performance at 9.30am. Queue from 8.30am or before to be sure of a chance of a seat.

Backstage Tours

One of the best ways of discovering more about the theatre is to go on a backstage tour. The three mentioned here also take you beyond the stage, into the auditorium and the changing rooms and give you a good potted history of the place. There's nothing more exciting—and daunting—than standing on the stage staring out into the footlights and beyond. The experience should sort out the serious from the dilettante aspiring thespians. **Drury Lane Theatre Royal**, Catherine St, WC2, 0171-494 5060; **National Theatre**, South Bank, SE1, 0171-633 0880; **Royal Shakespeare Company**, Barbican Centre, Silk St, EC1, 0171-628 3351.

Royal Shakespeare Company

BARBICAN CENTRE, SILK ST, EC2, 0171-638 8891,
U: BARBICAN.

As its name suggests, one of the main purposes of the Royal Shakespeare Company is to produce the works of the Bard, but it also embraces new plays and classics from the entire world repertoire. Originally based in Stratford, Shakespeare's birthplace, where it was founded nearly 120 years ago, the company now divides itself between its three theatres there and its two in the Barbican in London. The RSC is more of a repertory company than the National in that one team of actors plays first the Stratford theatres and six months later comes to London. The Artistic Director, Adrian Noble, has almost as wide a range of directors as the National, and productions are exciting and innovative.

The building itself is something of an architectural folly: it opened in 1982 but dates in conception from a futuristic vision of the 1960s. Inside the building it's easy to get lost—get there early. But the two auditoria are magnificent. The main theatre is almost spherical giving even those in the remotest seats—the 'gods'—a good view of the large stage. The Pit is also impressive: it is small with a capacity of only 180-240, with the action three-quarters in the round so the audience feels a real involvement. Unfortunately the RSC has decided to spend six months every summer away from London touring provincial cities. The management of the Barbican has responded imaginatively to this blow and every summer mounts a festival of international theatre, together with some dance and small-scale opera including the Royal Opera (see above). British theatre is sometimes accused of being parochial so the annual presence in London of the world's leading companies is a stimulus hugely to be welcomed.

Royal Court

DOWNSTAIRS: DUKE OF YORK'S, ST. MARTINS LANE, WC2, UPSTAIRS: AMBASSADORS, WEST ST, WC2, 0171-565 5000,
U: Leicester Sq.

Another beneficiary of the National Lottery is the renowned Royal Court Theatre. Its two auditoria in Sloane Square are being rebuilt, and it is temporary based at two West End theatres. The 'Upstairs' at the Ambassadors is particularly intimate with only 60 or 70 seats arranged in the circle of one of London's tiniest theatres.

In 1999 they are scheduled to return to their permanent home in Chelsea's Sloane Square (next to the tube station of that name). Built in 1888, it has always been an important venue for new writers. Once it was George Bernard Shaw, Sir Arthur Pinero and Granville Barker, then in the 1950s John Osborne and the revival of realistic English drama, and since 1998 it has had a new, exciting, young Artistic Director, Ian Rickson. The minute studio Theatre Upstairs will continue to be an important venue for radical new writing.

Buying Tickets

The most convenient way is by phone direct to the theatre box office; only rarely is a booking charge made and tickets can be paid for by credit card or reserved up to 30 minutes before curtain-up. Most theatres are centrally located so you can often stop by in person to buy your tickets and check seat locations. For sell-out musicals try reputable theatre ticket agencies who make a booking charge (enquire the percentage). The cheapest way to buy tickets for many shows is at the **Leicester Square Half Price Ticket Booth**. Theatres with a surplus of unsold tickets deliver them for sale at half price plus a £2 service fee or £1 for tickets with a face value of £5 or less. Tickets go on sale for the day of performance only at 12noon for matinees and from 1pm to 6.30pm for evening performances, with a limit of 4 tickets per person. You have no choice of seats (you get the best available), but for the cost of a half hour in the queue this is a great way of economising on the cost. As seats for the English National Opera, The National and the RSC are often included the choice is wide. So successful is the official half price booth that unscrupulous competitors have set up on the streets leading into the square advertising similar offers, but delivering much less. Remember the genuine booth is inside the gardens of the Square itself on the south side opposite the Radisson Edwardian Hampshire Hotel.

West End Theatres

Plays—with the notable exception of The Mousetrap at St. Martin's Theatre—do not have long runs, but a few pointers as to what to look for can be given. Such is the excellence of the National and the RSC that transfers of their most popular productions can be amongst the best bets for quality serious theatre in the West End.

Donmar Warehouse

EARLHAM ST, WC2, 0171-369 1732,
U: Covent Garden.

This small theatre has been carved out of the upper floors of a magnificent Victorian warehouse in Covent Garden. Under the dynamic direction of the young Sam Mendes, it offers an exciting programme of mostly new plays with small scale, experimental musicals.

Haymarket (Theatre Royal)

HAYMARKET, SW1, 0171-930 8800,
U: Piccadilly Circus.

Second only to the Drury Lane Theatre Royal for a sense of history, the Haymarket was originally built in 1720 and rebuilt in 1821 by John Nash. A beautiful theatre is not in itself a reason to choose a production, but it is a wonderful bonus and the Theatre Royal's track record in choosing productions is good.

Piccadilly Theatre

DENMAN ST, W1, 0171-369 1734,
U: Leicester Square.

Since retiring from a long and distinguished reign over first the RSC then the National, Sir Peter Hall is now an independent producer of plays and opera. His preference is generally for classic works produced with clarity and style and with distinguished casts. Since 1997 he has built up a genuine and distinguished repertory company performing mainly classic plays. He is a brave and unsubsidised rival of the National and RSC, and deserves support and success. Some of his productions move on to other West End theatres, so check through the listings.

Fringe Theatre

The West End theatre is fed by the creative ferment of the fringe, London's equivalent of New York's 'Off Broadway'. It ranges from the well-established—indeed subsidised—theatre to small rooms in pubs.

Almeida

ALMEIDA ST, N1, 0171-359 4404,
U: Angel.

Since the artistic direction was taken over by actors Iain McDiarmid and Jonathan Kent, this tiny 1837 building has become acknowledged as the most exciting theatre outside the West End. It stages a mixture of premieres (by authors as notable as Harold Pinter) and the classics, adorned by stars who give their services for the Actors Equity minimum wage and directed by the two principals and celebrated guests. With a capacity of only 300 in an arena layout, intimacy as well as excitement is guaranteed. Located in Islington (near the Camden Passage Antique market) the theatre is an easy ten-minute walk from the Angel underground station.

Hampstead

SWISS COTTAGE CENTRE, AVE RD, NW3, 0171-722 9301,
U: Swiss Cottage.

Housed in a shed-like building, the Hampstead Theatre in its almost 30 years of existence has sent many successes to the West End. Most productions are of new plays so prediction of what you might see is impossible, but this is the sort of venue always worth giving the benefit of the doubt. With permanent tiered seating this is an unusually comfortable way of visiting the Fringe. The theatre is adjacent to Swiss Cottage underground station. Hampstead has made an application for Lottery money to fund a major expansion so if it is lucky, 1999 or 2000 may see a brief interruption of activities.

King's Head Islington

115 UPPER ST, N1, 0171-226 1916,
U: Angel.

This is deservedly the most famous of all London's pub theatres. It puts on a broad repertoire of new plays in a cramped room where you can eat beforehand (honest, good-value-for-money, ordinary food). The atmosphere is special and on the right night can offer great excitement. It is located in Upper Street 100 yards before Almeida Street.

Theatre Royal, Stratford East

GEORGE RAFFLES SQUARE, E15, 0181-534 0310, *U: Stratford.*

A tiny Victorian theatre located deep in the East End of London but conveniently close to Stratford tube station and subsidised mostly by local government, this theatre caters primarily for the local community. But it also has a long history of developing popular works which transfer to the West End from its days as the Theatre Workshop under Joan Littlewood in the 1960s through to the present. Often the work will be of only parochial interest, but look out for their enjoyable and traditional Christmas pantomimes (a strange mixture of fairy tales, comedy and modern bawdy that is uniquely English). This theatre is another beneficiary of Lottery funds and enjoyed a well merited refurbishment in 1998.

Tricycle Theatre

269 KILBURN HIGH RD, NW6, 0171-328 1000, *U: Kilburn.*

Another intimate theatre with an excellent track record of producing exciting new plays often with an Irish or Caribbean background.

MUSIC

London offers daily more than a dozen chances to listen to classical or contemporary music with artists varying from international stars to ambitious students.

Major Venues

Barbican

BARBICAN CENTRE, SILK ST, EC2, INFORMATION AND BOOKINGS 0171-638 8991
U: Barbican.

Anything from full-scale symphonies in the main concert hall to performances of chamber and folk music in the various foyers.

Royal Albert Hall

KENSINGTON GORE, SW7, 0171-589 8212
U: High St Kensington.

A beautiful round building with everything from Eric Clapton to the best symphony concerts. It's probably best known, in Britain at least, as the home of the annual BBC Promenade concerts ('the Proms'). Tickets for the Proms can be bought on the day of performance, but long queues build up early, so take a cushion or camping stool with you. The 'Promenaders' then sit in the middle of the hall or high up in the balconies. It's the thing almost every English person will have done once.

St. John's Smith Square

SMITH SQUARE, SW1, 0171-222 1061
U: St. James's Park/Westminster.

Chamber and symphony orchestras play in this converted church. Concerts are frequently recorded by the BBC and the atmosphere is very special.

South Bank Centre

SOUTH BANK, SE1, 0171-960 4242
U: Waterloo.

Three halls with music from pop to Prokofiev. The Royal Festival Hall is the biggest venue with good acoustics for symphonies or great choral works. The Queen Elizabeth Hall is smaller, suitable for chamber music and visiting opera productions. The Purcell Room seats under 400 people and is used for recitals, readings and debut concerts by new artists. Book shops, bars, cafés, exhibitions and foyer concerts make the South Bank Centre a pleasant place for a concert-goer.

Wigmore Hall

36 WIGMORE ST, W1, 0171-935 2141
U: Bond St.

The refurbished Wigmore Hall is an intimate and pleasant place for small-scale concerts. Good acoustics and a friendly atmosphere have made it probably the most loved of London's classical venues. There is music every night.

Other Regular Music Venues

London's cathedrals all offer wonderful church music with magnificent choirs and organists, and many churches hold frequent secular concerts, particularly in the summer when the **City of London Festival** (0171-377 0540) stages concerts in St. Paul's Cathedral and many of Sir Christopher Wren's beautiful City churches. The principal music colleges' concerts give you the chance to enjoy young talent for a modest cost.

British Music Information Centre

10 Stratford Pl, W1, 0171-499 8567
U: Bond St.

The BMIC, which promotes contemporary British music and has a music library, also hosts small concerts and recitals of 20th century music on Tuesdays and Thursdays at 7.30pm. Telephone for programmes.

Christ Church, Spitalfields

Commercial St, EC1, 0171-344 0287
U: Aldgate East.

Nicholas Hawksmoor's magnificent church is the scene of a very fine musical festival every June and a series of concerts leading up to Christmas.

Guildhall School of Music

Barbican Centre, Silk St, EC2, 0171-628 2571
U: Barbican.

This prestigious music school holds regular concerts and events by students, mostly free. Telephone for programmes.

Royal Academy of Music

Marylebone Rd, NW1, 0171-873 7373
U: Baker St.

One of London's trio of outstanding schools of music that gives regular concerts.

Royal College of Music

Prince Consort Rd, SW7, 0171-589 3643
U: South Kensington.

The place for students' showcase concerts of a very high quality. Telephone for programmes.

St. James Piccadilly

197 Piccadilly, W1, 0171-381 0441
U: Piccadilly Circus.

A lovely church in a convenient location which holds regular lunch time concerts.

St. Mary-le-Bow

Cheapside, EC2, 0171-248 5139
U: St. Paul's.

They hold series of concerts on Thursday lunch times at 1.05pm.

St. Martin-in-the Fields

Trafalgar Square, WC2, 0171-839 8367
U: Charing Cross/Leicester Square.

St. Martin's is world-famous for its concerts which range from lunchtime recitals to Mozart by candle light in the evening. On the east side of Trafalgar Square, the church is one of London's landmarks.

OPERA AND DANCE

Britain's National Lottery devotes part of its income to the Arts and a part to celebrating the Millenium. A bizarre result of this largesse is that two of London's three major opera and dance venues, **The Royal Opera House** and **Sadler's Wells**, are currently closed for rebuilding, the former until 1991 and the latter until 2000.

Coliseum

St. Martin's Lane, WC2, 0171-632 8300
U: Leicester Square.

London's largest theatre, with 2,356 seats, has been home to the English National Opera (ENO) since 1968. Built in 1904 by prolific theatre architect, Frank Matcham, the Coliseum was originally a variety theatre, then home to lavish spectaculars and briefly a down-at-heel cinema before its rebirth as an opera house. ENO's present singular character stems from its origins as a touring company with the mission to bring opera to new audiences in the provinces. To do this it needed a permanent company, mostly British—soloists as well as chorus—and it chose to sing everything in English for greater accessibility. Today it has turned these traditions to good effect: its soloists are drawn from a small but increasingly excellent pool of largely British talent. Because they work closely together more of an ensemble feel has developed, and with it a more committed acting style than is normal in opera.

Royal Opera House

Bow St, WC2, 0171-304 4000
U: Covent Garden.

When 'Covent Garden', (as the Royal Opera House is invariably known), re-opens in the year 2000 only the auditorium will remain of the original 1858 building. Everything backstage is being rebuilt, and a new foyer and experimental small scale venue are being added at a cost of £75 million. In the meantime, you must seek out the Royal Opera and Royal Ballet companies in such venues as the Barbican Theatre (now rebuilt in to include an orchestra pit), the Shaftesbury Theatre, Labbatts Apollo in Hammersmith or in concert performances at the Royal Festival Hall on the South Bank or the Royal Albert Hall.

None of these venues are as traditional or as opulent as the 'Garden', but because some are smaller, the repertoire has been enlarged to include more intimate and rarely seen seventeenth- and eighteenth-century works. Bernard Haitink remains musical director through this traumatic period, so you can be assured of the highest standards being maintained.

Sadlers Wells at the Peacock Theatre

PORTUGAL ST, WC2, 0171-314 8800
U: Holborn.

The first theatre to take advantage of a Millenium grant to expand was Sadlers Wells, home to touring companies visiting London. Until at least mid 1999, the Rosebery Avenue theatre will be closed and Sadlers Wells will operate from the Peacock Theatre. It will continue to put on a broad repertoire featuring major companies in all forms of musical theatre from dance (Adventures in Motions Pictures is a successful modern dance company who visit regularly), opera (Glyndebourne Touring Company) and revivals of musicals (*Calamity Jane* was a great success). Just round the corner from the Aldwych, it is always worth checking what Sadlers Wells is putting on at the Peacock.

EXPERIMENTAL VENUES FOR MUSIC AND DANCE

The Place

17 DUKES RD, WC1, 0171-387 0031,
U: Euston.

The principal experimental venue for dance.

The Drill Hall

CHENIES ST, WC1, 0171-637 8270,
U: Warren St.

For small-scale opera, dance and off beat drama often with a gay orientation, this offers an exciting and innovative programme.

OUT OF LONDON

CONTENTS

INTRODUCTION

The visitor to London has more than the capital to explore. With **Bath** a mere 90 minutes away by train, **Oxford** and **Windsor** about an hour and **York** only two hours away, it's worth taking a day trip in this green and pleasant countryside. But once there, you may well find so much to see that you decide to stay longer. So here we make some suggestions: where to stay, what to do, what to see and of course, where to eat.

On the practical side: we have indicated hotel prices, and where breakfast is included. You will find, however, that there are so many special weekend/weekday/Champagne breaks, and that prices vary so much according to the season and availability, that the prices printed here are more an indication of what you might expect to pay than exact prices.

BATH

The onset of Spring transforms the English countryside. Hedgerows begin to blossom, crocuses, daffodils and tulips fill rural gardens, apple blossoms appear and the countryside takes on that glorious fresh lime green colour. But the weather, particularly in March, can be cruel, so if you choose to go to one of the great steeplechasing race meetings of the year, Cheltenham for the Gold Cup, make sure you go prepared. Whether you choose this sporting event in early Spring, or book for the **Bath International Music Festival**, the great Roman city of Bath is wonderful at any time.

It's a mere two-hour drive to Bath. Drive out of London to Andover then to Salisbury. The tiny village of **Pitton** is a good place for a country lunch stop. **The Silver Plough** was a farmhouse until it became a pub. Traditionally decorated, it serves honest pub food, from ploughman's to pan-fried fish with Mediterranean influences. There are two afternoon possibilities. **Wilton House** is a wonderful seventeenth-century mansion still owned by the Earls of Pembroke, the neo-classical interiors of architect Inigo Jones echoed in the pretty Palladian bridge standing in the grounds. **Stonehenge** is Europe's most famous and complex prehistoric monument-still presenting a mystery to scholars as to its original purpose.

Then it's on to Bath and a spectacular stay in the heart of the city. As Bath is a mere 90 minutes by train, you can stay for a weekend without a car. Either way, base yourself at one of two hotels, the **Royal Crescent Hotel**, or the **Queensberry**.

Bath has been a visitor destination since Roman times when the discovery of hot springs led to a complex of baths plus a temple to the goddess Minerva in the city the Romans called Aqua Sulis. By AD 410 the Romans had abandoned their most northerly province of Britain, the baths fell into disuse and the Roman buildings were plundered for their valuable stone. It wasn't until the early eighteenth century that Bath was once again on the map, put there by Queen Anne who was advised by her doctors that the waters were a great cure for gout. Three men were largely responsible for the city we see today: Ralph Allen, a stone quarry owner, and the architects John Wood the Elder and John Wood the Younger. Together they set about building the most splendid new Georgian city, with terraces and crescents and circles of houses in mellow, golden Bath stone. Throughout the eighteenth century, fashionable society came here to take the waters and enjoy the balls and assemblies. In the early nineteenth century, the young and fashionable followed the Prince Regent to the newly discovered seaside resort of Brighton for their summers, and Bath once again was left to the staid and the elderly. But in 1879, when digging out new sewers, the borough engineer discovered the remains of the Roman Baths. Extensive excavations were made and ever since, tourists have flocked to Bath.

The city's attractions are many and varied. For a true historical taste, start at the **Roman Baths** themselves, sulphurous, smoky and subterranean. A light lunch in the nearby **Pump Room** keeps you rooted in the past, so an afternoon visit to the **Museum of Costume** and the perfect Georgian interior of **No. 1 Royal Crescent** fits the mood perfectly.

Bath is famous for many things, not least the Bath Bun which you can buy at any bakery. For something equivalent, try Sally Lunn's buns at—where else?—**Sally Lunn's Refreshment House**, which claims to be the oldest house in Bath and certainly has one of the most interesting cellars and original bakeries.

There are several possibilities for dinner, from the musically inclined (both in terms of decor and pianist during dinner) **Clos du Roy** next to the Theatre Royal offering good classic French cooking to the gutsy flavours of the **Hole in the Wall**, one of Britain's best known and much loved restaurants. Also recommended is **Woods**, near the Assembly Rooms, a good, cheerful brasserie with modern cooking. Top of the list, however, is **Lettonie**, which moved from Bristol to Bath and has remained consistently very good indeed.

Bath is a good city to walk around, the beautifully proportioned streets and crescents full of plaques to the famous and infamous who came here for the waters and for the entertainment—aristocratic gamblers, architects, statesmen, Sir William Herschel, the potter Josiah Wedgwood, the soldier General Wolfe. A walk over Pulteney Bridge takes you to the **Holburne of Menstrie Museum** with its collection of great English paintings, furniture and silver. The no.18 bus drops you at The Avenue and a ten-minute walk to the unusual **American Museum in Britain**, showing domestic life in America from colonial times to the end of the 19th century. It's a delightful manor house, with good grounds and a café for light lunches. If you're in the centre of Bath, you might try **The Moon & Sixpence**—a pleasant, light and airy place with a summery feel. You can just spend a day in Bath, which will give you a tantalising glimpse of the place and the desire to return, but to get the full flavour of this historic city, take a few days.

One delightful further option is to stay at The Vineyard at Stockcross near Newbury, some 50 miles or so from London and about the same from Bath. It is best known for its first-class restaurant, but the 33 bedrooms attached are of a very high standard indeed. Near London, Bath, Southhampton, Heathrow and Gatwick, this is a supberb location for visiting any or all of these areas. The hotel will meet you from any location within reasonable distance.

HOTELS

Not To Be Missed:

Royal Crescent Hotel

16 ROYAL CRESCENT, BATH, BA1 2LS, 01225-739955, FAX 01225-339401

26 Rooms £170-£220, 16 suites £370-£675. Dinner for two is around £90.

A P *Holistic spa.*

In the centre of Bath's most famous crescent, the Royal Crescent Hotel is set up high enough to give wonderful views over the city and out to the rolling countryside beyond. There are four-poster beds as well as antique furniture everywhere in this period hotel which preserves many of its historic features intact. Dinner in **Pimpernel's**, reached across a pretty garden, is an experience in good modern British cooking.

Queensbury Hotel

RUSSEL ST, BATH, BA1 2QF, 01225-447928, FAX 01225-446065

Double from £135, four-poster from £195. Dinner for two is around £60.

This stylish townhouse hotel, privately owned by Stephen and Penny Ross, is delightful and in a residential street near the centre. It's welcoming and gracious with eighteenth-century features retained from the original house, and its restaurant, **The Olive Tree**, offers good modern British cooking.

Also Recommended:

The Priory Hotel

WESTON RD, BATH BA1 2XT, 01225 331922, FAX 01225 448276

21 rms £160-£310.

A *(English breakfast)*

RESTAURANTS

Not To Be Missed:

Lettonie 16/20

FRENCH

35 KELSTON RD, BATH, 01225 446676, FAX 01225 447541

5 rooms, £95-£165.

Lunch & Dinner Tues.-Sat. £££

A

Since moving from their first small place in Bristol to this pleasant restaurant with rooms in Bath, Siân and Martin Blunos' enterprise has really taken off. As before, Martin Blunos' culinary genius is at once apparent in a menu which fizzes with inventiveness and reassures with its self-confident cooking. The menu remains intact; if you haven't already tasted it, try the unusual scrambled duck egg with sevruga caviar on top served with blinis and washed down with a glass of properly iced vodka. Complex mixings come again with the scallop, grey mullet and aubergine mille feuille with piquant tomato, peppers, olives and basil oil. Main courses appear a little less exuberant, though try the contrasting textures of pan-fried wild salmon with crisped nettle fritters offset in a cream sauce; or a wonderful roast squab pigeon with spiced pears cooked in its jus. Desserts please, from a deceptively simple hot caramel and almond sponge tart to a perfectly judged bitter dark chocolate mousse with a robust prune and Armagnac ice cream. The wine list is mainly French and mainly pricey. The service is delightful. Long may this delightful place thrive. Set lunch £25, Set menu £44.50.

Also Recommended:

Clos du Roy

FRENCH/BRITISH

1 SEVEN DIALS, SAW CLOSE, BATH, 01225 444450

Lunch and Dinner daily. £ Set lunch and dinner, 6pm-7.15pm, £9.95-£13.95, Set dinner £16.50-£19.50.

Near Newbury:

The Vineyard at Stockcross

INTERNATIONAL 14/20

STOCKCROSS, BERKS

01635 528 770, FAX 01635 528 398

Daily lunch and dinner, £££

This lovely dining room features well spaced tables, a lantern-style glass roof and a view of William Pye's outside sculpture 'Fire and Water' blazing in the pool. It's an elegant setting for some very fine dishes from David Sharland, ex Savoy Grill, who produces an eclectic, perfectly balanced style of cuisine. For starters, pan-fried scallops were delicately cooked, and the carpaccio of beef with Parmesan shavings tender. Equally as good choices include foie gras accompanied by apple, rhubarb and beetroot. The lobster in a saffron nage was a masterly entrée, while a dish of breast of duck came with a generous sprinkling of girolles and a piece of meltingly tender foie gras on a crisply cooked French bean salad, with a veal jus. The Vineyard's chocolate assiette was a glorious rendering of three different chocolate desserts. Accompanying all this is one of the most interesting wine lists to be found. The owner, Sir Peter Michael, also owns the Peter Michael Winery in Sonoma Vally which since 1987 has been producing top California wines. Six whites are on the list, including the Cuvée Indigene which can compete with the best Chardonnays around. Of the two reds, the superb Les Pavots 1989 and the Point Blanc 1993 can only be drunk at The Vineyard. It might seem ironic to come to England for a Californian wine not available in its state of origin, but it's a great talking point. Ask the head sommelier, Edoardo Amadi, about the list which extends to some 300 wines. Business Lunch £33; Fusion menu of an amuse bouche, six courses and four glasses of wine £70.

Woods

MODERN BRITISH

9-13 ALFRED ST, BATH, 01225 314812

Lunch and Dinner daily. ££

Set lunch £6, £7, £14, Set dinner £11.50-£15.50, Set dinner(Sat) £19.95.

PUBS & CAFÉS

Silver Plough

PITTON, WILTSHIRE, 01722 712266

Meals Lunch and Dinner daily, exc Sun evening.

Lunch for two is from £15 to £30. Sunday lunch 3 courses £13.95.

Sally Lunn's Refreshment House & Museum

4 NORTH PARADE PASSAGE, BATH, 01225 461634

Daily 10am-11pm (closed Monday evening in winter).

OXFORD

Oxford is a bustling, lively place at any time of the year with a life independent of the university for which the city is famous. You can get here easily by train; alternatively it's about a one-hour drive from London. If time is short, take the M40 motorway; otherwise go by the prettier road to **Henley**, then through some charming countryside through **Nettlebed** and **Dorchester**. If you're based in Oxford, stay either at the **Old Parsonage Hotel**, a creeper-clad old stone house, once Oscar Wilde's base and furnished in a delightful English style, or at **Bath Place**, right in the heart of medieval Oxford in its own small alleyway off Holywell street. The alternative many go for is one of Britain's best country-house hotels, **Le Manoir aux Quat'Saisons**, with an internationally renowned restaurant.

Oxford is well known for Frank Cooper's Oxford Marmalade (no longer made here), Oxford University Press, the covered market, which nobody should miss, and lately for the fictional but oh-so-believable Inspector Morse, and of course its ancient university which is the main visitor attraction. If you want a guide, the **Oxford Information Centre** organises walking tours of the colleges and the city conducted by Blue Badge Guides which last two hours. Or you can wander at will through the halls, quads and gardens of the medieval and later buildings. Oxford's beauty is not so immediate as that of its rival university town, Cambridge; you have to seek it out down small passages, through gateways into College quads (at Cambridge they're called 'courts') and along semi-hidden alleyways.

Now with 35 colleges, the University began when a group of English students were expelled from Paris in 1167. But it was not until 1249 that the first college, **University College** was founded. For a good walk, start at the centre of the old city, **Carfax** ('the crossing of the four ways'). South along St. Aldate's you come to **Christ Church**, the grandest college and the home of Alice in Wonderland; Lewis Carroll—a mathematics don here—wrote it for Alice Liddell, the dean's daughter. Along Blue Boar Street, you come to **Corpus Christi College**, founded in 1517 and the first college at which Greek was taught. Nearby **Merton College** possesses some of the oldest buildings in Oxford; its gateway tower was built in 1418, the chapel was built in the last decade of the thirteenth century. The library is one of the oldest medieval libraries in England (1371-78), and was the first to store books upright in shelves instead of lying them flat in presses.

Along the **High Street** (east of Carfax) you come across the university church of **St. Mary's**. It's well worth climbing up the spire high above the rooftops. From here you look over the mellow buildings and understand the nineteenth-century poet Matthew Arnold who described Oxford as 'That sweet city with her dreaming spires'.

Behind the church there's a cluster of buildings: **Brasenose College** (so called after its brazen or brass door knocker), and **All Souls College**, founded in 1438 by King Henry VI and dedicated to the souls of all those who fell in the Hundred Years War against the French. The **Sheldonian Theatre** was the first work of Sir Christopher Wren and was built 1663-1669. Impossible to miss is the splendid **Radcliffe Camera**, built to house Dr Radcliffe's science library, and now part of the world famous **Bodleian Library**, one of the six copyright libraries in Britain.

Oxford is a city where you wander at will, either discovering new sights or if you are a frequent visitor, rediscovering your favourites. Try to see **New College** in New College Lane, founded in 1379, with a particularly fine chapel adorned with Epstein's statue of Lazarus, and gardens bounded by the old city wall. **Magdalen College** (1458) is worth seeking out for its famous fifteenth-century Bell Tower, lawns, river walk and deer park, as well as its three quads; **Worcester College** (1713) for its delightful gardens and lake.

If colleges pall, Oxford has other attractions. The **Botanical Garden** in the High Street—the oldest in Britain—was founded as a 'Physic Garden' in 1621. The **Ashmolean Museum** in Beaumont Street contains the university's art and archaeological collections. The **Pitt Rivers Museum** is one of the world's great anthropological collections in an extraordinary Victorian setting. **Blackwell's** book shop in Broad Street is a large and comprehensive book shop, a delight to browse through. And **The Oxford Story** gives you the chance to take a ride through scenes from the University's past.

There's plenty of choice for lunch or dinner, all within easy reach. Down by the river, **Cherwell Boathouse** offers a cosy atmosphere and a modern British menu, accompanied by a good wine list. **15 North Parade** offers gutsy cooking and a brasserie-style atmosphere, while **Gee's**, in a large Victorian greenhouse, is at its most enjoyable in the evening. Pretty **Whites** is comfortable, and Raymond Blanc's **Le Petit Blanc** is an all-day brasserie with its finger on the culinary pulse. **Browns**, which has branches in London and in other cities, is consistently reliable and also open all day.

Oxford, also, has its fair share of pubs. Try the **Eagle and Child**, 49 St. Giles, known locally as the Bird and Baby. J R Tolkein used to drink here, as did C S Lewis; the firelit parlours are very welcoming. In the ancient **Turf Tavern**, Bath Place, tall customers bang their heads on the picturesque beams. **The Bear**, Alfred St, behind Christ Church, dates from 1242 and has a collection of 3,000 ties from schools, colleges, clubs and regiments.

Oxford can easily occupy you for a whole weekend, but if you want to see a little of the English countryside, go out to **Woodstock**, a typical old market town, slightly sleepy but kept permanently on the visitor map by the splendid palace of **Blenheim**, a huge baroque edifice built by Sir John Vanbrugh for the first Duke of Marlborough. Lunch at **The Feathers Hotel** is a delight, the welcoming hotel offering both bar snacks and more substantial meals and, should you decide to stay here, peace and quiet in the centre of the small town.

Further information from the **Oxford Information Centre**, St. Aldate's, 01865 726871.

HOTELS:

Not to be Missed:

Le Manoir aux Quat'Saisons

CHURCH RD, GREAT MILTON, OXFORD OX44 7PD

01844 278881, Fax 01844 278847; e-mail: lemanoir@oxfordshire.co.uk; toll free (from USA only) 1-800 845 4274. 29 rooms: £210-£435. Most rooms air cond.

A P *nearby*

Le Manoir, an old, mellow stone manor house in the small country village of Great Milton eight miles south east of Oxford, presents a tranquil façade to the world, and is rightly considered one of Britain's top country house hotels. But Le Manoir is by no means set in aspic, for Raymond Blanc is a forward thinker, who believes that the flowery English chintz style—which can be so overpowering—has had its day, and that to survive, the country house hotel has to reflect a contemporary ethos and the aspirations of a new generation. This philosophy does not however, translate into a rejection of the past; here are the mullioned windows, the English gardens, a perfect round dovecot, working fireplaces and rooms that fit perfectly into the old house. Bedrooms are named after flowers: Hollyhock, for instance, is a faithful replica of Elizabethan style with its four-poster bed, elegant dark wood furniture and flax-coloured carpet. But in the new wing contemporary inspiration has re-interpreted the past. Behind a pure traditional exterior are a series of rooms where imagination has taken off and produced a very different style and feel from the main house. So, here is a room predominantly decorated in silvers and greys, with geometric snowflake reproduced on the walls, and shimmering mirrors and glass. You prefer something with a touch of decadence, and a feel of the Renaissance? Try the Venetian room with its silhouettes of masked figures. The Chinese room is decorated in rich reds and golds; the Provençal-style farmhouse rooms are beamed; there is even a room devoted to a great courtesan. The rooms have their own gardens which give an extraordinary sense of privacy. The English country house party, devoted to the pleasures of life, found its greatest expression in the Edwardian era at the turn of the century; Le Manoir has taken on that same mantle a century later.

Highly Recommended:

Old Parsonage Hotel

BANBURY RD, OX2 6NN

01865-310210, FAX 01865-311262;

E-mail oldparsonage@dial.pipex.com

26 Rooms: £125-£160. 4 stes £185-£200. A meal for two in the bar is around £50.

A P

Bath Place Hotel

5 BATH PL, HOLYWELL ST, OXFORD OX1 3SU

01865-791812, FAX 01865-791834

12 Rooms: £75-£125.

Restaurant: Set lunch £18.75, Sun lunch £21.50, Set dinner £28.50, an à la carte meal for two is around £85.

 P

RESTAURANTS:

Not to be Missed:

Le Manoir aux Quat' Saisons

FRENCH 19/20

CHURCH RD, GREAT MILTON, OXFORD OX44 7PD, 01844 278881, FAX 01844 278847

e-mail: lemanoir@oxfordshire.co.uk

TOLL FREE (FROM USA ONLY) 1-800 845 4274

Lunch & Dinner daily. ££££

A

Raymond Blanc's all-consuming enterprise never appears to slow down, and Le Manoir, with its new private dining and cookery school wing, bedroom courtyard with a further 10 rooms, and more planting and outdoor lighting in the already delightful gardens, moves into the next century with panache and style. The improvements have led to practical advantages, too, as in a vastly enlarged and better organised kitchen and separate bakery section. For the diner, there's a new conservatory, a charming spacious room made light and airy by a cane-covered glass roof, with large windows looking out over the green sweep of lawn, cream cotton covers to the dining chairs and splendid, robust green conservatory plants. It is a suitable stage for the immense talents of this energetic man and his new head chef Jonathan Wright, who has ably taken over the mantle of Clive Fretwell. The à la carte is relatively short, some seven hors d'oeuvres, four fish courses, five meat courses and two from the rôtisserie. However, for a real taste of Raymond Blanc's genius, the best bet is the £72 menu gourmande which offers an appetiser plate, two starters, perhaps fish and asparagus, a main fish dish, a main meat dish, two desserts and petits fours. In the last edition, we referred to Raymond Blanc's moves towards the Orient. But now his ever prolific imagination has taken him back to a classicism which has been further refined by his former love affair with the East. Take his confit of wild salmon fillets, the salmon of the most delicate, lightly flaked texture, on thin slices of salt cod, mouli and cucumber salad with a light horseradish sauce; or an apparently uncomplicated chilled essence of tomato with a red pepper ravioli which surprises with a small morsel of marinated Picaudon cheese; each hors d'oeuvre startling in its varied contrast of tastes. This love and understanding of the complex mixing of tastes and spices leads to dishes like roasted Scottish scallops, with a fennel fondue in red wine jus and a light liquorice sauce, or a masterly red mullet served on a risotto of squid ink, squids with lemon and coriander and a saffron jus. Raymond Blanc's preoccupation with only using the finest ingredients brings an Agen, not a Bresse, squab cooked in its own juices with the freshest of vegetables from his own extensive vegetable garden; and a perfectly cooked roasted best-end and braised knuckle of milk-fed lamb with a simple sage jus. Desserts might simply refresh as in a mango soup with its own bitingly fresh sorbet, or indulge extremely as in a hot chocolate fondant with bitter almond cream served with pistachio ice cream. The cheese board offers an object lesson in how to choose and present a wide variety of cheeses, both well known and unusual. The wine list is long, predominantly French and extremely good, but the young wine waiter knows his stuff and will offer some interesting suggestions, as in a delightful and unknown 1995 Vin de Pays du Var from Triennes followed by a more recognisable 1994 Chateauneuf-du-Pape, Domaine Font de Michelle. Not all will break the bank. Le Manoir's young team are a delight, and are clearly at one with the overriding passion of Raymond Blanc, which is to present the very best in the most enjoyable way. Set lunch from £32. Menu Gourmande £72.

Recommended:

Browns

INTERNATIONAL
5-11 WOODSTOCK RD, OXFORD, 01865-511995
Lunch & Dinner daily. £

Cherwell Boathouse

MODERN BRITISH
BARDWELL RD, OXFORD, 01865-52746
Lunch Tues.-Sun., Dinner Tues.-Sat. £
Set lunch £10-£17.50, Set dinner £18.50.

Pubs

The Bear

ALFRED ST, OXFORD, 01865 721783
Mon.-Sat. noon-11pm, Sun. noon-6pm. Lunch daily.

Eagle and Child

49 ST. GILES, OXFORD, 01865 310154
Mon.-Sat. 11am-11pm, Sun. noon-10.30pm.
Lunch & Dinner Mon.-Thurs., Lunch Fri.-Sun.

Woodstock:

The Feathers Hotel, Restaurant & Whinchat Bar

MARKET ST, WOODSTOCK, OXFORDSHIRE, OX20 1SX, 01993-812291, FAX 01993-813158
3 stes £215-£260, 16 rms £88-£169.

WINDSOR

Windsor Castle, where the kings and queens of England have lived for 900 years, dominates the small town and the surrounding countryside. First a wooden fortress built by William the Conqueror in 1066—a day's march, or twenty miles from his other castle, the Tower of London—the present collection of buildings is a mixture of architectural styles. Three sections—**Upper, Middle and Lower Wards**, give dramatic views over the river and countryside. Within the castle, you see the little houses of the Military Knights of Windsor, an order founded by King Edward III as the

'Poor Knights of Windsor', and **St George's Chapel**, begun in 1478. Reminscent of King's College Chapel, Cambridge, it is full of tombs (ten monarchs are buried here), and monuments to various royal figures. But most visitors come to see the **State Apartments**, the formal rooms used by the reigning monarch for ceremonial, State and official occasions. Open to the public when the Royal Family is not in residence, they are now beautifully restored after a huge and very destructive fire. Some of the Queen's impressive art collection is on display on the walls. Also within the castle is the delightful **Queen Mary's Dolls' House**, created by the architect Sir Edwin Lutyens for the young Queen Mary and given to her by the nation in 1923. It's a wonderful world in miniature. You can combine a trip to Windsor with a trip to the **Waterside Inn at Bray**, one of Britain's best restaurants and with rooms attached.

Windsor is about 27 miles west of London and a short car journey. Trains from Waterloo Station run regularly and take about 45 minutes.

NOT TO BE MISSED:

Bray-on-Thames:

Waterside Inn

FRENCH 17/20

FERRY RD, BRAY-ON-THAMES, NR WINDSOR, 01628 20691, FAX 01628 620691

Lunch Wed.-Sun., Dinner Tues.-Sun. ££££

A

It is over 20 years since Michel Roux was awarded the Meilleur Ouvrier de France in Paris, and there are those who have felt over the period since then that the Waterside may have been guilty of coasting a little. Only one thing can silence such quibbles, and that of course is present excellence, and that—we are happy to report this time—is not in dispute. The plain fact is that this is one of the top restaurants in the UK, and well worth the journey from London, if your schedule can encompass an away-day .

For one thing, there is the setting, as idyllic as ever and a world away from city hubbub. Bray is a pretty enough village, but the name of this restaurant-with-rooms reflects its location on the bank of the Thames—right on it. Aperitifs may be taken under the drooping branches of a willow, or there is a little gazebo if the sun feels too fierce. The dining room itself is airy and sunny, encouraging relaxation. Prices dropped somewhat this summer, but only because service is no longer included, but is now an extraneous addition at 12.5%, a bad old British habit that seems a curiously retrogressive step for a place such as this. It is all the more difficult to understand, given that nobody expects a restaurant like this to be bargain-priced anyway. What you get for your money is a carte of broad range and impeccable technique or a fixed-price whole-table deal for £69.50. The spring carte offered, among much else, scrambled eggs with crabmeat and asparagus; sautéed scallops on rocket leaves with wild mushrooms and apple julienne; grilled turbot with sauce choron, and a grand dish of veal three ways—medallions stuffed with a duxelle of ceps, a grilled kidney on braised lettuce and the sweetbreads en croûte, the whole dish unified with a white wine jus. It is the intensity of flavour that most impresses: our breast of guinea fowl sauced with a rich truffled cream was a masterpiece of restrained power. At dessert stage, raspberry gratin with a Grand Marnier sauce or the famous mirabelle plum soufflé, are joined by a grande assiette of six items for those who can't make up their minds. The cheeses, too, are superb, and include some British examples among the French classics. The self-effacing and highly proficient service helps to make the Waterside a true delight. Set lunch £30.50, Set dinner £69.50 (5 courses).

ALSO

Fat Duck

FRENCH

1 HIGH ST, BRAY-ON-THAMES, BERKS, 01628 580333, FAX 01628 776188

Lunch Tues.-Sun., Dinner Tues.-Sat. ££

A

Shinfield

L'Ortolan

FRENCH 16/20

THE OLD VICARAGE, CHURCH LANE, SHINFIELD, 0118 9883783, FAX 0118 9885391

Lunch Tues.-Sun, Dinner Tues.-Sat. ££££

A

This pleasant old red-brick vicarage has been somewhat refurbished, and now presents a more sophisticated, comfortable dining room, with the conservatory a delightful adjunct. Consequently L'Ortolan remains one of the restaurants of pilgrimage for those after an exquisite meal served in such pleasant surroundings. The chef/owner, John Burton-Race, is a perfectionist, whose cooking is firmly based on French classic haute-cuisine. Technical refinement and a masterly grasp of the various layers of taste result in dishes like marinated wild salmon layered with a horseradish cream on which is placed a little Beluga caviar, or the assiette of salmon teriyaki with a lightly battered tempura of langoustine and scallop. Ingredients are of the finest, the flavours enhanced by a delicate saucing. Flavours, though, become rich in many of the main dishes, like the veal fillet roasted and glazed in its own juices with grilled veal kidney in a sweet-and-sour sauce and pan-fried sweetbreads with a truffle cream. This is complex cooking of a very high standard indeed, and some of the dishes are advertised as needing 15, 18, 20 minutes' cooking. Desserts reveal the same sureness of touch—cherries flambéed in kirsch are served in a light pancake with a vanilla ice cream; summer fruit sorbet come with a tart lime sauce and rich candied berries. Service is French and can be extremely solicitous. The wine list, predominantly French, has a good New World section, though expect to pay dearly. There is a good house selection from £15, though with this level of cooking and pricing, it is better to go prepared for a hefty bill. Set menu 3 courses £42, Menu Gourmand £150 for 2 (including wines).

YORK

Of all Britain's great historic cities, York is the one which inspires a huge amount of admiration and devotion in Brits and visitors alike. One of Britain's best preserved medieval cities, it's only two hours from London by train. But that apart, it's also an extremely friendly city and an easy one for visitors to get to know quickly. Put that together and you have a magical experience.

There are three possible places to stay. **Middlethorpe Hall**, built in 1699, is a mile or so south of the city centre, easily reachable by taxi and overlooking delightful York racecourse. It stands in its own extensive grounds and welcomes you into the stone-flagged entrance hall with blazing log fires. It has an excellent restaurant, particularly good for dinner where a gourmet menu is served along with the regular à la carte. A little more central, the **Grange Hotel**, with a good and popular restaurant, just outside the city walls, was originally an elegant Regency townhouse.

York is a city for walking, another of those places where you discover its corners only on foot. Founded by the Romans in AD 71 as a fortress to quell the rebellious northerners, York was first known as 'Eboracum'. With the departure of the Romans successive invasions followed, but it was the Vikings who left the greatest mark on the city, not least by the fact that the gates are still called bars and the streets are called gates. (The Danish word for street is gaten). The eleventh-century Norman conquerors found a thriving little city which they promptly sacked but they did build the magnificent city walls which you can still walk on today. In the Middle Ages York became the most important city in the north as its massive Minster church—the largest north of the Alps—testifies. By the eighteenth century, York was also the most fashionable, welcoming the 'Beau Monde' from far and wide for the balls and assemblies, who found graceful Georgian houses to stay in. By great good fortune, the Victorian Industrial Revolution largely passed York by, and instead the city became a refuge for the mill owners of the neighbouring towns, leaving it wonderfully preserved and unspoilt by Victorian 'improvements'.

The best way to start a visit to this intriguing city is to walk around the walls which enclose the 263 acres of medieval York. From here you look down on the web of narrow streets whose names read like a history lesson: **Spurriergate** named after the spur makers, the **Shambles** from 'fleshammels' (once a row of butchers' shops), and the curiously named **Whip-Ma-Whop-Ma Gate**, derived from a whipping post where criminals were thrashed. Dominating the skyline is the great **York Minster** which took over two hundred years to build. It has some of the finest medieval stained glass in Britain and is a 'must' for any visitor to York. One of the most exciting developments in recent years was the excavation of the Viking settlement in **Coppergate** and the opening of the **Yorvik Centre**. The visitor boards a 'time car' and is whisked back through history to a reconstruction of the Viking community of over 1,000 years ago. The car passes through the actual excavation site and finally the visitor walks through an exhibition of everyday items from the 'dig': woollen socks, shoes and, rather surprisingly, hornless Viking helmets.

No visit to York is complete without seeing the **Castle Museum**. Partly housed in the old prison, the visitor sees the highwayman Dick Turpin's cell (the residents of York are particularly proud of this famous resident), and walks through reconstructed Victorian streets. It is essentially a museum of everyday life and some of the twentieth-century exhibits—vacuum cleaners, television sets and so on from the recent past—bring a pang of nostalgia. Medieval buildings such as the **Merchant**

Adventurer's Hall, scores of churches, narrow streets, the **National Railway Museum**, the eighteenth-century **Fairfax House**, the city walls and gates, the Minster, the Yorvik Centre and excellent shops make York a city with something for everyone.

York has several good restaurants. **Melton's** remains one of our favourites, its simple decor and good cooking matched by reasonable prices. **19 Grape Lane** is in the heart of medieval York and serves modern British food. Of the pubs, the **Black Swan**, timber-framed and dating back to the fifteenth century, is everyone's idea of an ancient pub. The **Olde Starre** is another popular place, in one of York's prettiest streets and the city's oldest licensed pub (1644). One great northern institution should be indulged in in York: afternoon tea at **Bettys**, a quintessential English tearoom where they serve excellent pastries (Bettys was founded by a young Swiss confectioner in Harrogate in the 1920s and has gone on to spawn younger versions like the one in York).

Further information from **York Tourist Office**, De Grey Rooms, Exhibition Sq, York, 01904-621756.

HOTELS

Not to be Missed

Middlethorpe Hall

BISHOPSTHORPE RD, YORK, YO2 1QB, 01904-641241, FAX 01904-620176
7 stes £175-£230, 23 rms £99-£155.

Recommended

Grange Hotel

1 CLIFTON, YORK, YO3 6AA, 01904-644744, FAX 01904-612453
1 ste £190, 29 rms £99-£160.

RESTAURANTS

Middlethorpe Hall

MODERN BRITISH
BISHOPSTHORPE RD, YORK, YO2 1QB, 01904-641241, FAX 01904-620176
Lunch and Dinner daily. Set lunch £12.50 and £14.50, Set dinner £27.95.

Melton's

INTERNATIONAL
7 SCARCROFT RD, YORK, 01904-634341, FAX 01904 635115
Lunch Tues.-Sun., Dinner Mon.-Sat. ££
Set lunch £15, set dinner £14.50-£19.50.

19 Grape Lane

MODERN BRITISH
19 GRAPE LANE, YORK, 01904-636366
Lunch & Dinner Tues.-Sat. ££

PUBS AND CAFÉS

Bettys

CAFÉ
6-8 ST. HELEN'S SQ, YORK, 01904-659142
Daily 9am-9pm.

The Black Swan Pub

PEASEHOLME GREEN, YORK, 01904-625236
Mon.-Sat. 11am-11pm, Sun. noon-10.30pm.

The Old Starres

PUB
STONEGATE, YORK, 01904-623063
Mon.-Sat. 11am-11pm, Sun. noon-10.30pm.

BASICS

CONTENTS

ARRIVING IN LONDON

The London Tourist Board's official Internet site for London is **www.LondonTown.com**

Getting into London from any of the three major airports is relatively easy.

FROM HEATHROW

(15 MILES FROM LONDON):

The **Heathrow Express**, a dedicated high-speed rail link takes passengers from the airport to **Paddington Station** every 15 minutes between 5.20am and 11.40pm. The trip takes 15 minutes from Terminals 1, 2, & 3 and around 20 minutes from Terminal 4. Paddington Station will have full airline passenger and luggage check-in facilities beginning in March 1999.

The **Piccadilly Line** underground departs for London every five minutes; the trip takes about 50 minutes. But note: that there are only escalators to get you down to the trains at Heathrow and few stations in central London have lifts, so if you have lots of luggage, this can present problems.

The **Airbus A1** takes about one hour to **Victoria Station**. **Airbus A2** takes about one hour to **King's Cross**. The Airbuses depart approximately every thirty minutes, stop at various places en route and cost £6 single, £10 open return. Signs at the airport indicate the route and the stops.

A **taxi** will cost around £45. Beware mini cabs or private drivers touting for custom in the airport; they can be expensive, so you should only take a licensed black cab.

FROM GATWICK

(29 MILES TO LONDON):

Fast and frequent **train service** takes 30 minutes into **Victoria Station** (£9.50 single, £19 return, valid for one month).

Flightline Buses 777 depart at 5am and 6.30am, then about every hour until 5.40pm. The last bus is at 8.10pm. The bus trip takes around 75 minutes depending on the time of day and costs £7.50 single, £11 return.

A **taxi** will cost around £65 and take from an hour-and-a-half to two hours.

FROM STANSTED

(32 MILES TO LONDON):

A **train** departs every 30 minutes on the hour and the half hour and takes 45 minutes to **Liverpool Street Station** (£10.40 single, £20.80 return, but there are special deals). A **taxi** will cost around £50 and takes about 90 minutes.

The Eurostar from Paris or Brussels via the Channel Tunnel:

The trip is around 3 hours, with trains arriving at **London Waterloo International Station**. For information tel: 0345-303030.

GENERAL ENQUIRIES

Heathrow—0181-759 4321
Lost Property—0181-745 7727
Gatwick (general inquiries and lost property)—01293-535353
London City Airport—0171-474 5555
Stansted—01279-680500

GETTING AROUND

PUBLIC TRANSPORT SYSTEM

London's public transport system is one of the biggest, oldest and most complex in Europe, so expect overcrowding at peak times—between 8am and 9.30am and 4.30pm to 6.30pm. For information telephone 0171-222 1234.

It is also expensive compared to other cities. The most economical tickets are ***Travelcards***—daily, weekly or monthly passes giving you unlimited travel on all forms of transport in set zones. Make sure you get the right ticket for the right zone as there are six which stretch from city centre into outer suburbia. Most major sights are contained within Zones One and Two. You can buy these tickets at underground stations and at newsagents showing a special Red Pass agent sign. Weekly and monthly passes require a passport-sized photograph. One-day Travelcards (no photo needed) cannot be used before 9.30am Monday to Friday. Central London bus and underground guides are available from underground stations and at Heathrow.

Recently introduced are ***The Carnet***, a book of ten single tube tickets for travel in Zone One costing £10 and saving £3; a ***Family Travelcard***, giving various savings on buses, the underground, Docklands Light Railway and some trains within the greater

London area; and a ***Weekend Travelcard*** offering a 25 percent discount.

For overseas visitors various options of cards to buy in advance are available from British Rail International offices.

NO SMOKING on London Transport—you can be fined up to £1,000 for the offence.

AIR CHARTER

Aerostar— 0181-897 6021
Heathrow Jet Charter—0181-759 5560
International Sky Charter—0171-242 9501
Southern Air—01273-461 661

BUSES

The nicest way to travel around London is by bus. Bus stops are either compulsory stops (London Transport signs on a white background), or request stops (signs on a red background). At the latter, hold out your hand to indicate to the driver to stop.

Most new buses are one-man operated and you pay your fare to the driver as you get on. Do not try to pay with large notes—you risk the wrath of the queue. Night Buses exist on several popular routes from 11pm to 6am. The routes are prefixed with the letter 'N'. One day Travelcards do not operate on night buses.

If you want to take a bus to almost anywhere outside central London, from Aberdeen to Athens, you'll probably go from the main coach station on Buckingham Palace Road (about five minutes walk from Victoria railway station). The two main companies for national travel are: ***Green Line***, 0181-668 7261, and ***National Express***, 0990-808080.

CARS

Driving in London can be a nightmare if you don't know your way around. And there is the added hazard of possible clamping for illegal parking or overrunning time on a meter. If you plan to go outside London into the countryside, hiring a car is a good idea, particularly from an airport.

Alamo —03800-272300
Avis—0990-900500
British Car Rental—01203-716166
Budget—0800-181181
Eurodollar—0990 365365
Europcar—0171-834 8484
Hertz—0171-730 8323
Hertz Worldwide Reservations—0990-996699
Thrifty—0171-262 2223

TAXIS

There are taxi ranks at railway stations and throughout London. You can hail a cab on the street whenever you see the yellow 'Taxi' or 'For Hire' sign lit up. A tip of between ten and fifteen percent of the cost of the journey is usual. You can call a taxi on ***Radio Taxicars***, 0171-272 0272 and ***Computer Cabs***, 0171-286 0286.

TRAINS

To get to outer London and beyond, trains run every day except Christmas Day and Boxing Day (December 25 and 26). For all national enquiries, telephone 0345 48 49 50. Please note that all mainline stations share the national enquiry number.

Charing Cross Station—Strand, WC2. For connections to south London and the southeast of England.

Docklands Light Railway (DLR)—0171-363 9700. Connects Docklands with the City, Stratford and Greenwich. Also available are 'Sail and Rail' tickets combining a day's unlimited travel on DLR, visit to Greenwich, discount on entry to the National Maritime Museum and return trip by riverboat.

Euston Station—Euston Rd, NW1. For connections to northwest London and northwest England, the Midlands, North Wales, Scotland and Ireland via Holyhead.

King's Cross Station—Euston Rd, NW1. For connections to northeast London, the east and northeast of England, and the east coast of Scotland.

Liverpool Street Staion—Bishopsgate, EC2. For connections to east and northeast London, Essex and East Anglia.

Paddington Station—Praed St, W2. For connections to west London, Oxford, Bristol, Plymouth, the west of England, South Wales and Ireland via Fishguard.

Thameslink Service—Connects Luton Airport with south London, Gatwick Airport and Brighton via West Hampstead and Blackfriars.

Victoria Station—Buckingham Palace Rd, SW1. For connections to south London, Gatwick airport, southwest England and the Channel ports for Europe.

Waterloo Station—Waterloo Rd, SE1. For south London and the south of England

Waterloo International—Waterloo Rd, SE1. For connections to Paris, Brussels and other European destinations via the Channel tunnel.

UNDERGROUND

Known as the 'tube', the London underground has eleven lines and 270 stations and is the oldest in the world, having opened on January 10, 1863. Tube trains run every day except Christmas Day from around 5.30am to just after midnight, but this is not always the case on lines running to outlying stations. Get tickets either from a ticket office or an automatic machine which indicates whether it will give change or not. Keep your ticket as you will need it at the end of the journey. Tel for information on 0171-222 1234.

LONDON TRANSPORT

London Buses andUnderground—
0171-222 1234
Lost Property—200 Baker St, NW1,
0171-486 2496

TOURS

BY BUS/COACH

A good way to see London is from the top of a special double-decker open-topped bus. **The Original London Sightseeing Tour** (0181-877 1722) runs from four central London departure points close to underground stations: Baker Street, Marble Arch, Haymarket and Victoria Station. Buy tickets on the bus, from any London Transport station, or London Tourist Board Information Centres and at many central London hotels.

The Big Bus Company (0181-944 7810) offers much the same service, a two-hour tour in an open-top bus, departing from Marble Arch, Green Park Underground (by The Ritz Hotel), Victoria (Royal Westminster Hotel) and Victoria Coach Station. Prices are £12 for adults, £6 for children for a two-hour tour .

Other companies offering bus tours lasting from two hours to a full day include: **London Pride**, 01708-631122; **Frames Rickards**, 0171-837 3111; **Harrods**, 0171-581 3603.

If you want to go outside London, try **Visitors Sightseeing**, 0171-636 7175, which includes trips around Britain, as well as London half-day tours.

BY CHAUFFEURED CAR OR LIMOUSINE

Alamo Chauffeur Service—0345 886688
Avis—0171-917 6703
Berkeley Square Chauffeur Services—
0171-629 3939
Camelot Chauffeur Drive—0171-235 0234
Chauffeurdrive—0541 536537
Europcar Interent—0171-834 6701
Kensington & Chelsea Cars—
0171-603 6660
Masterdrive—0541-536537

By Private Car & Driver-Guide

Take-a-Guide Ltd
43 Finstock Rd, W10—0181-960 0459, Fax 0181-964 0990. One of the oldest and best driver-guide companies.

Good Company
48 Prince of Wales Rd, NW5—0171-267 5340, Fax 0171-284 0765. Or try this smaller company.

James & Company
POBox 549, SW18—Tel & Fax 0181-875 0755; website: www.jamestours.com; e-mail: james@jamestours.com. London and Paris based service for Britain and Europe.

BY RIVER & CANAL

Travelling through London by river is a wonderful experience as you see the riverside buildings from a different angle and travel effortlessly. The 'hop-on, hop-off' ferry operates in the city between 11am and 5pm, calling at Tower Pier, London Bridge Pier, HMS Belfast, Butlers Wharf and St. Katharine's Dock, and running either every 30 minutes or 15 minutes depending on the time of year. Fares are adults £2, children £1 for an all-day ticket including discount vouchers for several places of interest.

Other trips go from Westminster Pier and Charing Cross Pier regularly, winter and summer. They take twenty minutes to the Tower of London and 50 minutes to Greenwich. You can just go to the piers and take the next boat; they depart every 30 to 45 minutes, depending on the time of year and cost around £5-£6 single to the Tower of London, £6-£7 return, and around £7 single to Greenwich, £7 return. For general information call 0839-123432. For information on specific companies, call **Catamaran Cruiser**, 0171-987 1185, **London Launches**, 0171-930 3373, **Turk Launches**, 0181-546 2434 (summer only), or **Westminster Passenger Service Association**, downriver on 0171-930 4097, and upriver on 0171-930 4721.

Bateaux London/Catamaran Cruisers—Charing Cross Pier, Victoria Embankment, WC2, 0171-839 3572, Fax 0171-839 1034. A restaurant cruiser offering lunch (£21-£27) and dinner (£54) cruises. Telephone or fax for details and booking. Board at Temple Pier on Victoria Embankment.

Silver Sturgeon—Savoy Pier (by the Savoy Hotel), Embankment, SW1, 0171 878 2002. Luxury restaurant river boat with bars, dance floor and two restaurants offering dinner on Mon., Wed., Fri., Sat., £54 per person.

The Regent's Park Canal is worth seeing. Narrow boat cruises on *Jason's Trip* start opposite 60 Blomfield Rd, Little Venice, W9, daily at regular intervals, 0171-286 3428. From Camden Town, try the *Jenny Wren* at Camden Lock.

The same company runs *My Fair Lady*. You get a good lunch (Sundays only) or dinner and a trip past the **London Zoo** to **Little Venice** and back. *My Fair Lady*, 250 Camden High St, NW1, 0171-485 4433 or 0171-485 6210. The costs vary from around £6 to £29.95.

France Vacations

Don't let the name fool you. This excellent tour company offers many affordable packages that combine Paris and London—two great cities, two great cultures—via Eurostar. Their vacation options are very reasonably priced, and include airfare, hotel accommodations and daily breakfast. In London, they offer rooms at a wide array of hotels—from economy-class to top-of-the-line. France Vacations will also arrange for theatre tickets, museum passes and car rentals (in U.S. 310-645-3070 or 800-332-5332).

BY TAXI

Black Taxi Tours—Tours last 2 hours and cost £65 per taxi cab (maximum of 5 people). They can pick you up and return you to your hotel and give you a real insider's knowledge and point of view.

GUIDE BOOKING AGENCIES

GUILD OF REGISTERED TOURIST GUIDES:

The Guild House—52d Borough High St, SE1, 0171-403 1115, Fax 0171-378 1705

Professional Guides—0181-874 2745

Tour Guides—57 Durham St, W1, 0171-495 5504, Fax 0171-495 5323

TOURIST INFORMATION CENTRES

Britain Visitor Centre
1 Regent St, SW1 (no tel). Open Mon.-Fri. 9am-6.30pm, Sat., Sun. 10am-4pm (May-Sep Sat. 9am-5pm).

Canary Wharf Tourist Information Centre
Ground Floor, Cabot Place West, E14, 0171-512 9800. Open Mon.-Fri. 9am-6pm, Sat., Sun., Bank hol Mon. 10am-5pm.

City of London Tourist Information
St. Paul's Churchyard, EC4, 0171-332 1456. Open Mon.-Fri. 9.30am-5pm, and in summer also Sat., Sun., 9.30am-5pm.

Greenwich Tourist Information Centre
46 Greenwich Church St, SE10, 0181-858 6376. Open Apr-Sep daily 10.15am-4.45pm. In winter open daily with reduced hours.

Heathrow Terminals 1, 2, 3
Underground Station Concourse, Heathrow Airport, Middlesex. Open daily 8am-6pm.

Islington Tourist Information Centre
44 Duncan St, N1, 0171-278 8787. Open 1 Apr-end Oct: Mon. 2pm-5pm, Tues.-Sat. 10am-5pm (closed Sat. 1.30pm-2.30pm).

Liverpool Street Underground Station
EC2. Open Mon.-Fri. 8am-6pm, Sat., Sun. 8.45am-5.30pm.

London Tourist Board & Convention Bureau
26 Grosvenor Gdns, SW1. No personal callers. Instead the LTB runs various information lines which you can reach by telephone only. Check in the London telephone book for details of services like:

Accommodation Information, 0891-505487; *Changing the Guard*, 0839123411; *Events This Week*, 0839-123400.

Southwark Tourist Information Centre
Unit 4, Lower Level, Cotton's Centre, Middle Yard, SE1, 0171-403 8299. Open Mon.-Fri. 10am-5pm, Sat., Sun. 11am-5pm.

Victoria Station Forecourt
Victoria Station, SW1, Open Mon.-Sat. 8am-6pm, Sun. 8.30am-4pm.

Waterloo
Waterloo Station, SE1, Open daily 8.30am-9pm.

USEFUL ADDRESSES & PHONE NUMBERS

BUREAUX DE CHANGE

Almost every bank in central London operates a bureau de change, and there are numerous private enterprises which change money also. Exchange rates vary widely, sometimes with differences at branches of the same bank. Otherwise try:

American Express—Haymarket, SW1, 0171-930 4411 or **24-hour Travellers Cheque Refund**—0800-521313

EMBASSIES

Australian High Commission
Australia House, Strand, WC2, 0171-379 4334

Canadian High Commission
Macdonald House, 1 Grosvenor Square, W1, 0171-258 6600

French Consulate General
21/23 Cromwell Rd, SW7, 0171-201 1000

New Zealand High Commission
New Zealand House, 80 Haymarket, SW1, 0171-930 8422

United States Embassy
24 Grosvenor Square, W1, 0171-499 9000

EMERGENCY PHONE NUMBERS

Emergency Dentist—Guy's Hospital Dental School, 0171-995 5000

Emergency Doctor—Doctorcall, 0171-225 1111; Medcall, 0800 136

Emergency Optician—Opticall, 0171-495 4915

Lost Credit Cards—American Express, 01273 696 933; Diners Club, 01252 513 500; Mastercard/Eurocard, 01268 298178; Visa, 01604 230 230

Lost property in taxis—0171 833 0996

Police, Fire and Ambulance Services—999

LATE OPENING PHARMACISTS

Bliss Chemist—5 Marble Arch, W1, 0171-723 6116, Open daily 9am-midnight.

Boots the Chemist—Piccadilly Circus, W1, 0171-734 6126, Open Mon.-Sat. 8.30am-8pm, Sun. noon-6pm.

MONEY TRANSFER

Western Union—0800-833 833.

PHOTOGRAPHIC DEVELOPMENT

Compton Photos—Old Compton St/Wardour St, W1, 0171-437 7329

Joe's Basement—113-117 Wardour St, W1, 0171-439 3210 (24 hours).

RELIGIOUS SERVICES

Baptist—London Baptist Association, 1 Merchant St, E3, 0181-980 6818

Buddhist—The Buddhist Society, 58 Eccleston Sq, SW1, 0171-834 5858

Jewish—Liberal Jewish Synagogue, 28 St. John's Wood Rd, NW8, 0171-286 5181; United Synagogue (Orthodox), 735 High Road, N2, 0181-343 8989

Moslem—Islamic Cultural Centre, 146 Park Rd, NW8, 0171-724 3363

Protestant—Church of England, St. Paul's Cathedral, EC4, 0171-248 2705, Information line 0171-236 0752

Quakers—Religious Society of Friends, 173-177 Euston Rd, NW1, 0171-387 3601

Roman Catholic—Westminster Cathedral, Victoria St, SW1, 0171-798 9055, Service information 0171-798 9099

TRANSLATION SERVICES

All Languages Ltd—0171-739 6641
Berlitz International—0171-629 7360
Multilingual Services—0171-836 2979
Universal Translations—0171-248 8707

TAX-FREE SHOPPING

Value added tax (VAT) of **17.5%** is charged on almost all goods in Britain except, most notably, on books, food and all children's clothes, and is almost always included in the advertised price. Non-European Community visitors to Britain staying for less than three months can claim back VAT. Take your passport with you when shopping. You must fill in a form in the store when you buy the goods and then give a copy to Customs when you leave the country. You may also have to show the goods to Customs, so make sure they are accessible. The tax refund will either be returned by cheque or attributed to your credit card although in that case you may pay a service charge. Most stores have a minimum purchase threshold, often £50 or £75. If your goods are shipped directly home from the shop, VAT should be deducted before you pay.

Jet Vacations

A terrific tour operator for the independent traveller, Jet Vacations features air, hotel and car rental packages that combine London with excursions to the English countryside—in all price ranges. Among their most popular options: theater packages, countryside train tours, barge cruises, walking tours, golf packages, and stays in coaching inns and country-house hotels. They also arrange stays on the Channel Islands of Jersey and Guernsey (in U.S. 800-JET-0999).

CALENDAR OF EVENTS

There is so much going on in London it is difficult to decide what to see, but here we give a brief summary.

English National Holidays: January 1, Good Friday, Easter Monday, the first and last Mondays in May, last Monday in August, December 25, 26. When December 25, 26 fall on a weekend, extra holidays are given on the preceding Friday or following Monday/ Tuesday. If New Year's Day falls on a weekend, the first Monday in January is usually a Public Holiday.

JANUARY

- **London International Boat Show**—Earl's Court Exhibition Centre, SW5, 0171-385 1200. Huge exhibition of large and small craft.
- **World of Drawings and Watercolours**—The Dorchester Hotel, Park Lane, W1. One of the biggest and most prestigious international art fairs.
- **Contemporary Art Show**—Business Design Centre, Upper St, Islington, N1, 0171-359 3535. Annual exhibition of work by living artists from around the world producing some wonderful surprises. Prices range from £50 to £20,000.
- **Decorative Antiques & Textiles Fair**—The Marquee, Riverside Terraces, Battersea Park, SW11. Wonderful decorative fair giving you plenty of ideas for your home.
- **West London Antiques & Fine Art Fair**—Kensington Town Hall, Hornton St, W8. Vetted fair with plenty of stands and a good range of items and styles.

FEBRUARY

- **Chinese New Year**—Celebrations throughout Chinatown, around Gerrard St, W1.

MARCH

- **British Antique Dealers' Fair**—Duke of York's Headquarters, SW3, 0171-589 4128 Run by one of the two official antique dealers' organisations, the BADA show is a popular, excellent antiques fair with an international clientele.
- **Little Chelsea Antiques Fair**—Chelsea Old Town Hall, King's Rd, SW3, 0171-352 1856. Vetted and fun, with a good range.
- **London Original Print Fair**—Royal Academy of Arts, Piccadilly, W1, 0171-439 7438. The longest-running event of its kind in the world, attracting print dealers from around the world.

APRIL

- **Oxford and Cambridge Boat Race**—From Putney to Mortlake, a 4 1/4 mile course.
- **The Decorative Antiques & Textiles Fair**—The Marquee, Riverside Terraces, Battersea Park, SW11. Another of the decorative fairs (see January).

MAY

- **Royal Windsor Horse Show**—Home Park, Windsor, 01753-860633. A long-running ever popular event with show-jumping, dressage and Country Fair.
- **Chelsea Flower Show**—Royal Hospital, Chelsea, SW3, 0171-828 1744. Probably the most famous flower show in the world and one of the most difficult to get tickets to. Contact the Royal Horticultural Society for details (0171-834 4333) or the special show telephone number (see above).

JUNE

- **Beating the Retreat by the Massed Bands of the Household Division**—Horse Guards Parade, SW1, 0171-839 5323. A wonderful piece of pageantry with various regiments taking part.
- **Trooping the Colour**—Horse Guards Parade, SW1, 0171-414 2479. Celebration of the Queen's official birthday on June 11.
- **Antiquarian Book Fair**—Olympia 2, Kensington Olympia, W14. A huge antiquarian book fair with dealers offering a great range of subjects and prices.
- **Fine Art & Antiques Fair**—Olympia, Kensington, W14, 0171-603 3344. One of the great fine arts fairs held this month.
- **Stella Artois Championship**—Queen's Club, W14, 0171-225 3733. The 'run-up' to Wimbledon—small and delightful.
- **Royal Academy Summer Exhibition**—Royal Academy of Arts, Piccadilly, W1, 0171-439 7438. One of the largest public art exhibitions in the world and the event that, in the days when such things mattered, announced the beginning of the London social season.
- **Grosvenor House Art and Antiques Fair**—Grosvenor House Hotel, Park Lane, W1, 0171-499 6363. The most prestigious antiques and fine art fair in the world, with top dealers mainly from Europe and the United States. Not to be missed.
- **International Ceramics Fair and Seminar**—The Park Lane Hotel, Piccadilly, W1, 0171-499 6321. This ceramic fair of the most commonly collected of all antiques combines the best dealers and an interesting lecture programme.
- **Royal Ascot Race Meeting**—Ascot, Berks, 01344-22211. One of the best flat race meetings in the world.
- **Wimbledon Lawn Tennis Championships**—All England Lawn Tennis Club, SW19, 0181-946 2244. One of the world's major sports events always the last week of June and the first of July.

JULY

- **Henley Royal Regatta**—Henely-on-Thames, Oxfordshire, 01491 572153.
- **Royal Tournament**—Earl's Ct, SW5, 0171-385 1200. When the army shows off in a wonderful display of might and skill, orchestrated so well it puts many operatic directors to shame.
- **Hampton Court Palace International Flower Show**—Hampton Court Palace, East Molesey, 0171-828 1744. This new event has become one of the major UK horticultural events of the year. The largest of its kind in the world, it features landscaped garden displays, marquees, water gardens, crafts and more.

AUGUST

- **Notting Hill Gate Carnival**—Notting Hill Gate, W8. A celebration of Caribbean culture and music in London.

SEPTEMBER

- **Chelsea Antiques Fair**—Chelsea Old Town Hall, SW3, 0171-352 1856. A popular antiques event stretching over ten days and held twice a year (also March).
- **20th Century British Art Fair**—Royal College of Art, Kensington Gore, SW7. Important view of the contemporary art scene, much sought after by serious collectors and those interested in today's artists.

OCTOBER

- **Horse of the Year Show**—Wembley Arena, Wembley, 0181-900 1234. Show-jumping from the world's top competitors.
- **Chelsea Crafts Fair**—Chelsea Old Town

Hall, King's Rd, SW3, 0171-352 1856 One of the most important crafts fair in Europe, stretching over two sessions with different craftspeople in each, offering a huge range of very high quality items from jewellery to textiles.

- **City of London Antiques Fair**—Honourable Artillery Company, Armoury House, City Rd, EC1. Large fair in the City offering plenty of choice.
- **LAPADA (London & Provincial Antique Dealers' Association) Arts and Antiques Fair**—Royal College of Art, Kensington Gore, SW7, 0171-823 3511. The biggest London fair from this antique dealers' association.
- **Kensington Antiques & Fine Art Fair**—Kensington Town Hall, Honrton St, W8. Great fair with around 70 stands, dateline to 1914.

NOVEMBER

- **Chelsea Book Fair**—Chelsea Old Town Hall, SW3. Vetted, high quality antiquarian and second hand book fair, vetted, no dateline.
- **The Fine Art & Antiques Fair**—Olympia, W14, 0171-603 3344. One of London's prestigious arts events.
- **RAC London to Brighton-Veteran Car Run**—Hyde Park, London to Brighton. When the 'old crocks' gather to drive in stately manner to Brighton from Hyde Park.
- **Lord Mayor's Show**—The new Lord Mayor parades through the streets of the City of London. It always takes place on the second Sunday in November, with fireworks along the river at the end of the day.
- **Remembrance Sunday Ceremony**—Cenotaph, Whitehall, W1. Ceremony attended by the Queen and the Royal Family commemorating the dead of both world wars.
- **World Travel Market**—Earl's Ct, SW5, 0171-385 1200. One of the biggest travel trade shows in the world.
- **Little Chelsea Antiques Fair**—Chelsea Old Town Hall, King's Rd, SW3, 0171-352 1856. Autumn equivalent of the Spring fair.

DECEMBER

- **Olympia International Show Jumping Championships**—Olympia, W14, 0171-373 8141. A great show-jumping international event.

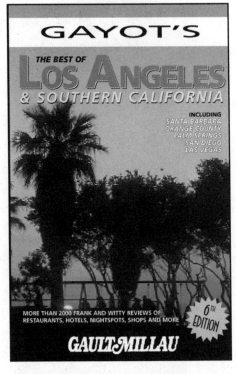

MENU SAVVY

CONTENTS

MENU SAVVY

A Guide to International Food Terms

FRENCH

Agneau: lamb

Aïoli: garlicky mayonnaise

Américaine or armoricaine: sauce of white wine, Cognac, tomatoes and butter

Andouille: smoked tripe sausage, usually served cold

Anglaise (à l'): boiled meats or vegetables

Ballottine: boned, stuffed and rolled poultry

Bâtarde: sauce of white roux (a mixture of flour and butter or other fat, usually in equal proportions, cooked together slowly and used to thicken sauces and soups).

Béarnaise: sauce made of shallots, tarragon, vinegar and egg yolks, thickened with butter

Béchamel: sauce made of flour, butter and milk

Beurre blanc: sauce of wine and vinegar boiled down with minced shallots, then thickened with butter

Beurre noisette: lightly browned butter

Bière: beer

Bigarade: bitter orange used in sauces and marmalade

Bisque (crayfish, lobster, etc.): rich, velvety soup, usually made with crustaceans, flavored with white wine and Cognac

Blinis: small, thick crêpes made with eggs, milk and yeast

Boeuf: beef

Boeuf bourguignon: beef stew with red wine, onions and lardons (Lardoon; larding fat cut into long strips and threaded through lean cuts of meat by a special larding needle in order to moisten the meat as it cooks).

Bombe glacée: molded ice cream dessert

Bordelaise: fairly thin brown sauce of shallots, red wine and tarragon

Borscht: thick Eastern European soup of beets and boiled beef, often garnished with a dollop of sour cream

Boudin noir: blood sausage

Bouillabaisse: various fish cooked in a soup of olive oil, tomatoes, garlic and saffron

Bourride: sort of bouillabaisse, usually made with large white fish, thickened with aïoli; served over slices of bread

Brie: cow's milk cheese with a soft, creamy inside and a thick crust, made in the shape of a disk and sliced like a pie

Brioche: a soft loaf or roll, often sweetened and used for pastries

Brochette: on a skewer

Canapé: small piece of bread topped with savory food

Canard: duck

Carbonnade: pieces of lean beef, first sautéed then stewed with onions and beer

Carré d'agneau: rack of lamb

Cèpes: prized wild mushroom, same family as the Italian porcini

Chanterelles: prized wild mushroom, trumpet-shaped

Charcutière: sauce of onions, white wine, beef stock and gherkins

Charlotte: dessert of flavored creams and/or fruit molded in a cylindrical dish lined with ladyfingers (if served cold) or strips of buttered bread (if served hot)

Chasseur: brown sauce made with shallots, white wine and mushrooms

Chèvre: goat cheese

Choucroute: sauerkraut; often served with sausages, smoked bacon, pork loin and potatoes

Citron: lemon

Chou-fleur: cauliflower

Clafoutis: a dessert of fruit (usu. cherries) baked in an

eggy batter
Confit: pork, goose, duck, turkey or other meat and sealed in its own fat
Coquilles St-Jacques: sea scallops
Côte d'agneau: lamb ribs
Coulis: thick sauce or purée, often of vegetables or fruit
Court-bouillon: stock in which fish, meat and poultry are cooked
Crème chantilly: sweetened whipped cream
Crêpe Suzette: crêpe stuffed with sweetened mixture of butter, Curaçao, tangerine juice and peel
Croque-monsieur: grilled ham and cheese sandwich
Croûte (en): in pastry crust
Crudités: raw vegetables
Daube: beef braised in red wine
Ecrevisses: crayfish
Entrecôte: "between the ribs"; steak cut from between the ribs
Epinards: spinach
Escalope: slice of meat or fish, flattened slightly and sautéed
Escargots (à la bourguignonne): snails (with herbed garlic butter)
Financière: Madeira sauce enhanced with truffle juice
Florentine: with spinach
Foie gras: liver of a specially fattened goose or duck
Fondue: a bubbling pot of liquid into which which pieces of food are dipped—most commonly cheese and bread; can also be chocolate and fruit or various savory sauces and cubes of beef. Also, vegetables cooked at length in butter and thus reduced to pulp
Forestière: garnish of sautéed mushrooms and lardons (Lardon; larding fat cut into long strips and threaded through lean cuts of meat as it cooks).
Frangipane: almond pastry cream used to fill thick crêpes
Galantine: boned poultry or meat, stuffed and pressed into a symmetrical form, cooked in broth and coated with aspic
Galettes and crêpes (Brittany): galettes are thin pancakes made of buckwheat flour and are usually savory. Crêpes are made of wheat flour and are usually sweet
Gâteau: cake
Gelée (en): in aspic (gelatin usually flavored with meat, poultry or fish stock)
Génoise: sponge cake
Granité: lightly sweetened fruit ice
Gratin dauphinois: sliced potatoes baked in milk, sometimes with cream and/or grated Gruyère
Grenouille: frog (frogs' legs: cuisses de grenouilles)
Hollandaise: egg-based sauce thickened with butter and flavored with lemon
Jambon: ham
Julienne: vegetable soup made from a clear consommé, or any shredded food
Lait: milk
Langouste: rock or spiny lobster
Langoustine: saltwater crayfish
Lapin: rabbit
Lièvre: hare
Limon: lime (also, **citron vert**)
Lotte: monkfish or anglerfish; sometimes called "poor man's lobster"
Madrilène (à la): garnished with raw, peeled tomatoes
Magret (Maigret): breast of fattened duck, cooked with the skin on; usually grilled
Médaillon: food, usually meat, fish or foie gras, cut into small, round pieces
Moules marinière: mussels cooked in the shell with white wine, shallots and parsley
Nantua: sauce of crayfish, white wine, butter and cream with a touch of tomato
Noisettes: hazelnuts; also, small, round pieces of meat (especially lamb or veal)
Nougat: sweet made with roasted almonds, egg whites, honey and sugar
Oeufs: eggs
Pain: bread
Parfait: sweet or savory mousse; also a layered ice cream dessert
Parisienne: garnish of fried potato balls
Paupiettes: thin slices of meat stuffed with forcemeat and shaped into rolls
Pissaladière: tart with onions, black olives and anchovy filets
Poires: pears
Pommes: apples
Pommes de terre: potatoes
Poulet: chicken
Profiteroles: small puffs of choux paste often filled with

whipped cream of crème patissiere and piled high in a dish with chocolate sauce poured over
Provençale (à la): with garlic or tomato and garlic
Quiche: tart of eggs, cream and various fillings (such as ham, spinach or bacon)
Ratatouille: stew of eggplant, tomatoes, bell peppers, zucchini, onion and garlic, all sautéed in oil
Rémoulade: mayonnaise with capers, onions, parsley, gherkins and herbs
Rissoles: type of small pie filled with forcemeat
Rouille: sort of mayonnaise with pepper, garlic bread soaked in bouillon, olive oil and possibly saffron
Sabayon: fluffy, whipped egg yolks, sweetened and flavored with wine or liqueur; served warm
Saint-Pierre: John Dory, a white-fleshed fish
Salade niçoise: salad of tomatoes, hard-boiled egg, anchovy filets, tuna, sweet peppers, celery and olives (also can include green beans, potatoes, basil, onions and/or broad beans)
Sole meunière: sole dipped in flour and sautéed in butter with parsley and lemon
Soissons: garnished with green beans
Sorbet: sherbet
Spätzle: round noodles, often made from eggs
Steak au poivre: pepper steak; steak covered in crushed peppercorns, browned in a frying pan, flambéed with Cognac; also sauce deglazed with cream
Tapenade: a paste of olives, capers and anchovies, crushed in a mortar with lemon juice and pepper
Tartare: cold sauce for meat or fish; mayonnaise with hard-boiled egg yolks, onions and chopped olives
Tarte: tart, round cake or flan; can be sweet or savory
Tarte Tatin: upside-down apple tart
Tortue: turtle; also, a sauce made with various herbs, tomato, Madeira
Tournedos Rossini: beef sautéed in butter, served with pan juices, foie gras
Truffe: truffle; highly esteemed subterranean fungus, esp. from Périgord
Vacherin: ice cream served in a meringue shell; also, creamy, pungent cheese from Switzerland or eastern France
Viande: meat

Italian

Acciughe: anchovies
Aceto: vinegar
Aglio: garlic
Agnello: lamb
Agnolotti: crescent-shaped, meat-filled pasta
Agrodolce: sweet-and-sour
Amaretti: crunchy almond macaroons
Anatra: duck
Anguilla: eel
Aragosta: spiny lobster
Arrosto: roasted meat
Baccalá: dried salt cod
Bagna cauda: hot, savory dip for raw vegetables
Bierra: beer
Biscotti: cookies
Bistecca (alla fiorentina): charcoal-grilled T-bone steak (seasoned with pepper and olive oil)
Bolognese: pasta sauce with tomatoes and meat
Bresaola: air-dried spiced beef; usually thinly sliced, served with olive oil and lemon juice
Bruschetta: toasted garlic bread topped with tomatoes
Bucatini: hollow spaghetti
Calamari (calamaretti): (baby) squid
Calzone: stuffed pizza-dough turnover
Cannellini: white beans
Cappelletti: meat- or cheese-stuffed pasta ("little hats")
Carbonara: pasta sauce with ham, eggs, cream and grated cheese
Carciofi (alla giudia): (flattened and deep-fried baby) artichokes
Carpaccio: paper thin, raw beef (or other meats)
Cassata: ice-cream bombe
Cavolfiore: cauliflower
Ceci: chickpeas
Cipolla: onion
Conchiglie: shell-shaped pasta
Coniglio: rabbit
Coppa: cured pork filet encased in sausage skin
Costata: rib steak
Costoletta (alla milanese): (breaded) veal chop
Cozze: mussels
Crespelle: crêpes
Crostata: tart
Fagioli: beans

Fagiolini: string beans
Farfalle: bow-tie pasta
Fegato: liver
Fegato alla veneziana: calf's liver sautéed with onions
Fichi: figs
Finocchio: fennel
Focaccia: crusty flat bread
Formaggio: cheese
Frittata: Italian omelet
Fritto misto: mixed fry of meats or fish
Frutti di mare: seafood (esp. shellfish)
Funghi (trifolati): mushrooms (sautéed with garlic and parsley)
Fusilli: spiral-shaped pasta
Gamberi: shrimp
Gamberoni: prawns
Gelato: ice cream
Gnocchi: dumplings made of cheese (di ricotta), potatoes (di patate), cheese and spinach (verdi) or semolina (alla romana)
Grana: hard grating cheese
Granita: sweetened, flavored grated ice
Griglia: grilled
Insalata: salad
Involtini: stuffed meat or fish rolls
Lenticchie: lentils
Maccheroni: macaroni pasta
Manzo: beef
Mela: apple
Melanzana: eggplant
Minestra: soup; pasta course
Minestrone: vegetable soup
Mortadella: large, mild Bolognese pork sausage
Mozzarella di bufala: fresh cheese made from water-buffalo milk
Noce: walnut
Orecchiette: ear-shaped pasta
Osso buco: braised veal shanks
Ostriche: oysters
Pane: bread
Panettone: brioche-like sweet bread
Panna: heavy cream
Pancetta: Italian bacon
Pappardelle: wide, flat pasta noodles
Pasta asciutta: pasta served plain or with sauce
Pasticceria: pastry; pastry shop
Pasticcio: pie or mold of pasta, sauce and meat or fish
Patate: potatoes
Pecorino: hard sheep's-milk cheese
Penne: hollow, ribbed pasta
Peperoncini: tiny, hot peppers
Peperoni: green, red or yellow sweet peppers
Pesca: peach
Pesce: fish
Pesce spada: swordfish
Pesto: cold pasta sauce of crushed basil, garlic, pine nuts, parmesan cheese and olive oil
Piccata: thinly-sliced meat with a lemon or Marsala sauce
Pignoli: pine nuts
Polenta: cornmeal porridge
Pollo: chicken
Polipo: octopus
Pomodoro: tomato
Porcini: prized wild mushrooms, known also as boletus
Prosciutto: air-dried ham
Ragú: meat sauce
Ricotta: fresh sheep's-milk cheese
Rigatoni: large, hollow ribbed pasta
Riso: rice
Risotto: braised rice with various savory items
Rucola: arugula
Salsa (verde): sauce (of parsley, capers, anchovies and lemon juice or vinegar
Salsicce: fresh sausage
Saltimbocca: veal scallop with prosciutto and sage
Sarde: sardines
Semifreddo: frozen dessert, usually ice cream, with or without cake
Sgombro: mackerel
Sogliola: sole
Spiedino: brochette; grilled on a skewer
Spumone: light, foamy ice cream
Tartufi: truffles
Tiramisú: creamy dessert of rum-spiked cake and triple-crème Mascarpone cheese
Tonno: tuna
Torta: cake
Tortelli: pasta dumplings stuffed with greens and ricotta
Tortellini: ring-shaped dumplings stuffed with meat or cheese and served in broth or in a cream sauce
Trenette: thin noodles served with potatoes and pesto sauce
Trota: trout
Uovo (sodo): egg (hard-boiled)
Uva: grapes
Uva passa: raisins
Verdura: greens, vegetables
Vitello (Tonatto): veal (in a tuna and anchovy sauce)
Vongole: clams
Zabaglione: warm whipped egg yolks flavored with Marsala
Zafferano: saffron
Zucchero: sugar
Zucchine: zucchini
Zuppa: soup
Zuppa inglese: cake steeped in a rum-flavored custard sauce

Spanish & Latin American

Because there are so many regional dialects in Spain and Latin America, the term for one food product might easily have four or five variations. We've chosen a simple list of those ingredients and dishes most often found in Southern California restaurants.

Aceite: oil
Ajo: garlic
All-i-oli: aïoli; garlicky mayonnaise
Arroz: rice
Bacalao: dried, salted codfish
Bullabesa: Catalán fish stew similar to bouillabaisse
Burrito: soft, wheat-flour tortilla rolled and stuffed with various meats, refried beans, cheese and vegetables
Caldo: broth
Camarones: shrimp
Carne: meat
Cerveza: beer
Chalupa: a small, thick corn tortilla folded into a boat shape, fried and filled with a mixture of shredded meat, cheese and/or vegetables
Chilequile: flat tortilla layered with beans, meat, cheese and tomato sauce
Chile relleno: large, mild chile pepper, stuffed with cheese and fried in an egg batter
Chorizo: spicy pork sausage flavored with garlic and spices
Conejo: rabbit
Cordero: lamb
Empanada: pie or tart filled variously with meat, seafood or vegetables
Empanadita: a small empanada
Enchilada: a tortilla, fried and stuffed variously with meat, cheese and/or chiles
Entremeses: appetizers
Flan: a baked custard with a caramel coating (also **crema caramela**)
Frito (frita): fried
Gambas: shrimp
Garbanzo: chick pea
Gazpacho: Andalusian; a cold soup of fresh tomatoes, peppers, onions, cucumbers, olive oil, vinegar and garlic (also celery, breadcrumbs)
Guacamole: an avocado dip or filling, with mashed tomatoes, onions, chiles and citrus juice
Higado: liver
Huachinango: red snapper
Huevos: eggs
Huevos rancheros: tortillas topped with eggs and a hot, spicy salsa
Heuvos revueltos: scrambled eggs
Jalapeño: very common hot chile pepper, medium size
Jamón: ham
Licuado: fruit milkshake
Lima: lime
Limón: lemon
Linguiça: garlicky pork sausage
Mantequilla: butter
Mariscos: shellfish
Masa: cornmeal dough; essential for making tortillas
Menudo: a stew featuring tripe
Mole: sauce; most often a thick, dark sauce made with mild chiles and chocolate
Nachos: a snack dish of tortilla chips topped with melted cheese and chiles
Nopales: leaves of the prickly pear cactus; simmered and used in various dishes
Ostras: oysters
Paella: a dish of saffron-flavored rice studded with meat (chicken, ham, sausages, pork), shellfish and vegetables
Papas: potatoes (also, **patatas**)
Papas fritas: literally "fried potatoes "; french fries
Parrillada: grilled
pechuga de pollo: chicken breast
Pescado: fish
Pez espada: swordfish
Pimiento: red chile pepper; can be sweet or hot
Plátano: plantain; a starchy, mild-tasting variety of banana popular in Latin American; usu. cooked and served as a side dish
Pollo: chicken
Poblano: large, mild, dark green chile pepper; used for chile rellenos
Puerco: pig
Pulpo: octopus
Quesadilla: a soft, folded tortilla filled with cheese (and/or other savory stuffings) and toasted or fried
Queso: cheese
Salchicha: sausage
Salsa: sauce; also, an uncooked condiment employing fresh tomatoes, onions and chiles
Salsa borracha: "drunken sauce "; salsa made with tequila
Sangría: Spanish drink made with red wine, soda water, chopped fresh fruits and sugar, often with a touch of brandy; served on ice
Seviche: raw fish marinated in citrus juice (also, **cebiche**)
Sopa: soup
Sope: a small cornmeal bun

cooked and filled with savory stuffing

Taco: a folded, fried tortilla filled with ground beef (or other meats or fish), refried beans, shredded lettuce, tomatoes, onion, cheese and salsa

Tamale: Corn dough made with lard, filled with a savory stuffing, wrapped up in a piece of corn husk, and steamed

Tapa: appetizer, Spanish in origin; usu. enjoyed with an apéritif such as dry sherry

Tortilla: a flat, unleavened, crêpelike bread made with cornmeal flour (masa) or wheat flour

Tostada: a fried tortilla topped with a saladlike mix of ground beef or chicken, beans, lettuce, tomato, guacamole

Asian

Chinese

Bao bun: dim sum item; small, steamed buns, white in color, stuffed with a variety of minced fillings (often chicken, shrimp, pork or lotus beans)

Bird's-nest soup: soup that has been thickened and flavored with the gelatinous product derived from soaking and cooking the nests of cliff-dwelling birds

Bok choy: Chinese white cabbage

Chop suey: strictly a Chinese American dish; meat or shrimp and vegetables (mushrooms, water chestnuts, bamboo shoots, bean sprouts) stir-fried together and served over rice

Chow mein: strictly a Chinese American dish; meat or shrimp and vegetables (mushrooms, water chestnuts, bamboo shoots, bean sprouts) stir-fried and served over crispy egg noodles

Dim sum: figuratively, "heart's delight"; a traditional meal featuring a variety of small dumplings, buns, rolls, balls, pastries and finger food, served with tea in the late morning or afternoon

Egg roll: thiulike wrapper stuffed with pork, cabbage or other vegetables, rolled up, and deep-fried or steamed

Fried rice: cooked, dried rice quickly fried in a wok with hot oil, various meats or vegetables and often an egg

Hoisin: a sweet, rich, dark brown sauce made from fermented soy beans; used as a base for other sauces

Lo mein: thiu, steamed wheat-flour noodles stir-fried with bean sprouts and scallions and either shrimp, pork, beef or vegetables

Lychee: small, round, fleshy fruit; used fresh, canned, preserved and dried

Mu shu: a delicate dish of stir-fried shredded pork and eggs rolled up in thin pancakes

Oyster sauce: a thick, dark sauce of oysters, soy and brine

Peking duck: an elaborate dish featuring duck that has been specially prepared, coated with honey and cooked until the skin is crisp and golden; served in pieces with thin pancakes or steamed buns, and hoisin

Pot sticker: dim sum item; dumpling stuffed with meat, seafood or vegetables, fried and then steamed

Shark's fin soup: soup thickened and flavored with the cartilage of shark's fins, which provides a protein-rich gelatin

Shu mai: dim sum item; delicate dumpling usu. filled minced pork and vegetables

Spring roll: a lighter version of the egg roll, with fillings such as shrimp or black mushrooms

Szechuan: cuisine in the style of the Szechuan province, often using the pepper-corn-like black Chinese pepper to make hot, spicy dishes

Thousand-year-old eggs: chicken, duck or goose eggs preserved for 100 days in ashes, lime and salt (also, **100-year-old eggs**)

Wonton: paper-thin, glutinous dough wrapper; also refers to the dumpling made with this wrapper, stuffed with minced meat, seafood or vegetables

Wonton soup: a clear broth in which wontons are cooked and served

Japanese

Amaebi: sweet shrimp

Anago: sea eel

Awabi: abalone

Azuki: dried bean; azuki flour is often used for confections

Ebi: shrimp

Enoki (Enokitake): delicate mushrooms with long stems and small caps

Hamachi: yellowtail
Hibachi: small, open charcoal grill
Hirame: flounder
Ikura: salmon roe
Kaiseki: Multicourse menu of luxury dishes reflecting the seasons with the use of seasonal foods and artistic dinnerware and presentation
Kani: crab
Kappa: cucumber
Kobe beef: cattle raised in exclusive conditions (frequent massages and a diet featuring large quantities of beer), which results in an extraordinarily tender, very expensive beef
Konbu: dried kelp; used in soup stock, for sushi and as a condiment
Maguro: tuna
Maki: rolled
Mako: shark
Mirugai: giant clam
Miso (soup): soybean paste from which a savory broth is made, usu. served with cubes of tofu or strips of seaweed
Ono: wahoo fish; a relative of the mackerel often compared in taste to albacore
Ramen: Chinese soup noodles
Saba: mackerel
Sake: salmon
Saké: traditional rice wine served hot or cold
Sashimi: thinly sliced raw fish on rice, usually served with soy sauce and wasabi
Shabu shabu: similar to sukiyaki; beef and vegetables cooked tableside in a broth
Shiitake: Prized cultivated mushroom, dark brown with a large cap
Shoya: soy sauce
Soba: buckwheat noodles
Sukiyaki: braised beef and vegetable dish with broth added after cooking
Sushi: Rounds of vinegared rice wrapped in dried seaweed with a center of raw rish or vegetables, served with wasabi and soy
Tai: snapper
Tako: octopus
Tamago: egg
Tamari: dark sauce similar in composition and taste to soy; often used for dipping
Tempura: deep-fried, batter-dipped fish or vegetables
Teriyaki: A marinade of soy and sweet sake, used on meats, fish and poultry
Tofu: bean curd, processed into a liquid and then molded into large cubes
Toro: fatty belly cut of tuna
Udon: wheat noodles
Unagi: freshwater eel
Uni: sea-urchin roe
Wasabi: a hot, spicy condiment made from the roots of Japanese horseradish, chartreuse in color
Yakitori: a dish of pieces of chicken and vegetables, marinated in a spicy sauce, skewered and grilled

Thai

Kaeng (or **Gaeng**): large and diverse category of dishes; loosely translates as "curry"
Kaeng massaman: a variety of coconut-milk curry
Kaeng phed: a red, coconut-cream curry
Kaeng som: a hot-sour curry
Kapi: fermented shrimp paste; vital ingredient in **nam phrik**, or dishes flavored with hot chili sauce
Kai (or **Gai**): chicken
Khai: egg
Khao: rice
Khao suai: white rice
Khao phad: fried rice
King: ginger
Kung: prawns
Lab (or **Larb**): dish of minced meat with chilies and lime juice
Mu: pork
Nam: sauce
Nam pla: fish sauce
Nam phrik: a hot chili sauce
Nuea: beef
Ped: duck
Phad: fried
Phad king: fried with ginger
Phad phed: fried hot and spicy
Phad Thai: pan-fried rice noodles with chicken, shrimp, eggs, peanuts and bean sprouts
Phrik: chili pepper
Pla: fish
Si racha (or **Sri racha**) spicy chili condiment
Tom: boiled; often refers to soups
Tom kha kai: chicken coconut-cream soup flavored with lemongrass and chilies
Tom yam kung: hot-sour shrimp soup flavored with lemongrass, lime and chilies
Yam: flavored primarily with lime juice and chilies, resulting in a hot-sour taste; usually "salads" but can also be noodle dishes or soup
Yam pla: raw fish spiked with lime juice, chili, lemongrass, mint and fish sauce

General Index

A

B

D

I

J

M

S

T

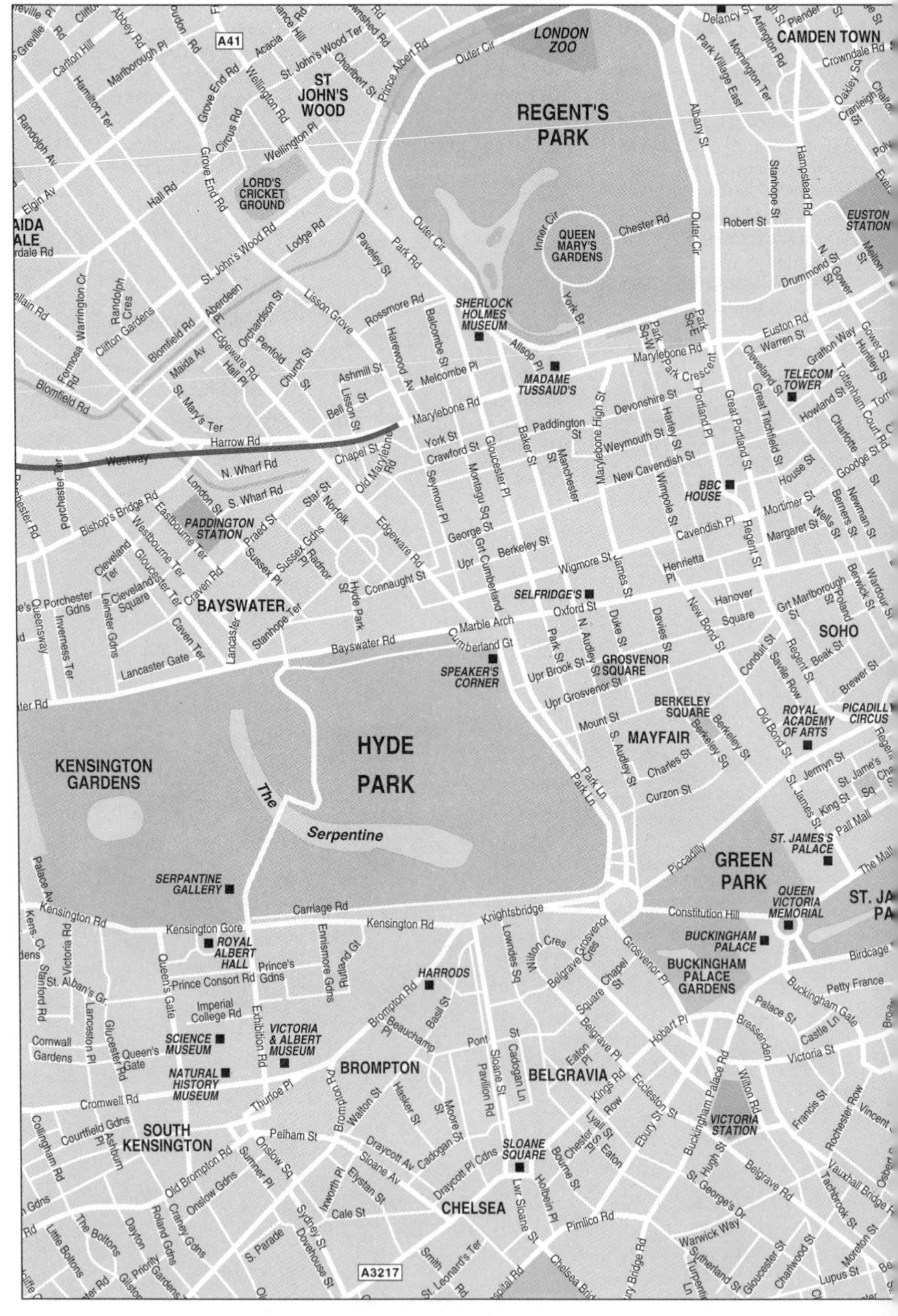
A41
LONDON ZOO
CAMDEN TOWN
ST JOHN'S WOOD
REGENT'S PARK
LORD'S CRICKET GROUND
QUEEN MARY'S GARDENS
EUSTON STATION
SHERLOCK HOLMES MUSEUM
MADAME TUSSAUD'S
TELECOM TOWER
BBC HOUSE
PADDINGTON STATION
BAYSWATER
SELFRIDGE'S
SOHO
SPEAKER'S CORNER
GROSVENOR SQUARE
BERKELEY SQUARE
ROYAL ACADEMY OF ARTS
PICADILLY CIRCUS
MAYFAIR
HYDE PARK
KENSINGTON GARDENS
The Serpentine
ST. JAMES'S PALACE
GREEN PARK
SERPANTINE GALLERY
QUEEN VICTORIA MEMORIAL
BUCKINGHAM PALACE
BUCKINGHAM PALACE GARDENS
ROYAL ALBERT HALL
HARRODS
SCIENCE MUSEUM
VICTORIA & ALBERT MUSEUM
NATURAL HISTORY MUSEUM
BROMPTON
BELGRAVIA
VICTORIA STATION
SOUTH KENSINGTON
SLOANE SQUARE
CHELSEA
A3217
Abbey Rd
Carlton Hill
Hamilton Ter
Marlborough Pl
Grove End Rd
Circus Rd
Wellington Rd
Wellington Pl
St. John's Wood Ter
Charlbert St
Prince Albert Rd
Outer Cir
Inner Cir
Chester Rd
York Br
Park Village East
Mornington Ter
Arlington Rd
Delancy St
Crowndale Rd
Oakley Sq
Albany St
Stanhope St
Hampstead Rd
Robert St
Drummond St
Euston Rd
Warren St
Grafton Way
Gower St
Huntley St
Howland St
Tottenham Court Rd
Charlotte St
Goodge St
Randolph Av
Elgin Av
Hall Rd
St. John's Wood Rd
Lodge Rd
Paveley St
Park Rd
Lisson Grove
Rossmore Rd
Balcombe St
Harewood Av
Melcombe Pl
Allsop Pl
Marylebone Rd
Park Crescent
Portland Pl
Great Portland St
Cleveland St
Great Titchfield St
Devonshire St
Harley St
Weymouth St
New Cavendish St
Wimpole St
Marylebone High St
Paddington St
Baker St
Manchester St
Gloucester Pl
Montagu Sq
Crawford St
York St
Seymour Pl
George St
Upr Berkeley St
Grt Cumberland Pl
Wigmore St
James St
Cavendish Pl
Mortimer St
Margaret St
Wells St
Berners St
Newman St
Henrietta Pl
Regent St
Hanover Square
Oxford St
Grt Marlborough St
Poland St
Berwick St
Wardour St
Davies St
Duke St
N. Audley St
New Bond St
Conduit St
Savile Row
Beak St
Brewer St
Old Bond St
Marble Arch
Cumberland Gt
Bayswater Rd
Upr Brook St
Upr Grosvenor St
Park St
Mount St
S. Audley St
Charles St
Berkeley Sq
Berkeley St
Curzon St
Park Ln
Jermyn St
St. James's St
King St
St. James's Sq
Pall Mall
Piccadilly
The Mall
Constitution Hill
Birdcage Walk
Harrow Rd
Westway
N. Wharf Rd
S. Wharf Rd
London St
Bishop's Bridge Rd
Eastbourne Ter
Westbourne Ter
Praed St
Sussex Gdns
Norfolk Sq
Star St
Chapel St
Old Marylebone Rd
Edgeware Rd
Connaught St
Hyde Park St
Sussex Pl
Radnor Pl
Craven Rd
Gloucester Ter
Cleveland Square
Cleveland Ter
Porchester Ter
Porchester Gdns
Queensway
Inverness Ter
Leinster Gdns
Lancaster Gate
Caven Ter
Stanhope Ter
Maida Av
Aberdeen Pl
Orchardson St
Penfold St
Church St
Ashmill St
Bell St
Lisson St
Hall Pl
St. Mary's Ter
Blomfield Rd
Formosa St
Warrington Cr
Randolph Cres
Clifton Gardens
Carriage Rd
Kensington Rd
Kensington Gore
Knightsbridge
Palace Av
Victoria Rd
Kens. Ct
Stanford Rd
St. Alban's Gr
Launceston Pl
Gloucester Rd
Queen's Gate
Prince Consort Rd
Prince's Gdns
Ennismore Gdns
Rutland Gt
Imperial College Rd
Exhibition Rd
Cornwall Gardens
Lowndes Sq
Wilton Cres
Grosvenor Cres
Belgrave Sq
Chapel St
Grosvenor Pl
Petty France
Buckingham Gate
Palace St
Castle Ln
Bressenden Pl
Victoria St
Brompton Rd
Beauchamp Pl
Basil St
Pont St
Sloane St
Cadogan Ln
Pavilion Rd
Eaton Pl
Belgrave Pl
Hobart Pl
Eccleston St
Kings Rd
Lyall St
Chester Row
Buckingham Palace Rd
Wilton Rd
Francis St
Rochester Row
Vincent Sq
Cromwell Rd
Thurloe Pl
Walton St
Hasker St
Moore St
Cadogan St
Draycott Av
Sloane Av
Draycott Pl
Cdns
Courtfield Gdns
Ashburn Pl
Collingham Rd
Pelham St
Onslow Sq
Old Brompton Rd
Sumner Pl
Onslow Gdns
Ixworth Pl
Elystan St
Cale St
Lwr Sloane St
Holbein Pl
Bourne St
Chester Pl
S. Eaton Pl
Ebury St
Hugh St
Belgrave Rd
St. George's Dr
Vauxhall Bridge Rd
Tachbrook St
Pimlico Rd
Warwick Way
Sutherland St
Gloucester St
Charlwood St
Moreton St
Lupus St
Turpentine Ln
Chelsea Bridge Rd
Ebury Bridge Rd
Little Boltons
The Boltons
Dayton Gr
Roland Gdns
Priority Gardens
Cranley Gdns
S. Parade
Sydney St
Dovehouse St
Smith St
St. Leonard's Ter
Royal Hospital Rd

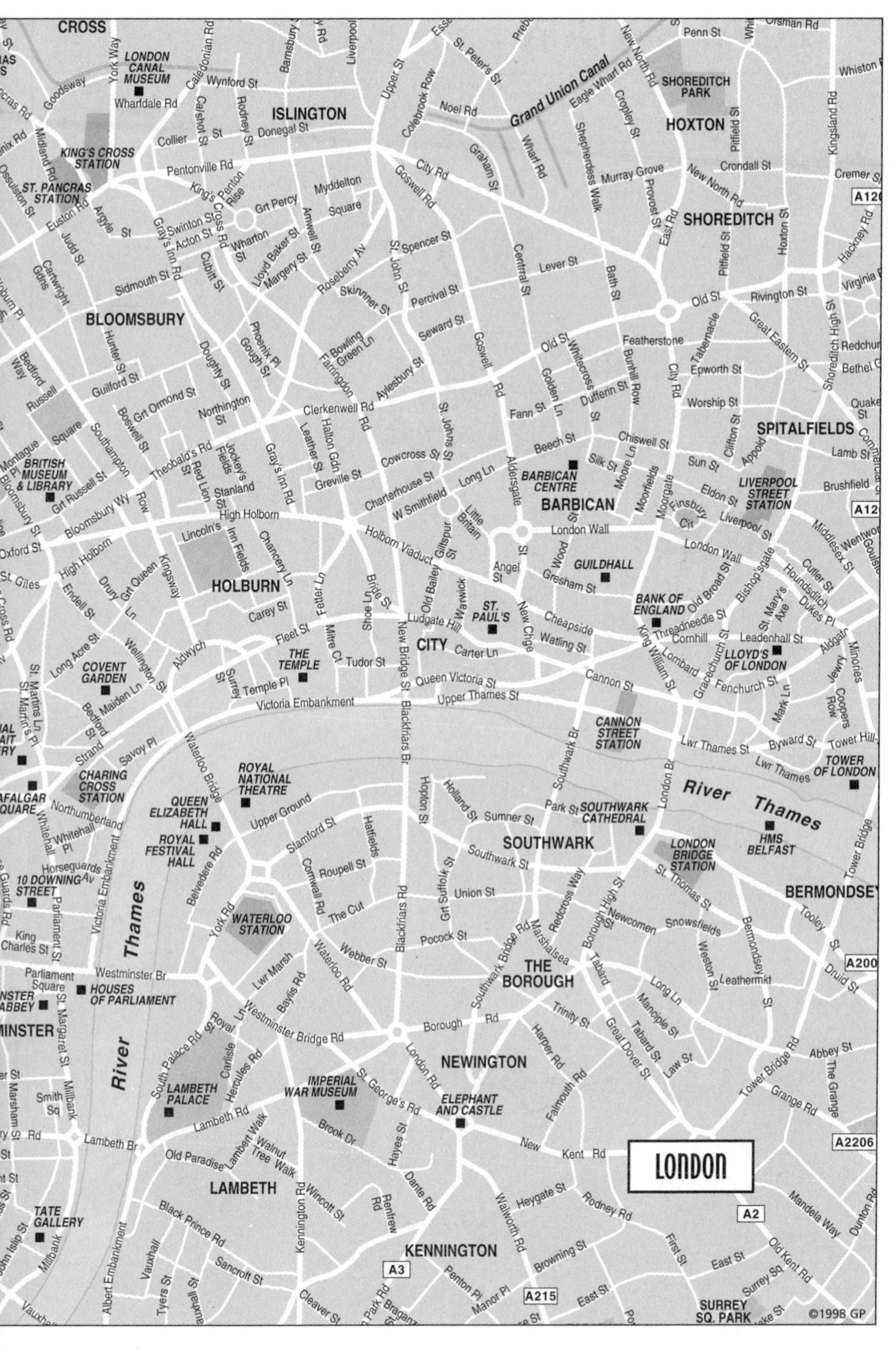
CROSS
LONDON CANAL MUSEUM
Wharfdale Rd
Goodsway
York Way
Caledonian Rd
Wynford St
Barnsbury
Liverpool
Upper St
St. Peter's St
Penn St
Orsman Rd
Whiston Rd
New North Rd
Grand Union Canal
Eagle Wharf Rd
SHOREDITCH PARK
HOXTON
Kingsland Rd
ISLINGTON
Donegal St
Collier St
Calshot St
Rodney St
Noel Rd
Colebrook Row
Wharf Rd
Shepherdess Walk
Cropley St
Pitfield St
Midland Rd
KING'S CROSS STATION
ST. PANCRAS STATION
Pentonville Rd
Penton Rise
Myddelton Square
City Rd
Goswell Rd
Graham St
Murray Grove
Provost St
New North Rd
Crondall St
Cremer St
A120
Ossulston St
Euston Rd
Argyle St
King's Cross Rd
Grt Percy
Swinton St
Acton St
Wharton St
Gray's Inn Rd
Lloyd Baker St
Amwell St
Margery St
Rosebery Av
Spencer St
Central St
Lever St
Bath St
East Rd
SHOREDITCH
Pitfield St
Hoxton St
Hackney Rd
Judd St
Cartwright Gdns
Sidmouth St
Cubitt St
Skinner St
Percival St
St. John St
Old St
Rivington St
Virginia
BLOOMSBURY
Hunter St
Phoenix Pl
Gough St
Doughty St
Bowling Green Ln
Farringdon Rd
Seward St
Aylesbury St
Goswell Rd
Whitecross
Golden Ln
Featherstone
Bunhill Row
Tabernacle
Epworth St
Great Eastern St
Shoreditch High St
Redchurch
Bethel
Bedford Way
Russell Square
Guilford St
Grt Ormond St
Northington St
Clerkenwell Rd
St. Johns St
Fann St
Dufferin St
City Rd
Worship St
Quaker St
Boswell St
Southampton Row
Theobald's Rd
Jockey's Fields
Leather St
Halton Gdn
Cowcross St
Beech St
Chiswell St
Clifton St
SPITALFIELDS
Commercial St
Lamb St
Montague Pl
BRITISH MUSEUM & LIBRARY
Grt Russell St
Red Lion St
Stanland St
Gray's Inn Rd
Greville St
Charterhouse St
Long Ln
BARBICAN CENTRE
Silk St
Moore Ln
Moorfields
Moorgate
Sun St
Appold
Eldon St
LIVERPOOL STREET STATION
Brushfield
A12
Bloomsbury St
Bloomsbury Wy
High Holborn
W Smithfield
Little Britain
BARBICAN
Wood St
Finsbury Cir
Liverpool St
Middlesex St
Wentworth
Oxford St
Lincoln's Inn Fields
Chancery Ln
Holborn Viaduct
Giltspur St
London Wall
London Wall
St. Giles
High Holborn
Endell St
Drury Ln
Grt Queen
Kingsway
HOLBURN
Fetter Ln
Bride St
Old Bailey
Warwick
Angel St
GUILDHALL
Gresham St
Old Broad St
Bishopsgate
Cutler St
Houndsditch
Dukes Pl
Carey St
Shoe Ln
ST. PAUL'S
New Chge
Cheapside
BANK OF ENGLAND
Threadneedle St
St. Mary's Axe
Long Acre St
Wellington St
Aldwych
Fleet St
Mitre Ct
New Bridge St
Ludgate Hill
Watling St
Cornhill
Leadenhall St
Aldgate
Minories
COVENT GARDEN
THE TEMPLE
Tudor St
CITY
Carter Ln
King William St
Lombard
Gracechurch St
LLOYD'S OF LONDON
Jewry
St. Martins Ln
St. Martin's Pl
Maiden Ln
Bedford St
Surrey St
Temple Pl
Queen Victoria St
Cannon St
Fenchurch St
Mark Ln
Coopers Row
Victoria Embankment
Upper Thames St
Blackfriars Br
Strand
Savoy Pl
Waterloo Bridge
CANNON STREET STATION
Southwark Br
Lwr Thames St
Byward St
Tower Hill
CHARING CROSS STATION
ROYAL NATIONAL THEATRE
Hopton St
Holland St
London Br
Lwr Thames
TOWER OF LONDON
River Thames
Northumberland Av
QUEEN ELIZABETH HALL
Upper Ground
Sumner St
Park St
SOUTHWARK CATHEDRAL
Whitehall
Whitehall Pl
ROYAL FESTIVAL HALL
Stamford St
Hatfields
SOUTHWARK
HMS BELFAST
Horseguards Av
Belvedere Rd
Cornwall Rd
Roupell St
Southwark St
Gt Suffolk St
LONDON BRIDGE STATION
Tower Bridge
10 DOWNING STREET
Parliament St
Victoria Embankment
Thames
WATERLOO STATION
York Rd
The Cut
Union St
Redcross Way
Borough High St
St. Thomas St
Newcomen St
BERMONDSEY
Tooley St
King Charles St
Pocock St
Snowsfields
Weston St
Bermondsey St
Webber St
Blackfriars Rd
Southwark Bridge Rd
Marshalsea
THE BOROUGH
A200
Druid St
Westminster Br
Parliament Square
HOUSES OF PARLIAMENT
Lwr Marsh
Waterloo Rd
Tabard
Leathermkt
Long Ln
ABBEY
MINSTER
St. Margaret St
Baylis Rd
Westminster Bridge Rd
Royal St
Borough Rd
Trinity St
Mancipal St
Harper Rd
Great Dover St
Tabard St
Law St
South Palace Rd
Carlisle Ln
Hercules Rd
River
London Rd
NEWINGTON
Abbey St
The Grange
Tower Bridge Rd
Smith Sq
Marsham St
Millbank
LAMBETH PALACE
IMPERIAL WAR MUSEUM
St. George's Rd
ELEPHANT AND CASTLE
Falmouth Rd
Grange Rd
Lambeth Rd
Brook Dr
Lambeth Br
Lambeth Walk
Walnut Tree Walk
Old Paradise
Hayes St
New Kent Rd
A2206
LONDON
Dante Rd
LAMBETH
Kennington Rd
Wincott St
Renfrew Rd
Walworth Rd
Heygate St
Rodney Rd
Mandela Way
Dunton Rd
A2
TATE GALLERY
Black Prince Rd
John Islip St
Millbank
Albert Embankment
Vauxhall
KENNINGTON
Sancroft St
First St
Old Kent Rd
East St
A3
Penton Pl
Browning St
Surrey Sq
Tyers St
Manor Pl
A215
East St
Cleaver St
Park Rd
SURREY SQ. PARK
©1998 GP

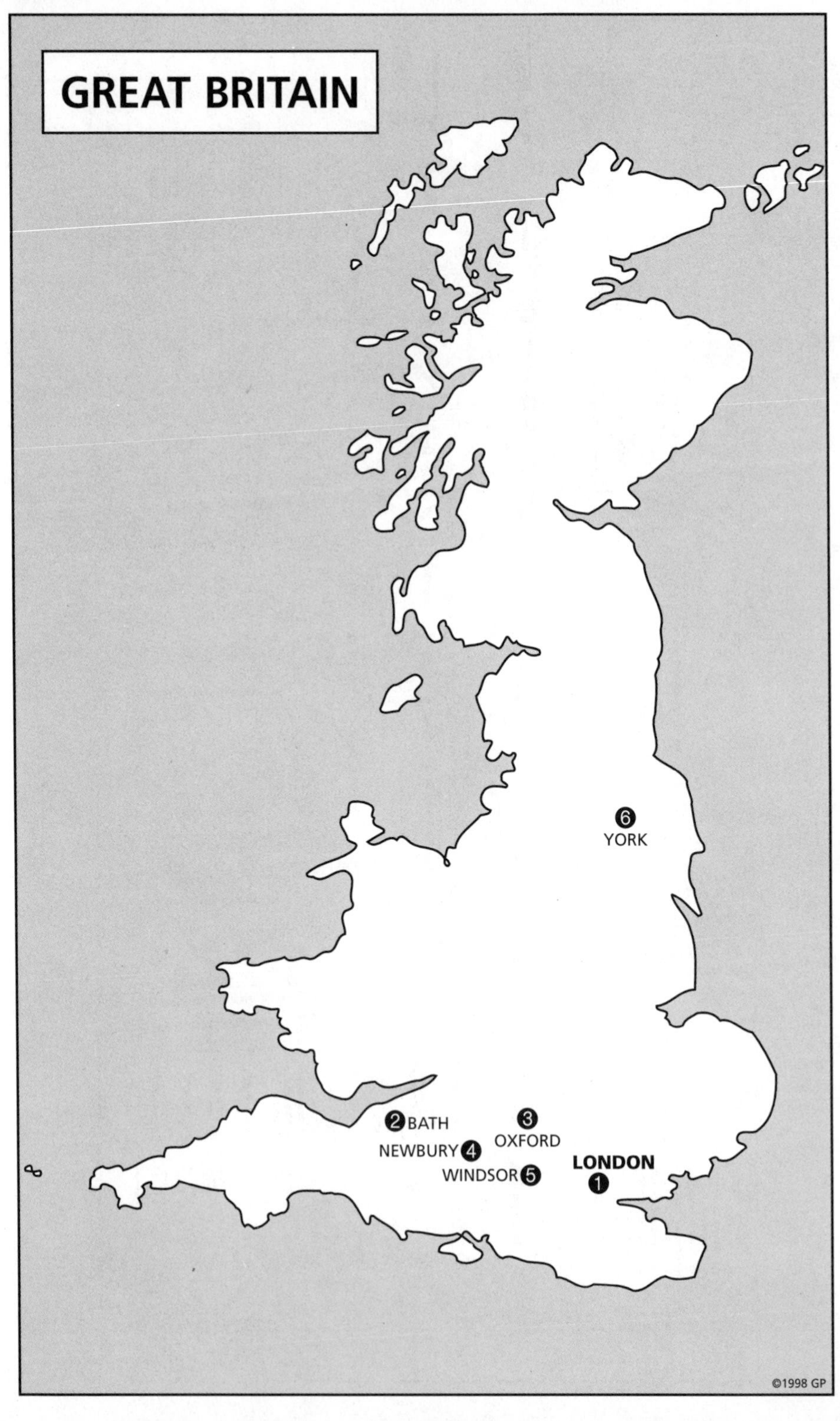
GREAT BRITAIN
6 YORK
2 BATH
3 OXFORD
NEWBURY 4
LONDON
1
WINDSOR 5
©1998 GP

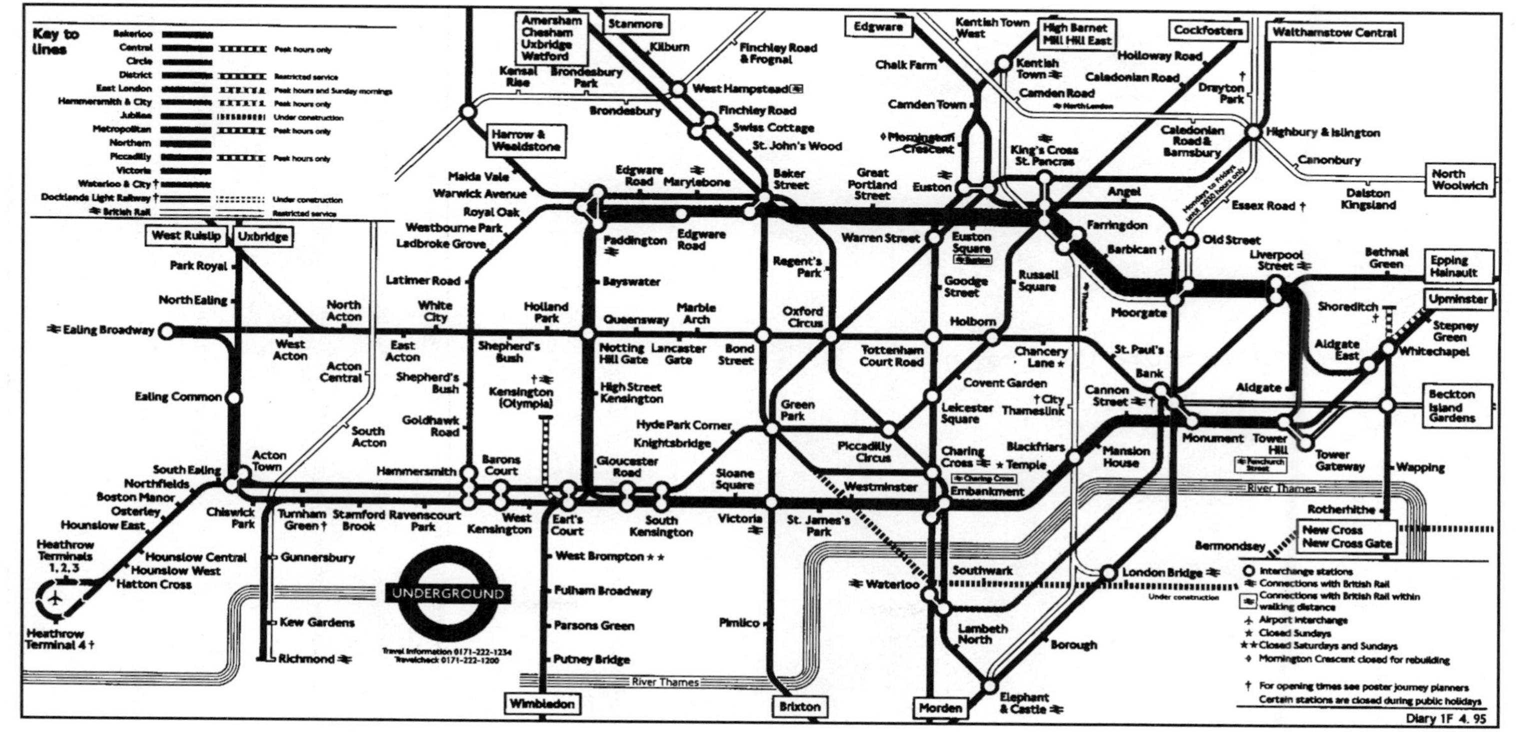

Key to lines
Bakerloo
Central — Peak hours only
Circle
District — Restricted service
East London — Peak hours and Sunday mornings
Hammersmith & City — Peak hours only
Jubilee — Under construction
Metropolitan — Peak hours only
Northern
Piccadilly — Peak hours only
Victoria
Waterloo & City †
Docklands Light Railway † — Under construction
British Rail — Restricted service
Amersham Chesham Uxbridge Watford
Stanmore
Kilburn
Finchley Road & Frognal
Kensal Rise
Brondesbury Park
West Hampstead
Brondesbury
Finchley Road
Swiss Cottage
St. John's Wood
Harrow & Wealdstone
Maida Vale
Warwick Avenue
Royal Oak
Westbourne Park
Ladbroke Grove
Latimer Road
Edgware Road
Marylebone
Baker Street
Paddington
Edgware Road
Bayswater
Queensway
Marble Arch
Notting Hill Gate
Lancaster Gate
Bond Street
High Street Kensington
Holland Park
Shepherd's Bush
Kensington (Olympia)
West Ruislip
Uxbridge
Park Royal
North Ealing
North Acton
White City
Ealing Broadway
West Acton
East Acton
Acton Central
Shepherd's Bush
Goldhawk Road
Ealing Common
South Acton
Acton Town
South Ealing
Northfields
Boston Manor
Osterley
Hounslow East
Heathrow Terminals 1, 2, 3
Hounslow Central
Hounslow West
Hatton Cross
Heathrow Terminal 4 †
Chiswick Park
Turnham Green †
Stamford Brook
Ravenscourt Park
Hammersmith
Barons Court
West Kensington
Earl's Court
Gloucester Road
South Kensington
Hyde Park Corner
Knightsbridge
Sloane Square
Victoria
Gunnersbury
Kew Gardens
Richmond
UNDERGROUND
Travel Information 0171-222-1234
Travelcheck 0171-222-1200
West Brompton ★★
Fulham Broadway
Parsons Green
Putney Bridge
River Thames
Wimbledon
Pimlico
Brixton
Edgware
Chalk Farm
Camden Town
Mornington Crescent
Kentish Town West
High Barnet Mill Hill East
Kentish Town
Camden Road
North London
Great Portland Street
Euston
King's Cross St. Pancras
Warren Street
Euston Square
Regent's Park
Goodge Street
Russell Square
Oxford Circus
Tottenham Court Road
Holborn
Green Park
Piccadilly Circus
Leicester Square
Covent Garden
Chancery Lane ★
City Thameslink †
Thameslink
Charing Cross
Charing Cross
Temple ★
Blackfriars
Westminster
Embankment
St. James's Park
Waterloo
Southwark
Lambeth North
Elephant & Castle
Morden
Borough
Cockfosters
Holloway Road
Caledonian Road
Drayton Park †
Caledonian Road & Barnsbury
Walthamstow Central
Highbury & Islington
Canonbury
North Woolwich
Dalston Kingsland
Essex Road †
Mondays to Fridays until 2030 hours only
Angel
Farringdon
Barbican †
Old Street
Moorgate
Liverpool Street
Bethnal Green
Epping Hainault
Upminster
Shoreditch †
Stepney Green
Whitechapel
Aldgate East
Aldgate
St. Paul's
Bank
Cannon Street †
Mansion House
Monument
Tower Hill
Fenchurch Street
Tower Gateway
Beckton Island Gardens
Wapping
River Thames
Rotherhithe
New Cross New Cross Gate
Bermondsey
London Bridge
Under construction
Interchange stations
Connections with British Rail
Connections with British Rail within walking distance
Airport interchange
★ Closed Sundays
★★ Closed Saturdays and Sundays
Mornington Crescent closed for rebuilding
† For opening times see poster journey planners
Certain stations are closed during public holidays
Diary 1F 4.95

RECEIVE
3 FREE
ISSUES OF

(A $15 VALUE)

BY FILLING OUT THIS QUESTIONNAIRE, YOU'LL RECEIVE 3 COMPLIMENTARY ISSUES OF "TASTES," OUR INTERNATIONAL NEWSLETTER.

NAME ____

ADDRESS ____

CITY ____________________________ STATE ______________

ZIP ____________________ COUNTRY _____________________

PHONE (   )   -

The Gayot/GaultMillau series of guidebooks reflects your demand for insightful, incisive reporting on the best that the world's most exciting destinations have to offer. To help us make our books even better, please take a moment to fill out this anonymous (if you wish) questionnaire, and return it to:

GaultMillau, Inc., P.O. Box 361144, Los Angeles, CA 90036;
Fax: (323) 936-2883.

1. How did you hear about the Gayot guides? Please specify: bookstore, newspaper, magazine, radio, friends or other.

2. Please list in order of preference the cities or countries which you would like to see Gayot cover.

3. Do you refer to the AGP guides for your own city, or only when traveling?

A. (Travels) ....   B. (Own city) ....   C. (Both) ....

(Please turn)

4. Please list by order of preference the three features you like best about the Gayot guides.

A. ....

B. .... C. ....

5. What are the features, if any, you dislike about the Gayot guides?

6. Please list any features that you would like to see added to the Gayot guides.

7. If you use other guides besides Gayot, please list below.

8. Please list the features you like best about your favorite guidebook series, if it is not Gayot/GaultMillau.

A. ....

B. .... C. ....

9. How many trips do you make per year, for either business or pleasure?

Business: International .... Domestic ....

Pleasure: International .... Domestic........................

10. Please check the category that reflects your annual household income.

$20,000–$39,000 .... $40,000–$59,000 ....
$60,000–$79,000 .... $80,000–$99,000 ....
$100,000–$120,000 .... Other (please specify) ....

11. If you have any comments on the AGP guides in general, please list them in the space below.

12. If you would like to recommend specific establishments, please don't hesitate to list them:

Name ***City*** ***Phone***

13. Do you often/sometimes use the Internet to buy goods & services? ❑ Yes ❑ No

We thank you for your interest in the Gayot guides, and we welcome your remarks and recommendations about restaurants, hotels, nightlife, shops, services and so on.

309/98

GAYOT PUBLICATIONS

THE BEST OF LONDON

We wish to thank our generous sponsors for their invaluable contributions which made this book possible

- **22 Jermyn Street**
  www.22jermyn..com
- **About Family Travel**
- **Blakes Hotel**
- **Forbes FYI**
  www.forbes.com
- **France Vacations**
  www.France-Vacations.com
- **Jet Vacations**
  www.jetvacation.com
- **London Hilton**
  www.hilton.com/hotels/LONHITW/
- **Radisson Edwardian Hotel**
  www.radisson.com
- **The Vineyard at Stockcross**
  www.the-vineyard.co.uk
- **Rail Europe Eurostar**
  www.raileurope.com